Empathy Reconsidered

Empathy Reconsidered
NEW DIRECTIONS IN PSYCHOTHERAPY

EDITED BY

ARTHUR C. BOHART AND LESLIE S. GREENBERG

American Psychological Association, Washington, DC

Published by
American Psychological Association
750 First Street, NE
Washington, DC 20002

Copies may be ordered from
APA Order Department
P.O. Box 92984
Washington, DC 20090-2984

In the UK and Europe, copies may be ordered from
American Psychological Association
3 Henrietta Street
Covent Garden, London
WC2E 8LU England

Typeset in Goudy by Maryland Composition Company, Inc., Glen Burnie, MD

Printer: United Book Press, Baltimore, MD
Jacket Designer: Anne Masters Design, Washington, DC
Technical/Production Editor: Edward B. Meidenbauer

Library of Congress Cataloging-in-Publication Data
Empathy reconsidered : new directions in psychotherapy / edited by
    Arthur C. Bohart and Leslie S. Greenberg.
        p.   cm.
    Includes bibliographical references and index.
    ISBN 1-55798-410-7 (alk. paper)
    1. Empathy.   2. Psychotherapist and patient.   I. Bohart, Arthur
C.   II. Greenberg, Leslie S.
RC489.E46E48   1997
616.89'14—dc21

                                                                    97-3398
                                                                    CIP

British Library Cataloging-in-Publication Data
A CIP record is available from the British Library

Printed in the United States of America
First edition

To Carl Rogers and Heinz Kohut, two pioneers in the study of empathy.

CONTENTS

PART III: EXPERIENTIAL PERSPECTIVES

PART IV: PSYCHOANALYTIC PERSPECTIVES

PART V: OTHER RECENT PERSPECTIVES

CONTRIBUTORS

Godfrey T. Barrett-Lennard, Visiting Fellow in Psychology, Murdoch University, Australia.

Jerold D. Bozarth, Department of Counseling and Human Development Services, University of Georgia, Athens.

Morris Eagle, Derner Institute, Adelphi University, Garden City, New Jersey.

Robert Elliott, Department of Psychology, University of Toledo, Ohio.

Norma Deitch Feshbach, Department of Education, University of California, Los Angeles.

Adelbert H. Jenkins, Department of Psychology, New York University.

Judith V. Jordan, Department of Psychology, McLean Hospital, Belmont, Massachussetts.

Marsha M. Linehan, Department of Psychology, University of Washington, Seattle, Washington.

David S. MacIsaac, Private practice, Englewood, New Jersey.

Alvin R. Mahrer, School of Psychology, University of Ottawa, Ontario, Canada.

Maureen O'Hara, Vice President for Academic Affairs, Saybrook Graduate School, San Francisco.

Crayton E. Rowe, Jr., Private practice, New York, New York.

John Shlien, Professor Emeritus, Harvard University, Cambridge, Massachusetts.

Robert D. Stolorow, Faculty member and Training and Supervisor Analyst, Institute of Contemporary Psychoanalysis, Los Angeles. Core faculty member, Institute for Psychoanalytic Study of Subjectivity, New York, New York.

Karen Tallman, Department of Educational Psychology and Technology, University of Southern California, Los Angeles.

Jeffrey L. Trop, Faculty member and Training and Supervisor Analyst, Institute of Contemporary Psychoanalysis, Los Angeles. Assistant Clinical Professor of Psychiatry, UCLA, School of Medicine.

Greet Vanaerschot, Counseling Centrum, Leuven, Belgium.

Margaret S. Warner, Illinois School of Professional Psychology, Chicago.

David L. Wolitzky, New York University Psychology Clinic, Department of Psychology.

PREFACE

Our goal in developing this book was to bring renewed attention to the topic of empathy in psychotherapy for clinicians, theoreticians, and researchers. On the one hand, empathy is an important research topic for developmental and social psychologists, and programs are being developed to train school children in empathy for the purposes of promoting prosocial behavior and reducing aggression. On the other hand, there are only scattered new books on empathy in psychotherapy. Furthermore, there has been very little recent research. Empathy as a key element in psychotherapy is being downplayed by many who adopt a manualized, technological, or "managed care" view of what psychotherapy is all about. It is included as a background characteristic for building the therapeutic relationship but is not seen as an important therapeutic ingredient in its own right. In addition, as one well-respected clinician recently suggested to the first author, most clinicians do not believe there is much new to know about empathy—they think that they already know what it is. Yet we agree with John Shlien, who suggested as a title for this book: "Empathy and Psychotherapy: Not What You Think."

We believe empathy is important in the intensely human activity of psychotherapy, and we also believe that there is much that is not known about it. A good deal of new significant writing is being done on the topic, but we do not believe all clinicians and theoreticians are aware of these developments. Our goal in this volume was to bring together writers from a variety of perspectives who are making active contributions to the development of our understanding of what empathy is and how it plays a role in psychotherapy. We hope that by bringing contributions together from diverse perspectives we will restimulate interest in the topic, particularly among researchers.

This volume is unique in that there has never been a book on empathy in which writers from different perspectives were represented. Because empathy is most emphasized in client-centered, psychodynamic, and experiential approaches, most of the chapters come from writers from these traditions. In this volume there are contributions from the perspectives of psychodynamic self psychology, psychodynamic intersubjectivity theory, psychodynamic theory in general, client-centered theory, varying experiential approaches, feminist self-in-relation theory, a psychodynamic–humanistic perspective on empathy with people of color, a postmodern view of empathy, a view of empathy from an eclectic–integrative perspective, a view on a related variable—validation—from a cognitive–behavioral perspective, and a chapter from a developmental perspective. The recent trend toward psychotherapy integration is also heavily represented, as chapters by Bohart and Tallman, Eagle and Wolitzky, Greenberg and Elliott, Jenkins, Jordan, Linehan, Mahrer, O'Hara, Vanaerschot, and Warner are integrative in various ways.

We hope that by bringing together these diverse perspectives we will contribute to further theoretical work in clarifying this very interesting and important variable. We especially believe this volume is timely at a moment when the human relationship in psychotherapy threatens to be lost under the onslaught of managed care. We hope that, while empathy is increasingly being emphasized in many other areas of life, we will continue to examine this important variable in that most intimate of helping relationships—psychotherapy. As we have noted, we especially hope that the volume will stimulate new research efforts. We had hoped to have more research in the volume but discovered that relatively little new had been done.

There are two generic groups of questions we wanted our authors to explore. The first consists of questions related to the nature of empathy—what is it? There are many different conceptualizations and definitions, as you will see when you read the different chapters. The second set of questions deals with how empathy functions in therapy. Once again, there is a large diversity of views. In our last chapter, we try to analyze, schematize, and integrate the different perspectives provided in the book.

We asked our authors, with the exceptions of Eagle and Wolitzky, Shlien, and Feshbach, to (a) provide a definition of empathy, (b) discuss how empathy functions in their approach to therapy, (c) give a case example, and (d) provide research if available. Eagle and Wolitzky and Shlien wrote general commentaries on empathy from their perspectives. Shlien's commentary is enriched by his first-hand knowledge of how Carl Rogers developed his interest in empathy. Feshbach's chapter gives a general overview of empathy in developmental psychology, with implications for psychotherapy.

We wish to thank our former editor, Joy Chau, and Ted Baroody for their help in developing the volume. We also wish to thank Yvonne Lucius for her last-minute help with getting the manuscript ready.

I
INTRODUCTION

1

EMPATHY AND PSYCHOTHERAPY: AN INTRODUCTORY OVERVIEW

ARTHUR C. BOHART AND LESLIE S. GREENBERG

We live in a paradoxical age. On the one hand, empathy is an important area of study in developmental and social psychology. Popular books argue that "emotional intelligence," which includes empathy, may be more important than IQ (Goleman, 1995). In line with this view, a number of significant programs have begun to train schoolchildren in empathy (e.g., Feshbach, Chapter 2, this volume). Empathy training is also being used in medicine and in business.

Despite this and despite evidence that the therapeutic relationship is the best predictor of success in psychotherapy, opinions in academic psychology as well as the influence of managed care often minimize the importance of the relationship in therapy, treating it as a background variable and assuming all clinicians know how to establish a therapeutic relationship. Rogers' work on the relational conditions specifies that empathy is one of the key ingredients in creating a therapeutic relationship and that fundamentally it is the therapist's empathic attitude that is crucial. This relational view has not been endorsed in a "fix-it" culture in search of interventions that produce specific effects. Therapeutic technology, in which the therapist is an active dispenser of differential treatment, has sometimes been viewed as more appealing than the empathic facilitation of clients' own problem-solving capacities. Therapy is seen by many as the application of a technological procedure that can be manualized. Those who follow these beliefs, however, often do hold that the therapist should be empathic. For some

3

of them, however, empathy is primarily a soothing background variable used to establish a relationship so that the client will comply with the therapist's treatment prescriptions. In these manuals, the attainment of the skills to establish the necessary true empathic base in which these need to be embedded is often overlooked in the search for specific or differential tools. This neglect of the curative effects of relational empathic skills is occurring despite the fact that most of our psychological models of the genesis of psychopathology emphasize relationship deficits.

Simultaneous with this neglect of empathy in psychotherapy, there has also been a resurgence of interest in empathy. The original "heyday" of interest was during the 1960s and early 1970s, during which there was a great deal of research activity testing Carl Rogers's hypothesis that three therapeutic conditions—unconditional positive regard, empathy, and genuineness—were necessary and sufficient for therapeutic change. By the late 1970s, evidence accumulated by Charles Truax and his colleagues (Truax & Carkhuff, 1967; Truax & Mitchell, 1971) had suggested correlations between empathy and therapeutic outcome. However, inconsistencies in this research led many to conclude that the contention that the three conditions were necessary and sufficient had not gathered sufficient empirical support to be accepted. One of the criticisms of this research with regard to empathy was that it had been equated with a specific response technique—empathic reflection—that was primarily relevant to the Rogerian approach.

Nevertheless, empathy did come to be seen as useful in establishing a relationship, and at one level, most therapists accepted the importance of empathy. At another level, the stronger contention that empathy was a powerful "curative agent" in its own right was generally not believed. Paradoxically, the form of empathy adopted, and trained in communications-skills programs, was often that of empathic reflections, the very definition of empathy criticized in some of the attacks on the research by Truax and his colleagues.

As a result of a variety of the factors above, research on empathy in the 1980s began to dwindle. Aside from a few studies, there have been no recent more sophisticated attempts to specifically investigate empathy and its components and their relationship to client process and outcome. At the same time, thanks largely to the development of psychoanalytic self psychology, a renewed theoretical interest in empathy blossomed in the 1980s. In addition, feminist self-in-relation theory stressed the fundamental importance of empathy.

Currently, it seems that many therapists conceive of empathy as little more than a kindly and supportive posture (Snyder, 1992). For them, there may be nothing more important to know about empathy. After all, most therapists, with a little effort, can show that they care. What's all the fuss about? In contrast to the view of empathy as akin to establishment of rapport, most of the authors in this volume conceive of empathy as far more central to therapeutic change and far more than just acknowledging the client's perspective and being warm and supportive. Rather, they see it as a major component of the healing process. They also see it as consisting of far more "depth." First, empathy includes the making of deep and sustained psychological contact with another in which one is highly attentive to, and aware of, the experience of the other as a unique other. In an empathic way of being, one appreciates the other's experience as it is, as an idiosyncratic expression of the other in his or her difference. A genuine meeting of persons can occur. Second, empathic exploration includes deep sustained empathic inquiry or immersing of oneself in the experience of the other. This can lead to sensitive interpretations that help clients access unconscious experience. Third, empathic exploration includes a resonant grasping of the "edges" or implicit aspects of a client's experience to help create new meaning.

Empathy, seen not as a mere background characteristic but as a central variable in its own right, is not incompatible with the use of technology. If one learns more about it, one can create truly powerful human interactions in which both relational attitudes and technology are also used in the service of clients. We hope this volume will further this aim. In this regard, we believe that all practitioners can benefit from learning more about this central ingredient of psychotherapeutic change.

In the chapters to come, authors discuss some of the enduring issues in the study of empathy and raise novel issues. Some of the persistent issues concern the nature of empathy and whether or not empathy is an attitude or a behavior. Some see empathy as closer to affect contagion in which the therapist actually feels some of what the client is feeling, whereas others see it as more of a hermeneutic process for knowing the mind of the other. In relation to its operation, some believe any behavior can be empathic provided the therapist's attitude is correct, whereas others believe specific types of behavior best implement an empathic way of being. Other perennial issues concern the degree to which unconscious processes are involved in being empathic and are the target of empathy as well as the degree of inference or interpretation involved. Novel and postmodern views concern themselves with the issues of the coconstruction of meaning in empathy as well as reconceptualizing empathy in self-in-relation and other relational ways of viewing of human functioning in which connectedness precedes or predominates over separateness as a criterion of healthy functioning. In addition, the centrality of empathy in relation to treatment in cross-cultural and multicultural contexts is discussed.

Although the definition and mechanisms are still somewhat unclear, we see empathy as an essential ingredient of therapeutic practice and a key concept in attempts to understand how therapy works. The empathic process in which therapists steep themselves in the world of the other attempting to understand how others see and experience themselves and their worlds, putting this into words and checking their understanding, appears to us to be curative. Empathy is a process of coconstructing symbols for experience. Clients' process of symbolizing their experience in awareness promoted by empathic responding to their internal experience appears to us to be a universal core ingredient of the therapeutic process. Being able to name an experience first makes the previously implicit explicit, thereby providing an improved sense of facilitation and comprehension of how one knows what one is experiencing. This in and of itself provides some clarity—and relief from earlier confusion. Once one has a handle on what is felt, one can then also begin to reflectively operate on what has been symbolized in awareness: reorganizing, explaining, and exploring further, thereby creating new meaning and new narrative constructions. This process of becoming aware of internal experience, putting it into words and reorganizing it once it has been symbolized, is healing and leads to greater self-understanding and improved self-organization. Empathy thus helps us make sense of our experience (Greenberg & Paivio, in press; Watson & Greenberg, 1996). Rather than simply conceptually understanding oneself, empathy helps clients become more compassionate and empathic to themselves. An important change then is one of moving from a stance of negative evaluation, rejection, or disavowal of experience to accepting one's experience as one's own. This occurs by a shift in stance to empathic self-understanding through being treated as a self that is an authentic source of experience. Empathy helps clients learn to articulate their own experience and to see themselves as agents of that experience. In this sense, empathy is the therapist's contribution to the basic self-articulation and narrative-formation process that has been shown to be therapeutic in studies of journaling and of account making after trauma (Harvey, Orbuch, Chwalisz, & Garwood, 1991; Pennebaker, 1990). In this book, further differentiations of how empathy heals will be offered, but we see them as variations of the core process of symbolizing to create meaning and promotion of a shift to greater self-understanding and self-acceptance that are universal processes of human psychological change and development.

EMPATHY AND PSYCHOTHERAPY

Empathy in Client-Centered Therapy

Much of the general popularity of empathy in psychology can be traced to Carl Rogers's influence (Wispé, 1987). For Rogers (1959), empathy was defined as an ability to "perceive the internal frame of reference of another with accuracy and with the emotional components and meanings which pertain thereto as an ability if one were the person, but without ever losing the 'as if' condition" (p. 210). However, in contrast to the psychoanalytic emphasis on empathically grasping the unconscious structure of experience that underlies the client's ways of being in the world, for client-centered therapists empathy involves focusing on the client's presently available moment-to-moment meanings and experiencing. The therapist tries to non-judgmentally understand the client's immediate frame of reference in the moment and to communicate that understanding back to the client. In essence, empathy in practice is careful "communicative attunement" (to borrow a term from Orlinsky, Grawe, & Parks, 1994). The therapist attempts to imaginatively enter the client's experience of struggling to articulate, share, and dialogue with the therapist, as well as to try to grasp the content of what the client is striving to communicate. To quote Brodley (1996), client-centered empathy responses emphasize "the client's perceptions and the ways in which the client as a self is an agency or an active force and a source of meanings, reactions and other experiences" (p. 23). Raskin (1974) defines empathy as "an understanding of what the client is aware of and trying to convey to the therapist, so if the latter is accurate in his empathic endeavor, the client will feel and may say, 'Yes, that's it! That's how I feel! That's what I meant!' " (p. 11).

Empathy is not the same as unconditional positive regard (liking and prizing the client). Nor is it being sympathic or compassionate. Empathy is one of the three "therapeutic conditions" that Rogers (1957) postulated as necessary and sufficient for therapeutic change to occur. According to Rogers, empathy, combined with unconditional positive regard and congruence, operates by contributing to a safe climate where clients heal themselves through their own self-actualization tendencies. No specific "effect" of empathy is postulated, other than that it plays a role in the therapist's being a nondirective companion on the client's journey.

During the 1950s, empathy was the major ingredient in client-centered therapy (Hart, 1970) and was expressed largely through a technique often referred to as "reflection of feeling." Empathic reflections differed from psychodynamic interpretations in that reflections addressed themselves to the client's immediately available internal world of experience, whereas interpretations addressed themselves to aspects of the unconscious. However, Rogers (1986) rejected the idea that empathy was to be equated with reflection and held instead that it was an attitude. In his later writing, he emphasized the idea that what he was doing was "checking" his understanding of the client.

The client-centered perspective was fertile in spawning a number of developments in training empathy. One was the skills-training approach to empathy (Carkhuff, 1971; Egan, 1982; Goodman, 1984; Guerney, 1984), which emphasized empathic reflections as the primary response tool for conveying empathy. The focus on empathic reflections also became a part of a focus on the use of different response modes in therapy in general (e.g., Stiles, 1986). Empathic reflections subsequently became a staple of communications-skills training programs (e.g., Bolton, 1979). Despite the contributions of skills-training approaches, one inadvertent side effect was that they led, as we have mentioned previously, to empathy being equated with the reflection technique, even though, as we have noted, Rogers himself objected to this equation. As a result, many therapists came to think that they understood what empathy is—empathic reflections—and missed the richer complexities of the concept in both the client-centered and psychodynamic literatures. Specifically, empathic reflections can be done in a programmatic, mechanistic way; for client-centered therapy, this misses the importance of really trying to understand the other person in terms of the richness of his or her own perspective.

Recent Developments in Client-Centered and Experiential Therapies

In the past 20 years, there has been an evolution of client-centered and other existential–humanistic approaches. Client-centered therapy has become the "person-centered approach." At the same time, a whole new group of therapies, called "experiential" (Greenberg, Lietaer, & Watson, in press; Mahrer & Fairweather, 1993) have appeared. Experiential therapies differ from their predecessors in (a) their more explicit emphasis on working at the experiential and emotional level and (b) their more specific emphasis on how particular therapist operations can facilitate specific client processes at specific times.

The four experiential perspectives represented in this volume are integrative. Vanaerschot's approach is an integration of client-centered and Gendlin's (1974) experiential therapy. The process-experiential approach of Greenberg, Rice, and Elliott (1993) integrates ideas and procedures from client-centered therapy, Gendlin's experiential therapy, Gestalt therapy, and cognitive theory. Warner's approach integrates client-centered and Gendlin's experiential therapy with psychodynamic self psychology. Mahrer's (1995) experiential psychotherapy comes out of an existential tradition and integrates influences from psychodynamic and behavioral sources.

Two major lines of thought on empathy have continued from the original client-centered emphasis. In the person-centered approach, empathy has a single intention: to convey understanding to promote safety and trust in the self. In this line the major evolution has been toward increasing flexibility in how empathy is conveyed (Bozarth, 1984; Chapter 4, this volume). Bohart (1991) and Rogers and Sanford (1984) have also suggested that one way empathy helps is that it provides a model for clients to learn how to relate to themselves, an idea developed in Chapter 5 of this volume by Barrett-Lennard.

In the other line of thought, developed by those in the experiential tradition, a more exploratory form of empathy is emphasized. The intentions for therapeutic responding are differentiated and varied and go beyond understanding alone (Greenberg & Elliott, Chapter 8, this volume; Wexler & Rice, 1974). Empathy both functions to establish a good therapeutic alliance and is an intervention in its own right (Watson & Greenberg, 1994). Different kinds of empathic responses may be used at different times. In a related vein, Vanaerschot (Chapter 7, this volume) and Warner (Chapter 6, this volume) discuss how empathic responses can specifically facilitate the client's experiencing process and repair damage to it from childhood.

Mahrer's (Chapter 9, this volume) use of empathy represents an independent line of development. For Mahrer empathy is aligning with the client's experience and then "becoming" that experience. This kind of deep empathic "joining" is seen as facilitating clients' accessing of their own deep experiencing potential.

Some writers from the client-centered and experiential tradition, in keeping with psychodynamic and feminist therapists, have also begun to stress a relational view of empathy (Barrett-Lennard, 1993; O'Hara, Chapter 14, this volume; Snyder, 1994) in which the connecting function of empathy is emphasized. Relational units such as couples, families, or groups are seen as having a higher order existence in their own right, and empathy is a fundamental way of being together in such units.

Empathy in Psychoanalysis

Although not as a major variable for psychoanalysis, Freud did mention empathy. For him it was a way for the therapist to know the mind of the client. The analyst tuned his or her unconscious to that of the patient and then noticed what inner resonances were set up. The analyst also listened with "evenly hovering attention," that is, suspended judgment so as to hear the client more fully.

In classical psychoanalysis, empathic listening served only one function. It provided clues about the patient's unconscious dynamics. This facilitated making effective interpretations. That, in turn, led to the patient's gaining insight. The therapist's empathic understanding was not directly shared with the analysand, and there was no attempt to use empathy to establish a relationship in which a corrective emotional experience could take place. Freud thought the relationship between analyst and analysand should be cordial but advocated that the analyst adopt a relatively cool, analytic, and even "surgical" perspective.

Some modern analysts (e.g., Buie, 1981a) are skeptical of the idea of a warm, empathic atmosphere that can provide a corrective emotional experience. They are concerned that emotionally reacting to the client in an affectively empathic way is countertransferential. Other classical analysts reject the idea that the analyst can intuit himself or herself into the experience of the client. They are concerned that a focus on empathy as the primary way of knowing about the client undermines the scientific status of psychoanalysis (Buie, 1981a; Shapiro, 1984). They argue that empathy involves conceptual inference, just as other ways of developing conceptualizations about the client do.

Recent Developments in Psychoanalytic Thought

Empathy moved from being a peripheral player on the psychoanalytic stage to being central with the development of Heinz Kohut's self psychology (Kohut, 1971, 1977, 1984). Kohut became convinced that the "experience distant" way analysts understood their patients was not helpful. By "experience distant," Kohut meant a way of knowing the patient in which the analyst observed the patient's free associations and then used those observations in combination with analytic theory to infer patterns of unconscious meaning and organization. In contrast, Kohut came to believe that it was important for the analyst to try to comprehend what was going on with the client in an "experience near" way. This meant that the analyst was to try to place himself or herself, through a process of "vicarious introspection," into the experience of the client.

In addition to facilitating insight, Kohut observed that expressing empathic understanding sometimes facilitated the therapeutic process by making patients more open to receiving interpretations. He developed a theory that held that empathic failures in childhood led to failures in the self-structuralization process in the client. Empathic responsiveness in therapy created a corrective context in which particular types of transferential feelings toward the analyst related to empathic failures in the past could develop. In this context, occasional empathic failures on the part of the analyst provided an opportunity for clients to learn and to strengthen defects in their self-structures. In this volume, MacIsaac (chapter 11) and Rowe (chapter 12) carry forward work on empathy from a self-psychological point of view. Their discussion of understanding and expanding attunement has parallels to client-centered communicative attunement.

Modern psychodynamic theory in general has shifted from an emphasis on sexual and aggressive drive to an emphasis on relationships and their role in both the development and the remediation of psychopathology (e.g., Luborsky, 1984; Mitchell, 1988; Stolorow & Atwood, 1992; Strupp & Binder, 1984; Wachtel, 1993). Correspondingly, empathy or its lack has come to be seen as an important component in both development and psychotherapy. For some, the primary function of empathy in therapy is to provide a supportive context for other therapeutic work. For others, empathy has intrinsic healing capacities in its own right (i.e., it provides a corrective emotional experience for the wounds suffered in childhood). Still others continue to view its function primarily as providing material for interpretation. In Chapter 13 of this volume, Trop and Stolorow write from a modern relational approach. Jordan (Chapter 16), writing on self-in-relation theory, and Jenkins (Chapter 15), writing on empathy with people of color, also come from relational psychodynamic orientations.

The psychodynamic use of empathy for the purposes of illuminating the unconscious seems different from the client-centered focus on empathy as "communicative attunement." In psychodynamic theory the ultimate goal is to enter into the client's experience to grasp an overall sense of what it is like to be the client, to understand how the client experiences and behaves in the world in a general sense. To do this, the analyst must acquire information beyond what the client is immediately communicating in the moment. Ideally, the analyst will help the client access warded-off experiences that help flesh out this understanding. If the therapist is successful, the therapist could say something like, "No *wonder* you see things the way you do, and feel the way you do, given your experiences" (e.g., Havens, 1986).

Despite the modern emphasis on the importance of empathy in psychoanalysis, there are many unresolved questions about its role in theory and psychotherapy, such as how one can empathize with experience that is unconscious and how empathy and countertransference relate to each other. Some of these are addressed by Eagle and Wolitzky (Chapter 10, this volume) in their critical overview of the topic.

Achievement of Empathy

Many analytic models of achieving empathy stress the idea of forming a "trial identification" with the client. However, keeping a clear sense of one's boundaries is also stressed. Getting too identified with the client's experience could be countertransferential. One must be careful not to project one's own concerns and experiences onto the client.

One commonly mentioned model for achieving empathy is that of Buie (1981b). For Buie, empathy is based on a process by which one observes the behavior of the other, searches one's own memories for configurations of experience that might lead to similar behavior if one expressed them, and then draws inferences to the internal experience of the other. In engaging in this process, one uses a working conceptual model of the patient, one's own imagination and fantasies, one's own evoked experiences in response to the client's communications, and what is called "resonant empathy." Resonant empathy is experiencing a temporary kind of merger in which the therapist has similar emotions as the client. This also includes feelings of warmth and closeness.

Empathy in Behavioral and Cognitive Perspectives

In recent years behaviorists have come to acknowledge the importance of the therapeutic relationship and of empathy in particular (Franks, 1994). For behaviorists empathy is one of two things. First, it is a nonspecific variable whose function is to help establish a good therapeutic alliance so that clients will be more likely to use the procedures offered by the therapist. Second, empathy and its components can be used as interventions. Linehan's (Chapter 17, this volume) concept of validation is closely related to empathy. Linehan delineates six different types of validation strategies in her work with borderline personality disorder. Christensen, Jacobson, and Babcock (1995) emphasize acceptance and use a variety of strategies to facilitate "empathic joining" in their behavioral approach to couples therapy. These include a positive reframing of couples' problems and an encouraging of "soft" rather than "hard" self-disclosures by each member of the couple.

Cognitive therapists such as Beck (e.g., Beck, Rush, Shaw, & Emery, 1979) also emphasize the importance of the therapist's being empathic. For them empathy is primarily a relationship-building variable. On the other hand, the interpersonal cognitive approach of Safran and Segal (1990) suggests that empathic responding can be used to facilitate the challenging of dysfunctional beliefs.

Empathy in Postmodernist Thought

Postmodern thought emphasizes the multiplicity of different ways humans can construct reality (Mahoney, 1991). The idea that the experience of the Western White (heterosexual) man forms the paradigm for how all humans experience is forcefully rejected. Instead, feminists, multiculturalists, gay men, and lesbians have argued that the experience of diverse groups is different and needs to be understood in its own terms. Constructivists argue for the multiplicity of reality (e.g., Neimeyer & Mahoney, 1995).

Because there is no one "objective" reality, the therapist's ability to empathize becomes particularly important. If reality is multiple and we construct our own realities, then empathy becomes the fundamental way of knowing across diverse personal realities. Empathy is not merely an intervention but also a fundamental way of meeting another person from a different experiential reality. It is only through this genuine "meeting" that therapeutic interventions can be helpfully used. Stone Center theorists (Jordan, Chapter 16, this volume) see therapy as fundamentally relational. Empathy is something that exists between therapist and client, not within one or the other. Therapy is the restoring of connection with others, rather than the developing of a separate autonomous "Western" self.

The idea that empathy is something between people, and that the relationship unit in therapy forms a kind of gestalt that transcends and includes the two parties involved, is also found in recent relational approaches to psychoanalysis (e.g., Stolorow & Atwood, 1992), client-centered therapy (Barrett-Lennard, 1993), and Gestalt therapy. For instance, Gestalt therapists propose a field theoretic view of interpersonal contact. They emphasize working at the "contact boundary" between therapist and client (Wheeler, 1991; Yontef, 1994). They also emphasize the emergent moment between two people as transcending the existence of separate entities. In this volume, O'Hara (Chapter 14) describes a relational view of empathy that emphasizes the emergent nature of groups as a whole.

Empathy, the Therapeutic Alliance, and Eclectic Therapeutic Practice

Empathy has recently been somewhat subsumed under the concept of the *therapeutic alliance* (Bordin, 1979; Horvath & Greenberg, 1994). The therapeutic alliance consists of the establishment of a bond between therapist and client and an agreement between them on tasks and goals. A good initial therapeutic alliance provides the context within which the therapist can use other interventions to achieve therapeutic effect. The tearing and repair of the ongoing alliance is viewed as curative (Bordin, 1979). Although empathy is acknowledged as an important aspect of securing the bond in the alliance, it is not always seen as a primary agent of therapeutic change. Nor is it seen as uniformly important across all relationships. For some eclectic therapists, empathy is a quantity to be titrated in amounts appropriate to meeting the needs of particular clients. It has also been suggested that empathy can make some clients deteriorate (Beutler, Crago, & Arizmendi, 1986), a finding we shall consider in more detail in our concluding chapter.

On the other hand, Bohart and Tallman (Chapter 18, this volume) argue that empathy is an essential component of eclectic therapeutic practice. Not only does it strengthen the bond, but it is also the core component in the therapeutic "art" of sensitively applying techniques and procedures from any perspective.

Conclusions

From our brief review, it can be seen that empathy has been postulated to serve diverse psychotherapeutic functions. Furthermore, different writers mean different things by empathy, so when therapists universally acknowledge its importance, they are not talking about the same thing. Briefly, we suggest the following schematization of therapeutic empathy. The first general category we call "empathic rapport." This is the person on the street's view of empathy and is also what many practitioners mean by it. Empathy is primarily kindliness, global understanding, and tolerant acceptance of the client's feelings and frame of reference. The therapist shows that he or she recognizes what the client is feeling. He or she also recognizes that it makes sense that the client feels as he or she does given his or her perspective on the situation. He or she may further even identify with the client to some degree. However, this understanding is at a general level, in which the therapist applies his or her knowledge of human experience to "understand" that it makes sense that if the client feels rejected he or she will feel sad, or if the client feels neglected he or she will feel angry, and so on.

Empathy at this level does not involve any active attempt to "dig into" the client's frame of reference and to grasp it in a more deeply differentiated way and help make sense of it.

The second category is "experience-near understanding of the client's world" Here the focus of the therapist's empathy is to try to grasp the whole of the client's perceived situation. The therapist wants to empathically understand what it is like to be this client based on knowing about the client's perceived world—what it is like to have the problems the client has, to live in the life situation the client lives in, and so on. In the first sense of this, the therapist explores the factors involved in the client's present world, such as details of the client's relationships, job, or values. If the client says he or she is depressed about his or her spousal relationship, the therapist wants details on how he or she perceives that relationship to help understand what it would be like to be the client. In the second sense of this, the therapist explores both conscious and unconscious elements of the client's life history to attain a deeper understanding of what it is like to be him or her. The therapist's ideal response here is be able to say "No wonder you're feeling the way you do—given how you experience your current life situation and given the earlier life history experiences you have had." This type of empathic activity is most characteristic of psychodynamic approaches and involves a recursive cycle of exploring client experience, both conscious and unconscious, and using this to achieve a differentiated understanding of how the client experiences his world.

The third category of empathy is "communicative attunement" and is most emphasized by client-centered therapy. This involves moment-by-moment attunement and frequent understanding responses. The therapist tries to put himself or herself in clients' shoes at that moment, to grasp what they are consciously trying to communicate at that moment, and what they are experiencing at that moment. In essence, it is to share, connect, or "be in the moment with" the client's active struggle to understand himself or herself, access his or her experience, shape it into words and concepts, and communicate it to another person. This is similar to what Stern (1985) has studied with parents and their infants at a nonverbal level. Good mothers apprehend what the child is experiencing in the moment, and what the child is trying to share with them, and respond accordingly. They respond with appropriate nonverbal language to the child's efforts to share his or her excitement, surprise, or sadness. They also "hear" the child's frustration with a game that the child and the mother are playing and terminate or change the game in an attuned fashion. At the adult level, the communicatively attuned therapist actively and effortfully enters into the client's world at the moment to sense or grasp the client's struggles to understand himself and to communicate self. The therapist is attuned to the quality of the experience, the intensity, the degree of fragility, and the rhythm of expression, as well as to the content and nuances of meaning being expressed.

In addition, the therapist may try to grasp the implications or trajectories in what the client is trying to say and to help the client articulate and explore further. A good therapist response leads to the client saying "you took the words right out of my mouth!" Here empathy is helping clients symbolize, organize, and make sense of their ever-emerging experience. More advanced levels of communicative attunement between therapist and client lead to the kind of interactional empathy stressed by relational theorists in this volume (e.g., Jordan, Chapter 16, and O'Hara, Chapter 14).

These three forms of therapeutic empathy are not levels of empathy but rather types, and each may be helpful at different times. Empathic rapport is the most global form. It can be therapeutic in a relationship-building sense, but it does not lead to the deeper levels of understanding and interpersonal meeting that the other two forms of empathy do. Experience-near entry into the client's world and communicative attunement, although having different foci (understanding the client's life situation in addition to there-and-then experience versus understanding the client's immediate experience), are not mutually exclusive, although they are differentially emphasized by different approaches.

RESEARCH ON EMPATHY IN PSYCHOTHERAPY

During the 1960s and 1970s, inspired by Carl Rogers's (1957) hypothesis that therapists' unconditional positive regard or "warmth," empathy, and congruence or genuineness were "necessary and sufficient" for therapeutic change to occur, a variety of researchers began to study empathy and its companion conditions. The work of Truax and his colleagues (Truax & Mitchell, 1971) appeared to show strong relationships between these conditions and positive change. However, during the 1970s, the Truax findings faced challenges, and interest in that approach to research on empathy waned.

Since then, research on empathy has been sporadic. Both Greenberg, Elliott, and Lietaer (1994) and Orlinsky et al. (1994) note the recent sparsity of research on empathy. Orlinsky et al. note only five studies since 1985, and Duan and Hill (1996) note only eleven. Furthermore, very little research has addressed anything but the most general question about empathy: its overall relationship to therapeutic outcome. Research in the area has generally been plagued by confusion over operational definitions and lack of adequate measures (Duan & Hill, 1996). Below, we first review issues of empathy measurement. Then we review findings on empathy in therapy. Finally, we discuss directions for further research.

Measurement

How one measures empathy has depended heavily on the kinds of research questions one has asked. Developmental and social psychologists have been primarily interested in studying the relationship of empathy to prosocial and helping behavior. They have focused on measures that access an individual's ability to feel, experience, or perceive the affective state of another or their compassion for someone in distress. This makes sense if one believes that it is the detection of distress in another that motivates helping.

In contrast, empathy as measured in therapy has typically focused on in-therapy behavior. There have been four general classes of measures. First, therapists have rated their own empathy. Second, clients have rated the level of empathy provided by their therapists. Barrett-Lennard's (1986) Relationship Inventory provides scales for measuring both of these. Sample items from the client scale include "He (she) usually understands the whole of what I mean," "When I am hurt or upset, she (he) can recognize my feelings exactly without becoming upset herself," and "Sometimes he (she) thinks I feel a certain way, because that's the way he (she) feels" (p. 442).

A third way empathy has been measured is to use Interpersonal Process Recall (Elliott, 1986; Johnson, Geller, & Rhodes, 1994; Kagan, 1984). Clients listen to tapes of their own therapy sessions and rate the therapist's responses for degree of empathy or misunderstanding.

A fourth way empathy has been measured is to have objective raters listen to or observe tapes of therapy sessions and rate the therapist for degree of empathy. The most well-known of these approaches was the work done by Truax, Carkhuff, and their colleagues (Carkhuff & Berenson, 1967; Truax & Carkhuff, 1967). In their systems, short (2- to 4-min) samples of therapy sessions were rated on 5- to 9-point scales for degree of empathy shown by the therapist.

Most of the research done in the 1960s and 1970s on empathy used either ratings of client perceptions or objective ratings. In recent years only a few new operational definitions of empathy have been developed. One is by Elliott et al. (1982). They developed a multicomponent rating scale for measuring empathy, based on the work of Hargrove (1974) and Cochrane (1974). In Elliott et al.'s work, objective raters rated individual responses of counselors on nine different components: the intention to enter the client's frame of reference, the degree to which the counselor makes perceptual inferences and clarifications of the client's frame of reference, the accuracy–plausibility of the counselor's inference, reference to what the client is experiencing in the here and now, the degree to which the counselor refers to the centrality of the topic the client is focusing on, the kinds of words the counselor uses (e.g., rich, metaphoric), the voice quality of the counselor, the exploratory manner, and the impact (does the therapist's response facilitate exploring, or block the client?). The study found that reliability for all components except voice quality and exploratory manner was good. A factor analysis found that there were two general factors: a depth-expressiveness factor and an empathic exploration factor. The most important component, based on client ratings of therapist responses, was the centrality component.

There is evidence that different perspectives on empathy do not necessarily correlate. There are relatively low correlations between therapist's and client's perceptions (Gurman, 1977; LaCrosse, 1977) on the Barrett-Lennard Relationship Inventory. Caskey, Barker, and Elliott (1984) found that therapists and clients did not agree on the perception of the intention to understand in specific therapist responses either. Correlations between observer ratings of empathy on the Truax and Carkhuff scales with client perceptions have generally been low. For instance, Kurtz and Grummon (1972) correlated seven different measures of empathy and found that the correlations ranged from -.24 to .66. Client and therapist perceptions of empathy correlated .21, and client perceptions correlated .31 with judge's tape ratings, leaving the construct validity of the measures open to question. Similarly, Gladstein and his colleagues (1987) found low correlations between measures of cognitive and affective components of empathy. On the other hand, as Barrett-Lennard (personal communication, September 1996) has noted, if empathy is a multidimensional construct, as both he (Barrett-Lennard, 1993) and we suggest, then low correlations are not surprising.

Furthermore, Elliott et al. (1982) found significant but small correlations between objective ratings of empathy on a response-by-response basis and the client's subjective rating of how empathic a response was. When responses were aggregated, either over episodes or over the whole session, correlations between objective ratings and client's subjective perceptions increased substantially. Correlations between specific response modes and client's total ratings of empathy were also found. For example, interpretations and reflections correlated .49 and .48 with empathy ratings, whereas small but statistically significant negative associations were found between empathy and questions (-.19) and advisement (-.09).

Empathy and Outcome

Early research on the relationship of therapist empathy to therapeutic outcome was highly encouraging. On the basis of studies using objective tape ratings, Truax and Mitchell (1971) claimed that, in general, there was a strong relationship among Rogers's therapeutic conditions of warmth, empathy, and genuineness on the one hand, and positive therapeutic outcome on the other. However, a number of subsequent analyses of studies that use objective tape measures led to more cautious conclusions (Mitchell et al., 1977). First, the relationships did not necessarily hold up in studies with non-client-centered therapies. For instance, Sloane, Staples, Cristol, Yorkston, and Whipple (1975) found no relationship between therapist empathy and client success in their study of psychodynamic and behavioral therapies. Part of the reason for this lack of relationship may have been that the Truax definition of empathy tended to equate it with the response *form* of empathic reflections, making this definition more appropriate to how client-centered therapists demonstrated empathy than for how therapists of other persuasions might have demonstrated it.

A second problem with the Truax and Mitchell (1971) results was that reanalyses of their data suggested that results were more inconsistent than had been claimed (Mitchell et al., 1977). A third problem was that some questioned aspects of the methodology (Chinksy & Rappaport, 1970), such as how Truax and his colleagues calculated the reliability of the empathy measurements. Overall, the conclusion from these reanalyses was that the relationship between empathy in particular, and the therapeutic conditions in general, and therapeutic change was positive but weaker than originally thought. The idea that the three therapeutic conditions were both necessary and sufficient was held to be unsupported by the data. However, these conclusions have been contested by some Rogerians (Patterson, 1984; Watson, 1984). They have argued, among other things, that Truax's "objective" tape ratings of empathy, regard, and genuineness were not appropriate operational definitions of Rogers's "necessary and sufficient conditions" hypothesis. Rogers had stressed client perceptions of the therapeutic conditions. Evidence on the relationship between client perceptions of empathy and therapeutic outcome has generally been positive (Gurman, 1977).

Although there has been little recent research, what has been done has continued to find correlations between therapist empathy and outcome. Orlinsky et al. (1994) conclude that 54% of 115 studies done over many years show a positive relationship between empathy and outcome (a meta-analysis needs to be done, but a chi-square shows this to be significant at $p < .001$). The number rises for studies where empathy is measured with client perceptions (72%). For instance, Lorr (1965) found that clients' ratings of their therapist as "understanding" correlated more highly with improvement than any other variable. Orlinsky et al. also note that a related variable "communicative attunement" has been found to positively relate to outcome (we have borrowed and adapted the term *communicative attunement* for one of our categories of therapeutic empathy). Communicative attunement is the degree to which therapist communications are attuned to client communications. As an example, Sachse (1990) has found that therapist responses that respond to the centrality of the client's message are more likely to facilitate client process.

In other studies, Miller, Taylor, and West (1980) found that in an alcoholism treatment program therapist rank on empathy correlated .82 with outcome as measured 6 to 8 months later. Lafferty, Beutler, and Crago (1991) found that client ratings of empathy were the best predictor of therapist effectiveness. Burns and Nolen-Hoeksema (1991) found that the client's perception of therapist empathy correlated with outcome in cognitive therapy. Elliott, Clark, and Kemeny (1991) found that clients and therapists felt that being understood was the most important variable in therapy. Greenberg and Watson (in press) have shown that an empathically based client-centered therapy was effective in reducing depressive symptoms at termination and at follow-up. Vaillant (1994) reports that several studies have demonstrated the value of empathic responses versus confrontive responses in short-term dynamic therapy.

Nature of Empathy

Empathy can be studied either as a general attitudinal or "climate" variable, not equated with specific therapist responses, or in terms of specific dimensions of empathy responses and their potential specific effects. In looking at empathy as a general climate or attitudinal variable, one important question is: Is empathy unique or distinct from other positive qualities in the therapeutic relationship? Early research (Truax & Carkhuff, 1967) that used objective ratings of tapes found that empathy generally correlated positively with measures of unconditional positive regard and genuineness. However, there was also evidence that they did not always positively correlate.

However, earlier factor analyses of the Barrett-Lennard Relationship Inventory (Barrett-Lennard, 1986) suggested that empathy was a separate factor. On the other hand, a recent study on the Relationship Inventory found high correlations among regard, empathy, and congruence (Salvio, Beutler, Wood, & Engle, 1992). Salvio et al. also found that the Relationship Inventory correlated highly with a measure of the therapeutic alliance. These authors conclude that these two measures and their components may be measuring the same underlying factor, which they call "Strength of the Therapeutic Alliance." In other words, empathy may simply be a component of a general strength of therapeutic alliance factor.

In contrast, Horvath and Greenberg (1986) found that empathy correlated more highly with the "bond" component of the therapeutic alliance than with the task or goal component, suggesting some differentiation between empathy and different components of the alliance (Watson & Greenberg, 1994). Overall, these findings suggest that some sort of relationship exists between empathy and other positive qualities of the therapeutic relationship, including the therapeutic alliance, but the exact nature of the relationship has yet to be worked out.

Looking at research that takes a more differentiated view of empathy, Bachelor (1988) asked clients to report on their experience of empathy. She found that clients reported four different types of empathy: cognitive, affective, shared, and nurturant. Cognitive empathy was feeling that the therapist understood the client's subjective experience. Affective empathy was feeling that the therapist shared some of the clients' affective experience. Shared empathy was that the client experienced the therapist as demonstrating empathy through self-disclosure. Nurturant empathy was perceiving the therapist as nurturant, supportive, and attentive. She further found that clients were generally unable to identify what behaviors of the therapist led them to feel that a therapist was empathic and that experiences of empathy were not tied to any particular ways of therapist responding. Clients reported that empathy was helpful to them for a variety of reasons including self-validation, facilitation of self-exploration, and feelings of support and safety.

Barkham and Shapiro (1986) investigated therapist response modes associated with client's experience of empathy. They found that exploratory responses, in which therapists tried to understand clients' experience as the two cocreated an emerging, shared frame of reference, led clients to feel more understood than did either reflection or interpretation. On the other hand, Elliott (1986) reports results indicating that the experience of empathy could not be equated with specific response forms such as reflection, although, as we have noted, Elliott et al. (1982) did find some association between response forms and the client's experience of being understood.

Recently, the work of Greenberg and his colleagues (Greenberg & Elliott, Chapter 8, this volume) have begun to differentiate kinds of empathy and the kinds of therapeutic intentions that they serve. For instance, evocative empathy responses may be used to heighten and evoke experience to help clients work through problematic reactions (Rice & Saperia, 1984). Empathic prizing may be used to help clients who are feeling highly vulnerable, and empathic exploration may be used to help clients who are ready to explore their experience.

Gendlin and his colleagues (Gendlin, 1968; Klein, Mathieu-Coughlan, & Kiesler, 1986) have suggested that empathy is best characterized in experiential terms. Experiential responses are defined as responses that point to the immediate experience of the client, help symbolize it, and help carry it forward. On the basis of Gendlin's theorizing, a "therapist experiencing scale" has been developed. This scale rates the degree to which the therapist's responses engage the client's experiencing process. At present there is little research on this scale. However, in a conceptually related study, Tallman, Robinson, Kay, Harvey, and Bohart (1994) found in a therapy analogue that empathy responses phrased in abstract nonexperiential ways were responded to less quickly and rated less positively by clients than "experiential" empathy responses.

Sachse (1990) has studied depth of patient processing. He has developed a scale that rates patient processing of material from superfical to "deep" levels. He has argued that therapist responses should be viewed as "processing proposals," responses that move clients to deeper levels of processing. He found that therapist responses that were at a less complex or more superficial level than the client's did not facilitate the client's ability to go deeper. This was also true of therapist responses that were essentially interchangeable with the client's level of depth. He concluded that therapist's responses can deepen the client's exploratory process. This depends on the quality of the therapist's empathic understanding responses, and this is a function of the therapist responding to the centrality of the client's message.

In a therapy analogue study, Bohart et al. (1993) studied "present-centered" versus "future-oriented" empathy responses. Present-centered empathy responses were reflections that focused on the here and now experience of the client, whereas future-oriented empathy responses focused on the "trajectory" toward the future embedded in the client's current experience. They found future-oriented responses led clients to rate themselves as feeling more empowered after the short analogue session in comparison with present-centered responses.

Tausch (1988) studied the therapy responses of a cognitive therapist and Carl Rogers. It was found that the cognitive therapist's responses focused predominantly on the cognitions of the client and relatively little on the emotions. In contrast, Carl Rogers's responses were more balanced, with about two thirds focusing predominantly on cognitive aspects of the client's experiences and one third either on emotion or on both cognition and emotion. It was further found that client responses tended to follow suit. That is, with the cognitive therapist clients came to focus predominantly on their cognitions, whereas with Carl Rogers clients focused both on cognition and emotion.

In a similar manner, Brodley and Brody (1990) studied the empathic understanding responses of Carl Rogers. They found that 92% of Rogers's responses were what they called empathic checking responses, done by Rogers to check his understanding of the client. They also found, based on the client's responses, that in 99% of the cases where Rogers checked his understanding of the client's communication, he received confirmation from the client that he had understood. They also found that Rogers used feeling words in only 24% of his empathic responses. In 76% there were no feeling words. Instead, many responses referred to what Brodley and Brody have called "action of the personality" on the part of the client—subjective actions existing in the mind and experience of the person, such as "You realize it has lost that special significance" (p. 7). Brodley and Brody concluded that, for client-centered work, "it may be more accurate to refer to the therapist's goal of understanding the client's perceptions and the personal meanings of things to the client" (p. 9), rather than focusing on feelings.

In contrast to studying therapist empathy, therapist misunderstanding has recently come under investigation (Johnson et al., 1994; Johnson et al., 1995; Rennie, 1990; Rhodes, Hill, Thompson, & Elliott, 1994). For instance, Johnson et al. studied the effects of therapist misunderstandings through an interpersonal process-recall procedure. Clients identified episodes in therapy in which they felt misunderstood. It was found that feeling misunderstood was associated with a variety of negative emotions, such as feeling helpless, confused, embarrassed, and guilty. It was also found that in some cases, where the misunderstanding was worked through, clients reported feeling good afterwards. Johnson and colleagues speculate that the working through of misunderstandings could be a powerful and important part of therapy.

Similarly, Rennie (1990) studied how clients react to "discordant therapist operations," such as misunderstanding. Clients may be afraid of criticizing the therapist and so keep their feelings to themselves, they may pursue covert self-focused meaning paths without sharing them with the therapist, or they may try to put the therapist "off the scent" by changing the topic. How much of the client's reactions are shared with the therapist depends on the therapeutic relationship. Interestingly, Rennie notes that clients try to understand the therapist's frame of reference in making their decisions on how to respond to therapist interventions.

Is Empathy Primarily a Therapist-Provided Variable?

Some research has attempted to identify correlates of therapist empathy. Goldstein and Michaels (1985) review research suggesting that higher levels of cognitive functioning and flexibility relate positively to therapist empathy. They also cite research suggesting that levels of training, experience, and personal therapy have been found to relate to empathy.

However, it is not clear that the level of empathy provided is primarily a function of the therapist. Truax and Carkhuff (1967) argued that levels of empathy provided by the therapist did not vary significantly across clients. However, Gladstein et al. (1987) found that counselor-offered empathy was affected by client behaviors and that counselors offered more empathy with compliant clients (Ham, 1987). In a similar manner, Henry, Schacht, and Strupp (1986) found that the level of empathy provided by the therapist varied from client to client.

A related question is: Is empathy primarily a function of what the therapist says, or do the therapist's nonverbal behaviors contribute? Some research (e.g., Smith-Hanen, 1977; Tepper & Haase, 1978) found that client perceptions of empathy depended in part on a variety of therapist nonverbal behaviors. Tepper and Haase found that the nonverbal components accounted for twice as much of the variance as did the verbal message. However, their findings were based on ratings of very short therapy segments and may not generalize to clients' experience in real therapy. The question is important, however, and merits further research in deciding if empathy is primarily a background, relationship-building characteristic or whether empathic responses are specific interventions in their own right.

Conclusion

Much empirical work on the nature of empathy in psychotherapy needs to be done. At the present time about all that can be said is that there is a global relationship between client perceptions of therapist empathy and client outcome, and it is not clear what that means. The use of measures of empathy in more context-sensitive ways to study the moment-by-moment effects of empathy (i.e., when does which kind of empathy have what kind of effect) seems one important direction for research to take. Effects of different kinds of therapist empathy and of their different intentions seems important. Is empathy primarily a relationship builder, or does it have specific effects? Is there a difference between empathy and being compassionate and kind?

Second, at a more macro level it would seem worthwhile to study some of the hypothesized relationships between empathy and client outcome. For instance, using measures of the internalization of the functions of the self, the self-psychological hypothesis that therapist empathy facilitates self-structuralization seems like an important new direction to follow. The centrality and exploratory depth of empathy seem to be two important aspects that merit further study. We make further recommendations at the end of the final chapter of this volume.

EMPATHY IN DEVELOPMENTAL PSYCHOLOGY

Since our focus in this book is on empathy in psychotherapy, we shall only briefly comment on the study of empathy in developmental and social psychology and leave it to Feshbach to elaborate on this further in the following chapter. In these fields empathy has become an increasingly important topic. Most developmental researchers have been interested in studying the relationship between empathy and prosocial behavior, such as altruism and morality, and antisocial behavior, such as aggression (Eisenberg & Miller, 1987). These researchers tend to see empathy as having an emotional response similar to the response the other person is having. No strong distinction between empathy and sympathy is drawn. For instance, Hoffman (1987) sees empathy as responding affectively to the distress of another person, and Hoffman's interest has been in how that can lead to the development and practice of morality and altruism. For him, empathy is most basically affective, but cognitive factors play a role in mediating empathic experiences as the child matures. Empathy also has motivational properties in that it motivates altruistic and moral behavior.

Feshbach (1987) has proposed a three-component model of empathy, which includes the cognitive ability to discriminate affective cues in another, the more mature cognitive skills involved in taking the role or the perspective of another, and the ability to experience emotions. Once again, empathy is most centrally seen as the capacity to experience the emotions of the other.

Overall, research on empathy in developmental and social psychology has used a wide range of measures (see Feshbach, Chapter 2, this volume) and has found mixed results in the relationship of empathy to prosocial behavior. However, there does appear to be a relationship (Eisenberg & Miller, 1987). In addition, relationships between parental empathy, or the lack thereof, and various behavioral outcomes in children have also been found (Feshbach, Chapter 2, this volume; Feshbach, 1987).

Psychoanalytic Research on Empathy and Development

In the psychoanalytic literature, Stern (1985), Beebe (e.g., Beebe, Jaffe, & Lachmann, 1988), and others have begun to study the effects of attunements by the mother on the development of the child. Attunements are in the family of empathy-related constructs but are more similar to the form of empathy, which we have called communicative attunement above, than to empathy as a broad attempt to understand "where the client is coming from," or what we have called above "experience-near entry into the client's world." The mother trying to attune to the infant is not necessarily "trying to put herself in the shoes" of the infant. Rather, she is reading the infant's emotional and need states and reacting in an immediate, interactive way to confirm these states. For instance, if mother and infant are playing a game leading to increasing emotional arousal on both parts (for instance, giggling and laughing), an attuned mother will de-escalate her level of emotion-arousing interaction if the infant begins to exhibit signs that he or she is getting overloaded. Stern and Beebe and her colleagues suggest that it is such attuned or nonattuned interactions that create prerepresentational structures of expectancies for perceiving the world. Thus, a form of empathy is presumed to play an important role in how infants develop their initial models of interpersonal realities.

Psychotherapeutic Versus Developmental Views of Empathy

A major discrepancy exists between how writers on psychotherapy view empathy and how developmental psychologists view it (Eisenberg & Strayer, 1987; Gladstein et al. 1987). For developmental psychology, the core component of empathy is experiencing the same emotion as another (Olmstad, 1995). Some writers even argue that empathy should be distinguished from cognitive activities such as perspective taking (Olmstad). Other developmentalists include cognition in their models of empathy (Davis, 1993; Feshbach, 1987; Hoffman, 1987). Nonetheless, empathy is still primarily the ability to perceive and feel the emotions of another.

However, for psychotherapists, the emphasis has been on empathic understanding (Orlinsky et al., 1994). We have noted research showing that the majority of Carl Rogers's responses addressed themselves to understanding the personal meanings of the client's experience more than to predominantly emotional aspects. Emotional resonating or emotional sharing with the other can play a role in helping the therapist achieve empathy, but it works by enhancing the therapist's understanding of the client's subjective world or by facilitating the making of psychological contact. Furthermore, although therapeutic empathy is based on therapists' experiencing with the client, that experiencing can include many aspects, not just sharing similar emotions. To feel the same feelings, in fact, might be dangerous. It could lead to the therapist's emotionally over-identifying with the client. This could lead to counterproductive attempts to "rescue" the client or to a failure to differentiate the client's experience from that of the therapist, with the therapist imposing his or her view of the situation on the client. In this regard, both client-centered and psychodynamic therapists, in contrast to developmental psychologists, draw a sharp distinction between empathy and sympathy, usually explicitly cautioning the therapist against adopting a sympathic stance.

REFERENCES

Bachelor, A. (1988). How clients perceive therapist empathy: A content analysis of "received" empathy. *Psychotherapy, 25,* 227–240.

Barkham, M., & Shapiro, D. A. (1986). Counselor verbal response modes and experienced empathy. *Journal of Counseling Psychology, 33,* 3–10.

Barrett-Lennard, G. (1986). The Relationship Inventory now: Issues and advances in theory, method, and use. In L. Greenberg & W. Pinsof (Eds.), *The psychotherapeutic process* (pp. 439–476). New York: Guilford.

Barrett-Lennard, G. (1993). The phases and focus of empathy. *British Journal of Medical Psychology, 66,* 3–14.

Beck, A. T., Rush, A. J., Shaw, B. F., & Emery, G. (1979). *Cognitive therapy of depression.* New York: Guilford.

Beebe, B., Jaffe, J., & Lachmann, F. (1988). A dyadic systems view of communication. In N. Skolnick & S. Warshaw (Eds.), *Relational perspectives in psychoanalysis* (pp. 61–81). Hillsdale, NJ: Analytic Press.

Beutler, L. E., Crago, M., & Arizmendi, T. G. (1986). Therapist variables in psychotherapy process and outcome. In S. L. Garfield & A. E. Bergin (Eds.), *Handbook of psychotherapy and behavior change* (3rd. ed., pp. 257–310). New York: Wiley.

Beutler, L. E., Machado, P. P. P., & Neufeldt, S. A. (1994). Therapist variables. In A. E. Bergin & S. L. Garfield (Eds.), *Handbook of psychotherapy and behavior change* (4th ed., pp. 229–269). New York: Wiley.

Bohart, A. (1991). Empathy in client centered therapy: A contrast with psychoanalysis and self psychology. *Journal of Humanistic Psychology, 31,* 34–48.

Bohart, A., Humphrey, A., Magallanes, M., Guzman, R., Smiljanich, K., & Aguallo, S. (1993). Emphasizing the future in empathy responses. *Journal of Humanistic Psychology, 33,* 12–29.

Bolton, R. (1979). *People skills.* New York: Simon & Schuster.

Bordin, E. (1979). The generalizability of the psychoanalytic concept of the working alliance. *Psychotherapy: Theory, Research and Practice, 16,* 252–260.

Bozarth, J. D. (1984). Beyond reflection: Emergent modes of empathy. In R. F. Levant & J. M. Shlien (Eds.), *Client-centered therapy and the person-centered approach* (pp. 59–75). New York: Praeger.

Brodley, B. T. (1996). Empathic understanding and feelings in client-centered therapy. *The Person-Centered Journal, 3,* 22–30.

Brodley, B. T., & Brody, A. F. (1990, August). *Understanding client-centered therapy through interviews conducted by Carl Rogers.* Paper presented at the annual convention of the American Psychological Association, Boston, MA.

Buie, D. (1981a). Discussion. In J. Lichtenberg, M. Bornstein, & D. Silver (Eds.), *Empathy* (Vol. 1, pp. 129–136). Hillsdale, NJ: Analytic Press.

Buie, D. (1981b). Empathy: Its nature and limitations. *Journal of the American Psychoanalytic Association, 29,* 281–307.

Burns, D. D., & Nolen-Hoeksema, S. (1991). Coping styles, homework compliance, and the effectiveness of cognitive behavioral therapy. *Journal of Consulting and Clinical Psychology, 59,* 305–311.

Carkhuff, R. R. (1971). *The development of human resources.* New York: Holt, Rinehart, & Winston.

Carkhuff, R. R., & Berenson, B. (1967). *Beyond counseling and therapy.* New York: Holt, Rinehart, & Winston.

Caskey, N., Barker, C., & Elliott, R. (1984). Dual perspectives: Clients' and therapists' perceptions of therapist responses. *British Journal of Clinical Psychology, 23,* 281–290.

Chinsky, J. M., & Rappaport, J. (1970). A brief critique of the "accurate empathy" ratings. *Psychological Bulletin, 73,* 379–382.

Christensen, A., Jacobson, N. S., & Babcock, J. C. (1995). Integrative behavioral couple therapy. In N. S. Jacobson & A. S. Gurman (Eds.), *Clinical handbook of couple therapy* (pp. 31–64). New York: Guilford.

Cochrane, C. T. (1974). Development of a measure of empathic communication. *Psychotherapy: Theory, Research and Practice, 11,* 41–47.

Davis, M. H. (1993). *Empathy: A social-psychological approach.* New York: Brown & Benchmark.

Duan, C., & Hill, C. E. (1996). A critical review of empathy research. *Journal of Counseling Psychology, 43,* 261–274.

Egan, G. (1982). *The skilled helper* (2nd ed.). Monterey, CA: Brooks/Cole.

Eisenberg, N., & Miller, P. (1987). Empathy, sympathy, and altruism: empirical and conceptual links. In N. Eisenberg & J. Strayer (Eds.), *Empathy and development* (pp. 292–316). New York: Cambridge University Press.

Eisenberg, N., & Strayer, J. (1987). Critical issues in the study of empathy. In N. Eisenberg & J. Strayer (Eds.), *Empathy and development* (pp. 3–16). New York: Cambridge University Press.

Elliott, R. (1986). Interpersonal Process Recall (IPR) as a psychotherapy process research method. In L. S. Greenberg & W. M. Pinsof (Eds.), *The psychotherapeutic process* (pp. 503–528). New York: Guilford.

Elliott, R., Clark, C., & Kemeny, V. (1991, July). *Analyzing clients' postsession accounts of significant therapy events.* Paper presented at the Society for Psychotherapy Research, Lyon, France.

Elliott, R., Filipovich, H., Harrigan, L., Gaynor, J., Reimschuessel, C., & Zapadka, J. K. (1982). Measuring response empathy: The development of a multi-component rating scale. *Journal of Counseling Psychology, 29,* 379–387.

Feshbach, N. D. (1987). Parental empathy and child adjustment/maladjustment. In N. Eisenberg & J. Strayer (Eds.), *Empathy and development* (pp. 271–291). New York: Cambridge University Press.

Franks, C. M. (1994). Behavioral model. In V. B. Van Hasselt & M. Hersen (Eds.), *Advanced abnormal psychology* (pp. 93–110). New York: Plenum.

Gendlin, E. T. (1968). The experiential response. In E. Hammer (Ed.), *Use of interpretation in treatment* (pp. 208–227). New York: Grune & Stratton.

Gendlin, E. T. (1974). Client-centered and experiential psychotherapy. In D. A. Wexler & L. N. Rice (Eds.), *Innovations in client-centered therapy* (pp. 211–246). New York: Wiley.

Gladstein, G. A., & Associates. (1987). *Empathy and counseling: Explorations in theory and research.* New York: Springer-Verlag.

Goldstein, A. P., & Michaels, G. Y. (1985). *Empathy: Development, training, and consequences.* Hillsdale, NJ: Erlbaum.

Goleman, D. (1995). *Emotional intelligence.* New York: Bantam.

Goodman, G. (1984). SASHAtapes: Expanding options for help-intended communication. In D. Larson (Ed.), *Teaching psychological skills* (pp. 271–286). Monterey, CA: Brooks/Cole.

Greenberg, L. S., Elliott, R., & Lietaer, G. (1994). Research on experiential psychotherapies. In A. Bergin & S. Garfield (Eds.), *Handbook of psychotherapy and behavior change* (4th ed., pp. 509–539). New York: Wiley.

Greenberg, L. S., Leitaer, G., & Watson, J. (in press). *Experiential psychotherapy: Differential interventions.* New York: Guilford.

Greenberg, L. S., & Paivio, S. (in press). *Working with the emotions.* New York: Guilford.

Greenberg, L. S., Rice, L. N., & Elliott, R. (1993). *Facilitating emotional change: The moment-by-moment process.* New York: Guilford.

Greenberg, L. S., & Safran, J. D. (1987). *Emotion in psychotherapy.* New York: Guilford.

Greenberg, L. S., & Watson, J. (in press). Experiential therapy of depression: Differential effects of client-centered relationship and active experiential interventions. *Psychotherapy Research.*

Guerney, B. G. (1984). Relationship enhancement therapy and training. In D. Larson (Ed.), *Teaching psychological skills* (pp. 171–206). Monterey, CA: Brooks/Cole.

Gurman, A. S. (1977). The patient's perception of the therapeutic relationship. In A. S. Gurman & A. M. Razin (Eds.), *Effective psychotherapy* (pp. 503–543). New York: Pergamon.

Ham, M. A. (1987). Client behavior and counselor empathic performance. In G. A. Gladstein & Associates (Eds.), *Empathy and counseling: Explorations in theory and research* (pp. 31–50). New York: Springer-Verlag.

Hargrove, D. S. (1974). Verbal interaction analysis of empathic and nonempathic responses of therapists. *Journal of Consulting and Clinical Psychology, 42,* 305.

Harvey, J. H., Orbuch, T. L., Chwalisz, K. D., & Garwood, G. (1991). Coping with sexual assault: The roles of account-making and confiding. *Journal of Traumatic Stress, 4,* 515–531.

Hart, J. (1970). The development of client-centered therapy. In J. T. Hart & T. M. Tomlinson (Eds.), *New directions in client-centered therapy* (pp. 3–22). Boston: Houghton-Mifflin.

Havens, L. (1986). *Making contact: Uses of language in psychotherapy.* Cambridge, MA: Harvard University Press.

Henry, W. P., Schacht, T. E., & Strupp, H. H. (1986). Structural analysis of social behavior: Application to a study of interpersonal process in differential psychotherapeutic outcome. *Journal of Consulting and Clinical Psychology, 54,* 27–31.

Hoffman, M. L. (1987). The contribution of empathy to justice and moral judgment. In N. Eisenberg & J. Strayer (Eds.), *Empathy and development* (pp. 47–80). New York: Cambridge University Press.

Horvath, A. O., & Greenberg, L. S. (1986). The development of the Working Alliance Inventory. In L. S. Greenberg & W. M. Pinsof (Eds.), *The psychotherapeutic process: A research handbook* (pp. 529–556). New York: Guilford.

Horvath, A. O., & Greenberg, L. S. (1994). *The working alliance.* New York: Wiley-Interscience.

Johnson, B., Geller, J. D., & Rhodes, R. (1994). Nonverbal profile analysis in psychotherapy: Markers of client-identified misunderstandings. *Psychotherapy Bulletin, 29,* 54–59.

Johnson, B., Taylor, E., D'Elia, J., Tzanetos, D., Rhodes, R., & Geller, J. D. (1995). The emotional consequences of therapeutic misunderstandings. *Psychotherapy Bulletin, 30,* 54–58.

Kagan, N. (1984). Interpersonal process recall: Basic methods and recent research. In D. Larson (Ed.), *Teaching psychological skills* (pp. 229–244). Monterey, CA: Brooks/Cole.

Klein, M., Mathieu-Coughlan, P., & Kiesler, D. J. (1986). The experiencing scales. In L. Greenberg & W. Pinsof (Eds.), *The psychotherapeutic process* (pp. 21–72). New York: Guilford.

Kohut, H. (1971). *The analysis of the self.* New York: International Universities Press.

Kohut, H. (1977). *The restoration of the self.* New York: International Universities Press.

Kohut, H. (1984). *How does analysis cure?* Chicago: University of Chicago Press.

Kurtz, R. R., & Grummon, D. L. (1972). Different approaches to the measurement of therapist empathy and their relationship to therapy outcomes. *Journal of Consulting and Clinical Psychology, 39,* 106–115.

LaCrosse, M. B. (1977). Comparative perceptions of counselor behavior: A replication and extension. *Journal of Counseling Psychology, 24,* 464–471.

Lafferty, P., Beutler, L. E., & Crago, M. (1991). Differences between more and less effective psychotherapist: A study of select therapist variables. *Journal of Consulting and Clinical Psychology, 57,* 76–80.

Lorr, M. (1965). Client perceptions of therapists. *Journal of Consulting Psychology, 29,* 146–149.

Luborsky, L. (1984). *Principles of psychoanalytic psychotherapy.* New York: Basic Books.

Mahoney, M. (1991). *Human change processes.* New York: Basic Books.

Mahrer, A. R. (1996). *The complete guide to experiential psychotherapy.* New York: Wiley.

Mahrer, A. R., & Fairweather, D. R. (1993). What is "experiencing"? A critical review of meanings and applications in psychotherapy. *The Humanistic Psychologist, 21,* 2–25.

Miller, W. R., Taylor, C. A., & West, J. C. (1980). Focused versus broad-spectrum behavior therapy for problem drinkers. *Journal of Consulting and Clinical Psychology, 48,* 590–601.

Mitchell, K. M., Bozarth, J. D., & Krauft, C. C. (1977). A reappraisal of the therapeutic effectiveness of accurate empathy, nonpossessive warmth, and genuineness. In A. S. Gurman & A. N. Razin (Eds.), *Effective psychotherapy.* New York: Pergamon.

Mitchell, S. (1988). *Relational concepts in psychoanalysis.* Cambridge, MA: Harvard University Press.

Neimeyer, R. A., & Mahoney, M. J. (Eds.). (1995). *Constructivism in psychotherapy.* Washington, DC: American Psychological Association.

Olmstad, B. L. (1995). *Cognitive appraisal, emotion, and empathy.* Mahwah, NJ: Erlbaum.

Orlinsky, D. E., Grawe, K., & Parks, B. K. (1994). Process and outcome in psychotherapy—noch einmal. In A. E. Bergin & S. L. Garfield (Eds.), *Handbook of psychotherapy and behavior change* (4th ed., pp. 270–378). New York: Wiley.

Patterson, C. H. (1984). Empathy, warmth, and genuineness: A review of reviews. *Psychotherapy, 21,* 431–438.

Pennebaker, J. W. (1990). *Opening up.* New York: William Morrow.

Raskin, N. J. (1974). *Studies of psychotherapeutic orientation: Ideology and practice* (Research Monograph No. 1). Orlando, FL: American Academy of Psychotherapists.

Rennie, D. L. (1990). Toward a representation of the client's experience of the psychotherapy hour. In G. Lietaer, J. Rombauts, & R. Van Balen (Eds.), *Client-centered and experiential therapy in the nineties* (pp. 155–172). Leuven, Belgium: Leuven University Press.

Rhodes, R. H., Hill, D. E., Thompson, B. J., & Elliott, R. (1994). Client retrospective recall of resolved and unresolved misunderstanding events. *Journal of Counseling Psychology, 41,* 473–483.

Rice, L. N., & Saperia, E. P. (1984). Task analysis and the resolution of problematic reactions. In L. N. Rice & L. S. Greenberg (Eds.), *Patterns of change.* New York: Guilford.

Rogers, C. R. (1957). The necessary and sufficient conditions of therapeutic personality change. *Journal of Consulting Psychology, 21,* 95–103.

Rogers, C. R. (1959). A theory of therapy, personality and interpersonal relationships as developed in the client-centered framework. In S. Koch (Ed.), *Psychology: A study of a science* (Vol. 3, pp. 184–256). New York: McGraw-Hill.

Rogers, C. R. (1986). Reflection of feelings. *Person-Centered Review, 2,* 11–13.

Rogers, C. R., & Sanford, R. C. (1984). Client-centered psychotherapy. In H. I. Kaplan & B. J. Sadock (Ed.), *Comprehensive textbook of psychiatry* (Vol. 4, pp. 1374–1388). Baltimore: Williams & Wilkins.

Sachse, R. (1990). Concrete interventions are crucial: The influence of the therapist's processing proposals on the client's intrapersonal exploration in client-centered therapy. In G. Lietaer, J. Rombauts, & R. Van Balen (Eds.), *Client-centered and experiential psychotherapy in the nineties* (pp. 295–308). Leuven, Belgium: Leuven University Press.

Safran, J. D., & Segal, Z. V. (1990). *Interpersonal process in cognitive therapy.* New York: Basic Books.

Salvio, M. A., Beutler, L. E., Wood, J. M., & Engle, D. (1992). The strength of the therapeutic alliance in three treatments for depression. *Psychotherapy Research, 2,* 31–36.

Shapiro, T. (1984). Empathy: A critical reevaluation. In J. Lichtenberg, M. Bornstein, & D. Silver (Eds.), *Empathy* (Vol. 1, pp. 103–129). Hillsdale, NJ: Analytic Press.

Sloane, R. B., Staples, F. R., Cristol, A. H., Yorkston, N. J., & Whipple, K. (1975). *Psychotherapy versus behavior therapy.* Cambridge, MA: Harvard University Press.

Smith-Hanen, S. S. (1977). Effects of nonverbal behaviors on judged levels of counselor warmth and empathy. *Journal of Counseling Psychology, 24,* 87–91.

Snyder, M. (1992). The meaning of empathy: Comments on Hans Strupp's case of Helen R. *Psychotherapy, 29,* 318–322.

Snyder, M. (1994). The development of social intelligence in psychotherapy: Empathic and dialogic processes. *Journal of Humanistic Psychology, 34,* 84–108.

Stern, D. (1985). *The interpersonal world of the infant.* New York: Basic Books.

Stiles, W. B. (1986). Development of a taxonomy of verbal response modes. In L. S. Greenberg & W. M. Pinsof (Eds.), *The psychotherapeutic process* (pp. 161–200). New York: Guilford.

Stolorow, R., & Atwood, G. E. (1992). *Contexts of being.* Hillsdale, NJ: Analytic Press.

Strupp, H. H., & Binder, J. L. (1984). *Psychotherapy in a new key.* New York: Basic Books.

Tallman, K., Robinson, E., Kay, D., Harvey, S., & Bohart, A. (1994, August). *Experiential and non-experiential Rogerian therapy: An analogue study.* Paper presented at the annual Convention of the American Psychological Association, Los Angeles.

Tausch, R. (1988). The relationship between emotions and cognitions: Implications for therapist empathy. *Person-Centered Review, 3,* 277–291.

Tepper, D. T., & Haase, R. F. (1978). Verbal and nonverbal communication of facilitative conditions. *Journal of Counseling Psychology, 25,* 35–44.

Truax, C. B., & Carkhuff, R. R. (1967). *Toward effective counseling and psychotherapy.* Chicago: Aldine.

Truax, C. B., & Mitchell, K. M. (1971). Research on certain therapist interpersonal skills in relation to process and outcome. In A. E. Bergin & S. L. Garfield (Eds.), *Handbook of psychotherapy and behavior change* (1st ed., pp. 299–344). New York: Wiley.

Vaillant, L. M. (1994). The next step in short-term dynamic psychotherapy: A clarification of objectives and techniques in an anxiety-regulating model. *Psychotherapy, 31,* 642–655.

Wachtel, P. (1993). *Therapeutic communication.* New York: Guilford.

Watson, J., & Greenberg, L. S. (1994). The alliance in experiential therapy: Enacting the relationship conditions. In A. Horvath & L. S. Greenberg (Eds.), *The working alliance: Theory, research, and practice.* New York: Wiley-Interscience.

Watson, J., & Greenberg, L. S. (1996). Emotion and cognition in experiential therapy: A dialectical constructivist perspective. In H. Rosen & K. Kuehlwein (Eds.), *Constructing realities* (pp. 253–276). San Francisco: Jossey-Bass.

Watson, N. (1984). The empirical status of Rogers' hypotheses of the necessary and sufficient conditions for effective psychotherapy. In R. F. Levant & J. M. Shlien (Eds.), *Client-centered therapy and the person-centered approach* (pp. 17–40). New York: Praeger.

Wexler, D. A., & Rice, L. N. (Eds.). (1974). *Innovations in client-centered therapy* (pp. 49–116). New York: Wiley.

Wheeler, G. (1991). *Gestalt therapy reconsidered.* New York: Gardner Press.

Wispé, L. (1987). History of the concept of empathy. In N. Eisenberg & J. Strayer (Eds.), *Empathy and development* (pp. 17–37). New York: Cambridge University Press.

Yontef, G. (1994). *Awareness, dialogue, and process: Essays in Gestalt therapy.* New York: Gestalt Journal Press.

2

EMPATHY: THE FORMATIVE YEARS IMPLICATIONS FOR CLINICAL PRACTICE

NORMA DEITCH FESHBACH

David, observing his friend Alex searching for a lost dog, experiences a twinge of sadness and offers to help Alex look for the dog. David is manifesting empathy.

A mother takes her 3-year-old to the pediatrician for an inoculation. The mother winces as her daughter is administered the injection and comments that injections can really be painful. On returning home, the daughter eagerly asks her mother to read to her from her favorite book. As the daughter smilingly responds to the mother's reading, the mother beams and remarks how comforting and fun it is to listen to stories! In each instance the mother has responded empathically to her child's feelings and has communicated her empathic response to the child.

Empathy is a basic form of social communication that can occur in many different social contexts. The examples given above reflect rather simple social contexts in which manifestations of empathic communication occurred. The social and emotional situation eliciting empathy can become quite complex depending on the feelings experienced by the observed and the relationship of the observed to the observer. The presence and degree of empathy with a student who aspires to success but is fearful of risking failure may differ for that student's parent, teacher, friend, and therapist. Empathic responsiveness in this context requires greater cognitive and affective sophistication. Regardless of the complexity of the social situation and context, empathy plays an important role in social interaction. Empathy can be conceived of as an interaction between any two individuals, with one experiencing and sharing the feeling of the other. This shared affective correspondence can occur in any interpersonal interaction: between parent and child, between teacher and student, between psychotherapist and client, between friends, and even between strangers.

Contemporary psychological literature reflects the importance of the process or construct of empathy for the development of the child and for the psychotherapeutic situation. However, theory and research bearing on the role of empathy in the child's development and that bearing on the role of empathy in psychotherapy have largely followed two independent paths. The two separate streams have rarely intersected. This is unfortunate because results obtained from social, developmental, and educational psychology investigations could illuminate issues and problems presented by the client, potentially informing the psychotherapist regarding optimal therapeutic interventions for particular clients. Another critical area of mutual interest relates to issues bearing on therapist attributes that maximize effective treatment outcomes. Factors that contribute to environmental influences on empathy, and empathy-related characteristics and behaviors—a research thrust of developmentalists—are also of reciprocal concern.

Also, the psychotherapeutic context is potentially an ideal arena to study the empathic process and to evaluate the role of empathy in informing the therapist, the role of empathy or the lack of empathy in the client's socialization history, and the role of empathy as a positive force in the mental health status of the client. I hope the twain will meet.

This chapter will be primarily devoted to issues of empathy as they have emerged in developmental psychology, including the following: the various meanings of the concept; its biological, cognitive, and affective roots; its socialization antecedents; theoretical anticipated correlates such as aggression and prosocial behavior, as well as additional cognitive and personal correlates; empathy's role as a protective factor; and measurement issues and the training of empathy. I will draw heavily on studies carried out in our research laboratory at the University of California, Los Angeles, primarily with children and sometimes with parents. Where possible and appropriate, the implications of the developmental literature for the clinical enterprise will be discussed.

THE CONSTRUCT OF EMPATHY

Empathy is frequently referred to as an elusive concept, difficult to define and even more difficult to measure. The multidimensionality of the construct and the internal properties of its components make it less amenable to traditional methods of study and investigation. Although it shares with the study of emotion similar problems regarding investigation and definition, the complexity of the construct of empathy increases the diversity of its meaning. Also ambiguous are the various roles attributed to empathy in the social development of the child and even to its place in the social fabric of our society. Empathy has been linked by theory or research to have a regulatory effect on aggression; a motivating effect on prosocial behaviors such as generosity, cooperation, helping, and other altruistic actions; a facilitating effect on communication and social relationships; an organizing role in development and adjustment. Perhaps, as a consequence, the definition of empathy has been confounded with its functions, the effects of empathy often becoming interwoven with the concept.

Empathy has also been likened to compassion, love, nurturance, caring, altruism, and social understanding. In the psychological literature, as well as the popular literature, empathy and sympathy are often used synonymously. Occasionally, the difference is carefully articulated (Eisenberg, Shea, Carlo, & Knight, 1991). For the very young child, manifestations of distress are sometimes labeled as empathy (Zahn-Waxler & Radke-Yarrow, 1982) and cited by others as evidence of its congenital beginnings (Hoffman, 1982). As we have indicated elsewhere (Feshbach & Feshbach, 1986), empathy in humans may have its origins in the distress behaviors manifested by some of our mammalian forebears in response to the distress of another individual to whom they are attached. But empathy in humans, early in the developmental process, becomes a more complex phenomenon, involving aspects of the child's cognitive and emotional development. Although in some individuals empathy may appear to be an almost automatic primitive process, for most it is a consequence of learning, socialization experiences, and social interaction.

In general, empathy refers to an emotional response that emanates from the emotional state of another individual, and although empathy is defined as a shared emotional response, it is contingent on cognitive as well as emotional factors. This definition is compatible with but not identical to the various developmental conceptions of the phenomenon. In addition, many but not all theorists distinguish empathy from sympathy, defining the latter as consisting of feelings of sorrow or concern for others (Eisenberg, Fabes, et al., 1991; Feshbach, 1978; Hoffman, 1982; Zahn-Waxler & Radke-Yarrow, 1990). Both empathy and sympathy are distinguished from personal distress, an emotional state that is characterized by anxiety and aversion to another's pain. Hoffman (1982) and Zahn-Waxler and Radke-Yarrow (1990) distinguish mature empathy from personal distress but equate personal distress with empathy in the toddler (Zahn-Waxler & Radke-Yarrow, 1990) and with empathy in the infant (Hoffman, 1982).

The age at which empathy emerges is another critical issue in understanding and studying empathic responsiveness in children. Is empathy innate—present at birth—albeit in a more rudimentary form? Because the role and salience of the cognitive component of empathy varies in different theoretical approaches so does the age at which empathy is thought to be present. Self–other differentiation appears to be a requirement for empathy to occur in the writings of Eisenberg (Eisenberg, Fabes, et al., 1991), Feshbach (1982), and Zahn-Waxler and Radke-Yarrow (1990) but not for Hoffman (1982).

THE STRUCTURE OF EMPATHY

Systematic investigations of the development of empathy in children are relatively recent. Theoretical conceptions of empathy have varied in crude parallel with variations in dominant theoretical themes in psychology. Major theoretically controversial issues regarding empathy have been concerned with cognitive versus affective mediators, degree of cognitive complexity entailed in the empathic response, biological versus socialization roots, trait–state of the construct, and stage–age of early manifestations of empathy. What empathy is, does, and relates to is very much a function of a particular theoretical position and a particular procedure of measurement. In this regard, it may be noted that current conceptions of empathy reflect increasing consensus regarding its defining features.

Early formulations of empathy were predominantly cognitive (Mead, 1934) or affective (Berger, 1962; McDougall, 1908; Stotland, 1969; Sullivan, 1953). Later cognitive definitions conceptualized empathy in terms of role taking, perspective talking, or social comprehension. Formulations and descriptions of measures used in these early cognitive approaches to measuring empathy in children are found in the writings of Borke (1973); Chandler (1973); Chandler and Greenspan (1972); Chandler, Greenspan, and Barenboim (1974); Deutsch and Madle (1975); and Shantz (1975).

The theoretical controversy that occurred in the 1970s, when research on children's empathy first began to flourish, as to whether the nature of the internal response was cognitive or affective has subsided. Today the general consensus is that empathy entails both affective and cognitive elements, the relative role of each varying with the situation, age and personal characteristics of the child (Eisenberg, Fabes, et al., 1991; Feshbach, 1972, 1978, 1982; Hoffman, 1982; Zahn-Waxler & Radke-Yarrow, 1990). Although empathy is defined as a shared emotional response between observer and other person, it is contingent on cognitive factors. In the integrative cognitive–affective model I have proposed elsewhere (Feshbach, 1975a, 1978), the affective empathy reaction is postulated to be a function of three component factors: (a) the cognitive ability to discriminate affective cues in others; (b) the more mature cognitive skill involved in assuming the perspective and role of another person; and (c) emotional responsiveness, that is, that the affective ability to experience emotions (Feshbach, 1972,

1975a, 1978; Feshbach & Roe, 1968). Implicit in this and other models of empathy is the critical requirement of differentiation of self from object.

Hoffman's (1982, 1984) developmental model of empathy also has three components—cognitive, affective, and motivational—and focuses on empathic responsiveness to distress in others as the motivation for altruistic behaviors. For Hoffman, empathic arousal is already reflected in infant behavior, and he ascribes reflexive and innate origins to the emergence of empathy. Empathy is also acquired through associative, conditioning experiences and through imagination. Within this approach, empathic behavior is primarily affective but subsequently becomes transformed when the cognitive system of the child develops (Hoffman, 1982).

Eisenberg and her colleagues (Eisenberg, Shea, et al., 1991), building on the Feshbach (1978; Feshbach & Roe, 1968) and Hoffman (1982, 1984) models, further delineate four modes of cognitive responding: conditioning–association, labeling, retrieving elaborated cognitive network, and role taking. There is only modest empirical support for this hierarchial delineation of the cognitive components of empathy. However, there is some empirical support between role taking and empathy and between role taking and sympathy (Toi & Batson, 1982).

THE MEASUREMENT OF EMPATHY IN CHILDREN

Although interest in empathy that focuses on the sharing of another person's feelings has had a long history, interest in early emergence and development has occurred only during these past two decades. Research in this area has recently burgeoned, yet there is still a wide hiatus between the critical role afforded to empathy in regard to the child's cognitive, affective, and social development and the database that provides information on many theoretical and developmental issues. Because of the inferential nature of the task, assessing empathy is very difficult. A variety of procedures, varying in modality and orientation, have been developed. Inconsistencies in the literature relating empathy to other variables may be in part attributed to measurement matters.

Although there are a growing number of assessment procedures for children and adolescent empathy, we are still striving for a measure that fully taps the internal, multidimensional nature of the construct. Assessment procedures for children's empathy can be classified in a number of ways. They can be categorized as primarily cognitive (e.g., Borke, 1973; Chandler, 1973); as primarily affective (Bryant, 1982); as primarily integrative (Davis, 1983; Davis & Franzoi, 1991; Feshbach, 1980; Feshbach & Roe, 1968; Strayer, 1987); as predictive (Dymond, 1949) and as situational (Borke, 1973; Feshbach, 1980). They can be categorized on the basis of stimulus modality such as stories (Borke, 1973); audio tapes (Deutsch & Madle,

1975; Rothenberg, 1970); cartoons (Chandler, 1973); paper and pencil (Bryant, 1982; Feshbach, Socklowski, & O'Leary, 1991); slides and narration (Feshbach & Roe, 1968); and audio-video tape; (Feshbach, 1980, 1982). They can also be categorized by type of response modality, including reflexive crying (Sagi & Hoffman, 1976) and self-report (Borke, 1973; Bryant, 1982; Feshbach, 1980, 1982; Feshbach & Roe, 1968). Hoffman (1982) has categorized empathy measures as automatic (including such parameters as skin conductance and heartrate); somatic (facial expression, posture, and gaze); and verbal indexes (including both pictorial stimuli and questionnaires). Eisenberg and Lennon (1983), on the other hand, organize extant measures as story–picture; psychological; facial, gestural, or vocal indexes; and self-or-other report measures.

More recently, measures of physiological arousal such as heart rate and electro-dermal responses are being used to assess empathy (Eisenberg, Fabes, Schaller, & Miller, 1989). In addition, facial-musculature responsiveness to affective states in others are being coded on the basis of neuro-anatomical systems (Brothers, 1989, 1990; Levenson & Rief, 1992). These physiological- and neuroscience-based procedures are being hailed by many as more "objective" measures of empathy. In my judgment, these more "objective" measures contribute to the assessment of empathy but, in themselves, do not resolve the problem of measuring empathy. As past research using psycho-physiological measures of emotion have demonstrated, there are considerable individual differences in the pattern of physiological response to an emotion arousing stimulus. Therefore, one would anticipate similar individual differences in physiological manifestations of empathy. More important, the meaning of physiological measures is provided by the "subjective" reports and behavioral concomitants associated with the physiological response.

In summary, the breadth of measures used to evaluate children's empathy is expanding like the research base itself. The measures themselves vary in focus, stimulus characteristics, and response modality. Perhaps a multimeasure approach to its assessment combining "subjective" self reports and "objective" physiological measures is not only inevitable but also mandatory. Such an approach allows for differentiation between affective reactions that result from emotional contagion, projection, and loss of self–other boundaries from empathy that reflects cognitive understanding and discriminating emotional responsiveness. The ambiguity and inconsistencies in obtained relationships between empathy and other behaviors discussed below may be a function of differences in measures used to evaluate empathy, in the general problems inherent in the measurement of empathy, and in the validity of the psychological relationship itself.

The definition and theoretical model of empathy proposed in this chapter and that has guided the more recent developmental research on empathy asserts that empathy has both cognitive and affective components.

This conception of empathy differs in an important respect from the original Rogerian concept of therapist empathy that prevailed for many years. For Rogers (1961), therapeutic empathy entailed taking the perspective and role of the client. The therapist displays empathy by communicating a perception of the client's situation as the client perceives it. Also, in Rogerian usage, there is the related implication that empathy is a skill that enables the therapist to assume the perspective of the client.

The developmental usage of empathy is in accord with the Rogerian usage but with the important caveat that affect does not enter into the Rogerian model of empathy. Whether it is clinically important for the therapist to share, in a controlled, bounded manner, the affective experience of the client is an issue that needs to be explored in clinical research.

In my judgment, the incorporation of the affective component in the therapist's responses is likely to enhance the effectiveness of the therapeutic interchange. The patient should experience the therapist's efforts at empathic communication as more genuine. At the same time, the empathic feeling component may provide the therapist with an important cue as to feelings and perceptions of the client that may have been apprehended but not fully cognized by the therapist. One may raise a concern regarding the possible emotional burden that the experience of shared affect may create for the therapist. This would be the case if the therapist fails to maintain self boundaries, with excessive affective sharing being the consequence. However, the maintenance of clear boundaries between therapist and client that the assumption of empathy entails allows for a modulated, controlled sharing of affect. The latter may result in some experience of pain but not so intense or sustained as to interfere with the therapist's functioning.

THE EMERGENCE OF EMPATHY

The position one assumes regarding the age–stage emergence of empathy or "empathylike" behavior is controversial and depends to some extent on one's theoretical concept of empathy. Innate–physiological versus environmental–socialization accounts of empathy roughly correspond to the emphasis placed on the affective–spontaneous or the cognitive–reflective component of empathy. Although the contemporary concept of empathy is integrative and synthetic, including both cognitive and affective facets, the relative salience of each varies markedly.

One cannot easily turn to empirical data for a clear picture of the ontogenetic pattern of empathy. Research findings are inconsistent and vary with the definition of the construct and the measurement instrument. There are only a few longitudinal studies that have focused on empathic behavior as a main variable (Eisenberg, Fabes, Schaller, Carlo, & Miller, 1991; Zahn-Waxler & Radke-Yarrow, 1982). Infant responsiveness to the crying of other infants has been noted in infants as young as 2 weeks by a number of investigators (Buhler, 1930; Sagi & Hoffman, 1976). Other studies conducted with infants 6 months and older also reflect an awareness by many babies of the emotional distress of others (Radke-Yarrow, Zahn-Waxler, & Chapman, 1983). Studies concerned with differentiation of affective cues, similarly reflect that, before 1 year of age, infants can respond differentially to faces depicting differential affective states.

A variety of studies reflect some facet of empathy or a related behavior to distress signs in others during the preschool years (Radke-Yarrow et al., 1983). Zahn-Waxler and Radke-Yarrow's (1982) observations of toddler's responses to naturalistic and simulated distresses indicate that by age 2, children respond in a differentiated prosocial fashion to cues of emotional distress in others.

In an effort to study empathy and caring in a naturalistic setting, we observed preschool children's responses to peer crying in day-care settings (Phinney, Feshbach, & Farver, 1986). In 80% of the cases, crying was ignored by peers. Prosocial responses occurred in 13.4% of the events and were divided approximately equally among the following categories: approaches, comments, mediates, and consoles. Responses to crying were most significantly related to whether the cause of crying was peer- or adult-related or whether the child was alone at the time of the incident. These findings are more constricted than those reported by Zahn-Waxler, Radke-Yarrow, and King (1979), in which somewhat younger children were included and the distress incidents were manifested in the context of the child's home and reported by the mothers.

The most impressive empirical support for the early emergence of empathy is reflected in the studies carried out by Zahn-Waxler and Radke-Yarrow (1982). In their studies very young children exhibited empathylike behaviors. We refer to these behaviors as empathylike because many of the behaviors exhibited by the toddlers could easily be categorized as helping and altruistic. There appears to be a close theoretical and empirical relationship between empathy and prosocial behavior (Feshbach, 1982; Feshbach & Feshbach, 1987). However, empathy is distinct and theoretically should not be considered as synonymous with helping, caring, sharing, and other prosocial behavior. On the basis of their and other empirical findings, Zahn-Waxler and Radke-Yarrow (1990) believe that children at 2 years of age reflect a pattern of competencies and cognitive capacities that facilitate the manifestations of empathy, cognitive capacities, emotional capacity, and the behavioral repertoire to alleviate discomfort in others.

The question of the ontogenetic pattern of empathic development is unresolved. If the requirement is that the affective response reflect cognitive role-taking skills, then empathic responsiveness emerges during the preschool period. If infant cries to peer crying is considered as empathic behavior, rather than behavioral contagion, then empathy can be said to emerge almost congenitally. Is this latter behavior "true" empathy or a precursor to later empathic behavior? One's theoretical stance about the nature of empathy determines one's answer to this question about the ontogeny of empathy.

In spite of the equivocalness of the data regarding the emergence of empathy, a number of generalizations can be made. Children at a very early age discriminate emotional signs in others. A cluster of empathy-related skills appear very early in the child's development but become more differentiated and purposeful with additional years. Children at any age vary in empathic responsiveness, the source of which may be biologically–temperamentally or situationally–environmentally determined.

SOCIALIZATION ANTECEDENTS OF EMPATHY

A number of issues and questions regarding socialization influences have been of interest to researchers of children's empathy. Is there a cluster of parental child-training practices and attitudes that enhance the development of empathy in children? Are these effects similar for boys and girls? How does empathy relate to other parental child-training techniques? What are the effects of a high degree of parental empathy or a low degree of parental empathy on the child's social and emotional development?

Is empathic parenting positive for the child? According to the theoretical model I have presented, an empathic parent should be more understanding of a child's perspective and feeling than the parent low in empathy and be less punitive because pain inflicted on one's child will be vicariously shared and experienced by the parent. Excessive parental empathy can be damaging if it blocks the parent from appropriating child-training behavior, if it fosters intrusiveness, and if it is self-centered rather than child-centered. Thus, the affective response of the parent to the child's emotional experience can have divergent consequences for the child's development. If the parent's emotional reaction is exaggerated and it arises out of diffuse boundaries between parent and child, the child's socio-emotional development will be impeded. However, if the affective response is modulated, it has a positive impact on both parent and child.

For the parent, empathy can amplify and strengthen the cognitive understanding that gave rise to the shared affective response. For the child, it serves as a cue that the parent comprehends and shares the child's experience. In addition to facilitating understanding of the child and sensitivity to the child's feelings, parental empathy can influence the child's development of self through validation and reinforcement of the child's experiences.

Overall, empathy should function as a positive influence in the socialization process and should facilitate the child's development of adaptive behaviors. Moreover, parental empathy does not function in isolation from other parental attributes but should be associated with parental warmth, sensitivity, low punitiveness, and positive involvement with the child. Parental empathy should also affect the attachment relationship.

The research findings that I will present reflect the fact that empathy in parents is an integral part of a constellation of socialization factors. The research strategy that I have followed in my investigations of parental empathy has had two major directions. One direction has been the study of the relationship of parental empathy to parental personality and socialization attributes to which parental empathy should be theoretically linked (Feshbach & Feshbach, 1987). The second has been an examination of child attributes and behaviors that theoretically should be influenced by the degree of parental empathy (Feshbach, 1987). In addition, in some studies, the relationship between child attributes and parental attributes that are empirically or theoretically linked to parental empathy were examined, this latter approach constituting a closely related third direction in our research program (Feshbach, 1975b). To facilitate our study of parent empathy, a self-report measure was developed in which attitudes toward spouses as well as children were assessed (Feshbach, 1987, 1995).

Four investigations were carried out. The first examined the relationship between father and mother socialization practices and empathy in 6- and 7-year-old boys and girls (Feshbach, 1975b). The second study compared attitudes and behaviors of preschoolers and their mothers with a history of physical abuse and clinic attendance to those of controls (Feshbach & Howes, 1995). A third study looked at family and socialization practices in fathers and mothers and the child's development at age 9 to 11 (Feshbach & Feshbach, 1987). The fourth study was concerned with the relationships among maternal empathy, socialization practices, and child empathy in 4-year-olds (Feshbach, Socklowski, & Rose, 1996).

A summary of the findings from the four investigations reflect a consistency across studies regarding the relationship between parent empathy and other significant parent attributes and training behaviors as well as between parent empathy and child empathy. In one or more studies, maternal empathy is linked to other parent attributes as maternal involvement, affection, low hostility, low punitiveness, low inhibition of emotions, nurturance, acceptance, and low repressiveness. In contrast, low maternal empathy relates to such maternal and family attributes as hostility, punitiveness, repression, restrictiveness, low autonomy, family conflict and dysfunction, and even child abuse. Moreover, maternal empathy appears to influence important child characteristics, including and transcending empathy. Empathy in children is related to parent empathy and is also related to parent behaviors that are linked to parent empathy.

Mothers low in empathy are more likely to be the parents of children who show greater aggression, hyperactivity, depression, and anxiety. Moreover, children of mothers of low maternal empathy are more likely to be less compliant and less self-controlled and to show less positive and more negative affect. In addition to reflecting less psychoneurotic symptoms, children of high empathy mothers appear to be higher achievers, happier, and certainly less aggressive. An opportunity to study prospectively the influence of parent practices on the development of empathy is provided by data from a longitudinal study originally initiated by Sears, Maccoby, and Levin (1957). Koestner, Franz, and Weinberger (1990) related mother reports of parent practices when the children were age 5 to empathic concern when the children were grown up at age 31. Parental involvement in child care and maternal tolerance for dependent behavior most strongly predicted adult empathy. Marginal significance was also found for maternal inhibition of aggression and maternal role satisfaction in predicting adult empathy. In an interesting but surprising finding for the authors, maternal and parental warmth were unrelated to empathic concern in their offspring. Other findings from the study included predicted relationships between empathy and the need for affiliation and between empathy and prosocial values, the latter finding being relevant to the next section of this chapter.

There are a number of caveats regarding the generalization regarding parental empathy. Very few relationships were obtained between father empathy and other aspects of father behavior and between father empathy and child behavior. Thus, empathy as an interlocking factor in the socialization matrix appears to apply predominantly to mothers and their daughters.

Sex Differences in Empathy

The literature regarding sex differences in empathy tends to show modest differences in this attribute between boys and girls and men and women. Although some of these differences found in the literature can be accounted for by methodological and measurement factors, our data suggest that empathy may be structurally and functionally different in men and women. The role of maternal empathy reflected in the four studies, is different than the role of paternal empathy. More important, the effects of maternal empathy and lack of maternal empathy has a broader and more intense effect on girls than on boys.

The findings from our studies reflect that empathy in girls emerges from a socialization history that is punctuated by positive parenting rather than a family constellation fraught by distress, conflict, and discord as has been proposed (Hoffman, 1982). Eisenberg and her coauthors (Eisenberg, Fabes, et al., 1991) also report that, among their findings, parental sympathy was positively related to low levels of personal distress in same-sex children. It may be that empathy in boys, which is a less role-syntonic relationship, may emerge from different socialization experiences and roots than in girls.

Emotional–Affective Component of Empathy

Another important exception to the consistency of the findings relates to the role of the affective-expression empathy factor, one of the factors to emerge from the factor analysis of the Parent/Partner Scale (Feshbach, Socklowskie, O'Leary, 1996). Empathy, as has been indicated previously, is acknowledged to be both cognitive and affective in structure. The affective-expression factor is part of empathy. When affect is buttressed by cognitive understanding, empathy may occur. Affect, unsupported by cognition, may be egocentric and symbiotic rather than empathic. Cognitive understanding, devoid of emotion, is not empathy either. However, the deleterious effects of emotional diffuseness may be more serious than any negative effects of "cold" cognition, especially when the emotionality may be accompanied by impulsiveness—witness our findings on physically abusive mothers.

In our study in physically abusing mothers, the affective-expression factor was strongest. This same factor, correlated inversely with child compliance, self control, and child positive affect and directly with child negative affect. These findings suggest that, although parental empathy has positive socializing implications, the affective-expression component, untempered by other empathy components, may function as emotional contagion and may have negative consequences for the child's adjustment. Also, in another vein, studies on the impact of maternal depression in young children indicate that depressed mothers appear less likely than nondepressed mothers to adopt empathic-interaction strategies with their offspring and are less responsive to their children's concerns (Cox, Puckering, Pound, & Mills, 1987). Studies of the intensity of maternal affective expression and children's responses to distressed peers reflect complex relationships between maternal affective intensity and the child's reaction to distress in others, the relationship depending on other maternal attributes (Eisenberg & Miller, 1987; Fabes, Eisenberg, & Miller, 1990; Miller & Eisenberg, 1988).

Additional research is needed to explore more deeply the meaning and functions of empathy in the child-training process, especially for fathers and sons. Nevertheless, there is already sufficient data and consistent findings from these and other studies that enable us to make inferences and recommendations regarding programs for parents, teachers, and children.

Clinical Implications

Both the socialization and the gender differences data suggest that low empathy is more of a problem for women than men. Although empathy is a positive attribute for men, low empathy does not seem to be indicative of maladjustment in men, whereas low empathy in women appears to be indicative of emotional and behavioral problems.

A rather different clinical issue concerns the implications of the developmental and gender-difference data for empathy as conceptualized by Kohut (1971, 1977). Is the empathic mother or parent that Kohut wrote about the same empathic mother or parent that is studied in the laboratory? Because there have been relatively few studies integrating clinical and developmental approaches to empathy, it is not clear whether Kohut's concept of empathy, a core concept in his construction of the integrated self (Kohut, 1971, 1977), is compatible with the developmentalist's conception of empathy or with "vicarious emotional responding" as Eisenberg and her colleagues (Eisenberg, Shea, et al., 1991) term and conceive empathy. However, it seems to me that when Kohut uses the term *empathy*, he does not mean a shared emotional match. Rather, in the examples he cites, the portrait is drawn of a validating, supportive parent. Although validating and supportive parenting may be behavioral consequences of empathy, strictly speaking they are not identical processes. In a similar vein, the reciprocal, interactive parent–child sequences discussed by Stern (1987), labeled by him as *atunement,* may be akin to the concept of empathy but may not be identical to empathy or "vicarious responsiveness." However, in a constellation of variables or behaviors that correspond to a pattern of positive, parental characteristics fostering positive mental health aspects in children, we should expect parent empathy; atunement; and validating, supporting parenting behaviors to be associated with one other and with personally competent children.

The empirical findings of the socialization antecedents of empathy appear to be at some variance with the traditional psychoanalytic-object relations formulations of the mother–child bond relationship that focuses on conflict, aggressive tendencies, and distress. Infant research, in general, and the data we have observed support the "mutality" and "fit" between mother and child offered by neo-psychoanalytic approaches (Kohut, 1977; Lichtenberg, Bornstein, & Silver, 1984; Stern, 1987). The variables that seem to enhance the development of empathy appear to be congruent with the factors contributing to a healthy attachment, especially in girls. Longitudinal studies relating attachment to mother and father to empathy would be of theoretical and clinical interest.

EMPATHY AND PROSOCIAL BEHAVIOR

There are a number of theoretical and empirical factors that link empathy to prosocial behavior. The definition of prosocial or moral behavior is closely related to theoretical assumptions and principles. In this chapter, prosocial behavior will be defined as behavior that reflects caring and concern for others. Our discussion includes, but does not limit itself to, such prosocial acts as helping, cooperating, donating, sharing, and other altruistic behaviors.

Findings relating empathy to prosocial behavior in adults are generally positive. Individuals who rate themselves as empathic on self-report measures tend to manifest more helping behavior than individuals who rate themselves as less empathic (Batson et al., 1988; Toi & Batson, 1982). In children the relationship between empathy and prosocial behavior is somewhat inconsistent, the direction and significance of the relationship varying with the measure used to assess empathy, the specific prosocial behaviors addressed, the age of the sample, and the context of the study (Eisenberg & Miller, 1987). Some research paradigms more clearly indicate consistency between empathy and prosocial behavior in children. These are studies that focus on the relationship between empathy and cooperation (Levine & Hoffman, 1975; Marcus, Telleen, & Roke, 1979; Marcus, Roke, & Bruner, 1985) and studies that attempt to develop empathic skills through training procedures (Iannotti, 1978). A series of experimental studies carried out by Barnett and his associates (Barnett, Howard, King, & Dino, 1981; Barnett, Howard, Melton, & Dino, 1982; Barnett, King, & Howard, 1979; Howard & Barnett, 1981) in which either cognitive or affective facets of empathy were manipulated also showed moderate but somewhat inconsistent effects in regard to the enhancement of generosity and other prosocial behaviors. The Feshbach and Feshbach Empathy Training Study (Feshbach, 1983, 1984; Feshbach, Feshbach, Fauvre, & Ballard-Campbell, 1983), to be described at some length in a later section, also reflected increased prosocial behaviors following training. Although there is a dynamic interrelationship between prosocial behavior and empathy, the correlation between empathy and prosocial behavior is hardly perfect. For Hoffman (1984), prosocial behavior seems to be an inevitable consequence of empathic arousal, and to a lesser degree, this is also true for Zahn-Waxler and Radke-Yarrow (1990). The extant empirical literature on empathy and prosocial behavior is attenuated by psychometric limitations of the empathy measures and situational limitations of the prosocial behavior measures. However, there are other factors that may also attenuate the relationship between empathy and prosocial behavior. These will be elaborated on when I review the relationship of aggression to empathy.

EMPATHY AND AGGRESSION

The inverse relationship between empathy and aggression, which Seymour Feshbach and I have been concerned with for a number of years, may be a somewhat more reliable phenomenon, particularly for men. Our findings from an early study indicating that 6- to 8-year-old boys high in aggression were low in empathy (Feshbach & Feshbach, 1969) have been supported in a number of different studies that use variable measures of empathy and aggression and were carried out with similar or older age groups (Feshbach & Feshbach, 1982; Mehrabian & Epstein, 1972; Miller & Eisenberg, 1988). Sometimes a particular component of empathy was evaluated, such as perspective taking (Chandler, Greenspan, & Barenboim, 1973), and sometimes a general index of empathy such as the Feshbach and Roe Affective Situation Test (1968), the Bryant (1982) measure, or the 1982 Feshbach measure is employed. Assessments of aggressiveness include teachers' ratings of aggression, cruelty, competitiveness (Barnett, Matthews, & Howard, 1979), and delinquency. One study, contrary to the predominant pattern, reported positive correlations between perspective-taking skills and disruptive, difficult classroom behavior in elementary-school children (Kurdek, 1978).

The three-component model of empathic behavior suggests several mechanisms that should result in lower aggression and greater prosocial behavior in the empathic child relative to the less-empathic child. The ability to discriminate and label the feelings of others is a prerequisite to taking into account others' needs when responding to social conflicts. The more advanced cognitive skill entailed in examining a conflict situation from the perspective of another person should result in the reduction of misunderstandings, accompanied by a lessening of conflict and aggression and a greater likelihood of cooperative and other prosocial responses. The assumption of a process of this kind underlies the rationale for the many types of therapy, "dialogue," and comparable interpersonal communication procedures that have been applied to the resolution of conflict situations.

The affective component of empathy has a special relationship to the regulation of aggression. Aggressiveness implies the infliction of injury that may cause pain and distress. The observation of pain and distress should elicit distress in an empathic observer, even if the observer is the cause of the aggression. Thus, the painful consequence of an aggressive act through the vicarious response of empathy should function as an inhibitor of the instigator's own aggressive tendencies (Feshbach & Feshbach, 1969; Feshbach & Feshbach, 1986). An important property of empathic inhibition is that it applies to instrumental as well as anger-mediated aggressive behavior. Thus, one could predict that children high in empathy should be less aggressive than those low in empathy. One source of the difference between the relation of empathy to prosocial behavior and its relation to aggressive behavior is the nature of the mediating process. Empathy is presumed to affect aggression through inhibition. No other response is required. However, for prosocial behavior to occur when the child is empathic, the prosocial response must be in the child's repertoire and occur in the situation. This factor has implications for training, and perhaps empathy training must be accompanied by prosocial behavioral-transaction training.

Still another factor complicating the association between empathy and prosocial behavior is the general issue of the circumstances under which empathy is likely to be evoked. Even highly empathic individuals are not empathic in all situations. Some situations are ambiguous, and the affects experienced by the protagonists may be unclear. Or there may be conflicting affective and social cues. Still other factors may reduce empathic responsiveness through interference with role taking and perspective taking. For example, it may be difficult to assume the perspective and adopt the framework of an individual whom one intensely dislikes, with whom one is in sharp disagreement, or with whom one has very little in common. Yet other situational factors may have such affective-laden significance that they may overstimulate or, conversely, even block affective responses. All these situational contingencies reduce the likelihood of an empathic response and of prosocial behaviors that might be mediated by empathy.

The inverse relationship that has been explored between empathy and aggression is further discussed in the next section that reviews the issue of training empathy in children. The theoretical basis of the association and the empirical findings provide an important rationale for our endeavors in the training of empathy.

CORRELATES OF EMPATHY

The functions of empathy transcend its relationships to prosocial behavior and to lowered aggression. Its multifaceted structure, encompassing cognitive and affective dimensions, links it to other important domains of behavior, such as communication, adjustment, and achievement. In a short-term longitudinal study investigating the relationship between affective processes and academic achievement, we found a positive relationship between empathy at age 8 and 9 and reading and spelling skills at 10 and 11 years of age. Empathy at age 8 and 9 predicted reading and spelling achievement at 10 and 11, as well as empathy at this older age, the finding holding predominantly for girls (Feshbach & Feshbach, 1987).

It has also been proposed that empathy may function as a coping skill or serve as a protective factor in reactions to stress. The findings from a number of studies that examined the role empathy might play in children's managing postdivorce stress suggest that interpersonal reasoning and emotional empathy may serve as important resources in personal adjustment (Amato & Kieth, 1991). Thus, a component of empathy—the ability to take the perspective or role of another—was positively associated with children's and adolescents' postdivorce adjustment (Kurdek, Blisk, & Siesky, 1981). Work and Olsen (1990) also found that children's interpersonal understanding and emotional empathy predicted fewer adjustment problems in school. Also, Mutchler, Hunt, Koopman, and Mutchler (1991) found in postdivorce female adolescents an inverse relationship between cognitive empathy and anxiety.

Findings evaluating the potential of empathy serving as a protective factor for maltreated children were provided in a study carried out by Heidi Gralinski and myself in which physically maltreated, middle-elementary-age children were observed on empathy, self-perceptions, and self-concept rating scales (Gralinski & Feshbach, 1991, 1992). Maltreated girls, on average, were more empathic that their nonmaltreated peers. However, within the maltreated group high empathy was associated with low aggression, high social self-perception, and high self-acceptance. Consequently, although in general, physical maltreatment may significantly increase psychological risk, particularly for girls, empathy may play a role in mediating the negative social–emotional consequences of physical maltreatment.

Further research is needed to clarify these findings and to systematically explore the functions of empathy in maltreated children's perceptions of others and in other clinical groups as well. Research being carried out with atypical children on emotion recognition and empathy should also yield insights regarding the role of empathy in children's emotional and social development (Kasari, Hughes, & Freeman, 1995).

EMPATHY TRAINING

The issue and procedures of empathy training have been explored for children, nurses, and clinicians and less so for teachers, other educators, and parents. Goldstein and Michaels (1985) review criteria for developing and assessing training programs for clinicians and counselors. Parent programs, specifically those focusing on the training of empathy, have yet to be articulated but potentially could be derived from a counselor–clinician didactic model. Goldstein and Michael offer a six-stage prescriptive model for the training of empathy that involves readiness training (including imagination, observation, and flexibility skills); perceptual training (focusing on perceptual accuracy and sensitivity); affective reverberation training (including mediation and other somatopsychic methods); cognitive analysis training (such as discrimination-training procedures, i.e., analyzing facial features); communication (including modeling, role playing, behavior rehearsal); and transfer and maintenance training (which would include generalizability skills to the "real world").

Empathy-training programs for children have, in general, focused on more singular aspects of empathy. Many of these child-training programs have focused on role-taking and perspective-taking skills and have been carried out in the context of a laboratory setting with elementary-age and early-adolescent youngsters (Chandler et al., 1973, 1974; Howard & Barnett, 1981; Iannotti, 1978; Midlarsky & Bryan, 1967). Occasionally, acting-out, aggressive youngsters (Feshbach, 1979, Feshbach & Feshbach, 1982); "emotionally disturbed" children (Chandler et al., 1974); and delinquents (Chandler, 1973) have been the object of empathy training experimentally carried out in the context of the field.

I believe the most sustained effort of this kind was carried out by Seymour Feshbach and myself and our colleagues (Feshbach, Feshbach, Fauvre, & Ballard-Campbell, 1984). Building on our earlier research efforts and using the conceptual model of empathy described above, we developed 30 hours of training exercises and activities. The exercises were designed for use in small groups of four to six children age 8, 9, and 10. Each activity lasts from 20 to 30 minutes. Activities included problem-solving games; story telling; listening to and making tape recordings; simple written exercises; group discussions; and more active tasks such as acting out words, phrases, and stories. Several exercises involved videotaping children's enactments and replaying them for discussion. To increase skill in affect identification and discrimination, children were asked to identify the emotions conveyed in photographs of facial expressions, tape recordings of affect-laden conversations, and videotaped pantomimes of emotional situations. The children themselves role-played in a wide range of games and situations in which they acted out and guessed feelings. To foster children's ability to assume the perspective of another person and to take another's role, training exercises included a variety of games and activities that become progressively more difficult as training proceeds. They were asked to imagine the preferences and behavior of different kinds of people: for example, "What birthday present would make each member of your family happiest?" and "What would your teacher, your older brother, your best friend, a policeman do if he. . . ?" Children listened to stories, then recounted them from the point of view of each character in the story. Imagination exercises were also included to facilitate visual perspective taking.

Children who participated in the Empathy Training Program reflected a more positive self-concept than children in the Problem Solving Program or those with no training. They also showed significant changes in aggression and prosocial behavior. Empathy training proved to be critical in regard to positive shifts in prosocial behavior. Although the children who received problem-solving training showed a decrease in aggression, only those children who participated in empathy-enhancing activities showed an increase in such prosocial behavior as cooperation, helping, and generosity. It would appear that empathy training helps to bring about more positive social behaviors and a more positive self-evaluation in aggressive and nonaggressive children (Feshbach & Feshbach, 1982).

More recently, Seymour Feshbach and I have been involved in preliminary efforts to implement empathy training within a broader curriculum framework. The Empathy Training Program was carried out with small groups of children within a school setting but outside the classroom. Our more recent efforts have focused on activities within the classroom. We have developed a set of transformational principles based on the three-component model of empathy previously discussed. The object of this transformational guide is to heighten the empathic potential of the elementary- and middle-school curriculum for the purpose of promoting, in general, interpersonal sensitivity in children and, specifically, to enhance ethnic understanding and decrease prejudice among children (Feshbach & Feshbach, in press). We anticipate that the more focused application of empathy principles will result in more profound changes with regard to aggression and prosocial behaviors, particularly in relation to interethnic interactions.

Empathy and Attachment

There are other potential positive consequences of empathy-type training programs being implemented in educational settings that have clinical implications. There is an interesting and important relationship between empathy and attachment—the experience of a positive bond between oneself and another person. Although there is little research data bearing on this relationship, experience suggests that the stronger one's attachment to a person, the easier it is to empathize with that individual. Empathy, in turn, through the shared emotional experience it entails, should help sustain and contribute to the social bond or attachment to that other person. In addition, the perception by that individual of one's empathic response increases with their attachment to oneself. Thus, there appears to be a reciprocal and mutually sustaining interaction between empathy and attachment. This reciprocal-interaction process suggests that a classroom program designed to enhance children's empathy should contribute to positive attachments among the children and between the children and the teacher.

The fostering of empathy seems to be a natural step to pursue in any long-term approach to the problem of interpersonal violence. However, there is much about children's empathy to learn. Research in this area is still relatively recent, and there is not a substantial body of knowledge regarding the development of empathy and its dynamics. We know that similarity between observer and a stimulus person facilitates empathy (Feshbach, 1978; Feshbach & Roe, 1968), and this factor should be introduced into training activities. Much more precise data are required regarding the particular dimensions of similarity that are relevant to an empathic response. There is also much to learn about the factors that block empathy and interfere with the understanding and sharing of another's perspective and experience.

Clinical Implications

The research data indicate that, with some qualifications, the attribute of empathy is related to prosocial behavior in both boys and girls and to lower aggression, especially in boys. From a societal perspective, empathy is clearly related to desirable social behaviors. From a clinical perspective, there may be some who are unpersuaded by social criteria and culturally based values and who would prefer to focus on more personally oriented adaptive-behavioral correlates. These clinicians may be more persuaded by the albeit-limited data relating empathy to academic achievement, self-esteem, and resilience to stress.

However, the fostering of the processes mediating empathy, in and of themselves, would appear to be desirable. The three components of empathy entail skills that the individual can use in a variety of situations. These skills involve the ability to identify emotions in oneself and others; the ability to assume the perspective of others; and the ability to express emotion in a controlled, articulated manner. These are adaptive skills for children and for adults, although the cognitive complexity and affective sensitivity that are involved varies with developmental level.

Promoting empathy in clients should be a desirable therapeutic objective, whether the client is a child, parent, or patient. The empathy-training studies indicate that empathy is an attribute that can be enhanced through the training of its component skills. One does not directly train individuals to share another person's affect. Rather, the clinician should use procedures that address sensitivity to and identification of affect, the controlled expression of affect, and perspective and role taking. Mothers who physically abuse their children should be provided interventions that orient them to their children's perspective and feelings. Couples who engage in continued and mutual verbal attacks should learn to see the perspective and feelings that underlie their partner's behavior as well as their own perspective and feelings.

Although the data cited have been primarily based on studies of children, both theory and clinical experience suggest that adults can also profit from similar, but age-appropriate, empathy training. Furthermore, studies with both children and adults point to the importance of similarity between the observer and the observed as a mediator of empathy. The curriculum-transformation project uses the process of similarity as a means of enhancing ethnic understanding and reducing ethnic conflict. The role of similarity in this context is a subtle one because one is also addressing diversity among ethnic groups. Although the curriculum-transformation project helps children understand differences in behavior and in perspectives that are associated with the different historical experiences of diverse ethnic groups, it also enables children to appreciate the fundamental psychological similarities between these diverse groups. Clients in therapy can also profit from understanding differences between people that reflect important distinctions and differences that are alternative modes of expressing basically similar feelings and values.

Enhanced empathy is a desirable attribute for clinicians. The clinician's empathic response can serve as a cue to help make explicit feelings of the client that the clinician has subconsciously perceived, and communication to the client of the clinician's empathy provides a validating experience for the client. The experience and communication of empathy, whether between parent and child or clinician and client, fosters attachment in a relationship. Client attachment to the therapist contributes to trust of the therapist and, when appropriately used, contributes to the effectiveness of the therapeutic interaction.

These remarks regarding clinician–therapist empathy suggest that aspects of empathy training could be fruitfully incorporated in the training of clinicians. The student clinician should be encouraged to be sensitive to his or her own feelings as well as the client's feelings. The student should be trained to perceive situations from the perspective of the client and to be able to communicate that perspective and those of others. The third recommendation—namely, that the student clinician should be trained to express, in a controlled manner, empathic feelings—may be more controversial, but it is, in my judgment, important and therapeutic.

A Final Note

Empathy is an important but subtle mechanism of human communication that is difficult to capture in empirical studies. Nevertheless, the research on empathy has provided suggestive evidence of its significant role in social understanding and in social relationships. The research on empathy as a personality attribute indicates that it is associated with positive social behaviors and psychological adjustment. However, what seems to be lacking are studies of empathy in naturalistic settings, contexts in which a melange of affects are aroused and in which observed and observer interact and have affective reactions toward each other.

The clinical setting is precisely such a context. The concepts and theory that have guided research on the development of empathy should be incorporated in research on empathy in the clinical situation. Alterations in methods and measures will be required that are appropriate to the study of empathy in the interaction between therapist and client. Appropriate methods and measures are not readily available, and their implementation presents a difficult research challenge. However, the relevance of empathic understanding and communication for the clinical interaction merits the effort entailed in meeting this challenge.

REFERENCES

Amato, P. R., & Kieth, B. (1991). Parental divorce and the well-being of children: A meta-analysis. *Psychological Bulletin, 110,* 26–46.

Barnett, M. A., Howard, J. A., King, L. M., & Dino, G. A. (1981). Helping behavior and the transfer of empathy. *Journal of Social Psychology, 115,* 125–132.

Barnett, M. A., Howard, J. A., Melton, E. M., & Dino, G. A. (1982). Effect of inducing sadness about self or other on helping behavior in high and low empathic children. *Child Development, 53,* 920–923.

Barnett, M. A., King, L. M., & Howard, J. A. (1979). Inducing affect about self or other: Effects on generosity in children. *Developmental Psychology, 15,* 164–167.

Barnett, M. A., Matthews, K. A., & Howard, J. A. (1979). Relationship between competitiveness and empathy in 6- and 7-year-olds. *Developmental Psychology, 15,* 221–222.

Batson, C. D., Dyck, J. L., Brandt, J. R., Batson, J. G., Powell, A. L., McMaster, M. R., & Griffith, C. A. (1988). Five studies testing two new egoistic alternatives to the empathy–altruism hypothesis. *Journal of Personality and Social Psychology, 55,* 52–77.

Berger, S. M. (1962). Conditioning through vicarious instigation? *Psychological Review, 69,* 450–456.

Borke, H. (1973). The development of empathy in Chinese and American children between three and six years of age: A cross-cultural study. *Developmental Psychology, 9*(1), 102–108.

Bretherton, I., Fritz, J., Zahn-Waxler, C., & Ridgeway, D. (1986). The acquisition and development of emotion language: A functionalist perspective. *Child Development,* 529–548.

Brothers, L. (1989). A biological perspective in empathy. *American Journal of Psychiatry, 146*(1).

Brothers, L. (1990). The neural basis of primate social communication. *Motivation and Emotion, 14*(2).

Bryant, B. (1982). An index of empathy for children and adolescents. *Child Development, 53,* 413–425.

Buhler, C. (1930). *The first year of life.* New York: Day.

Chandler, M. J. (1973). Egocentrism and antisocial behavior: The assessment and training of social perspective-taking skills. *Developmental Psychology, 9*(3), 326–332.

Chandler, M. J., & Greenspan, S. (1972). Ersatz egocentrism: A reply to H. Borke. *Developmental Psychology, 7*(2), 104–106.

Chandler, M. J., Greenspan, S., & Barenboim, C. (1973). Judgments of intentionality in response to videotaped and verbally presented moral dilemmas: The medium is the message. *Child Development, 44,* 315–320.

Chandler, M. J., Greenspan, S., & Barenboim, C. (1974). The assessment and training of role-taking and referential communication skills in institutionalized emotionally disturbed children. *Developmental Psychology, 10*(4), 546–553.

Chisholm, K., & Strayer, J. (1995). Verbal and facial measures of children's emotion and empathy. *Journal of Experimental Child Psychology, 59*(2), 299–316.

Chlopan, B. E., McCain, M. L., Carbonell, J. L., & Hagen, R. L. (1985). Empathy: Review of available measures. *Journal of Personality and Social Psychology, 48*(3), 635–653.

Cialdini, R. B., Schaller, M., Houlihan, D., Arps, K., Fultz, J., & Beaman, A. L. (1987). Empathy-based helping: Is it selflessly motivated? *Journal of Personality and Social Psychology, 52,* 749–758.

Cicchetti, D., & Schneider-Rosen, K. (1986). An organizational approach to childhood depression. In M. Rutter, C. Izard, & P. Read (Eds.), *Depression in young people: Clinical and developmental perspectives.* New York: Guilford.

Cohn, J. K., Campbell, S. B., Matias, R., & Hopkins, J. (1990). Face-to-face interactions in postpartum depressed and non-depressed mother–infant pairs at 2 months. *Developmental Psychology, 26,* 15–23.

Cox, A. D., Puckering, C., Pound, A., & Mills, M. (1987). The impact of maternal depression in young children. *Journal of Child Psychology and Psychiatry, 28,* 917–928.

Davis, M. (1983). Measuring individual differences in empathy: Evidence for a multidimensional approach. *Journal of Personality and Social Psychology, 44,* 113–126.

Davis, M. (1994). *Empathy: A social psychological approach.* Madison, WI: Brown & Benchmark.

Davis, M., & Franzoi, S. (1991). Stability and change in adolescent self-consciousness and empathy. *Journal of Research in Personality, 25,* 70–87.

Deutsch, F., & Madle, R. A. (1975). Empathy: Historic and current conceptualizations, and a cognitive theoretical perspective. *Human Development, 18,* 267–287.

Dymond, R. F. (1949). A scale for measurement of empathic ability. *Journal of Consulting Psychology, 14,* 127–133.

Eisenberg, N., & Fabes, R. A. (1990). Empathy: Conceptualization, measurement, and relation to prosocial behavior. *Motivation and Emotion, 14*(2).

Eisenberg, N., Fabes, R. A., Miller, P. A., Fultz, J., Shell, R., Mathy, R. M., & Reno, R. (1989). Relation of sympathy and personal distress to prosocial behavior: Multi-method study. *Journal of Personality and Social Psychology, 57,* 55–66.

Eisenberg, N., Fabes, R. A., Schaller, M., Carlo, G., & Miller, P. A. (1991). The relations of parental characteristics and practices to children's vicarious emotional responding. *Child Development, 62,* 1393–1408.

Eisenberg, N., Fabes, R. A., Schaller, M., & Miller, P. A. (1989). Sympathy and personal distress: Development, gender differences, and interrelation of indexes. In N. Eisenberg (Ed.), *Empathy and related emotion responses* (New Directions in Child Development No. 44. pp. 107–126). San Francisco: Jossey-Bass.

Eisenberg, N., & Lennon, R. (1983). Sex differences in empathy and related capacities. *Psychological Bulletin, 94,* 100–131.

Eisenberg, N., & Miller, P. A. (1987). The relation of empathy to prosocial and related behaviors. *Psychological Bulletin, 101,* 91–119.

Eisenberg, N., Miller, P. A., Shell, R., McNalley, S., & Shea, C. (1991). Prosocial development in adolescence: A longitudinal study. *Developmental Psychology, 27*(5), 849–857.

Eisenberg, N., Shea, C., Carlo, G., & Knight, G. (1991). Empathy-related responses and cognition: A "chicken and the egg" dilemma. In W. Kurtines &

J. Gewirtz (Eds.), *Handbook of moral behavior and development*. Hillsdale, NJ: Erlbaum.

Ekman, P. (1984). Expression and the nature of emotion. In D. Scherer & P. Ekman (Eds.), *Approaches to emotion* (pp. 319–344). Hillsdale, NJ: Erlbaum.

Fabes, R. A., Eisenberg, N., & Miller, P. A. (1990). Maternal correlates of children's vicarious emotional responsiveness. *Developmental Psychology, 26*(4), 639–648.

Feshbach, N. D. (1972). *A cognitive process in the self regulation of children's aggression: Empathy.* Invited address presented at the National Institute of Mental Health Conference on Developmental Aspects of Self Regulation, La Jolla, CA.

Feshbach, N. D. (1973, August). Empathy: An interpersonal process. In W. Hartup (Chair), *Social understanding in children and adults: Perspectives on social cognition.* Symposium presented at the meeting of the American Psychological Association, Montreal.

Feshbach, N. D. (1975a). Empathy in children: Some theoretical and empirical considerations. *The Counseling Psychologist, 5*(2), 25–30.

Feshbach, N. D. (1975b). The relationship of child-rearing factors in children's aggression, empathy and related positive and negative social behaviors. In J. DeWit & W. W. Hartup (Eds.), *Determinants and origins of aggressive behavior.* The Netherlands: Mouton.

Feshbach, N. D. (1978). Studies of empathic behavior in children. In B. A. Maher (Ed.), *Progress in Experimental Personality Research* (Vol. 8, pp. 1–47). New York: Academic Press.

Feshbach, N. D. (1979). Empathy training: A field study in affective education. In S. Feshbach & A. Fraczek (Eds.), *Aggression and behavior change: Biological and social processes* (pp. 234–249). New York: Praeger.

Feshbach, N. D. (1980, May). *The psychology of empathy and the empathy of psychology.* Presidential address, 60th Annual Meeting of the Western Psychological Association, Honolulu, HI.

Feshbach, N. D. (1982). Sex differences in empathy and social behavior in children. In N. Eisenberg (Ed.), *The development of prosocial behavior* (pp. 315–338). New York: Academic Press.

Feshbach, N. D. (1983). Learning to care: A positive approach to child training and discipline. *Journal of Clinical Child Psychology, 12*(3), 266–271.

Feshbach, N. D. (1984). Empathy, empathy training, and the regulation of aggression in elementary school children. In R. M. Kaplan, V. J. Konecni, & R. Novoco (Eds.), *Aggression in children and youth* (pp. 192–208). The Netherlands: Martinus Ijhoff.

Feshbach, N. D. (1987). Parental empathy and child adjustment/maladjustment. In N. Eisenberg & J. Strayer (Eds.), *Empathy and its development* (pp. 271–291). New York: Cambridge University Press.

Feshbach, N. D. (1995). Parent empathy: A key element in the mother–child relationship. *Advances in Early Education and Day Care, 7,* 3–26.

Feshbach, N. D., & Feshbach, S. (1969). The relationship between empathy and aggression in two age groups. *Developmental Psychology, 1*(2), 102–107.

Feshbach, N. D., & Feshbach, S. (1982). Empathy training and the regulation of aggression: Potentialities and limitations. *Academic Psychology Bulletin, 4*, 399–413.

Feshbach, N. D., & Feshbach, S. (1987). Affective processes and academic achievement. *Child Development, 58*, 1335–1347.

Feshbach, N. D., & Feshbach, S. (in press). Toward reducing aggression in the schools: Enhancing ethnic identity and ethnic understanding. In P. K. Tricket & C. Schellenbach (Eds.), *Violence against children in the family and the community*. Washington, DC: American Psychological Association.

Feshbach, N. D., Feshbach, S., Fauvre, M., & Ballard-Campbell, M. (1984). *Learning to care: A curriculum for affective and social development.* Glenview, IL: Scott, Foresman.

Feshbach, N. D., & Howes, C. (1995). *Parent empathy, family attributes, and parent-child interactions in abusing and clinic referred families.*

Feshbach, N. D., & Roe, K. (1968). Empathy in six and seven year olds. *Child Development, 39*(1), 133–145.

Feshbach, N. D., Socklowskie, R. J., & O'Leary, E. (1991). *The utility of a new child questionnaire measure of perspective taking and empathy.* Presented at Third Annual Convention of the American Psychological Society, Washington DC.

Feshbach, N. D., Socklowskie, R., & Rose, A. (1996). *The relationship of parental empathy and parental child training attributes to empathy in four year olds: A reliable pattern.* Manuscript in preparation.

Feshbach, S., & Feshbach, N. D. (1986). Aggression and altruism: A personality perspective. In C. Zahn-Waxler, M. Chapman, & M. Radke-Yarrow (Eds.), *Aggression and altruism: Biological and social origins* (pp. 189–217).

Field, T. M. (1985). Neonatal perception of people: Maturational and individual differences. In M. Field & N. A. Fox (Eds.), *Social perception in infants* (pp. 31–52). Norwood, NJ: Ablex.

Field, T. M., Woodson, R., Greenberg, R., & Cohen, D. (1982). Discrimination and imitation of facial expressions by neonates. *Science, 218*, 179–181.

Goldstein, A. P., & Michaels, G. Y. (1985). *Empathy: Development training and consequences.* Hillsdale, NJ: Erlbaum.

Gralinski, J. H., & Feshbach, N. D. (1991). *Protective and risk patterns in maltreated children's self-conceptions and attitudes and empathy.* Paper presented at the biennial meeting of the Society for Research in Child Development, Seattle, WA.

Gralinski, J. H., & Feshbach, N. D. (1992). *The role of empathy in the cycle of interpersonal aggression: Children as victims and perpetrators.* Paper presented at the meeting of the International Society for Research on Aggression, Sienna, Italy.

Hoffman, M. L. (1975). Developmental synthesis of affect and cognition and its implications for altruistic motivation. *Developmental Psychology, 11*, 605–622.

Hoffman, M. L. (1982). Developmental prosocial motivation: Empathy and guilt. In N. Eisenberg (Ed.), *The development of prosocial behavior* (pp. 218–231). New York: Academic Press.

Hoffman, M. L., (1984). Interaction of affect and cognition in empathy. In C. E. Izard, J. Kagan, & R. B. Zajonc (Eds.), *Emotions, cognition, and behavior* (pp. 103–131). New York: Cambridge University Press.

Howard, J. A., & Barnett, M. A. (1981). Arousal of empathy and subsequent generosity in young children. *Journal of Genetic Psychology, 138*, 307–308.

Iannotti, R. J. (1978). Effect of role-taking experiences on role taking, empathy, altruism, and aggression. *Developmental Psychology, 14*, 119–124.

Kasari, C., Hughes, M. A., & Freeman, S. (1995). Emotions recognition of young children with Down syndrome. In M. Lewis & M. Sullivan (Eds.), *Emotional development of atypical children.* Mahwah, NJ: Erlbaum.

Koestner, R., Franz, C., & Weinberger, J. (1990). The family origins of empathic concern: A 26-year longitudinal study. *Journal of Personality and Social Psychology, 58*(4), 709–717.

Kohut, H. (1971). *The analysis of the self.* New York: International Universities Press.

Kohut, H. (1977). *The restoration of the self.* New York: International Universities Press.

Kozeki, B., & Berghammer, R. (1991). The role of empathy in the motivational structure of school children. *Personality and Individual Differences, 13*(2), 191–203.

Kurdek, L. A. (1978). Relationship between cognitive perspective taking and teachers' ratings of children's classroom behavior in grades one through four. *Journal of Genetic Psychology, 132*, 21–27.

Kurdek, L. A., Blisk, D., & Siesky, A. E., Jr. (1981). Correlates of children's long-term adjustment to their parents' divorce. *Developmental Psychology, 17*, 565–579.

Kurdek, L. A., & Sinclair, R. J. (1988). Adjustment of young adolescents in two-parent nuclear, stepfather, and mother-custody families. *Journal of Consulting and Clinical Psychology, 56*, 91–96.

Levenson, R., & Rief, A. (1992). Empathy: A psychological substrate. *Journal of Personality and Social Psychology, 63*(2).

Levine, L. E., & Hoffman, M. L. (1975). Empathy and cooperation in four-year-olds. *Developmental Psychology, 11*, 533–534.

Lichtenberg, J., Bornstein, M., & Silver, D. (Eds.). (1984). *Empathy* (Vols. 1–2). Hillsdale, NJ: Analytic Press.

Marcus, R. F., Roke, E. J., & Bruner, C. (1985). Verbal and nonverbal empathy and prediction of social behavior in young children. *Perceptual and Motor Skills, 60*, 299–309.

Marcus, R. F., Telleen, S., & Roke, E. J. (1979). Relation between cooperation and empathy in young children. *Developmental Psychology, 15*, 346–347.

McDougall, W. (1908). *An introduction to social psychology.* New York: Barnes & Noble.

Mead, G. H. (1934). *Mind, self, and society.* Chicago: University of Chicago Press.

Mehrabian, A., & Epstein, N. A. (1972). A measure of emotional empathy. *Journal of Personality, 40*, 523–543.

Midlarsky, E., & Bryan, J. H. (1967). Training charity in children. *Journal of Personality and Social Psychology, 5*, 408–415.

Miller, P. A., & Eisenberg, N. (1988). The relation of empathy to aggressive and externalizing/antisocial behavior. *Psychological Bulletin, 103*, 324–344.

Mutchler, T. E., Hunt, E. J., Koopman, E. J., & Mutchler, R. D. (1991). Single-parent mother/daughter empathy, relationship adjustment, and functioning of the adolescent child of divorce. *Journal of Divorce and Remarriage, 17*, 115–130.

Phinney, J., Feshbach, N. D., & Farver, J. (1986). Preschool children's response to peer crying. *Early Childhood Quarterly, 1*, 207–219.

Radke-Yarrow, M., Zahn-Waxler, C., & Chapman, M. (1983). Pro social dispositions and behavior. In E. M. Hetherington (Ed.), *Handbook of child psychology: Socialization, personality and social development* (Vol. 4, pp. 469–545). New York: Wiley.

Rogers, C. R. (1961). *On becoming a person.* Boston: Houghton Mifflin.

Rothenberg, B. B. (1970). Child's social sensitivity and the relationship to interpersonal competence, intrapersonal comfort and intellectual level. *Developmental Psychology, 2*(3), 335–350.

Sagi, A., & Hoffman, M. L. (1976). Empathic distress in the newborn. *Developmental Psychology, 12*, 175–176.

Sears, R. R., Maccoby, E. E., & Levin, H. (1957). *Patterns of childrearing.* Evanston, IL: Row Peterson.

Shantz, C. U. (1975). The development of social cognition. In E. M. Hetherington (Ed.), *Review of child development research* (Vol. 5). Chicago: University of Chicago Press.

Squires, M. F. (1979). Empathic, nurturant, and abusive behavior of normal and abnormally reared girls. *Dissertation Abstracts International, 40*, 937B.

Stern, D. (1987). *The interpersonal world of the infant.* New York: Basic Books.

Stotland, E. (1969). Exploratory investigations of empathy. In L. Berkowitz (Ed.), *Advances in experimental social psychology* (Vol. 4). New York: Academic Press.

Straker, G., & Jacobson, R. S. (1981). Aggression, emotional maladjustment, and empathy in the abused child. *Developmental Psychology, 17*(6), 762–765.

Strayer, J. (1987). What children know and feel in response to witnessing affective events.

Sullivan, H. S. (1953). *The interpersonal theory of psychiatry.* New York: Norton.

Toi, M., & Batson, C. D. (1982). More evidence that empathy is a source of altruistic motivation. *Journal of Personality and Social Psychology, 43*, 281–292.

Work, W. C., & Olsen, K. H. (1990). Evaluation of a revised fourth grade social problem solving curriculum: Empathy as a moderator of adjustive gain. *Journal of Primary Prevention, 11*, 143–157.

Zahn-Waxler, C., Emde, R. N., & Robinson, J. L. (1992). The development of empathy in twins. *Developmental Psychology, 28*(6), 1038–1047.

Zahn-Waxler, C., & Radke-Yarrow, M. (1982). The development of altruism. In N. Eisenberg (Ed.), *The development prosocial behavior* (pp. 109–137). New York: Academic Press.

Zahn-Waxler, C., & Radke-Yarrow, M. (1990). The Origins of Empathic Concern. *Motivation and Emotion, 14*(2), 107–130.

Zahn-Waxler, C., Radke-Yarrow, M., & King, R. (1979). Child rearing and children's prosocial initiations toward victims of distress. *Child Development, 50*, 319–330.

II

CLIENT-CENTERED PERSPECTIVES

3

EMPATHY IN PSYCHOTHERAPY: A VITAL MECHANISM? YES. THERAPIST'S CONCEIT? ALL TOO OFTEN. BY ITSELF ENOUGH? NO.

JOHN SHLIEN

In the English language, the word *empathy* is an abstract noun, of a peculiarly Germanic origin and influence. Being abstract, many definitions of empathy are afloat. As a personal quality, it is widely distributed, perhaps on the order of the distribution of eyesight. Everyone who experiences empathy is entitled to propose a definition. Mine is simple. Empathy is one of several essential forms of intelligence, an experiential form of such importance to adaptation that social and physical survival depends on it. It is a normal, natural, commonplace capacity, almost constant and almost unavoidable. Its nature does not determine its use. It is not in itself a "condition" of therapy, but probably a precondition.

Empathy is an enabler. It may be necessary, but it is certainly not sufficient. Because it is not a rarity, it cannot be a private preserve of professional practice, but may be part of our professional vanity. Those who think, like Kohut, that it is a "definer of the field" must then consider the majority of human beings as operatives in this field—a welcome thought to those of us who believe that principles of psychotherapy are simply refinements of the best in ordinary human relations. Those who think that empathy assures gentleness, benevolence, or reciprocity should consider that empathy can be an instrument of cruelty. The sadist, and especially the sado-masochist, makes intense use of empathy, albeit without sympathy. The sadist knows your pain, and takes pleasure in it. The hunter who "leads" his flying target soars with the bird to kill it. Empathy does not always go hand in hand with sympathy.[1]

It can, in fact, be a weapon of war, an advantage in every form of competition as well as in cooperation. The quarterback who throws the football goes with the ball, runs along with his receiver, who in turn may stand with the one throwing the ball to him. Unlike the hunter and bird, this empathy is interactive and relatively benign. The champion tennis player knows where a well-hit ball will land before it gets there and feels the tension of the strings, the sound and compression of the ball, and the hopelessly out-of-place position of his or her opponent. In short, empathy may be used to help or to harm, and it does not automatically communicate its activity or intention. It may not have any "intention" of its own, other than to function, like any vital organ.

The manner in which this noun was invented is one source of confusion. It begins in a linguistic system that permits the combination of more than one word into a single new entity. For example, there is feeling, and there is the feeling of, or with, and so on. In the case of empathy, there is "feeling in," or feeling into. In German they are combined into one word, a style for which the language is made famous in jokes, but which may have a real effect on the manner of thought, as well. When "in-feeling" became a single combination, it was immediately capitalized (*Einfühlung*), as are all German nouns, and thus became a new word, instantly, as if it were a new idea. Package is to concept as medium is to message. But *empathy*, the English translation of the active or verblike noun *Einfühlung*, is inert at its beginning. It will have to work its way up (or down) to the active form *empathize*.

We posit a universal human capacity for empathy. Surely the French do not lack for it, as a nation or as a culture. But, as in many cultures, there is no such word in their language, just as there was none in German prior to the combined-word *Einfühlung* or in English prior to the introduced translation "empathy". Following World Wars I and II, and given the cultural antipathy to anything less than French (especially German), French translators have struggled with the word. "A sympathetic penetration" is one phrase (in Swiss French). "Affection" is another. The current solution is simply to spell the word *empathie*, meaning whatever English speakers mean by that. The Italians have long used the word *simpatico* in a general way, much as we now use empathy, and it may be that the more expressive climates and cultures did not need to invent a word to represent their sensitivities, as did the Teutonic German and British Anglo-Saxon tribes with their more brusque or formal manners.

---

[1] Surely on the highway you have met that other driver who knows exactly what you want to do—change lanes, pass, or turn—and deftly, persistently prevents you from doing it. That is empathy without sympathy.

Language influences thought, and thought influences action—sometimes the influence runs in reverse directions—but when a word is translated from its original setting, where it may have some specificity, it loses that specific meaning and becomes even more abstract. How and when did we get our version? This happened circa 1910 when E. B. Titchener, living in the United States, translated *Einfühlung* as empathy. Although Titchener was English, he studied in Leipzig with Wundt (the name of Wundt comes up constantly as a central influence in the culture that gave us *Einfühlung*). It was Wundt who defined the subject matter of psychology as "immediate experience," and Titchener who spent most of his life investigating "introspection," which are both viewpoints of great import in the floundering advancement of clinical psychology. Titchener's was sometimes called "existential psychology."

Empathy was a somewhat playful word at the beginning. Titchener considered that it exercised "the muscles of his mind." (He mixed his metaphors, as well). *Einfühlung* was not related to pain so much as to appreciation, or even enjoyment. The "pathy" in empathy introduced a significantly different association: with "patheos": illness, suffering, or "to suffer with." Thus, although nicely clinical, it also appeared to have some distance from the word and idea of "sym-pathy," and so offered psychologists an operation somewhat distinct from ordinary sympathetics by ordinary people. Then as empathy spread into the popular culture, it moved from being a noun to becoming a modifier, "empathic" (as in empathic understanding), and from this, to becoming a verb, "to empathize." The Cartesian credo, "I think, therefore I am," which had undergone so many transformations in psychology and comedy (I talk, therefore I feel; I dream, laugh, therefore . . .) turned into the vulgar psychological misconception of "I empathize, therefore I am therapeutic." What an unfortunate mistake. A noun has changed into a verb, and an attitude into a technique. How? It is done by the extraction and mechanization of procedures.

It may help to go back to another example, again from sports—good clean fun with no hidden psychological undercurrents. It is active, therefore visible in ways that intellectual empathy is not. An archer travels with her arrow; and this travel starts before the arrow flies, as she estimates distance, trajectory, strength, and so on. From the moment of release, the archer is in the space between arrow and target. Empathy is involved throughout the process of shooting an arrow.

However, there are machines that will compute the factors of speed, power, distance, and wind, as well as fire the shot. This is not empathy; this is sheer and mere performance. It is based on experience and knowledge derived from empathy, much as a thermometer is based on subjective human response to gradients of hot and cold, but it is merely derivative, cannot adjust, or invent, or even tell right from wrong performance.

When attitude becomes technique, empathy becomes a product in the marketing of psychology, a part of the entertainment vocabulary, and a sort of performance art for therapists. They have "extracted the procedures." Those who believe they are well-equipped with empathic sensitivity boast about it, and those who feel ill-equipped consider it a "deficiency syndrome" to be repaired by sensitivity training. In our time, psychotherapy is featured in theatrical venues—professional films, TV talk shows, and dramatic cinema—that lead to the unfounded belief that what is most dramatic is most effective. Empathy is now a popular, if vulgarized, form of support and unreliable sincerity. The adolescent putative father in a sitcom tells his pregnant girlfriend who fears an abortion, "I really empathize with that." The president tells his TV audience of unemployed, "I feel your pain." A Columbia professor of law advises the prosecution in a televised murder trial to "try to empathize more with the victims." What does he have in mind? Empathy with the dead? Why not? It's something to think about. Or is he just confused, thinking that it is the same as sympathy?

Therapists and others now talk less about how well they understand someone. Instead, they perform "feats of empathy." Take, for example, Paul Goodman, a brilliant writer, theoretician, and sponsor of The Living Theater, one of the authors of the book *Gestalt Therapy* (Perls, Hefferline, & Goodman, 1951). He writes that when, as a therapist, he is dealing with jealousy, "I empathize completely. I can predict the next sentence" (Stoehr, 1994, p. 200). This is one of the more benign examples of "empathy as performance art." And it must be said that Goodman is worth serious attention as one of the more intelligent and articulate people in the field, even though he is an unconventional representative of it. He is really no more unconventional, no more theatrical, than his colleague Fritz Perls, whose ideas *became* conventions, except for his lesser-known original theory of "Dental Aggression" (Stoehr, p. 82). In that connection, and not incidentally, Perls studied theater direction under Berthold Brecht in Berlin, where Brecht wrote, in *The Three Penny Opera*, "What keeps a man alive? He feeds on others" (Brecht & Weill, 1934). Nor is this to suggest that the theatrical inclination is only in Gestalt therapy circles.[2] Sometime in the late 1950s, when Carl Rogers had become famous enough to be interviewed by *Time* magazine, the writer–editor asked what category this material would best fit. Rogers considered the available choices; art, literature, business, medicine, and so on, and said, only half-jokingly, "How about, theater?"

True, there is often high drama in psychotherapy. Too often that is exploited as entertainment. It does not excuse those therapists who boast

---

[2] Neither is it mere conjecture. Taylor Stoehr's book (1994) provides explicit testimony from Lore Perls that Fritz Perls's "first love was the theater" and, in my opinion, it is evident that he never left it but imported that interest into his practice of psychotherapy. The same book presents a number of comments on the exercises in Dental Aggression: "You had to see him in action, eating his patients alive, to understand what dental aggression was all about" (p. 134).

about how empathic, or congruent they are. They have too easy a time of it with their self-proclaimed performance. And because it is their internal state, we have to take their word for it. Furthermore, even though it may indeed be true that a high degree of empathy is present, empathy is not enough. Empathy is not a theory of therapy, not even one of the "conditions" proposed by Rogerians. It does not require "contact between two people, one of whom is anxious." It does not require two people; empathy is exercised in flying a kite. So, although empathy is an important and perhaps essential factor in the service of understanding, it is not in itself the hoped-for consequence of understanding.

Nor is empathy difficult to achieve. It happens. The problem is how to use it wisely and well. In my opinion, empathy has been overrated, underexamined, and carelessly though enthusiastically conceived—in short, treated like the Holy Grail, as "received knowledge." It may instead be a sort of dodge, a "therapeutic costume," an act heavily tinged with pride and vanity. Empathy has been taken as both a means and end; it has become an easy substitute for the real motive, and the real work in therapy—sympathy and understanding.

Sympathy—"feeling for"—is a type of commitment. Empathy is not. Is it perhaps time to call sympathy "an unappreciated way of being"? In my view, it works at a higher stage of moral development than empathy. In fact, empathy may have no more moral status than does the circulatory system. Understanding is a volitional effort and a service that empathy is not; if there is "empathic" understanding, then it is the understanding that promotes the healing from within (within being the only possible source). The difficult task is to understand. Empathy alone, without sympathy, and even more, without understanding, may be harmful.

It is important to give recognition to empathy for all that it is, but it is also important to make sure that it does not, by thoughtless substitution, undermine and even obliterate the positive values of sympathy and understanding. This effect goes beyond the realm of psychological practice. A whole society is currently affected, slowly losing the vocabulary and consciousness of compassion. Insofar as concepts and practices in psychotherapy create this loss, they are helping to cause the illnesses they mean to cure.

INNOCENCE ABROAD: HISTORY RIDES IN A DUMBWAITER

Partly by accident, a coincidence of timing and interest, I was privileged to be a participant observer, a sort of bystander and witness, to the development of the theory of empathy as it took place at the University of Chicago after World War II. The university was a neighborhood composed of unique circumstances. George Herbert Mead, who had studied in Germany with Wilhelm Dilthey, had left his "social interaction" tradition there, with Blumer and others who had compiled his posthumous collection of lectures into the book *Mind, Self, and Society* (Mead, 1934). The Division of Social Sciences was full of intellectual and interdisciplinary ferment. Bruno Bettleheim, who lived a few doors away, made a local name for himself as a master of antipathy, which actually helped define empathy by way of demonstrating its contrast. Heinz Kohut was just arriving from Austria (and lived in the next block), although it would be several years before he published his thoughts on empathy. He had not studied with Freud directly but did see him once at the train station in Vienna, when Freud was leaving under great duress to take his daughter Anna to safety in London, along with parts of his library, which contained some writings of Theodore Lipps. In addition, Martin Buber lectured in Rockefeller Chapel a few years later. With all of this, the university was a setting for the conjunction of several stars, who by and large avoided one another, sending their lines of influence through students. I was one of those.

Carl Rogers, already a major figure there, was beginning one of his most productive periods. He had a keen intelligence, a great talent for recognizing and assembling ideas and research findings, and a rather new theory and practice of psychotherapy that gave him such prominence that his advocacy would assure wide attention to a new idea. As the artist historian Ewa Kuryluk said, "Sometimes history hibernates; at times it runs like a gazelle." This was the time of the gazelle.

My special interest was cultural anthropology, particularly the "sociology of knowledge." Rogers and his school of thought, about which I was skeptical, were tempting opportunities. It was the period in which he was formulating and compiling his book *Client-Centered Therapy* (Rogers, 1951), which contained a major theoretical statement and a powerful philosophical position. I attended some of his courses and seminars and, through this, had the privilege of many casual meetings with him. His honesty, forthrightness, and decency won my respect to such a degree that I felt it would be a sort of betrayal to analyze this material from a sociological framework, which would have missed the most important substance of his work.

So, my interests turned back to prior questions: What do we know, how do we know it, and how does anyone understand another person? At our next meeting, I handed Rogers the book *The Philosophy of the AS-IF* (Vaihinger, 1924). It is a theory of knowledge and of the treatment of ideas as fictions that we must imagine as being real, in order to discover their meanings. It was my hunch that there was value in this theory and that Rogers would have a better grasp than mine. At the same meeting, I also told him about another reading that had struck me as hilarious, written by or about the ideas of a psychologist named Lipps. To illustrate the idea, the writer, whose name I cannot recall, used the example of Viennese gentlemen who carried walking sticks and rolled umbrellas while they strolled the avenues. Why the canes? To replace the tails men had lost as they evolved from monkeys—extensions of themselves that they needed to feel their surroundings. We thought it funny, and we laughed at the writer's need to relate social science to that most-respected scientific establishment, Darwinism. But two things in the discussion were serious. One was the idea of extending oneself, found in both Vaihinger and Lipps. The other was the word used by Lipps, *empathy*. It caught our attention like a magnet, much as it currently has for the field of psychology. It seemed a word we dimly knew or recognised, or were waiting to hear.

It was in the air, but new to me, and I believe to Rogers, too. We talked about it, and we talked about the "couvade," and the yawn, and so on. We had both seen the photographs in *Social Psychology* (Allport, 1923/1937) showing spectators who lifted one leg and strained with the pole vaulter as he tried to clear the bar above their heads. So we knew of empathy as "ideo-motor," or sympathetic imitation, or something of that sort. We also knew of Titchener's work on introspection, but we certainly had not heard of his invention of this term or of any of his descriptions of empathy. It would have surprised us.

In my self-absorbed way, I took the idea of "extensions" to heart and recalled such experiences as my juvenile-delinquent driving days. With friends, we drove cars through narrow passages, trying to barely "click" the fenders against walls, trees, and other fenders. How can that be done? Your body, your self, extends into the body of your car. You are spread out into its dimensions, its wheels, fenders, and even the engine. You are in the machine. A scrape against the car is a scrape against yourself. In fact, you have such a sensitive feel for the speed of the engine and of the transmission that you sense the moment of synchronization of those two and can shift gears silently, without even using the clutch. I explained this to Rogers. He was interested but dubious—a more careful and methodical driver one seldom sees—and he was more interested in concepts and in people.

The next time we met, it was Rogers who was excited. Though wearing hat and coat and ready to leave, he beckoned me into his office, handed me the Vaihinger book without comment, and said, "You know what we were talking about the other day? You ought to read Martin Buber, *I and Thou*. Have you heard of that?" I had not, but he pushed me out the door, saving me a confession of ignorance. The book was checked out of the Divinity Library, and by Russell Becker, a close friend and colleague of Rogers, the husband of Rogers' loyal secretary. Actually, it was the wrong book. The relevant work was Buber's *Man to Man* (Buber, 1933). Three paragraphs from that work were circulated to the staff a few weeks later (and will shortly be reproduced here to illustrate a significant difference between Rogers and Buber). What was not reproduced was Buber's statement on the page following these paragraphs, which contained his rather scornful dismissal of empathy. Speaking of his idea of "inclusiveness," which is the relation between humans, and also between man and God (cf. Karen

Armstrong's recent book, *The History of God,* 1993), Buber wrote, "It would be wrong to identify what is meant here with the familiar but not very significant word 'empathy.' Empathy means, if anything, to glide with one's own feeling into the dynamic structure of an object, a pillar, or a crystal or the branch of a tree, or even an animal or man, and as it were, to trace it from within" (Buber, 1933, p. 97). But I did not read this page until some years later, nor did Rogers. Buber was far ahead of us, closer to the original usage of the word empathy, and unlike psychologists, not in need of a "clinical" view of this term.

Now we began to meet with a more regular focus on empathy. Rogers was engrossed in finishing his book and in some difficult clinical work as well. My work was to collect more ideas, more material for discussions. Late in 1948 a 1,000-page book on personality was sent by its author, Gardner Murphy, to Rogers, and this stupendous tome was handed to me. It had considerable information on empathy and sympathy, stating that the two were "difficult to separate" (Murphy, 1947), a point that did not sit well with Rogers. He had deep misgivings about the idea of sympathy, basically because he thought it smacked of "feeling sorry for, or looking down upon," both of which were reprehensible, or at least disrespectful attitudes, in his view. He also feared that being overly sympathetic might lead to an "indulgent" attitude on the part of the therapist. Above all, he wanted to avoid any tendency to pity, which he considered to be not a kindness, but something approaching contempt. He spoke of the lasting effect of his visit to China as a young man with a missionary group, where he saw humans treated as animals, beasts of burden, and humans as prisoners who groveled. It made him sick with rage and made him "wish he had a gun."

I was taking a course with Professor Blumer to study the ideas of G. H. Mead. To my mind, it was a great and influential theory, which espoused "taking the role of the other," but Rogers particularly disliked the notion of a "role." Although Mead used the term *sympathy* throughout, never empathy, I thought then and still do think that he was describing, early on and in wonderfully astute observations, an empathic process in every phase; he was describing the learning of the language and rules of the game, of social customs, in short, the whole of being human.

I brought in material from still another seminar, this one with the great biopsychologist Heinrich Kluver. Like Mead, he had studied in Germany, but of course he was born there, and knew Wundt, Titchener, Wertheimer, Koffka, and many others, including even Lipps. He was a man of enormous sophistication and modesty. In fact, he was quite shy. Like Kohut. Like Rogers. Intimate and expressive relationships were an effort, but also a delight to them. The class took place in his animal laboratory, where he studied the phenomenology of perception, working mainly with monkeys, to locate the neurological sites and mechanisms of perception. Sometimes he used himself as an experimental subject and related some of his experiences (Kluver, 1966). One afternoon in New Orleans, he had taken the drug mescaline and had gone for a walk. He had looked up at a wrought iron balcony, and felt himself "becoming that wrought iron. I took its shape. I WAS that wrought iron."

We five students stared. This was 1949, and we had never heard of "psychedelics." But was this empathy too? I reported to this class, and then to Rogers, an incident from my childhood, around the age of 9 or 10, when I had become a leaf. Resting on the grass, reading the *Wizard of Oz,* I had looked up to see a curled leaf, in a boatlike shape, slowly floating down from a high branch. As it rocked and turned in the air, I had become that leaf. I had understood why, given my shape and weight, I had to fall with a rocking motion. It was a physical and conceptual experience, that is, I had learned physics and logic from it. When the leaf landed, I became separate from it, happy and content. This had not seemed extraordinary. Didn't everyone do this? (I think so.)

Rogers did not like this story. He admired Kluver but may not have approved of drug use. I am certain that he did not at that time like the idea of self-induced hallucination. (Thirty years later, perhaps, yes). He was working with two clients who were experiencing hallucinations. One of them, the "easy" one, I later "inherited." The other, unbeknownst to me, was causing him a terrifying degree of stress. (That would have some bearing on his reservations—the "as-if"—about empathy, and the distinction between Rogers and Buber.)

Meanwhile, in another section of the university, empathy was a concept commonly read about and discussed by graduate students (my wife among them) in art history. One assigned reading was *Empathy and Abstraksion* (Worringer, 1908/1948), first published a year before Titchener introduced the term in the United States. Its concept and language is quite explicit and well-thought-out within its field, even dealing with "negative" as well as positive empathy. However, because it deals with art, which is considered by most to be "inanimate," the idea of empathy did not make its way across the Quadrangles—about 600 yards—from one department to the other. If only we had known. The Foreword in Worringer's book describes his chance meeting with Georg Simmel at a museum in Berlin, where they talked about the idea of empathy. Georg Simmel! My hero! Revered as the Leonardo of sociology, he was first translated by Albion Small, a founder of the Department of Sociology at the University of Chicago. Our work in psychology might have been enlightened years earlier if Art and Science had been exchanging ideas, for Wispé's superb chapter (Wispé, 1994) on the history of empathy dates the idea back to 1873, with the work of Vischerin, again in the field of aesthetics.

None of this meant much, it seemed, to Rogers. For one thing, he did not care much about history, or origins, or social science in general, for that matter. He cared about individual psychology and contemporary meanings, some of which he was trying to create. At the same time, he was under intense personal pressure. I was not yet an "insider" and did not know much of this until a few years later. Nor did I comprehend the greater effect until still later, when it was published in the biography *On Becoming Carl Rogers* (Kirschenbaum, 1979). (I did, however, know enough to avoid being interviewed by Kirschenbaum, not wanting to discuss or withhold material that Rogers himself, to my surprise, had chosen to reveal in the book.) In that, the reader can learn of a period, somewhere "during the years 1949 through 1951" when Rogers was afraid that he might be going insane, and might be "locked up and start to hallucinate" (which may have some bearing on his negative reaction to Kluver) and in desperation, "ran away" on a trip with his wife that lasted over 2 months (Kirschenbaum, 1979, pp. 191–192). He speaks of his work with a client with whom he "felt trapped" (how true) and felt that

> many of her insights were sounder than mine, and this destroyed my confidence in myself, and I got to the point where I could not separate my "self" from hers. I literally lost the boundaries of myself. The situation is best summarized by one of her dreams in which a cat was clawing my guts out, but did not wish to do so. (Kirschenbaum, 1979, p. 192)

Reading these pages some time after 1980 was a shock to me. I already knew about the case, having been told about it by some older staff members. And I had actually met this woman; what is more, in my own mind I had always referred to her as "the cat woman." She had stepped out of Rogers' office, and we passed in the hall. She'd said she "had to come back to see Carl again in a couple of hours" and invited me to lunch. She seemed both beseeching and commanding. I did not like her face. She once had perhaps been beautiful, but now in early middle age, she appeared seductive and menacing, with her flat, symmetrical face, and dark-blue, slanted eyes. I made some excuse about lunch. She had followed me to the first-floor research room and there talked about some research she had recently completed. She was very astute. It was a great study of learning, under conditions of actual practice compared with imaginary practice. I thought she must be Carl's research colleague from another university (Canadian, perhaps) and made a note about the research for future quotation. Although she timidly was seeking friendship, she was oddly possessive about the Counseling Center, the arrangement of the desks, the dirty curtains, and so on. This so annoyed me that I later told Carl about the research, meaning to get her academic address, but also complained about her possessiveness, and said, "Who the hell does she think she is?" He looked stricken. I will never forget his eyes. He shook his head, wiped the cup of his famous thermos bottle, screwed it on, and quietly said to come back for a talk next week. A few days later, he was gone. What a blunder, mine.

To get some idea of "who she thought she was," one can read that section of the biography (Kirschenbaum, 1979). Writing this 45 years later, I have a much more sympathetic understanding of this intelligent woman, trying to make her place in the world and to find recognition, trying to find relationships in a strange place, this being perhaps at the period of her final visits, while she probably had a sense of losing her struggle. She may well have been feeling as much desperation and anxiety as was her therapist.

How does this relate to Rogers' ideas about empathy? In the book *Client-Centered Therapy*, Rogers makes his first published statement about empathy. There he describes the act of assuming "the client's frame of reference" and calls it "empathic understanding" (Rogers, 1951, p. 29). This is not empathy per se, but a particular type of understanding, distinct from the types of understanding that come from external frames, such as diagnostic, or judgmental, or suspicious interrogation. Furthermore, the counselor must *communicate something of this empathic understanding to the client* [italics added]. Rogers then quotes a passage from a previously unpublished, but now deservedly famous, statement by Raskin, which is about a kind of understanding that represents "the non-directive attitude." Although it does not use the term *empathy*, the description forecasts the present-day concept.

Raskin concludes with the words, "because he (the counselor) is another, and not the client, the understanding is not spontaneous but must be acquired, and this through the most intense, continuous and active attention to the feelings of the other, to the exclusion of any other type of attention" (Rogers, 1951, p. 29). Important to note, such understanding is an act of attention, an effort, and not at all the kind of instant, immediate, spontaneous understanding that many associate with the word *empathy*. Rogers (1951) then adds to Raskin's statement a most interesting qualification, saying that this

> experiencing with the client . . . is not in terms of emotional identification . . . , but rather an empathic identification, where the counselor is perceiving the hates and hopes and fears of the client through immersion in an empathic process, but without himself, as counselor, experiencing those hates and hopes and fears. (p. 29)

Plainly, empathic is still a modifier, adjective, or adverb, not the supposedly active noun *empathy*. But the difference between "emotional" and "empathic" is not clear, then or now. What is clear is that Rogers is putting distance between the feelings and experiences of the client and his own. Later, he would entirely abandon the idea of identification of any kind, when, around 1956, he drafted the "as-if" clause (Koch, 1959). I do not know the exact timing of his thoughts as he made these distancing revisions in published writing, but they do follow his experience with the client about whom he was so disturbed, and when his own identity was so threatened.

Turning back to Buber, here are the three paragraphs that so impressed Rogers around 1949 to 1950.

> A man belabors another, who remains quite still. Then let us assume that the striker suddenly receives in his soul the blow which he strikes; the same blow; that he received it as the other who still remains still. For the space of a moment he experiences the situation from the other side. Reality imposes itself upon him. What will he do? Either he will overwhelm the voice of the soul, or his impulse will be reversed.
>
> A man caresses a woman, who lets herself be caressed. Then let us assume that he feels the contact from two sides—with the palm of his hand still, and also with the woman's skin. The two-fold nature of the gesture, as one that takes place between two persons, thrills through the depth of enjoyment in his heart and stirs it. If he does not deafen his heart he will have—not to renounce enjoyment—but to love.
>
> I do not in the least mean that the man who has had such an experience would from then on have this two-sided sensation in every such meeting—that would perhaps destroy his instinct. But the one extreme experience makes the other person present to him for all time. A transfusion has taken place after which a mere elaboration of subjectivity is never again possible or tolerable to him.[3] (Buber, 1933, p. 196)

Reference has already been made to the theme of "inclusiveness" in Buber's approach to an "empathic" relationship. In 1957, he and Rogers met, and that meeting is published (Anderson & Kissna, in press). In it, Rogers asks Buber, "How have you lived so deeply . . . and gained such an understanding . . . without being a psychotherapist?" (Laughter). It is indeed a funny "throwaway" question from Rogers, the former Divinity School student, who knows and welcomes the fact that many "untrained" humans have keen sensitivities, to the theologian who also knows and welcomes that. Buber explains that he did in fact study three terms in psychiatry,—"first in Leipzig, where there were students of Wundt" (again, Wundt) and afterwards in Berlin with Mandel and Bleuler. He did not intend to become a therapist:

> It was just a certain inclination to meet people. And as far as possible to, just to change if possible something in the other but also let me be changed by him. At any event, I had no resistance . . . put no resistance to it. I began as a young man. I felt I had not the right to change another if I am not open to be changed by him, as far as it is legitimate. I cannot say to him, "NO! I'm out of the play. You are mad."

---

[3] It is my hope that the reader will study Buber's words more than in one reading, to imagine, reflect on, visualize, and perhaps remember. These words express profound levels of thought. Rogers wanted to move closer to this position, but something prevented that, at least in early writing. Also, note that Buber's second paragraph is, in part, about sexuality. It is strange that psychologists, so preoccupied with both sex and empathy, have little to say about their connection. One exception is in *The Talk Book*, by Gerald Goodman (1988), who expands on the above paragraph by Buber in a more prosaic paraphrase.

He then describes more experiences in which he was suffering for a friend who had been killed in the war, "imagining the real," feeling it not just in an optical way of imagining but "just with my body" (pp. 42–45). Most telling, most relevant to this comparison, is the description of "a tragic incident" in which a young man came to seek his advice. Buber was preoccupied and talked with him but did not really "meet" him. The young man went away and committed suicide.

For Buber, there is no "as-if." He does not want that. It would preclude the possibility of the "I-Thou." Buber is willing to be changed by the other. That is the choice of "inclusiveness." His tragedies—grief, guilt—and his fears, hates, and hopes are not the same as those of Rogers. Thus, for one person, Rogers, it was essential to preserve boundaries; for the other, Buber, it was to dissolve them. Therefore, these two, among the greatest humanists of our time, espouse different theories of empathic understanding. If there is nothing else to be drawn from this, we can at least conclude that all personality theory is autobiographical. Variations on a theme stem from differences in personal experience. Everything is personal.

In addition, if they do not know each other's particular experience of tragedies, hopes, and fears, they will not readily understand the basis or meaning of each other's theories of self-in-relationship, although they might have had (in fact, they did have) more theoretical similarities than are apparent in their writings and in these dialogues.

Finally, it is worth noting that when Rogers became involved with large "person-centered" groups around 1970, and no longer felt such personal responsibility for the individual client, or need for such detachment, he was sometimes so moved that, as he put it, he "wept buckets of tears." Not "as-if" but quite real tears, I am sure. And with both Rogers and Buber, we have seen that reaction to failure or disappointment with self sometimes determined theory that later influenced the professions and the world at large. Fortunately, this only applies to the subsidiary issue of the "as-if" not the general theory of empathy. Unfortunately, there is no such general theory.

A CASE OF "REVERBERATIVE" EMPATHY

Although empathy works as a more or less constantly active system, found everywhere in daily life, clinicians look for special displays in "clinical cases" as if they were exceptional. Here is a bit of such material. Why this particular case? Because it has been published—cited as an "exquisite" example of empathy, most of it recorded, dramatic to the point of obscuring its defects—and because it contains a special theory of psychological disintegration in the psychotic state (Shlien, 1961). When Rogers read it for the second time, some years after his experience in the Wisconsin "Schizophrenia Project," he called the theory "a work of genius." So it is, this theory being taken directly from the writings of a certified genius, Jean-Paul Sartre, in his study of the lie, self-deception, and the consequent loss of self (Sartre, 1956).

During months of strenuous therapy, I learned many things that enter into the experience of empathy—the smell of fear, for instance. That smell is stark, intense, and common to the patients who are subjected to electro-convulsive shock. Many expect to die, strapped down and helpless, to lose consciousness, and never regain it. This patient felt that way. He thought I had ordered that treatment (although I had distinctly forbidden it, a ward physician ordered it to subdue violent outbursts), and Mike, the pa-tient–client, wanted to kill me in return. I didn't blame him.

Lacking space, not much can be reported here. Mike was a former Navy frogman, very strong, a carpenter by trade, and usually good-natured. Easily goaded into foolish escapades, he had been in two other hospitals before his parents committed him (after promising him it was "just a visit") to the rather gruesome state institution where I consulted. He heard his thoughts coming out of the television set. His mind was transparent; he was the object of an experiment by the FBI; he raged, wept, begged, denied, was sly, and was life-threatening. Often during interviews, guards were sta-tioned outside my office door by the hospital director (who was also my client). Mike and I went through hell together—he in his own hell, I in mine with my own fears, and both hells intermingled. Eventually there came a time when he understood that much more about his life and had so much more control that he was given a grounds pass, and we could meet on the lawn, alone and safe.

At some point during the last of these meetings, he began to cry softly, saying, "They talk about love and affection. I know what that means. The only good thing I ever had (his engagement to a girl) was taken away from me, broken up." He blew his nose, dropped his handkerchief, and as he picked it up, glanced at me. He saw tears in my eyes. He offered me the handkerchief, then drew it back because he knew he had just wiped his nose on it and could feel the wetness on his hand. We both knew this, and each knew the other knew it; we both understood the feel and the meaning of the handkerchief, the stickiness and texture, the sympathy of the offering and the embarrassment of the withdrawal, and we acknowledged each other and the interplay of each one's significance to the other. It is not the tears, but the exquisite awareness of dual experience that restores consciousness of self" (and not a word was spoken during this episode) (Shlien, 1961, p. 316).

In our final meeting on the lawn, Mike said, "I went to church yester-day, Doc, and I said a prayer that this would never happen again. I said a little prayer for you, too, that you could help me and always be well your-self." Of course I was touched, as he was, but did not simply express our mutual appreciation. I said, "It sounds like you are trying to say goodbye, Mike, and to leave us feeling OK about each other." Without this, there would have been only empathy, not empathic understanding. Yes, he explained, he absolutely had to get out of here and could not come to see me at the university. Where he lives, "a person has to be goofy to go to a psychiatrist." He was discharged before I could see him again.

The significant empathy in this was relational, interactive empathy. The rest—the kite, the straining rope, the rendering of meaning to art—is only basic. What you see in this episode on the hospital lawn is a series of mutual, reciprocal, complex "reverberations." Although it need not be wordless, it is, and takes place at a speed beyond our ability in speech. I know his sincerity, his fear, his desperate hope, and his recognition of my caring for his welfare and know that he cares for mine. There is something full of grace in his gesture with the snotty handkerchief and something ungainly, not "graceful," about it at all. It has the ambivalence that characterizes most of life. He knows that I saw his offer, wanted and did not want to accept it, and why, and that I understood, he understood—we understood, in a series of "bouncing between us" consequences, for each and for both.

What does this mean to us? It means public confirmation, and internally, self-affirmation. These "reverberations," in infinite regress (or progress) tell Mike that he can know, he does know, he can be known, understood, and can reciprocate in kind. For Mike, knowing means sanity, no less. To me, it suggests that, although "growth motive" is a wonderful and spirited idea, it is more elementary—that the animal lives to grow, but the relationally construed person lives to know. Knowing confirms being, existence, and humanity, and for the insane, confirms the restoration of sanity. But knowing takes some degree of communicated confirmation.

In silent empathy, those bouncing "reverberations" not only take up a large portion of consciousness but also cost us subterranean uneasiness and a good deal of energy for the storage of these unsettled and unconfirmed understandings. It is almost like living with half-truths; hard to make use of these largely voiceless, invisible, unconfirmed signals. What is more, the organ of empathy is not so familiar, not so palpable, or distinct. It takes the whole of the mind–body composite, and it is often wordless. This most certainly does not mean thoughtless. Quite the opposite! True, empathy is more sensational than perceptual, but that only means it requires still more in extra effort of "cognitive processing" for humans who want to examine and understand their experience, rather than simply to have it.

Empathy operates on data such as smell, sight, and sound: the smell of fear; the sight of tears, of blushing, and of yawning; and the sound of cadences, tone, sighs, and howls. It operates at what we might think of as primitive levels, cellular, glandular, olfactory, chemical, electromagnetic, autonomic, postural, gestural, and musical–rhythmical, more than lexical.

If such modalities seem far-fetched, consider the pupil of the eye. For a long time, it had a status less observed than was sweating, or flaring of the nostrils. But in folk-psychology, gem traders were said to watch the pupils of the buyer's eyes for signs of special interest. In academic psychology, the pupil was well-known mainly for the phenomenon of contraction when exposed to light; it was a favorite in the laboratory because so readily conditioned. Only a few decades ago Eckhard Hess (Hess, 1975) and colleagues demonstrated with unmistakable evidence what those shrewd jade dealers had noticed. The pupil dilates when one sees what is interesting, attractive, and lovable, such as when a mother sees an infant or when a man sees a beautiful woman. Even more relevant in this latter case, when her pupils are dilated, her face looks softer, more beautiful, and above all, his pupils will dilate in response. Neither (unless they are trained observers) is likely to be aware of this. It just happens. It is involuntary. It is a routine, though seldom-recognized, example of the theory of empathy, in action. Like blood pressure, heart rate, and ovulation, some individuals can sense pupillary reactions, and even control them, but for most, it is subliminal. Because the interactions of our pupils come from such an unrecognized source, some imagine it to be "intuition"—a lazy as well as false explanation. The fact is, the information is clear and direct, replicable, and easily visible (especially in blue eyes).

Ideas about "intuition" confuse and mislead, as do other lures such as metaphors and myths. They are especially damaging to our less-obvious psychological realities, such as empathy. We say that someone "speaks from the heart" if he is sincere, "decides with her heart" if she seems romantic. Really, hearts do not speak. They inform, by clenching, racing, and so on, in response to some experience. A friend had his heart replaced with a pump. He still spoke with the same values, convictions, and sincerity as before. Where was his "heart"? In the hospital garbage, long gone. But that was only his flesh and blood heart, not his "real" heart. Perhaps he "speaks from his pump"? That is no more likely and much less poetic. There is a "psychological organ" we call "heart." It has a memory of heart experience, with functional autonomy, which is a functional equivalent of the flesh and blood organ. It is in this sense that empathy is an organ, as well as a form of intelligence. If it is an organ related to intelligence, it is organ-as-agency of intelligence (i.e., gathering information). Why this design? Perhaps it is an experience-seeking part of the therapist, or other humans, in the way that some other species or artificial models are heat seeking or phototropic. Empathy is like a guidance system: It gets you to the airport but makes no decisions about what to do once you are there.

We may have doubts about these and other subtle "ingredients" in spite of the evidence from such phenomena as the pupils of the eye. Electromagnetic? It sounds impossible. Yet it alters our cells and body chemistry. Try for yourself a crystal radio in an AM frequency. You act as an antenna.

There will be tiny changes in the amplitude of your body. The crystal will change dimensions. You may hear music (or voices) with low-frequency headphones. Change your position or temperature, and the reception will change. Other such effects remain to be discovered, or uncovered (as with pupils), and while some will be false leads, some even too ephemeral to study, modalities now hidden will surface. However subtle, these mind-body interrelationships are more substantial than some notions of the physical world in which we place considerable confidence. The electron is only a theory. But it works so well, that is, explains so much (but not all) that it seems real.

Empathy, on the other hand, is not much of a theory, explains hardly anything, tells us nothing of the "mechanisms," but it is an experiential actuality for many people, and generally considered an established fact. That "fact" is so recently discovered and named that it seems new and fashionable. Without doubt it is primitive, quite ancient. Whole flocks of birds do it, bees do it, even recent PhD's do it. When domestic animals do it, humans call them "smart." When humans do it, they consider it elementary, from the heart, a sort of "gut reaction," and a saving grace to counter the psychologists' suspicion of "over-intellectualization". This attractive subscribing to the "wisdom of the body" is onesided and unfortunate. Empathy should not be a denial of the brain. Some of our most advanced modern ideas may rely on empathy. Einstein's "thought experiments" demonstrate the launching of an imaginary object into space, accompanied by the genius (as the archer goes with the arrow?) and upon return to earth, there is new understanding of time and space.

Does this exercise of empathy restore the supremacy of brain over body? Oddly, it cannot favor either, because, now we know, they are one. It is new but public knowledge that a part of the neural tube, forming in the neonate, is squeezed down into the lower cavity, creating the "enteric nervous system" (Blakeslee, 1996, p. B5). The brain is not only that encased in the skull. A part, connected by the vagus nerve, is actually in the abdominal tissue. Biological study finds the same neurons and transmitters in each part, both formed by the original neural crest. When the theory of empathy is developed, it will support the restoration of the "whole person"—an idea too long submerged by poorly informed mind–body disputes.

REFERENCES

Allport, F. (1937). *Social psychology*. Boston: Houghton Mifflin. (Original work published 1923)

Anderson, R., & Kissna, K. N. (in press). The Martin Buber–Carl Rogers dialogue: A new transcript with commentary. Albany: State University of New York Press.

Armstrong, K. (1993). *A history of God.* New York: Ballantine Books.

Blakeslee, S. (1996, January 23). Complex and hidden brain in the gut makes cramps, butterflies and valium. *The New York Times,* pp. B5, B10.

Brecht, B., & Weill, K. (1934). Ballad of Mack the Knife. On *Three penny opera* [record]. New York: Columbia MasterWorks.

Buber, M. (1933). *Between man and man.* London: Kegan Paul.

Goodman, G. (1988). *The talk book.* New York: Rodale Press.

Hess, E. H. (1975). *The tell-tale eye.* New York: Van Nostrand Reinhold.

Kirschenbaum, H. (1979). *On becoming Carl Rogers.* New York: Dell.

Kluver, H. (1966). *Mescal and mechanisms of hallucinations.* Chicago: University of Chicago Press.

Koch, S. (Ed.). (1959). *Psychology: A Study of a Science* (Vol. 3). New York: McGraw-Hill.

Mead, G. H. (1934). *Mind, self, and society.* Chicago: University of Chicago Press.

Murphy, G. (1947). *Personality: A biosocial approach.* New York: Harper & Brothers.

Perls, F., Hefferline, R. F., & Goodman, P. (1951). *Gestalt therapy.* New York: Julian Press.

Rogers, C. R. (1951). *Client-centered therapy.* Boston: Houghton Mifflin.

Sartre, J. (1956). *Self deception and falsehood.* In W. Kaufman (Ed.), *Existentialism from Dostoevsky to Sartre.* New York: Meridian Books.

Shlien, J. (1961). A client-centered approach to schizophrenia: First approximation. In A. Burton (Ed.), *The psychotherapy of the psychoses.* New York: Basic Books.

Stoehr, T. (1994). *Here, now, next: The origins of Gestalt therapy.* San Francisco: Jossey-Bass.

Vaihinger, R. (1924). *The philosophy of the "AS-IF."* London: Rutledge Kegan Paul.

Wispé, L. (1994). History of the concept of empathy. In N. Eisenberg & J. Strayer (Eds.), *Empathy and its Development.* Cambridge, England: Cambridge University Press.

Worringer, W. (1948). *Abstraksion and empathy.* New York: International Universities Press. (Original work published 1908)

4

EMPATHY FROM THE FRAMEWORK OF CLIENT-CENTERED THEORY AND THE ROGERIAN HYPOTHESIS

JEROLD D. BOZARTH

This chapter examines Rogers's unique conceptualization of empathy as it has evolved in relationship to client-centered theory (Rogers, 1959) and to the Rogerian hypothesis, or "integrative" statement, of the necessary and sufficient conditions for therapeutic personality change (Rogers, 1957). Rogers's (1951, 1957, 1959, 1975, 1980, 1986a, 1986b, 1987; Rogers & Sanford, 1989) conception of empathy is central to client- and person-centered theory and to the Rogerian hypothesis. Although it was Rogers (1975) and Kohut (1959, 1984) who perpetuated empathy's central importance in psychotherapy, Rogers's view of empathy is different from Kohut as well as from others. Rogers considered empathy to be (a) a central therapeutic construct rather than a precondition to other forms of treatment, (b) a therapist's attitude toward and experiencing of the client rather than any particular therapist behavior, (c) an interpersonal process grounded in a nondirective attitude, and (d) a part of a whole attitude wherein the experience of empathic understanding is intertwined with the therapist's congruence and the experiencing of unconditional positive regard toward the client. Rogers also brought attention to a particular way of communicating the empathic attitude that he referred to as "Reflection" or "Reflection of Feelings." Rogers's unique view of empathy is discussed in the context of his theory and his written comments.

It is my conclusion that Rogerian empathy is (a) a concept integrally intertwined with congruence and unconditional positive regard as they exist

81

within his hypothesis; (b) a process that intends only to understand the client's frame of reference rather than to achieve any particular therapeutic goal and, as such, communicates unconditional positive regard; and (c) an attitude rather than any particular way of responding.

It has been suggested that Rogerian empathy is primarily the purest way to communicate unconditional positive regard. Rogerian empathy is, in fact, inseparable from unconditional positive regard, and I suggest that they are ultimately the same condition.

THEORETICAL FRAMEWORK

Rogers's basic assumption is that human thought, feeling, and behavior are motivated and directed by one constructive force, the actualizing tendency that is inherent in the organism (Bozarth & Brodley, 1991). His theory of the process of personality disturbance purports that individuals develop psychological problems because of the introjections of conditional acceptance from parents and other significant people. These introjections of conditional regard create incongruence between organismic experiencing and the self concept. As the self becomes laden with conditions of worth, a person becomes anxious and vulnerable. The theory asserts that when the person perceives unconditional positive regard in the context of empathic understanding from a congruent individual (the therapist), then the actualizing tendency of the client is promoted (Rogers, 1959). It is from this theoretical base that the "necessary and sufficient" conditions were posed as the therapeutic attitudes for the therapist to embody. Rogers's (1959) statement concerning the conditions within client-centered theory are as follows:

1. That two persons are in contact.
2. That the first person, whom we shall term the client, is in a state of incongruence, being vulnerable or anxious.
3. That the second person, whom we shall call the therapist, is congruent in the relationship.
4. That the therapist is experiencing unconditional positive regard towards the client.
5. That the therapist is experiencing an empathic understanding of the client's internal frame of reference.
6. That the client perceives, at least to a minimal degree, Conditions 4 and 5, the unconditional positive regard of the therapist for him, and the empathic understanding of the therapist. (pp. 238–239)

Rogers (1957) lists the same conditions with slight variations in his integrative statement. The definitions for the attitudinal qualities are similar in both the theory and the integration statement. He defines them as follows

Congruence: . . . discrepancy between the actual experience of the organism and the self picture of the individual insofar as it represents that experience. [For the therapist:] It means that within the relationship he (or she) is freely and deeply him (her) self, with his (or her) actual experience accurately represented by his/her awareness of him/herself. (pp. 98–99)

Unconditional Positive Regard: To the extent that the therapist finds him (or her) self experiencing a warm acceptance of each aspect of the client's experience as being a part of that client, he (or she) is experiencing unconditional positive regard. (p. 100)

Empathy: To sense the client's private world as if it were your own, but without ever losing the "as if" quality. (p. 101)

In addition, Rogers hypothesizes that "the client perceives, to a minimal degree, the acceptance and empathy which the therapist experiences for him (or her)" (p. 102).

It can readily be seen from Rogers's six-point statement that the conditions are integrally related as one hypothesis—especially the therapist's experiencing of and the client's perception of empathic understanding and unconditional positive regard.

DELINEATION OF ROGERIAN EMPATHY

Examination of Rogers's historical and evolutionary delineation of empathy suggests that empathy in client-centered theory is a concept that is integrally integrated with the conditions of congruency and unconditional positive regard. It exists within a context of nondirectivity and is predicated on the foundation block of the actualizing tendency.

Rogers brought a distinct view to the concept of empathy by making it central to the therapeutic change process; that is, if only the therapist experiences an empathic understanding and unconditional acceptance of clients, the clients who perceive the conditions will be better able to understand themselves, accept themselves, make behavioral changes that enhance their lives, and be more able to relate constructively in their social world.

Rogers's (1942) first major theoretical work on nondirective therapy did not mention the term *empathy*; however, a number of his comments paved the way for the conceptualization. For example, in his discussion of a good therapist he refers to "a capacity for sympathy . . . a generally receptive and interested attitude, a deep understanding which will find it impossible to pose moral judgments" (p. 254). He also refers to "a degree of sympathetic identification with (the client) as him (or her), on his (or her) own level of adjustment" (p. 255). As well, he voiced the nondirective element in empathy, describing the therapy relationship as expressing "warmth of acceptance and absence of any coercion or personal pressure" (pp. 113–114). He asserted that the therapist "takes no responsibility for directing the outcome of the process" (p. 115).

Early in his career, Rogers (1939) asked the question, "What, if anything, do all these therapeutic approaches have in common?" (Kirschenbaum, 1979, p. 96). At that time, Rogers identified the four qualifications of the therapist for effective therapy with children as objectivity, respect for the individual, understanding of self, and psychological knowledge. Rogers elaborates on these qualifications:

1. *objectivity*, in which he included a capacity for sympathy which will not be overdone, a genuinely receptive and interested attitude, a deep understanding which will find it impossible to pass moral judgments or be shocked and horrified.
2. *a respect for the individual*: the aim is to leave the major responsibilities in the hands of the child as an individual going towards independence.
3. *understanding of the self*, to which he allied the therapist's ability to be self-accepting as well as self-aware.
4. *psychological knowledge*, by which he meant a thorough basis of knowledge of human behaviour and of its physical, social and psychological determinants (Thorne, 1992, p. 10)

Rogers's attempting to identify the core and crucial qualifications of the therapist in work with children appears to be an early forerunner to his general hypothesis of the necessary and sufficient conditions for personality change in all therapies and all therapeutic approaches.

Rogers first labeled his theory *nondirective therapy*. He also focused on the technique of "reflection of feelings," which he cautioned not to be practiced as a simple technique. Rogers wrote in the mid-1940s that

> to create a psychological climate in which the client feels the kind of warmth, understanding and freedom from attack in which he may drop his defensiveness, and explore and reorganize his life style, is a far more subtle and delicate process than simply "reflecting feeling." (Kirschenbaum, 1979, p. 160)

It is clear that "understanding" of the client was couched in, if not subsidiary to, "warm acceptance" and an atmosphere of freedom toward the client. Although Rogers focused on the therapist's activity as one that was meant to clarify the feelings of individuals, he used the terms *clarification, reflection,* and *reflection of feelings.* The role of the therapist's action was that "reflection of feelings communicates to the client that whatever his feelings and behavior are or have been, no matter how troubling or frightening or socially disapproved of, he is still accepted as a worthy human being by the therapist" (Kirschenbaum, 1979, p. 120). Much of Rogers's work at the University of Chicago, although grounded in the attitudinal principles, focused on therapists' responses. Out of the scientific method and with a behavioral context, Rogers and his colleagues examined the effect of specific client behaviors to specific responses of the therapist. It was not until Rogers became concerned about the misunderstandings of reflection and the use of reflection techniques that he talked about the client's frame of reference and began to use the term *empathy*. Empathy provided Rogers with a more comprehensive meaning that emphasized attitude rather than a response repertoire or skills model.

As Rogers (1951) began to explicitly use the term *empathy*, he described it as the therapist's development of an interest in and receptivity to the client and a search for a deep nonjudgmental understanding. It involved identification with the client, respect for the client as a whole person, and acceptance of the person as he or she is. The search, through interaction with the client and close attention to the client, was and is considered a nondirective process. Indeed, the empathic therapist is responsible for his or her attitudes and responsiveness to the client and not for the outcome of the therapy. Later, Rogers's (1980) descriptions of the empathic process focus on the therapist's empathic intention:

> to sense the hurt or the pleasure of another as he (or she) senses it, and to perceive the causes thereof as he (or she) perceives them. (p. 210)
>
> [and it involves] . . . lay[ing] aside all perceptions from the external frame of reference. (p. 29)
>
> It means entering the private perceptual world of the other . . . being sensitive, moment by moment, to the changing felt meanings which flow in this other person. . . . It means sensing meanings of which he or she is scarcely aware, but not trying to uncover totally unconscious feelings. (p. 142)

This is the kind of understanding required in client-centered therapy, namely:

> the therapist's sensitive ability and willingness to understand the client's thoughts, feelings and struggles from the client's point of view. This ability to see completely through the client's eyes, to adopt his frame of reference . . . is the basis for the use of the term "client-centered." (Kirschenbaum, 1979, p. 164)

In these explanations of empathic understanding, Rogers's focus on understanding empathy per se is directed toward the therapist's activity and does not include explicit reference to his fundamental therapeutic change agent of unconditional positive regard. Rogers's implicit, and often explicit, assumption in his definition of empathic understanding is that it is integrally related to the unconditional positive regard of the therapist for the client. Indeed, empathic understanding is the unconditional acceptance of the individual's frame of reference.

It should be noted that Rogers was quite insistent that one should perceive the internal frame of reference from the person's view without losing the "as if" condition. This seemed particular important to Rogers. Perhaps this was related to a difficulty in which he had approached a "psychotic" breakdown while working with a "psychotic" client (Kirschenbaum, 1979, p. 191). He did, as previously noted, identify "objectivity" as one of the qualifications of the therapist in his early speculations about common therapist qualities, even though it was couched in the idea of helping the therapist to not pass moral judgments on the client. Whatever the reason, he seemed particularly concerned that the therapist not identify with the client but maintain the as-if dimension. It is, perhaps, this concern that was part of the reason for Rogers's ostensible literal and logical–rational verbal focus of responding to clients.

The Integrative Statement

Rogers's (1957) formal statement of the necessary and sufficient conditions for therapeutic personality change accounts for therapeutic personality change as it occurs in all therapy, not only in client-centered therapy (Stubbs & Bozarth, 1996). In this statement, as well as in his formulation of client-centered theory, Rogers (1959) asserts the necessity that the client perceive the therapist's experiencing of acceptant empathic understanding for therapeutic change to occur. Neither Rogers's theory of therapeutic change nor the hypothesis of the necessary and sufficient conditions are expressed in terms of behavior. This is a crucial point in understanding Rogerian empathy, particularly because most explanations of it and models developed from Rogers's hypothesis (e.g., Carkhuff, 1971; Corey, 1982; Cormier & Cormier, 1991; Egan, 1975) have cast the concept into a behavioral framework. The frequent focus on techniques and the therapist's behavioral strategies has been responsible for the misunderstanding and trivializing of client-centered therapy and its concept of empathy (Bozarth & Brodley, 1986; Stubbs & Bozarth, 1996). Rogers's theory is expressed in terms of the therapist's attitudes. There is no specific behavior or pattern of behavior that can be considered to be an inevitable expression of empathy nor a necessarily true expression of an empathic attitude. The role of attitudes is conveyed in Rogers's (1957) statement:

> There is no essential value to the therapy of such techniques as interpretation of personality dynamics, free association, analysis of dreams, analysis of transference, hypnosis, interpretation of life style, suggestion and the like. Each of these technique may, however, become a channel for communicating the essential conditions. . . . But just as these techniques *may* communicate the elements which are essential for therapy, so any one of them may communicate attitudes and experiences sharply contradictory to the hypothesized conditions of therapy. (p. 101)

There is, in fact, no specific form of communication of the therapeutic attitudes that can describe client-centered therapy or communicate the necessary and sufficient conditions (Bozarth, 1984; Rogers, 1957, 1959; Stubbs & Bozarth, 1996). Although empathic understanding responses (Brodley, 1993), earlier referred to as "reflection of feelings" responses (Rogers, 1986b), have been identified with client-centered work, such responses are not to be confused with empathy. The limited importance of specific responses is emphasized by Rogers (1957) in his comment concerning techniques:

> The techniques of the various therapies are relatively unimportant except to the extent that they serve as channels for fulfilling one of the conditions. In client-centered therapy, for example, (even) the technique of "reflecting feelings" . . . is by no means an essential condition of therapy. To the extent . . . that it provides a channel by which the therapist communicates a sensitive empathy and an unconditional positive regard, then it may serve as a technical channel by which the essential conditions of therapy are fulfilled. . . . Feeling may (however) be reflected in a way which communicates the therapist's lack of empathy. (pp. 102–103)

Rogerian empathy is fundamentally the same in his theory and his integrative statement.

EMPATHY AS THE THERAPIST'S ACTIVITY

The therapist has a deliberate and abiding intent to empathically understand and accept the immediate frame of reference and experience of the client while being integrated and congruent in himself or herself. The attitudinal action component of the therapist is that of empathy. The therapist's activities involve several categories that are commented on in this section.

The Nondirective Attitude

The nondirective attitude is rarely mentioned in recent literature concerning the client-centered and person-centered approach. It is, however, implicit in the theory and suggests that there is, in essence, no room for directivity in Rogers's conceptions of therapy and the therapist's role. Nondirectivity casts a major influence on Rogers's conceptualization of empathy.

Although the concept of nondirectivity is not explicit in Rogers's generic theoretical statements (Rogers, 1951, 1959; Rogers & Sanford, 1989) or the integrative statement (Rogers, 1957), it is implied in nearly all of Rogers's writings. Rogers was explicit that he had no goals for clients.

As he stated, "the goal has to be within myself, with the way I am" (Baldwin, 1987, p. 47). He contended that therapy is most effective "when the therapist's goals are limited to the process of therapy and not the outcome" (p. 47). He indicated, "I want to be as present to this person as possible. I want to really listen to what is going on. I want to be real in this relationship" (p. 47). He continued, "Am I really with this person in this moment?. . . [These are] suitable goals for the therapist" (p. 48). The nondirective attitude is explained by Rogers as he quotes an unpublished article by Raskin, who coined the term. Raskin (as cited in Rogers, 1951) states:

> There is a level of . . . response which . . . represents the nondirective attitude . . . participation becomes an active experiencing with the client of the feelings to which he (or she) gives expression . . . he (or she) tries to get within and to live the attitudes (of the client) expressed instead of observing them, to catch every nuance of their changing nature; in a word, to absorb himself (or herself) completely in the attitudes of the other. And in struggling to do this, there is simply no room for any other type of counselor activity or attitude; if he (or she) is attempting to live the attitudes of the other, he (or she) cannot be diagnosing them . . . cannot be thinking of making the process go faster. (p. 29)

In an analysis of the essence of client-centered therapy, Bozarth (1990b) asserts that the implications "are staggering" and states:

> It (the essence) is a functional premise that precludes other therapist intentions. The therapist goes with the client—goes at the client's pace—goes with the client in his/her own ways of thinking, of experiencing, of processing. The therapist can not be up to other things, have other intentions without violating the essence of CC/PC therapy. To be up to other things—whatever they might be—is a "yes" but reaction to the essence of the approach. (p. 63; italics in original)

The essence of Rogerian therapy is embedded in nondirective empathy. The foundation block of the theory is the actualizing tendency. The change agent is unconditional positive regard.

Therapist Techniques and Communications

Rogers's theory is resistant to the systematic use of techniques. His "techniques" are always embedded in the therapeutic attitudes—that is, grounded in the inner experiences of the therapist in response to the client's frame of reference.

Rogers's contribution to techniques is a paradoxical one. The formalization of reflection, reflection of feelings and the restatement rule (Teich, 1992) provides a powerful tool for the therapist to attain empathic understanding. Shlien (Rogers, 1986b) has suggested that client-centered therapy would have never progressed without the development of the technique of reflection. Even so, Rogers was clear that the technique was of little value if not embedded in the attitudes of the therapist. Rogers (1980), in fact, referred to the "appalling consequences" of the schematization of the principle of reflection into a schema of a technique. Brodley and Brody (1996) purport that techniques can be used if they are part of the response to client questions or responses. However, they respond, "Not if they are the result of the therapist's having a diagnostic mind set that determines which goals and techniques are indicated" (p. 369). Bozarth (1996b) believes that the theory reacts against the use of techniques but their use may be consistent with the theory if the techniques emerge from the blending of the therapist and client. According to Bozarth, "the primary reason for involving techniques in a client-centered frame of reference is to help the therapist to clear his/her barriers to absorbing the client's perceptual world" (p. 367).

To Rogers, empathy is a mode of the therapist's experiencing of another person to an extent that is more than a technique, formula, form, or cognitive schema. It is integrally intertwined with trusting the client (in the theory, it is expressed as the actualizing tendency) within a nondirective context. Rogerian empathy and unconditional positive regard are inseparable.

UNCONDITIONAL POSITIVE REGARD AND EMPATHY

I assert that the empathic and unconditional acceptance of the therapist is, in essence, the same experience. Unconditional positive regard is the crucial client perception in the client's change process and is conveyed by empathy (Bozarth, 1996a). This is clear in Rogers's early speculations and conceptualizations before he used the term *empathy*. In Rogers's (1959) theory of personality reintegration, discussed above, his view is that learned conditions of worth and consequent incongruence between the self and organismic experiencing are reversed by the growth process inherent in the client (i.e., the process of the actualizing tendency). This inherent process is activated when the client perceives the therapist's unconditional positive regard and develops unconditional positive regard toward himself or herself. Such regard is communicated through the therapist's acceptant empathic understandings in the context of the therapist's congruence in the relationship. Rogers (1975) states the role of the combined acceptant and empathic attitudes in terms of the processes that take hold in the client as follows:

(1) The non-evaluative and acceptant quality of the empathic climate enables the client, as we have seen, to take a prizing, caring attitude toward himself. (2) Being listened to by an understanding person makes it possible for him to listen more accurately to himself, with greater empathy towards his own visceral experiencing, his own vague felt

meanings. But (3) his greater understanding of, and prizing of, himself opens up part of a more accurately based self. His self is now more congruent with his experiencing. Thus, he has become, in his attitudes toward himself, more caring and acceptant, more empathic and understanding, more real and congruent. (pp. 7–9)

Rogerian empathy involves the therapist in a personal commitment to experience acceptance toward the client and to experience the client's inner world. In client-centered work, empathy is both a manifestation of and a communication vessel for unconditional positive regard. The consequences of such empathy for the recipient is twofold, according to Rogers (1980). Empathy "dissolves alienation" and helps the recipient to feel "valued, cared for, accepted as the person that he or she is." When this occurs, "true empathy is always free of any evaluative or diagnostic quality" (pp. 151–155). The nonevaluative and acceptant quality Rogers ascribes to empathy is, in fact, the same as his definition of unconditional positive regard, wherein the therapist experiences "a warm acceptance of each aspect of the client's experience as being a part of that client" (Rogers, 1957, p. 93).

RESEARCH FINDINGS AND ROGERIAN EMPATHY

An overview of relevant research findings related to Rogerian empathy suggests that, to a significant extent, current outcome research substantiates Rogers's conceptualization of empathy in relation to effective psychotherapeutic outcome.

In his classic article on empathy, Rogers (1975) cites several general statements about empathy that emerge from research. The following statements, Rogers believed, could be stated with assurance:

(1) The ideal therapist is first of all empathic. They (therapists of many different orientations) are in high agreement in giving empathy the highest ranking out of twelve variables. (2) Empathy is correlated with self-exploration and process movement. (3) Empathy early in the relationship predicts later success. . . . (4) The client comes to perceive more empathy in successful cases. (5) Understanding is provided by the therapist. . . . (6) The more experienced the therapist, the more likely he is to be empathic. (7) Empathy is a special quality in a relationship, and therapists offer definitely more of it than even helpful friends. . . . (8) The better integrated within himself, the higher the degree of empathy the therapist exhibits. (9) Experienced therapists often fall far short of being empathic. (10) Clients are better judges of the degree of therapy than are therapists. (11) Brilliance and diagnostic perceptiveness are unrelated to empathy. (12) An empathic way of being can be learned from empathic persons. (pp. 5–6)

Rogers continues in this statement to report that there is "overwhelming" evidence that empathy is clearly related to positive outcome with individuals diagnosed as schizophrenic, with students, with counseling-center clients, with teachers in training, and with individuals diagnosed as neurotic in the United States and Germany. The common thread in all of these research conclusions concerning the impact of empathy is that, when a person experiences himself or herself as being empathically understood with warm acceptance, a set of growth-promoting therapeutic attitudes is developed toward himself or herself.

Research (e.g., Bohart & Rosenbaum, 1995; Lambert, Shapiro, & Bergin, 1986) provides the soil for renewed consideration of Rogers's hypothesis. Of particular interest is Stubbs and Bozarth's (1994) qualitative study of the reports of psychotherapy outcome literature over four decades of outcome research. Of five emergent temporal categories of focus, the abiding relationships to outcome that emerged in some form center on those that Rogers (1957) identified in his classic integrative statement as necessary and sufficient for therapeutic personality change (i.e., congruence, unconditional positive regard, and empathic understanding).

Duncan and Moynihan (1994) present an intriguing argument for what is, in essence, Rogerian empathy when they propose a model predicated on recent conclusions concerning the research on psychotherapy outcome. They point out that the research suggests the utility of intentionally using the client's frame of reference. Indeed, they resonate the Rogerian view:

> Empathy, then, is not an invariant, specific therapist behavior or attitude (e.g. reflection of feeling is inherently empathic), nor is it a means to gain a relationship so that the therapist may promote a particular orientation or personal value, nor a way of teaching clients what a relationship should be. Rather, empathy is therapist attitudes and behaviors that place the client's perceptions and experiences above theoretical content and personal values (Duncan, Solovey, & Rusk, 1992); empathy is manifested by therapist attempts to work within the frame of reference of the client. When the therapist acts in a way that demonstrates consistency with the client's frame of reference, then empathy may be perceived, and common factor effects enhanced. Empathy, therefore, is a function of the client's unique perceptions and experience and requires that therapists respond flexibly to clients' needs, rather than from a particular theoretical frame of reference or behavioral set. (p. 295)

Duncan and Moynihan (1994), like many researchers, dismiss Rogerian empathy because they identify it with specific behaviors rather than with the bedrock of the empathic attitude in the theory. As such, they apparently do not realize that they are actually proposing an operational concept predicated on psychotherapy outcome research that is essentially the same as Rogers's conception of empathy. The potency of Rogerian empathy as a complete dedication to and acceptance of the client's perceptual world is reasserted by psychotherapy outcome research.

THE EMPATHIC STANCE

One of the prominent questions concerning Rogerian empathy is, "How do you do it?" It is contended (Bozarth, 1992; Bozarth & Brodley, 1986; Brodley, 1993) that one of the greatest sources of misunderstanding of the person-centered approach is that of focusing on "how to do it." This suggests that Rogerian empathy is not necessarily the same as "communication" of empathy or "empathic responses."

The therapist-provided conditions for therapeutic change are, in fact, all attitudes—inner, subjective experiences. Any behavior that has the appearance of a therapeutic attitude may or may not implement the attitude. Behaviors that do not appear to fit the descriptions of the attitudes may, in fact, be expressions of the therapeutic attitudes. Alternatively, such behaviors may be perceived by a client as expressions of the attitudes.

Mindell (1992), from his own theoretical perspective, suggests that it is not the response skills that are truly important but the metaskills that underlie the responses. Metaskills, in Roger's theory and hypothesis, refer to the attitudinal qualities of the therapist. One possibility for future investigation of the complex phenomena of ways of being empathic may be Neville's (1996) use of Gebser's structures of consciousness model. This model suggests several levels of empathy ranging from total union of the individuals to rational verbal kinds of responses.

In discussions of Rogerian therapy, the technique of reflection is often equated with empathy. The fact that reflection statements might be empathic contributes to this confusion. Bozarth (1984) responds to this issue as follows:

1. Reflection is a way for the therapist to become empathic, to check whether or not he or she understands the client, and to communicate this understanding to the client.
2. Reflection is primarily for the therapist and not for the client. Reflection is one way for the therapist to enter the world of the client. It is the walk in the world of the client that assists the client toward growth.
3. Reflection is not empathy. It is a way to help the therapist become more empathic.
4. Empathy is not reflection. Empathy is a process of the therapist entering the world of the client "as if" the therapist were the client. Reflection is a technique that may aid the process.
5. Other modes of empathy have not been considered. Other modes are usually not as easily observed and analyzed as are the verbal forms of reflective statements. The dedication of Rogers to quantitative, scientific inquiry influenced the nature of what would be examined by others, although his major

thrust of inquiry has been a qualitative, heuristic examination of the nature of things. (p. 69)

Particular kinds of responses may or may not be representative of empathic understanding of the individual's frame of reference.

Empathic Responses

As noted earlier, one of Rogers's contributions was the development of a way for communicating empathy. This was once identified by him as reflection or reflection of feelings. In his last statement about reflective responses, Rogers (1986b) identified such statements as being attempts to test his understandings with the client. In later writings, he referred to *attitudes* and, still later, to the *relationship* rather than to the method or *reflection.* Rogers consistently referred to empathic responses as those that captured the client's internal frame of reference. These forms of empathic responses, verbal or nonverbal, are responses that attempt to represent the client's internal frame of reference in the immediate interaction. Thus, whatever their means of expression or form, these empathic responses are a kind of as-close-as-possible following of the client as he or she narrates and expresses himself or herself. Also, all empathic responses are inherently tentative, implying the therapist's asking the client, "Is this accurate?" As such, the actual responses come in a variety of forms. Films delineating Rogers's demonstrations of client-centered therapy (e.g., Rogers, 1965; Rogers & Segel, 1955) reveal an almost constant flow of expressive movement accompanying verbal empathic communications.

Responses to Questions and Requests

Another basic therapist–client interaction that often occurs in therapy is when the client asks the therapist a question or makes a request. When the therapist is being addressed and something is being directly asked of the therapist, the values and attitudes of client-centered theory require the therapist to adapt to this situation and express the therapeutic attitudes, often by honestly answering questions. The values of respect for people and of trust in the inherent constructive self-directive capabilities of people that are so basic in client-centered theory (Rogers, 1951) require that the client's voice (Grant, 1990) be respected and trusted. This means that the therapist should be inclined to address clients' questions by being genuine and open to honoring their requests, as well as offering empathic responses to verify the therapist's experiences of empathic understanding during the interaction process. It is a manifestation of the therapeutic attitudes, of acceptant empathic attunement to the client, to treat the client's questions and requests respectfully.

Empathic-Understanding Response Process

There is a well-developed and -demonstrated process that seems to me to be a more elaborate conceptualization of the method of reflection that Rogers focused on in his years at the University of Chicago. Brodley (1977, 1986) espouses the concept of the "empathic-understanding response process." This concept allows concrete examples of the therapist's responses to be identified in relation to the client's process. This process can be considered as a likely implementation of the client-centered therapist's acceptant empathic attitude. The empathic-understanding response process is the process often modeled by Rogers in demonstrations and examples of his therapy (e.g., Rogers, 1965; Rogers & Segel, 1955). It is inherently nondirective without goals for the client. Examples of Rogers and others demonstrating client-centered therapy often illustrate the empathic-understanding response process and are readily available for review (e.g., Bozarth, 1990a; Bozarth & Brodley, 1991; Brodley, 1993; Brodley & Brody, 1993; Brody, 1991; Ellis & Zimring, 1994; Merry, 1996; Raskin & Rogers, 1989; Rogers, 1986a). For some, it may be the best way to hold an empathic stance and one of the best ways to learn to trust the client. Again, this response process must be understood as expressive of the therapeutic attitudes, not as a technique or strategy.

Empathic Reactions

Rogers's responses can most often be classified as empathic-understanding responses. Nevertheless, he often discussed other aspects of the implementation of the attitudes. Rogers's presence in the relationship seemed to permit him to respond in ways consistent with the client. Although he often responded with the reflection method that fit him best, he also reacted in various ways in which he felt himself to be empathic and present to the client. Kirschenbaum (1979) notes that during Rogers's 12 years at the University of Chicago, he "moved from the *method* to the *attitudes* to the *relationship* as the key ingredient in the therapeutic process" (p. 202). The earlier review of the development of Rogerian empathy in this chapter suggests that Rogers's first references to empathy are nonspecific. He did not use the term until the late 1940s. The therapists' qualifications were more clearly couched in the attitudes of genuineness and unconditional positive regard in his earlier works. Understanding was important but subsidiary to acceptance of the individual's feelings. He, then, functionally took a behavioral focus in much of his practical work at the University of Chicago. This behavioral focus was related to the method of quantitative inquiry rather than to any behavioral intention. This is not to say that Rogers and his colleagues operated with any behavioral intent. However, there was clear focus on, "What does the client do when the therapist responds in a certain way?" Hence, how should the therapist respond? It was when Rogers realized the technological (and possibly behavioral) interpretations given to his work that he used a broader reference than the reflection of feelings and referred to "adopting the client's frame of reference" (Kirschenbaum, 1979, p. 164). It was only at this time that Rogers started to use the term *empathy* and developed it in his own unique formulation while popularizing it as a clinical concept in the helping professions.

Later in his life, Rogers (1980) was more explicit in his flirtation with holistic experiential blending with clients. He notes, for example, that when he could be in touch with the unknown in himself during a therapy session, whatever he might do "seems to be full of healing" (p. 129). He felt that his sometimes strange and impulsive way in a relationship turned out "to be right, in some odd way: it seems that my inner spirit has reached out and touched the inner spirit of the other" (p. 129). Rogers said that when he was "intensely focused on a client, just my presence seems to be healing" (Baldwin, 1987, p. 45). He further reflected, "Perhaps it is something around the edges of those conditions that is really the most important element of therapy—when myself is very clearly, obviously present" (p. 45).

During much of Rogers's life, there was an inner conflict between observing an individual from the outside and understanding a person from the person's frame of reference. The former view was important to him in research and the latter view in his clinical work. The two perspectives, however, pervaded his work until his personal involvement in quantitative research diminished during the last two decades of his life. His experiences in encounter groups and large community groups affected his view of empathy by his realization that there "is not even hope of understanding what is going on" in any given large group. However, he suggests, "by surrendering yourself to the process, certain things happen" (Baldwin, 1987, p. 50). Rogers has provided the foundation for the importance of empathic reactions as well as of more obvious empathic responses. The therapist may experientially and holistically "absorb" the experience without worrying about providing particular empathic responses. Indeed, in groups, Rogers learned even more to trust individuals to help themselves and, in addition, for them to help others. In fact, Rogers's emphasis on empathic reaction was not new. As early as the Miss Mun (Rogers & Segel, 1955) sessions, he referred to what goes on in therapy as a willingness for the therapist to go with the client in his or her separate feeling as a person. In less didactic terms, he concluded that "what the individual experiences in therapy is the experience of being loved."

He referred to empathic reactions in the classic *Gloria* (Rogers, 1965) film as:

> I find myself bringing out my own inner experience statements which
> seem to have no connection with what is going on but usually prove

to have a significant relationship to what the client is experiencing . . .
I simply know I was very much present in the relationship, that I lived
it in the moment of its occurrence.

There is often discussion about one of Rogers's responses to Gloria. At one
point, she says that she would like Rogers for her father. Rogers replied by
saying, "You look to me like a pretty nice daughter" (Rogers, 1965). Some
discussants think that he had a particular intention. Many say that this
might have been helpful but that it was not an empathic response. His
response, however, might be viewed as an empathic reaction if we consider
Rogers's reference to his inner experience that he claimed to come from
some unidentifiable source. It was his presence in the relationship and to
the client that stimulated him to respond in this way. Although his comment might not meet the criteria for a valid empathic-understanding response, it could well be considered an empathic reaction (that is, coming
from Rogers's presence in the relationship while giving total attention to
the individual and having no particular intent).

Bozarth (1984) has provided some examples of idiosyncratic empathy,
including the following response preceding a longer monologue to a client's
question, "What did you do this weekend?" The therapist responded, "when
I took my Volkswagen engine out, the car rolled down the hill, hit the
rabbit pen" (p. 70).

The client later verified the therapists' monologue as being empathic.
Her previous session had been laden with tenseness and difficulty, and she
needed a reprieve from such struggle to allow her to assimilate her experience
of that previous session. The therapist's reaction, according to the client,
relieved her whole psychologically exhausted state.

The concept of empathic reactions theoretically suggests that there is
an integral link between congruence and empathy. Congruence became the
most important of the conditions to Rogers, who periodically referred to it
as "transparency." Rogers increasingly referred to transparency of the therapist in the relationship with the other person and, concomitantly, to the
importance of the person-to-person encounter in the relationship. He also
periodically, albeit more tentatively, referred to the use of intuition of the
therapist. Taking these thoughts into account, Bozarth (1984) states:

> The basic premise is that the role of the person-centered therapist is that
> of being transparent enough to perceive the world nonjudgmentally, as
> if the therapist were the other person, in order to accelerate the forma-
> tive tendency of the other person toward becoming all that he or she
> can become. (p. 69)

Hence, the therapist must continuously be aware of his or her own feelings
as though they were the feelings of the client, perhaps "as is" rather than
"as if." The therapist's congruence is viewed as being integrally intertwined
with empathy. That is, the more congruent and the more transparent the

therapist in the relationship, the higher will be the empathy. Bozarth (1996b) contends that if the therapist is authentically and deeply attuned to the client, then most of the therapist's experiences, even bizarre fantasies, will have therapeutic relevance to the client and the client–therapist relationship. Empathic reactions of this nature of "oneness" seem closer to Basch's definition of *Einfühlung* as "searching one's way into the experience of another without specifying or limiting the means whereby this occurs" (pp. 110–111).

Bozarth (1996b) and Stubbs and Bozarth (1996) contend that empathic understanding responses as well as empathic reactions may emerge from the search into the experience of the interaction between the client and the therapist. Indeed, the empathic response repertoire may be gleaned from the client's way of understanding (i.e., *Einfühlung*). The contention is that if the therapist's intent is totally (as much as humanly possible) dedicated to acceptant understanding of the perceptions and experiences of the client, nearly everything the therapist does is meant to achieve this goal and to prepare himself or herself to be in the relationship in that way. It might, then, entail any form of response or reaction that is idiosyncratic to the client, therapist, and dyadic interaction (Bozarth, 1984). Spahn (1992) suggests that the person-centered model of therapy "is particularly conducive to the separateness giving way to unity . . . in that the therapist is free to devote his or her entire being to attending to the client" (p. 35). Rogers refers to such moments in several of his later writings (Rogers, 1980) and interviews (Baldwin, 1987) and, as well, to the use of self in therapy. Analyses (Brodley & Brody, 1996; Merry, 1996) reveal that Rogers practiced empathy in a way that was "simple, economical and idiosyncratic in the sense of personal or individual" (Merry, 1996, p. 280) and that "there is evidence that Rogers responded to different clients in different ways; the underlying intention appears to be a consistent intent empathically to follow and hence to understand each client afresh" (p. 281). Transcripts of his sessions reveal that he primarily practiced with verbal empathic-understanding responses. I surmise that this was his primary way of reacting to his absorption of clients' experiences and the most prevalent way that he checked his experience of empathic understanding with them.

Rogerian empathy is fundamentally different from other conceptualizations of empathy in its convergence with other attitudinal qualities and in its role in bringing the self of the therapist to the self of the client without presuppositions and theoretical speculations concerning the client.

SUMMARY

Rogerian empathy is grounded in self-empowering principles, operationalized on a behavioral schema; it is a flirtation with holistic experiential blending with another individual. This chapter has discussed empathy from the frame of reference of client-centered theory and the Rogerian hypothesis. Empathy from this framework is considered unique from other conceptualizations of empathy in that Rogers considered empathy to be (a) a central therapeutic construct rather than a precondition for other forms of treatment; (b) an attitude and experience toward the client rather than a particular behavior; (c) an interpersonal process grounded in a nondirective attitude; and (d) a part of a whole attitude, wherein the experience of empathic understanding is intertwined with congruence and unconditional positive regard of the therapist for the client.

I have presented several assertions in relation to Rogerian empathy:

Assertion 1. Empathy in client-centered theory is a concept that is integrally integrated with the conditions of congruency and unconditional positive regard. It exists within a context of nondirectivity and is predicated on the foundation block of the actualizing tendency.

Assertion 2. There is, in essence, no room for directivity in Rogers's conceptions of therapy and the therapist's role. Nondirectivity casts a major influence on Rogers's conceptualization of empathy.

Assertion 3. Rogers's "techniques" are always embedded in the therapeutic attitudes—that is, grounded in the inner experiences of the therapist in empathic response to the client's frame of reference.

Assertion 4. The empathic and unconditional acceptance is, in essence, the same experience.

Assertion 5. To a significant extent, current outcome research substantiates Rogers's conceptualization of empathy in relation to effective psychotherapeutic outcome.

Assertion 6. Rogerian empathy is not necessarily the same as "communication" of empathy or "empathic responses."

Rogers was involved simultaneously and continuously in developing client-centered and person-centered theory and formulating his hypothesis concerning the necessary and sufficient conditions for therapeutic personality change in general. Rogerian empathy is a central component to both of these efforts. As such, Rogerian empathy is integrally related to the theory and also a unique conceptualization of empathy to all therapies and interpersonal relationships.

Rogers's early focus on method provided his theory with a form of response that helped to establish the theory and the man. He, however, discovered that the *method* was misinterpreted as technique and often used as a form that did not capture the principles that he espoused. It was then that Rogers used the term *empathy* in his reference to the importance of the *attitudes*. This allowed more variation of form but also opened the way for the contamination of his idea of empathy when it was distorted by others to serve directive intention.

Rogers more recent evolution to the *relationship* has never been fully developed. It is a "formless form" more akin to Basch's (1985) reference to *Einfühlung* or "feeling into" (i.e., "finding" or "searching" one's way into the experience of another without specifying or limiting the means whereby this occurs," pp. 110–111). It is predicated on the person-to-person blending of the therapist enmeshed in the world of the client with empathic reactions and "total" attunement to the other. It is, perhaps, as Shlien (1971) noted, "the exquisite awareness of dual experience that restores consciousness of self. A self *being*, the self-concept can change" (p. 164) Rogerian empathy is a unique contribution to psychotherapy, clinical work, and interpersonal relationships in general. In addition, Rogers's conceptualization of empathy is on the threshold of new explorations and meanings.

REFERENCES

Baldwin, M. (1987). Interview with Carl Rogers on the use of the self in therapy. In M. Baldwin & V. Satir (Eds.), *The use of self in therapy* (pp. 45–52). New York: Haworth Press.

Basch, M. F. (1985). Empathic understanding: A review of the concept and some theoretical considerations. *Journal of the American Psychoanalytic Association, 31*, 101–126.

Bohart, A., & Rosenbaum, R. (1995). The dance of empathy: Empathy, diversity, and technical eclecticism. *The Person-Centered Journal. 2*(4), 5–9.

Bozarth, J. D. (1984). Beyond reflection: Emergent modes of empathy. In R. F. Levant & J. M. Shlien (Eds.), *Client-centered therapy and the person-centered approach: New directions in theory, research and practice* (pp. 59–75). New York: Praeger.

Bozarth, J. D. (1990a). The evolution of Carl Rogers as a therapist. *Person-Centered Review, 2*(1), 11–13.

Bozarth, J. D. (1990b). The essence of client-centered therapy. In G. Lietaer, J. Rombouts, & R. Van Balen (Eds.), *Client-centered and experiential psychotherapy in the nineties* (pp. 59–64). Leuven, Belgium: Leuven University Press.

Bozarth, J. D. (1992). Coterminous intermingling of doing and being in person-centered therapy. *The Person Centered Journal, 1*(1), 15–35.

Bozarth, J. D. (1996a). A reconceptualization of the necessary and sufficient conditions for therapeutic personality change. *The Person Centered Journal, 3*(1), 25–45.

Bozarth, J. D. (1996b). Techniques in person-centered therapy. In R. Hutterer, G. Pawlowsky, P. Shmid, & R. Stipsits (Eds.), *Client-centered and experiential psychotherapy: A paradigm in motion* (pp. 363–368). New York: Peter Lang.

Bozarth, J. D., & Brodley, B. T. (1986). Client-centered psychotherapy: A statement. *Person-Centered Review, 1*(3), 262–271.

Bozarth, J. D., & Brodley, B. T. (1991). Actualization: A functional concept in client-centered therapy. *Journal of Social Behavior and Personality. 6*, 45–60.

Brodley, B. T. (1977). *The empathic understanding response process.* Unpublished manuscript.

Brodley, B. T. (1986, May). *Client-centered therapy: What it is? What it is not?* Paper presented at the First Annual Meeting of the Association for the Development of the Person-Centered Approach, Chicago.

Brodley, B. T. (1988, May). *A client-centered psychotherapy practice.* Paper presented at the Third Annual Meeting of the Association for the Development of the Person-Centered Approach, New York.

Brodley, B. T. (1993). Some observations of Carl Rogers' behavior in therapy interviews. *Person-Centered Journal, 1*(1), 37–47.

Brodley, B. T., & Brody, A. F. (1993). *A rating system for studying client/person-centered interviews.* Unpublished manuscript.

Brodley, B. T., & Brody, A. F. (1996). Can one use techniques and still be client-centered? In R. Hutterer, G. Pawlowsky, P. Shmid, & R. Stipsits (Eds.), *Client-centered and experiential psychotherapy: A paradigm in motion* (pp. 369–374). New York: Peter Lang.

Brody, A. F. (1991). Understanding client-centered therapy through interviews conducted by Carl Rogers. Unpublished manuscript, *Illinois School of Professional Psychology,* Chicago, IL.

Carkhuff, R. R. (1971). *The development of human resources.* New York: Holt, Rinehart & Winston.

Corey, G. (1982). *Theory and practice of counseling and psychotherapy* (2nd ed.). Monterey, CA: Brooks/Cole.

Cormier, W. H., & Cormier, S. (1991). *Interviewing strategies for helpers.* Belmont, CA: Brooks/Cole.

Duncan, B. L., & Moynihan, D. W. (1994). Applying outcome research: Intentional utilization of the clients frame of reference. *Psychotherapy, 31,* 294–301.

Duncan, B. L., Solovey, A., & Rusk, G. (1992). *Changing the rules: A client-directed approach to therapy.* New York: Guilford.

Egan, G. (1975). *The skilled helper: A model for systematic helping and interpersonal relating.* Belmont, CA: Wadsworth.

Ellis, J., & Zimring, F. (1994). Two therapists and a client. *The Person-Centered Journal, 1*(2), 79–92.

Grant, B. (1990). Principled and instrumental nondirectiveness in person-centered and client-centered therapy. *Person-Centered Review, 5*(3), 77–88.

Kirschenbaum, H. (1979). *On becoming Carl Rogers.* New York: Delta/Dell.

Kohut, H. (1959). Introspection, empathy, and psychoanalysis. *Journal of the American Psychoanalytic Association, 7,* 459–483.

Kohut, H. (1984). *How does analysis cure?* Chicago: University of Chicago Press.

Lambert, M. J., Shapiro, D. A., & Bergin, A. E. (1986). The effectiveness of psychotherapy. In S. L. Garfield & A. E. Bergin (Eds.), *Handbook of psychotherapy and behavior change* (Rev. ed., pp. 157–212). New York: Wiley.

Merry, T. (1996). An analysis of ten demonstration interviews by Carl Rogers: Implications for the training of client-centered counselors. In R. Hutterer, G.

Pawlowsky, P. F. Schmid, & R. Stipsits (Eds.), *Client-centered and experiential psychotherapy: A paradigm in motion* (pp. 273–283). New York: Peter Lang.

Mindell, A. (1992). *The leader as martial artist: An introduction to deep democracy.* San Francisco: Harper.

Neville, B. (1996). Five kinds of empathy. In R. Hutterer, G. Pawlowsky, P. F. Schmid, & R. Stipsits (Eds.), *Client-centered and experiential psychotherapy: A paradigm in motion* (pp. 437–453). New York: Peter Lang.

Raskin, N. J., & Rogers, C. R. (1989). Person-centered therapy. In R. J. Corsini & D. Wedding (Eds.), *Current psychotherapies* (pp. 155–194). Itasca, IL: F. E. Peacock.

Rogers, C. R. (1939). *The clinical treatment of the problem child.* Boston: Houghton Mifflin.

Rogers, C. R. (1942). *Counseling and psychotherapy: New concepts in practice.* Boston: Houghton Mifflin.

Rogers, C. R. (1951). *Client-centered therapy: Its current practice, implications, and theory.* Boston: Houghton Mifflin.

Rogers, C. R. (1957). The necessary and sufficient conditions of therapeutic personality change. *Journal of Consulting Psychology, 21,* 95–103.

Rogers, C. R. (1959). A theory of therapy, personality and interpersonal relationships, as developed in the client-centered framework. In S. Koch (Ed.), *A study of science. Study 1. Conceptual and systematic. Vol. 3. Formulations of the person and the social context* (pp. 184–256). New York: McGraw-Hill.

Rogers, C. R. (1965). Transcript of Rogers and Gloria. In E. L. Shastrom (Producer), *Three approaches to psychotherapy. Part I: Client-centered therapy* [Film and transcript]. Corona del Mar, CA: Psychological and Educational Films.

Rogers, C. R. (1975). Empathic: An unappreciated way of being. *The Counseling Psychologist, 5,* 209–220.

Rogers, C. R. (1980). *A way of being.* Boston: Houghton Mifflin.

Rogers, C. R. (1986a). The dilemmas of a South African White. *Person-Centered Review, 1*(1), 15–35.

Rogers, C. R. (1986b). Reflection of feelings. *Person-Centered Review, 2*(1), 11–13.

Rogers, C. R. (1987). Client-centered/person-centered? *Person-Centered Review, 2*(1), 11–13.

Rogers, C. R., & Sanford, R. C. (1989). Client-centered psychotherapy. In H. I. Kaplan, B. J. Sadock, & A. M. Friedman (Eds.), *Comprehensive textbook of psychiatry* (4th ed., pp. 1482–1501). Baltimore: William & Wilkins.

Rogers, C. R., & Segel, R. H. (1955). *Psychotherapy in process: The case of Miss Mun* [film]. State College: Pennsylvania State University Psychological Cinema Register.

Shlien, J. (1971). A client-centered approach to schizophrenia: First approximation. In C. R. Rogers & B. Stevens (Eds.), *Person to person* (pp. 149–165). New York: Pocket Books.

Spahn, D. (1992). Observations on healing and person-centered therapy. *The Person-Centered Journal, 1*(1), 33–37.

Stubbs, J. P., & Bozarth, J. D. (1994). The dodo bird revisited: A qualitative study of psychotherapy efficacy in research [special issue]. *Journal of Applied and Preventive Psychology, 3,* 109–120.

Stubbs, J. P., & Bozarth, J. D. (1996). The integrative statement of Carl Rogers. In R. Hutterer, G. Pawlowsky, P. Shmid, & R. Stipsits (Eds.), *Client-centered and experiential psychotherapy: A paradigm in motion* (pp. 25–33). New York: Peter Lang.

Teich, N. (Ed.). (1992). *Rogerian perspectives: Collaborative rhetoric for oral and written communication.* Norwood, NJ: Ablex.

Thorne, B. (1992). *Carl Rogers.* London: Sage.

5

THE RECOVERY OF EMPATHY—
TOWARD OTHERS AND SELF

GODFREY T. BARRETT-LENNARD

The aim of psychotherapy has many faces; even the purposes of a single broad approach lend themselves to differing emphases (Barrett-Lennard, 1990, p. 128). This chapter explores an aspect widely focused on as a crucial feature of therapist response but largely neglected as an axis of client change. In the perspective developed here, an impairment of empathy for others can be both an effect and a cause of suffering, and is frequently an implicit issue for the person seeking relief and help through psychotherapy. The voluntary client usually experiences deprivation in some form and anxiety or conflict within the self. He or she is likely to feel in fear of or unable to call on aspects of self. In other language, there are areas in which the person is not open to experience. One might say further that there is a loss or lack of self-empathy.

To be able to speak carefully about self-empathy, an accompanying focus on the way that "self" is conceived is necessary. Building on prior person-centered thought, some fresh distinctions are worked out in the early part of this chapter. These lay the ground for inquiry into the process of self-empathy and its relation to interpersonal empathy. The growth of empathic engagement with self and others is viewed as a crucial potential effect of therapy and further explored in this context. Available evidence from research bearing on issues and ideas set forth is considered, and a plea is made for more directly pertinent studies.

To the very vulnerable and guarded self, others are always a potential threat, and the consequent narrowing of perception leaves little scope for responsive empathy. It might be said that such a person is seldom in a mood state with others in which their latent capacity for empathy can be exercised. Of course it is also possible that there has been a failure in the development of the potential for empathic response. In any case, those who give little attention to their own inner stirrings, or who anxiously ward off impulses or other patterns within the self, are not likely to be very receptive to the felt inner experiencing and meanings of others.

SELF AND AWARENESS

The concept of openness to experience (versus denial to awareness) has a long history in client-centered thought. Rogers singled this quality out as a primary characteristic of the "fully functioning person." Such openness implies that every stimulus is "freely relayed through the nervous system," triggering or connecting with other information and having the property of being available to awareness (Rogers, 1961, p. 188; 1963, pp. 18–19). The term *availability* was not used lightly. Indeed, Rogers took pains to stress that sensory and integrative processes often register in the human organism without being discriminated; the important feature is that the way is open, not blocked, for their conscious representation. Rogers (1963) states directly that the fully functioning individual would not be conscious of everything that was going on within, would not be "like the centipede that became aware of all of his legs":

> On the contrary, he would be free to live a feeling subjectively, as well as be aware of it. He might experience love, or pain, or fear, living in this attitude subjectively. Or he might abstract himself from this subjectivity and realize in awareness, "I am in pain," "I am afraid," "I do love." (pp. 19–20)

This distinction by Rogers (although difficult) is suggestive. Two levels or kinds of inner process are implied. First is the level of primary, unselfconscious experience. This experience is felt, the person is living it, and it is reflected in spontaneous behavior. It may well have sensory components but is integrated beyond the level, say, of brainstem activation. The other level, that of articulate consciousness, involves a rendering of the primary subjective experience in symbolic form. In the well-functioning person, symbolic discrimination of inner process follows and matches the primary experience. A quality of attention and receptivity to the underlying substance and flow of experience is implied.

A further, linked property of the fully functioning person, in Rogers's conception, is that he or she is said to "live in an existential fashion" (1963,

p. 20). In principle, each experience is new, and the person engages in a nonrepetitive process of becoming. Central to this process is the idea that:

> the self and personality would emerge from experience, rather than experience being translated . . . to fit a preconceived self-structure. It means that one becomes a participant in and an observer of organismic experience rather than being in control of it. (Rogers, 1963, p. 20)

Who is the "one" in this passage? Evidently, it is the I-self identified with articulate consciousness, an I in this case that is receptive rather than seeking to dictate. Receptive to whom or to what? Again, it is the person's underlying—or organismic—experience. The term *organismic* suggests not merely a flow but a whole that is like an organism. I would prefer to term this underlying whole *the organic self*. Rogers (1963) speaks also of the person's

> total organism, his consciousness participating, [being able] to consider each stimulus, need, and demand, its relative intensity and importance, and out of this complex weighing and balancing, discover that course of action which would come closest to satisfying all his needs in the situation. (p. 20)

His language remains consistent with the notion of the person in a total sense being *more than one*, even when fully functioning and not in conflict within the self.

Only a year after the long-delayed publication of his concept of the fully functioning person, Rogers (1964) produced a freshly worked out exploration and analysis of "the valuing process in the mature person." The attention to values does not restrict the scope of his discussion, which is concerned broadly with preferential and intentional behavior. It is Rogers's fullest account of integrative "organismic valuing" versus the living out of introjected values, the latter seen as acquired through a kind of force-feeding from significant social others. The infant is portrayed as first engaging in organismic valuing and then, typically, acquiring superimposed values at odds with the organismic tendency. These values result from what parents, teachers, and others reject as unacceptable and what they hold up before the child as desirable or virtuous. The psychic cost can be high:

> By taking over the conceptions of others as our own, we lose contact with the potential wisdom of our own functioning. . . . We have in a very basic way divorced ourselves from ourselves. . . . This is a part of the fundamental estrangement of modern man from himself. (Rogers, 1964, p. 163)

In describing the process of recovering this inner wisdom, Rogers uses language that draws on Gendlin's (1962) early formulations. The person, Rogers (1964) writes, now "uses his experiencing as a direct referent to which he can turn in forming accurate conceptualizations and as a guide to his behavior" (p. 163). Gendlin had discussed in detail the process of "direct reference" to felt meaning. He focused on the function of this indwelling in leading on to awareness as inner statement carrying a quality of "recognition" of the primary felt experience. Where in the person does such recognition reside, and where is the felt meaning or sense? For Gendlin, it is clear that, although the latter can be evoked by words and other signs, its origin is preconceptual and bodily. He soon afterward named this self-dialogue "focusing," referring to it as "the whole process which ensues when the individual attends to the direct referent of experiencing" (Gendlin, 1964/1970, p. 141)[1]

THE DUALITY OF SELF

Although the notion of self was pivotal in Rogers's thought, it remained relatively undifferentiated. Much fruitful attention was given to the self-concept and to distinguishing this perceived actual self from the desired or ideal self, but the self itself was, in principle, one for each person. Even in a self torn by conflict, this conflict resulted either from contradiction within the self or from incongruence between the conscious self and a more basic given—the person as living organism. In his closest account of client-centered theory and its development, Rogers (1959) wrote: "We began to see the development of self as a criterion by which the organism screened out experiences which could not comfortably be permitted in consciousness" (p. 200). A basic duality within the person is, again, strongly implied. Rogers stresses that his theory is an abstraction from the phenomena, which might be reconstrued: "One of our group is working on a definition of self which would give more emphasis to its process nature. Others have felt that a plural definition, including many specific selves in each of various life contexts, would be more fruitful" (p. 203). Such thought could complement the notions he advanced himself.

The well-functioning person may be more integrated than the self in conflict, not because he or she contains less diversity (is literally more of a single unit) but because the component self-systems are working in partnership. Differentiation is a feature of any complex system. Humans on a biological level have a great array of organs and systems with very distinct functions, yet in the healthy person these work in intricate, cooperative, and interdependent harmony. Given this great physical complexity, is it

---

[1] Gendlin's (1964) original account of the process was a breakthrough. The descriptions (e.g., Gendlin, Beebe, Cassens, Klein, & Oberlander, 1968) made clear that a special quality of open inner attention and listening was involved, a process more embracing and wide-angle than the term *focusing* might suggest. Later, in working to specify this process as concretely as possible (Gendlin, 1981), the textured versatility of the original inquiry and conception suffered. Focusing was portrayed as a sequence of laid-out steps to follow. Some exponents actively resist a technique quality and argue for a responsive focusing "attitude" added to other basic therapist attitudes stressed by Rogers (Leijssen, 1990).

plausible to expect experiential–mental life to be vastly simpler, literally one indivisible whole if the person is healthy? Or is it more plausible to look for a differentiation of levels and functions in this domain also? I pose these questions in order to dismiss them as rhetorical. On their face, the first question calls for a "no" response, and the second invites a "yes".[2]

A person is both one and many. A first-order division involves the duality of (a) articulate consciousness and the I-self and (b) a preconceptual, but sentient, organic self. The idea and language of having a relationship with oneself was once quite perplexing to me, but is no longer. A person might say, after therapy or any experience of growth, "I now have a more comfortable relationship with myself." Outside the context of therapy, one hears remarks starting with "I am" or "I feel" and ending "about myself" or "with myself." The words in between might be negative or positive in thrust. In each case, a relation is implied between the two components referred to as "I" and "myself." Distinctions between a mental–experiential and a physical–organic self are also endemic in everyday discourse. The idea of a person being dual is in no way novel. A particular, careful way of viewing this duality, and the implications relating to empathy that flow from it, is my concern here.

The view advanced is that a person has, on the one hand, an articulate, reflective, doing self, a self with values, goals, and intentions, a self that speaks for itself and for the *bodymind* whole, a self that refers to itself as "I," and sees itself as the responsible agent and life center of being as a person. It is the seat of volition and individual identity. This regnant self is constantly receiving information and/or influence from other components and levels of process in the total organism. (It is not necessarily receptive to all of this information, and may resist or screen out parts of it.) These other levels, inherent in the person's biological being, may be collectively referred to as the organic self.[3]

The organic self is not a conglomerate of tissue, not mere machinery, but a living, sentient system of interwoven elements and subsystems dynamically knit in a union of such exquisite complexity that it supports and gives rise to the conscious, symbolizing, self-knowing, articulate self. This latter self, while existing in intricate interdependent and communicative relation with the organic self, has its own distinct nature and functions and does not operate in any simple lockstep with the underlying biological systems. It has open system properties in its own right; if this were not so, the whole person–organism would go in a singular direction with consciousness in the

---

[2] In the presentation of his "model of positive health," Seeman (1989) provides a searching, integrative analysis of the intricately interdependent working of systems from a biochemical to interpersonal level in states of wellness.

[3] The articulate I-self has a "left hemisphere" quality. In effect, it is the self Descartes implied in reasoning, "I think, therefore I am" (*cogito ergo sum*). The organic self, on the other hand, inclines more to a right hemisphere quality.

role of onlooker, not of integrator with initiating capacity. The organic self on some of its many levels (that of sensory nerve signals, for example) has a fairly direct route to the conscious self. This I-self can be highly attentive and receptive in relation to its inner constituents, or precommitted to a "policy direction" at odds with voices and needs of the organic self and formed perhaps with little self-consultation in the first place. The potential for inner listening—as in the case of empathic listening to another person—goes further than "consultation" implies. It involves a form of empathy turned inward, if and as the articulate I-self devotes special listening attention to the wider underlying organic self.

EMPATHY DIRECTED INWARD

The phasic process of interpersonal empathy as I have delineated it (Barrett-Lennard, 1981, 1993) can be readily adapted to the case of what I am calling self-empathy. A precondition for empathy to occur is to listen personally with truly interested attention and nonjudging receptivity. This is manifested in the self-empathy case as a respectful inner listening, with readiness to take seriously whatever signals arise internally. One is not at the time submerged in or literally swept along by what is being experienced as, for example, in a rush of emotion that possesses the person in whom it is occurring. The construing I is fully present, although not obtrusive, and open to being taken by surprise. It seeks direct awareness of inner flow, an experiential knowing of whatever is felt, sensed, and new or connected in meaning.[4]

The person's organic being is in living motion all the time, a motion that implies a constant flow of interlevel and lateral signals. Signals that reach and activate higher integrative centers in the nervous system, in effect, then have a voice with the potential to be heard in articulate consciousness. The situation is analogous to the person who expresses feelings and personal meaning and, in this expressive mode, has clear potential to be responded to empathically. In the latter case, this potential is realized only in the presence of another person who is closely attending and able to register and respond in an inner human echo of recognition. If there is mostly no such listener in the person's life, he or she may cease expecting to be received and reach forth self-expressively less and less. It is possible that inner signals of a kind that could be heard in consciousness become muted in the absence of self-empathy, but they do not disappear unless the

---

[4] Cutting through differences in thought context and implied specifics of practice, I see resemblance between this quality (a condition for self-empathy to occur) and the intent of what Gendlin (1981) refers to under the heading of "clearing a space." In the interpersonal case, I have used the term *empathic set* to refer to an immediate, active openness to knowing the other person in their inner experiencing and subjectivity (Barrett-Lennard, 1993, p. 6).

organism is literally running down. When there is deeply receptive attention by the construing I-self (however this comes about), the signals can flow through strongly and be encoded in articulate consciousness. Now they are in dynamic interplay with other elements in awareness and can play a part in the person's directly communicative and other intentional behavior.

The first phase of empathic response, called empathic resonation in the interpersonal case (Barrett-Lennard, 1981, 1993), needs a different designation in the inward-focused case. The term *formative recognition* seems apt for its various connotations. In both cases, there tends to be a quality of energy arousal as the meaning forms and comes to life, in a clear sense of recognition and contact. In self-empathy, the forming recognition arises from indwelling attention to signals from the organic self. (Many physiological processes clearly have no direct line to consciousness but may activate intermediate and higher level processes with potential to be heard.) The energizing and satisfying quality of such recognition may be compared to the "aha" experience in classical accounts of insight, such as the case where Archimedes reportedly leapt from his bath, with a basic physical law new born in his awareness. In self-empathy, a felt something comes to the edge of awareness from a deeper level of being and is apprehended in a literal process of formative recognition where form and sense unite.

Although there is no full counterpart in the case of self-empathy to the ensuing, communication phase of interpersonal empathy, the formulating process itself works as an inner communication. It may catch the exact nuance of what is sensed or initially be a crude approximation. Full reception and accurate recognition by the attending self yields by its effect the clearest indication of feedback to the level of the organic self. It seems that where signals are only half heard, perhaps obscured by anxiety or over-eagerness, any feedback to the organic self is muted and with little effect. The attending, articulate self, especially with prior experience of the fruits of such attention, may become aware that it is not yet on target and perhaps is not in the fully receptive mode that would be needed.

In the interpersonal domain, when empathic resonation has occurred and is effectively communicated, the recipient person is aware of being companioned in experiential understanding. This is the culminating phase of "received empathy" (Barrett-Lennard, 1993, pp. 5–6). In the case of self-empathy, the impact of recognizing and accurately articulating the message of signals from a deep, precognitive, level of inner being seems to radiate through the whole person–organism. At that moment, the dual self is one; there is a peak of integration or wholeness. It is unity not of structure but of immediate process of inner connection and communication (Seeman, 1995). The underlying, organic self effectively has been heard and is influenced by this opening to articulate consciousness. The effect of the inner communication is not only a greater unity in the moment but also a fresh affirmation of a partnership of selves within the total human person.

Awareness arising from very distinct experience has a compelling quality that leads naturally to adjustments in behavior. In the present case, the extended awareness by the articulate self is not that of a separate individual but that of an alter ego sharing literally the same life as the self of which it is more deeply aware. This deepening of awareness may be assisted by another empathically responsive person. But the effect of received empathy goes further than any given content of self-knowledge. A self-empathic process is activated or enhanced through the experience of sustained, multi-level empathic sensitivity and response from any caring human source. Self-empathy, in turn, plausibly brings the potential for a wider scope of sensitive attunement to others in the person's life.

INTERRELATION OF INTERPERSONAL AND SELF-EMPATHY

Multilevel empathic response (from a therapist, say) is tuned both to the articulate self, who experiences being fully heard and received, and to the more implicit voices of the organic self. The closely attuned and perceptive listener registers what is expressed, staying close to visible cues of the other's experience—cues that include but are not confined to direct verbal expression. Although these signs are not all immediately in the client's articulate consciousness, their existence makes them potentially accessible to discriminate awareness. Rogers (1966) by no means an advocate of interpretation, spoke eloquently on the issue of responding to a wider flow than the client's immediate consciousness. It is not the case, he wrote,

> that the client-centered therapist responds only to the obvious in the phenomenal world of the client. If that were so, it is doubtful that any movement would ensue in therapy. Indeed, there would be no therapy. Instead, the client-centered therapist aims to dip from the pool of implicit meanings just at the edge of the client's awareness. (p. 190)

Rogers uses the term *implicit meanings*, but the context makes it clear that he is referring to what is stirring in the person on a felt level and which acquires or has meaning in articulated form. What Rogers does not go on to spell out here (1966) is that movement in therapy is more than achieving a new level of self-awareness. It can amount to fundamental change in the way an individual works in relation to felt experience or, as I would now put it, the way the person relates self to self, both inwardly and in relationships. Rogers' closest approach to this issue is found in his later paper centered on empathy: "Being listened to by an understanding person makes it possible for [a person] to listen more accurately to himself, with greater empathy toward his own visceral experiencing, his own vaguely felt meanings" (Rogers, 1975, p. 8).[5]

It is evident that an individual may ruminate, introspect, and interpret his or her reactions, question self endlessly, anxiously watch over daily bodily functions, or otherwise be self-attentive, without having the quality of self-empathy. If self-empathy flows strongly, the person's construing articulate self tends to be open and receptive as a matter of course to signals originating at an organic preconscious level. Such experiential openness and sensitivity would not only be self-referent but also manifest outwardly, especially in engaging with another person communicating from their experience. Put another way, the person who is at home with the subjective stirrings of his or her own inner being tends to be sensitive to the inner felt world of others and is not afraid of responding from this awareness.

These observations highlight the proposition that self-empathy opens the way to interpersonal empathy. This does not preclude influence the other way round. The refinement of interpersonal empathy, for example, through therapy training, challenges individuals to be in fuller listening contact with their own precognitive experiencing. Indeed, left to themselves, it seems that trainees within a context that emphasizes development of empathic sensitivity and responsiveness mostly choose at some point in this training to enter therapy themselves.[6] If (for example) they are consciously uneasy about felt issues not formerly in awareness they will want to work through and beyond this anxiety.

THE RECOVERY OF EMPATHY THROUGH THERAPY

Facilitation of self-empathy is implicit in or compatible with most forms of psychotherapy, perhaps most clearly so in the case of client-centered and related experiential therapies (Gendlin, 1974; Leijssen, 1990; Raskin, 1985; Rogers, 1961, 1975, 1980, interview excerpts). In a classic paper, Rogers cites a simple example, from a late stage in therapy, that closely fits the picture given here of a self-empathic mode. In moments of puzzlement the particular client "would put his head in his hands and say 'Now what is it that I'm feeling? I want to get next to it.' Then he would

---

[5] In his 1960s book on empathy, Katz, too, implies the idea of linkage between interpersonal and self-empathy. Whether in the position of therapist or client, he wrote, one requires the capacity "for being in touch with one's own inner experience and for being in touch with the inner experience of others" (Katz, 1963, p. 103).

[6] An instance is my own experience at the University of Chicago Counseling Center, during Rogers' tenure there. My strong impression is that all of the graduate students who continued in counseling training and supervision beyond a first year opted to enter a personal therapy experience at some stage in their training.

wait quietly and patiently, trying to listen to himself, until he could discern the exact flavor of the feelings he was experiencing" (Rogers, 1964, p. 164).

Snyder (1992) notes that the "self-observing abilities of the client are strengthened in the act of listening to an empathic response" (p. 320). It is evident that she does not mean a process of looking at self in an external-ized way. Her implication is that the client's receptivity and attunement to the inner, deeper-lying self is strengthened through the enabling example and impact of the therapist's empathic response. In a study concerning the "internalization of therapeutic relationships," Quintana and Meara (1990, p. 130) propose that self-referred clients are seeking" an interpersonal rela-tionship that they are not providing for themselves (e.g., self-affirmation and self-empathy)."[7] Empathy is not one form of response. It might be argued that asking a client "to direct his attention inwards and let a total feeling about the problem arise" (Leijssen, 1990, p. 232) can be a sensitively attuned suggestion expressive of empathy. This would be a matter of debate in client-centered circles. However, both for therapists who are devotedly client-centered and for those who use focusing as a method (positions that Leijssen works to bridge), receptive inner listening is a key element in therapy. In the perspective developed here, it is vital to the nuclear process of self-empathy.[8]

Clarke (1991) closely examines what she calls "creation of meaning" events, drawing this term from Gendlin's original work. Her particular focus is on episodes of strong and uncomfortable feeling accompanying experience that is sharply discrepant with beliefs cherished by the individual. The experience is viewed as information that does not fit existing "cognit-ive–emotional schemata" (p. 396). By implication, these schemes encom-pass value constructs that are part of the I-self concept. As for the internal origin of the discrepant experiential information, Clarke refers to it as "emo-tional experience which was previously out of awareness, or automatically processed" (p. 396)—thus arising, it would seem, from the organic self. In Clarke's account, following the emotional arousal, a fruitful creation of meaning episode entails attending to the emotion, seeking and then finding an adequate symbolization, this then followed by "accommodation" and emotional relief (p. 396, Figure 1). A form of self-empathic process is im-plied.

Various authors have advanced or implied the view that the capacity for interpersonal empathy is an attribute of mental health (e.g., Jahoda,

---

[7] The idea is implicit, but this parenthetical use of the term *self-empathy* is its only direct mention by these investigators. I have not encountered any previous systematic and elaborated focus on self-empathy in the literature.

[8] For followers of Gendlin's work, I would suggest that a self-empathic process lies at the heart of fruitful inner dialogue and connection, through focusing or otherwise. Self-empathy encompasses responsive engagement of the articulate and organic selves that occurs spontaneously as well as that which is more deliberate. In the helping context, a new "equation of therapy" suggests itself: Crucial process conditions include those that enable the use and development of self-empathic potential.

1958, pp. 52–53; Katz, 1963, p. 102 ff.; Kohut, 1977, 1984; Snyder, 1994). One advocate has taken the further step of suggesting that "the progress of a client can often be measured in terms of an increase in the capacity for empathy" (Katz, 1963, p. 102). Kohut (e.g., 1984, p. 66) certainly implies a similar view. Katz also sees low or impaired empathy as an underlying motivation for therapy (pp. 109–112) and has tabulated a range of contexts in which "empathic skill" is vital in everyday relational life (pp. 105–106). Writing from the context of group psychotherapy, in Germany, Mente and collaborators viewed the interactive working, facilitation, and development of client empathic understanding as core features of the process (Giesekus & Mente, 1986; Mente, 1990; Mente & Spittler, 1980).

Kohut (1977, 1984) made empathy and the development of self the cornerstones of his radically innovative departures from prior psychoanalytic thought. In discussing the "curative process" in his last book, he speaks of the defining aim and result of this cure as being "the opening of a path of empathy between the self and selfobject" (effectively, between self and significant other). This path is two way, involving "the establishment of empathic in-tuneness between self and selfobject in mature adult relationships" (Kohut, 1984, p. 66). No esoteric language is called on in defining empathy as "the capacity to think and feel oneself into the inner life of another person" (p. 82). However for Kohut, too, empathy can be inward focused; it is not solely interpersonal. He notes, for example, that "the patient's empathy with himself" is at times superior to that of the analyst (p. 72).[9]

Snyder (1994) builds on another source, G. H. Mead's fertile thought (e.g., 1934, p. 141), in freshly articulating the thesis that the capacity for empathy is a central feature of social intelligence. During the normal course of development, as well as in therapy, personal meaning grows in large measure out of communicative encounter and inward "observation" interwoven. In respect to the helping encounter, Snyder suggests that a primary function of the therapist is:

> to model and facilitate the capacity . . . to enter one's own life world and to do this. . . on a level that includes keen attention to our embodied emotions, the continual formation of meanings, and the capacity to constitute and interpret experience in a way different than we habitually or reflexively do. (p. 90)

In a word, the therapist is fostering self-empathy, later mentioned directly by Snyder (1994): "The ability to deepen one's own awareness," she

---

[9] Kohut (1984) also observes that a helpful interpretation has two-sided impact, that it "not only broadens and deepens the patient's *own empathic-accepting grasp of himself*, [italics added] but strengthens the patient's trust in the reality and reliability of the empathic bond between himself and his analyst." This strengthening results, in his view, from the patient experiencing "the full depth and breadth of the analyst's understanding of him" through the sharing of an accurate psychodynamic construction crafted through many instances of empathic contact (p. 105).

writes, "is self-empathy—that is, the attitude of compassion and curiosity regarding one's own experience that enables one to be simultaneously conscious of feelings and detached from them" (p. 97). Her language and nuances are distinctive, the general direction of meaning by now familiar. With social intelligence as her focus, Snyder advances several particular modes of being helpful. Crucially, one of these is "the therapist's ability to facilitate the client's ability to put himself or herself in the places of others" (p. 91), in a word, to enhance interpersonal empathy. Such heightened sensitivity to the perspectives and feelings of others may at first stress the person in another way, and a complementary aspect of helping is identified. This entails supporting the client through the period of feeling exposed or vulnerable to a stage of more integrated and secure sensitivity (pp. 95–96). This second aspect is an acknowledgment that there can initially be costs, as well as gains, in being empathically sensitive.

There is broad agreement, variously formulated, that fear or denial on the part of the acknowledged I-self toward reactions and inclinations of the organic self gradually dissolve in successful therapy. Responsive empathy by the therapist not only helps to bring particular experience into clearer view but also contributes to a different inner receptivity to and processing of experience, a change effectively toward enhanced self-empathy. The new quality of self-engagement is at best not an adopted technique but represents an individualized discovery by the client, a discovery both of how to tune in receptively to information available from his or her own organic and intuitive being and of the difference it makes to draw on this knowledge in a spirit of partnership with self. This perspective flows especially from practice observation, reflection, and theory. Directly pertinent empirical research is distinctly lacking, so far.

RESEARCH DIRECTIONS, NEED, AND POTENTIAL

There are a few studies, illustrated below, that examine change in empathic communication in couple relationships, associated with conjoint therapy or marital enrichment programs. Research on group therapy and process contains some marginally relevant work. There are studies concerned with person-by-person change in empathic forms of communication. There appears at present to be no published empirical research (at least in English) that directly centers on change in client or patient empathy as a concomitant of individual psychotherapy. Since self-empathy has not in the past been a systematic construct, what work there is centers on interpersonal empathy, either within particular relationships *or* treated as an ability or trait.

Tangentially Relevant Existing Research

A smorgasbord of studies has focused on effects of direct training in patterns of responding behavior purported to be indicative of empathy. In this work, empathy is treated as a behavioral skill, susceptible to development by shaping and reinforcement through highly structured communication training procedures (see Mitchell, Bozarth, & Krauft, 1977, p. 494 ff.). If such an approach were applicable to therapy clients and actually produced recovery of empathy in all its aspects, confirming that intensive therapy was an avenue to such change would be of no great practical consequence. As it is, this work appears to have largely confused particular forms of response with the essence of empathy, which connotes experiential engagement pivoting on inner resonance (further discussed in Barrett-Lennard, 1993, pp. 7–8). I mention the work to acknowledge its existence and as a lead-in to one study in particular.

Hines and Hummel (1988) employed several empathy-training formats in a carefully controlled study with married couples. They found that rated empathic ability was significantly higher for each trained group than for a control group which met for assessment only. (Assignment to groups was random.) No substantial effect was detected, however, on the other two outcome indices used (Hines & Hummel, p. 328, Table 3). Didactic training and modeling, psychodramatic doubling, and practice in reflective empathic responding, were variously used in the training sessions, which ran to about 8 hours over 4 weeks. The ratings of empathic ability were based on 10-minute audiotapes, each tape assessed blind on an anchored four-point scale. In addition, the empathic understanding scale of the Relationship Inventory (Barrett-Lennard, 1986) yielded an index of "perceived spousal empathy" and the Locke and Wallace (1959) test gave a measure of marital satisfaction.

In discussing the lack of effect on the two latter measures, Hines and Hummel (1988) explain that participant use of the new-found empathy skills outside the training setting was not assessed and might not have occurred (p. 333). A plausible extension of this explanation is that such training can effect intentional performance but may do little to help the trainee become a more empathic person. It is hardly surprising if 8 hours of structured training does not, by itself, have this effect. However, another study broadly in the same genre yielded somewhat different findings.

Wampler and Sprenkle (1980) examined effects of the Minnesota Couple Communication Program (MCCP). Three groups were compared, the last a no-treatment control. One group began with the 6-week MCCP followed by a similar interval of lecture–discussion sessions, and then a waiting period before follow-up testing. A second group reversed this sequence, beginning with the lecture–discussion phase and then the MCCP. Effects were studied using the whole Relationship Inventory and a behavioral measure of open versus closed communication style. (Responding in open style, encompassing both receptive and expressive aspects, was a focus of the learning program.) The first group shifted to a more open style, specifically during the MCCP, but then reverted. Presuming a similar MCCP effect, the second group also reverted. However, the experienced quality of relationship rose and held, except for the controls, with significant pretest to follow-up differences on the empathy and other RI scales. Thus, change toward a more open style did not persist, but enhanced relationships evidently did (Wampler & Sprenkle, 1980, p. 581). All test-point comparisons were made only for those persons who stayed with the project over the 33-week period, suggesting both a high level of motivation and time for more empathic relationships to develop.

The results obtained in the aforementioned studies are compatible with viewing empathic communication as multichannel, not tied to particular forms of responding, an issue directly addressed in an ingenious dissertation study by Brown (1981). Each of three experienced therapists, diverse in orientation, met once each with five volunteer "clients." The videorecorded interviews were replayed to clients who, wherever they had a distinct sense of being understood or misunderstood, recorded a rating. This was done by pressing one button to note a sense of being understood completely, a second button if mostly understood, a third if feeling very little understood, and so on. Interviews were separately analyzed to identify the form of therapist behavior at each point of rated interaction. The results "suggested that clients associate empathy with questions, reflections of feeling, interpretations, . . . summaries, suggestion for activity outside therapy, and expert opinions" (Brown, abstract). No single category of behavioral response stood out as a clear primary determinant of perceived personal understanding.

Mente and Spittler (1980) developed a nine-point scale for the rating of client empathic understanding (CEU), then applied to member interaction samples from a number of long-running therapy groups. Ratings of self-exploration (S-E) were also used. For the sample overall, CEU was significantly associated with change on six clinical Minnesota Multiphasic Personality Inventory (MMPI) scales, and all other measures of therapy outcome used. (A subsample of clients with initially low levels of CEU developed higher levels over the course of therapy.) S-E ratings were a much weaker predictor than the client empathy measure: they correlated with change on only two MMPI scales and did not show significant linkage with the other outcome measures (see Giesekus & Mente, 1986, pp. 166–167). The results are compatible with viewing interclient empathy as a therapeutic condition in the client-centered group therapy context.[10]

---

[10] For the reader of German, these results are presented much more fully by Mente and Spittler (1980, e.g., pp. 130–151) than in the English summary I have drawn on here (Giesekus & Mente,

Guerney, Coufal, and Vogelsong (1981) used the small-group medium in more structured form, with help-seeking clients consisting of mothers and their adolescent daughters. Treatment ran for about three months, with weekly group meetings and homework sessions. Clients were randomly assigned to either a no-treatment control condition, a "traditional" group, or a parent–adolescent relationship enhancement (PARD) group. Significant change in "empathic skills" and "expressive skills" in the mother–daughter interaction was found for the PARD group only (pp. 933–935). Increases in relationship quality, as more broadly assessed by questionnaires, were detected in the treatment groups of both kinds. Interestingly, "self-feeling awareness"—possibly flowing from self-empathy—was subsumed under expressive skills. The effects overall seemed to reflect greater sensitivity and receptivity as well as (in the PARD case) mastery of new patterns of response. Whether the changes lasted or extended to other relationships are issues not directly addressed in the research.[11]

One reason for the dearth of outcome research on empathy is that an enhanced quality of relationships has been generally regarded as a spin-off of successful therapy rather than its primary aim. The main focus has been on personality or self change. Self-empathy, however, does fall in the personality domain, can be seen to have a theoretically crucial role in healthy functioning, and plausibly has close interdependent linkage with interpersonal empathy. Alienation and loneliness (Barrett-Lennard, 1996), and impersonality in human relations, are tragic, dangerous problems of our time, ones that imply low levels of empathic contact. For all of these reasons both kinds of empathy warrant priority targeting in research on effects of psychotherapy.

Possible Future Directions

Measures of interpersonal empathy encompass a broad spectrum and can be variously classified. Some are relationship-specific, and others are conceived as measuring a trait or generalized ability. Some are skills-oriented, focusing on particular forms or patterns of behavior. Others center on the experience of being understood and the inner process of feeling-with another person. When empathy is viewed as a multiphase process sequence—inner resonance, communicative expression of this awareness,

---

1986). The wider context of practice in which the research was done is also the focus of a report in English (Mente, 1990).

[11] Kleinberg (1991) reports on a pragmatic approach to assessing the capacity for empathy of prospective members of a therapy group before their final selection for the group medium. The rationale was that with low capacity the individual would not contribute to an empathic, mutually facilitating climate in the group. Kleinberg attributes low empathy for others to an inability to recognize and articulate one's own feeling states, in effect, to a deficit in self-empathy (p. 142).

and empathy as received—it is not surprising that measures tapping different phases and frames of reference tend to correlate weakly, and sometimes not at all (Barrett-Lennard, 1993; Kurtz & Grummon, 1972). Useful measurement of client empathy in the study of therapy outcome would hinge on both a clear defining conception and the versatile use of measures expressive of this concept. A number of levels seem important to consider. One is in the realm of values: Is the client more predisposed to respond empathically to others? Has such attunement become a more significant priority and source of meaning than before?

Another level would target the individual's empathic sensitivity as experienced by significant others, asking: "Has the person's level of responsive empathy changed as a concomitant of therapy"? One investigative approach would be to ask clients to nominate other individuals whom they "understand" (or understand better than others). These understood persons would be called on pretherapy and posttherapy to provide their view of the client's response to them in empathy-relevant ways. This might be done using the empathy scale of the RI (a simple item reads "S/he understands me"). Client self-perceived understanding could also be tapped using the parallel, MO, form of the RI ("I understand him/her"). After therapy, presuming the client has become more open to experience, perceptions from these two vantage points should, in theory, be more congruent than before. Plausibly, also, after a healing and growthful therapy experience, clients will themselves feel more expressive and understandable to others in important life relationships.

If a convincing measure of general empathic ability were devised, this obviously would be relevant also. It appears to me that, in practice, we typically display greatly varying empathy across differing contexts of relationship, circumstance, and inner state. If one does venture to posit an underlying capacity or tendency, the manifestation is always in relationships. Self-empathy, on the other hand, is in principle an individual process and resource. Planning a specific measure is beyond my scope here, but one approach would involve careful design of exercises that evoke a self-empathic process. These test exercises would permit the use both of external–observational frames of reference and of self-report information in establishing the self-empathy measure. Whether by fleshing out this suggestion, or creative discovery of an alternative, significant new paths of research could go forward.

RETROSPECT

Empathy as responsive recognition of the other's felt experiencing and meanings is fundamental to connection between persons. Without activation of empathy, the individual lives in isolation. Caring (or desire) may be felt but unseeing. Perception of the other's feeling is a projection from self, or an intellectual process. Society with high incidence of such patterns is a milieu with little cohesion or sense of "we." Empathic relations may occur but mostly within small familial groups. The social collective is a community in name only, vulnerable to erratic behavior and deep division.

Empathy or its lack not only has profound bearing on relations with others but also has a crucial role in the person's inner world. Thus, it is treated in the present work as a twin phenomenon. The "twins" are familial, not identical, but closely interdependent. One twin is empathy between persons, a concept familiar from customary usage and in accord with my own prior formulations. The other twin, in counterpoint to the first, pivots on quality of communication within the individual, especially between the conscious, recognized self and the person's underlying organic being. Isolation and even intense loneliness arises from being out of touch "on the inside" (Barrett-Lennard, 1996), as well as from unempathic relations with others.

It is remarkable that client change in respect to empathy has not been a significant axis of research. On the occasions it has been a focus, participant relationships in couple and family therapy or in helping groups have been the context. Therapist-to-client empathy, now studied for nearly four decades, is largely accepted either as integral to the helping process or as a foundation for other operative factors. The disposition or ability of the client to respond empathically, viewed as an effect of therapy or as part of the malaise and motivation for change, lies "waiting" for empirical investigation. A serious beginning to research in this sphere would be one consummation of the thought advanced here. Another would be to carry forward and build on the freshly delineated conception of self-empathy to realize its integrative potential in psychotherapy theory, practice, and research.

REFERENCES

Barrett-Lennard, G. T. (1981). The empathy cycle: Refinement of a nuclear concept. *Journal of Counseling Psychology, 28,* 91–100.

Barrett-Lennard, G. T. (1986). The Relationship Inventory now: Issues and advances in theory, method and use. In L. S. Greenberg & W. M. Pinsof (Eds.), *The psychotherapeutic process: A research handbook* (pp. 439–476). New York: Guilford.

Barrett-Lennard, G. T. (1990). The therapy pathway reformulated. In G. Lietaer, J. Rombauts, & R. Van Balen (Eds.), *Client-centered and experiential psychotherapy in the nineties* (pp. 123–153). Leuven, Belgium: Leuven University Press.

Barrett-Lennard, G. T. (1993). The phases and focus of empathy. *British Journal of Medical Psychology, 66,* 3–14.

Barrett-Lennard, G. T. (1996). *Levels of loneliness.* Manuscript submitted for publication.

Brown, J. T. S. (1981). Communication of empathy in individual psychotherapy: An analogue study of client perceived empathy. *Dissertation Abstracts International, 41*, 2748B. (Doctoral dissertation, University of Texas at Austin, 1980.)

Clarke, K. M. (1991). A performance model of the creation of meaning event. *Psychotherapy, 28*, 395–401.

Gendlin, E. T. (1962). *Experiencing and the creation of meaning.* New York: Free Press.

Gendlin, E. T. (1964). A theory of personality change. In P. Worchel & D. Byrne (Eds.), *Personality change* (pp. 206–247). New York: Wiley. Reprinted in J. T. Hart & T. M. Tomlinson (Eds.) (1970), *New directions in client-centered therapy* (pp. 129–173). Boston: Houghton Mifflin.

Gendlin, E. T. (1974). Client-centered and experiential psychotherapy. In D. A. Wexler & L. N. Rice (Eds.), *Innovations in client-centered therapy* (pp. 211–246). New York: Wiley.

Gendlin, E. T. (1981). *Focusing* (Rev. ed.). New York: Bantam Books.

Gendlin, E. T., Beebe, J., Cassens, J., Klein, M., & Oberlander, M. (1968). Focusing ability in psychotherapy, personality and creativity. In J. M. Shlien, H. F. Hunt, J. D. Matarazzo, & C. Savage (Eds.), *Research in psychotherapy* (Vol. 3, pp. 217–238). Washington, DC: American Psychological Association.

Giesekus, U., & Mente, A. (1986). Client empathic understanding in client-centered therapy. *Person-Centered Review, 1*, 163–171.

Guerney, B., Coufal, J., & Vogelsong, E. (1981). Relationship enhancement versus a traditional approach to therapeutic/preventative/enrichment parent–adolescent programs. *Journal of Consulting and Clinical Psychology, 49*, 927–939.

Hines, M. H., & Hummel, T. J. (1988). The effects of three training methods on empathic ability, perceived spousal empathy, and marital satisfaction of married couples. *Person-Centered Review, 3*, 316–336.

Jahoda, M. (1958). *Current concepts of positive mental health.* New York: Basic Books.

Katz, R. L. (1963). *Empathy: Its nature and uses.* Glencoe, IL: Free Press.

Kleinberg, J. L. (1991). Teaching beginning group therapists to incorporate a patient's empathic capacity in treatment planning. *Group, 15*, 141–151.

Kohut, H. (1977). *The restoration of the self.* New York: International Universities Press.

Kohut, H. (1984). *How does analysis cure?* Chicago: University of Chicago Press.

Kurtz, R. R., & Grummon, D. L. (1972). Different approaches to the measurement of therapist empathy and their relationship to therapy outcomes. *Journal of Consulting and Clinical Psychology, 37*, 106–115.

Leijssen, M. (1990). On focusing and the necessary conditions of therapeutic personality change. In G. Lietaer, J. Rombauts, & R. Van Balen (Eds.), *Client-centered and experiential psychotherapy in the nineties* (pp. 225–250). Leuven, Belgium: Leuven University Press.

Locke, H. J., & Wallace, K. M. (1959). Short marital adjustment and prediction tests: Their reliability and validity. *Marriage and Family Living, 21*, 251–255.

Mead, G. H. (1934). *Mind, self, and society.* Chicago: University of Chicago Press.

Mente, A. (1990). Improving Rogers' theory: Toward a more completely client-centered psychotherapy. In G. Lietaer, J. Rombauts, & R. Van Balen (Eds.),

Client-centered and experiential psychotherapy in the nineties (pp. 771–778). Leuven, Belgium: Leuven University Press.

Mente, A., & Spittler, H-D. (1980). *Erlebnisorientierte Gruppenpsychotherapie: Eine wirksame methode der klienten-zentrierten behandlung von verhaltensstörungen* [Experience-oriented group psychotherapy: An effective method of client-centered handling of behavioral disturbances] (Vol. 2). Paderborn, Germany: Junfermann.

Mitchell, K. M., Bozarth, J. D., & Krauft, C. C. (1977). A reappraisal of the therapeutic effectiveness of accurate empathy, non-possessive warmth and genuineness. In A. S. Gurman & A. M. Razin (Eds.), *Effective psychotherapy: A handbook of research* (pp. 482–502). New York: Pergamon.

Quintana, S. M., & Meara, N. M. (1990). Internalization of therapeutic relationships in short-term psychotherapy. *Journal of Counseling Psychology, 37,* 123–130.

Raskin, N. J. (1985). Client-centered therapy. In S. J. Lynn & J. P. Garske (Eds.), *Contemporary psychotherapies: Models and methods* (pp. 155–190). Columbus, OH: Charles E. Merrill.

Rogers, C. R. (1959). A theory of therapy, personality, and interpersonal relationships as developed in the client-centered framework. In S. Koch (Ed.), *Psychology: A study of a science. Vol 3. Formulations of the person and the social context* (pp. 184–256). New York: McGraw-Hill.

Rogers, C. R. (1961). *On becoming a person: A therapist's view of psychotherapy.* Boston: Houghton Mifflin.

Rogers, C. R. (1963). The concept of the fully functioning person. *Psychotherapy: Theory, Research and Practice, 1,* 17–26.

Rogers, C. R. (1964). Toward a modern approach to values: The valuing process in the mature person. *Journal of Abnormal and Social Psychology, 68,* 160–167.

Rogers, C. R. (1966). Client-centered therapy. In S. Arieti (Ed.), *American handbook of psychiatry* (pp. 183–200). New York: Basic Books.

Rogers, C. R. (1975). Empathic: An unappreciated way of being. *The Counseling Psychologist, 5*(2), 2–11.

Rogers, C. R. (1980). Client-centered psychotherapy. In H. I. Kaplan, B. J. Sadock, & A. M. Freedman (Eds.), *Comprehensive textbook of psychiatry* (3rd ed.). Baltimore: Williams & Wilkins.

Seeman, J. (1989). Toward a model of positive health. *American Psychologist, 44,* 1099–1109.

Seeman, J. (1995). *A human-system model of psychotherapy.* Manuscript submitted for publication.

Snyder, M. (1992). The meaning of empathy: Comments on Hans Strupp's case of Helen R. *Psychotherapy, 29,* 318–322.

Snyder, M. (1994). The development of social intelligence in psychotherapy: Empathic and dialogic processes. *Journal of Humanistic Psychology, 34*(1), 84–108.

Wampler, K. S., & Sprenkle, D. H. (1980). The Minnesota Couple Communication Program: A follow-up study. *Journal of Marriage and the Family, 42,* 577–584.

III

EXPERIENTIAL
PERSPECTIVES

6

DOES EMPATHY CURE?
A THEORETICAL CONSIDERATION OF
EMPATHY, PROCESSING, AND
PERSONAL NARRATIVE

MARGARET S. WARNER

Self psychology and client-centered therapy both place great emphasis on empathy as a central element of therapeutic change. Yet the precise way that empathy, in and of itself, generates positive change has tended to remain vague in both traditions. In this chapter I will explore the reasons for this ambiguity and present a more precise account of the way empathic understanding, in and of itself, is able to effect deep and lasting change in the lives of clients.[1]

EMPATHY DEFINED IN CLIENT-CENTERED AND
PSYCHODYNAMIC TRADITIONS

To begin this exploration, we need to consider the complex definitional history of the word *empathy* within psychology. In its everyday meaning, empathy is taken to be an "intellectual identification with or vicarious
experiencing of feelings, thoughts, or attitudes of another person" (*Random*

An earlier version of this chapter was presented at the Third International Conference on Client-
Centered and Experiential Psychotherapy (Gmunden, Austria, September 1994).
[1] I have used the word *cure* in the title in a parallel to Heinz Kohut's *How Does Analysis Cure?* By
cure I mean the capacity to effect deep and lasting change; I do not mean to imply that clients are
sick in a medical sense of the word.

125

House College Dictionary, 1988, p. 433). Metaphorically, empathy is often described as an experience by which one is able to "walk in the other person's shoes" or to see a situation "through the other person's eyes." Empathy is usually seen as involving both cognitive perspective taking and emotional resonance in some sort of interaction with each other.[2] Understanding another person's world view enables one to feel what particular experiences must be like for that person; feeling with the person enables one to learn about the person's world view. Yet, as many observers point out, the emotional resonance involved in empathy is not so intense or undifferentiated that the person loses track of the distinction between his or her own experience and that of the other person. Up to this point, most scholars agree on the use of the term.

However, an interesting divergence emerges in the use of the word *empathy* among clinical psychologists. If empathy involves deeply understanding the inner world of another person, does this involve the phenomenological world of the person—the world as the person would construe it him or herself? Or, does it involve a psychologically interpretive view of the person's inner world—the world as the person *would* view it if fully aware of his or her experience or motives as construed by expert observers? This is a crucial distinction that leads to considerable confusion in the literature because some authors assume the first meaning, some the second, and some alternate between the two without clarification.

Because writers in the psychoanalytic tradition see the therapist's primary role as one of uncovering, conveying, and helping analysands assimilate material emerging outside of awareness, they tend toward the second meaning of the word *empathy*. Empathy, then, is a way that the analyst can become aware of material that the client is not aware of himself or herself. Freud (1912/1958) initiated this usage with his comment that empathic connectedness can allow analysts to experience associations and primary process material within themselves that analysands have blocked from their own awareness. This awareness can be used to construct interpretations and evaluate analytic strategies. Roy Schafer (1983) summarizes this position, suggesting that by general analytic consensus, empathy includes:

1. constructing a mental model of the analysand
2. being alert to signal affects and shared fantasies in response to analysands' associations
3. being prepared to use these responses reflectively as cues to the emotional aspects and significance of the analysand's activity in the analysis. (p. 36)

Clearly, the primary process material that emerges in the consciousness of the analyst through this sort of interaction might initially be surprising or

---

[2] See, for example, A. Goldstein and G. Y. Michaels (1985, pp. 12–61) for a summary of this literature.

foreign to the analysand if conveyed to him or her. Given this usage of the word *empathy*, the analyst would not need to assume that the interaction was less "empathic" as a result of such discrepancies.

Carl Rogers, on the other hand, is quite clear that he is using the word *empathy* to refer to the client's own phenomenologically based experience. He notes that

> the state of empathy or being empathic is to perceive the internal frame of reference of another with accuracy and with the emotional components and meanings which pertain thereto as if one were the person, but without ever losing the "as if" condition. Thus, it means to sense the hurt or the pleasure of another as he senses it and to perceive the causes thereof as he perceives them, but without ever losing the recognition that it is as if I were hurt or pleased and so forth. (1959, pp. 210–211)

This understanding of the word is apparent from Rogers's style of empathic responding, in which he conveys his understanding of the client's meaning to check whether it fits with the client's own understanding. If his expressed understanding diverges from that of the client, he sees this as a failure of empathy on his part.

Kohut seems to use the word *empathy* in both of these ways at different times without noting the distinction. In his communication with narcissistic clients in early phases of therapy, he is clearly trying to put words to the analysand's situation in such a way that the analysand feels understood in his or her own terms. He is deliberately not trying to interpret or convey new information of any kind to the analysand—however true or useful such information might be—because he assumes that such communications would be experienced as narcissistically wounding and retraumatizing for the client. (See, for example, Kohut, 1984, pp. 84–85.)

On the other hand, Kohut (1982, pp. 84–85) uses empathy as an "information-gathering activity" that allows him to formulate an "experience near" model of the client's inner dynamics. Here he sees empathy as a theoretically informed way of understanding the selfobject needs that the client is not aware of within himself or herself. In his theoretical explanations, then, he follows the traditional analytic usage, ignoring the fact that his actual practice often follows the first usage of the word.

EMPATHY IN THE CLIENT-CENTERED AND SELF-PSYCHOLOGY TRADITIONS

Although both self psychology and client-centered therapy (Kohut, 1971, 1977, 1984; Rogers, 1957, 1959) emphasize empathic responding as a core aspect of their therapy practices, both traditions have remained vague as to the exact ways that empathy, in and of itself, functions to create positive change. Some client-centered theorists such as Brodley (1990) and Bozarth (1984) believe that therapists' individual ways of manifesting empathy and clients' ways of undergoing change are varied enough that any attempts to generalize are likely to limit a spontaneous, naturally occurring process. Several client-centered theorists—Eugene Gendlin (1964, 1968), Laura North Rice (1974), and David Wexler (1974)—have proposed models of optimal client-centered processes that often emerge under empathic conditions. Yet these models have not been integrated with one another. And each of these theorists have advocated ways of stimulating such optimal client processes when they do not occur spontaneously. As a result, it is often unclear how and to what degree they believe that empathy, in and of itself, is a powerful instigator of such change processes.

While eloquently advocating empathy with narcissistically disturbed clients, Heinz Kohut (1984) remained curiously doubtful that empathy, in and of itself, generates positive effects. In his chapter on empathy in *How Does Analysis Cure?* (p. 177), he proposes exclusive reliance on empathic responding for substantial periods of time with narcissistic clients. Yet he suggests that the positive force for change comes from those moments when the therapist fails in his or her attempts at empathy, creating empathic breaks that result in new structuralization (Kohut, 1984, pp. 66–67). Or he notes that positive effects of empathy result from the "optimal frustration" clients feel when the therapist understands but does not actually meet the client's infantile needs (1984, pp. 102–103). As a "value-neutral tool of observation," the therapist's empathy allows him or her to form interpretive hypotheses. Although not having an impact in themselves, such empathically informed hypotheses do form the background for personal interactions that Kohut does see as highly significant and curative.

In his last essay, Kohut (1982) notes that

> . . . empathy is never by itself supportive or therapeutic. It is, however, a necessary precondition to being supportive or therapeutic. In other words, even if a mother's empathy is correct and accurate, even if her aims are affectionate, it is not her empathy that satisfies her child's selfobject needs. Her actions, her responses to the child do this (p. 85).

When Kohut (1982) acknowledges direct benefits of empathy, he does so with the greatest reluctance. In the same last essay, he notes that, he thinks that empathic interactions do have *some* positive effects. He seems to see this as a highly controversial position to take within the psychoanalytic movement because he expresses the fear that he will have aroused the "suspicion of abandoning scientific sobriety and entering the land of mysticism or of sentimentality" in presenting this view (p. 85). He does not elaborate further on the nature of that positive bond and the ways that it might be involved in client change.

Thus, although both the client-centered and self-psychology traditions have offered substantial insights into the functioning of empathy within psychotherapy, I do not believe that either tradition has offered a fully articulated account of how empathic interaction, in and of itself, creates positive effects. In addition, the proponents of both traditions often remain quite isolated from each other's work. Real differences of theory, language, and tradition often stop theorists from seeing ways that elements of the two traditions could complement each other in significant ways.

In this chapter I will offer an integrated view of how empathic interaction has a direct effect on client change.[3] In creating this overall model, I am heavily indebted to the work of various client-centered and self-psychology theorists.[4] Yet, because I am combining elements from a number of independently developed systems, the theorists themselves might or might not agree with the particular synthesis that I am proposing.

PHENOMENOLOGICALLY BASED EMPATHY AND CLIENT CHANGE

I believe that phenomenologically based empathy of the sort described by Rogers (and often practiced by Kohut and others) has substantial change-inducing potential at both an immediate problem-solving level and a longer-term characterological levels. This change-inducing potential operates in therapies that rely almost exclusively on empathic responding as well as in those therapies that are empathically grounded but include some amount of feedback and interpretation in the therapy process.

I propose that the following qualities are characteristic of such phenomenologically based empathy. (I will elaborate my reasons for advancing these propositions in subsequent sections.)

1. The communication of empathy, in and of itself, tends to foster positive, self-directed processing of experience.
2. Although there is considerable individual variation, this self-directed processing takes common forms that can be described and are deeply grounded in human nature. Empathic responding creates a particular kind of experiential recognition that tends to bring up new facets of experience, allowing clients' life narratives to be reformulated.

---

[3] Throughout this chapter, I am assuming that effective empathic interaction also meets Carl Rogers other "necessary and sufficient" conditions—that the therapist is genuine and prizing of the client in his or her responses and that these conditions are perceived by the client to some degree.
[4] Although I am focusing on therapeutic processes here, the phenomena I am describing apply equally well to empathic interactions in everyday life.

3. Caretaker empathy is a crucial selfobject function[5] that operates as a precursor to mature abilities to hold and process experience.
4. Empathic relating within therapy tends to reactivate thwarted selfobject functions and challenge early decisions about one's own and others' way of relating to one's experience.
5. Clients who have suffered early empathic failure are likely to have a fragile style of processing experience. As a result, they have difficulty holding experiences in attention at workable levels of intensity or taking in the perspectives of others without feeling that their own experience has been annihilated.

EMPATHY AND EXPERIENTIAL RECOGNITION

A commonsense question arises: How could the communication of empathy generate change when, by definition, nothing has been added to the client's or analysand's experience in the process? The answer that I would give is implicit in a great deal of empathic practice and theory but seldom stated fully. The communication of empathy tends to facilitate change because it generates a particular sense of experiential recognition within the receiver—both the sense of being recognized in one's experience of the moment by another human being and the sense of recognizing one's own experience in the moment. This experience of recognition is of value in itself as a form of human connection, and it also tends to shift one's relation to implicit, bodily felt, nonconscious aspects of experience, opening these to awareness and change. Let me first examine the nature of this experience of recognition in some depth and then consider its impact on relationships with others and with one's own experience.

The phenomenological sense of recognition that I am referring to here is a simple and virtually universal human experience. Yet the capacities involved in generating such an experience are complex and deeply grounded in early childhood experience. I am speaking of the sense of recognition that one has when one feels that another has grasped—in words or in some other way—the essence of one's situation as it is currently experienced, in the absence of a sense of threat or judgment about the experience.[6] This kind of recognition is often accompanied with a sense of slight release or relief at being seen. At an everyday level, a person might feel this sense of

---

[5] By "selfobject function," I mean a function necessary to the maintenance of the coherence and stability of an individual's experience that is performed by two people in a relationship partnership as a precursor to being internalized as a relatively independent capacity.

[6] This, of course, is complex because being understood or seen may be experienced in itself as threatening under some circumstances. However, in a noninterpretive, empathic relationship the client has the option of shifting to less self-revealing material should the level of threat feel to high.

recognition when someone notices that he or she has been waiting in line for service or if someone says, "You look like you are tired of all of this," when this is in fact true. Most people experience a fuller version of this experience of recognition at certain rare and valued moments in life. Often in a personal crisis, while many people try to say helpful things, a close friend is able to say something that captures one's experience so deeply that one could say, "Yes, that's exactly how I feel," or "This person understands exactly what I mean."

In this experience of recognition, a person momentarily lessens his or her sense of existential aloneness in the world, and that which the person is experiencing has some matching, some comprehensibility, to another human being. Or, even within one's experience, the fact of finding words that fit one's experience and make sense of it can give one the confidence that there is a matching between one's experience and some account of that experience that is comprehensible.

What kind of processing goes into that friend's knowing what is central to one's experience in the moment? Certainly, there is no explicit formula that could tell a person how to create that experience of interpersonal understanding. The friend may well be responding to things one had said in the moment or nonverbal cues. But, he or she would also be responding out of a whole lifetime of general understandings, perhaps a history of knowing this person in particular, various culturally grounded understandings, and the like.

Eugene Gendlin's theory of experiencing offers some clues as to how this experiential sense of recognition might occur. In his 1964 article, "A Theory of Personality Change," he notes that "we employ explicit symbols only for very small portions of what we think. We have most of it in the form of felt meanings" (p. 112).

He notes that explicitly symbolized aspects of our experience exist in relationship with a "direct referent" or "felt meaning":

> For example, someone listens to you speak, and then says: "Pardon me, but I don't grasp what you mean." If you would like to restate what you meant in different words, you will notice that you must inwardly attend to your direct referent, your felt meaning. (1964, p. 112)

In discussing such felt referents, Gendlin is not referring to experiences that are unconscious but to states of consciousness that may or may not be made the focus of attention at any given moment:

> When felt meanings occur in interaction with verbal symbols and we feel what the symbols mean, we term such meanings "explicit" or "explicitly known." On the other hand, quite often we have just such felt meanings without a verbal symbolization. (1964, p. 112)

He notes that such implicit and explicit meanings are different in nature, "As we have shown, a felt meaning can contain very many meanings and can be further and further elaborated. Thus, the felt meaning is not the same in kind as the precise symbolized explicit meaning" (1964, p. 113). The experience of recognition, then, would tend to occur when another person's account of one's experience resonates with one's own implicit sense of that experience, generating an immediate subjective feeling of rightness.

Of course, there is no such thing as one's "real" experience, only an actively constructed account of one's life situation, grounded within one's social and cultural milieu. I could give any number of accounts of my experience at a given moment; I might give quite a different set of accounts if I reflected on my experience a week or a year later. An outsider can sensibly challenge me to whether my account of my experience makes sense. Indeed, Gendlin (1964) notes, "even when a meaning is explicit (when we say 'exactly what we mean') the felt meaning we have always contains a great deal more implicit meaning than we have made explicit" (p. 113).

Yet not all accounts of one's experience offer this experience of matching with one's explicitly or implicitly felt meaning—this sense of experiential recognition. And no account of one's experience—however valuable in other ways—is fully satisfying until it does correspond with one's subjective sense of oneself in this way.

To understand the function of empathy, it is crucial to see that this sense of experiential recognition of one's own meaning is different from the experience of receiving new and perhaps useful information from outside one's frame of reference. For example, a person might be angry at someone he or she is close to. A good friend might respond from an external frame of reference and say, "You think that you are angry, but I think that you are really scared of being hurt and you don't want to admit it." This comment might (or might not) be experienced as right and useful by the person receiving it. But to take it in, a person needs to let go of his or her current way of experiencing the situation, take in a new idea or perspective, and relate that in some way to his or her own experiencing.

Empathic understanding that is aligned with the person's internal frame of reference tends to lead to a subjective sense of being recognized in the quality of one's experience at that very moment. It does not require a person to let go of attention to the immediacy of the experience as would the response given in the above example. As a result, I believe that these two sequences are quite different in the kinds of subsequent experience that they generate and in the ways they are received by different sorts of clients.

How, then, would this experience of recognition generate positive change processes? Again, the answer is implicit in a great deal of empathic theory and practice but seldom fully stated. In having one's experience recognized and received by another person, one becomes able to recognize and receive one's own experience, both in a broad sense and in one's particular ability to receive one's own moment-to-moment experiencing. A shift in the way one receives one's moment-to-moment experiencing opens a number of natural processes by which one integrates and differentiates the meaning of one's experience.

A number of theorists have noted that when people hold their experience in empathic attention they tend to spontaneously reorganize their understanding of these experiences (Gendlin, 1964; Rice, 1974; Wexler, 1974). This internal reorganization occurs, in large part, because, as a person holds an experience in attention, new experiences come into awareness. Typically, these are related but previously unattended memories, thoughts, feelings, and images. As such new material is attended to, the individuals are opened to the possibility of construing their situations in new and more meaningful ways. When emotions are evoked in the process, they often intensify, go through transformations, and ultimately resolve themselves into experiences of much less intensity (as when sadness becomes grief and sobbing and ultimately changes into a feeling of peace).

Gendlin (1968, 1974), Rice (1974), and Wexler (1974) have each noted that this process of spontaneously generating and integrating new experience happens particularly strongly when clients attend to aspects of their experience that they have not yet clearly articulated to themselves. Each of these theorists has emphasized a different sort of unclearness—Gendlin (1968, 1974), the bodily felt senses clients have about situations; Rice (1974), the vivid scenes or images that come up in clients; and Wexler (1974), the themes and facets that clients have not fully worked out within themselves. These theorists are less clear as to why empathic understanding, in and of itself, would lead clients to explore such less-articulated and possibly threatening aspects of their experiences.

I believe that the following sequence occurs in empathic interactions. As an intrinsic part of human nature, people have an attraction to experiences that offer a subjective sense of aliveness and they have an impulse to make sense of experiences that are discrepant with what they feel that they know about the world. At the same time, they have a sensible fear of the unknown.[7] Experiences that are symbolized, articulated, and integrated into one's sense of oneself offer a reassuring sense of order and predictability, even if negative. (For example, a person may say, "I'll probably die an alcoholic like my father," and feel quite at home with a well-established view of himself or herself.) Yet such familiar, well-articulated experiences tend to be felt as having less immediacy and aliveness than experiences that are less familiar and have not been integrated into one's sense of self.[8]

In a relationship that is new or threatening, a person is likely to stay with the relative safety of only expressing familiar, well-articulated aspects

---

[7] Certainly, these impulses seem evident in the earliest infant exploration as documented by recent research. As such, it seems likely that they are deeply embedded in the biology of the human organism. See Stern (1985) for a summary of this research.

[8] Rice and Sapiera (in Rice & Greenberg, (1984, p. 42) make a similar point, noting that the immediacy or vividness of problematic situations tends to lead clients to spontaneously search for what is salient in such situations.

of experience. But the very risk and aliveness of sharing less-articulated experience tends to make the experience of being understood in these moments feel more personal and more meaningful.

Empathic responding offers the reassurance that one's experience is comprehensible to another human being. This tends to lessen one's fear of the unknown in one's experience. Under these circumstances, the sense of aliveness present in less-integrated and articulated aspects of experience increases its intrinsic attractiveness.[9] Holding these "alive" aspects of experience in attention tends to bring up other, related facets of experience and stimulates a reorganization of one's understanding of them. This openness to an ongoing experiencing allows a continuing revision of one's life narrative and the "scripts" by which experiences are organized and interpreted, making possible more mature, differentiated ways of living in relationship with others.

THE DEVELOPMENT AND INTERNALIZATION OF THE CAPACITY TO HOLD EXPERIENCE IN ATTENTION

Rogers (1975) notes that therapists' empathy toward all aspects of the clients' experiencing tends to be internalized by the clients as a way of relating to their own experiences: "Being listened to by someone who understands makes it possible for persons to listen more accurately to themselves, with greater empathy toward their own visceral experiencing, their own vaguely felt meanings" (p. 159).

Notably, the process of internalization that Rogers describes in therapy parallels a crucial aspect of optimal child development. Children relate meaningfully to their own experience only after they have first lived in a "good enough" parent–child dyad in which their experiences are responded to and named by another. They are initially completely reliant on such two-person relationships to create meaning and to stabilize their experience, and in this sense these partnerships can be seen as selfobject relationships. Ideally, such relationships lead to an internalization of the ability to hold one's own experience in empathic attention and to respond empathically to the experience of others. This initial reliance on others to empathically understand and to name one's experience could be seen as one aspect of the holding–soothing and mirroring selfobject functions described by Kohut. Or it could be seen as an independent selfobject function.[10]

---

[9] Butler and Rice (1963, p. 102) and Wexler (1974, p. 78) make related points in an information-processing format.
[10] The capacity to hold experience in attention could also be described as a developing function of the ego. I use the term *selfobject* because it emphasizes the intensity of the relational partnerships that occur as people who have difficulty holding experience in attention try to maintain a sense of coherence and stability in their lives and the degree to which the loss of such relationships can threaten the person's ability to function.

Initially, an infant's experience can be seen as entirely constituted by Gendlin's (1964) directly felt, implicit meanings because the infant has no ability to symbolize in words: "the 'implicit' or 'felt' datum of experiencing is a sensing of bodily life. As such it may have countless organized aspects, but this does not mean that they are conceptually formed . . . we complete and form them when we explicate" (pp. 113–114). Still, the infant engaged in such implicit experiencing relates and undergoes change within relationship. Gendlin notes, "it is often the case that there is an ongoing experiencing process without verbal symbols. In fact, most situations and behaviors involve feeling in interaction with nonverbal events" (p. 130).

Thus, Gendlin said that:

> Interpersonal events occur before there is a self. Others respond to us before we come to respond to ourselves. If these responses were not in interaction with feeling—if there were nothing but other peoples' responses as such—the self could become nothing but the learned responses of others. (p. 135)

Certainly, in this initial "implicit" relating, an infant is active in initiating and responding to interactions with adults. Daniel Stern (1985) eloquently describes the nonverbal "affect attunement" central to early phases of infancy that cultivates a sense of efficacy in relating to another. And, caretakers' overall ability to eliminate trauma and to create a benign ratio between positive and negative experiences undoubtedly contributes to an infant's overall association of his or her experiences with "goodness" or "badness" (Demos, 1984).

Early on, most parents begin to engage in a particular sort of empathic interaction in which they begin to name infant's experiences and to offer hypothesized reasons for these experiences—perhaps saying that the baby is "tired" when he or she cries or that he or she thinks "spinach is disgusting" when the baby spits it out. Essentially, parents are offering verbal symbols that *could* carry the infant's implicitly felt experience forward into explicit meaning if the infant had words. At some point, children come to recognize a matching or mismatching between words and their own felt experience.

I remember seeing such a moment of dawning recognition in my 3-year-old nephew. His mother had left the room to pay attention to his younger brother, and he had begun throwing his toys. I said, "You feel angry." He looked at me with a sense of surprise and discovery and tried on the words "I feel angry." He threw his toys a few more times, saying the words with greater conviction each time. Then he went into the kitchen to tell his mother triumphantly about his new discovery, that he felt "angry."

Of course, there is great variation in the quality of parental empathy in this early naming of infant experience and the clarity of reasons offered for such experiences. Some parents are relatively inattentive or have difficulty leaving their own perspectives. Hence, experiences may go unnamed or be systematically misnamed. Particular sorts of experiences such as unhappiness or anger may be threatening in some families and may be routinely labeled as something else. Or children of a very volatile or insecure parent may learn to label their experience in the way they find most calming or least threatening to that parent (Lee, 1988). As result of such empathic failure, children may never develop a capacity to hold experience in attention to check the felt rightness of its meaning. In the process they are likely to rely on more external or socially conventional cues as criteria for labeling experiences. Their personal sense of experiential recognition, or the lack of it, may be unattended to or actively avoided and disparaged (Stern, 1985, pp. 162–182). Such experiences that have never been received empathically in childhood are likely to feel unreal or, in some mysterious way, bad or poisonous to the person as an adult.

Therapists who offer empathic understanding, then, can be seen as offering a particular aspect of optimal parental interaction. By expressing their best understanding of the client's experience in the moment, therapists are valuing the version of the client's experience that generates a sense of immediate experiential recognition within the client. The intrinsic satisfaction of this sense of experiential recognition is strong enough that clients are likely to internalize the therapists' stance toward their experience—attending to and valuing the version of their own experience that offers an internal sense of rightness or recognition.

By activating the deeply human wish to have one's experience recognized and received by another, such empathic interaction is likely to bring up client's reactions and beliefs related to any lack of such empathic recognition in earlier nurturing relationships. As a result, it tends to reopen early relationship decisions about intimacy and self-worth—with all of the attendant deep wishes, fears, and vulnerabilities that go with such early developmental issues.

PROCESSING AND THE REVISION OF LIFE NARRATIVES

Human beings have the ongoing capacity to reconstrue the meaning of their lives and the strategies with which they choose to organize experience. The sort of processing that I have been exploring in this chapter offers one of the main ways that this ongoing reformulation of life meanings takes place.

One can, of course, adopt a life narrative wholesale from the culture or others' preconceived ideas about one's self. Yet such preformed narratives will be dry and detached—creating a false self experience—if they have not been integrated with one's organismically felt responses to life. Processing allows a dialectic between the intricacy of lived experience and the ways that lived experience might be construed within one's culture and life circumstances.[11]

This creation of a personally grounded life story is neither totally determined nor totally open to choice. There is always more than one sensible account that one could offer of one's life history. A person has a considerable amount of existential freedom in deciding what to make of his or her life and what strategies to adopt in approaching the future. Yet not all versions of a person's life story—however outwardly sensible—ring true to the person himself or herself. Renditions of one's life narrative create a sense of experiential recognition, or the lack of it, much the way that responses to smaller units of meaning do.

HOW DOES EMPATHY CURE?

Virtually all people live within a life narrative that leaves some aspects of their experience poorly explicated. Some experiences that are felt organismically are not named or are named in ways that do not function well in helping to make sense of one's situation. One's acknowledged reasons for doing things may contradict one another, or they may contradict important aspects of reality as seen by other people. And, even if people's articulated understandings of themselves were fully congruent with all of their lived experience, they would still be likely to generate new life goals and aspirations that would need to be integrated with their experiences in life thus far. To the degree that empathic understanding stimulates the processing of experience and the reworking of life narratives, it is likely to be valuable to virtually all people throughout their lives.

However, I believe that empathic understanding plays a particularly crucial role in therapy with clients who have suffered empathic failure in childhood to the point that their ability to hold and process their own experience has been severely compromised. I believe that such people are likely to experience a "fragile" style of processing as adults.[12] Without having had the sustained experience of empathy from significant adults, they are unlikely to have internalized the capacity to hold their own experience in empathic attention. I suspect that this ability to hold experience in attention is essential to the development of later skills such as the ability to moderate the intensity of one's experience or to attend to the experience of another person without losing the ability to return to one's own experience.

---

[11] Gendlin (1990, pp. 213–214) makes a similar point.
[12] A fuller consideration of this subject can be found in Warner (1991).

Clients who have a fragile style of processing tend to experience core issues at very high or low levels of intensity.[13] They have difficulty starting or stopping experiences that are personally significant or emotionally connected, and they are likely to have difficulty taking the point of view of another person while remaining in contact with their own experiences.

Empathic understanding responses are often the only sorts of responses people with a fragile style of processing can receive without feeling traumatized or disconnected from their experience. The ongoing presence of a soothing, empathic person is often essential to the person's ability to stay connected without feeling overwhelmed. In a certain sense, clients in the middle of fragile process are asking if their way of experiencing themselves has a right to exist in the world. Any misnaming of their experience or suggestions that they look at the experience in a different way is experienced as an answer of "no" to the question and is likely to be felt as an annihilation of their right to exist at all.

I believe that such fragile processing accounts for much of the intensity of negative reaction to interpretive comments that Kohut observes in analysands diagnosed as narcissistic. At the same time, it accounts for much of the intensity of dependence and selfobject transference such clients initially experience with therapists who do provide an ongoing climate of empathic understanding.

For clients with fragile styles of processing, an empathic relationship may well create the *only* place in the world that they are able to exist in an existential sense because it is the only place they are able to hold experiences without being traumatized. Understandably, such clients would feel frantic at the idea of losing the therapist or being away for even moderate periods of time.

Ongoing empathic interaction is directly curative for such clients in that it offers the sort of empathic, selfobject relating that was missing in childhood. Clients with fragile process are initially able to hold only their experience in an ongoing empathic relationship with another person—and that with considerable difficulty. The experience of holding their experience in a selfobject partnership with another tends to reengage with the natural developmental sequence by which the capacity to hold and process experience is internalized.

Related capacities—such as the ability to modulate the intensity of experiences and the ability to take in another person's perspective without feeling that one's own has been annihilated—tend to develop spontaneously. This fits with Kohut's (1984) observation that after a period of exclusively empathic responding to his analysands they become able to take

---

[13] Most people have a somewhat "fragile" style of processing when they are exploring vulnerable edges of their experience. Clients who have experienced severe empathic failure in childhood tend to experience this sort of process more intensely and over a broader range of issues.

in experience-near observations without feeling that the empathic bond with the therapist has been ruptured.

In summary, then, empathy is curative in the sense that it encourages clients to hold their own experiences in attention in ways that tend to stimulate a deep reworking of personal life issues. And for those clients who have experienced particularly severe empathic failure in childhood, it allows them to reconnect with previously thwarted developmental processes. Within an ongoing empathic relationship, such clients are likely to develop and strengthen capacities that are central to psychological relating—the capacity to hold and process their own experiences and the capacity to take in the experiences of others without annihilating their own.

REFERENCES

Bozarth, J. D. (1984). Beyond reflection: Emergent modes of empathy. In R. F. Levant & J. M. Schlein (Eds.), *Client-centered therapy and the person-centered approach: New directions in theory, research, and practice* (pp. 59–75). New York: Praeger.

Brodley, B. T. (1990). Client-centered and experiential: Two different therapies. In G. Lietaer, J. Rombauts, & R. Van Balen (Eds.), *Client-centered and experiential psychotherapy in the nineties.* Leuven, Belgium: Leuven University Press.

Butler, J. M., & Rice, L. N. (1963). Adience, self-actualization and drive theory. In J. M. Wepman & R. W. Heine (Eds.), *Concepts of personality.* Chicago: Aldine.

Demos, V. (1984). Empathy and affect: Reflections on infant experience. In J. Lichtenberg, M. Bornstein, & D. Silver (Eds.), *Empathy II.* Hillsdale, NJ: Analytic Press.

Freud, S. (1958). Recommendations to physicians practicing psychoanalysis. In *The standard edition of the complete psychological works of Sigmund Freud* (Vol. 12, pp. 111–120). London: Hogarth Press. (Original work published 1912)

Gendlin, E. T. (1964). A theory of personality change. In P. Worchel & D. Byrne (Eds.), *Personality change* (pp. 100–148). New York: Wiley.

Gendlin, E. T. (1968). The experiential response. In E. Hammer (Ed.), *Use of interpretation in therapy* (pp. 208–227). New York: Grune & Stratton.

Gendlin, E. T. (1974). Client-centered and experiential psychotherapy. In D. Wexler & L. N. Rice (Eds.), *Innovations in client-centered therapy* (pp. 211–246). New York: Wiley.

Gendlin, E. T. (1990). The small steps of the therapy process: How they come and how to help them come. In G. Lietaer, J. Rombauts, & R. Van Balen (Eds.), *Client-centered and experiential psychotherapy in the nineties.* Leuven, Belgium: Leuven University Press.

Goldstein, A. P., & Michaels, G. Y. (1985). *Empathy: Development, training, and consequences.* Hillsdale, NJ: Erlbaum.

Kohut, H. (1971). *The analysis of the self.* New York: International Universities Press.

Kohut, H. (1977). *The restoration of the self.* New York: International Universities Press.

Kohut, H. (1982). Introspection, empathy, and the semicircle of mental health. *International Journal of Psychoanalysis, 63,* 395–408.

Kohut, H. (1984). *How does analysis cure?* Chicago: University of Chicago Press.

Lee, R. (1988). Reverse selfobject experience. *American Journal of Psychotherapy, 42,* 416–424.

Random House college dictionary (Rev. ed.). (1988). New York: Random House.

Rice, L. N. (1974). The evocative function of the therapist. In D. A. Wexler & L. N. Rice (Eds.), *Innovations in client-centered therapy* (pp. 289–311). New York: Wiley.

Rice, L. N., & Greenberg, L. S. (Eds.). (1984). *Patterns of change.* New York: Guilford.

Rogers, C. R. (1957). The necessary and sufficient conditions of therapeutic personality change. *Journal of Consulting Psychology, 21,* 95–103.

Rogers, C. R. (1959). A theory of therapy, personality and interpersonal relationships, as developed in the client-centered framework. In S. Koch (Ed.), *Psychology: A study of a science: Vol. 3. Formulation of the person and the social context* (pp. 184–256). New York: McGraw-Hill.

Rogers, C. R. (1975). Empathic: An unappreciated way of being. *The Counseling Psychologist, 5*(2), 2–10.

Schafer, R. (1983). *The analytic attitude.* New York: Basic Books.

Stern, D. N. (1985). *The interpersonal world of the infant.* New York: Basic Books.

Warner, M. S. (1991). Fragile process. In Lois Fusek (Ed.), *New directions in client-centered therapy: Practice with difficult client populations* (Monograph Series 1). Chicago: Chicago Counseling and Psychotherapy Center.

Wexler, D. A. (1974). A cognitive theory of experiencing, self-actualization and therapeutic process. In D. A. Wexler & L. N. Rice (Eds.), *Innovations in client-centered therapy.* New York: Wiley.

7

EMPATHIC RESONANCE AS A SOURCE OF EXPERIENCE-ENHANCING INTERVENTIONS

GREET VANAERSCHOT

Over the years, Rogerian core conditions have become recognized by various therapeutic schools as the basic relationship skills necessary for the creation of a climate that makes therapeutic work possible. In this context, empathic listening is generally considered to be a means of ensuring relational safety—decreasing the client's defensiveness and thus strengthening a working alliance. Although these are important aspects of an empathic relationship, the danger exists of restricting the role of empathic listening to one of only providing a relationship context for other supposedly important processes such as confrontation and interpretation. This view overlooks the essence of empathy.

This chapter describes empathy as a curative process that engenders, by itself, processes leading to personality change. Empathy is a way of interacting, originating in the therapist's own empathic-resonance process, and has a process-enhancing effect on the client's experiencing process in those areas where the client's process has become stuck or fails to proceed adequately. I will first briefly discuss the client-centered view of the experiencing process and proceed to a description of the resonance process as an experiencing process with specific characteristics. Finally, I will illustrate by means of clinical and research material how an offer of an empathic interaction facilitates the client's experiencing process.

THE EXPERIENCING PROCESS

The term *experiencing process* refers to the act of experiencing; the term *experience* refers to what is experienced and is the product of the experiencing process. Experiencing is the process of attributing (implicit) affective meaning and arises from the interaction between person and environment—from a person's way of knowing and sensing his or her situation. It means perceiving something and also noticing how that something impacts yourself (i.e., how something moves you or "gets" you). It results in a fully felt internal sense of yourself in relation to the situation.

Gendlin (1970) introduces the notion "experiencing" in order to underline the process-quality of the experience (p. 138). His intensive study of the ways in which successful clients proceed in their exploration resulted in a better understanding of the experiencing process and specifically of the way of experiencing, which is at the basis of personality change. The following description of the experiencing process will thus be based on Gendlin's writings (1968, 1970, 1974, 1981, 1990; Gendlin & Lietaer, 1983).

Experiencing: An Interactional Process

Two levels of interaction can be distinguished in the experiencing process (Depestele, 1984; Gendlin, 1970; Van Balen, 1991).

The first level refers to the bodily implicitly felt whole concerning a situation and originates in the interaction between person and situation or environment, thus in the way people take in various situations. For example, late one evening a young woman goes to a parking garage to get her car. She does not hear anybody; the garage seems deserted. Suddenly, someone appears from a dark corner and approaches her. She becomes frightened. Then she notices that the person appears to be a man who needs coins for a parking meter and needs change. On arriving home, she tells a friend in detail what went on in her mind during the few seconds after the man appeared and before she knew what he wanted: She initially worried that he could be dangerous and that his actions were ambigous, but it finally became clear that he needed some change. Her listener may wonder: "And you thought all this in a few seconds?" Of course, she did not "think" all this in this few seconds, but she had all this, and perhaps much more, inside of her, in an implicit, bodily felt way. Experiencing is a process, anchored in the body; it is an act of the sentient body. The interaction between body and situation gives rise to an implicit, bodily felt sense, which is preconceptual and undifferentiated. It is a knowing without words: a knowing that precedes words and from which words emerge. It is concrete because anybody can experience it and have direct access to it. The bodily feeling of the interaction, the feeling of oneself-in-the-situation, is implicit, not only in the sense of not explicit but also in the sense of implying more, implying further—implying something that presses for expression. Thus, the woman in the above example is likely to express her reaction—at first primarily a bodily one—as "I became frightened." Chances are, during the ride home, the feeling persisted. Perhaps the feeling will still exist when she arrives home, and it may linger as long as she has not verbalized it. A implicit meaning is incomplete, it is the feeling of something unsolved, something that looks for completion through interaction with verbal symbols (for a more thorough discussion, see Depestele, 1984, 1986).

This leads us to the second level of interaction, which is the one between the bodily sensing and symbols (such as words) through which explicit meanings are formed from preconceptual, implicit, and incomplete meanings. When this interaction occurs, access to conscious knowledge takes place (Van Balen, 1991). Once explicated, the person experiences the implicit in a new and more complete way because it is now understood (Depestele, 1984). By *symbols,* I mean everything that interacts with the implicit, be it that which awakens the felt sense or that through which the felt sense unfolds or is carried further.

Conscious or explicit meanings are products of this process that have as a referent an implicit whole of felt meanings. The felt sense contains many more meanings than those made explicit. The explicit meaning is not a previously hidden or repressed one that now becomes clear, but one that is formed in the interaction between felt sense and symbols. A correct verbalization is one that brings about an experiential effect: a physical feeling of relief and a more intense and precise awareness of a facet of the felt sense. A correct verbalization arises from a shift at the implicit level; the essential carrying forward occurs at the implicit level—the new meaning as bodily knowledge—and, in this sense, verbalization is a by-product. Following a correct symbolization, a new sense forms, a new implicit feeling of oneself in the situation. This process of forming anew follows a particular order. Thus, the woman in our example, after having put into words that she was afraid, can now feel how threatened she felt; she may then become aware of her confusion, her feelings of helplessness and resourcelessness, her panic at being at someone else's mercy, and eventually her urge to run away. Only after putting into words one aspect of her feelings can new aspects be felt and become available for interaction and symbolization. This is a step toward change. In this way, experience is carried further and is completed. Change comes about by many small steps carrying the experience forward.

Healthy Mental Functioning: An Adequate Experiencing Process

Healthy mental functioning implies a constant and flexible interaction at both of these levels, by which experience is continuously carried further.

An adequate way of experiencing is characterized by reflective attention to the felt sense about a situation. To busy oneself only with the explicit does not lead to anything new or to any change; instead, one's experiencing process stagnates. Indeed, the explicit is only that already formulated and not new, but the implicit implies more.

To function in a healthy way, one should not view experiences "as if they were set, shaped units with their own set structure (Gendlin, 1970, p. 154). One should not consider the explicits as fixed and unalterable end products. Instead, one should view experiences as temporary constructions to be transcended by further experience, to be changed or replaced by new constructions that will, in turn, enter into interaction with the forever changing implicit experiencing of the moment. Thus, in an adequate experiencing process, symbolization always results in a hypothesis that needs to be put to the test.

What has been learned and experienced in the past functions implicitly in the present, concretely felt experience. Previous experiences that cannot function implicitly interfere with a fresh and rich experience of the present moment. The experience is then structure-bound, the present situation or certain aspects of it evoking only an already formed experience pattern with a fixed unchangeable and repetitive structure. In that case, the experience is a "frozen whole" (Gendlin, 1970, p. 154), and interaction with the multiple aspects of the present moment is impossible. To the extent that experiencing is structure-bound, the person experiences the same thing over and over. Implicitly functioning experiences, on the other hand, are felt as a complex preconceptual whole, carrying a multitude of implicit meanings that can interact with the present situation. To return to our example, suppose the young woman had recently been a victim of assault and had not yet come to terms with it. Chances are, the suddenly emerging person would reactivate the experience of the assault. One would not be surprised if she immediately ran away, yelled, or prayed for the man not to hurt her, instead of waiting and hearing the man's innocent request. Her experience of the present would be distorted by the past, and the man would have had to go through considerable trouble to convince her of his innocent intentions.

This description shows how a person's way of experiencing may deviate from the mentally healthy—and therapeutically desirable—processlike experiencing. Indeed, the interaction may be blocked or hindered at both levels of interaction. I will illustrate this further on in this chapter with clinical vignettes.

EMPATHIC RESONANCE

A Process of Knowing

The empathically listening therapist's inner process, which we call empathic resonance after Barrett-Lennard (1981), can be seen as a specific way of knowing (see also Vanaerschot, 1990a, 1990b; Vanaerschot & Van Balen, 1991). Of course, one can never know another person's world directly. By "*knowing*" I mean, in this context, that the therapist's inner experience, which he or she can perceive directly, has come to resemble as closely as possible the client's or may indeed be almost identical with it. The therapist can generate hypotheses about the client's inner experience. These hypotheses are the result of a range of comparisons between the client's verbal or nonverbal clues and the inner referents the therapist has at his disposal. These inner referents, such as experiences and feelings similar to the client's, or experiential knowledge acquired from literature, movies, previous therapy, or psychopathology, function as internal resources that are available for this process of comparison. The therapist then tests these hypotheses against the client's phenomenological world. Therefore, from the therapist's point of view, the empathic response is primarily in the service of tuning in to the client. Indeed, the client's reaction to the therapist's intervention allows the therapist to adjust his or her experience and to attune it better and more precisely to the client's.

The process of knowing described above implies a specific way of being or functioning that differs somewhat from the "usual" interpersonal contact. The difference does not lie in the therapist putting the self aside—as Rogers' (1975) description of empathy as "putting oneself aside" could perhaps erroneously suggest—but rather in a way of using the self. Indeed, the therapist "uses" himself or herself so as to be maximally receptive to and open to being corrected by what the client presents. This presupposes a processlike way of experiencing.

Process Functioning as Basic Condition for Empathy

Empathic Resonance: Eliciting a Felt Sense

Empathic resonance refers to a way of experiencing whereby what the client expresses (what is said, what is not said, how it is said, and what the body language is) elicits a bodily felt sense in the therapist. In other words, certain aspects of the therapist's implicit experience come to be in process, the client's expressions being symbols that interact with the therapist's experiencing. The therapist will then focus on his or her own felt sense and try to explicate aspects of it. This is then submitted to the client for testing. An empathic process can take place only when this interaction develops between the client's symbols and the therapist's implicit experiencing.

Helpful in developing this process of resonance is asking oneself how someone relating these experiences would feel inside. To listen with this question in mind can be helpful in understanding the experience at the root of the client's expression. This becomes all the more important as the client's symbols are less evocative or adequate. For example, a client says,

"Someone puts an electric current through me. It hurts." The empathic therapist will consider these words as a (clearly inadequate) symbolization of a meaningful implicit experience and will try to make contact with his or her own felt sense, which may correspond to the client's underlying, but at present inaccessible, experience. The therapist could, for example, intervene with, "As if you were sensing a destructive energy in yourself, something painful and destructive? And it feels as if someone were doing it to you?" Such an intervention aims to acknowledge the underlying experience as meaningful and give the client a chance to develop it into more adequate symbols. The therapist's empathic attitude implies that all the client's experiences are taken seriously. With this example, I hope to clarify that the therapist should not simply accept each symbol at face value.

Congruence as Upper Limit

The quality of a therapist's process of empathic understanding will be determined by the extent of his or her contact with his or her own constantly changing, ongoing experiencing. While seeing a client, a therapist should thus make sure that he or she is open to his or her own experiencing: he or she should be congruently present. A therapist will, of course, try to develop this process quality mainly outside of the sessions, through personal therapy or supervision, but being attentive to one's own experience during the session remains crucial. Thus, an important aspect of any empathic therapist's listening attitude is reserving time and space to feel how the client's words affect him or her. In this way, a felt sense develops in the therapist, in tune with the client's discourse.

Incongruence, Lack of Containment, and Structure-Bound Functioning

A therapist's difficulty allowing this process of empathic resonance to take place is often related to the inability to admit certain experiences, thus with a lack of congruence. This is especially the case with painful and hard-to-tolerate experiences. In this sense, congruence has a lot in common with the notion of "containment" (Cluckers, 1989). For the therapist to be able to contain painful client experiences, the therapist must be able to be congruent with his or her painful experiences.

Incongruence refers to a structure-bound way of experiencing, in which experience is related to through rigid preset structures of meaning. The quality of the process of empathic understanding will largely be determined by the degree to which the therapist's experiences can function in a non-structure-bound or "optimally implicit" manner (Gendlin, 1974). When this is the case, he or she will be able to use his or her experiences in a way that is detached from the specific structure and context that they have for him or her. Not only does the therapist then have thousands of implicitly functioning aspects of meaning at his disposal for interaction, but he or she also remains open to correction in the light of new information—in this case new symbols coming from the client. And this is precisely what is needed to arrive at a new meaning or, in the case of empathy, at the meaning that the client is trying to convey. On the other hand, the more structure-bound the therapist's manner of experiencing, the less attuned his or her experience will be to the client's and the less possible it will be for him or her to correct personal experience as a function of the client's new symbols. In this sense, a structure-bound manner of experiencing becomes the source of a countertransferential reaction.

Characteristics of Empathic-Process Functioning

It is clear that process functioning is a basic condition for empathy. However, the specific characteristics of empathic-process functioning still remain to be clarified.

Typical of empathy is the therapist's attempt to attune his or her implicitly felt sense to the client's felt sense. Therefore, the therapist's implicit experiencing should be made to correspond to the felt sense from which the client speaks. The word *correspond,* however, does not mean "be identical to." Should the therapist's implicit experiencing be identical to the client's, then therapy would be impossible. Indeed, therapy can be effective only if the therapist is capable of living the situation more fully than the client. This experiencing more fully can occur at both levels of interaction. First, the therapist can be more fully aware of those aspects of the client's implicit experiencing that are present but largely overlooked by the client and can carry them forward by symbolizing them. Here, the therapist intervenes at the second level of interaction and helps to unfold the implicit experiencing through helping to give words to the client's experience (Gendlin, 1970, p. 144). Even aspects that are not yet part of the client's ongoing interaction process, however, may be active in the therapist's implicit experiencing. These can be used to help the client unblock those aspects "stuck" in a structure-bound manner of functioning. In this last case, the therapist intervenes at the first level of interaction, which is that of reconstituting the experience (Gendlin, 1970, p. 156). He can sense directions implicit in what the client is now experiencing and help organize and unfold them.

It should be pointed out that, at this last level of more fully experiencing, the criterion of differentiating between internal and external frames of reference, traditionally held to be important in judging the existence of empathy, is irrelevant. It is traditionally held that, if the therapist responds from his or her perspective, he or she is responding from an external frame of reference and not being empathic. To be empathic he or she must respond from his or her perception of the client's internal frame of reference. However, the degree of empathy in a therapeutic interaction is not determined by an imaginary dividing line between internal and external frames of reference but by the therapist's way of handling the experience elicited in himself or herself. The empathic character of a therapeutic interaction is determined by letting the empathic-resonance process develop within the therapist and then by tuning into the client's inner experience to check for an ultimate test of accuracy to see how close the therapist is.

The criterion of accuracy of the therapist's responses is the client's and not the therapist's felt sense—the degree to which the response carries the client's experiencing a little forward. Thus, the therapist should use the "more" that he or she implicitly feels insofar that it suits the client's process. Indeed, the experiencing process has its own order: Something can start functioning implicitly only after other already implicitly functioning aspects have been carried forward by symbols. Introducing new elements before the client's experiencing process had reached the point where these elements can start functioning implicitly is of no help to the client. The client cannot do anything with them, and the experiencing process cannot yet be furthered by them.

In much the same way, psychoanalysts will talk about "premature" interpretation. This makes specific demands on the therapist's experiencing process. The therapist has to refrain from precipitous conceptualization of his or her felt sense. He or she has to strive for, and learn to tolerate, a state of deliberate not-knowing to a greater extent than he would in everyday interpersonal functioning. This includes being able to prolong one's experiential process at the level of implicit experiencing. Several authors have described this essential characteristic of empathic functioning. Rice (1974) spoke about "avoiding closure." From a psychoanalytic point of view, Olinick (1969) called it "regression in the service of the other" and "regressive openness and receptivity," whereas Freud (1912/1958) called it "free-floating attention." Margulies (1984) stressed the importance of the empathic therapist's "negative capability" referring to a therapist's need to tolerate ambiguity, uncertainty, and lack of differentiation.

What this really amounts to is that empathic functioning is essentially: the therapist putting his or her proficiency in process experiencing at the client's disposal; that the client is offered a more adequate way of experiencing in those areas where his functioning is structure-bound or where his experiencing process does not come to completion. In analogy to Wexler's therapist as "surrogate information processor" (Wexler, 1974, p. 97), I would call the therapist a "surrogate experiencer."

EMPATHIC INTERACTION IN CLINICAL PRACTICE: ILLUSTRATIONS FROM A QUALITATIVE STUDY

As a basic principle of the therapeutic effect of empathy, I postulate that the therapist's own process functioning offers a correction or completion of those aspects of the client's experiential process that are blocked or do not proceed adequately. I will illustrate this with therapy excerpts and interview data gathered during a research project on the role and meaning of empathy in experience-oriented therapy (Vanaerschot, in preparation). In this study, a number of cases were studied intensively. All sessions were recorded on audiotape and videotape. A number of these sessions were selected for detailed study by means of the Interpersonal Process Recall method (IPR; Elliott, 1986). This method consists of intensive postsession questioning of both therapist and client about a session fragment labelled as *important* by either client or therapist in a postsession questionnaire. The questioning takes place during or immediately after reviewing the fragment on videotape. I selected two such IPR fragments judged to be "very empathic" to illustrate this chapter. I transcribed the core part of the recording together with therapist's and client's comments during the IPR interview. I have added my own comments as a researcher.

Illustration 1: "We Have Good Mothers"

Fragment

This is a client-selected fragment from the eighth session of a client-centered therapy.

Prior to this fragment, the client, a young woman, gave a number of examples illustrating how she is second to her mother in a number of areas, and how those areas in which she excels are either not noticed or are minimized by her mother.

The peak interventions in this fragment—those labelled as *very important* by the client while reviewing the tape—are in italics. The selected fragment starts with the 44th therapist intervention of the session.

> T44:[1] I sit here, thinking, but perhaps it is largely something [C laughs] that comes from myself, . . . *a mother who does not see the good in her child and does not bring it out* . . .
>
> C44: [interrupts] But did not see it in her husband either.
>
> T45: Yes, that too.
>
> C45: This, I find more terrible still.
>
> T46: *To me, these are just aspects of "loving someone really"* . . . *of* [C: Yes] *seeing the good parts and bringing them out.* [12 sec. of silence; client starts crying.]
>
> C46: [crying] Yes, I think so too . . .
>
> T47: Is this perhaps something [client blows her nose] which you not only think but also wonder a little, feel a little, something like: Did she really love me?
>
> C47: As a child, I always had the impression of being born in the wrong family. [T: Yes. Hmmm.] But that was when I was

very little [T: Hmmm]. Later, this ebbed away. But, as a small child, I always had the impression that . . . my brother and sister did . . . wrong things; they were the wild ones and did not meet the requirements, whereas I kept always trying and . . . [T: Hmmm].

Therapist's View

During the IPR interview, the therapist describes her intervention as a confrontation, therefore an intervention from her own frame of reference.

The following is the therapist's answer to follow the question: "What exactly did you feel during the fragment we just watched?"

Before the intervention (T44) I felt something like . . . how she kept heaping up examples of how mother does this better and mother does that better. I found it terrible, the way she kept doing more of the same, always stressing what mother did better. I felt I wanted to straighten the balance somehow, yes, not to repeat again what the client herself kept saying over and over. I probably particularly took stock of my own experiences as a mother and of my views on loving as well. I find this strange to always emphasize to one's children what one does best. This, for me, jars with what I consider: loving my children . . . Personally, I had the feeling that I took a risk by filling it in as I did. I was acutely aware that, at that moment, I was pushing her own views totally aside and was picking up something of which I felt that it could touch on something very painful.

The following is the therapist's answer to the subsequent question: "Did you do anything here which, in your experience, strikes you as helpful?"

With this client, I have the feeling that limiting myself to empathic translation would do too little to get her out from where she was stuck. I have the feeling that I have to tap my own frame of reference. Thus, I believe, I am confronting here out of my own frame of reference.

Client's View

During the IPR interview, the client mentioned that, in that fragment, she felt the therapist understood at a deep level something that she herself did not yet dare to feel fully, nevermind state explicitly.

The following is the client's answer to the question: "What exactly did you feel during this fragment?"

The awareness of not being loved . . . it is difficult when someone else tells you that you don't have a good mother. But worse is that you realize it yourself. That is the worst, I think, when someone else says it and you don't even defend yourself any longer; you just find it true . . .

> I do not like to admit it, but . . . she is right. It just is that way. And that is painful.

She answered the question: "What did you do, or what did you try to do during this fragment?" in the following way:

> Swallow a lump in my throat . . . let it all penetrate, face the truth in it, be sad . . . and let it settle in the sense of, yes, now the words have been spoken. And also something like: And damn it! she found out. You may give as many examples as you wish but as long as nobody puts it into words or defines it clearly, you can still hope that it has not been fully heard. But once it has been that precisely defined, there is something like: It had to come to this and it did come to this . . . and she found out.

Later, the client stated that she sometimes tells similar things to her friend, but they always allow her to escape, whereas this is no longer possible with the therapist. She also stated that the process was difficult and painful, but later, she felt some sort of relief:

> Something like braving the waves or so. What you minimize all your life or put aside or find too difficult, or . . . what you feel will make you sad if you go on with it, you then realize that, indeed, it now makes you sad; but later on, you experience some sort of relief.

Discussion

This fragment illustrates how the client's story evoked, in keeping with the numerous examples preceeding the fragment, a felt sense in the therapist. The therapist then tapped her own inner referents—her own views on motherhood—and used these to tune into her client. The therapist refers to her own felt sense, in which her interventions originated, as her "own frame of reference." I do not believe this to be entirely the case, however. I see the therapist as being more aware of the client's implicit experience than the client was herself. In the felt sense evoked in the therapist, which is partly colored by her own experiential world, implicit aspects are present that the client does not express. These aspects are then explicated by the therapist in the form of a personal view. Another therapist may have expressed it as an empathic guess, such as: "In all the examples you give, something painful sounds through as if you were asking yourself 'did she really love me?' " Why did this particular therapist choose this particular wording? She answers the question herself in the IPR interview, when asked: "Why did you intervene in the way you did at that moment (T44)? What was your intervention a reaction to, and what was your intention?"

> I reacted to a whole series of statements in which her mother stressed above all else, how her way of being was the best. And how the client

apparently had to fight hard in order to be allowed to exist on her own terms. Thus, it is in fact . . . my summary of the tale. My intention was to break through something. And perhaps also to stop the tale. I wanted to get away from her level of telling it and get to a deeper level, something like, what did it really do to her? . . . I did not have the impression that she was very frightened but rather that she recognized something on a deeper level; that I had touched on something which she also felt but did not dare put into words. And which she then picked up again in her statement about not belonging to the family or something like it. But that was her translation, which was still somewhat weaker than mine. . . . I have the feeling that, if I did not go on confronting her, I would not really get through this; that I have to somehow . . . sometimes dare to adopt a confronting way, otherwise it is all so obvious.

The client indicated that she had vaguely sensed, somewhere, the implicit aspects expressed by the therapist but did not dare to feel them fully and certainly did not dare to express them. The client gives the therapist many examples in the hope, but at the same time fearing that, these implicit aspects will be heard.

Some of the client's statements in the IPR interview suggest that structure-bound concepts ("We have good mothers") stood in the way of a complete experience of the situation.

Not to feel loved. When this is said from a mother, then . . . that always sounds incredible, something like: but every mother loves her child. . . . Here, in this room, to dare saying what a bad mother I had, what she did to her children . . . While this does not really fit in with our social background [laughing]: we have good mothers. . . . I will, so to speak, not stop any more saying such negative things about my mother. This . . . pot has been opened and everything is running out.

Daring to say negative things about her mother feels like something that was previously closed but is now open. The client mentioned that what happened in that session—the implicit that has been completed—was in fact already set in motion in the previous session. She called the first 6 sessions "exploratory, preparatory" and said that it would have made her very mad had the therapist told her that in the first session. This would indicate that those aspects of implicit experiencing that were expressed in the session, and had previously functioned in a structure-bound way, were able to start functioning implicitly by what had happened in the previous sessions.

This fragment illustrates how certain aspects of experience had slowly started functioning implicitly by what had happened in previous sessions, and how, in this present session, the therapist's empathic interaction, which was precisely aimed at these implicitly functioning aspects, has helped to unfold the client's experiencing.

Illustration 2: "It Is Enough to Chop Off Your Head"

The following fragment illustrates how the therapist's empathic responses help the client to develop a felt sense or help her stay in contact with it, thus preventing the client pushing back her experience into formlessness. The therapist relies on her own experiential sense to frame a response (e.g., the first peak moment), shows her interest in the experiences of her client (e.g., the second peak moment), and restates what her client has said to clarify the meaning of it (e.g., the third peak moment). These responses make the client feel understood, make her feel the value of her experience, and thus stimulate further development of a felt sense (e.g., the first peak moment). Also shown is how the therapist's interest and her restatements are experienced by the client as a confirmation of the meaningfulness of the experiencing process itself (e.g., second and third peak moment).

Fragment

The fragment was selected by a female client from the 18th session of psychoanalytic therapy. From the 30-minute fragment, she selected five therapist peaks and five client peaks (in italics in the transcript). To clarify the meaning of the empathic intervention, a fairly long excerpt is given here, the first 15 minutes or so. It contains the 5 therapist peaks.

Prior to the fragment, the client expressed concern about the value of therapy. She questioned it because she felt overwhelmed by grey, depressive feelings, more pronounced during the sessions than in real life. The feelings were formless, and she could not explain them. She experienced the therapist's pauses and silences as threatening, oppressive, and compelling, urging her to say something. She believed that therapy works for other people because they have something to say, know more precisely what they feel, what they think, and what is wrong, whereas she herself does not. The client described her habitual way of dealing with this greyness as consciously doing something, any activity, to chase away the grey.

> C26: And then you think: yeah, when things work that way . . .
> It all happens in your head anyway and it is enough to put in another slide or something like that. [17 seconds of silence; the client is using the image of a slide projector to describe what is going on in her head.]
> T26: I thought you were going to say: it is enough to chop off your head. [laughs]
> C27: [laughs] Yes, sometimes. [5 seconds of silence] I did imagine it that way: that I just could . . . shove aside my head; then all this . . . all that buzz would be gone. [26 seconds of silence]

Having the feeling of having to be continuously distracted in order to rid yourself of this. [12 seconds of silence]

T27: It is painful to tolerate the confusion, the grey and the lack of structure . . .

C28: Yes.

T28: Until a structure emerges, right? A bit as if you were saying: I don't believe in that any more, or I doubt that it is possible. The best system is to put in another slide, or whatever else you count doing with your head: hang it somewhere on something artificial until it is cleaned, and then it will take some time until it gets filled again or something like that, but . . . [C laughs] [11 seconds of silence]

C29: No, I sometimes find it so unbearable, ugh . . . that I am happy in the morning when I can say: for x hours now I have not been busy with anything that I can remember. [6 seconds of silence]

T29: Thus, you have worked without a head . . . or been busy.

C30: Yes, I have been, well . . . absent.

T30: And you find this a relief or . . . ?

C31: I find this a relief, yes. [9 seconds of silence]

T31: Thus, that being busy with your head or what happens in it, has a paralyzing effect. [5 seconds of silence]

C32: I don't know how to call it. [7 seconds of silence] But where do we go from here? [23 seconds of silence] I think, since all this can be interpreted . . . [5 seconds of silence] I may just as well . . . give it another interpretation . . . which has more form or simply is better.

T32: Could you make this more concrete? [7 seconds of silence]

C33: For example you say . . . you try to get some structure in there . . . And, yeah, you try to have as little as possible left over. [7 seconds of silence] Until you simply start concentrating on, well . . . everyday things. [11 seconds of silence] I cannot even tell what in particular I'm thinking of. [53 seconds of silence] I think that I try to avoid [10 seconds of silence], perhaps precisely these structures. Or these facts. [32 seconds of silence] That everything simply becomes liquid . . . [7 seconds of silence], and then that everything simply . . . I mean, overflows, with all the consequences thereof. [48 seconds of silence] Sometimes I think: I simply make it terribly complicated for myself, and . . . everything, well, seems simple or appears simple. [5 seconds of silence] But isn't so, I find. [106 seconds of silence] When you talk about putting that head aside . . . sometimes I have to do this very consciously . . .

with good results. This means, for example, . . . I go swimming a lot, simply . . . [laughing] because I can put my head under water . . . And, well . . . this creates a pressure on your head and you hear nothing any more. [11 seconds of silence]

T33: How do you feel when you swim? [7 seconds of silence]

C34: I find this exceptionally . . . relaxing and . . . I even find it . . . well, in a certain sense . . . sacred.

T34: Sacred? [5 seconds of silence]

C35: Sacred, or, well, yes, I experience this as a ritual . . . when I can concentrate on it, when I do not have to busy myself with my little nephew or so . . . [6 seconds of silence] Sacred, well, purifying. [23 seconds of silence] This is almost addictive, really. [11 seconds of silence]

T35: Could you describe that a little more? Which elements are in there, or how does this . . . feel exactly?

C36: That swimming?

T36: Yes, yes, and what you experience around it, right? [7 seconds of silence]

C37: I think simply, the feeling that you . . . dissolve. Thus that, that you simply become part of . . . of the water . . . of the silence . . . and, . . . all this mobility, all this freedom. [15 seconds of silence] Simply the very calming effect of it. [61 seconds of silence] If I were not coming here, I would, would find . . . [7 seconds of silence] the thought of it, well, simply very pleasant. But when I tell it now . . . it takes on such proportions, I find, which do not at all, well, I mean, which evoke a counter-weight. [10 seconds of silence]

T37: How is that?

C38: Well . . . [6 seconds of silence] that these experiences become all so very big and are always, well, placed opposite to something else which . . . well, is in contrast with it. [5 seconds of silence]

T38: A little as if these experiences were taken away from you in this way . . . [7 seconds of silence]

C39: Perhaps in a certain sense, yes. [21 seconds of silence]

T39: And against what is this image of swimming, against what contrasting thing is that then placed? [6 seconds of silence]

C40: This unity thus of, of water, the whole atmosphere of unity, well . . . becomes very big and all the rest becomes, well, very shattered, broken to pieces and sharp. [5 seconds of silence] I think: You only have to think it and it is there.

T40: What?

C41: Whatever. [T: Hmmm?] Whatever. [11 seconds of silence]

T41: Do I understand you correctly when you say: When you think or speak, then it's nothing but loose bits and pieces that come out? [10 seconds of silence]

C42: No, when I talk about it like that, now, well, then [10 seconds of silence]—how shall I say it?—then all the rest throws itself much more at you.

T42: What rest?

C43: Everything which stands opposite to it, . . . well, this confusion and this, this rubbish. [9 seconds of silence]

T44: Something like: One should not talk about the sacred lest it should become profane? [6 seconds of silence]

Therapist's and Client's Views: General Comments

The therapist describes the first part of the session as "dysphoric" and vague. She has the feeling that her crude image (T26: "chop off your head") encourages the client to express her experience with images, to bring forward something more lively and pictorial. The therapist experiences the transition from dysphoric to pictorial as a relief. During this fragment, she tries essentially to understand better what occupies the client's mind.

The client leads off with the slide image (C26). From that moment on, the vague—which the client describes as "you feel physically that it gets fatter and fatter and that you have to do something"—becomes more concrete.

> It becomes more concrete on account of the images and because I can see more clearly what I do to balance it (the grey). In that way, something starts moving. This whole clump does not just keep hanging there; it feels that something starts moving, yes. Then I see it as: click click, before my eyes (these slides changing). . . . When I say: "everything happens in your head," then a lot can happen. But when I bring in these slides, then it is already framed, right? Well, I don't really think about it too much during the session but I realize it afterwards. And that is perhaps why I did not feel so stuck any more. . . . I was so relieved that something was moving. Especially when I think about something being projected, and it going on that way; that you don't have to pin yourself down to something which has no shape, or anyway, something which isn't framed.

Within the fragment, the client picks out three peak moments in which the above-mentioned feeling of "something starting to move, having a shape, being framed is clearly present." In between, the feeling slowly ebbs away and sinks back into the grey. These peak moments are: C26 to T28, C33 (from the client peak moment) to T35, and T41 to T44.

When reviewing the fragment on videotape, the client talks as follows about the selected peaks:

When I imagine this as a diagram, then the peaks are like points sticking out. I think, if they were not there, then perhaps I would be too far gone to come back. These words (peaks) always seem to occur before I am about to sink into the grey

I will now show how the empathic therapist interventions retrieve the concrete feeling in each fragment. I will also quote the therapist's comments during the IPR interview about the origin of the peak interventions. The question I asked was: "Why did you intervene in this way at that moment? What did you react to by this intervention and what was your intention?"

Detailed Analysis of the Peak Moments

Peak Moment 1: Chop Off Your Head (C26–T28)

T26: I thought you were going to say: it is enough to chop off your head.
T27: It is painful to tolerate the confusion, the grey and the lack of structure.

Therapist's view on therapist peaks.

> [On T26] I think I reacted to "put in another slide" (C26). I thought I understood that she was still thinking and thinking again, and then concluded: "one could do it differently." And I thought: "differently," that would mean "not thinking at all." But she says "put in another slide." Thus, my words were really contradicting hers. I really meant to tell her: another slide, that is, not thinking any more. And that is really what she does: does the washing-up and various chores which will numb her thinking. I really thought she would say: I could just as well amputate my head, really; I do away with all psychic life and go on like a robot. If I did not have any psychic life any more, then I would continue automatically and there would not be any problems. By ironically exaggerating this solution, I wanted to arrive somehow at the possibility of "thinking differently," not that brooding sort of thinking any more. By using a bit of irony, by almost laughing a little at what she says: Can you image running around like a vegetable, washing-up and so on, with your head next to you? Come on, you know better! You will anyway have to use your head, and instead of putting in another slide, you could perhaps try to let your head go its own way.

Later in the interview, the therapist said that she often almost senses what a person will say after they have worked together for a while. Here, this was clearly the case:

> [On T27] This is something which I know quite well myself: getting active when depressing, dysphoric feelings lurk, in order not to think about them any more. Thus, I recognize this very well as a way of escaping. And I only tried to say here what one tries to escape from: the sadness and the pain in it all. Not that it is instructured and vague but that it is so difficult and painful.

Client's views on the peak moment. Client states that, during this part, she experienced mostly amazement:

> [On T26] How is it possible that you understand me! I don't even say anything! . . . Chop off the head, that was really . . . If she had not said it, I would surely have. Then I thought: You take the words out of my mouth. This certainly gave me the feeling that she knew well where I am at. Or perhaps even better than I know it myself. Thus, I thought, when you use images, and these images are still standing there waiting (in me), because I want to say something about them, too, then this is a sign, at any rate, that you know well what I am talking about. She sees precisely what comes next. This gives me the feeling that I'm not just sitting here talking nonsense; there is someone who will surely have an answer to it. I had simply been under the impression that I was telling nothing at all. It did not even matter much, really.
>
> [On T27] I have the feeling that, in there, there are the same words (as what I am experiencing) with the exact same meaning. And this while I find it (my experience) just meaningless, really. And then she says something like that and I think: how is it possible? She says or experiences it as I do. I think: Yes, it is, after all, being taken seriously. Simply that you have the certainty that someone comes along in the same direction. And I think: What a relief! Or: she doesn't try to corner me with questions such as: What do you mean by that? What are you trying to say? . . . To me it feels as if she was giving it a bonus value because I don't value it at all. Or that I am perhaps continuously in doubt, something like saying to myself: "What are you cooking up there?" And then this (T27) almost sounds refreshing.

After this part of the fragment, the above-described feeling slowly ebbs. The client comments about that:

> I know what I am talking about in that piece, but I can imagine that someone would need more information. . . . I see it clearly before me but don't have any words ready for it. . . . Then I arrive again at the conclusion that I cannot give any more information about it. I feel I'm saying the same thing all the time; I do not add anything new. . . . Until the moment comes when I think: "Come on, we just forget it and switch to simple things about which I do have something to say." And then, I think, it switches to the swimming pool because that is something concrete and anybody can evoke images.

Peak Moment 2: The Swimming Pool (C33–T35)

> T33: How do you feel when you swim?
> T35: Could you describe that a bit more? Which elements are in there, or, how does this feel exactly?
>
> *Therapist's views on the therapist peaks.*
>
> [On T33] I was simply interested in hearing some more about her experience while swimming.

[On T35] I think my reaction came from my uncertainty about the meaning of "addictive." I could just as well have repeated: addictive, too? I found that addictive announced yet another element than what she had said about the purifying aspect.

Client's view on the peak moment. Through the swimming pool image the client gets back in touch with a crisper, fresher feeling:

I got into the swimming pool atmosphere right away. I felt something was lifting up; felt all my senses getting fresher. . . . Thus, I will quote an example, I thought; I will take one in which things are at their clearest for me. (When I wondered whether the feeling was one of "here I caught something, I have something concrete which I can shape," the client enthusiastically agreed).

[On T33] I thought: What could anybody ask about a swimming pool? "Do you want to go there?" or something. But the therapist simply asks: "How do you feel there?" Yes, then a whole pack of feelings come to the surface, you only have to choose. . . . And I also think: When someone asks you, "How do you feel?" then he also asks himself the question, "How would I feel?" When someone asks such a question, then he is busy with that himself. And that is reassuring.

[On C34] I almost could not pronounce the word *sacred.* I was a bit worried to say it. I thought: The hell! Sacred! Who will now say that swimming is sacred? Or, how will I have to explain this again? There we have it again: Something very abstract. . . . When you pronounce such a word, that is more loaded, yes? Yes, it was taking a risk because I knew I would have difficulty explaining it; . . . because I know very well that a whole area is lying there, waiting to be filled in. And also because I always think that such combinations are senseless. "In a swimming pool, how do you feel in there? Sacred." Something like: Enter a convent! You can just as well be laughed at or something. Right? I think: When I come here anyway, then I just have to do it without asking myself, "What is now to the point and what is not?" These terms simply don't apply.

The client has the feeling (in C35) that she is trying to weaken the notion of "sacred," that she is running away again and that the therapist may have noticed and makes her next intervention (T35) on that basis. She experiences this intervention as important because it "pulls that string again. Do not run away! Come here!"

What follows is experienced by the client as a new phase of ebbing.

Peak Moment 3: Speaking Chops It Up (T41–T44)

T41: Do I understand you correctly when you say: When you think or speak then it's nothing but loose bits and pieces that come out?

T44: Something like: One does not talk about the sacred lest it should become profane?

Therapist's views on therapist peaks.

[On T41] I did not understand what was chopped up, and I tried to clarify it myself: The telling itself chops it up. I tried to say it with a question mark, as if asking: Is that what you mean? But she denies.

[On T44] I continue with my idea: The act of speaking chops it up, and this time I put it differently. And she does pick up on it and refers to something else than "chopped up," but really she keeps denying it. Right?

Client's views on the peak moment.

[On T41] It is important that she says that because I still feel that she is coming along.

[On T44] I think she sensed already quite a while how I wanted to get rid of it. And when she said that, it was a cut and dried remark which was really right on. . . . I think: Yes, simply, that is it. I do know this indeed but haven't put it across clearly. But indeed, that is it.

Discussion

This fragment illustrates the significance of intervening empathically with a client who is not sure whether or not she has the right to have a personal experiencing process. Although it is concrete relationship problems that brought her to therapy, these cannot be discussed as a separate problematic area precisely because they are related to her basic doubt about the possibility of others recognizing her inner world as equally valid as that of others. This doubt also blocks the experiencing process in therapy. The client comes face to face with her problem right away in her relationship with the therapist, whose trustworthiness she has not yet assessed, the problem being whether or not the therapist will assign her the right to her own experience and will thus acknowledge her.

The depressive, grey feeling experienced by the client all her life is felt very strongly during therapy; she speaks of it being "cultivated." The question arises as to how this "grey" is to be understood theoretically. The client's descriptions of this feeling as "grey, formless, confused, vague, liquefy till everything overflows" may be understood as not letting a clear physical sense develop. The client's description of this feeling as "a clump which remains hanging there" and "feeling stuck" suggests that she is dealing with a structure-bound manner of experiencing. The term *buzz* could refer to her sensing the underlying, not yet clearly implicitly formed or tangible, meaning. The depressive, rotten aspect of the feeling refers, I think, to "sheer emotion." Sheer emotion is experiencing an emotion without the accompanying felt or associated meanings. It is an emotional response that prevents awareness of the implicit meaning, namely of that about which she feels depressed (Gendlin, 1974, p. 149).

In the above-described peak moments, the client contacted the felt sense and expressed one or several facets of it, thus carrying the experiencing further. She found, or received from the therapist, words that could express it. At the same time, these words served as handles[1] that helped to stay with the implicit experience and thus helped symbolization to occur. Thus, the slide image refers to the client's way of dealing with the implicit experience of the grey, which is her implicit experience pushed back into formlessness. The therapist's subsequent interventions (T26 and T27), which are clearly based on her client-oriented implicit experience, not only provided the client with a feeling of being understood, to her own surprise, but also supported and confirmed the value and sense of what she is experiencing. Without this affirmation, the experiencing process would stop, and this is precisely what threatened to happen after this first peak fragment. In C33, she described how she tries without success to make explicit her implicit experience ("you try to get structure in it") and how she also feels that she is trying to avoid this expression ("I think that I am trying to avoid, perhaps, precisely those structures"). The interview and the second part of the fragment—not given here—make it clear that she is afraid that symbolization other than her own may be given to her experiences, either by herself or by others, and that would ultimately destroy her experience. In this sense, interrupting the experiencing process can be understood as an attempt to safeguard her inner world.

The swimming pool image brought the client into contact with how it feels when there is interactional experiencing. The immediate sensual–bodily experience of swimming refers to a way of experiencing that feels good and is characterized by a feeling of wholeness. Analysts may be inclined to interpret it after its content, for example as longing for fusion, and thus as a regressive feeling. Within the experiential frame of reference, it is seen positively as having a longing for an interactional, fresh, and immediate manner of experiencing that contrasts strongly with the own deficient interpersonal experience. The therapist's question (T33: How do you feel when you swim?) not only stimulates the development of a bodily felt sense ("then a whole pack of feelings come to the surface") but also supports the experiencing process itself because asking about an experience means that one values it. The implicit experience of swimming unfolds through the word *sacred*. Although this word expresses the client's implicit experience, she has doubts about its communicative value. She was afraid of not being understood and having to justify herself, which means having to express her experience in other people's words, or else being laughed at. She had thus the urge to interrupt her experiencing process at that point. The therapist's subsequent request to describe her experience a bit more (T35) was understood as an invitation to continue ("Do not run away!

---

[1] Gendlin (1984) calls a word that helps the client hold onto the felt sense a *handle* (p. 86).

Come here!"). The interview data show how the therapist peaks T41 and T44 supported the experiencing process in the same way as described above: Namely, that the feeling that somebody "comes along" with her confirmed the meaningfulness of the experiencing process.

For the experiencing process to take place at all, the client has to clearly receive the message from the therapist that it is meaningful and worthwhile; she has to have the feeling that her words are received and are acknowledged as meaningful, significant products of her experiencing process, as her own creations that have a meaning for the therapist and will not be destroyed. When the client does not feel this, she keeps her experience implicit and thus incomplete.

The way in which the empathic therapist peaks operated is summarized as follows by the client:

> When there is a sign of weakening or so, then strings are pulled a bit tighter. Also by her asking more details, or simply by insisting on something which you don't think you can clarify or elaborate on. Also that you start with something very ill-defined, unframed, and then hear a remark which confronts you immediately with the feeling, or which perhaps renders the feeling more concrete or more serious, or gives it more value just by naming it, by clarifying it in a certain sense by means of a single sentence. Something for which I need, I don't know how many sentences. Thus, starting from a hazy, muddy situation, from something undefined, and getting a definition out of it. And also the feeling of: So far we are still on the same wavelength. Because when she says nothing, then you think: Nothing is said because there simply isn't anything to say.

At this point, we may be tempted to conclude that therapy should be an uninterrupted chain of peak fragments. However, the client denied this in the IPR interview. She found alternating between peak fragments and doubt fragments important because of "the fact that you are, in a way, being challenged to make something of it yourself, with the certainty that you are being followed in this [e.g., by the therapist]."

In summary, this fragment illustrates how empathic interventions operate in an experience-enhancing way by recognizing and confirming the value and meaningfulness of the experience, which enabled the client—by making it safe enough—to let a felt sense develop and to let symbolization take place.

CONCLUSION

We saw how interventions originating in the therapist's empathic-resonance process influence the client's experiencing process in a process-enhancing way. Judging from two fragments, interventions act on the experiencing process precisely in those areas in which it does not proceed adequately.

A noteworthy observation in the study of these empathic fragments is that, in their formal aspect, empathic interventions are not limited to reflections of feelings. Thus, interventions that could be called self-expressive can apparently be highly empathic as well.

The theoretical views and supporting evidence from qualitative research presented in this chapter constitute a framework in which to understand and place the various kinds of effects, traditionally attributed to empathy. (For an overview of the effects traditionally ascribed to empathy, see Vanaerschot, 1993, 1996; Vanaerschot & Van Balen, 1991). In this framework, the effects of empathy as climatic factor or as primary relationship variable (Rice, 1983) can be seen as furthering the first level of interaction in the experiencing process, which is the implicit experiencing, and as encouraging the communication of private symbols. The effects of empathy as task-oriented relationship variable or the concrete empathic response, on the other hand, seem to refer to the unfolding of the implicit experiencing, and thus to the second level of interaction.

Identifying and describing the various forms of interaction between therapist and client, and of the specific way in which they enhance the client's experiencing, is, we believe, an important area in psychotherapy research. It leads not only to a better theoretical understanding of the way in which experiential change occurs but also to a more differentiated process-diagnostic way of thinking. Furthermore, a better knowledge of process signals may make the practicing psychotherapist more sensitive to what happens in the here and how, so that he or she can direct his or her interventions at those aspects of the client's experiential process that need attention. I do not want to promote a technical form of therapy comparable to establishing the right connection in a telephone exchange, but I do want to promote a more conscious use by the psychotherapist of his or her own implicit experiencing of the client's discourse. Finally, I hope that a better knowledge of process signals indicative of specific deficiencies in the experiential process will contribute to a better understanding of "strange" or "difficult to understand" clients.

REFERENCES

Barrett-Lennard, G. T. (1981). The empathy cycle: Refinement of a nuclear concept. *Journal of Counseling Psychology, 28,* 91–100.

Cluckers, G. (1989). "Containment" in de therapeutische relatie: De therapeut als drager en zingever ["Containment" in the therapeutic relationship: The therapist as a holder and sense-giver]. In H. Vertommen, G. Cluckers, & G. Lietaer (Eds.), *De relatie in therapie* (pp. 49–64). Leuven, Belgium: University of Pers Leuven.

Depestele, F. (1984). Ervaringsgerichtheid en Gendlins begrip "felt sense" [Experientialness and Gendlin's concept "felt sense"]. In G. Lietaer, P. H. van Praag, & J. C. A. G. Swildens (Eds.), *Client-centered psychotherapie in beweging* (pp. 87–110). Leuven, Belgium: Acco.

Depestele, F. (1986). Het lichaam in psychotherapie [The body in psychotherapy]. In R. Van Balen, M. Leijssen, & G. Lietaer (Eds.), *Droom en werkelijkheid in client-centered psychotherapie* (pp. 87–123). Leuven/Amersfoort, Belgium: Acco.

Elliott, R. (1986). Interpersonal Process Recall (IPR) as a process research method. In L. Greenberg & W. Pinsof (Eds.), *The psychotherapeutic process* (pp. 503–527). New York: Guilford.

Freud, S. (1958). Recommendations to physicians practising psychoanalysis. In J. Strachey (Ed. and Trans.) *The standard edition of the complete psychological works of Sigmund Freud* (Vol. 12, pp. 109–120). London: Hogarth Press. (Original work published 1912)

Gendlin, E. T. (1968). The experiential response. In E. Hammer (Ed.), *The use of interpretation in treatment* (pp. 208–227). New York: Grune & Stratton.

Gendlin, E. T. (1970). A theory of personality change. In J. T. Hart & T. H. Tomlinson (Eds.), *New directions in client-centered therapy* (pp. 129–174). Boston: Houghton Mifflin.

Gendlin, E. T. (1974). Client-centered and experiential psychotherapy. In D. A. Wexler & L. N. Rice (Eds.), *Innovations in client-centered therapy* (pp. 211–246). New York: Wiley.

Gendlin, E. T. (1981). *Focusing.* New York: Bantam Books.

Gendlin, E. T. (1990). The small steps of the therapy process: How they come and how to help them come. In G. Lietaer, J. Rombauts, & R. Van Balen (Eds.), *Client-centered and experiential psychotherapy in the nineties* (pp. 205–224). Leuven, Belgium: University of Pers Leuven.

Gendlin, E. T., & Lietaer, G. (1983). On client-centered and experiential psychotherapy: An interview with Eugene Gendlin. In W. R. Minsel & W. Herff (Eds.), *Research on psychotherapeutic approaches* (pp. 77–104). Frankfurt, Germany: Peter Lang.

Margulies, A. (1984). Toward empathy: The uses of wonder. *American Journal of Psychiatry, 23*(1), 4–20.

Olinick, S. (1969). On empathy and regression in the service of the other. *British Journal of Medical Psychology, 42,* 41–49.

Rice, L. N. (1974). The evocative function of the therapist. In D. A. Wexler & L. N. Rice (Eds.), *Innovations in client-centered therapy* (pp. 211–246). New York: Wiley.

Rice, L. N. (1983). The relationship in client-centered therapy. In N. J. Lambert (Ed.), *Psychotherapy and patient relationship* (pp. 36–60). Homewood: Dow Jones-Irwin.

Rogers, C. R. (1975). Empathy: An unappreciated way of being. *The Counseling Psychologist, 5*(2), 2–10.

Vanaerschot, G. (1990a). The process of empathy: Holding and letting go. In G. Lietaer, J. Rombauts, & R. Van Balen (Eds.), *Client-centered and experiential psychotherapy in the nineties* (pp. 205–224). Leuven, Belgium: University of Pers Leuven.

Vanaerschot, G. (1990b). Empathie: Een proces gekenmerkt door vasthouden en loslaten [Empathy: A process characterized by holding and letting go]. *Tijdschrift voor Psychotherapie, 16*(4), 186–198.

Vanaerschot, G. (1993). Empathy as releasing several micro-processes in the client. In D. Brazier (Ed.), *Beyond Carl Rogers. Towards a psychotherapy for the 21st century* (pp. 47–72). London: Constable.

Vanaerschot, G. (1996). *Plaats en betekenis van empathie in belevingsgerichte psychotherapie. Theoretische en empirische exploratie* [Place and meaning of empathy in experiential psychotherapy]. K. U. Leuven, nietgepubliceerd proefschrift.

Vanaerschot, G., & Van Balen, R. (1991). Empathie. In J. C. A. G. Swildens, O. de Haas, G., Lietaer, & R. Van Balen (Eds.), *Leerboek gesprekstherapie. De cliëntgerichte benadering* (pp. 93–137). Amersfoort/Leuven, Belgium: Acco.

Van Balen, R. (1989). De therapeutische relatie bij C. Rogers: Enkel een klimaat, een dialoog of beide? [The therapeutic relationship to C. Rogers: Only a climate, a dialogue, or both?] In H. Vertommen, G. Cluckers, & G. Lietaer (Eds.), *De relatie in therapie* (pp. 27–48). Leuven, Belgium: University of Pers Leuven.

Van Balen, R. (1991). Theorie van de persoonlijkheidsverandering [Theory of personality change]. In H. Swildens, O. de Haas, G. Lietaer, & R. Van Balen (Eds.), *Leerboek Gesprekstherapie. De cliëntgerichte benadering* (pp. 139–167). Amersfoort/Leuven, Belgium: Acco.

Wexler, D. A. (1974). A cognitive theory of experiencing, self-actualization, and therapeutic process. In D. A. Wexler & L. N. Rice (Eds.), *Innovations in client-centered therapy* (pp. 211–246). New York: Wiley.

8

VARIETIES OF
EMPATHIC RESPONDING

LESLIE S. GREENBERG AND ROBERT ELLIOTT

The revival of interest in the importance of empathy in psychotherapy calls for the specification of what is being referred to in clinical practice by both clinicians and theorists when using the term *empathy*. We will argue that empathy is not a unitary construct and thus clarification and differentiation of the phenomena referred to by the concept are needed. We will initially discuss the nature of empathy and contrast it with interpretation to clarify the essential nature of empathy. Then we will suggest that a more componential view of empathic responding is required—one that is more differentiated than for example the dichotomy proposed between empathy and interpretation. Following this, we will discuss a variety of different types of empathic responses, empathic tasks, and principles, from the viewpoint of a process-experiential approach to treatment (Greenberg, Rice, & Elliott, 1993).

What is Empathy?

Empathy first and foremost is an attitude and is implemented by the taking of a specific type of vantage point or stance toward another. This means that the empathic therapist attempts to operate within the internal frame of reference of the client and to remain in empathic contact with the client's inner world. Empathy involves listening from the inside as if "I am the other," as opposed to occupying an outside vantage point. Empathy is not simply friendly rapport, sympathetic encouraging, listening, or being warm and supportive. Conflation of empathy with these common social responses, essentially forms of rapport, has resulted in one of the major persistant misunderstandings of the nature of empathy in some approaches that claim to be empathic. Empathy is the process of deeply contacting the inner world of another, being attuned to the nuances of feeling and meaning as well as the essence of another's current experience.

In understanding what empathy is, it is also important to distinguish between experiencing empathy and communicating empathic understanding (Barrett-Lennard, 1981). As we have said, being empathic involves entering the psychological world of the other and in some way experiencing what it is like to be that person in this moment. Communicating this understanding is a separate component of empathy, which must flow from empathic attunement but may be communicated in a variety of ways. In addition, one could be empathic (i.e., enter the other's frame of reference) but then use one's sense of the other's experience to manipulate the person. Thus, empathic communication differs from empathic contact or attunement, and, as we will discuss later, the communication of empathy can take a variety of forms.

The Function of Empathy

A variety of different functions have been outlined in the literature (Bohart, 1991). In client-centered therapy empathy has been viewed essentially as providing two different kinds of learning experiences. First, the therapist's communication of empathic understanding is viewed as helping clients come to trust and accept themselves. To facilitate this, the therapist's process goal is to follow the client, to be an accepting companion who helps break the psychological isolation experienced by the client. Here empathy is viewed as helping clients to be self-accepting and to find their own voice. In this view clients' increased trust in themselves then leads, among other things, to increased awareness.

The second type of learning occurs through exploration and discovery. In this view clients are seen as explorers who come to relate to their internal experience differently, to see things freshly and experience things more deeply. By paying attention to what they experience, they expand their awareness. The therapist's process goal here is to be a facilitator of exploration and a companion in the search, a co-explorer. The therapist does not lead the client but encourages the client to look carefully and to keep going where he or she might have feared to go. In this view discovery then leads to internal reorganization.

In our view, empathy involves the more or less immediate apprehension of the client's subjective world through imaginative entry into the experience of the other. This is an affective form of understanding that does not depend on labored reasoning and differs from conceptual understanding. In our view empathy does not entail actually feeling the feeling of the other "as if one were the other." Rather, it entails a complex process of emotional understanding of the other. This involves a felt apprehension of the other's situation as well as one's own affective response to this. All of this is then synthesised into a felt understanding. Thus, when a client feels pain or sadness, in being empathic the therapist does not necessarily feel pain or sadness. It is more complex than this. Often, the therapist may feel a reciprocal responsive feeling, such as compassion or concern. As opposed to feeling a "little" of what a client is feeling, a therapist often experiences a complex felt sense, a complex sense of understanding the felt meaning of the situation to the client. What is important is that it is something the therapist feels rather than just understands intellectually. Empathy is thus a feeling, or experiential process of understanding.

In terms of the communication of empathic understanding, we believe that the moment-by-moment communication of empathic understanding is important in providing a safe facilitative environment and promoting exploration. Another form of empathic communication, practised more consistently by self psychologists, involves offering at more spread-out intervals a more holistic understanding of a person's experience. This form of empathy is offered more as a summary or integrative understanding of what the client has been saying. This may even be offered only a few times a session. Thus, the therapist's activity level can vary quite dramatically in the empathic process, and we view a sustained active effort at communicating understanding as most helpful. In addition, in our view this form of sustained empathy serves the important function of enhancing affect regulation, in that symbolization of affect by an empathic response aids in its assimilation into meaning structures (Greenberg & Paivio, in press; Pennebaker, 1990; Pennebaker & Susman, 1988). Once symbolized, the emotion becomes more able to yield its meaning and is more amenable to reorganization (Greenberg & Paivio, in press).

DYNAMIC INTERPRETATION

Empathic responding will be contrasted with dynamic interpretation below to clarify some of their differences. First, however, we need to clarify the nature of dynamic interpretation.

What is Interpretation?

As defined by the Therapist Intervention Rating System (Piper, Azim, Joyce, & McCallum, 1991), for example, a dynamic interpretation is a therapist statement that (a) refers to a dynamic component (i.e., a wish, fear, defensive process, or dynamic expression), and (b) provides links between affect, thought, or behavior (e.g., "You felt guilty so you bought her a gift"). More broadly, interpretation in general has been defined as a therapist response mode that intends to give clients new information about self through offering connections, labels, or patterns (Hill, 1986).

In our view a key distinction between empathic and interpretive responding lies in the intention of the therapist when delivering the intervention rather than the behavior. The intention in interpretation is to point out something to the client or to "give news," to have the client see something he or she did not see before. This intention can be contrasted with the intention in empathic responding of conveying understanding or promoting exploration. Thus, it may be that the same words (e.g., "You're feeling angry because therapy is ending") could be either an interpretation or an empathic response, depending on the therapist's intention.

An additional feature of interest in distinguishing empathy and interpretation, and especially dynamic interpretations, is that the content of interpretations is more often theory derived, whereas the content of empathy is derived from the client's experience and is always checked back against the client's experience.

Comparison of Empathy and Interpretation

In our view empathic and interpretive responding can be compared profitably on the dimensions of (a) aim or intention, (b) function, (c) degree of inference, (d) target or focus, and (e) the created role relationship.

Aim or Intention

Three aims can be delineated that help distinguish empathic from interpretative responding: (a) to convey that one understands, (b) to promote exploration of the client's experience, and (c) to give news to clients about themselves. The first two intentions are compatible with empathy, whereas the third is not.

Function

The functions associated with these three intentions are: (a) Conveying understanding leads to reduction of isolation to improved affect regulation, to the experience of being confirmed, to greater trust in the self, and to a strengthening of the self. (b) Exploring leads to discovery and new awareness within a particular situation. This results in a new perceptual–experiential awareness of self and other, rather than a conceptual understanding (Greenberg et al., 1993). (c) Giving news involves explanation, results in insight, and generally leads to the client recognizing patterns of behaviors across situations. The result is that clients understand patterns or connections they did not see before.

Degree of Inference

Empathic responses are low on inference and focus on explicit and implicit meanings. They focus not only on what is in awareness but also on what is currently not attended to or is implicit. What is currently out of awareness is, however, regarded as being available to awareness by a shift in attentional focus. It is not repressed from consciousness by a barrier that can be broken only by interpretation. Empathic responding requires listening for what is being said or expressed and focuses on what is explicitly or implicitly meant. By contrast, interpretation is higher in inference. It brings what is not available to awareness into awareness. Interpretation listens more for what is not being said or is being defended against or avoided and focuses on what is hidden. It should be recognized that degree of inference is a continuum that ranges from very explicit on to low-level inference on to high-level inference on to totally unconscious client material.

Target or Focus

Three major targets of empathy have been delineated: (a) Feelings, with the focus on emotional experience; (b) self-concept, with people's views of themselves and their self-evaluations as the focus; and (c) dynamic elements and their connections, with the focus on underlying motivations and defenses, wishes, and fears.

Role Relationship

Three views of the therapist's expertise and directiveness can be delineated: (a) The client is treated as an expert on his or her own experience with the therapist following the lead of the client; (b) a coconstructive, collaborative form of interaction occurs between client and therapist. Neither leads or follows but both contribute to an evolving shared understanding; (c) the therapist is seen as the expert, sensitive to unconscious cues, who understands clients better than they understand themselves and explains them to themselves.

Clearly, empathic responding lends itself to certain of the above elements more than to others. It is best characterized as involving a more egalitarian or nonexpert role-relationship stance, lower level inference statements that focus on feeling, conveying of understanding to facilitate healthier affect regulation, trust in the self, and promotion of exploration. Ultimately, however, the false dichotomy between empathic responding and interpretation needs to be overcome, as does the view that empathic responding is solely client-centered and interpretation is solely psychodynamic. More differentiated analyses of therapist responding are needed. For example, what is the intention, the function, degree of inference, and the focus or target of the response, and what is the role relationship created by the response?

Differentiation and Specification of Empathy

A much more differentiated understanding of the many facilitative processes that therapists engage in in therapy is needed. Attempts to clearly label many therapist actions as either exclusively empathic or interpretive is fraught with difficulty. Although there are prototypic differences between empathic and interpretive interventions, in general the picture is more fuzzy.

The first author tested this view by asking 12 therapists to rate a set of responses as predominantly empathic or interpretive according to their own view of these constructs. This was done to test the hypothesis that a response would be categorized as either empathic or interpretive, as a function of the therapist's theoretical orientation (i.e., that the same responses that dynamic therapists would tend to label as *interpretations* would be viewed as empathic by experiential therapists). This would reveal how fuzzy the distinction is in defining the nature of many real therapeutic interactions. This hypothesis, however, was not borne out. Rather, no consistent pattern of response labelling within or across orientation was found. Particular responses were labelled by some as interpretation and by others as empathic, regardless of orientation. Many actual instances are, therefore, combinations of features that were difficult to label clearly as either empathic or interpretive. What is called empathic by one therapist may be called interpretation by another.

A Process-Experiential View of Empathy

On the basis of the above views, we have begun in our experiential approach to empathy (Greenberg et al., 1993) to make a number of distinctions about therapeutic actions that help specify what we actually do in our practice of empathy. First, we view each therapist statement as a momentary process facilitation or a processing proposal (cf. Sachse, 1992) that potentially has an effect on the client's next processing step. Each therapist statement has the potential to influence the form and content of the client's internal processing.

In conveying empathic understanding, we therefore view ourselves as engaging in both selection and reflection of client experience. Clients' communications are complex and everchanging, requiring the therapist to select what to listen for. A selective response focuses on specific parts of the message. One of the most important things to listen for is the client's current feelings and strong attitudes. The therapist listens particularly for what is live and most poignant and what is central in these messages. A second important element to listen for is what can be thought of as the client's growth possibilities (Greenberg et al., 1993). This type of growth-oriented response often has a future orientation (Bohart et al., 1993) and focuses on organismic needs and internal strengths or resources, whenever these emerge—even if only momentarily. What is possible, desired, or wanted by the client is constantly being picked up and confirmed by the therapist. Thus, it is the seeing by the therapist of the client's growth possibilities that is critical, and it is this that helps confirm the person's possibilities. Responses based on this type of empathic selection are process directive and are intended both to convey understanding and to promote exploration and growth. This can be contrasted with the purely nondirective attitude involved in classical client-centered reflection with its singular intention of conveying understanding of what is most alive or central. We believe that both types of responses are important but are useful at different times.

Below we will discuss different process-experiential principles of empathy, followed by a variety of different types of empathic responses, and empathic tasks that we have delineated.

Principles

In addition to specifying and attempting to measure different actions, we have delineated two higher-level principles governing empathic functioning (Greenberg et al., 1993). We distinguish between an empathic attunement principle, in which the therapist makes empathic contact with the client, and an empathic communication principle, in which the therapist communicates understanding and forms a warm supportive bond.

Empathic Attunement

The first principle of process-experiential therapy is empathic attunement. Empathic attunement begins with the therapist attempting to "step into the client's shoes" and continues as the therapist tries to follow closely in the client's "footsteps," "tracking" what is most important to the client as it evolves through the session. Making contact with and tracking the person's moment-by-moment experience is the fundamental activity. In empathic attunement, the therapist then directs his or her focal attention toward the client's current, immediate experiencing and attempts to "join" with the client in understanding what the client is currently experiencing. To do this, the therapist listens deeply to both what is said (content) and how it is said (manner), as this evolves from moment to moment. As we have said, empathy involves a complex process of apprehension and therapist experiencing but is not primarily feeling the client's feeling "as if" one were the client.

From the therapist's point of view, empathic attunement is an unmistakeable but difficult-to-describe experience. For this reason, a wide range of language has been used, with a number of basic metaphors seeming to capture different aspects of the experience: letting go, moving toward or into, resonating, sorting out or selecting, and grasping or taking hold. Each of these metaphors provides a variety of potentially useful ways of understanding and developing this crucial attitude.

Letting go involves setting aside preformed ideas, beliefs, expectations, or previous understandings of the other (cf. Vanaerschot, 1990). The therapist tries to let go of or "bracket" preconceptions of the client to make himself or herself more open to what the client is saying or revealing. To enter deeply into the client's world and pursue his or her evolving experiencing, the therapist must alternate between grasping and letting go of understanding (Vanaerschot). Moving into involves actively entering the other's world, becoming immersed in, dwelling in, or feeling into the client's experience. In empathizing with the client, the therapist experiences an active reaching out to enter into the client's world. Resonating with the other involves tuning into, being "on the same wavelength," feeling with (i.e., compassion), feeling similar to, or tasting the client's experiencing. Sorting out or selecting is another aspect of the therapist's experience, as he or she is often faced with a host of client's experiences to respond to empathically.

A final image or component experience is that of actively grasping or taking hold of what is important in the client's world (cf. Vanaerschot, 1990), as suggested by words such as apprehending, comprehending, getting (the point), assimilating, or perceiving. In other words, having entered into the client's world, the therapist then latches onto what is central, critical, alive, or poignant, sometimes with a sudden sense of insight into the other's experience.

Attunement also involves tracking the client's evolving moment-by-moment experiencing. As client experiencing develops and changes from moment to moment in the therapy session, the therapist listens carefully and responds to these small changes. Attunement to affect involves not only tracking the client's experiencing but also conveying an appreciation of the quality of the affect state, without imitating the exact behavioral expression of a person's inner state. This involves the manner in which one responds and is best explained in dynamic, kinetic terms. Thus, the therapist's tone or facial expression may catch the surging, fleeting, fading, or exploding quality of the client's affect. The response matches not only content but also intensity, time course, and shape or contour of the client's emotional experience, as when, for instance, the therapist speeds up a response and in a fast tempo and with an anxious look responds, "It's like they're gonna get me, they're gonna get me."

Not only is being empathically attuned to affect important but empathic understanding of empathic failure is also important. The therapist is at times bound to misunderstand or not grasp the client's experience. When the therapist is attuned to the possibility of misunderstanding and tries to grasp empathically how he or she has failed to grasp the client's world, the client realizes the therapist is with him or her. Thus, the creation of an empathic bond and its continual repair by empathic understanding of empathic failures is in our view an important curative agent.

Empathic Communication

The second principle of our approach is that the therapist's empathic attunement should be verbally communicated to clients. The varieties of forms in which this can be done will be discussed below. At the core of empathic communication is communicated accurate understanding. Understanding implies acceptance as well as confirmation of experience. Clients typically experience communicated therapist empathy as a supportive relationship message, indicating that the therapist is "on my side" (Elliott, 1985). In fact, in many instances clients are quite satisfied simply with the sense that their therapist is trying to understand, perceiving inaccurate but tentative reflections as empathic because of their intent.

Types of Therapist Empathic Responses

For purposes of specification and measurement, we have conceptualized empathy as consisting of qualitatively different types of empathic responses, of which empathic understanding is only one. Earlier conceptualizations of empathy measurement adhered to a unitary additive–subtractive model wherein empathic responses were rated according to their ability to access feelings at various depths of awareness (Truax, 1967). Instead we would rather define a number of different types of empathic responses and see them as guided by the two dimensions of (a) specific intentions directed selectively toward (b) different classes of targets, including different types of emotions and cognitions, rather than simply toward different levels of feeling (Campbell, 1988; Goldman, 1991; Greenberg et al., 1993).

We have delineated and attempted to measure five distinct forms of empathic responding: understanding, evocation, exploration, conjecture, and interpretation. These empathic forms of responding vary on whose frame of reference is being used in making the response and on the degree of new information that is added. The continuum of frame of reference (or degree or depth of inference) ranges from the client's frame of reference, through a shared frame of reference, to the therapist's frame of reference. The degree of new information increases from reflective empathic understanding, where no new information is added, to empathic interpretation, where the relatively highest degree of information is added.

In our view two major intentions serve to guide the choice of empathic form, either the intention to create an accepting, supportive environment, through conveying nonjudgmental understanding or the promotion of exploration and current growth possibilities by searching for newness. In both cases, manner of communication, especially vocal quality and facial features, are as important as content in achieving these aims. Finally, each of the empathic forms is directed toward a target of either different types of emotional process (primary or other emotions) or toward a target of different types of meaning (idiosyncratic meaning or core organizing belief). Using this system, it is therefore possible to code a response as, say, an empathic understanding of a primary emotion, or perhaps an empathic exploration of a nonprimary emotion, or an empathic conjecture about an idiosyncratic personal meaning. The forms of empathic responding and the targets shown in Table 1 are described briefly below.

Empathic Understanding

The therapist communicates understanding of explicit felt experience or of what is just implied but not yet stated. The therapist's communication is from within the client's frame of reference. The intention is to communicate an understanding of experience. The function is to strengthen and affirm the self and help build trust in the self.

Empathic Evocation

The therapist brings the client's experience to life through the use of metaphor, expressive language, evocative imagery, or speaking as the client. The therapist's communication is from within the client's frame of reference. The intention is to elicit, arouse, or evoke experience so that it is reexperienced in the moment. The function is to access new experiential information. There is no new information added by the therapist, but evocation enhances the possibility of accessing new information from the client's own experience. The therapist selectively attends to poignant information that seems suitable to evoke.

Empathic Exploration

The therapist encourages the client to search around the "edges" of his or her experience to symbolize it in a differentiated fashion. The therapist's communication is from within the client's frame of reference. The intention is to promote an experiential search for new internal information. The function is to promote discovery of some new aspect of experience, to see something in a new way. There is no addition of new information by the therapist, but the client is encouraged to search for new information. The

TABLE 1
Empathic Forms and Targets

Target form	Emotion				Cognition	
	Adaptive	Maladaptive	Secondary	Instrumental	Idiosyncratic meaning	Core belief
Empathic understanding	I hear how sad you feel	Just so shaky inside	Feeling really frustrated	Crying, saying "you've hurt me"	Unsure whether you can do it	Just feeling "I'm bad"
Empathic evocation	Just wanting to cry out, but no one will hear	Feeling wretched like a motherless child	—a	—	Like this means I'm fighting her ghost	Like whatever I touch will be cursed
Empathic exploration	Feeling so hurt you just want to . . . what?	So rotten inside like you might never feel good again	—	—	Does it mean something like I'll never be able to be me	You say "I'm bad" and then what's it like inside?
Empathic conjecture	My hunch is you're feeling sad	I guess it feels like, "I'll shatter"	—	—	Maybe it seems like "no one believes in me"	Maybe you believe you don't deserve to be happy
Empathic interpretation	Your sadness seems to belong to what you missed in the past	Your need to be loved also seems to drive your ambition	Your anger protects you from your sadness	The tears may be an attempt to get his comfort	This present threat seems so similar to the past defeat	Your belief that you're bad prevents your anger

a These empathic forms are not used for secondary and instrumental emotion targets.

therapist focuses on the expansion and differentiation of the client's current experience by either using reflections to focus the client's attention on the unclear edges of experiences or through open-ended questioning or even direct requests for more information about what is implicit or not yet explicitly stated. The therapist selectively attends to what is most poignant, unclear, idiosyncratic, or implicit in what the client is saying.

Empathic Conjecture

The therapist attempts to clarify the client's experience by tentatively offering information from his or her own perspective about what might be the client's current experience in the form of a hunch or a guess. The therapist encourages the development of a shared frame of reference by taking a nonauthoritarian and nondogmatic stance, thereby making it easy for the client to disagree if necessary. The therapist does not leave the client's frame of reference but rather is operating synergistically, neither leading nor following. The intention is to offer the client a possible symbol to capture an aspect of his or her current experience. The therapist creates the possibility of the addition of new information through focusing on an unstated aspect of the client's current experience. The conjecture functions to give form to an unstated but significant aspect of the experience, which, once clarified in this manner, serves to bring about acknowledgement of the experience.

Empathy-Based Interpretation

Here empathy is used to help the therapist build an internal model of the client to help understand unconscious dynamics. From this model the therapist then infers the nature of the client's experience and states aspects of the experience that are not available to the client's awareness. This response builds on empathy but goes beyond it by moving outside the client's frame of reference. The therapist's communication is now from within the therapist's frame of reference. The intention is to tell the client something new about himself or herself or to offer information to the client about his or her experience that is not already known by the client. The function is to promote links between aspects of experience. There is an explicit attempt to add new information about the client's experience. In addition, timing is important: The therapist interprets the client's experience in a sensitive and nonjudgemental fashion when the client seems ready to accept and assimilate this new information.

Targets of Empathic Responding

The second dimension of empathic responding is the empathic target, defined in categories drawn from our work on emotion and cognition (Greenberg & Safran, 1986; Greenberg et al., 1993).

Primary Emotional Processes

1. *Primary adaptive emotional processes.* The focus is on the basic feelings and needs and the associated adaptive responses to environment such as feelings of fear and sadness and the needs for protection or closeness and the associated action tendencies.

2. *Primary maladaptive emotional processes.* The focus is on core maladaptive feelings such as fear of abandonment, basic insecurity, or shame. These emotional experiences may have been adaptive in certain situations at one time but are now problematic.

Nonprimary Emotional Processes

(1) *Secondary emotional processes.* The focus is on feelings that are expressed in response to some more primary experience, such as when anger is expressed when fear is the primary feeling, when frustration or rage is experienced in response to disappointment, or when depressive feelings occur in response to self-criticism.

(2) *Instrumental emotional processes.* The focus is on emotional expressions used with the intention to influence others, such as crying to evoke sympathy.

Cognitive Processes

(1) *Idiosyncratic meanings.* The focus is on the client's subjective construal of the impact of a given situation or experience and on what an experience means to the client.

(2) *Core organizing belief.* The focus is on basic assumptions that organize meaning. These represents basic guiding values, standards, or beliefs about self and others.

On the basis of this reconceptualization, an empathy-measurement system was created that consists of operationalized definitions of the components of the empathic response forms and targets plus examples (Campbell, 1988; Goldman, 1991). In a test of this measure, two raters rated 26 samples of therapeutic empathy (Campbell). The overall agreement between the raters on forms was a Cohen's kappa of .4521. This indicates only fair agreement on empathic forms. Categories of empathic understanding $(k=.6119)$ and empathic conjecture $(k=.5667)$ showed stronger and moderate agreement respectively, but it was difficult to distinguish evocation from exploration. The overall agreement between raters on targets was $k=.3158$, indicating a less than fair agreement. The category of primary emotion $(k=.7417)$, however, showed strong agreement. Results indicate that the different components of empathic responding show promise and that collapsing into the three broader categories of understanding, exploration, and conjecture would be useful. The targets need further refinement.

Empathic Tasks

In addition to specifying higher-level principles and lower-level concrete actions, we have, at a level intermediate to these, delineated different types of empathic tasks. We have distinguished between the baseline task of empathic exploration and a specific task of interpersonal affirmation at a vulnerability marker (Greenberg et al., 1993). These are discussed briefly below.

Empathic Exploration of Experience

The key task in the process-experiential approach is the exploration and elaboration of client's experiences. In this task, the therapist attempts to facilitate client experiencing by helping the client focus on and explore the bodily felt sense of a particular domain of experience. While staying within a particular domain of client experiencing (e.g., memories of father), the therapist helps the client to re-experience, explore the edges of, and differentiate his or her experience. Here, the therapist listens for what is most important or poignant in what the client says. In addition, if the client is telling an external narrative, the therapist listens for "doors" into the client's internal experience, indicators of what the client is actually experiencing. Thus, the therapist looks for nonverbal signs of unspoken feelings or perhaps may stop the client to inquire, "I wonder, as you're telling me this, what you're feeling inside about it?" or, when the client continues to speak externally, the therapist may try to capture the sense of the client's stance in what is being narrated, perhaps one of watching with absorbed interest or even mild horror.

The therapist also attempts to help the client engage in various forms of exploration, including reexperiencing, attending to, and differentiating experience. In facilitating reexperiencing, the therapist attempts to evoke the past experience by having the client re-enter the original situations and relive it in the present, as when the therapist says, "Can you go back there, picking up the phone and dialing. What's it like? What happens for you as you begin to dial?" The therapist also encourages the client to explore the "edges" of experience by attending to what the client is groping toward. The therapist listens for what is sensed at the periphery of awareness but not yet said and for the direction in which the client is headed, but in which he or she may not yet know quite how to proceed. These edges may be variously sensed as unclear, troubling, or puzzling; fresh, incipient, or emerging; poignant, primary, or authentic; future- or possibility-oriented; or idiosyncratic or special (Rice, 1974). The therapist encourages the client to examine these experiences because they are likely sources of new experiencing, discovery, and growth.

An example of baseline empathic exploration task follows. At the level of action a variety of empathic forms are used, and these are indicated on the transcript.

The client in the following excerpt is a 30-year-old woman with some high-school education. She is the mother of two preschoolers, and her husband has a gambling problem. Her family believes she should stick by her husband whom she has unsuccessfully attempted to leave twice. The treatment of depression has focused, to this point, on her feelings of dependence on her husband and her parents and on her lack of self-worth. She has decided to become more independent of her husband by giving up on trying to save him from his gambling addiction. From her newly gained sense of independence, strong feelings of loneliness have emerged. This segment starts a few minutes into session nine and involves entry into her feelings of unsureness and difficulty "being herself."

T: So what's happening with you this week?

C: (Sigh) um—(crying) I'm sad today (T. mm hm), sad—I mean it's loneliness I find um this week I've been, eating a lot and I don't know if it's just—filling in an emptiness.

T: Uh huh, feeling empty [empathic understanding–reflection].

C: (Sniff) yeah as much as you know, my surrounding lately has been really good (T. uh huh) like having the support group (T. yeah), that's really good, I feel good about that but I still feel. . .

T: Still it's when you're (C: yeah [crying]) by yourself there's a real sense of just being alone [evocation].

C: Yeah like "why not, I'm important," and I can't because I have to be there for the kids (T. mm hm).

T: So it keeps you relating to something [understanding].

C: Yeah, um, I find it hard like I'm taking care of everybody, well you know, the kids and you know, and myself that's a that's a must, that comes with it—maybe I'm expecting something back.

T: So it feels like you're kind of giving and giving and (C: yeah) and sort of like, well "What about me?" or . . . [exploration]

C: Yeah that's right even though, you know, I feel content because um I do have friends now that I'll just sooner or later talk to (T. mm hm), but then that loneliness um creeps up when I'm alone.

T: There's just something about being alone right now that just really hard [exploration].

C: Yeah, I guess it's lonely no matter how much I understand you know I'm needed or I am wanted and I do count?

. . . .

C: Yeah it's like, well it's not hard, it's the loneliness is there, and I guess what I'm looking for is comfort (T: uh huh), um being told that I matter (T: yeah, that's what you'd like), reassurance I guess.

T: Yeah, somebody to say "Yeah, it's okay, Cindy." [evocative]

C: Yeah (crying), I'm just I guess to just hear from somebody else, and (T: uh huh) and um I mean just repeating to myself . . .

T: Uh huh, it's like hard to keep doing it on your own [exploration].

C: Yeah yeah, it is, that's right, it's like always there.

T: Sort of a constant feeling of wanting something [exploration].

C: Yeah yeah, that's always there (T: uh huh)—I guess I just need to reassure myself that you know it's going to be okay, (T: mm mm hm hm) you know that—you do have friends that care and um family and yeah I guess just reassurance (T: mm hm).

T: But just something there's there's something you want out there—some kind of reassurance [exploration].

C: Mm hm, yeah I guess I'm the type of person that needs to hear that or again because I've always been, always been giving and um not I guess I didn't get it back to me um that make makes me feel maybe like um you know I've been ripped off or . . . (T: mm hm)

T: So there's a feeling of being cheated, too (C: cheated, yeah). What's that like? "I've given and given and given and what have I got for this?" kind of thing [understanding/exploration].

C: Right yeah, "Why isn't it coming back to me?" or (T: mm hm) it's prolonging like it's been a very long time.

T: So you're getting a bit fed up with it like, "It's been a long time since I've been giving and putting out" [evocative].

C: Yeah, "When is it going to be my turn to?" not that I want to receive as in gifts stuff but just (T: yeah) to mean that I count that I'm there for a reason (T: yeah), to be told that (sniff).

T: Yeah like you've sort of become more aware now of what you need—right? [exploration]

C: Yeah, um and maybe this is why um I give because I guess the emptiness—it makes me feel good like when I do that but then inside um well it seems like a hole.

T: Yeah so you're saying you sort of would try to fill it before by giving and now that you're not doing it you're kind of left with this big open gap [understanding and evocation].

. . . .

C: That creeps up on me and you know I will think when you know um I've given and given "When is it my turn to receive?"

T: Yeah so it sounds like a little bit of almost anger or like (C: uh) it's like "What about me?" [empathic conjecture]

T: So you sort of (C: cut myself up) and tell yourself like—"No that wasn't nice (C: yeah), you're mean C." [understanding]

C: (Crying) so it's actually—I guess being myself you know why can't I just (crying) do that, why do I have to feel this, you know it's just common sense it's something that is minor.

T: So it's like just being yourself and saying what you want to say is difficult? [understanding & exploration]

C: Yeah (crying)(sniff)(T: try to take a breath) (crying) (T: yeah just breathe) I guess you just you just hit the spot like when you said (crying) um be myself (T: uh huh) (sigh).

T: There's something about being yourself that's difficult [understanding].

C: Yeah, it's like um I feel restrained (T: uh huh) um . . .

T: Is there some feeling of uh you're clamping down? [conjecture]

C: No (crying), you know it's bad to say what I think that or (T: uh huh) (sniff), but then it worries me because then I say to myself, you know, "Don't you have any respect for yourself?"

T: Uh huh, that's the other side of it, but there's something about it like it's bad to be yourself or . . . [exploration]

C: Yeah yeah, that's it, it's bad to speak your mind (T: uh huh) um again because (sniff) it's um getting it from my parents saying you know, don't and then getting it from V. (T: mm hm) I just have a hard time (sigh)—you know even though it's in my mind I want to express it but it's, I hold back (T: mm hm).

Empathic Affirmation of Intense Vulnerability

Some of the most powerful moments in therapy occur when therapists are able to convey genuine acceptance of client's expressions of strong, vulnerable, self-relevant emotions. Here, the task involves affirmation as opposed to the exploration of the previous task. Such emotions as deep hurt, intense shame, bitterness, despair about the future, or a sense of total isolation from others or an extreme sense of fragility are all felt as intensely personally defining. People feel extremely vulnerable about having these feelings. Clients often fear that if they reveal themselves and fully express these painful emotions, or other seemingly unacceptable aspects of themselves, that the therapist will not understand, will judge them, feel alienated from them, or even reject them. They fear that they will be viewed by the therapist as unacceptable, abnormal, defective, or even frightening. There is, thus, often an attempt to close down, or hold off, dreaded feelings or aspects of self and to avoid dealing with them. For some clients there is also the fear that, if they fully acknowledge these dreaded negative feelings, these emotions will be bottomless and engulfing, and they will lose control and will, themselves, be overwhelmed by them. They, therefore, feel extremely fragile.

A client's statement of intense vulnerability presents an important opportunity for an empathic and highly validating intervention by the therapist. This provides an affirming interpersonal experience with the therapist. If a client can fully express a feared, dreaded, unacceptable aspect of experience, such as intense despair or shame, and have it fully received by a therapist who is sensing the feeling in full intensity and is clearly valuing the client with no reservations, this can be a powerful experience that promotes change. The product of this event is the crucial interpersonal learning that one's experience is acceptable to another, and this validation leads to a stronger sense of self.

In this whole process, vulnerable clients are confirmed by making contact and being accepted as they are. They are helped to become unique selves by the therapist's confirming them in their uniqueness. It is the existence of the self as a separate centre of experience and agency that is confirmed by the therapist's empathic affirmation of the client's unique inner experience, however fragile. Accepting clients as they are in their vulnerability or despair does not imply accepting them as forever stuck; nor does it imply that the therapist has given up hope for their change. Instead, the continuing empathic affirmation of the whole person while they are experiencing and revealing these painful, fragile aspects of themselves helps them to differentiate this aspect of self from the total self. They cease to feel as overwhelmed by the vulnerability and can see the feared aspect as a part, rather than as all, of themselves. The person feels stronger and more able to cope. This strengthened sense of self makes possible further changes and growth. (For more on the task, see Greenberg et al., 1993).

CONCLUSION

The self speaks in a language of feeling, and empathy is the channel for understanding affect. The self is always in a constructive process of becoming, involving a dialectical process of symbolizing and constructing experience from internal complexity (Greenberg & Pascual-Leone, 1995, in press). People simultaneously discover and create themselves anew each moment (Greenberg et al., 1993). Self-organization is created in the moment from person and situation interactions, by integrating information from both inside and outside. Meaning arises in the moment out of the constituting activity of inwardly attending to and symbolizing one's internal complexity (Greenberg et al., 1993; Greenberg & Pascual-Leone, 1995). Empathic attunement to affect is one of the core ways of being therapeutic because empathic attunement and its communication are key aids in the construction of self experience. They help the client to symbolize inchoate emotional meaning, and this aids affect regulation and strengthening of the self as well as exploration and discovery.

In our view, to better understand empathy and its communication in therapy, empathy needs to be differentiated into a variety of different components, including both acts with different intentions and targets and different, more molar tasks with different processes and effects, as well as different higher-level principles that describe its functioning. Empathy, as therapist experience of attunement, needs to be differentiated from the communications that flow from the attunement. Communication can take many forms, of which empathic understanding is only one. Empathic exploration to promote discovery and conjecture to offer new symbols are other important forms of responding from an empathically attuned base. Future efforts at investigating empathy in psychotherapy need to be guided by differentiated questions such as what type of empathic communication, with what intent, at what target, in what specific context, with what interpersonal style and manner, has what type of effect? In addition, new attempts are needed to measure therapists' attunement to clients' changing states and their ability to track their clients' moment-by-moment experience and to design their interventions to fit the client's current experience. It is this skill that is probably at the core of effective therapeutic intervention.

REFERENCES

Barrett-Lennard, G. (1981). The empathy cycle: Refinement of a nuclear concept. *Journal of Counseling Psychology, 28,* 91–100.

Bohart, A. (1991). Empathy in client centered therapy. *Journal of Humanistic Psychology, 31,* 34–48.

Bohart, A., Magallanes, M., Guzman, R., Smiljanich, K., Aguallo, S., & Humphrey, A. (1993). Empathy in client centered therapy: A contrast with psychoanalysis and self psychology. *Journal of Humanistic Psychology, 33,* 12–29.

Campbell, K. (1988). *Empathy: Reconceptualization and development of a measure.* Unpublished honours thesis, York University, Toronto, Ontario, Canada.

Elliott, R. (1985). Helpful and nonhelpful events in brief counselling interviews: An empirical taxonomy. *Journal of Counseling Psychology, 32,* 307–322.

Goldman, R. (1991). *The validation of the experiential therapy adherence measure.* Unpublished master's thesis, York University, Toronto, Ontario, Canada.

Greenberg, L., & Paivio, S. (in press). Working with the emotions: Changing core schemes. New York: Guilford Press.

Greenberg, L., & Pascual-Leone, J. (1995). A dialectical constructivist approach to experiential change. In R. Neimeyer & M. Mahoney, *Constructivism in psychotherapy* (pp. 169–191). Washington, DC: American Psychological Association.

Greenberg, L., & Pascual-Leone, J. (in press). Emotion in the creation of personal meaning. In M. Power & C. Brewin (Eds.), *The transformation of meaning in psychological therapies.* London: Wiley.

Greenberg, L., Rice, L., & Elliott, R. (1993). *Facilitating emotional change: The moment by moment process.* New York: Guilford.

Greenberg, L., & Safran, J. (1986). *Emotion in psychotherapy.* New York: Guilford Press.

Hill, C. (1986). An overview of the Hill Counselor and Client Verbal Response Modes Coding Systems. In L. Greenberg & W. Pinsoff (Eds.), *The psychotherapeutic process: A research handbook* (pp. 131–154). New York: Guilford.

Pennebaker, J. (1990). *Opening up: The healing power of confiding in others.* New York: Morrow.

Pennebaker, J., & Susman, J. R. (1988). Disclosure of traumas and psychosomatic processes. *Social Science and Medicine, 26,* 327–332.

Piper, W. E., Azim, H. F. A., Joyce, A. S., & McCallum, M. (1991). Transference interpretations, therapeutic alliance and outcome in short-term individual therapy. *Archives of General Psychiatry, 48,* 946–953.

Rice, L. (1974). The evocative function of the therapist. In D. Wexler & L. Rice (Eds.), *Innovations in client centered therapy* (pp. 289–312). New York: Wiley-Interscience.

Sachse, R. (1992). Differential effects of processing proposals and content references on the explication process of clients with different starting conditions. *Psychotherapy Research, 2,* 235–251.

Truax, C. B. (1967). A scale for the measurement of accurate empathy. In C. Rogers, E. Gendlin, D. Kiesler, & C. Truax (Eds.), *The therapeutic relationship and its impacts: A study of psychotherapy with schizophrenics* (pp. 398–402). Madison: University of Wisconsin Press.

Vanaerschot, G. (1990). The process of empathy: Holding and letting go. In G. Lietaer, J. Rombauts, & R. Van Balen (Eds.), *Client-centered and experiential psychotherapy in the nineties* (pp. 269–294). Leuven, Belgium: Leuven University Press.

9

EMPATHY AS THERAPIST–CLIENT ALIGNMENT

ALVIN R. MAHRER

Here is the main point and invitation: (a) If you and the client are both fully attending to a compelling, important, feeling-arousing center of attention, rather than attending to one another; (b) if you are situated so that the client's words come from inside you, truly as if from some part of you, rather than from a separate person who is over there; and (c) if you are "aligned" in these two ways throughout most of the session, then (d) you can have virtually direct access to the most private, personal, sensitive world in which the person is living and being, both on the surface and more deeply and (e) you can probably be in direct touch with the feelings and experiencings occurring in the person, both at the surface level and much more deeply. Here is a way of being empathic by going "beyond empathy" and into therapist–client "alignment" (Mahrer, 1996; Mahrer, Boulet, & Fairweather, 1994).

What are the Aims and Goals of More or Less Traditional Empathy and of Empathy as Therapist–Client Alignment?

Empathy is generally acknowledged as brought into psychology and psychiatry by Theodore Lipps in 1897 and as probably first used in the diagnosis of mental disease by Southard in 1918 (Schilder, 1953; Schroeder, 1925). Since then, it has been acknowledged as playing a central role in many therapies (Brenner, 1982; Cox, 1988; Fox & Goldin, 1984; Freud,

1921/1955; Greenson, 1960; Kohut, 1959; Kramer, 1989; Rogers & Truax, 1967).

Empathy is generally understood as having two aims and goals. First, it is to enable the therapist to get inside the client's frame of reference, to see the client's world through the client's eyes, and to see the client's world the way the client does (Carkhuff, 1972; Egan, 1986; Havens, 1974; Mearns & Thorne, 1988; Rogers, 1951). Second, it is to enable the therapist to know, have, grasp, understand, sense, and share what the client is feeling, thinking, and experiencing both at a more surface level and at a deeper level (Berger, 1987; Jaffe, 1986: Kohut, 1978, 1984; Langs, 1982; Margulies, 1984; Schafer, 1959). In general, empathy or being empathic includes both of these components (Berger, 1984; Brammer & Shostrom, 1982; Brenner, 1982; Dymond, 1949; Fliess, 1942; Gladstein, 1977, 1983; Korchin, 1976).

The aims and goals of therapist–client alignment are essentially the same, and it is fair to say that being aligned is another way of being empathic.

What is a Definition of Empathy as Therapist–Client Alignment?

The therapist is aligned when (a) both therapist and person are mainly attending out there, onto something that is important, that is the center of their attention; and (b) the person's words seem to be coming from inside the therapist, from some part of the therapist, from in and through the therapist.

When the therapist and the person are doing these two things rather well, then there usually are two consequences, and these two consequences help define empathy as therapist–client alignment. The therapist lives, exists, in the immediately ongoing world of the person. The therapist can live in this world as much as, or even more than, the person. The therapist actually has, undergoes, the feelings and experiencings that are occurring in the patient, both at the more or less surface level and at a much deeper level.

This is the state the therapist is in throughout most of the session. It is not some state that the therapist dips in to and out of.

When therapists began writing about this state, they described it as merging or fusing with the patient. Although alignment shares much of the spirit of these two terms, what the therapist actually does and the defining consequences may be a little different than the pictures that might go with more poetic terms such as *merging* and *fusing* into the patient, although the spirit is similar.

WHAT DO YOU DO TO ACHIEVE EMPATHY AS THERAPIST–CLIENT ALIGNMENT?

There are explicit things you can do to get into and remain in this aligned state throughout the session.

How Can the Seating Arrangements Help Therapist and Client to Attend Mainly Out There and Help the Therapist to Live and Be in the Client's Personal World?

I like to use big, comfortable chairs, with high headrests and ample arm rests, where we can lean back and put our feet on large foot stools. Both chairs are quite close to each other, perhaps 1 or 2 feet apart, and facing in the same direction. I want the chairs close because I would like to be almost united with the person. I want the chairs facing the same direction because we will both be attending out there, at whatever it is, at the young fellow in the elevator, or her mother's frowning face, or the cancer in her lung.

To help me see what is out there, and to feel and experience what the person is feeling or experiencing, and to minimize all the interferences and problems of two people looking directly at each other, I close my eyes throughout the whole session. I also invite the person to do the same, for precisely the same reasons.

These seating arrangements are fine for most patients. However, many therapists have a hard time. To make it easier for these therapists, it usually helps if you sit at the usual angle with the person. Explain that it helps you to listen carefully if most of the time you are looking off, or away, or down, or out there, rather than directly face to face and that you may even close your eyes at times, to concentrate more on what the person is saying. Invite the person to do the same thing if he or she wishes. After all, this is what two people often do when they are both looking at the baby or the tennis racket or the faucet, when one is concentrating on what her mother actually said, or when both are recollecting the high-school teacher. Looking away, and even closing your eyes, are rather natural under these conditions, even though this does not happen much in most therapies.

Give Opening Instructions to Enable the Client to Attend Out There and to See Strong-Feelinged Scenes

In the beginning of each session, your opening instructions aim at enabling the person to look out there; to put most of his or her attention out there; and to see things, objects, times, or scenes of relatively strong feeling. You are candid in showing the person what he or she is to do and why.

You say something along these lines:

Put all your attention out there. Be ready to see something, maybe one or two things. . . . Just see the things that come to your mind, whether or not they have anything to do with what I say. You may see anything, or all sorts of things. It may be from recently or maybe from some time ago. . . . Ready? Are you all set? . . . Think of the thing that bothers you, that really troubles you, that makes you feel rotten, awful, worried, terrible, the thing that drives you crazy, worries you more than anything. . . . Think of the times when you have strong feelings. You know that the strong feeling is in you, even if it came and went in a flash. A time when the feeling in you is very bad, awful, rotten, or maybe just wonderful, feels great. . . . Think of the kind of strong feeling that you have, one you like, feels wonderful. Or one that feels terrible, bad, awful. Now think of some time when you have this feeling. . . . All right, what did you see, whatever it was?

You may get a little more specific by naming particular topics that help the person see a scene of strong feeling. You say,

Think of when you had one of the worst feelings you ever had. . . . Think of one of the worst things about you, that thing about you, since you were little, the thing about you that you just can't get away from, and it makes you feel bad, and it's always been the kind of person you are. . . . When is it that you felt so scared or troubled or just awful? . . . What is on your mind now, and when you think of it you feel rotten, depressed, torn apart? . . . What is the thing that bothers you so much, worries you? . . . When is it that you feel good, great, just wonderful . . . or awful, terrible, the worst? . . . There, so what comes to mind? No matter what it was, what did you see?

When you give the opening instructions well, and when the person is ready and willing, she will be looking mainly out there, she will be seeing scenes of at least moderate feeling, and she will be having at least moderate feelings.

Both Therapist and Person are Fully and Continuously Attending Out There Rather Than Mainly to Each Other

From the moment you start the session, as you give the opening instructions, and throughout the entire session, your attention is mainly directed out there. The patient's attention should likewise be mainly out there. Showing him or her how to do this is one of the purposes of the opening instructions. Accordingly, throughout the whole session, both of you are attending predominantly out there, onto whatever it is, and not mainly at each other, as is the usual posture (Havens, 1986; Mahrer, 1978, 1982, 1986, 1989a, 1989c, 1996; Major & Miller, 1984; May, 1989; Rothenberg, 1987).

Both of you are looking at some scene, some incident, or some particular thing such as the flower or the toy truck or the bird, or something inside such as the cancer or the headache. Even when you address the person, your attention is always and continuously directed out there. In this stance, you rarely attend mainly to the patient. This model has essentially no place for the two of you to be face to face, mainly attending to each other.

What the Patient Says and Does Come From Inside the Therapist

With your attention mainly out there, and with your eyes closed, posture yourself so that the patient's words are coming from inside you. It is as if the person is a part of you, and what is being said, including how it is being said, is coming from within you. It is as if your outer boundary has stretched to include the patient, or as if the patient is an enlivened, speaking part of you, or as if the two of you are within an encompassing, larger personality. With the two of you sitting so close, with both of you attending out there, with your eyes closed, it is easy to receive what the patient says and does as if it is originating from within you and occurring in and through you. Quite literally, you are both saying these words, and in this way. Beyond your "talking along with the patient" (Rothenberg, 1987, p. 451), the patient's words are almost literally your words, literally coming from you (Mahrer, 1986, 1989a, 1989c).

Put your attention out there, and let the person's words be as if they are coming from inside you, coming in and through you, said by you: "I love my mother. I would do anything for her . . . I never show my feelings, and I think that's the way the whole family is." Practice until the patient's words are your words.

What Are the Necessary and Just-About-Sufficient Conditions for You to Be Aligned With the Person?

Three of these conditions have already been mentioned. You have to give opening instructions so that the person and you direct most of your attention out there, on some scene that is accompanied with relatively strong feeling. Second, both you and the person are to be attending mainly out there. Third, you are positioned so that what the person says and does comes from inside you.

Fourth, you must be sufficiently competent and skilled to give the instructions, to attend out there, and to let the person be inside you. Just knowing what to do is not enough; you have to be competent and skilled. Fifth, both you and the person must be quite ready and willing to attend mainly out there. If either of you is not fully ready and willing, you cannot be aligned. Usually, it is much harder for therapists than for clients to put most of their attention out there and to stay in this posture throughout the session. The willingness to throw oneself fully into attending out there usually represents the turning point between a therapist who can't quite be aligned and one who is good at being aligned. Finally, it is necessary that the aligned posture makes sense and seems to fit with your picture of psychotherapy. When these conditions all seem to be nicely present, then it is almost certain that you are being aligned.

Can You Be Aligned With Just About Any Person, or Are There Particular Clients and Client Qualities That Make Alignment Difficult?

If you are competent and skilled, and if the client is quite ready and willing, you can be aligned with just about any client. None of the categorizations by which most therapists describe patients seem to make any difference. It makes little or no difference if therapists describe the person as psychotic, having this or that mental disorder, being autistic, emotionally labile, character disordered, resistant, unmotivated, controlling, borderline, acting out, paranoid, or a paragon of abhorrent qualities. When you are skilled at letting yourself be aligned, you can be aligned with just about any person; there are essentially no limits.

Nor does the likelihood of being aligned have much to do with the relative goodness of fit between your characteristics and the patient's. You may be Black, young, female, slender, short, upper class, and beautiful. You still can be aligned with a patient who is White, old, fat, tall, lower class, and ugly. Although there may be some extreme examples, you can be aligned even if you have not been through the history, background, or experiences the person has been through. Most of the usual restrictions make little or no difference when the person is ready and willing and you are skilled and competent at being aligned.

There are mainly two ways that clients can make alignment almost impossible, at least in this session. One is that the person is neither ready nor willing to follow the instructions and to put most of his or her attention out there, on whatever is accompanied with relatively strong feelings. The other is when the person is insistent on attending mainly to you and not to whatever is out there. When patients are either of these two ways, alignment is almost certainly difficult, at least in that particular session.

Can Just About Any Therapist Be Aligned, or Does Alignment Seem to Call for Certain Therapist Qualities and Characteristics?

I have been wrong so often that I don't even try to predict which therapists will be able to learn the skills of attending out there and letting the patient's words come from inside the therapist. To learn the skills of being aligned, the therapist needs to be able to learn the skills of being aligned.

What does seem to be important is that the very notion of being aligned with patients makes psychotherapeutic sense. If it does make sense, you can learn the skills. If, alternatively, what seems much more sensible is for you and the patient to be face to face, attending almost exclusively to each other, then it could be very hard to be aligned. The very idea would grate, especially because you would be sacrificing all the supposed advantages, role relationships, and personal experiencings that go with attending mainly to each other in a face-to-face posture (Mahrer, 1978, 1989a, 1995).

Being able to be aligned seems to have little or nothing to do with the kind of person that you are. You would think that being able to be aligned would depend on the degree you can have many different feelings or you have been through the kinds of experiences the patient has been through. Although there may be some extreme exceptions, I find that when you are truly skilled, you can be aligned, even though, in contrast to this client, you have not been pregnant, tried to kill yourself, been beaten up by a violent stranger, been truly alone, felt absolutely crazy, been with a friend who died in your arms, or grew up as the only boy with four older sisters. When you are truly skilled, the range of who and what you can be is about as great as when you become something or someone in a dream.

Except for being skilled and having alignment make sense, I know of few if any personal qualities or characteristics that mean a therapist probably can or cannot be aligned with this patient.

The Consequence is That You Live in the Patient's Immediate World

The consequence of being aligned is that you will see all sorts of things. You will live and be in scenes and situations that are from the person's immediate and conscious world or from farther in and deeper (Havens, 1978, 1986; Mahrer, 1978, 1989a, 1996; May, 1989). What you see may be fleeting or more lasting, real or unreal, vivid and detailed or softly diffused and cloudy, immediate or remote, mundane or dramatic or big whole situations or tiny objects.

You are a little girl, walking with grandmother in the park, with your right hand raised, rhythmically squeezing her hand as the two of you walk along. You are seeing your neighbors huddled together and eying you with evil intentions. You are lying in bed lightly kissing the neck of your lover. You are seeing the cancer in all its fatal glory. You are witnessing the "depression" attacking you whenever it chooses. You are seeing your self, walking along the street, bloated with fluids of all kinds.

The payoff is seeing, living, and being in this scene, in the patient's immediate world.

The Consequence is That You Have the Feeling and the Experiencing Occurring Inside the Person

When you are living and being in the person's world, and when the person's words come from inside you, the consequence is that something happens inside you. You have a feeling or experiencing (Buie, 1981; Furer,

1967; Havens, 1972, 1973, 1978, 1986; May, 1989; Mearns & Thorne, 1988; Vanaerschot, 1990). You may be having this feeling or experiencing just a little bit or fairly fully and intensely. But you can undergo, sense, share, resonate with, and have whatever feeling or experiencing goes with your saying these words in this way and in living and being in this scene. You will feel aroused, critical, silly, or cruel, like you had better get out of here, or like bathing in the glory of his or her looking at you that way.

There is a special added bonus when you and the person have discovered the precise moment of strong feeling, when both of you are living and being in this moment of strong feeling and when you are quite fully aligned with the person. The bonus is that you can go beyond the more or less surface feeling or experiencing. You can sense, receive, and have experiencings that are deeper within the person. Finding and being in these precious moments of quite strong feeling seem to be a royal road into what lies deeper inside the person (Mahrer, 1982, 1986, 1989a, 1989b, 1989c, 1996: cf. Major & Miller, 1984; May, 1989; Mearns & Thorne, 1988; Vanaerschot, 1990).

How can you be reasonably confident that this is indeed the surface experiencing or perhaps even the inner, deeper experiencing? What makes you believe that the inner, deeper experiencing is of winning, beating, being the best? The experiencing may be held in reasonable confidence provided that you are well and truly aligned. Once you have fully allowed the person's words to come from inside you, and once you are fully living and being in the evoked scene, then you may confidently trust the experiencings you get.

The Consequence is That You Virtually Let Go of Your "Self," Your Stream of Private Thoughts, and the Face-to-Face Relationship With the Patient

When you are thoroughly aligned, you have essentially stepped outside your own continuing sense of self, your identity, the continuing person who you are. You are mostly disengaged from your own troubles and worries, your own sense of who and what you are, your own way of thinking about things, and your own personal world. Instead of being a therapist with this patient, you have disengaged from that you, and you no longer have that continuing ordinary sense of self.

Being aligned means that you have essentially let go of the usual stream of private thoughts. There is virtually no removed stream of inferences, no executive monitoring of what is going on, and no private observations. There are essentially no private thoughts about how to phrase what you intend to say, whether to deal with this particular matter now or a bit later, what topic to pursue next, and how what the patient is saying is similar to what he said in previous sessions. You are no longer in a position to have this stream of private thoughts.

When you are aligned, almost all your attention is out there, and almost all of the patient's attention is out there. This means that there is little if any of the two of you attending mainly to each other. The vaunted therapist–patient "relationship" is all but washed away. You have stepped away from helping alliances, transferences, and relationships in which each party is attending mainly to the other. Even when you address the patient, it is generally with most of your attention out there, on something other than mainly that person. When you are aligned, the two of you have departed from the mutual attending to and relating to each other.

These are the ways to achieve empathy as therapist–client alignment. We now turn to how to use this state of alignment, how to use the scenes of your living in the person's world, and how to use the feelings and experiencings that you have.

HOW DO YOU USE EMPATHY AS THERAPIST–CLIENT ALIGNMENT?

Once you are in a state of alignment, how do you use that state? Suppose that you are living and being in the person's world, how do you use that? Suppose that you have the person's feeling and experiencing, how do you use that?

You Can Stay in This Aligned State Throughout the Entire Session

You can use the state of therapist–client alignment by remaining in this state. Throughout virtually the whole session, most of your attention is out there, and you are positioned so that the person is inside you, talking from in and through you. This is your normal, ordinary, continuing position from the very beginning to the end of the session. You do not dip into and out of this posture, this state.

You Can Be the Voice of the Person's Experiencing

One of the most useful consequences of being aligned is that you sense, you undergo, and you are the very experiencing that is occurring in the person. You speak as this experiencing, you are the embodiment of this experiencing, and you are the live expression of this experiencing. You think, feel, and behave as this experiencing. This experiencing is the kind of person that you are.

Typically, you are on much better terms with the experiencing than the person is. You can be more welcoming, more appreciating, and more loving of it. You relate to it much more wholesomely. It feels good being this experiencing. Whether it is an experiencing that is more on the surface or deeper, you probably can like the experiencing more than the person does. You can be better friends with it. You can also be the inner experiencing more openly, fully, easily, and spontaneously. Quite often, the person draws back from it as something awful, twisted, and dangerous and sees it as appropriately awful, twisted, and dangerous. In contrast, the experiencing that you are is softer, nicer, more fun, gentler, friendlier, more gracious, good-feelinged, and different.

You are the voice and the being of the person's caring, nurturing, and loving; you are the person's sensuality, sexuality, and eroticism; you speak as the person's being superior, accomplished, and better than. If the experiencing shifts about, especially in the first step of each session, you shift the experiencing to which you give voice. Whatever the nature of the experiencing, you are its voice. Essentially, empathy as therapist–client alignment defines and tells you who you are throughout the session.

You Can Enable the Person to Live and Be in Feelinged Scenes, Rather Than Attending Mainly to You

Throughout the whole session, your attention is mainly out there, and you are living and being in scenes of relatively strong feeling. This means that the person can also be attending mainly out there and, likewise, can live and be in scenes of relatively strong feeling. If you can do this, so can the person. When you are ready and able to do this, the chances are good that the person can also do this. When the person is attending out there, living and being in feelinged scenes, the person is thereby not attending mainly to you. In this aligned state, the person is able to go through the steps of experiential change, and the person can avoid the traps of attending mainly to you.

You Can Get the Information You Need for Experiential Change

For the person to go through experiential change, you mainly need to discover the deeper experiencing that is inside, and you need to know the scene or situation that is out there, the one in which the person is living. This is the main information you need to proceed with your work. The aligned posture is explicitly designed to enable you to get this kind of information. If you are mainly face to face with the patient, attending mainly to each other, it will probably be much harder to get this information.

The common face-to-face way of being with clients can provide all sorts of other information and is probably better if you want to get such information as how the client does on hundreds of tests, what kind of mental disorder the client has, what the client's demographic information is, what the client's medical histories is, how far the client went in school, what previous treatments entailed, what jobs the client has had, how often the client has sex and with whom, which parts of the country the client lives in, and lots of other information. However, if you want to get the kinds of information you need for experiential change, the face-to-face way of being with a client is probably much less useful than the aligned posture.

You Can Use the Therapist–Client Alignment to Help in Finding the Deeper Potential for Experiencing

Finding the deeper potential means that both of you must first find a scene of strong feeling. Then you both are to enter into this scene, to live and be in this scene, and to try to find the precise moment of strong feeling in this scene. Once you are living and being in this precise moment of strong feeling, you can be in a position to access, to receive, the deeper potential. There are various methods of accessing and receiving the deeper potential, once you are in the moment of strong feeling, but all of these methods depend on your being aligned with the person. Indeed, just about everything that you do to find the deeper potential for experiencing requires that you be in this state of alignment.

Once You Find the Deeper Potential, You Can Use the Therapist–Client Alignment

Once you discover the deeper potential, your being aligned with the person enables you to accomplish some valuable kinds of therapeutic changes.

In Enabling the Person to Welcome and Appreciate the Deeper Potential

Once the deeper potential is accessed and discovered, it is possible for the person to achieve a radical change in the way the person relates to this particular deeper potential. Instead of fearing it; hating it; running from it; and keeping it hidden, distant and barricaded, there can be a magnificent change so that the person welcomes and appreciates the deeper potential, enjoys it, feels good about it, and relates more integratively toward it.

There are lots of specific methods both the therapist and the person can use to help enable this kind of change. The aligned state is just about essential in using the methods for enabling the person to welcome and appreciate the deeper potential.

In Enabling the Person to Be the Deeper Potential in the Context of Earlier Life Scenes

Once the person welcomes and appreciates the deeper potential, the person is in a position to undergo a radical change of disengaging from the ordinary, continuing person and entering into or "being" the deeper potential. This is accomplished when the person can be the deeper potential within the context of earlier life scenes. These scenes may be relatively recent or from some time ago. The methods for accomplishing this qualitative change virtually require that the therapist be aligned with the person, that the therapist live and be in these earlier scenes right along with the person, and that the therapist likewise make the momentous shift into being the deeper potential. The therapist is to take on the identity of the deeper potential, is to be the voice of the deeper potential, and is to join with the person in being the deeper potential in these earlier life scenes.

In Enabling the Person to Be the New Person in the Present

The final step in each session gives the person a chance to be a whole new person right now, in the present, after the session, in the extratherapy world. The person ends the session and, I hope, goes into the extratherapy world as this new person and as someone who is now relatively free of the bad-feelinged scenes from the beginning of the session.

Accomplishing this fourth step calls for particular methods that depend on the therapist and person being aligned. Being aligned, by itself, does not accomplish this fourth step. But just about all of the methods rely on the therapist being aligned.

How do you use empathy as therapist–client alignment? Being aligned with the person, both attending out there, with the words of the person coming from inside you—these are essential ingredients for you to enable the person to access the deeper potential, to have a good relationship with the deeper potential, to actually be the deeper potential in the context of past scenes, and to become the new person in the present.

HOW DOES EMPATHY AS THERAPIST–CLIENT ALIGNMENT RELATE TO SOME OTHER MEANINGS AND METHODS OF EMPATHY IN OTHER APPROACHES?

Answering this question enables us to take a closer look at this meaning of empathy. At the same time, we can get a more careful picture of how this meaning of empathy may differ from some other meanings in some quite explicit ways.

Therapist and Client Both Attend Mainly to the Focal Center of Attention Versus They Attend Mainly to Each Other

In the aligned model, both therapist and client spend almost the whole session attending out there, both concentrating on the scene, the thing, the focal center of attention. The actual content of this third thing, this focal center of attention, generally shifts quite a bit throughout the session, but they both are attending mainly out there, onto the focal center of attention.

In most other approaches, therapist and client spend just about the whole session with most of their attention on each other. Even when most therapists are being empathic, their attention is mainly on the client. Of course there are some exceptions. Therapists may not be attending mainly to the client when the client is free associating or looking over a symptom checklist, but almost always most therapists studiously attend to the client even when therapists are being empathic. This is why it is understandable that so much is made of the relationship and the interaction. From moment to moment throughout most sessions, most therapists and most clients are attending mainly to each other. The two models differ immensely on this point.

The Methods of the Aligned Model are Generally Outside the Methods of the Face-to-Face Models

In the aligned model, the therapist attends mainly out there, seeing what is out there, living and being in those scenes, and doing so along with the client. In the aligned model, the therapist allows the words of the client to come from inside the therapist. These two methods, and the specific techniques and procedures for doing these two things, are generally outside the methods of face-to-face approaches. A list of the empathic methods, in the face-to-face models, would seldom include our two methods. In teaching students the methods of empathy, our two methods are not standard fare. They are almost certainly outside the boundaries of most face-to-face therapists.

Which Model Is More Useful for Enabling the Therapist to Let Go of One's Self, Therapist Identity, Private Thoughts, Inferences, and Preconceptions About the Client?

Some therapists talk about a state of being so naive, so open to what comes from the person, and so sensitively receptive to the person that this state earned its own name of *recipathy* (Murray, 1938). Other therapists talk about the empathic state as one in which the therapist is relatively free of the sense of self, of personal identity, and of having few if any private thoughts or inferences and virtually no preconceived ideas about the client. Some refer to this as a state of Husserlian "phenomenological reduction" in which you are free of what is you and you are almost wholly open to the phenomenon itself. In this general state, you are essentially free of your own self-awareness, your identity, and your preconceived notions of the person's history, personality, your feelings about this person, and the treatment program for this session. In general, many therapists see this as an essential ingredient in being empathic (Buie, 1981; Chessick, 1992; Freud, 1912/1953; Greenson, 1967; Margulies, 1984; Margulies & Havens, 1981).

The aligned model places high premium on this state. Its methods enable you to achieve this state. You achieve this state when you attend fully to what the person's words put out there for you to focus on and to live and be in. You achieve this state when the person's words are your words, when how and what the person says are how and what is coming from inside you.

The Aligned Therapist Has and Is the Experiencing Occurring in the Person Versus the Therapist Retains One's Own Identity or Self

The aligned therapist is almost fully undergoing the experiencing that is occurring in the person. Rather than having this experiencing just a little bit and being keenly aware of your being a therapist who is having this experiencing, you are the self or identity who is this particular experiencing. You are literally being the experiencing of defiance, refusal, and standing one's ground. You are much less a therapist who says, "I, the therapist, sense an experiencing of defiance, refusal, standing one's ground. How interesting this is! This explains why he is treating me like this." There is little or no conscious awareness of being you, a therapist, with your own identity and self, and that you are being with a patient who is over there. There is, in other words, a washing away of the self–other distinction (Vanaerschot, 1990). It is as if the two of you now occupy the same physical space (Rothenberg, 1987), and you literally take on the experiencing identity or self that is the other person (cf. Buie, 1981; Corcoran, 1982; Havens, 1978; Major & Miller, 1984; May, 1989; Olden, 1953).

In contrast, in most face-to-face therapies, the empathic therapist is to keep a firm grip on one's own sense of identity or self. Tiptoe out a bit, venture toward the client's self or identity, but do this "as if" you are being the patient. Do not go too far, do not become the client too much, and beware against losing your own stable identity or self (Airing, 1958; Beres & Arlow, 1974; Blackman, Smith, Brokman, & Stern, 1958; Cooper, 1970; Lichtenberg, 1984; Mearns & Thorne, 1988; Rogers, 1959; Schafer, 1968; Schroeder, 1925; Stewart, 1956).

In the same way, most face-to-face empathic therapists want to know the feelings and experiencings going on in the patient, but there are plenty of warnings against actually undergoing the patient's feeling and experiencings, and certainly against having them "too much" (Beres & Arlow, 1974; Cooper, 1970; Rogers, 1959; Rogers & Truax, 1967; Rowe & Isaac, 1991; Schafer, 1959; Szalita, 1976; Truax, 1967). Havens (1973) is clear in describing Freud as being penetratingly drawn toward knowing what is going on inside the patient, the feelings and experiencings, but as clearly not wanting to undergo them.

The Aligned Therapist Lives in the World of the Patient Versus the
Face-to-Face Therapist Remains Safely Outside the World of the Patient

The aligned therapist actually lives in the scenes created by the words of the patient. So much of the therapist's attention is directed out there, and so ready is the therapist to live and be in these scenes, that the therapist is typically living in the patient's world at least as much or more than the patient. The therapist is wholly living in a scene in which she and her mother are having coffee together, or he is writhing in sexual feelings on the bed, or he is slapping the other guy on his shoulder and laughing in camaraderie, or she is holding the infant on your lap and feeling her right index finger pushing your lower lip down.

In contrast, most face-to-face therapists are warned against living in the patient's world "too much" or entering in "too far," or becoming caught or lost in the patient's world (Airing, 1958; Blackman et al., 1958; Cooper, 1970; Mearns & Thorne, 1988; Rogers, 1959, 1975; Schafer, 1959; Stewart, 1956; Vanaerschot, 1990). The face-to-face model's emphasis on generally retaining one's self and identity is not especially useful to allow the aligned therapist to live and be in the patient's immediately ongoing world.

The Aligned Therapist Joins With the Patient in Going Through the Steps of Therapeutic Change Versus the Empathic Face-to-Face Therapist Is Unlikely to Join With the Patient in Going Through the Steps of Therapeutic Change

The aligned therapist shows the patient what to do and how to do it, in going through the actual steps of therapeutic change. More important, the aligned therapist is exceedingly ready, willing, and able to accompany the patient so that both go through therapeutic changes, therapist and patient together.

In contrast, most empathic, face-to-face therapists apply interventions. They engage in relationships with their clients. They use methods and techniques that are either part of being empathic or deemed helpful in accomplishing what the face-to-face therapist seeks to accomplish. However, these interventions, methods, and techniques, these therapist–client relationships, generally do not include joining with the person in going through the actual steps of therapeutic change. Being empathic does not typically mean going through the changes right along with the patient, in the face-to-face model of empathy.

The Aligned Therapist Loses Most of What Is Provided by the Relationship, Therapist Roles, and Personal Experiencings

The aligned therapist tries to be fully aligned throughout most of the session. This means that the therapist sacrifices a great deal of what this model sees as fueling most empathic, face-to-face therapists, namely, the relationship in which the therapist attends mainly to the client and the client attends mainly to the therapist; this occurs before, during, and after those times when the face-to-face therapist is being empathic. To a very large extent, the aligned therapist loses this therapist–patient relationship, and this is a loss of what may be regarded as crucial, or at least almost essential, in most face-to-face therapies.

In addition, the aligned therapist loses the whole array of therapist roles and personal experiencings that may be a major feature in most face-to-face therapies. The aligned therapist generally loses the opportunity of being the patient's best friend, someone the patient looks up to, someone who provides valuable insights and understandings, a trusted confidante, someone with wisdom about life, an exemplar of mental health, a solid rock of reality, someone who values and treasures the patient's preciousness, the rescuer from catastrophic psychopathology, the expert in behavior change (Mahrer, 1996).

The aligned therapist tends to sacrifice a great deal that is provided by the therapist–patient relationship and by many therapist roles and highly personal experiencings.

Will the Aligned Model and the Traditional Empathic Model Yield Similar or Different Feelings and Experiencings and Worlds, Scenes, and Situations?

In one sense, this is a payoff question. If both the aligned model and the face-to-face model of empathy are designed to get at what the person is feeling and experiencing, and the world, scene, or situation in which the person is living, then it makes a big difference if both models come up with similar or different things. It seems to me that the two models will typically come up with quite different things.

The Aligned Model and the Face-to-Face Model Would Probably Select and Use Altogether Different Patient Statements

In the aligned model, the therapist is aligned throughout the session, from beginning to end. This means that the therapist uses just about every patient statement to grasp the feeling or experiencing and to know the world or scene that is present. In the face-to-face model, there may be some approaches that select and use a high proportion of patient statements, notably an orthodox client-centered approach. However, it is my impression that most face-to-face therapists do not select and use most of the patient's statements for purposes of empathy. Instead, I believe that only a relatively small proportion of particular kinds of patient statements are so selected and used, perhaps closer to 5%. If these impressions are even somewhat accurate, then it seems that the aligned model and the face-to-face model would likely come up with quite different empathic payoffs because they select and use altogether different patient statements for explicitly empathic purposes.

What the Patient Says and Does Would Almost Certainly Be Quite Different in the Aligned Model as Compared With the Face-to-Face Model

To be able to see if the aligned therapist and the face-to-face therapist get similar empathic payoffs, it would probably help if the comparison were done on just about the same patient statements. The trouble is that what the patient says and does in the aligned model would almost certainly differ from what the patient says and does in the face-to-face model. In the aligned model, the patient is mainly attending out there, living and being in some scene as he says, "Why are you doing this?" "I think it's changing!" "What am I going to do about you?" It may occur, but it is not so very common, that in the face-to-face model the patient is attending mainly to the cancer, to her sister, and that she is living and being in some scene, rather than talking mainly to the therapist about this or that. Symmetrically, what the patient ordinarily says and does in attending mainly to the face-to-face therapist is generally not what a patient says and does in the aligned model.

If this difference is exaggerated, it is like comparing one way of being empathic, when the patient is actually undergoing sexual intercourse, with another way of being empathic, when the patient is attending mainly to a therapist and merely telling about having had intercourse. The aligned model and the face-to-face model would probably come up with different empathic payoffs, if only because the patient is likely saying and doing different things in the two models.

The Altogether Different Positions and Locations of the Aligned and Face-to-Face Therapists Would Likely Provide Altogether Different Empathic Payoffs

Even when listening to ostensibly the same words, said in ostensibly the same way, it is almost certain that the empathic payoffs would be quite different because the two therapists are located in such different positions. The aligned therapist is positioned so that he is saying these words right along with the person and is living and being in the scene created by the words. In contrast, the face-to-face therapist might typically be external to and separated from the patient, attending to and observing the patient.

The patient says, "That depression won't go away! I can't get rid of it. It's too strong!" The face-to-face therapist reasons that the patient is depressed, is perhaps overwrought about her depression. In contrast, the aligned therapist says these words right along with the person, sees a form or shape that is the depression, a thing that is strong and defiant enough to refuse to go away, and the therapist experiences a sense of pride, admiration, approval of that objectified depression.

The patient says, "Sarah is only a week old, and she knows that I made a mistake in telling my mother to stay with me and help. Sarah knows everything that is best for me. She's divine. She'll show me what to do." The external, face-to-face therapist may have trouble trying to be empathic because she is impelled by thoughts about the patient's psychopathology, paranoid thinking, and mentally disordered condition. In contrast, the aligned therapist is attending to the newborn baby Sarah and is experiencing a sense of secure trust, being taken care of, and entrusting oneself.

The exaggerated extreme is if the patient were to say, "Uh, I don't quite know if I should say this, but, your fly is open." The face-to-face therapist is entitled to be the object or brunt or target of what the patient is saying, and any attempt to be empathic may be set aside as the therapist checks his fly. In contrast, if the therapist is aligned, he is saying these words right along with the patient, talking to the waiter in the posh restaurant, and the experiencing might be a risked nastiness, devilishness, and wickedness.

In general, both the aligned and the face-to-face therapists may get empathic payoffs, but the chances are that the payoffs would be somewhat different because of the altogether different positions and locations of the therapists.

When the Person Refers to Feelings and Emotions, It is Likely That the Aligned and Traditionally Empathic Therapists Will Arrive at Different Feelings, Experiencings, and Scenes

Ordinarily, when a patient says he is having a feeling or emotion, the traditionally empathic therapist concludes that he is having that feeling or emotion. If the patient says, "I feel irritated," the therapist may well conclude that the patient is feeling irritated. When the patient says, "I really feel proud of my son," it is easy to conclude that he is feeling a sense of pride. It seems generally true that the therapist will accept that the person is having the feeling he or she says he has. There are exceptions, such as when the patient is in the throes of hilarious laughter as she blurts out the words, "I feel irritated," or he may be conspicuously fearful and scared as he is breathing hard and saying, "I am relaxed, not worried. Yes, I feel relaxed." But most empathic therapists accept that when the patient says she is feeling relaxed or irritated she is truly feeling relaxed or irritated.

It is even easier when the patient says something about the justifying circumstances. So she says, "I feel irritated when I get home and there is a big mess in the kitchen. Everything's all over!" When the person adds words such as these, it is easier to conclude that she is having the feeling she says she is having, especially because the circumstances seem to justify that feeling.

In rather sharp contrast, the aligned therapist will get some idea of the feeling or experiencing by seeing what is occurring as the words come in and through him, and as the aligned therapist sees whatever scenes are put there by the words. Accordingly, if the person says, "I feel irritated," with the words coming through him in a particular way, and in the context of a particular scene, the therapist just might have a feeling or experiencing of moderate surprise and delight, or perhaps a feeling or experiencing of tightly bound coldness and control, or maybe a feeling or experiencing of being irritated. There is usually a big difference between the feeling or experiencing that is talked about or referred to, and the feeling or experiencing in the person who is talking about or referring to the feeling or experiencing.

In the same way, when patients "talk about" feelings, there is almost certainly a big difference in the scenes that the therapist gets, depending on whether the therapist is face-to-face or aligned. Patients often talk about feelings. "I feel irritated, and I don't like that feeling. I have tried to put a lid on that feeling." As these words come in and through the aligned therapist, she may see the feeling of irritation. Perhaps the therapist sees the feeling looking demurely innocent, unfairly accused, unjustifiably disliked, not deserving a lid put on it. Aligned therapists can easily see such things as feelings, especially when the person refers to it, attends to it, has feelings about it, and thereby paints it as a seeable thing, an object that can be looked at.

The net result is that when the person refers to feelings and emotions, it seems quite likely that the aligned and traditionally empathic therapists will arrive at substantially different feelings, experiencings, and scenes.

What the Aligned Therapist Gets is Actually and Immediately Felt, Undergone, Experienced, Rather Than Something Different, Arrived at by Figuring Out, Inferring, Using a Private Stream of Thoughts

He is attending to the expression on his aunt's face as they are sitting in her living room, talking about her deceased husband. "She closes her eyes for a few seconds, and she's gonna cry. Her lower lip's quivering like, and I just look her over, watch her, just look her over. We're all alone. She really trusts me. She can tell me anything and I understand."

What the face-to-face therapist gets is usually from combining, or going back and forth between, an empathic stance and a private stream of thoughts or clinical inferences. The face-to-face therapist may thereby arrive at a conclusion that the patient is really talking about his or her therapist and is thereby communicating a wish to have a trusting relationship with the therapist who is to understand and accept everything that the patient says. Or the therapist reasons that the aunt is mother's younger sister, that the patient does not feel close with his mother, and is displacing this wished-for relationship onto his aunt. Or the therapist has clinical inferences that the patient rarely cries and is coming closer to regarding crying as acceptable. What the face-to-face therapist gets is substantially through use of a stream of private thoughts. The therapist is not actually feeling any of these things. Instead, the therapist arrives at things that are figured out, inferred, and reached by means of a private stream of thoughts.

What the aligned therapist gets is not through figuring it out, or inferring, or using a private stream of thoughts. The aligned therapists gets what is present as the therapist is actually feeling something and actually undergoing or experiencing something. Living in this immediate situation with the aunt, saying these words, something happens inside the therapist. She may undergo a sense of incredible caring, being concerned about, nurturing. She senses herself holding the aunt's hands and being so very caring and concerned. Or the therapist may, perhaps unaccountably, be undergoing strong sexual feelings, feelings of being aroused, being filled with the experiencing of being sensual. These feelings or experiencings are present. They are occurring. The face-to-face therapist probably did not get these kinds of feelings or experiencings any more than the aligned therapist got what the face-to-face therapist got.

The chances are pretty good that what the therapist gets is quite different if one therapist gets it through its being immediately felt, undergone, and experienced and the other therapist gets it by figuring out, by inferring, and by using a private stream of thoughts.

Will the aligned and the traditional empathic models yield similar or different feelings and experiencings and worlds, scenes, and situations? Each of these considerations suggests that the two models will almost certainly yield altogether different feelings and experiencings and altogether different worlds, scenes, and situations.

This conclusion is important, and it makes for very different practical consequences. What the face-to-face, traditionally empathic therapist gets can be crucial for what he tries to accomplish with this patient, how he describes the patient, and what he does in the course of this and subsequent sessions. Much of the basic data and information about the patient may be provided by what you get from being empathic. If what you get varies considerably with whether you are aligned or face to face, then the significant differences can make for even more significant differences. It is perhaps inviting to believe that each way of being empathic gives you essentially similar payoff data and information. It is a whole different ball game when you accept that the aligned model and the traditional empathic, face-to-face model will almost certainly yield altogether different feelings and experiencings and altogether different worlds, scenes, and situations.

Which Empathic Model Will Yield Feelings, Experiencings, and Scenes That Are More Objective, Trustworthy, and Accurate?

Both the aligned and the traditionally empathic models seek to get at the feelings and experiencings that are going on in the person, and both try to get at the kinds of worlds, situations, and scenes in which the person is living and being. Is one model more objective, trustworthy, and accurate than the other? This question is especially important if the two models do provide different kinds of supposed feelings and experiencings and different kinds of worlds, scenes, and situations.

What Each Model Gets May Be Equally Objective, Trustworthy, and Accurate, Yet Different

One position you can take is that there is only one answer that is objective, trustworthy, and accurate. Compare traditional models and the aligned model, and then see which one is closest to the right answer. See which one gets at the objective, trustworthy, and accurate feeling or experiencing or the scene in which the person is living, being, or talking about. One answer must be better, more objective, trustworthy, and accurate. You may accept this position, but I do not. I prefer a position that recognizes different possible answers from different perspectives. A skilled and competent therapist, using a traditional model of empathy, may come up with one notion of what the person is feeling and experiencing and the world in which the person is living. An equally skilled and competent therapist, using the aligned model, may come up with a different answer. I accept that there can be several answers, each quite different from the other, and each quite objective, trustworthy, and accurate. Accordingly, my conclusion is that both the traditional and the aligned models can be objective, trustworthy, and accurate, even though their answers are quite different.

It is Hard to Find a Single Criterion Against Which Both Models Can Be Tested

There may be a criterion answer that is objective, trustworthy, and accurate when you are using the aligned model and a different criterion answer using the traditional empathic model. But I find it very hard to find some single criterion against which both models could be tested. Whether we ask some empathic experts, a group of judges, the patient, or a group of researchers to serve as criterion, they would almost certainly have to use some model. Whatever they come up with is what is yielded by some particular model rather than a criterion against which both may be compared. I know of no scale, inventory, or instrument that can be the criterion for all models. Even if there were some, they would almost certainly have to favor one of the models rather than being a separate criterion against which all the models may be compared. In general, I cannot picture some single criterion against which all the models may be compared in any useful, practical way.

The Challenge is That What the Aligned Model Gets is More Objective and Trustworthy Because the Therapist Actually Undergoes It

I believe that the aligned model is better than traditional empathic models in providing data that are real, objective, and trustworthy. The aligned model produces evidence that is real, objective, and trustworthy, whereas the traditional models produce evidence that is loose, vague, diffuse, much softer and unscientifically unreal, unobjective, and untrustworthy (cf. Havens, 1973; Mahrer, 1996; Mahrer et al., 1994; May, 1989; Mearns & Thorne, 1988; Vanaerschot, 1990).

When the aligned therapist gets a feeling or experiencing, the hard evidence is in the form of real, objective, and trustworthy bodily sensations. The therapist actually has shivers down her back, actually has perspiration on her forehead, and actually has a clutching up sensation in the belly. He actually has an erection, is actually dizzy in the head, and actually has an electrical tingling in the skin across his chest. When the aligned therapist sees the world out there, she actually sees a little baby, actually sees the elevator doors that are locked, and actually sees the knife with blood on it. The aligned model's evidence is relatively real, objective, and trustworthy.

In contrast, what the traditional empathic model yields is far more hypothetical, inferential, conceptual-bound, and cognitive. The face-to-face therapist may infer a sense of the patient's feeling sexual toward the child, but it is much less likely that the therapist is having bodily sensations of sexual excitement, is having an erection or warm oozing sensations in the genitals, is literally being here with the child, and is seeing the child. Compared to the face-to-face, empathic therapist, the challenge is that what the aligned model gets is more objective and trustworthy because the aligned therapist actually undergoes it.

Which Model Is More Useful, Objective, Trustworthy, and Accurate in Getting at Inner Deeper Experiencings?

It is very hard to answer this question because of at least two considerations. One is that you would have to value the identifying of inner, deeper material and specifically material that consists of experiencings. Not every approach values material that is held to be deep inside the person, well beyond the person's awareness. Nor would all approaches accept that what is deeper inside consists of inner experiencings. Second, even with approaches that valued identifying inner, deeper experiencings, the aligned model is expressly designed to yield this material, and the face-to-face model is not especially designed to get at what may be described as the person's inner deeper experiencings. Accordingly, it seems difficult to examine which model is more useful, objective, trustworthy, and accurate in getting at this particular kind of empathic yield.

How Can Research Contribute to Empathy as Therapist–Client Alignment?

I know of no research on empathy as therapist–client alignment. If there is to be research on this way of being empathic, perhaps an easy question for researchers is to see which model is more effective. Both the face-to-face model and the aligned model want to get inside the client's frame of reference; to see the client's world through the client's eyes; and to know, grasp, understand, sense, share, and have what the client is feeling, thinking, and experiencing, both at a more surface level and at a deeper level. Why not see which is better?

There are several answers as to why such research is hardly doable in a constructively useful way. One reason is that there is no criterion of the real or true or accurate or objective goals of empathy. There is no single criterion of what the client is seeing or feeling, especially at the deeper level. A second reason is that each model is almost certainly going to adopt its own criterion of exactly what it is trying to attain and of its success in attaining it. A third reason is that the two models would almost certainly not agree on precisely which client statements the contest should be held. It seems hard to decide who wins. Even if a researcher declares one the winner, it is unlikely that many proponents of the losing side would switch models.

My preference is for research that contributes to the increasing effectiveness of each model. If the model is made better, more further developed, and more carefully used, I find such research more helpful than trying to see which model wins out over the other. If researchers are drawn toward contributing to empathy as therapist–client alignment, research may focus on improving the nuts and bolts of the method. What can therapists do to put most of their attention out there on whatever the client is attending to or creating out there? How can clients put most of their attention on scenes and focal centers that are accompanied with strong feeling? How can therapists join with or align with the client so as to maximize the extent to which the client's words can seem to come from a part of the therapist? How can therapists be taught how to align fully and completely, quickly and efficiently, regardless of who and what kinds of people the client and therapist are? My preference is for research that makes each model better, rather than trying to have a contest between the various models of empathy.

CONCLUSIONS

1. There are several models or ways of trying to know (a) what the person is feeling and experiencing, both more or less on the surface and at the inner, deeper level; and (b) the scenes, situations, and focal centers that the person is attending to, living and being in. In other words there are several models of what is called *empathy*. One of these models or ways may be called being "aligned" with the person.

2. There are two relatively explicit methods and procedures to enable the therapist to be aligned with the person: (a) Both client and therapist attend mainly to a third focal center, rather than mainly to one another. The therapist's attention is fully and consistently out there, on the third focal center of attention. (b) The therapist is postured so that the words of the client come in and through the therapist, with the therapist and client as two parts of a larger single person. When the person is talking, it is also a part of the therapist who is talking.

3. The aligned therapist is able to attain the aims of empathy, namely to know what the person is feeling and experiencing, and to know the world in which the person is being. In addition, the aligned therapist is in a sensitive and powerful position to discover and to access inner, deeper experiencings in the person, to enable the person to welcome and appreciate this accessed inner, deeper potential, to enable the person literally to disengage from the continuing person, and to be a qualitatively new person who is free of the bad-feelinged scenes that were front and center in the session. These are the in-session aims and goals of experiential psychotherapy (Mahrer, 1996).

4. The aligned model is a powerful, sensitive method of achieving the above aims and goals. Practitioners seeking to achieve these aims and goals are invited to adopt the aligned model.

5. The aligned model seems to differ from most face-to-face models of empathy in some ways that may be considered significant, basic, and fundamental. It is a rather radical departure from and alternative to most face-to-face models. The aligned model seems to differ from the face-to-face models in such fundamental dimensions as (a) the role, posture, and self or identity of the therapist; (b) the nature of the relationship between therapist and person; (c) the concrete working methods of empathy; (d) the specific working aims and purposes of empathy; and (e) the actual nature and content of the empathic feelings, experiencings, scenes and worlds, especially at the inner, deeper level of personality.

REFERENCES

Airing, C. (1958). Sympathy and empathy. *Journal of the American Medical Association, 167,* 448–452.

Beres, D., & Arlow, J. A. (1974). Fantasy and identification in empathy. *Psychoanalytic Quarterly, 43,* 26–50.

Berger, D. M. (1984). On the way to empathic understanding. *American Journal of Psychotherapy, 38,* 111–120.

Berger, D. M. (1987). *Clinical empathy.* London: Jason Aronson.

Blackman, N., Smith, K., Brokman, R., & Stern, J. (1958). The development of empathy in male schizophrenics. *Psychiatric Quarterly, 32,* 546–553.

Brammer, L. M., & Shostrom, E. L. (1982). *Therapeutic psychology.* Englewood Cliffs, NJ: Prentice-Hall.

Brenner, D. (1982). *The effective psychotherapist.* Elmsford, NY: Pergamon.

Buie, D. H. (1981). Empathy: Its nature and limitations. *Journal of the American Psychoanalytic Association, 29,* 281–307.

Carkhuff, R. R. (1972). *The art of helping.* Amherst, MA: Human Resource Development Press.

Chessick, R. D. (1992). Phenomenology of the emerging sense of self. *Psychoanalysis in Contemporary Thought, 15,* 57–88.

Cooper, L. (1970). Empathy: A developmental model. *Journal of Nervous and Mental Diseases, 154,* 169–178.

Corcoran, K. J. (1982). An exploratory investigation into self–other differentiation: Empirical evidence for a monistic perspective on empathy. *Psychotherapy: Theory, Research and Practice, 19,* 63–78.

Cox, M. (1988). *Structuring the therapeutic process.* London: Jessica Kingsley.

Dymond, R. F. (1949). The measurement of empathic ability. *Journal of Consulting Psychology, 13,* 127–133.

Egan, G. (1986). *The skilled helper.* Monterey, CA: Brooks/Cole.

Fliess, R. (1942). The metapsychology of the analyst. *Psychoanalytic Quarterly, 11,* 211–227.

Fox, R. E., & Goldin, P. C. (1984). The empathic process in psychotherapy: A survey of theory and research. *Journal of Nervous and Mental Diseases, 138,* 323–331.

Freud, S. (1953). Recommendations to physicians practising psycho-analysis. In J. Strachey (Ed. and Trans.), *The standard edition of the complete psychological works of Sigmund Freud* (Vol. 12). London: Hogarth Press. (Original work published 1912)

Freud, S. (1955). Group psychology and the analysis of the ego. In J. Strachey (Ed. and Trans.), *The standard edition of the complete psychological works of Sigmund Freud* (Vol. 18). London: Hogarth Press. (Original work published 1921)

Furer, M. (1967). Some developmental aspects of the superego. *International Journal of Psychoanalysis, 48,* 277–280.

Gladstein, G. A. (1977). Empathy and counseling outcome: An empirical and conceptual review. *Counseling Psychologist, 6,* 70–79.

Gladstein, G. A. (1983). Understanding empathy: Integrating counseling, developmental, and social psychology perspectives. *Journal of Counseling Psychology, 30,* 467–482.

Greenson, R. R. (1960). Empathy and its vicissitudes. *International Journal of Psychoanalysis, 41,* 418–424.

Greenson, R. R. (1967). *Technique and practice of psychoanalysis* (Vol. 1). New York: International Universities Press.

Havens, L. L. (1972). The development of existential psychiatry. *The Journal of Nervous and Mental Diseases, 154,* 309–331.

Havens, L. L. (1973). *Approaches to the mind.* Boston: Little, Brown.

Havens, L. L. (1974). The existential use of the self. *The American Journal of Psychiatry, 131,* 1–10.

Havens, L. L. (1978). Explorations in the uses of language in psychotherapy: Simple empathic statements. *Psychiatry, 41,* 336–345.

Havens, L. L. (1986). *Making contact: Uses of language in psychotherapy.* Cambridge, MA: Harvard University Press.

Jaffe, D. S. (1986). Empathy, counteridentification, countertransference: A review, with some personal perspectives on the "analytic instrument." *Psychoanalytic Quarterly, 55,* 215–241.

Kohut, H. (1959). Introspection, empathy, and psychoanalysis: An examination of the relationship between mode of observation and theory. *Journal of the American Psychoanalytic Association, 7,* 459–483.

Kohut, H. (1978). *The search for the self* (Vol. 1). New York: International Universities Press.

Kohut, H. (1984). *How does analysis cure?* Chicago: University of Chicago Press.

Korchin, S. J. (1976). *Modern clinical psychology.* New York: Basic Books.

Kramer, P. D. (1989). *Moments of engagement.* New York: Norton.

Langs, R. (1982). *Psychotherapy: A basic text.* New York: Jason Aronson.

Lichtenberg, J. D. (1984). The empathic mode of perception and alternative vantage points for psychoanalytic work. In J. D. Lichtenberg, M. Bornstein, & D. Silver (Eds.), *Empathy II* (pp. 113–135). Hillsdale, NJ: Erlbaum.

Mahrer, A. R. (1978). The therapist–patient relationship: Conceptual analysis and a proposal for a paradigm shift. *Psychotherapy: Theory, Research and Practice, 15,* 201–215.

Mahrer, A. R. (1982). Humanistic approaches to intimacy. In M. Fisher & G. Stricker (Eds.), *Intimacy* (pp. 141–158). New York: Plenum Press.

Mahrer, A. R. (1986). *Therapeutic experiencing: The process of change.* New York: Norton.

Mahrer, A. R. (1989a). *Experiencing: A humanistic theory of psychology and psychiatry.* Ottawa: University of Ottawa Press. (Original work published 1978)

Mahrer, A. R. (1989b). *Experiential psychotherapy: Basic practices.* Ottawa: University of Ottawa Press. (Original work published 1983)

Mahrer, A. R. (1989c). *How to do experiential psychotherapy: A manual for practitioners.* Ottawa: University of Ottawa Press.

Mahrer, A. R. (1996). *The complete guide to experiential psychotherapy.* New York: Wiley.

Mahrer, A. R., Boulet, D. B., & Fairweather, D. R. (1994). Beyond empathy: Advances in the clinical theory and methods of empathy. *Clinical Psychology Review, 14,* 183–198.

Major, R., & Miller, P. (1984). Empathy, antipathy, and telepathy in the analytic process. In J. Lichtenberg, M. Bornstein, & D. Silver (Eds.), *Empathy II* (pp. 227–248). Hillsdale, NJ: Erlbaum.

Margulies, A. (1984). Toward empathy: The uses of wonder. *American Journal of Psychiatry, 141,* 1025–1033.

Margulies, A., & Havens, L. L. (1981). The initial encounter: What to do first? *American Journal of Psychiatry, 138,* 421–428.

May, R. (1989). *The art of counseling.* New York: Gardner.

Mearns, D., & Thorne, B. (1988). *Person-centered counseling in action.* London: Sage.

Murray, H. A. (1938). *Explorations in personality.* New York: Oxford University Press.

Olden, C. (1953). On adult empathy with children. In B. Charles (Ed.), *The psychoanalytic study of the child* (Vol. 8, pp. 111–126). New York: International Universities Press.

Rogers, C. R. (1951). *Client-centred therapy.* Boston: Houghton Mifflin.

Rogers, C. R. (1959). A theory of therapy, personality, and interpersonal relationships, as developed in the client-centred framework. In S. Koch (Ed.), *Psychology: A study of a science* (Vol. 3, pp. 184–256). New York: McGraw-Hill.

Rogers, C. R. (1975). Empathic: An unappreciated way of being. *The Counseling Psychologist, 5,* 2–10.

Rogers, C. R., & Truax, C. B. (1967). The therapeutic conditions antecedent to change: A theoretical view. In C. R. Rogers (Ed.), *The therapeutic relationship and its impact* (pp. 97–108). Westport, CT: Greenwood.

Rothenberg, A. (1987). Empathy as a creative process in treatment. *International Review of Psycho-Analysis, 14,* 445–463.

Rowe, C. E., Jr., & Isaac, D. S. (1991). *Empathic attunement.* Northvale, NJ: Jason Aronson.

Schafer, R. (1959). Generative empathy in the treatment situation. *Psychoanalytical Quarterly, 28,* 342–373.

Schafer, R. (1968). *Aspects of internalization.* New York: International Universities Press.

Schilder, P. (1953). *Medical psychology.* New York: International Universities Press.

Schroeder, T. (1925). The psycho-analytic method of observation. *International Journal of Psychoanalysis, 6,* 155–170.

Stewart, D. (1956). *Preface to empathy.* New York: Philosophical Library.

Szalita, A. B. (1976). Some thoughts on empathy. *Psychiatry, 39,* 142–152.

Truax, C. B. (1967). A scale for the rating of accurate empathy. In C. R. Rogers (Ed.), *The therapeutic relationship and its impact* (pp. 555–568). Westport, CT: Greenwood.

Vanaerschot, G. (1990). The process of empathy: Holding and letting go. In G. Lietaer, J. Rombauts, & R. Van Balen (Eds.), *Client-centred and experiential psychotherapy in the nineties* (pp. 267–293). Leuven, Belgium: Leuven University Press.

IV

PSYCHOANALYTIC PERSPECTIVES

10

EMPATHY:
A PSYCHOANALYTIC PERSPECTIVE

MORRIS EAGLE AND DAVID L. WOLITZKY

Our aim in this chapter is to discuss the nature of empathy and its role in psychoanalytic theory and practice. We will begin with a consideration of the definition of *empathy* and the different uses of the term.

Definition of Empathy

We start with a general and commonsense working definition of empathy that, we assume, will be more or less shared by other contributors to this volume. A good place to begin is to cite Mead's (1932–1934) statement that "adequate empathy involves the ability to take the attitude of another" (p. 318). Thus, empathy refers to one's putting oneself in another person's shoes and getting a sense (i.e., a cognitive–emotional grasp) of that person's perspective and what he or she is experiencing, feeling, and thinking. Put very simply, empathy entails taking the role of the other and seeing the other from his or her internal frame of reference.

The preceding general definition is quite compatible with the conceptions of empathy in psychotherapeutic and psychoanalytic contexts. For example, in a much discussed article on empathy as a mode of

217

psychoanalytic listening, Schwaber (1981) defines empathy as "that mode of attunement which attempts to maximize a singular focus on the patient's subjective reality, seeking all possible cues to ascertain it" (p. 378). In this mode of listening, one will be attentive to all the cues that will enable one to understand the experience and the subjective reality of the other. For Schwaber, when one is listening to a patient empathically, the basic questions that orient one's listening are: What is the patient's experience? What is the nature of his or her subjective or perceptual reality?

According to Schafer (1959), empathy involves "the inner experience of sharing in and comprehending the momentary psychological state of another person" (p. 345). However, he also appears to define empathy much more broadly when he describes it as a sharing and comprehension of "a hierarchic organization of desires, feelings, thoughts, defenses, controls, superego pressures, capacities, self-representations, and representations of real and fantasied personal relationships" (p. 347). We will return to this issue of broad versus narrow conceptions of empathy.

Greenson (1960), embracing the narrower definition, wrote that "to empathize means to share, to experience the feelings of another person" (p. 148). He stresses the dangers of both inhibited empathy and the loss of control of empathy seen in overidentification with the patient. Both Greenson and Schafer (1959) emphasize the idea of an optimal distance from the patient and the development of an internal working model of the patient as an important guide to empathic responsiveness.

In further refining the meaning of empathy, we should perhaps speak about what empathy is not. As has been said many times, empathy is not identical to sympathy. One can understand the feelings, thoughts, and attitudes of another without having sympathy for the person having them. And conversely, one can feel sympathy for another without a deep understanding of that person's subjective reality. According to Schwaber (1981), another thing that empathy is not is "what *we* would feel if *we* were in [another's] shoes" (p. 385).[1] Hoffman (1984) refers to this stance as "egocentric empathy." In short, when one takes an empathic stance one tries to understand the other as an experiencing subject, whereas when one takes an external perspective one understands the other as a behaving object.

---

[1] We believe that Schwaber's statement is too strong. Although putting oneself in another's role involves trying to imagine what the other person is feeling, it seems inevitable that one aspect of this process will include one's own imagined feelings and experiences in a similar situation. We implicitly assume that we are sufficiently like the other so that what *we* would feel in that person's shoes is similar to what he or she feels. (See Basch, 1983, which will be discussed later.) Indeed, empathy is probably facilitated by the greater similarity between two people.

Uses of the Concept of Empathy[2]

There at least six different uses of the term *empathy*:

Empathy as a Genetically Based Capacity for Understanding, Relating to, and Reacting to Others in Particular Ways

According to this view, empathic capacity unfolds developmentally along a continuum. Thus, Hoffman (1984) refers to "global empathy," already present in the first year of life and manifested, for example, in the distress cries of infants that are elicited by hearing other infants' distress cries (Sagi & Hoffman, 1976). That infants as young as 6 weeks can imitate an adult's facial acts (Meltzoff & Moore, 1994) also suggests early precursors of empathy.

Hoffman (1984) understands empathy as one aspect of a genetically based capacity for altruism. Thus, he interprets the distress cries of the infants in the Sagi and Hoffman (1976) study as a primitive form of feeling distress in reaction to another's distress. As noted, Hoffman refers to this reaction as "global empathy." A later stage in the development of empathy identified by Hoffman is referred to, in what seems like an oxymoron, as "egocentric empathy," which is expressed in the behavior of people giving to others "what they themselves find most comforting" (p. 287).[3] It is also clear that Hoffman views such egocentric behavior as empathic because it involves caring and concern for the other—remember that, according to Hoffman, a genetic tendency for altruism is the basis for empathy—and an attempt to understand what the other is experiencing and needs, even if the attempt is based on the egocentric assumption that the other is just like oneself. Thus, central in Hoffman's conceptualization of empathy is not so much accuracy of understanding but an altruistic concern and caring for the other that leads one to at least attempt to understand or make assumptions regarding what the other is experiencing and needs.

Empathy as a genetically based and developmentally unfolding capacity to understand and relate to another implies an ability to conceptualize and experience another as having inner mental states. That is, one cannot take the attitude of another unless one implicitly assumes that another has attitudes. One cannot imagine what another feels, thinks, and believes

---

[2] Holt (1969) writes about five kinds of phenomena to which the concept of empathy is applicable: (a) "aesthetic empathy" in which one "feels into" a work of art. This is derived from the original use of the term introduced by Lipps around the turn of the century; (b) "autistic (or magical) participation" (Murphy, 1947), more familiarly known as "body English"; (c) "basic species" identity by which Holt means "the automatic and unconscious identification of every normal human being with any other he encounters" (p. 606); (d) "emotional contagion"; and (e) "mature empathy," which according to Holt, requires a secure sense of identity that enables one to "let go of his own immediate interests and to participate imaginatively in someone else's world" (p. 610).
[3] See footnote 1.

unless one implicitly assumes that others feel, think, and believe. In short, one can say that empathy implies a tacit theory of mind.

It is interesting to observe that at the core of a currently influential theory of autism is the idea that autistic individuals are impaired in their ability to think about or imagine another's state of mind or to attribute mental states to others (e.g., Baron-Cohen, Tager-Flusberg, & Cohen, 1993). In contrast to normal children who show a progressive development in their capacity to perceive other people as having subjective mental states, autistic children do not develop this capacity or develop it only to a minimal degree. In short, they are relatively incapable of empathic understanding of others (as well as of themselves).

The issue of autism aside, it is likely that there is a wide range of individual differences in people's ability and tendency to think about and imagine another's state of mind, let alone the ability to do so accurately. It is a common observation that very egocentric, self-absorbed, and narcissistic individuals have difficulty with, as well as little apparent interest in, thinking about and being concerned with the other's state of mind. And if they do have an interest in the other's state of mind, it is only in those particular thoughts and feelings that pertain to themselves. There is the well-known joke in which the egocentric and narcissistic Hollywood director is going on endlessly about himself in his "conversation" with a young starlet. In a rare moment of seeming self-awareness, he says, "I've been talking only about myself. That's enough about me. Let's talk about you. What do you think of me?"

Empathy as a Method of Observation and Data-Gathering

This idea is clearly illustrated by Kohut's (1984) definition of psychoanalysis as a discipline that bases its observations on introspection and empathy (which he refers to as "vicarious introspection"). According to Kohut, physical phenomena are grasped by our senses, while psychological, or at least psychoanalytic data, are understood by introspection and empathy.

The distinction made by Kohut derives from the distinction, associated with Dilthey (1961) and other post-Kantians, between *Geisteswissenschaften* (which can be very roughly be translated as "human sciences") and *Naturwissenschaften* (which can be translated as "natural sciences"). According to this point of view, in contrast to disciplines that deal with physical phenomena and are concerned with explanation, disciplines that deal with human behavior are primarily concerned with understanding (*Verstehen*). Furthermore, the primary means of understanding another's mental states and actions is to put oneself in the place of the other to grasp his or her feelings, thoughts, motives, intentions, aims, and so on.

Empathy as a Mode of Listening

Empathy can be understood as a mode of listening that according to Schwaber (1981), characterizes (or should characterize) the analyst's listening orientation. As noted earlier, according to Schwaber, when one listens empathically one focuses on the person's subjective reality, on what that person is feeling and experiencing. In the clinical situation and in the context of transference, an implicit and abiding question that guides the therapist's listening and focus of attention is: What is the patient feeling and experiencing in relation to me, the therapist? It seems to us that, as described by Schwaber, an empathic mode of listening is not so much a special method of observation and data gathering as a particular perspective—as a kind of listening in which one is always trying to understand the other's subjective reality.

Empathy as a Developmental Need

Kohut (1971, 1977) views empathy as a universal developmental need. That is, he maintains that the infant's experience of the caregiver's empathic mirroring is a necessary ingredient in the development of a cohesive self and, conversely, that traumatic failures in the provision of empathic mirroring play a critical causal role in the development of self defects and pathology. Concepts such as "attunement" between infant and mother (e.g., Beebe & Lachmann, 1988) and the caregiver's "sensitive responsiveness" (e.g., Ainsworth, 1974), although not identical to the concept of empathy, certainly bear a family resemblance to it, and perhaps one can say that they both involve the use of empathy.

Empathy in Communication

Here the emphasis is on how one communicates one's understanding to another, whatever the methods used in acquiring that understanding. Thus, even if the methods used in gaining understanding of another may not have especially involved empathy, one can communicate that understanding empathically or nonempathically. In the former case, one will communicate one's understanding in a way that takes account of how the other is likely to react and is reacting to one's communication. We think there would be little dispute with Schlesinger's (1981) statement that "the capacity to communicate empathically with patients is the basis of psychoanalysis and psychodynamic psychotherapies" (p. 415). We would add that it is also the basis of a wide range of psychotherapies.

Empathy as a Curative Agent

Finally, we come to a conception of empathy as a central therapeutic or "curative" agent. In a psychoanalytic context, this idea is most closely associated with the work of Kohut (1971, 1977, 1984) and other self psychologists. It is well to remember, however, that quite a bit prior to Kohut's work, Rogers (e.g., 1951) had identified empathy (along with congruence and unconditional positive regard) as one of the primary growth-facilitating ingredients in psychotherapy. Rogers and Kohut also share in common the linkage between the idea of a developmental need for empathy and the nature of therapeutic "cure." We noted above that Kohut views empathy (i.e., to be treated empathically) as a universal developmental need and that traumatic failures to meet this need are held to be instrumental in generating self-pathology. We think it is fair to say that, according to Kohut, it is the therapist's success in meeting this need for empathic mirroring that is the primary factor in therapeutic change. One might say that the therapist fulfills a developmental need that was traumatically unmet by the parents.

Of the above different uses of the term *empathy*, we will focus mainly on the role of empathy in psychotherapy. We will discuss the following main topics: empathy as a method of observation in classical psychoanalytic theory, processes by which empathy operates, the validation of empathic understanding and knowledge, and empathy as a therapeutic agent.

EMPATHY AS A METHOD OF OBSERVATION AND DATA GATHERING IN CLASSICAL PSYCHOANALYTIC THEORY

Freud (1921/1955) wrote that "a path leads from identification by way of imitation to empathy, that is to the comprehension of the mechanism by means of which we are enabled to take up any attitude at all towards another mental life" (p. 110). This comment has been taken up by some to demonstrate that Freud was vitally concerned with the issue of empathy. For example, in his book *Clinical Empathy*, Berger (1987) cites this passage and notes that Freud refers to empathy (*Einfühlung*) a total of 15 times in the body of his work and that he views it as essential to the carrying out of treatment. Fifteen references in a total of 23 volumes of text hardly suggests an abiding interest in the issue. However, quite apart from the number of references, neither Freud's case histories, his other discussions, nor the logic of Freudian theory, including the Freudian theory of treatment, suggests that empathy plays a distinctive role as a method of data gathering in classical theory. We agree with Shapiro's (1981) judgment that "even though Freud mentioned empathy in his treatises on jokes (Freud, 1905/1960a) and group psychology (Freud, 1921/1955), he never attended to it as a central instrument of analysis" (p. 423). One certainly does not find in Freud's work the central and explicit role that is given to empathy in Kohut's writings. It will be recalled that the therapeutic stance that Freud (1912/1958d) frequently advocated is that of a "blank screen" and, on occasion, that of a surgeon who takes an entirely objective attitude toward the patient. Quite apart from the therapeutic rationale for this stance, the point to be noted in the present context is the degree to which such a stance suggests an understanding of the patient from an external perspective—from the "outside."

It seems clear that Freud viewed empathy not as a central and distinctive method of gathering analytic data or as a direct therapeutic agent, but as a background factor in at least two senses. He believed that empathy (*Einfühlung*)—that is, the ability to put oneself in another's place and imagine that he or she has mental states and reactions similar to one's own—is a prerequisite for a conception of other minds. He also believed that empathy was also a prerequisite in the context of treatment.

In "On Beginning Treatment," Freud (1913/1958b) states that "sympathetic understanding"—which, according to Pigman (1995) and to Shaughnessy (1995), is an incorrect translation of *Einfühlung* and is better translated as empathy—is a prerequisite for the patient's attachment to the therapist. Pigman goes on to say that, for Freud, "an empathic stance is thus a prerequisite for the curative agent of analysis, interpretation" (p. 246). As we shall see later, Pigman's view echoes Hamilton's (1995) claim that "empathy is an *enabling* rather than a curative factor. Pigman also notes Freud's cautious approach to empathy, particularly his concern that some analysts might invoke empathy to justify arbitrary interpretations.[4]

We believe it can be shown that Freud's cognitive style comprises a number of components that include inferences from cues that are loosely based on psychoanalytic "rules" and principles (e.g., of primary process thinking), pattern matching, intuitive thinking, and some elements of empathy. It is, of course, the case that all psychoanalytic thinking includes attempts to identify and understand the mental states (conscious and unconscious) of another (as well as of oneself). That one attempts to understand the feelings, thoughts, and, in general, mental states of another suggests that this understanding is obtained primarily through the operation of empathy. But that is not necessarily the case. For, as Schwaber (1981) has noted, one can try to understand another's mental state, so to speak, from the outside on the basis of inferences from verbal and nonverbal behavioral responses and cues. A good deal of the time this is what Freud does. As Eissler (1968, p. 168) observes, one can contrast an empathic mode with Freud's explanation of mental life based on observation of the patient's production and hypothetical reasoning. Let us provide one or two illustrative examples.

Consider first the well-known example of Freud's (1953a, 1960b) analysis of the *aliquis* slip. A young man quotes a Latin phrase and omits the

<hr />

[4] Contemporary Freudian analysts have no problem according a significant place to empathy as a part of the therapist's overall "analytic attitude." (See Beres & Arlow, 1974; Schafer, 1983.) For example, Beres and Arlow state, "empathy, which we consider of focal significance in our work as psychotherapists, is something that is easily taken for granted. We expect a good therapist to be empathic and we search for this quality in the candidates whom we select for training in psychoanalysis." They claim that "empathy is an essential tool in psychoanalytic work" (p. 47). They view empathy as a signal affect evoked in the therapist that leads to intuition based on psychoanalytic principles and knowledge and, in turn, to interpretations designed to promote insight.

word *aliquis*. He then associates to that word, and his associations include references to blood and a calendar. Freud then asks the young man whether he is worried that his girlfriend might have missed her menstrual period and might be pregnant, and, sure enough, the young man *is* concerned, even preoccupied, with that worry. Freud's thinking is very clever, highly intuitive, almost as if he can divine the content of the young man's mind. However, we would maintain that it is not an especially good example of empathic understanding. Rather, he *interprets* the meaning of a chain of verbal associations and makes an intuitively based inferential leap. Freud's clever conclusion is based on the reasoning (implicit or explicit) that, given the context of the Latin phrase (which is concerned with the idea of bringing forth, giving birth to a hero), the associations of blood and calendar can be interpreted to suggest a concern with someone being pregnant. Although the interpretation concerns the inner experience or subjective reality of another, it is not arrived at through an empathic mode, that is, through putting oneself in the place of the other. Thus, if one accepts Basch's (1983) idea that in empathic experience the "receiver experiences an affect identical with that of the sender" (p. 108), then Freud's interpretation hardly qualifies as an empathic experience.

Given certain basic concepts and tenets of the Freudian theory of psychopathology and of treatment, it is not surprising that empathy does not play a special and primary role for Freud in data gathering and in understanding another. In particular, we are referring to the emphasis on unconscious mental states and on inner conflict. It is the nature of repressed unconscious wishes that they are not accessible to conscious experience. Indeed, thoughts and feelings linked to these wishes are likely to be experienced as *ego-alien*, as "not me." Hence, empathy, defined as being in touch with what another is experiencing, would not constitute an especially valuable or indispensable tool in identifying and understanding mental contents that are barred from conscious experience. To understand another's unconscious mental states, at the very least, empathic listening would need to be supplemented by or perhaps even made secondary to the activity of interpretation that is based on both an intuitive and a theoretical understanding of such matters as the connections among associations, of primary process thinking, of compromise formations, and of other mental processes. Put perhaps in an over-simplified way, an understanding of the above sorts of processes is not so much a matter of putting oneself in the experiential shoes of the other, but of having a theoretical understanding of how the mind works generally and how it works in the case of a particular patient, given his or her particular unconscious wishes, conflicts, and defenses.

The centrality of conflict in classical psychoanalytic theory is also relevant to understanding the role of empathy insofar as one side of the conflict is often inaccessible to conscious experience. Thus, for one who views conflict as ubiquitous, one would want to ask, along with Schlesinger

(1981): With which side of the conflict is one being empathic? And as Schlesinger (1981) also notes, "since both sides of a conflict are not generally in consciousness together, a balanced intervention, to the extent that it alludes to an unlikely feeling state will, by definition, not be empathic" (p. 404). What Schlesinger is clearly saying here is that, when one (e.g., a therapist) attributes a feeling state (or, we would add, any mental state) to another to which that person does not have experiential access, it is difficult to imagine that the person will experience the attribution as empathic. That is, if the attributed unconscious mental state is defended against, and is therefore, by definition, ego-alien, the attribution may well not be experienced as empathic.

Narrow Versus Broad Conceptions of Empathy

In the discussion above, we have been implicitly defining empathy in terms of grasping another's conscious experience. One could say, however, with perhaps some justification, that in stressing the grasp of another's conscious experience as a hallmark of empathy, we are defining the concept too narrowly. Are definitions of empathy that speak of grasping another's "subjective reality" (Schwaber, 1981, p. 378) or of "the ability to take on the life world of another" (Snyder, 1992, p. 319) intended to limit empathy to conscious experience? The question is difficult to answer because of the imprecision of terms such as *subjective reality* or *life world*.

Let us begin with the question of whether empathy goes beyond grasping or understanding another's conscious experience. Some conceptions of empathy clearly claim to do so. For example, Berger (1987) explicitly states that "in dynamic or psychoanalytic psychotherapy, the therapist empathizes not only with the patient's present state of mind and concerns, but also with warded off contents and conflicts, and defensive operations, such as repression, denial, and regression" (p. 3). Berger, along with others, cites Freud's (1912/1958d) advice to the therapist that "he must turn his own unconscious like a receptive organ toward the transmitting unconscious of the patient" (p. 112). The fact is that Berger's extended definition seems to contradict his own more modest definition of empathy as "the capacity to know emotionally what another is experiencing from within the frame of reference of that other person, the capacity to sample the feelings of another or to put oneself in another's shoes" (p. 6). For, in one sense, when one focuses on another's warded-off contents, one is not putting oneself in his or her shoes (see Josephs, 1995).

As another example of an extended definition of empathy, Schafer (1959) writes that the therapist is expected to empathize with "a hierarchic organization of desires, feelings, thoughts, defenses, controls, superego pressures, capacities, self-representations and representations of real and fantasied personal relationships" (p. 345).

We think what Berger (1987) and Schafer (1959) implicitly have in mind (are we being empathic with them?) is the assumption that, because processes such as defensive operations, superego pressures, self representations, and so on refer to what is presumably going on within the person, it follows that knowledge and understanding of these processes and of the person in whom these processes are taking place constitute empathically gained knowledge. One is, the implicit reasoning goes, understanding the person "from the inside." Such reasoning, however, if we are correctly characterizing it, is somewhat problematic. For, by that reasoning, a cognitive scientist who posits, say, certain information-processing operations to understand another's memory or perceptual performance could also be said to be empathic and to gain his or her knowledge empathically. The cognitive scientist, too, is trying to understand the person from the inside, trying to understand what is going on inside that person's head.

It seems to us that too all-inclusive a conception of empathy tends to support Reik's (1948) early and somewhat exasperated conclusion that "the word empathy sometimes means one thing, sometimes another, until now it does not mean anything" (p. 35). If, as Berger himself defines it, empathy involves knowing "emotionally what another is experiencing" and "sampling the *feelings* of another" (p. 6; italics added), how can one empathize with unconscious defensive operations that are not and cannot be directly represented in experience and feelings?[5]

A narrower definition would restrict empathy to a cognitive–affective sharing of the patient's immediate, conscious affective experience, whereas a broader conception involves a view of empathy as an experience of the observer that goes beyond the patient's current emotional state and focuses on what Hoffman (1984) calls one's "general plight," or—even more broadly—on the person, including his or her goals, ambitions, inhibitions, limitations, and so on. Here we come close to talking about an "appreciation" of others, for instance their joys and sorrows and their life history and current circumstances. This is part of what Schafer (1983) refers to as the "appreciative attitude" toward the analysand in his explication of the "analytic attitude."

In the broader conception of empathy, one empathizes with a wide range of aspects of the other's mental life, including unconscious mental contents that the other is warding off. Although we have a good deal of sympathy with Josephs's (1995) reservation of the term *empathy* for communications directed to consciously accessible ego-syntonic mental contents, it is the case that many analysts, including Freudian analysts, use a more

---

[5] Holt (personal communication, July 20, 1996) notes that, the claims of classical psychoanalytic theory notwithstanding, we are often partly conscious of many of our defensive operations. Hence, in empathizing with what is referred to as another's unconscious defensive operations, we make a partial identification with that other person and recognize that we ourselves engage in very similar defensive operations.

extended conception of empathy. For example, as is clear from their case examples, Beres and Arlow (1974) appear to believe that a therapist can empathize with how the patient would feel *if and when* he or she became consciously aware of the unconscious wishes, conflicts, fantasies, and other mental contents that are being warded off.

Thus, in contrast to defining empathy or the empathic stance in terms of another's current conscious experience, one could say that it includes the attempt to imagine how someone would feel if he or she became aware of an unconscious mental content or even with how he or she might feel in reaction to a particular future event (e.g., graduation, job promotion, or the loss of a loved one). If one focuses on the patient's feeling of being understood as a meaningful test or criterion of whether the therapist's stance is empathic, then one can legitimately imagine something such as "conditional empathy" (i.e., a sense of how the patient would feel if and when *x* occurred). Also, in contrast to Josephs (1995), suggestion that the term *empathy* be reserved for interventions that address ego-syntonic experiences, one can legitimately say that a therapist is being empathic even when he or she is interpreting unconscious, ego-alien, or ego-dystonic material.

Limits to the Concept of Empathy

What are the reasonable limits, then, for the concept of empathy? It seems to us that a useful rule of thumb, even for a broad conception of empathy, is to limit the term to those mental contents and phenomena that *could*, in principle, be consciously experienced. According to this rule of thumb, insofar as they are inaccessible to conscious awareness, one could not empathize with another's automatic defensive processes, although one could empathize with the person's concerns and fears that motivated these defensive processes and with what the individual would feel and think if and when these defenses were no longer operating or were not operating to the same degree. Using this rule of thumb, one can avoid labeling as empathy every activity in which one is attempting to understand the mental processes and operations of another. Thus, as noted earlier, one would not describe the cognitive scientist's attempt to understand, say, the computational or representational processes of another as an empathic activity. To do so would truly render the term meaningless.

PROCESSES BY WHICH EMPATHY OPERATES

Assume for the moment that empathy is a special method of gaining knowledge of and understanding another. The very next question one would want to ask is: How does it operate? If, as Kohut (1971, 1977) maintains, it does not operate through our five senses, how does it operate? What specific processes are involved?

There have been a variety of answers—and debates over those answers—in the psychoanalytic literature. There is not sufficient space to review all this material with any degree of comprehensiveness, but they have covered a wide range. Some have suggested that the process of empathy is sufficiently mysterious that is cannot be specified any further. For example, Kohut (1966) writes that

> through empathy we aim at discerning, in one single act of recognition, complex psychological configurations which we could either define only through the laborious presentation of a host of details or which it may even be beyond our ability to define. (p. 262)

Other psychoanalytic writers have invoked somewhat mysterious unconscious communication or even telepathic communication (e.g., Major & Miller, 1984), but there are some notable exceptions to the somewhat obscurantist and mystifying accounts of empathy. For example, Buie (1984) describes "empathy as an inferential process that depends on ordinary observation of behavioral cues provided by the patient" (p. 131). Buie (1981) cites Freud's (1915/1958a) statement "that other people, too, possess a consciousness is an inference which we draw by analogy from their observable utterances and actions" (p. 169) and adds that "what Freud writes about our means of 'knowing' the consciousness of fellow human beings applies to our knowing anything at all about the content of another person's mind. We have no *direct* knowledge about the mental experience of another person" (p. 292).

As Beres and Arlow (1974) note, empathy requires the capacity to maintain stable self and object representations. Thus, empathy entails a partial, transient identification that is reflected in the therapist feeling not only *with* the patient but *about* the patient as well. Empathy requires an observation (or, a simultaneous experience) of being both an observing and an experiencing ego vis-à-vis the patient. There is no necessary antithesis between these two perspectives. Beres and Arlow emphasize the role of "signal affects" in the analyst, based on momentary identification with the patient, as a clue to what the patient may be experiencing. Although Beres and Arlow stress that the signal affect often is an important clue to the emergence of an unconscious fantasy, we may regard such signal affects as cues to a potential empathic grasp of any aspect of the patient's experience.

An especially serious attempt in the psychoanalytic literature to specify the processes through which empathic understanding is achieved has been made by Basch (1983). He speculates

> that because their respective autonomic nervous systems are genetically programmed to respond in like fashion, a given affective expression by a member of a particular species tends to recruit a similar response in

other members of that species . . . this is done through the promotion of an unconscious autonomic . . . imitation of the sender's bodily state and facial expression by the receiver. This then generates in the receiver the autonomic response associated with that bodily state and facial expression, which is to say, the receiver experiences an affect identical with that of the sender. (p. 108)[6]

Basch then goes on to say that one's own affective response that

is first identified as . . . resonance with another . . . leads to a reasoned, though not necessarily conscious, interpretation of what this means or says about the other; this postulated conclusion about the other's mental state is then subjected to validation or disconfirmation by testing against reality through further reflection, observation, or experimentation. (p. 111)

Both the content and the context of the above remarks make clear that Basch (1983) wants to counter and dispute the ideas that empathy excludes "inference, judgement, and other aspects of reasoning thought which are equally important to the concept of *Einfühlung*" (p. 110) and that empathy means "arriving at understanding of another person by experiencing or sharing his feelings with him" (p. 110). Instead, Basch wants to argue that empathic understanding involves inference, judgment, and confirmation or disconfirmation on the basis of "further reflection, observation, or experimentation" (p. 110).

Some additional comments that give one a sense of how Basch understands empathy include the following: "The analyst's facial expression and other bodily movements are in response to the patient's affective communications and represent a necessary precursor to reaching empathic understanding" (footnote 8, p. 113).[7] Empathy "is a considered judgement that there is a correspondence between what we are feeling and what, in the case of the analytic situations, the analysand is experiencing, consciously or unconsciously" (p. 114).

What is one to make of Basch's (1983) conception of empathy? Basch's formulation, because it constitutes a serious and sustained attempt to specify what he means by empathy and the processes involved in empathic understanding, reveals the confusions, questionable assumptions, and contradictions that characterize a good deal of the psychoanalytic literature in this area. Let us elaborate on this further. As we have seen, according to Basch, in empathy "the receiver experiences an affect *identical* [italics added] with

---

[6] Holt (personal communication, July 20, 1996) notes that any adequate explanatory account of empathy has to include consideration of individual differences in empathic performance. Basch's formulation focuses on a universal, species-wide tendency and does not appear to account for individual differences.

[7] As Holt (personal communication, July 20, 1996) points out, Basch's description does not seem to distinguish between emotional contagion and mature empathy (see Holt, 1969).

that of the sender" (p. 108).[8] But if the receiver's affect is *identical* to that of the sender, why is there any further need for reflection, judgment, confirmation, or disconfirmation? Were the receiver's affect identical to that of the sender, empathy would always and automatically be accurate—something that is often implied in the psychoanalytic literature.

We also question Basch's insistence that "facial expression and other bodily movements are . . . a necessary precursor to reaching empathic understanding" (footnote 8, p. 113). There is little empirical evidence that we know of that indicates that facial expression and bodily movements, in response to another's affective communication, regularly precede and are necessary precursors to empathic understanding.

An example of empathic experience involving neither facial expression and bodily movements nor direct affective communication is taken from a recent personal experience. One of the authors was informed that a good friend of his is suffering from a fatal illness. He imagined—including a visual image of what his friend would be experiencing—the pain, the fear, and the despair. One emotion-filled thought was, "My God, what he must be feeling," and this recurrent thought was accompanied by feeling small doses of what he imagined the friend was feeling. And whatever the psychoanalytic debate about whether or not identification, as technically defined in psychoanalytic theory, is involved in empathy, it is quite clear that, as defined commonsensically in ordinary discourse, he did identify with his friend. He certainly imagined what he would feel were he in his friend's situation. Furthermore, one can be fairly sure that the empathic sense of what his friend was experiencing is probably accurate and that the accuracy is based on knowledge of his friend, knowledge of how people generally react to such terrible news, and the feeling of what one would experience were one facing what this friend is facing. There is nothing mysterious in any of this, and we do not believe that it is necessary to appeal to a process involving the perception of one's own facial expression and body movements.

Countertransference and Empathy

We consider next the relation between countertransference and empathy. Much depends on how one defines countertransference. When the term is defined in the traditional way, referring to the therapist's unresolved conflicts and blind spots, countertransference reactions are antithetical to empathy. However, in the more recent "totalistic" conception of countertransference (see Eagle & Wolitzky, 1992), which includes any and all

---

[8] It is not clear why empathic understanding should be limited to affective experience. Can one not also try to gain an empathic understanding of another's way of thinking, intentions, goals, and so on?

affective reactions on the part of the therapist, countertransference logically has to comprise empathy as a sub-category. Let us explain what we mean. Recall that in Basch's (1983) conception of empathy, the therapist has an affective response that he or she then subjects to reflection and evaluation. But this is precisely how countertransference is frequently discussed in the recent psychoanalytic literature.

In many recent discussions, the therapist's countertransference reactions are held to be a valuable and even indispensable key to what is going on in the patient. Indeed, one sometimes gets the impression that for some the therapist's countertransference reactions are a certain and infallible indication of the mental state of the patient, requiring no further effort at validation or disconfirmation. Does this not begin to sound remarkably parallel to the claim that in empathic experience the therapist "experiences an affect identical with that of the sender"? It seems to us that in some accounts of countertransference, it is virtually indistinguishable, in certain respects, from empathy—which is quite ironic when one considers that in its original meaning countertransference is incompatible with empathic experience. The issue is an interesting one but cannot be pursued any further in this chapter because of space limitations.

Projective Identification and Empathy

One of the most extensive, systematic, and provocative discussions of the role of empathy as a means of understanding the patient is found in Tansey and Burke (1989). As the subtitle of their book, *From Projective Identification to Empathy*, suggests, Tansey and Burke maintain that "when empathy occurs, projective identification is always involved. The experience of empathy on the therapist's part always involves the reception and processing of a projective identification transmitted by the patient." (p. 195). In taking this position, Tansey and Burke obviously agree with Schafer (1994), who writes that "projective identification is . . . an essential constituent of empathy" (pp. 416–417). (Also see Grotstein, 1986.)

What do the authors who claim that projective identification and empathy are inextricably linked have in mind? In a sense, a good part of Tansey and Burke's (1989) book is devoted to answering this question. We can, however, try to present the essential components of their (and others') reasoning.

We begin with a definition of projective identification, which, according to Tansey and Burke (1989), and others, is an interactional phenomenon in which one person projects an aspect of the self or internal objects "into" another individual, and through "interactional pressure,"

> unconsciously elicits thoughts, feelings, and experiences within [this other] individual which in some way resemble his own. . . . [T]he projector may stir up within the therapist an experiential state that to

some degree matches or complements the projector's immediate self experience. (p. 45)

Borrowing from Racker (1968) and Deutsch (1926/1963), Tansey and Burke (1989) refer to the former as a "concordant" identification and to the latter as a "complementary" identification. A concordant identification is defined as one in which the therapist identifies with an aspect of the patient's self, and a complementary identification is one in which the therapist identifies with the patient's internal object. An example of the latter, taken from Schafer (1994), is one in which the therapist begins to feel critical toward the patient "after an internal critic has been projected 'into' the analyst" (p. 416). Presumably, through his or her communications ("interactional pressure"), the patient induces a particular set of affects, thought, and fantasies in the analyst.

What does projective identification, as described above, have to do with the process of empathy? At the risk of oversimplifying their complex discussion, Tansey and Burke's (1989) basic answer to the above question is as follows: An awareness and examination of one's own experiential state—insofar as it is closely related to the projected aspects of the patient's inner world (i.e., aspects of the self or internal objects) and has been induced by the patient through interactional pressure—becomes the primary "tool" for empathic understanding of the patient. That is, insofar as one's experiential state is either concordant with or complementary to the patient's self aspects and internal objects, the best means of achieving empathic understanding is by being aware of and examining one's own experiential state. This involves not so much *putting* oneself in another's place as *being* in another's place by virtue of the other's projection and interactional pressure (i.e., projective identification).

Tansey and Burke (1989) state that how one receives and processes the patient's projective identification will determine whether or not empathic understanding takes place. For example, if one is too threatened by the feeling and fantasies evoked or induced by the patient's projections and interactional pressure, one may block full access to one's experiential state and will thereby block an empathic understanding of the patient. One can sum up Tansey and Burke's point here by saying that every projection plus interactional pressure on the part of the patient must be met with an introjective identification and a processing of that identification on the part of the therapist for empathic understanding to occur.

Although one can understand from the above how projective identification can lead to empathic understanding, what is not clear and seems arbitrary to us is the stark and unqualified claim that "when empathy occurs, projective identification is always involved" (Tansey & Burke, 1989, p. 195). Can one not put oneself in the place of another, imagine what the other is feeling, and have feelings that resemble the other's feelings without a projection being involved or without the other exerting interactional pressure? In our earlier example of being empathic with a seriously ill friend, one finds neither projection nor interactional pressure. Among some of Tansey and Burke's (1989) own illustrations, they cite as an example of a concordant identification an analyst's suppressed impulse to cry in response to a patient's feeling of sadness after the latter's pet has died. One can certainly understand why Tansey and Burke refer to the analyst's experience as a concordant identification. However, how is projection involved and, for that matter, what kind of unconscious interactional pressure is being exerted by the patient? To assume that interactional pressure is being exerted simply by virtue of the patient's reporting that he or she is sad seems to us to stretch the concept to the point of meaninglessness.

VALIDATION OF EMPATHIC UNDERSTANDING AND KNOWLEDGE

In viewing empathy as a method of data gathering, one is making the claim that it is capable of generating knowledge. The nature of such a claim is that through imaginatively putting oneself in another's place, that is, through partial identification with another, one can acquire knowledge of another's mental states. But knowledge claims are just that, claims, and the question of their accuracy and validation needs to be considered. Given the intuitive conviction that often accompanies empathic experiences, this question is often overlooked. And, as we have seen earlier, the implicit and false assumption often seems to be made that empathically based knowledge is privileged and self-validating. Hence, it is not surprising that there is little in the psychoanalytic literature that deals specifically with the question of how one goes about validating or disconfirming claims of empathic understanding and of empathically derived knowledge. As we have seen, there is some talk (e.g., Basch, 1983) about subjecting empathic experience to the further tests of "reflection, observation, and experiment." But there rarely is a specific articulation of just how one would go about doing this.

Tansey and Burke (1989) devote an entire chapter to the issue of validation, that is, to "deciding whether or not the therapist's heightened experience of himself is a consequence of a patient's projective identification" (p. 47). In essence, their suggestions regarding validation consist in seeking "converging lines of inference in attempting to confirm [the therapist's] construal of both the source and the meanings of any given countertransference response" (p. 114).

Although Tansey and Burke's (1989) inclusion of validation issues is to be applauded, in our view, it is not likely to exert much of a restraining influence on those therapists who see projective identification everywhere and who tend to view uncritically their own experiential states as always having been induced by the patient and, therefore, as an unerring source of what is going on within the patient. Even Tansey and Burke, who are concerned with the issue of validation, cannot resist assuming the existence of projective identification when there seems to be no evidence for it and where it does not contribute to a clearer understanding of the phenomenon being described. Yet, they insist that "when empathy occurs, projective identification is always involved" (p. 195). It seems to us that this idea is based on a Kleinian vision, in which all human interactions, including or perhaps particularly those taking place in the therapeutic situation, are nothing but an unending sequence of bidirectional projections and introjections. Thus, according to this view (as expressed by Tansey and Burke), if I have an empathic sense of what you are feeling (a concordant identification), it is because (a) you have projected an aspect of yourself "into" me; (b) you have exerted interactional pressure on me; (c) I have introjected your projection and feel something very similar to what you are feeling; and (d) I process my experiential state "adequately" and achieve an emphatic understanding of you. A similar sequence holds for complementary identifications, the differences being that (a) you have projected an internal object "into" me instead of an aspect of your self; and (b) instead of feeling something that matches or is concordant with your feelings, I feel something complementary to your feelings. For example, if you are feeling masochistic (and are presumably projecting your sadistic internal object "into" me), I will feel sadistic toward you. However, in both concordant and complementary identifications, my processing and reflections on my experiential states will serve as a guide to your projections and interactional pressures—that is, to your inner world—and therefore, will serve as a source of my empathic understanding of you.

As noted above, Tansey and Burke (1989) do consider the possibility that the therapist's experiential state reflects largely or entirely his or her own preoccupations, conflicts, and so on and may not, therefore, be a product of the patient's projections and interactional pressures. However, and this is the critical point here, the possibility they do *not* consider is that the therapist's experiential state *is* indicative of what is going on in the patient but is *not* a consequence of projective identification. That is, contrary to their somewhat arbitrary assumption that "when empathy occurs, projective identification is always involved" (p. 195), in our view, it is commonplace for empathic understanding to occur *without* projective identification necessarily being involved. As noted, in the two examples of the therapist's impulse to cry in response to his patient's sadness and the individual's empathic resonance with a seriously ill friend, it is difficult to see how projection and interactional pressure are involved. And yet accurate empathic resonance and understanding were perfectly possible. Only a particular vision of the world of human interactions leads one to assume, in an a priori manner, that my empathic understanding of you always involves your projections "into" and interactional pressures on to me.

It seems to us that there are essentially three possible approaches to attempts to validate empathically derived knowledge, two of which are not essentially different from attempts to validate any knowledge claim. One is to use the traditional and reliable criterion of predictability. Put very simply, one says, in effect, that if your empathic understanding of P is valid or accurate, you should be able to predict somewhat successfully what P will feel, think, and do. The second way of attempting to validate empathic claims is the consensus of judgments of (usually trained) outside observers. The use of such clinical judgment in clinical research is, of course, quite familiar and has also been used in research on empathy (e.g., Elliot et al., 1982; Gurman, 1977). The third way of attempting to validate claims of empathically derived knowledge is to match such claims against the "receiver's" (e.g., the patient's) experience and report of being understood. (This has been referred to as "received empathy" by Barrett-Lennard, 1981). In effect, we have identified three validity criteria for empathic claims: (a) predictability, (b) clinical judgment of outside observers, and (c) agreement of the person with whom one is empathizing.

One of the problems in this area that emerges wherever one deals with multiple validity criteria is that there may not be a high degree of agreement among the different validity criteria. Thus, in the case of empathy, one may find that there is not much agreement, for example, between clinical judgments as to whether T empathically understands P (expressed empathy; Barrett-Lennard, 1981) and P's experience of being understood (received empathy; Barrett-Lennard, 1981).

For example, in his review of this literature, Gurman (1977) found correlations ranging from .00 to .88, with a mean of .24, between expressed empathy and the patients' received empathy. And Elliot et al. (1982) reported that although interrater reliability of ratings of therapists' empathy was quite high, the correlations between components of expressed empathy and client's ratings of feeling understood ranged from .10 to .27. When the different empathy components were combined to yield a mean empathy score, the correlation between the two rose to .42. The conclusion one can draw from research in this area is that the therapist's expressed empathy does not guarantee that the patient will experience being understood by the therapist.[9]

---

[9] One reason for these findings might be that "received empathy" is not a unitary, unidimensional experience. In this connection, Bachelor (1988), following Barrett-Lennard's (1981) five-phase model of empathy, focuses on the phase of "received empathy," that is, the manner in which the patient experiences the therapist's expressed empathy. She delineated four ways in which patients experience the therapist's empathy: cognitive (the patient feels understood), affective, sharing (the therapist discloses personal material), and nurturant (the patient experiences therapist as supportive). These ways of experiencing the therapist's empathy are not necessarily mutually exclusive. Also, they may or may not correspond to the therapist's intent or emphasis. Although the patients in this study reported that they felt that one or another of these modes of experiencing empathy facilitated their therapy, the study did not attempt to link these results to differential treatment outcomes.

All three validity criteria we have identified are precisely those that would be invoked in relation to any claim one would make regarding knowledge of another. Thus, although empathy may be a distinctive method of gathering data or of gaining knowledge, there is nothing special about validating empathically gained knowledge on more precisely, empathically gained knowledge claims. This has not been apparent because much of the psychoanalytic literature concerned with empathy has not dealt at all with validation issues but instead focuses almost exclusively on the empathic observer's experiences, on how empathy is experienced and how purported empathic knowledge is experienced and achieved. It seems to us that the failure to deal with validation issues flows directly from the basic philosophical idea, noted earlier, that *Verstehen,* or understanding, rather than prediction or explanation, is the proper goal for the *Geisteswissenschaften.* One implication that seems to have been drawn from this philosophical idea is that as far as the human sciences are concerned, it is the empathic observer's experience of *Verstehen* or understanding that is the sole validity criterion for evaluating an empathic knowledge claim. In this sense, any experience of empathy and any knowledge claim based on that experience is, in effect, self-validating. This becomes even clearer when one poses the following question: If the empathic observer's experience of *Verstehen* is the sole validity criterion for a knowledge claim, what would permit an outside judge to reach the verdict that an empathic observer's knowledge claim is invalid or not validated? The answer appears to be nothing at all.

There is very little in the psychoanalytic literature on the experience of the person who is the "object" of empathy (a major exception is the self-psychology literature that we will discuss later), that is, there is little on "received empathy" or what can just as easily be referred to as the other's experience of being empathically understood. The role of "received empathy" in validating empathic claims (in contrast to, for example, the role of "received empathy" in therapeutic outcome or effectiveness) intersects with a number of critical issues already discussed. For example, if one uses what we referred to earlier as the narrow conception of empathy—that is, a conception in which being empathic with another means empathically understanding another's conscious experiences, feelings, and thoughts—then it follows logically that "received empathy" is a necessary criterion for claims of "empathic resonance" and understanding. If, however, empathy is defined broadly—that is, as including another's unconscious defenses, wishes, and so on—then "received empathy" may not be a critical validity criterion. For it is possible, even commonplace, that for defensive reasons, patients may not experience "received empathy," that is, may not experience a therapist's communication as empathic despite the therapist's experience of "empathic resonance" and despite outside observers' consensus that the therapist has been empathic. If the patients' experience of "received empathy" cannot serve as a critical and indispensable criterion for determining whether or not the therapist has been empathic, what, then, can serve? As far as we can see, it cannot be solely or primarily the therapist's experience of "empathic resonance." This criterion, as we have seen, is self-validating. Also, what happens when two experiences or claims of "empathic resonance" directed toward the same person contradict (are not simply different, but contradict) each other? The two contradictory claims cannot both be correct or valid. If the experience of "empathic resonance" is also not an adequate validity criterion, what can serve? It seems to us that clinical judgement of "expressed empathy" remains as the rock bottom validity criterion for whether or not someone is being empathic or is expressing empathic understanding. It is difficult to see any alternative. (See also Tansey and Burke's, 1989, discussion of validation.)

One final issue needs to be addressed here. Above we referred to both someone (e.g., a therapist) feeling or experiencing "empathic resonance" and someone expressing empathic understanding. There is an important difference between the two. The latter concerns the communication of one's "empathic resonance." Of course, it is expressed empathy or communication of one's empathic understanding that clinical judges are judging. One empirical issue that emerges is the degree of relationship among empathic resonance (i.e., T's experience of empathically understanding P), expressed empathy (i.e., the communication of one's empathic understanding to P), and received empathy (i.e., P's experience of being understood). Our guess is that received empathy will be more highly correlated with expressed empathy than with empathic resonance. We would expect that how the therapist communicates his or her empathic understanding will be more important than his or her experience of empathic understanding in influencing the patient's experience of being understood. If this turns out to be true, it means that it is possible that even when the therapist experiences relatively little empathic resonance, he or she may show a high level of expressed empathy and may elicit a high level of received empathy. It would also suggest that the therapist's communicative style might be a critical determinant of the patient's received empathy. In any case, these issues are ones that can be investigated empirically.

There is an interesting epistemological issue here. When one puts the question of empathy aside, the general claim that one has knowledge of another does not require that the other feel understood or agree with or validate one's claim. For example, I may have knowledge about another person that is based on information about processes to which that person does not have access or that is based on cues and behaviors that I can better observe than the person himself or herself. The validity of my knowledge claims about the other in this case does not depend on his or her agreement, confirmation, or feeling understood. It depends, rather, on such criteria as predictability and consensus of qualified judges.[10]

It is clear that much empirical work needs to be done in this area. Such work would include, among other things, exploring the relationship among empathic understanding, the patient's experience of being understood, countertransference, and the therapeutic alliance. There are complex and difficult questions to be encountered here. To give but one example, the patient's sense of feeling understood does not necessarily mean that the therapist has offered an accurate interpretation. An inexact interpretation (Glover, 1955) might be warmly and appreciatively embraced if it promises to spare the patient from a more painful realization.

EMPATHY AS A THERAPEUTIC AGENT

Most analysts and therapists, classical or otherwise, would simply take it for granted that it is important for the therapist to have an empathic understanding of the patient's experience and psychic life. The issue is the therapeutic role given to such understanding. As noted earlier, Freud viewed empathy as a prerequisite for the therapeutic relationship rather than as a direct "curative" agent in psychoanalytic treatment. Thus, in classical conceptions of treatment, it plays what Hamilton (1981) refers to as an "*enabling*" role in treatment, which, in turn, permits the operation of the purported truly efficacious factors such as interpretation, insight, lifting repressions, awareness, and working through.

Thus, Hamilton (1995) writes,

> in the context of the therapeutic alliance, empathy is an *enabling* rather than a curative factor; that is, via empathic listening and observation, the analyst/therapist becomes aware of the patient's conflictual world, and in so doing, facilitates the passage from unconscious to conscious, which then permits the working through and structural revision of drive and object relations pathology through the vehicle of interpretation. (p. 534)

Hamilton (1995) makes explicit an assumption that is central to the classical view of treatment—namely, that the primary "curative" factors in psychoanalytic treatment have to do with interpretation, awareness, and insight, whereas other therapeutic factors—such as empathy and the therapeutic relationship—function primarily as "enabling" factors that facilitate the operation of the truly "curative" processes. The rejection of this assumption and the elevation of empathy to the status of a critical curative agent

---

[10] Because an empathic sense of another can often be experienced in an immediate and compelling way, it can contribute to the illusion that one has unmediated and infallible access to another's mental states. Such an experience can blind one to the possibility (or, as some would claim, to the inevitability) that it is theory-saturated or driven by undetected countertransference influences.

in treatment are central characteristics of psychoanalytic self psychology.[11] Kohut (1984) explicitly states that insight and increased awareness are not sufficient or even essential for therapeutic cure. As Kohut (1984) puts it, "self psychology does not find the essence of the curative process . . . when we say that the unconscious has become conscious . . . [nor] lying primarily in the expansion of the domain of the ego" (p. 64). He goes on to state that "while expansion of consciousness and verbalizable insight are often encountered in the late stages of successful analyses, some unqualified analytic successes include in the main neither of these gains" (Kohut, 1984, p. 76).

The essential therapeutic ingredients for Kohut (1984) are empathic understanding and what he calls "optimal failures" or "optimal frustration." According to Kohut (1984), therapeutic cure consists of "the opening of a path of empathy between self and self object, specifically, the establishment of empathic in-tuneness between self and self object on more mature adult levels" (p. 66). Furthermore, the goal of psychoanalytic treatment is not making the unconscious conscious or replacing id with ego (as in Freud's, 1905/1953b, "Where id was, there shall ego be," p. 266), but rather the building of psychic structure through "transmuting internalization" and the resumption of an arrested developmental growth.

These formulations and concepts are somewhat vague and abstract and raise a whole host of questions: How and why is empathic understanding therapeutic? What are "optimal failures," and how do they operate therapeutically? What is "transmuting internalization?" What does it mean to build psychic structure and to resume developmental growth? To deal with these questions, one must understand something about how Kohut views psychological development and his conception of the role of empathic mirroring in such development.

As noted earlier, according to Kohut, the need to experience empathic mirroring in infancy and childhood is universal. Its fulfillment facilitates the development of a cohesive self and the traumatic unfulfillment generates self defects. The experience of empathic understanding in the treatment, then, constitutes the partial meeting of an earlier unmet need. The meeting of this need, in turn, facilitates the resumption of developmental growth and the "repair" of self defects. Our description is quite telescoped and may be somewhat different from Kohut's language, but we believe that it captures the essential logic of Kohut's ideas and formulations.

How does the concept of "optimal failures" fit into the above account? According to Kohut (1971, 1977, 1984), the patient with self defects forms

---

[11] Not all analysts sympathetic to self psychology view empathy as a curative agent. Basch (1983) writes that "empathic understanding is not curative in the psychoanalytic sense; cure is the function of interpretation. By the same token, empathic understanding is not a substitute for interpretation; rather, it lays the groundwork that makes interpretation appropriate and effective" (pp. 123–124). It seems to us that Basch's views clearly differ from Kohut's in regard to both the therapeutic role given to empathic understanding and the implicit primary role given to insight by Basch.

a mirroring transference to the analyst, one aspect of which is the demand for perfect empathic mirroring from the analyst and the experience of rage and despair when this demand is not met. As Kohut observes, such a demand *cannot* be met—one cannot perfectly mirror or perfectly understand another. However, in successful treatment the analyst's empathic mirroring or understanding, although not perfect, will not constitute a traumatic failure (as was presumably the case in the patient's early life), but rather an optimal failure. That is, the less than perfect empathic understanding provided by the therapist, although perhaps initially eliciting rage, despair, and other related affective reactions, will become increasingly tolerable and useful to the patient and will ultimately permit the patient to avail himself or herself of the empathic resonance that is realistically available not only from the therapist, but from other "selfobjects" outside the therapeutic situation. As Kohut (1984) puts it, the analyst's "on the whole adequately maintained understanding leads to the patient's increasing realization that, contrary to his experiences in childhood, the sustaining echo of empathic resonance is indeed available in this world" (p. 78).

For the reader who is not familiar with Kohut's self psychology, the meaning of the term *selfobject,* used above, will not be clear. Hence, we need to take a brief detour to explain the meaning of that term. Kohut (1971) defines the term *selfobject* to refer to a way of relating to another in which one responds primarily to the other's role or function of shoring up one's self. Kohut (1984) defines selfobject as "that dimension of our experience of another person that relates to this person's function in shoring up our self" (p. 51). Thus, the other is not really a separate other, but rather represents a narcissistic function.

According to Kohut (1984), one does not lose one's need for selfobjects in the course of development. Indeed, as seen in the following passage, he compares the life-long need for selfobjects to one's life-long need for oxygen:

> A move from dependence (symbiosis) to independence (autonomy) in the psychological sphere is no more possible, let alone desirable, than a corresponding move from a life dependent on oxygen to a life independent of it. . . . The developments that characterize normal psychological life must, in our view, be seen in the changing nature of the self and its selfobjects, but not in the self's relinquishment of selfobjects. (p. 47)

The issue, then, for Kohut is not need for versus relinquishment of selfobjects, but rather archaic versus mature selfobjects. An archaic self–selfobject relationship is characterized by a demand for perfect empathic mirroring[12] and a slavish dependence on the selfobject for self-regulation and to avoid the feeling of self disintegration (what Kohut, 1971, refers to

---

[12] It is also characterized by the need for the analyst to be a perfect idealizable figure with whom one can merge and thereby gain strength. In this chapter, we deal only with the issue of empathic mirroring.

as "disintegration anxiety"). Contrastingly, a mature self–selfobject relationship is characterized by an ability to find and make constructive use of the empathic resonance that is realistically available in the world. In an important sense, therapeutic "cure" is marked by the patient's increasing ability to benefit from the less than perfect empathic mirroring and understanding that are realistically available both in and outside the treatment. The patient who has been successfully treated would move from a situation in which he or she "had originally been restricted to archaic modes of self–selfobject relationships" to one in which he or she would become "increasingly able to evoke the empathic resonance of mature selfobjects and to be sustained by them" (Kohut, 1984, p. 66). Furthermore, as noted above, such therapeutic change is, in large part, due to optimal failures that in turn lead to small and steady increments in the building of so-called psychic structure.

Note that, in Kohut's account of the therapeutic process, positive change is as much due to the therapist's failures (albeit optimal failures) in empathy, as to the therapist's provision of empathy. For it is the optimal failures and the patient's working through of his or her reactions to such failures (rage, despair, etc.) that, so it is claimed, ultimately lead to the increasing acquisition of psychic structure. (It should be noted that there is no systematic research investigating the relationship between optimal failures and therapeutic outcome.)

CONCLUSION

We have attempted to describe some current psychoanalytic views on the nature of empathy and its role in the therapeutic process. Some of our conclusions that emerge from this overview are: (a) Empathy is a complex and often confusing concept; (b) in view of the importance it is given in the therapeutic process, it is surprising that there are so few sustained efforts to clarify its meaning; (c) most contemporary analysts, explicitly and implicitly, emphasize the importance of empathy as a means for gaining knowledge about others, including the patient in the clinical situation; (d) although many or most analysts would likely agree that the accuracy and validity of empathic understanding cannot be taken for granted, the logic of some analysts' conceptions of empathy suggests that it has an epistemologically privileged status and is necessarily accurate and self-validating; (e) there is a division in the psychoanalytic literature between conceptualizing the role of empathy as a direct curative agent or as an "enabling" factor that permits the operation of the supposed primary therapeutic factors of interpretation and insight. In our view, this is a false dichotomy insofar as the two sets of factors are inextricably linked; (f) one finds narrow and broad conceptions in the psychoanalytic literature, the former limiting the term *empathy* to conscious and ego-syntonic experiences and the latter extending the term *empathy* to unconscious and ego-alien mental contents; (g) there are different components and aspects of empathy, including the empathic experience of the listener, received empathy, empathic communication, and so on; (h) empathy has been linked to the concept of projective identification that, in our view, detracts from rather than contributes to a clarification and understanding of empathy; and (i) the psychoanalytic literature on empathy is characterized by a virtual absence of research and of systematic empirical data.

REFERENCES

Ainsworth, M. D. S. (1974). Infant–mother attachment and social development: Socialization as a product of reciprocal responsiveness in signals. In M. P. Richards (Ed.), *The integration of the child into a social world*. Cambridge, England: Cambridge University Press.

Bachelor, A. (1988). How clients perceive therapist empathy: A content analysis of "received" empathy. *Psychotherapy, 25*(2), 227–240.

Baron-Cohen, S., Tager-Flusberg, H., & Cohen, D. I. (Eds.). (1993). *Understanding other minds: Perspectives from autism*. Oxford, England: Oxford University Press.

Barrett-Lennard, G. T. (1981). The empathy cycle: Refinement of a nuclear concept. *Journal of Counseling Psychology, 28*, 91–100.

Basch, M. F. (1983). Empathic understanding: A review of the concept and some theoretical considerations. *Journal of the American Psychoanalytic Association, 31*, 101–125.

Beebe, B., & Lachmann, F. (1988). The contribution of mother–infant mutual influence to the origins of self-object representations. *Psychoanalytic Psychology, 8*, 305–337.

Beres, D., & Arlow, J. A. (1974). Fantasy and identification in empathy. *Psychoanalytic Quarterly, 43*, 26–50.

Berger, D. M. (1987). *Clinical empathy*. Northvale, NJ: Jason Aronson.

Buie, D. H. (1981). Empathy: Its nature and limitations. *Journal of the American Psychoanalytic Association, 29*, 281–307.

Buie, D. H. (1984). Discussion. In J. Lichtenberg, M. Bornstein & D. Silver (Eds.), *Empathy* (Vol. 2, pp. 129–136). Hillsdale, NJ: Analytic Press.

Deutsch, J. (1963). Occult processes during psychoanalysis. In G. Devereaux (Ed.), *Psychoanalysis and the occult* (pp. 133–146). New York: International Universities Press. (Original work published 1926)

Dilthey, W. (1961). In H. P. Rickman (Ed.), *Meaning in history*. London: Allen & Unwin.

Dodge, K. A., Bates, J. E., & Pettit, G. S. (1990). Mechanisms in the cycle of violence. *Science, 250*, 1678–1683.

Eagle, M., & Wolitzky, D. L. (1982). Therapeutic influences in dynamic psychotherapy: A review and synthesis. In S. Slipp (Ed.), *Curative factors in dynamic psychotherapy* (pp. 349–378). New York: McGraw-Hill.

Eagle, M., & Wolitzky, D. L. (1992). Psychoanalytic theories of psychotherapy. In D. K. Freodheim (Ed.), *History of psychotherapy* (pp. 104–158). Washington, DC: American Psychoanalytic Association.

Eissler, K. R. (1968). The relation of explaining and understanding in psychoanalysis: Demonstrated by one aspect of Freud's approach to literature. *Psychoanalytic Study of the Child, 23,* 141–177.

Elliot, R., Filipovich, H., Harrigan, L., Gaynor, J., Reimschuessel, C., & Zapadka, J. K. (1982). Measuring response empathy: The development of a multicomponent rating scale. *Journal of Counseling Psychology, 29*(4), 379–387.

Freud, S. (1953a). Fragment of an analysis of a case of hysteria. In J. Strachey (Ed. and Trans.), *The standard edition of the complete psychological works of Sigmund Freud* (Vol. 7, pp. 3–124). London: Hogarth Press. (Original work published 1905)

Freud, S. (1953b). On psychotherapy. In J. Strachey (Ed. and Trans.), *The standard edition of the complete psychological works of Sigmund Freud* (Vol. 7, pp. 255–268). London: Hogarth Press. (Original work published 1905)

Freud, S. (1955). Group psychology and the analysis of the ego. In J. Strachey (Ed. and Trans.), *The standard edition of the complete psychological works of Sigmund Freud* (Vol. 18, pp. 65–144). London: Hogarth Press. (Original work published 1921)

Freud, S. (1958a). Observations on transference-love. In J. Strachey (Ed. and Trans.), *The standard edition of the complete psychological works of Sigmund Freud* (Vol. 12, pp. 157–171). London: Hogarth Press. (Original work published 1915)

Freud, S. (1958b). On beginning the treatment. In J. Strachey (Ed. and Trans.), *The standard edition of the complete psychological works of Sigmund Freud* (Vol. 12, pp. 123–144). London: Hogarth Press. (Original work published 1913)

Freud, S. (1958c). Papers on technique. In J. Strachey (Ed. and Trans.), *The standard edition of the complete psychological works of Sigmund Freud* (Vol. 12, pp. 83–171). London: Hogarth Press. (Original work published 1911–1915)

Freud, S. (1958d). Recommendations to physicians practising psychoanalysis. In J. Strachey (Ed. and Trans.), *The standard edition of the complete psychological works of Sigmund Freud* (Vol. 12, pp. 109–120). London: Hogarth Press. (Original work published 1912)

Freud, S. (1960a). Jokes and their relation to the unconscious. In J. Strachey (Ed. and Trans.), *The standard edition of the complete psychological works of Sigmund Freud* (Vol. 8, pp. 1–236). London: Hogarth Press. (Original work published 1905)

Freud, S. (1960b). The psychopathology of everyday life. In J. Strachey (Ed. and Trans.), *The standard edition of the complete psychological works of Sigmund Freud* (Vol. 6). London: Hogarth Press. (Original work published 1901)

Glover, E. (1955). The therapeutic effect of inexact interpretation. *International Journal of Psychoanalysis, 12,* 397–411. (Original work published 1921)

Greenson, R. R. (1960). Empathy and its vicissitudes. *International Journal of Psychoanalysis, 41,* 418–424.

Grotstein, J. (1986). *Splitting and projective identification.* Northvale, NJ: Jason Aronson.

Gurman, A. S. (1977). The patient's perception of the therapeutic relationship. In A. S. Gurman & A. M. Razin (Eds.), *Effective psychotherapy: A handbook of research.* New York: Pergamon.

Hamilton, J. W. (1981). Empathic understanding. *Psychoanalytic Inquiry, 1,* 417–422.

Hamilton, J. W. (1995). Some comments on Kohut's "The two analyses of Mr. Z." *Psychoanalytic Psychology, 11*(4), 525–536.

Hoffman, M. (1984). Interaction of affect and cognition in empathy. In C. Izard, J. Kagen, & R. Zajonc (Eds.), *Emotions, cognition, and behavior* (pp. 105–131). New York: Cambridge University Press.

Holt, R. R. (1969). Assessing personality. In I. Janis, G. F. Mahl, J. Kagan, & R. R. Holt (Eds.), *Personality* (pp. 575–801). New York: Harcourt, Brace, and World.

Josephs, L. (1995). *Balancing empathy and interpretation: Relational character analysis.* Northvale, NJ: Jason Aronson.

Kohut, H. (1966). Forms and transformations of narcissism. *Journal of the American Psychoanalytic Association, 14,* 243–272.

Kohut, H. (1971). *The analysis of the self.* New York: International Universities Press.

Kohut, H. (1977). *The restoration of the self.* New York: International Universities Press.

Kohut, H. (1984). *How does analysis cure?* Chicago: University of Chicago Press.

Major, R., & Miller, P. (1984). Empathy, antipathy and telepathy in the analytic process. In J. Lichtenberg, M. Bornstein, & D. Silver (Eds.), *Empathy* (Vol. 2, pp. 227–248). Hillsdale, NJ: Analytic Press.

Mead, G. H. (1932–1934). *Mind, self and society.* Chicago: University of Chicago Press.

Meltzoff, A. N., & Moore, M. K. (1994). Imitation, memory, and the representation of persons. *Infant Behavior and Development, 17,* 83–99.

Murphy, G. (1947). *Personality: A biosocial approach to origins and structure.* New York: Harper and Row.

Pigman, G. W. (1995). Freud and the history of empathy. *International Journal of Psychoanalysis, 76*(2), 237–256.

Racker, H. (1968). *Transference and countertransference.* New York: International Universities Press.

Reik, T. (1948). *Listening with the third ear.* New York: Grove Press.

Rogers, C. R. (1951). *Client-centered therapy.* Boston: Houghton Mifflin.

Sagi, A., & Hoffman, M. L. (1976). Empathic distress in the newborn. *Developmental Psychology, 12*(2), 175–176.

Schafer, R. (1959). Generative empathy in the treatment situation. *Psychoanalytic Quarterly, 28,* 342–373.

Schafer, R. (1983). *The analytic attitude.* New York: Basic Books.

Schafer, R. (1994). The contemporary Kleinians of London. *Psychoanalytic Quarterly, 63*(3), 409–432.

Schlesinger, H. J. (1981). The process of empathic response. *Psychoanalytic Inquiry, 1,* 393–416.

Schwaber, E. (1981). Empathy: A mode of analytic listening. *Psychoanalytic Inquiry, 1,* 357–392.

Shapiro, T. (1981). Empathy: A critical reevaluation. *Psychoanalytic Inquiry, 1,* 423–448.

Shaughnessy, P. (1995). Empathy and the working alliance: The mistranslation of Freud's *Einfühlung. Psychoanalytic Psychology, 12*(2), 221–231.

Snyder, M. (1992). The meaning of empathy: Comments in Hans Strupp's case of Helen R. *Psychotherapy, 29*(2), 318–321.

Strupp, H. H. (1992). The meaning of empathy: Reply to Maryhelen Snyder. *Psychotherapy, 29*(2), 323–324.

Tansey, M. J., & Burke, W. F. (1989). *Understanding countertransference: From projective identification to empathy.* Hillsdale, NJ: Analytic Press.

11

EMPATHY:
HEINZ KOHUT'S CONTRIBUTION

DAVID S. MacISAAC

Heinz Kohut died in 1981 just days after delivering his final address, "Reflections on Empathy," at the Berkeley Conference of the Psychology of the Self. In his remarks he summarized and clarified his many thoughts about a subject that had consumed most of his professional life. Debilitated by a terminal illness, Kohut strained to deliver his talk because he felt a sense of responsibility for the many misinterpretations of his meaning of the term that had been promulgated by supporters and critics alike. He was especially concerned that present and future generations understand that empathy as experience-near observation is not some way of being "nice" "kind," or "curing through love" but rather that it held the key to further advances in the in-depth understanding of the inner life of man.

Kohut had not always been committed to such a perspective, so what caused him to alter his thinking? As one steeped in the tenets of traditional psychoanalysis, he was highly respected and admired by his analytic colleagues because of his conservative theoretical views (Strozier, 1985); at the same time, he was a man of great integrity who placed commitment to those under his care before unflinching allegiance to theoretical dogmatism. Because of his concern for the large number of stalemated analyses and premature terminations among his caseload, he began to risk his newfound professional popularity that had won him the presidency of the American Psychoanalytic Association in 1964 by publishing papers (Kohut, 1966, 1968) that raised fundamental questions about the theoretical and technical principles that had guided his clinical work for so long. When asked by a fellow scientist what had altered his thinking, he readily admitted that he "had more and more the feeling that my explanations [to patients] became forced and that my patients' complaints that I did not understand them . . . were justified" (Kohut, 1974, pp. 888–889).

In particular, it was the case of Ms. F., a woman in her mid-20s, who insisted that he be perfectly attuned to her every word, that taught Kohut (1968, 1971) about empathy as experience-near observation. For example, whenever Kohut strayed from Ms. F's experience by offering an intervention that reflected even a slight revision to what she had arrived at on her own, she became enraged that he was ruining what she had accomplished and "wrecking" her analysis. By relinquishing his traditional theoretical assumption that her anger was an expression of her resistance to the analysis, which he recognized was impeding his ability to grasp the fullness of Ms. F's experience, Kohut learned to see and understand things exclusively from her viewpoint, terming this mode of observation *experience-near*. Thus, in these moments when he captured her experience of feeling misunderstood and communicated more or less accurately what she was thinking and feeling, he observed that her previous sense of well-being became quickly restored. In time, Kohut hypothesized that this sequence of disruption and reparation of the empathic connectedness between analyst and analysand is an inevitable part of any effective treatment process; at the same time, he suggested that if these disruptions of empathy are kept to an "optimal" level (vs. "traumatic") level, they not only are not harmful but, in fact, can also facilitate analytic cure.

These observations from an experience-near perspective led to Kohut's understanding of Ms. F's need for recognition, a need he viewed as a "developmental arrest" due to empathic failures of childhood and that he later theorized to be a mirror selfobject transference. Thus, it is this experience-near mode of observation that Kohut viewed as empathy.

EMPATHY: TWO DEFINITIONS

Kohut was not content with leaving any stone unturned when it came to defining exactly what he meant by this frequently misunderstood term. Many of his writings (Kohut, 1959, 1971, 1975, 1977, 1981, 1984) were devoted to refining his definition of empathy as well as to demonstrating in a hands-on way how it applied clinically. But what has made his explications more difficult to grasp is that he defines empathy on two different levels: the abstract and the more clinically relevant. Let's examine these definitions.

Abstract Definition

Kohut addressed the meaning of empathy on its most abstract level in his now acclaimed 1959 essay, "Introspection, Empathy, and Psychoanalysis: An Examination of the Relationship Between Mode of Observation and Theory." Although not well-understood when first presented in 1957, this paper was considered by Ornstein (1978) as pivotal to the development of Kohut's thought because it established the methodological foundation for his later theories.

Here, Kohut defined empathy as "vicarious introspection," by which he meant that only through introspection in our own experience can we learn what it might be like for another person in a similar psychological circumstance. By this, however, Kohut is not suggesting that our experience could ever be the same as another's, only that our similar experience allows us to approximate what it might be like for the other. For example, one does not have to experience physical and emotional abuse in childhood to know what it might be like for someone who has experienced pervasive maltreatment as a child. An awareness of our own attenuated experiences of abuse (i.e., being rejected, "put down," and feeling unwanted) is sufficient to allow us to empathize (vicariously introspect) with another's more severe abuse.

By defining empathy as "vicarious introspection," Kohut establishes it as the "tool," "instrument," or mode of observation by which the science of psychoanalysis collects its data. In other words, it is only by means of introspection in one self and vicarious introspection in another (i.e., empathy) that we are able to observe a person's inner life (i.e., thoughts, feelings, and other mental states). This methodology is in contrast to the physical sciences in which data is gathered with the senses and instruments that enhance the senses such as a microscope, telescope, and so on. Hence, Kohut establishes psychoanalysis as the only "pure psychology" when he defines it by the two components essential to every science: its field of study—that is, the complex states of a person's inner life, and its methodology (i.e., introspection and empathy).

But why did Kohut devote so much effort to these highly speculative, theoretical issues? It was because he had grown concerned that psychoanalysis had strayed from the original methodology used by Freud in his earliest discoveries of transference, countertransference, and resistance. He felt that certain essential concepts being used in contemporary psychoanalysis were "foreign" to the science because they had been derived through methodologies more appropriate to other sciences such as sociology, biology, and physics. For example, Kohut challenged the cornerstone of psychoanalytic theory when he questioned the concept of the sexual and aggressive "drive." Well-aware that this issue had been the basis of multiple schisms between Freud and his earlier disciples, he made it clear that he was not denying the observation of a psychological state of "drivenness" (i.e., a self "lusting after" or "wishing to kill"), which can be observed through introspection and empathy but objecting only to a concept that Freud (1957a) and his later followers assumed found its origin in certain somatic sources. In other words, Kohut believed that the "drive" concept belonged more appropriately to "bio-psychology" or "psycho-biology" than to the science of pure psychology, namely psychoanalysis.

Thus Kohut's 1959 essay stands as a turning point both in his own thinking and in the development of psychoanalysis because in it he convincingly establishes the vital link between theory in psychoanalysis and method of observation. Although he acknowledges that all theories, to a greater or lesser degree, are "experience-distant" because they are removed from actual observation, Kohut maintains that self psychology is an experience-near theory because its constructs are derived from data collected through introspection and empathy. Thus, Kohut proposes the theory of the self as an alternative to the psychic apparatus of traditional psychoanalysis because he believed the construct of the self more accurately reflects human experience than does the id, ego, and superego.

Clinically Relevant Definition

Kohut (1984) offers a more humanistic and pragmatic definition of empathy when he states that "it is the capacity to think and feel oneself into the inner life of another person" (p. 82). The precursor to this definition is found in the German term *Einfülung,* which Robert Vischer (1873; cited in Listowel, 1934) suggested was used in the aesthetic experience to mean humans' spontaneous projection of real psychic feeling in the people and things they perceive. At the turn of the century, Lipps (1903, cited in Wispé, 1987) organized and developed the theory of *Einfühlung* for psychology. He believed that *Einfühlung,* which was preceded by projection and imitation, allowed people to know and respond to each other and that as imitation of affect increases, so does *Einfühlung.* Thus, empathy came to connote "feeling into" or "searching one's way" into the experience of another (Basch, 1983). For Kohut, empathy is that which allows an individual to experience another's experience without losing one's ability to evaluate objectively another's mental states. In other words, empathy is simply experience-near observation and nothing more.

In attempting to immerse oneself in another's experience, there are numerous misunderstandings about the process that can lead to misperception and error (Rowe & MacIsaac, 1989). For instance, empathic immersion is not a process by which one guesses, intuits, or magically perceives—that is, it is not some form of extra-sensory perception. Nor, as indicated above, is it the same as we would feel if in a similar circumstance. It is also not the same as "identifying with" or "becoming" the other, so that one is "flooded by" or overwhelmed by the intensity of another's feelings. On the contrary, in the clinical setting, empathic immersion is a slow and "plodding," "trial and error," "long-term" process by which the self psychologist "tastes" to an attenuated degree the "flavor" of the patient's experience while maintaining his or her objectivity.

Finally, a very common error—and one seen more and more in the self-psychological literature—is the equation of empathy with an action. In this regard, Kohut was clear that empathy is not to be equated with a "deed," "act," or quality in a person's interactions that is commonly identified with love, compassion, or any other intense emotion[1] (Goldberg, 1980). At the same time, Kohut recognized that empathy is relevant to human interactions only if it results in a response or action (or nonresponse or nonaction) that follows directly from one's experience-near observations. Hence, Kohut links the two, while continuing to recognize their differences, when he states in his final address that "introspection and empathy are informers of appropriate action" (1981, p. 529). In other words, it is only when a person is able to "step into the shoes of the other," "to see the world through the other's eyes," that one is able to generate a response that is authentic, accurate, and fitting.

For example, a mother's empathy may inform her that the agitated cry of her infant signals hunger, but it is not her empathy that satisfies the infant's need. It is only the mother's actions, her offering the bottle or breast, that will sate the infant. Or, a salesperson uses his or her empathy to understand a person's indecisiveness in purchasing his or her first car. It is not empathy, however, but words of reassurance and encouragement that ultimately persuade the person to make the purchase. However, to respond appropriately, the mother's actions as well as those of the salesperson must be guided by correct and accurate empathy.

Thus, empathy per se, used spontaneously in everyday interactions between people or methodically in a therapeutic setting, is neither positive nor negative; it is value-neutral. At the same time, actions resulting from empathic observations can serve positive therapeutic and developmental purposes or clearly manipulative and sadistic aims. In other words, the particular use of empathy is determined by the nature of the relationship and the conscious and unconscious motivation of those involved. For example, we know that generally a parent will use empathy because he or she loves his child and wants his or her son or daughter to grow to be a strong,

---

[1] It is, of course, recognized that there are exceptional situations with particularly disturbed self disorders, in which with some action or parameter may be called for. Such was the case with Kohut's severely depressed suicidal woman, to whom he extended his two fingers during one particular difficult session in her analysis. Kohut (1981) was clear that he was not recommending such a response (even referring to it as a "doubtful maneuver") but was only trying to show that there are times in treatment when a particular patient may require more than understanding and explaining. In other words, such actions are exceptions and not the rule.

confident, and loving adult. Yet, we also know that a parent can use empathy to cajole, manipulate, and even emotionally "wound" the child. Paradoxically, Kohut emphasizes that, even in this latter instance (i.e., empathy used for sadistic purposes), the mere presence of empathy in the milieu has a more beneficial, humanizing affect than the indifference of an "emotionally absent" parent who is psychologically unable to extend empathy to his or her developing child. As Kohut (1980) states, "To be killed by someone who hates us is preferable to being exposed to the indifference of persecutors" (p. 502).

THE USE OF EMPATHY IN THE CLINICAL SETTING

The use of empathy in the clinical setting is primarily for the purpose of understanding and explaining. Let me briefly review this two-step process.

Understanding

By thinking and feeling his or her way into the patient's inner life, the analyst comes to know what the patient is experiencing in the moment and communicates in some verbal or nonverbal fashion that the experience has been understood. This initial step is what Kohut terms *understanding*. It is important to note that capturing a patient's experience does not always mean capturing a single feeling. On the contrary, an experience may encompass a complex blend of inner responses, including feelings, defenses against feelings, thoughts, dreams, and the unique way an individual organizes his or her world. For example, one patient may readily express feelings of anger, whereas another may be highly anxious about their expression. Whereas the former may require a response that captures a single feeling, the latter may require a response that captures a complex blend of experience such as anger, anxiety, and agitation. The nuances of these differences will be illustrated in the case of Ms. M.

The effect of this initial step, and one that allows the analyst to know that his or her understanding is more or less correct, is that the patient feels generally understood. Of course, it is acknowledged that there are certain individuals who, because of their own tenuous self-cohesion, have great difficulty tolerating an empathic response. The capacity to distinguish between a patient's reaction to faulty empathy from the side of the therapist versus an intolerance on the part of the patient for correct empathy is one that requires clinical experience and training.

Explaining

The second of the two-step process in psychoanalysis is that of explaining. Whereas the first step focuses on communicating simply that the experience of the patient has been grasped, the second step uses the accumulated understandings accrued over time to explain the meaning of the patient's experience as it relates to past experiences, to the intensity of inner forces, and to intrapsychic dynamics. Although certain very disturbed individuals may require only the initial step for long periods of the treatment, in time they may move comfortably to the two-step sequence of understanding and explaining.

For example, a man in his late 30s, who had been diagnosed with schizophrenia and seen by me in an outpatient setting, could initially tolerate treatment only on an biweekly basis. Although he had not worked for some 15 years, his sessions for over a year repetitively recounted his efforts to finalize the writing of his résumé. He would obsessively recount in each session minute aspects of the task. Although at first I found it difficult to immerse myself in his experience,[2] I soon came to understand the vital significance this task held for him, and I always attempted to communicate the nuance of what I was understanding in the moment. For example, "I'm coming to understand just how important it is to refine your c.v. so that it reflects accurately your job history." To my interventions, he generally responded with enthusiasm, seeming to feel buoyed by my understanding.

Early in the second year, after I had offered a similar intervention, my patient suddenly turned to me and asked, "Is this therapy?" Puzzled by his query, I responded, "It sounds as if you're not sure." To which he answered, "Yeah, because I don't think I've ever been in therapy before" (despite his having seen a number of different therapists in that particular setting for over 12 years prior to his seeing me). In time we came to understand his response to mean that he had never felt so understood before. Shortly afterwards, he asked to increase his sessions to once a week, which in turn led to his revealing far more intimate details of his life. In this instance, treatment moved from the initial step of understanding to that of explaining, triggered by the patient's curiosity to understand particular aspects of his life and how they related to the past, and so on.

Critics of psychoanalysis may argue that explanations per se are "experience-distant" interventions that inevitably lead to empathic failures between therapist and patient. Though an explanation is necessarily more "experience-distant" than the understanding response because it encompasses aspects of psychic experience that transcend the here and now and is formulated within a particular theoretical framework, in principle they are not any less empathic. How much an explanation captures the fullness of the patient's experience, however, is contingent on the following: First,

---

[2] It is not uncommon to hear complaints from young, and even some experienced, therapists in such instances that "it is boring to listen to such patients because they repeat the same thing over and over." However, a long-term empathic immersion in these repetitive themes always teaches us that what a person reveals in one moment is never the same as another, even when the content is basically the same.

the patient's conscious and unconscious readiness to hear a higher-level empathic intervention. In other words, the search for meaning begins with the patient, not the analyst. Second, the explanation is given with sensitivity to the patient's vulnerabilities, that is, it is not offered rotely and mechanically. In other words, the analyst is sensitive to the language used because it is recognized that certain words and phrases automatically evoke a feeling of being misunderstood. Third, the theory that the analyst uses is derived from experience-near data. In other words, the closer the theory is to the experience of the patient, the more accurate and effective the explanation.

Finally, it is important to note that, although understanding and explaining are discussed as discrete steps, in practice they overlap. For example, the process of grasping and communicating a patient's experience (understanding) is an ongoing part of coming to a fuller awareness of the meaning of the experience (explaining). At the same time explaining—necessarily more abstract than understanding—must include the experience-near ingredient (understanding) for it to encompass the fullness of the patient's experience.

Some might wonder if this two-step sequence is not the same as what the traditional analyst does, that is, he listens and then interprets to the patient what he has understood. As indicated earlier, it is similar to Freud's original introspective–empathic stance but differs from his later technical developments in which he held up to his followers the mode of the surgeon, "who puts aside all his feelings, even his human sympathy" (Freud, 1957b, p. 115).

Thus the experience-near empathic stance of self psychology differs from the traditional methodology in the following ways:

1. Empathic immersion focuses the analyst's attention on what it is like to be the subject, rather than on the analyst as "target" of the patient's sexual and aggressive impulses (Schwaber, 1979).

2. Empathic immersion takes the patient's experience as "bedrock," whereas traditional analysis looks on experience as a compromise formation (Brenner, 1982), that is, further reducible psychic phenomena.

3. Empathic immersion not only focuses on the content of what the patient says but also is attuned to the patient's experience of reporting it (Basch, 1980), that is, matter-of-factly and with little emotion, hesitantly and with anxiety, or freely and with enthusiasm.

4. Finally, the self psychologist operates with a theory of the self that is derived from experience-near data, different than the more experience-distant, structural theory of id, ego, and superego.

TREATMENT

Although Kohut's Theory of the Self is well known, a brief review of certain basic concepts is necessary for the later clinical discussion. Through his experience-near mode of observation during psychoanalysis, Kohut traced the development of the self not as a concept or representation of the mind as in object relations theory but as a "supraordinate" construct that encompasses the entire psychic structure. He came to understand that as a result of empathic failures in childhood—due not so much to traumatizing events as to the unmet narcissistic needs of parental figures—the self becomes fixated on certain unmet needs for recognition, idealization, and twinship. Within an empathic treatment milieu, these needs reemerge in the form of mirroring, idealizing, and twinship selfobject transferences. By selfobject, Kohut (1971, 1977, 1984) means the *experience* of another—more precisely, the experience of impersonal functions provided by another—as part of the self. Selfobject transference, therefore, is the patient's experience of the analyst as an extension or continuation of the self, that is, as fulfilling certain vital functions that had been insufficiently available in childhood to be transformed into reliable self structure. The selfobject transference is different than the traditional understanding of transference in which the analyst is thought of as a separate psychic entity, that is, an "object" from the past (a mother, father, and so on).

The growth-producing process by which an individual is able to internalize the needed selfobject functions and to acquire the missing self structure is termed *transmuting internalization.* Kohut (1984, p. 70) came to recognize that this process occurs through a two-step sequence. First, there must be a basic empathic intuneness between the self and its selfobjects. In the therapeutic setting this intuneness or bond is the emerging selfobject transference. Second, manageable and minor nontraumatic failures of the empathic bond must occur. Kohut referred to these failures as "optimal frustrations" and viewed them as inevitable, not because they are brought about by some technical manipulation on the part of the analyst to facilitate cure but because the analyst chooses to understand and explain the patient's needs rather than to try to meet them.[3]

It is the empathic process of understanding and explaining that allows the treatment to go forward and the self to acquire the missing structures in what Kohut (1984) describes as a three-step movement. First, there is the analysis of defenses against the emergence of the new editions of the selfobject transference. Second, there is the unfolding of the various selfobject transferences and their working through. Third, there is the making possible the establishment of an empathic intuneness between the self and its selfobjects on a more mature adult level. In other words, self psychology does not view the mature self as achieving an ideal state of "separation–individuation," as certain object-relations theory would suggest, but it maintains

---

[3] And for those who interpret optimal frustration as a technical prescription, Kohut (1987) clearly asserts his meaning when he responds, "There is *never* any need—and by never, I mean never—there is never any need to be artificially traumatic. Simply to give the best you can give is traumatic enough, because you cannot fulfill the real needs" (p. 91).

that even the mature self continues to have a need for mirroring, idealizing, and twinship selfobject experiences.

THE CASE OF MS. M.

I would now like to turn to a clinical case example that illustrates how the experience-near empathic stance of self psychology works in practice. In particular, I will attempt to show how the two-step empathic process evolves naturally over the course of the treatment, resulting in the working-through process and the emergence of the selfobject transference. Although the treatment lasted for 8 years, I will focus only on the early years, including the initial session, a treatment summary and history, and a vignette in the 4th year that demonstrates how a shift from understanding to explaining was instrumental in the development of the selfobject transferences.

The Initial Session

Ms. M., a single woman in her mid-20s, was seen by me in twice-weekly psychotherapy during the period of time discussed in this case. Prior to the initial consultation, the only information I had about her was what I learned during a brief phone contact: that she had been referred by a colleague who was seeing her fiancé and that she felt a certain urgency to speak with me.

When I entered my waiting room, my eyes were drawn to an attractive young woman with long brown hair, sitting motionless, with hands folded and head bowed. She was unaware of my presence. Concerned that I might startle her, I hesitated before announcing myself. In the few brief moments of observation, I sensed that she was deeply absorbed in her thoughts, like a child lost in a daydream. When I finally broke the silence, she winced, looked at me with a start, and jumped to her feet. She quickly moved toward me with hand extended while introducing herself, in what felt like a business call, "Hello, Doctor MacIsaac, I'm Ms. M. Nice to meet you." After shaking my hand rather mechanically, she rushed nervously by me and into my office. As she passed, I noticed for the first time her man-tailored blue suit that she wore with an open-collared, white blouse and loosely folded tie. In time I would come to learn that this was the "uniform" she was expected to wear at her work as a middle-management business executive for a large brokerage house.

Once in my office, she stood rigidly as if at attention, waiting for me to signal her. When I motioned to the chair, she eased herself down and for a few brief moments appeared ill at ease as she shifted back and forth in her chair. When she finally settled in, I detected a certain heaviness in her demeanor as her eyes became fixed on the floor.

In a low and minimally modulated tone, Ms. M. began to speak, "I guess you're wondering why I'm here?" Without pause, she answered her own question, "Well, I'm here because my boyfriend urged me to come. He felt I needed to speak with someone."

Without explanation of what she had done, she went on to say that "Jim, my fiancé, is so totally distressed with me that I wonder if he'll ever forgive me." With increasing intensity, she uttered what would become a refrain throughout the session," I feel terrible. . . I've done something horrible. . . I don't think he'll ever forgive me."

As she spoke, I was aware of diverse aspects of her experience. It was as if she experienced herself as despicable and loathsome while being wholly absorbed in her thoughts, oblivious to my presence. I was also aware of my own conflicting reactions, a growing concern that she had committed some heinous crime while having difficulty maintaining my alertness. Although I felt curious to know what she had done that was so terrible, I found my interest waning as she spoke in a haltingly meditative fashion. I had the distinct feeling that she might continue without interruption for the entire session.

She spoke glowingly and with affect of her fiancé Jim and how "he deserves better. . . . He loves me and is always so good to me. . . . Besides, he had an abusive, alcoholic father, who has always been so cruel to him. . . . He doesn't need more."

Until this point, her eyes had remained riveted on a single spot on the floor, but suddenly she glanced furtively in my direction. In time I would come to understand such a glance as Ms. M.'s way of "checking out" whether I was "with" her. If my eyes were focused on her, she felt assured; if they happened not to be on her, she felt "blown away" and distracted. For now, however, I sensed only that she was temporarily moving away from her self-absorbed dimension and that it might be an appropriate moment to offer my understanding of her experience.

"Yes," I said, "Jim's had a horrible life, and he deserves to be treated better than he has."

Ms. M.'s acceptance of my understanding seemed evident. For the first time, she looked directly at me as her eyes reddened and her face appeared flushed with embarrassment. Her voice choked back deep sobs as she recounted the incident that had brought her to therapy.

"Jim and I went to my office party. . . . I got slightly intoxicated. . . . and I kept flirting with this man who is my immediate supervisor. . . . Jim became so angry that he stormed out of the party and left me there alone. . . . We've spoken briefly since, but he is so depressed that he's not sure he wants to continue our relationship." No sooner had she confessed her "terrible" deed, than she began questioning why she had done what she had done. As if answering her own query, she began speaking about her sickly mother, whom she nursed for a number of years before her death 3 years earlier. She told of how she had to put her "own life on hold" to be there totally for her mother. It was a "bleak time" in her life, and she wondered how it might have affected her ability to form a relationship because she felt frightened of commitment.

As she spoke, I was aware of a noticeable shift from her earlier self-absorbed speaking. There was a modulation in her voice, an assertiveness in revealing important thoughts, and a deepening curiosity to understand why. At the same time, I was aware that I felt more alert and interested. In theoretical terms I postulated that she had moved away from the solitude of her self-absorbed thinking to a state of self-assertiveness. It might be said that there was a tentative emergence of her own grandiosity.

Except for a few interventions on my part that I felt appropriate, and to which she reacted in a similarly eager tone, Ms. M. spoke without interruption. Then, with just a few minutes to go before the end of the session and as Ms. M. continued to speak in her stronger tone, I indicated that the session would be drawing to a close. Immediately, I was aware that she was disturbed by my announcement as her face seemed to writhe in pain as she began apologizing profusely, "Oh, I'm sorry—I didn't mean to run over—I should have realized that my time was up." I was immediately aware that my words had shattered her newfound assertiveness, as she now retreated to a state of remorsefulness and penitence. It was as if she felt she had overstepped her bounds and gone too far.

When Ms. M. dropped into silence, I indicated that there were still some minutes remaining, which prompted her to resume speaking. Now, however, I noticed that her eyes were cast down and her words were spoken more tentatively and with greater reserve. I was reminded of her more distant and self-absorbed speaking that characterized the earlier part of the session. She continued in this manner until the end.

As result of this first session, I tentatively postulated that Ms. M. found a refuge from a pervasive psychic trauma to the autonomous and assertive dimension of her self in the isolation of her self-absorbed thinking. Outside the soothing comfort of this isolated world, she manifested an archaic form of idealization in which she experienced herself as abhorrent and subservient vis-à-vis a malignant idealized figure. Kohut characterized this as an archaic self–selfobject bond, the result of earlier empathic failures. At the same time, I realized that her acceptance of my understanding resulted in a tentative emergence of self-assertiveness, which appeared strong and lasting, as evidenced by her generally more upbeat voice and her affectively charged reflections on issues that felt more relevant and connected than her earlier self-absorbed speaking.

Treatment Summary: First 3 Years

I will summarize briefly Ms. M.'s treatment and then report a portion of a session early in the 4th year, just prior to her increasing her frequency to three sessions weekly. It is important to note that identifying data, without altering anything essential to the case, have been disguised to preserve confidentiality.

In the following session, Ms. M. requested a second session a week because she felt an urgency to deal with her concerns about Jim and their relationship. Although it was the relationship that was the frequent topic of the early sessions, it was her need for self-absorbed thinking that took center stage as treatment progressed. Though Ms. M. showed occasional glimpses of her more affectively connected self-assertiveness, she was unable to sustain this strength. No matter what the topic, Ms. M. lapsed into what she came to describe as her "default mode," that is, her distant and meditative mode of speaking, in which she was oblivious to the world around.

At the same time, it became increasingly clear that the slightest distraction would disrupt the solitude and comfort of her self-absorbed world. For example, when my intercom buzzer sounded or if in her occasional furtive glimpses in my direction she found my eyes not on her, I was aware that it would inevitably cause her to falter in her speech and to lose her train of thought. In time we came to understand that, in these moments, the quietude of her private world had been shattered, causing her to fall into what she labelled the "black hole of my psychic self-loathing."

An understanding response in these moments of empathic disruption (e.g., "Yes, it's painful when you don't feel I'm with you") would frequently bring momentary relief, which was quickly swallowed in a barrage of self-deprecating accusations because of what she characterized as her "unreasonable expectations." After all, she would add, "you have a right to occasionally look at the floor, or out the window, or at your clock." Though such remarks would appear reasonable and might even offer validation from an ego-psychology perspective that her reality-testing function was intact, we came to understand the experience of her self in these moments as "despicable and unworthy" represented archaic aspects of an idealizing self–selfobject configuration. After all, how could one "so undeserving" expect someone so exalted and powerful to understand and accept the fullness of her needs?

Following Kohut (1971), I came to learn that these states of self-absorbed thinking resulted from early selfobject fixations and were sought after to temporarily soothe her defective self. They represented a refuge from the burdens of her life as well as from her intense self-loathing that chronically arose in interactions with others. For example, Jim would frequently complain that on weekends she would prefer to be alone, rather than spend time with him. Although his complaints did not accurately reflect her feelings, she accepted them as valid, and, in turn, they seemed always to exacerbate her sense of self-loathing, triggering off her desire to retreat even more. For a time she found herself drinking alone, smoking marijuana, and compulsively masturbating to find relief from her intense self-disdain.

Early History

As Ms. M. felt more understood in treatment, she grew more curious to understand the roots of her fixations. She was an only child of parents who married later in life. It was a first marriage for the mother and a second for the father. Although Ms. M. had fond memories of her father, a highly successful business executive who died tragically in a automobile accident when she was only 13 years old, her recollections in the early years of treatment centered primarily on the mother. She was described as a "highly anxious, needy, and dependent woman," who relied on the father "for everything," while turning to her daughter to serve vital selfobject functions in his absence. When he was required to be out of the country on frequent business trips, the father invariably reminded his daughter when he kissed her goodbye, "Be a good girl and take care of Mom." His words always left Ms. M. feeling "big and important."

On the other hand, Ms. M. always felt that being at home with the mother in the years before school was "bleak and burdensome," and she wondered if the mother were depressed. Ms. M. thought of herself as her mother's "special possession." Only on occasion did she go out to play with friends, while most of her time was spent "shadowing" her mother as she went about doing the household chores. Whenever Ms. M. attempted to work along with her mother, she was told that she "wasn't big enough yet." However, a communication contradictory to the "you're-not-big-enough" message would be forthcoming from the mother whenever she and the father went away on trips related to his business. Staying with the maternal grandmother, Ms. M. received daily postcards or calls, in which the mother's message was always the same, "Hurry and grow up, so you can be with us." In time Ms. M. came to understand that this meant "hurry and grow up, so you can take care of me."

While Ms. M. did well in school and was a "favorite" of most teachers, she always felt relieved to see her mother at the end of the school day. This relief, however, quickly turned to "depletion" and "bleakness" as soon as she and her mother were together again in the house. It was in these years that Ms. M. found comfort in the solitude of her bedroom, the prototype of her self-absorbed thinking. There, among her "family" of dolls and stuffed animals, she could experience her power and grandiosity and find rejuvenation for her depleted and defective self.

As Ms. M. moved into preadolescence, the positive counter-balancing effect of her father's relationship became more significant. She felt "buoyed" by his presence and looked forward to being with him on weekends at a private field club, where they played tennis together. Needless to say, his sudden death "shocked" Ms. M. resulting in pervasive "heaviness" and "self-loathing." She remembered feeling "sick" about the father's loss and a deep sense of responsibility to care for her mother as the father had always urged. After the father's death, her interest in school faded, her grades fell, and a pall of "heaviness" settled over the home. In time Ms. M. left college to care for her "sickly mother," who emotionally deteriorated after the father's death and became physically ill when Ms. M. left home for school. For Ms. M., this period was the "darkest time" of her life, caring for her mother like a nurse until she died 4 years later.

Though Ms. M. eventually completed college and landed a job with a prestigious financial firm, she found that after her mother's death "life felt stagnant." She was not depressed, but it was as if the daily routine of living had become "wearisome," and her only relief was found in the refuge of her self-absorbed thinking. On weekends she pursued "excitement" with friends in the form of "drinking, smoking grass, and chasing after guys." She had a number of men who "pursued" her, but she "dreaded the thought" of dating one man because it represented both a burden and a loss of stimulation. In time she found her self in a relationship with Jim because he "just wouldn't take no for an answer." Eventually, it was the "pressure" of the relationship that caused her to seek help.

As treatment progressed, I sensed a subtle but significant shift in the transference over the early years. While she continued to speak in her self-absorbed manner, I sensed extended moments during sessions when she seemed able to move away from the self-soothing idealized dimension of her own isolated thinking to experiencing me as a more benign idealized (selfobject) figure, with whom she could speak in a more assertive and affectively connected way. Whereas she had been obsessed during the first year by her "horrible treatment of Jim," the harshness of her self-loathing gradually subsided as she spoke more analytically about her "fears" in both relationships and career.

Concurrently, as Ms. M. felt less self-loathing and greater confidence and expansiveness in her self, she manifested an increased capacity to express feelings of anger in treatment. For example, in one particular session early in the 2nd year when I answered my phone because of an emergency call, she cautiously expressed tentative feelings of anger toward me. She was greatly relieved, and even exhilarated, when I acknowledged the validity of her complaint and accepted her "rage" as an expression of her growth. Numerous experiences such as these resulted in Ms. M. feeling stronger and more assertive.

Vignette in the Fourth Year

In the beginning of the fourth year of treatment, Ms. M. spoke with greater urgency of "getting on with her life" because she felt she had been "stuck in neutral for many years," unable to risk moving on in her career or her relationship. Although she wanted "more" for her self, she felt "held back" by a pervasive sense of "dread." For the most part, treatment was dealing with her "fears and anxieties" of pursuing more realistic goals away from her self-absorbed state as well as feelings of "disillusionment" and "meaninglessness" whenever she dared to pursue what she felt was beyond what she deserved.

The following vignette is taken from a session in the middle of the 4th year of treatment and after months of Ms. M.'s trying to decide whether to marry or to break up with Jim and whether to pursue her master's of business degree. In the previous session, she spoke positively of treatment and how much she recognized it was helping her; she even expressed a desire to increase sessions from twice to three times weekly to "get more."

Ms. M. was 10 minutes late for her session. As she entered my office, I recognized that her walk was slower than usual and her eyes were cast down. There was a reluctance and timidity in her demeanor as she slumped into her chair. In general, she appeared preoccupied and anxious, but unlike other sessions in which she would begin speaking right away, she sat in silence. Her anxiety was mounting and she seemed to be increasingly uncomfortable. I felt I wanted to say something because I sensed an escalating anxiety and difficulty in speaking. I wished to communicate my sense of her experience, so I said, "It's not easy getting started today."

Shaking her head in agreement, she uttered in a low voice, "You're right. . . . I can't get myself going."

As she sat in silence, I sensed a hesitancy as she struggled to find words. Then, as if suddenly discovering newfound strength, she spoke more forcefully, "I didn't want to come today. . . . I guess that's why I'm late. . . . I had to push myself here. . . . I felt different than usual, but I don't know why." She fell silent once again.

Maintaining my focus on Ms. M.'s experience, I was aware of her emerging strength in confronting her reluctance to come to treatment as well as in speaking her mind, despite the uncertainty of my response, while puzzling over it all.

Consequently, I said, "I sense a new strength in your confronting your reluctance to come, in sharing with her your thoughts, even if you're anxious about how I might respond, and your desire to understand it all."

There was immediate relief as Ms. M. responded in an upbeat tone, "You're right! It wasn't easy because I was afraid you'd take it personally . . . like I didn't want to see you. . . . But I feel it has to do with me, and I don't understand why."

For several seconds she sat in silence, appearing to wrestle with her question. Then, as if the answer suddenly dawned on her, she began speaking, "I had a dream last night. When I awoke, I was scared and I wanted to tell you about it right away; but as the time for the session drew closer, I felt less and less like coming." After another pause, she told the dream:

> It was simple—I was in the bedroom of my childhood home and feeling excited to be among my dolls and stuffed animals when suddenly I was panicked by the sound of a noise outside the door. When I awoke, I felt frightened.

After recounting the dream, Ms. M. spoke of her fear as well as her feeling "strangely calmed" by the dream. Spontaneously, she recalled a recurring memory of childhood,

> I was alone in my bedroom, ensconced among my dolls and stuffed animals, powerful and alive, until I heard the sound of my mother outside my bedroom door. . . . Instantly, I scurried around the room in terror, straightening up before my mother barged in on me.

In those moments, she recalled a "sinking feeling" that made her feel "horrible," as if she had "done something terribly wrong." With a deliberateness, she added, "It's the same feeling that has stopped me all my life."

Suddenly, Ms. M.'s words lapsed as she appeared anxious and agitated. When she resumed speaking, her voice was barely audible: "I'm embarrassed—I feel like I'm speaking too much—like I overstepped my bounds." After another brief silence, she quickly added, "I feel that sinking feeling again—and the pull to my self-absorbed thinking—like I felt as a girl when I went off to my room." After another long deliberate pause, she spoke more forcefully and directly, "But I'm not stopping myself like I did—I'm freer and more spontaneous—I just feel stronger."

As Ms. M. spoke, I was coming to a deeper grasp of her experience, not only of the present moment but also of the accumulation of the many moments over time. I recognized that what I was observing was a most significant development, a shift from her archaic selfobject transference (i.e., her "self-loathing") that characterized so many years of the treatment, along with her tendency to retreat to her self-absorbed thinking, to a more mature self-selfobject relatedness (i.e., an emergence of her grandiose and exhibitionistic self) in which she was more able to resist the pull of the "sinking feeling" and hold on to her strength.

With the above in mind, together with Ms. M.'s increased awareness of how her present experiences were a recapitulation of the past, I wished to communicate my understanding. I, therefore, offered the following explanation: "You're allowing yourself to feel freer and more spontaneous in expressing and confronting your fears, even in the face of this terrible annihilation that has plagued you since childhood."

As I spoke, I sensed Ms. M. struggling to hold back tears. Then, in a choking voice she added,

As you speak, I'm feeling joyful and sad. Joyful because you've acknowledged a strength in me that, more and more, I'm feeling I want acknowledged. Sad because my mother could never give that to me—she told me she loved me, but she could never say she was proud of me. She could only give me recognition if my thoughts and opinions accorded with hers.

Following this session, Ms. M. described feeling a continuous joy that lasted for several days. In the months following, she increased her sessions to three a week while her analytic focus vacillated between intense feelings of rage and sorrow, at first toward her mother and then her father. In time she was able to acknowledge that the strength (i.e., the mirror selfobject transference) that eventually emerged in the treatment was associated to the selfobject father, who was able in his private moments with her to enjoy his daughter's independence and assertiveness. This led to a deep feeling of admiration and love for him because she was certain that if he had been alive he would be proud that she was "becoming a woman." She felt "fortunate" to have had their relationship, even though she acknowledged that it ended far too quickly and tragically.

In conclusion, Ms. M. completed her master's of business degree and went on to find another more satisfying and successful job with another company in the same field. She eventually broke off her relationship with Jim and, after a series of unsuccessful relationships, found a man who she felt offered her the kind of respect that she had come to feel for herself. She discontinued treatment because she felt ready to be on her own. She did not, however, preclude the possibility of returning at some future time.

CONCLUSION

The contributions of Kohut represent a major turning point in the history of psychoanalysis because they have shifted focus away from the embellishment of long-standing theories to the primacy of empathy as experience-near observation, the sole methodology by which we access and observe a person's inner life. Although Freud used introspection and empathy in the discovery of his original theories of transference and resistance, it might be said that Kohut has systematized this approach and made it the cornerstone on which psychoanalytic theory is built and treatment proceeds.

Although I have reviewed empathy's meaning on the various levels that Kohut considered, I have attempted to show in my vignette of Ms. M. how this approach is used in the clinical setting for the purpose of understanding and explaining patients' needs, not meeting them. In other words, the self psychologist is not using his or her experience-near approach, as some mistakenly suggest, to be "kind," "nice," or to "cure one's patients through love."

Similar to the great discoverers of the past who summoned their fellow humans to follow them into the uncharted waters beyond their view, Kohut has offered a comparable challenge. He has invited all who desire to explore the depths of human experience to plunge into that complex and obscure world. There may be a goldmine of riches, he suggests, if we are able to be free from the restraints of our various narcissistic predilections (i.e., personal, theoretical, social, and so on) to become immersed in the depths of a person's inner life. This is his legacy and our challenge.

REFERENCES

Basch, M. F. (1980). *Doing psychotherapy.* New York: Basic Books.

Basch, M. F. (1983). Empathic understanding: A review of the concept and some theoretical considerations. *Journal of the American Psychoanalytic Association, 31,* 102–126.

Brenner, C. (1982). *The mind in conflict.* New York: International Universities Press.

Freud, S. (1957a). Instincts and their vicissitudes. In J. Strachey (Ed. and Trans.), *The standard edition of the complete psychological works of Sigmund Freud* (Vol. 14, pp. 117–140). (Original work published 1915)

Freud, S. (1957b). Recommendations to physicians practicing psychoanalysis. In J. Strachey (Ed. and Trans.), *The standard edition of the complete psychological works of Sigmund Freud* (Vol. 12, pp. 111–120). (Original work published 1912)

Goldberg, A. (1980). Compassion, empathy and understanding. In J. Mishne (Ed.), *Psychotherapy and training in social work* (pp. 230–240). New York: Gardner Press.

Kohut, H. (1959). Introspection, empathy, and psychoanalysis: An examination of the relationship between mode of observation and theory. In P. H. Ornstein (Ed.), *The search for the self* (Vol. 1, pp. 205–232). New York: International Universities Press.

Kohut, H. (1966). Forms and transformations of narcissism. *Journal of the American Psychoanalytic Association, 14,* 243–272.

Kohut, H. (1968). The psychoanalytic treatment of narcissistic personality disorders, outline of a systematic approach. *The Psychoanalytic Study of the Child, 23,* 86–113.

Kohut, H. (1971). *The analysis of the self.* New York: International Universities Press.

Kohut, H. (1974). Letter of May 16, 1974. In P. H. Ornstein (Ed.), *The search for the self* (Vol. 2, pp. 888–891). New York: International Universities Press.

Kohut, H. (1975). The psychoanalyst in the community of scholars. In P. H. Ornstein (Ed.), *The search for the self* (Vol. 2, pp. 685–724). New York: International Universities Press.

Kohut, H. (1977). *The restoration of the self.* New York: International Universities Press.

Kohut, H. (1980). Selected problems in self psychological theory. In P. H. Ornstein (Ed.), *The search for the self* (Vol. 4, pp. 489–523). New York: International Universities Press.

Kohut, H. (1981). On empathy. In P. H. Ornstein (Ed.), *The search for the self* (Vol. 4, pp. 525–535). New York: International Universities Press.

Kohut, H. (1984). *How does analysis cure?* Chicago: The University of Chicago Press.

Kohut, H. (1987). *The Kohut seminars on self psychology and psychotherapy with adolescents and young adults.* New York: Norton.

Listowel, E. (1934). *A critical history of aesthetics.* London: Allen & Unwin.

Ornstein, P. H. (1978). Introduction: The evolution of Heinz Kohut's psychoanalytic psychology of the self. In P. H. Ornstein (Ed.), *The search for the self* (Vol. 1, pp. 1–106). New York: International Universities Press.

Rowe, C., & MacIsaac, D. (1989). *Empathic attunement: The "technique" of psychoanalytic self psychology.* Hillsdale, NJ: Jason Aronson.

Schwaber, E. (1979). On the "self" within the matrix of analytic theory: Some reflections and reconsiderations. *International Journal of Psycho-Analysis, 60,* 467–479.

Strozier, C. B. (1985). Glimpses of a life: Heinz Kohut (1913–81). In A. Goldberg (Ed.), *Progress in self psychology* (Vol. 1, pp. 3–12). New York: Guilford.

Wispé, L. (1987). History of the concept of empathy. In N. Eisenberg & J. Strayer (Eds.), *Empathy and its development* (pp. 17–37). New York: Cambridge University Press.

12

EXPANDING ATTUNEMENT: A CONTRIBUTION TO THE EXPERIENCE-NEAR MODE OF OBSERVATION

CRAYTON E. ROWE, JR.

There has been very little in the psychoanalytic literature that has addressed the technical issue of how we observe and perceive information from our patients. This lack of emphasis can seriously limit the opportunity for the development of the observational process and, as a consequence, limit the perception of data that could contribute significantly to the advancement of theory and technique.

This chapter highlights the importance of the in-depth attunement to the nuances of the patient's experience through a specific mode of analytic perception, "expanding attunement" (Rowe & MacIsaac, 1989). It follows on Kohut's (1959, 1968, 1977, 1981, 1984) teachings of the experience-near mode of observation, while emphasizing the ongoing development of perception during the treatment process to ensure the capturing of the patient's experience as fully as possible. In this chapter I have chosen to present an initial telephone communication, in addition to an initial session, to emphasize the clinical relevance of expanding attunement in a treatment situation where there is limited access to the patient's emotional life.

A version of this chapter was presented at the fourth National Conference of the National Membership Committee on Psychoanalysis in Clinical Social Work in Los Angeles, California, in October 1992.

THE EXPERIENCE-NEAR MODE OF OBSERVATION

Kohut was concerned that the field of psychology was moving away from what he referred to as the experience-near introspective mode of data gathering to an experience-distant mode of observation appropriate to other sciences but not to the understanding of complex mental states. This mode of observation requires the "commitment to a methodology of the observer's long-term empathic immersion in the psychological field—in particular, with regard to clinical phenomena, of his long-term, empathic immersion in the transference" (1977, pp. xxi-xxii). Kohut contrasts the experience-near mode of observing from within the patient's experience with that of the experience-distant mode of observing where the observer's focus is outside the patient's experience and on the patient's behavior or on the content of what the patient says or thinks (e.g., fantasies, thoughts, memories, and associations).[1]

Freud's Contribution to the Experience-Near Mode of Observation

Perhaps it would be more accurate to say that Kohut redirected attention to the importance of being attuned to the patient's experience because he repeatedly stated that it was the experience-near mode of observation that led Freud to his major theoretical discoveries. For example, Freud's experience-near introspective mode of observation with his patients led to the momentous discoveries of the unconscious, transference, the Oedipal configuration, primary narcissism, primary masochism, and infantile sexuality.

It is well-known that subjective reality became the domain of clinicians since Freud revised his thinking from the seduction theory to the fantasy theory as the source of neurosis. Freud (1916–1917/1963) wrote: "The phantasies possess *psychical* as contrasted with *material* reality, and we gradually learn to understand that *in the world of neuroses it is psychical reality which is the decisive kind*" (p. 368).

Earlier, Freud (1912/1958) gave us the technique of how to perceive the subjective world of the patient. He warned that the analyst must be all-encompassing in the listening process. The analyst "must turn his own unconscious like a receptive organ towards the transmitting unconscious of the patient. He must adjust himself to the patient as a telephone receiver is adjusted to the transmitting microphone" (p. 115–116).

---

[1] The term *experience-distant* used here refers to observations made from outside the patient's experience. Goldberg in his editor's note points out that Kohut seems to have expanded his meaning of the term to include how one has arrived at assumptions about normal growth and development and from a morally tinged posture (Kohut, 1984, Note 8, p. 226).

Experience-Near Observation as Empathy

The ability to observe another from the experience-near vantage point is the definition of empathy as translated from the German word *Einfühlung*, which refers to the ability of a person to come to know the experience of another. It is the "'feeling into,' i.e., 'finding' or 'searching' one's way into the experience of another without specifying or limiting the means by which this occurs" (Basch, 1983, pp. 110–111).

Kohut, more than Freud, developed and defined experience-near observation as empathy. From his early and more abstract definition of empathy as "vicarious introspection," he expanded his definition to the more clinically relevant *Einfühlung* meaning that emphasizes empathy as the capacity for experience-near observation. He stated, "the best definition of empathy—the analogue to my terse scientific definition of empathy as 'vicarious introspection'—is that it is the capacity to think and feel oneself into the inner life of another person" (1984, p. 82). By capacity, Kohut is speaking of an individual's unique endowment, inherited and developed, to perceive freely another's experience of mental and physical functioning in the moment and over time.

DEVELOPING ANALYTIC PERCEPTION THROUGH EXPANDING ATTUNEMENT

Implied in the views of Freud and Kohut is the assumption that the analyst has both unrecognized and unrealized capacities for perceiving and that these capacities can be developed.

Discovery of Capacities for Perception

A growing number of studies have shown evidence of unrealized capacities for perception in both infants and adults. Infant studies have challenged views that infants gradually construct schemas of the general properties of stimuli (Piaget, 1954). Studies by Spelke (1976, 1979) have shown that infants can recognize the temporal structure of visual and auditory events. When 4-month-old infants were shown two films simultaneously with one appropriate soundtrack, they looked at the film appropriate to the soundtrack. Later studies by Spelke, Breinlinger, and Macomber (1992) and Spelke (1994) have shown evidence for early developing capacities for knowledge (e.g., to represent physical objects and reason about object motion).

Studies on object permanence in infants call into question Piaget's (1954) beliefs about when object permanence occurs and what the processes are responsible for its emergence (Baillargeon, 1987, 1991; Baillargeon,

Spelke, & Wasserman, 1985). Studies have show a greater capacity for infant location memory (Baillargeon, 1988, 1989) and for seeking explanations of inconsistences than previously known (Baillargeon, 1994).

Adult studies on selective attention that dichotic presentation of material supported Kohut's assumption that long-term in-depth attention can be given to the experience of the patient without dividing one's attention (e.g., to theoretical concerns and meaning of the patient's behavior). These studies involved the use of stereo headphones to present different messages into each ear of subjects who were asked to attend to only one ear. Findings showed that (a) the subject's intention can be critical in determining what material becomes conscious (Cherry & Kruger, 1983); (b) one can consciously control the nature of attentional analysis (Johnston & Heinz, 1978; MacKay, 1973); and (c) cognitive resources can be allocated, and the allocation of these resources is under our control. We are able to shift cognitive resources onto important stimuli (Johnston & Heinz).

Numerous adult studies on divided attention have also focused on determining the extent of an individual's perceptual capacities (see especially Wickens, 1976, 1977a, 1977b, 1992).

Evidence of Development of Capacities for Perception

Perhaps the most striking evidence of one's ability to develop capacities for perception is the achievements of those who have lost their vision. It is common knowledge that adults who lose their vision or who are visually impaired can develop perceptual skills through the training of one sense to take the place of another (see especially Landau, Spelke, & Gleitman, 1984. See also Beggs, 1988a, 1988b, 1992, regarding training and psychological adjustment of the visually impaired).

Also especially significant was Dorothy Burlingham's (1961, 1964, 1965, 1967) work with blind children as part of the Educational Unit of the Hampstead Child-Therapy Course and Clinic. She has shown that blind children possess an extraordinary degree of memory as a result of their dependence on their inner world of experiences. She found that the children early on know not only their teachers, helpers, and visitors and where the furniture and toys are placed, but remember also cracks and unevenness in the wall or floor. Every sound, once noted, whether understood or not, was remembered to be referred to later. Burlingham (1965) thought that attention to detail has some similarity to what happens in analysis when certain highly cathected unconscious material is uncovered and details appear with photographic exactitude.

Development of Perception in the Analytic Situation

The above studies have given evidence to support Kohut's and Freud's assumption that the analyst has unrecognized capacities as well as the potential for developing perception.

I have attempted elsewhere with MacIsaac (Rowe & MacIsaac, 1989) to demonstrate how in the analytic situation one can develop one's potential for experience-near attunement through a mode of observation that we have succinctly termed *expanding attunement*:

> It requires continuous empathic immersion into the patient's shifting states of thinking and feeling. This is not only a matter of hearing the content of what the patient says, but is also an attunement to *how* the patient experiences what he or she says. . . . Expanding attunement is an intersubjective process whereby the analyst attempts as closely as possible to experience what the patient is experiencing, which incudes the patient's simultaneous experience of the analyst. It is not just an attunement to a specific affective coloring of a particular thought, idea, or fantasy expressed at a given moment; rather, it retains the cumulative moments of the patient's experience that the analyst has perceived and that continually widen and deepen the analyst's understanding. In this sense expanding attunement is the analyst's emotional canvas of the patient's shifting, changing, and widening experiences, which continually add new details to a slowly developing portrait. (pp. 136–137)

Intersubjectivity, as defined here, is the opening of two subjective worlds to each other as emphasized by Stolorow (Atwood & Stolorow, 1984; Stolorow, Brandchaft, & Atwood, 1987). However, our emphasis is on the continually changing and unfolding experiences of the patient experiencing the analyst experiencing the patient that take place within this intersubjective context. It is this developing, living portrait that adds to understanding and modifies what we have understood before. We might say we have before us the continually reforming portrait of the current summation of another's life. Oscar Wilde's descriptions of the changing portrait of Dorian Gray perhaps best captures how life experiences are carried forward into a continually evolving whole and can be understood only within the changing context of the whole. Attention to expanding our receptivity to the subtleties of our patients' experience of us as immersed in their experience simultaneously expands our receptivity to the subtleties of what the patient says (thoughts, wishes, fantasies, dreams, and so on) and to the patient's physical appearance and behavior. It is not unlike what is natural to all who desire to develop a deepening appreciation of works of art and music. We do this by immersing ourselves in the experience of the artist as reflected in a painting or in the rendition of a musical composition. Our attention to details and nuances is heightened as we capture the essence of what the artist has intended for us to experience. How common it is to see an individual standing for long periods in a museum before a painting to discover the yet-to-be-discovered subtleties of the many shades, textures, and colors that are blended and formed into the image of the artist's creation. Similarly, one can be reminded of the quiet, careful attention to an opera or a symphony. One listens sensitively to the familiar themes but not without attunement to the nuances of resonance, tone, and timing that have not been heard before. How much more could therapists learn from the experience of patients if they could bring similar empathic attention to the consulting room.

Of course, unlike capturing the creative experience of the artist as reflected in the work of art, immersion in the experience of a patient is an intersubjective one—where both analyst and patient mutually and continuously affect the experience of the other. It goes without saying that, although the process of empathic immersion is similar in its use for both artistic and clinical appreciation, the data or information obtained are used for different purposes.

The following is an example of how expanding attunement allows for a deepening awareness of the patient's subjective life. During a session, a patient suddenly sits up on the couch and forcefully turns to the analyst and says: "I would like to sit up."

From an outside observational view, the analyst will hear the content of what the patient is saying and perhaps acknowledge the patient's tone and inflection, the forcefulness of the patient's movements, the overall shift of affect, and so on. However, from a experience-near observational view with a focus of expanding one's attunement to the patient's experience, the analyst will be able to gain qualitatively different data. In addition to hearing the content of what the patient is saying and acknowledge the patient's affective states, the analyst will be attuned to the patient's inner life giving rise to the affects and content. The fact that the patient is anxious or angry is relative unimportant if the therapist does not capture as completely as possible the patient's continuous experience in the act of speaking and sitting. For example, the analyst may perceive a subtle fearfulness or hardly discernible moment of panic during the sitting and speaking, which is perhaps followed by a moment of relief after the forceful turning and looking. These experience-near data would point to the patient's behavior as evidence of vulnerability and fearfulness which might otherwise be understood as simply aggressive, hostile, angry, and so on.

It is important to note that expanding attunement to the nuances of the patient's experience heightens the therapist's cognitive awareness of the content of what the patient says, as well as of the patient's physical appearance and behavior. In other words, the therapist cannot be finely attuned to the patient's evolving experience without being aware of the ongoing translation into words, physical appearance, and behavior.

VIGNETTE

The following vignette illustrates how expanding one's attunement to the nuances of the patient's experience made it possible for me to become aware of a number of subtle yet highly critical aspects of the patient's experience in a taped telephone message. My awareness was critical in beginning the process of understanding the patient and making the beginning of treatment possible.

As stated earlier, I have chosen to present the initial telephone communication, in addition to the initial session, to emphasize the clinical relevance of expanding attunement where there is limited access to the patient. I have purposely attempted to describe in detail my efforts at expanding my attunement to demonstrate this mode of observation.

The Telephone Message: A Critical Beginning

Mr. X. left a brief message on my answering machine. He stated his name and said he wished an appointment. He learned of me through a friend and would like for me to return his call. He gave his phone number.

Though Mr. X.'s taped message was brief, I sensed that his speech seemed labored as if he were carefully choosing his words and modulating the tone and intensity of his voice. His frequent, short pauses seemed filled with what I tentatively sensed as moments of rising tension that he controlled by resuming speaking in his labored and measured way.

I am making an effort here to describe my experience-near attempt to immerse myself in Mr. X.'s taped experience. My attunement to Mr. X.'s message may seem to some like an aberration of the empathic process especially because only through prolonged immersion can we hope to gain meaningful understanding. However, I am suggesting that attention to the patient's first moments of communication—even a taped one—can be crucial to beginning the understanding process. For example, my attunement to Mr. X.'s message allowed me to be alert to a number of nuances of what I sensed he was experiencing: his guardedness, his rising tension at those times he paused, and his labored effort to continue speaking in an evenly measured pace and tone. It was the sum of these experience-near data that helped me to form a beginning impression of an individual who was experiencing considerable apprehension in leaving his message regarding an appointment.

Returning the Call

I returned Mr. X.'s call several hours later. His phone rang a number of times. Just as I thought no one would answer, I heard the click of the phone being picked up, but there was only silence. I waited to hear a voice, but I heard nothing. After some moments, I had the anxious impulse to break the silence with a "hello." However, I resisted the temptation as I kept in mind what I previously sensed Mr. X. was experiencing from his brief earlier message—that is, his seeming need to maintain a carefulness and evenly measured pace in speaking, as well as control of intensity and tone. I, therefore, thought to initiate the conversation might somehow be disrupting. I decided to continue waiting. After some moments, which seemed like minutes, Mr. X. said softly, "hello." I was aware that I experienced a feeling of relief when I heard his voice. I then quickly introduced myself and said that I was returning his call. I was also aware that at the moment I began to speak, I was removed from Mr. X.'s experience in that I was speaking out of my own frustration and need to move the conversation along. I had a particularly heavy schedule that day and was trying to fit the telephone call between appointments. I further thought that I might have even stopped Mr. X. from speaking after he said hello. Mr. X. was quiet for some moments and then in a barely audible voice said, "I'll have to call you back." He seemed shaken. I sensed he wished to get off the phone immediately. I tentatively understood that he was fearfully responding to my interrupting his carefully controlled pace. It goes without saying that my understanding could have been off the mark and that there might well have been many other explanations for his behavior. However, I chanced that my understanding was at least somewhat accurate as I wanted to communicate, before he hung up that, that I was aware that I had possibly imposed my pace on him. I spontaneously said, "I think I sound like a race horse."

Mr. X. said nothing, but I did not hear him hang up. Again, there were the seconds of silence that seemed like minutes. I was beginning to feel that my remark was pretty silly. I was also beginning to feel some embarrassment as I wondered how I could think of such a inane thing to say to a potential patient. Maybe he has already hung up and I didn't hear him hang up. I thought, "Maybe he was going to telephone me back . . . and I said that I sound like a race horse. How could he call me back now?"

As my embarrassment and discouragement began to mount, I reasoned I might as well say something to find out whether or not Mr. X. was still on the phone. But then, I heard a very faint sound. I couldn't tell whether it was a word or some extraneous background noise, but I realized that Mr. X. was still on the phone. Immediately, I felt relieved that maybe my remark was at least not as inane as I had begun to think. Perhaps it touched somewhat on Mr. X.'s experience, and, as a result, he felt understood to some extent and, perhaps, would give me another chance to speak with him.

Mr. X. began to speak in his characteristic slow and measured way. His tone seemed somewhat stronger and fuller than what I picked up in his earlier taped message. It certainly was in contrast to his anxious and barely audible voice when he told me he would have to call me back. Without pausing, he went on to say that he wanted a consultation with me and that any time I had available would do. Mr. X. then paused. Keeping within his experience, I sensed, unlike before, he was now waiting for me to respond. Still keeping within his experience and keeping in mind my understanding thus far of his vulnerability to my experience-distant input, I responded only to what he asked and told him a time that I could see him. Mr. X. said "fine" and that he had my address. He then hung up.

In reviewing my initial moments with Mr. X., I can say that my expanding attunement to the subtleties of his experience was critically necessary to provide me with the necessary data to begin to understand the severity of his vulnerability.

My beginning awareness of the nuances of his experience regarding my interrupting his pace made it possible for me to communicate my understanding that he felt that I was intrusive. It was this understanding that was pivotal in Mr. X.'s decision to make the appointment.

My immersion into the nuances of what I sensed he was experiencing not only gave me some beginning awareness of the complexities of his emotional life but also heightened my awareness to the content of what he said (e.g., his choice of words, phrasing of sentences, grammatical usage, and logic). These were important initial data that allowed me to arrive at a more complete picture of his mental functioning.

The First Session: Validation of the Telephone Impressions

Mr. X. rang the bell to my office at the exact time for his appointment. When I opened the door, he glanced at me momentarily then dropped his eyes and, without speaking, moved slowly and methodically into the waiting area. Without pausing, he continued into my office and sat in a small isolated desk chair close to the entrance.

My awareness of the severity of Mr. X.'s reactions to my lack of attunement and my interrupting him on the telephone alerted me to the critical importance of attunement to the nuances of his experience.

Mr. X. sat motionless in his chair, and I sensed a similar paniclike desperation as I did on the telephone. He was thin and appeared physically fragile. His face and arms were pale. I guessed from his slightly greying hair that he was in his 40s.

Mr. X. seemed to be immersed in a private world of feeling and thought. In view of my previous tentative understanding of Mr. X.'s vulnerability to interruptions, I decided against introducing myself. I also decided to angle my chair to align it with his rather than suggesting that he move to the consultation chair opposite my own.

Mr. X. continued to sit motionless and silently with his eyes to the floor. After about 2 minutes, I sensed that he was less tense. His breathing seemed more even, and he leaned back a bit on the chair. It was if he were slowly waking from a trancelike state. After another minute, he looked at me and, in a monotone and barely audible voice, said that it was almost impossible for him to come. In the past he wanted to make appointments with other therapists but almost always hung up the telephone when they began to ask questions. When he did manage to make appointments, he never kept them. Sometimes, he would leave his apartment to keep the appointment and then turn around and go home. On one occasion, he left after he rang the bell. After sharing these thoughts, he anxiously looked away from me, lowered his head, and seemed to return to his isolated state. However, I sensed that Mr. X. was not so rigidly immersed in his private world as before; he seemed to be more aware of my presence than when he entered and, perhaps to some extent, seemed to be waiting for a response from me. I thought that he might be accepting of my understanding of how difficult it was for him to keep his appointment. I said, "It was really very hard to come." Mr. X. said nothing, but after several moments he looked at me and shook his head in agreement. He said that somehow he felt different than the other times he tried to begin therapy. He did not feel "pushed."

Haltingly, and after frequent long pauses throughout the session, Mr. X. offered information about himself. He was 35 years old and knew that "life was passing him by." He felt he was becoming more and more fearful about leaving his apartment. He worked at home as an independent computer programmer, designing and redesigning existing programs for a major software corporation. He said he felt "used" by the corporation, which paid him well and then patented his programs under the corporation name. He thought of himself as being "too cowardly" to apply for his own patents, even though he had many computer programs that he was certain would sell. He had few friends and could not "bring himself to date," even though there were women interested in him whom he had met at his corporation's business meetings. On more than one occasion, he refused their invitations to attend social gatherings.

It was almost the end of the session, and Mr. X. fixed his eyes on the floor and returned to his motionless trancelike state. After some moments with his eyes still focused downward, he said he was surprised that he was able to talk. Even though his eyes remained fixed on the floor, I sensed that he felt a moment of accomplishment. I thought it important to communicate my recognition of his subtle response as part of my continuing effort to provide as full an understanding as possible.[2] I said: "I thought you gave me an important picture of how much you have struggled with feelings that kept you away from having the life you want." Mr. X. said that was true and, with some assertiveness in his voice, looked up at me and said he wanted to "get rid of the chains." I then said we would have to stop for

---

[2] The greater the analyst's perception of what the patient is experiencing, the more likely the analyst will be able to provide meaningful interventions, and the more likely the patient will feel understood. This is also true with those severely traumatized patients who are commonly referred to as having a negative reaction to empathy. I suggest that these patients, rather than having a negative reaction to empathy, are having a negative reaction to inadequate empathy, for if the analyst is sufficiently attuned to the patient's fragile inner life, the analyst will be less likely to impose unacceptable interventions.

now but we could meet at this same time next week if he wished. Mr. X., with the same tone of assertiveness, quickly said he wished to continue our discussion. He thought it might be easier for him to come next week.[3]

EXPANDING ATTUNEMENT:
A PRIORITY FOR UNDERSTANDING

Expanding attunement to the nuances of what Mr. X. was experiencing during his telephone contact with me led to a beginning understanding that I carried forward into the first session. For example, my awareness of his need to control his intensity and tone and to measure his pace in speaking helped me to be alert to his need to maintain emotional distance. This awareness led me to forego the usual introductions and the usual first-interview questions. My awareness also alerted me to his need to sit in a chair close to the entrance to my office and to be silent for extended periods of time. Expanding attunement made it possible for me to be aware of the continuum of his experiences from the first moment I heard his message on tape.

During the initial interview, Mr. X. began to feel a sense of trust. He was able to accept my understanding that coming to treatment was difficult. Much to his surprise, he began to share his concerns. Finally, he was able to accept my recognition of his being able to give me an important picture of himself and, by the end of the session, make the decision to continue our discussion the following week.

CONCLUSION

There has been little in the psychoanalytic literature that focuses on how the analyst observes and perceives data. This lack of emphasis limits the opportunity for the development of the observational process and, therefore, the understanding of the complexity of the patient's mental life. In this chapter, I have emphasized the importance of the ongoing development of one's perceptual capacities to perceive the easily overlooked nuances of the patient's experience. Research has shown convincing evidence of heretofore unrecognized perceptual capacities and that development of perceptual capacities is possible. Clinical vignettes of a taped message, a telephone discussion, and an initial session were provided to demonstrate the

---

[3] Mr. X. kept his next session and continued in once-per-week psychotherapy for 6 months. He then increased his sessions to twice-per-week. At the writing of this paper, Mr. X. has been in treatment for $2\frac{1}{2}$ years.

critical relevance of "expanding attunement" not only in engaging a highly vulnerable patient in treatment but also in developing attunement.

REFERENCES

Atwood, G., & Stolorow, R. (1984). *Structures of subjectivity: Explorations in psychoanalytic phenomenology.* Hillsdale, NJ: Analytic Press.

Baillargeon, R. (1987). Object permanence in 3½ and 4½ month old infants. *Developmental Psychology, 23,* 655–664.

Baillargeon, R. (1988). Evidence of location memory in 8-month-old infants in a non-search AB task. *Developmental Psychology, 24,* 502–511.

Baillargeon, R. (1989). Location memory in 8-month-old infants in a non-search AB task: Further evidence. *Cognitive Development, 4,* 345–367.

Baillargeon, R. (1991). Object permanence in young infants: Further evidence. *Child Development, 62,* 1227–1246.

Baillargeon, R. (1994). Physical reasoning in young infants: Seeking explanations for impossible events. *British Journal of Developmental Psychology, 12,* 9–33.

Baillargeon, R., Spelke, E. S., & Wasserman, S. (1985). Object permanence in five-month-old infants. *Cognition, 20,* 191–208.

Basch, M. F. (1983). Empathic understanding: A review of the concept and some theoretical considerations. *Journal of the American Psychoanalytic Association, 31,* 101–126.

Beggs, W. D. A. (1988a). Different approaches to training the low-vision client. In N. Neustadt-Noy, S. Merin, & Y. Schiff (Eds.), *Orientation and mobility of the visually impaired* (pp. 171–176). Jerusalem: Heiliger.

Beggs, W. D. A. (1988b). Training style. In N. Neustadt-Noy, S. Merin, & Y. Schiff, (Eds.), *Orientation and mobility of the visually impaired* (pp. 181–186). Jerusalem: Heiliger.

Beggs, W. D. A. (1992). Coping, adjustment, and mobility-related feelings of newly visually impaired adults. *Journal of Visual Impairment and Blindness, 86,* 136–140.

Burlingham, D. (1961). Some notes on the development of the blind. In R. S. Eisler, A. Freud, E. Glover, P. Greenacre, W. Hoffer, H. Hartmann, E. B. Jackson, M. Kris, L. S. Kubie, B. D. Lewin, R. Loewenstein, M. C. Putnam, & R. A. Spitz (Eds.), *The psychoanalytic study of the child* (Vol. 16, pp. 121–145). New York: International Universities Press.

Burlingham, D. (1964). Hearing and its role in the development of the blind. In R. S. Eisler, A. Freud, E. Glover, P. Greenacre, W. Hoffer, H. Hartmann, E. B. Jackson, M. Kris, L. S. Kubie, B. D. Lewin, R. Loewenstein, M. C. Putnam, & R. A. Spitz (Eds.), *The psychoanalytic study of the child* (Vol. 19, pp. 95–112). New York: International Universities Press.

Burlingham, D. (1965). Some problems of ego development in blind children. In R. S. Eisler, A. Freud, E. Glover, P. Greenacre, W. Hoffer, H. Hartmann, E. B. Jackson, M. Kris, L. S. Kubie, B. D. Lewin, R. Loewenstein, M. C. Putnam, & R. A. Spitz (Eds.), *The psychoanalytic study of the child* (Vol. 20, pp. 194–208). New York: International Universities Press.

Burlingham, D. (1967). Developmental considerations in the occupations of the blind. In R. S. Eisler, A. Freud, E. Glover, P. Greenacre, W. Hoffer, H. Hartmann, E. B. Jackson, M. Kris, L. S. Kubie, B. D. Lewin, R. Loewenstein, M. C. Putnam, & R. A. Spitz (Eds.), *The psychoanalytic study of the child* (Vol. 22, pp. 187–198). New York: International Universities Press.

Cherry, R. S., & Kruger, B. (1983). Selective auditory attention abilities of learning disabled and normal achieving children. *Journal of Learning Disabilities, 16,* 202–205.

Freud, S. (1958). Recommendations to physicians practicing psycho-analysis. In J. Strachey (Ed. and Trans.), *The standard edition of the complete psychological works of Sigmund Freud* (Vol. 12, pp. 111–120). London: Hogarth Press. (Original work published 1912)

Freud, S. (1963). Introductory lectures on psycho-analysis: Part III. General theory of the neuroses. In J. Strachey (Ed. and Trans.), *The standard edition of the complete psychological works of Sigmund Freud* (Vol. 16, pp. 358–377). London: Hogarth Press. (Original work published 1916–1917)

Johnston, W. A., & Heinz, S. P. (1978). Flexibility and capacity demands of attention. *Journal of Experimental Psychology: General, 107,* 420–435.

Kohut, H. (1959). Introspection, empathy, and psychoanalysis: An examination of the relationship between mode of observation and theory. In P. H. Ornstein (Ed.), *The search for the self* (Vol. 1, pp. 205–232). New York: International Universities Press.

Kohut, H. (1968). Introspection and empathy: Further thoughts about their role in psychoanalysis. In P. H. Ornstein (Ed.), *The search for the self* (Vol. 3, pp. 83–101). Madison, CT: International Universities Press.

Kohut, H. (1977). *The restoration of the self.* New York: International Universities Press.

Kohut, H. (1981). On empathy. In P. H. Ornstein (Ed.), *The search for the self* (Vol. 4, pp. 525–535). Madison, CT: International Universities Press.

Kohut, H. (1984). *How does analysis cure?* Chicago: University of Chicago Press.

Landau, B., Spelke, E. S., & Gleitman, H. (1984). Spatial knowledge in a young blind child. *Cognition, 16,* 225–260.

MacKay, D. G. (1973). Aspects of the theory of comprehension, memory, and attention. *Quarterly Journal of Experimental Psychology, 25,* 22–40.

Piaget, J. (1954). *The construction of reality in the child* (M. Cook, Trans.). New York: Basic Books.

Rowe, C., & MacIsaac, D. S. (1989). *Empathic attunement: The "technique" of psychoanalytic self psychology.* Northvale, NJ: Jason Aronson.

Spelke, E. S. (1976). Infants' intermodal perception of events. *Cognitive Psychology, 8,* 553–560.

Spelke, E. S. (1979). Perceiving bimodally specified events in infancy. *Developmental Psychology, 15,* 626–636.

Spelke, E. S. (1994). Initial knowledge: Six suggestions. *Cognition, 50,* 431–445.

Spelke, E. S., Breinlinger, K., & Macomber, J. (1992). Origins of knowledge. *Psychological Review, 99,* 605–632.

Stolorow, R., Brandchaft, B., & Atwood, G. (1987). *Psychoanalytic treatment, an intersubjective approach.* Hillsdale, NJ: Analytic Press.

Wickens, C. D. (1976). The effects of divided attention on information processing in manual tracking. *Journal of Experimental Psychology: Human Perception and Performance, 2,* 1–13.

Wickens, C. D. (1977a). The effect of divided attention on probe reaction time in multiple-task performance. *Canadian Journal of Psychology, 31,* 174–183.

Wickens, C. D. (1977b). Control theory measures of tracking as indices of attention allocation strategies. *Human Factors, 19,* 349–365.

Wickens, C. D. (1992). Visual scanning with or without spatial uncertainty and divided and selective attention. *Acta Psychologica, 79,* 131–153.

13

THERAPEUTIC EMPATHY: AN INTERSUBJECTIVE PERSPECTIVE

JEFFREY L. TROP AND ROBERT D. STOLOROW

In this chapter we describe the concept of empathy from an *intersubjective* viewpoint (Atwood & Stolorow, 1984; Stolorow & Atwood, 1992; Stolorow, Brandchaft, & Atwood, 1987). Intersubjectivity theory emphasizes the interaction between the differently organized subjective worlds of the therapist and the patient. The observational stance is always one within the intersubjective field being observed (Atwood & Stolorow, 1984). The theory of intersubjectivity shifts the psychoanalytic focus away from isolated pathological mechanisms located solely within the patient to the broader interactional field. Psychopathology is conceptualized in terms of the intersubjective context in which it emerges (Stolorow et al., 1987). Patient and therapist together form a psychological system, and investigating this system constitutes the essence of psychoanalytic inquiry.

The basic motivational principle of intersubjectivity theory is an overarching striving to organize experience. The intersubjective framework proposes that each person acquires unique organizing principles that automatically and unconsciously shape his experience. Atwood and Stolorow (1984) elaborate their concept of organizing principles as follows:

> The organizing principles of a person's subjective world are themselves unconscious. A person's experiences are shaped by his psychological structures without this shaping becoming the focus of awareness and reflection . . . In the absence of reflection, a person is unaware of his

role as a constitutive subject in elaborating his personal reality. The world in which he lives and moves presents itself as though it were something independently and objectively real. The patterning and thematizing of events that uniquely characterize his personal reality are thus seen as if they were properties of these events rather than products of his own subjective interpretations and constructions. (p. 36)

Transference, from an intersubjective perspective, is conceptualized as unconscious organizing activity (Stolorow & Lachmann, 1984–1985; Stolorow et al., 1987). Unconscious organizing principles that crystallize in the interactional system of child and caregiver form the basic building blocks of personality development (Stolorow & Atwood, 1992). Intersubjectivity theory thus adds a unique dimension to the concept of empathy. Empathic inquiry is defined "as a method of investigating and illuminating the principles that unconsciously organize a patient's experience" (Stolorow, 1994a, p. 45).

Empathy within an intersubjective framework is a *mode of investigation.* It is not the same as sympathy because the knowledge gained by empathic inquiry could be used for malevolent purposes. Empathy is also not the same as emotional responsiveness, although the understanding gained by sustained empathic inquiry may lead to vitalizing affective experiences for patients.

There has been confusion regarding the meaning and definition of empathy within psychoanalytic self-psychology (see Stolorow, 1994a). In an important paper delivered at the 11th annual Conference on the Psychology of the Self in Washington, DC, Brandchaft (1988) voiced certain concerns and caveats about the conflation of two uses of the concept of empathy appearing in Kohut's later writings. In one usage, consistent with his original pathbreaking essay (1959) on the subject, Kohut (1982) describes empathy as a "mode of observation attuned to the inner life of man" (p. 396), an *investigatory* stance that constitutes the "quintessence of psychoanalysis" (p. 398). In a second usage he depicts empathy as a "powerful emotional bond between people" (p. 397) and claims that "empathy *per se,* the mere presence of empathy, has . . . a beneficial, in a broad sense, a therapeutic effect—both in the clinical setting and in human life, in general" (p. 397). The same term, *empathy,* is being used to designate both a mode of psychological investigation and a mode of affective responsiveness and bonding.

In agreement with Brandchaft (1988), we have come to believe that such conflation of usages contains serious potential pitfalls, as do a number of otherwise valuable formulations, such as Bacal's (1985) concept of optimal responsiveness and Stolorow's (1983) previously proposed conception of optimal empathy. Many people who become psychotherapists have in their childhood histories a common element of having been required unduly to serve archaic psychological functions for a parent (Miller, 1981), a requirement that is readily revived in reaction to patients' archaic states and developmental longings. When empathy is equated with an ideal of optimal human responsiveness and, at the same time, rightfully claimed to lie at the heart of the therapeutic process, this can exacerbate the therapist's countertransference dilemma, which takes the form of a requirement to provide the patient with an unbroken, enhancing experience uncontaminated by painful repetitions of past childhood traumata—a requirement now invoked in the name of Kohut, Bacal, or Stolorow. As Brandchaft (1988) observes, when a therapist comes under the grip of such a requirement, the quintessential aim of investigating and illuminating the patient's inner experience can become significantly subverted.

Considerations such as these have led us to reaffirm Kohut's (1959) original conceptualization of therapeutic empathy as a unique investigatory stance. We have characterized this stance as an attitude of *sustained empathic inquiry,* an attitude that consistently seeks to comprehend the meaning of a patient's expressions from a perspective within, rather than outside, the patient's subjective frame of reference. We suggest the restriction of the concept of therapeutic empathy to refer to this distinctive investigatory stance and use some other term, such as *affective responsiveness,* to capture the "powerful emotional bond between people" that Kohut (1982, p. 397) believed can also produce therapeutic effects. By making this suggestion, we do not mean to imply that therapists should inhibit their natural affective responsiveness, although under some circumstances it might be desirable to do so. However, an essential ingredient of the therapist's attitude of empathic inquiry is his or her commitment continually to investigate the *meaning* of his or her affective responsiveness, or its absence, for the patient. After all, what is affective responsiveness for the goose might be something quite different for the gander. What the therapist experiences as affective responsiveness, the patient may experience as a covert seduction or a promise that revived archaic longings will literally be fulfilled in a concretized form. Alternatively, a therapist's emotional reserve can at times be experienced by a patient as a yearned-for haven of safety in which his or her own experience can be articulated free from the requirement to adapt to another's affectivity. Whether or not the therapist's affective responsiveness will itself have a beneficial or therapeutic effect will depend on its meaning for the patient.

We wish to stress that our emphasis on inquiry does not mean that the therapist is constantly asking questions. On the contrary, the therapist uses all the means at his or her disposal to facilitate the unfolding and illumination of the patient's subjective world, which may include prolonged periods of silent listening and reflection, in which the therapist searches his or her own world of experience for potential analogues of what the patient is presenting. Such analogues may be drawn from multiple sources, such as the therapist's own childhood history, personal therapy, recollections of other patients' treatments or of case reports by other therapists, readings of great works of literature, knowledge of developmental research, and studies of psychoanalytic theories. It is our view that psychoanalytic theories vary greatly in their capacity to enhance empathic access to the patient's subjective world and that differing psychoanalytic theories often address fundamentally different realms of experience (Atwood & Stolorow, 1993). When *any* theoretical system is elevated to the status of a metapsychology whose categories are presumed to be universally and centrally salient for all persons, then we believe such a theory actually has a constricting impact on therapists' efforts to comprehend the uniqueness of their patients' psychological worlds.

We also wish to emphasize that the attitude of sustained empathic inquiry is not to be equated with an exclusive preoccupation with conscious elements in a patient's experience, a common misconception voiced by critics. Indeed, as we have indicated, our conception of empathic inquiry emphasizes as a primary focus the elucidation of the principles that *unconsciously* organize a patient's experiences. Such unconscious principles become manifest, for example, in the invariant *meanings* that the therapist's qualities and activities recurrently come to acquire for the patient. Such meanings may contain defensive purposes, and failing to investigate unconscious defensiveness when a patient has shown a developmental readiness for such inquiry is *not* empathy (Trop & Stolorow, 1991).

We prefer the concept of sustained empathic inquiry to the commonly used phrase *prolonged empathic immersion* (Kohut, 1977) partly because the former underscores the therapist's investigative function. In addition, we believe that the idea of empathic immersion contains another potential countertransference pitfall, wherein the therapist feels required to immerse himself or herself completely in the patient's experience, banishing his or her own psychological organization from the therapeutic dialogue so that he or she can gaze directly on his patient's subjective world with pure and presuppositionless eyes—surely an impossible feat for even the most gifted of therapists. Such a requirement defies the profoundly intersubjective nature of the therapeutic process, to which the therapist's organizing principles, including those enshrined in the theory through which he or she attempts to order the clinical data, make an inevitable and unavoidable contribution.

We conceive of the development of psychoanalytic understanding as an intersubjective process involving a dialogue between two personal universes (Atwood & Stolorow, 1984). The process of arriving at an interpretation entails making empathic inferences about the principles organizing the patient's experience, inferences that alternate and interact with the therapist's acts of reflection on the involvement of his or her own subjective reality in the ongoing investigation. The attitude of sustained empathic inquiry, which informs the therapist's interpretations, must of necessity encompass the entire intersubjective field created by the interplay between the differently organized subjective worlds of patient and therapist. Thus, a more accurate characterization of the investigatory stance would be empathic–*introspective* inquiry because it includes the therapist's ongoing reflection on the contribution of his or her own organizing principles. The concept of an intersubjective field is well-suited to the methodology of empathic–introspective inquiry. What we investigate through empathy and introspection are the principles organizing the patient's experience (empathy), the principles organizing our own experience (introspection), and the psychological field formed by the interplay between the two (Stolorow, 1994b).

We now turn to a treatment conducted by one of us (see Trop, 1994) to illustrate the concept of empathy as a mode of investigation that seeks to illuminate the unconscious principles organizing the inner world of the patient. The case will also be used to sharpen the distinction between empathy and the provision of emotional responsiveness and support.

David was referred by his family physician at age 28 for symptoms of intense anxiety and panic precipitated by his having inhaled a small amount of a drug while celebrating his graduation from law school. In the first session, David, a strikingly handsome man of Scandinavian descent, appeared apprehensive, agitated, and fearful that he had some permanent damage from which he would never recover. As the therapist inquired about the incident, it became clear that David had become fearful and worried prior to smoking the drug and that his symptoms had developed immediately after attempting to inhale his first and only puff.

As the therapist listened to David describe the events, the therapist began to inquire about the details, and the patient became less pressured while talking about the incident. At the end of the first session, David asked the therapist what he thought. The therapist told him that he was very confident that no permanent damage would result from this episode and that David's fears did not seem grounded in anything that was inherent in the event. The therapist assured him that he had not harmed himself in any irrevocable way and told him that it would be valuable to try to understand how this event had unfolded in terms of its psychological meanings for him. David became visibly relaxed and said that he would very much like to come in and talk some more.

In the ensuing sessions, he gradually began to recount his history, and the initial episode began to recede as a source of concern to him. It was the therapist's belief at the time that his reassurance had supplied a calming and soothing function and that this had contributed to an underlying idealizing transference that unfolded in subsequent weeks.

David described an extremely tumultuous background. He was an only child, and his mother had abruptly left the family when he was 2 years old. His father continued to raise him by himself. David remembered his father's intermittent bouts of alcoholism, which were accompanied by rage and even beatings. These were intermittent and infrequent, but terrorizing to him. He also remembered his father as a man who was kind and loving when not drinking and who took him all over the city, pointing out beautiful landscapes and sunsets. His father died suddenly when David was 6 years old. He was told about his father's death in school, and he remembered feeling devastated. He was adopted by a brother of his father, who was married and had three other children. David's new parents attempted to integrate him into their family as an equal sibling. They were dedicated to giving him every economic and educational opportunity and were delighted at his graduation from law school.

In the first several months of treatment, David and his therapist tried to understand what had precipitated his initial feeling of panic. They discovered that his relationship to his adoptive parents was dominated by their reactions to issues concerning his expansiveness and health. His second father was preoccupied with drug abuse and used any opportunity to drum into David how dangerous drugs were and how one could "go crazy or become brain damaged with drugs." This "ammunition" was presented to David incessantly, long after it would have been useful to him from any educational perspective. There was also a more general feature of the relationship to his father that involved his father's reactions to David's states of expansiveness. David described how he would run exuberantly at the beach when he was growing up. His father would invariably be concerned and tell him repeatedly to settle down. Thus, it became clear that one of David's organizing principles was that states of intense excitement and aliveness were dangerous and that his father repeatedly conveyed this meaning to him. The therapist interpreted that the act of smoking a drug had taken on enormous symbolic meaning for David. He was at a party feeling excited and expansive and was unconsciously attempting to free himself of the relationship with his father and its constricting impact. He wanted to have his own experience of being alive and excited. He had, however, become reactively panicked. The therapist told him that taking the drug had not been recognized by him as an attempt to free himself from his father's view of him as fragile and vulnerable. He felt that the interpretation was correct, and he felt very relieved.

As patient and therapist talked together in the ensuing months, David began to describe a recurrent and painful experience in relationships. He had difficulty dating women and feeling at ease with himself. He felt wary of losing himself and being taken over in a relationship and had a pervasive feeling that he would not measure up. In particular, if he went out with a woman who was dating someone else, he would inevitably have a feeling that she would choose the other man, and he would act on this feeling by withdrawing morosely. He would be similarly threatened if he was talking to a woman and another male friend merely walked up to them. He would feel anxious, exposed, and unacceptable. Any situation involving a triangle with another man was organized by David as a threat and a confirmation that he would never be special. He described a relationship with a high-school sweetheart that had ended with her dating someone else on the side. He was thrown into turmoil and a sense of devastating betrayal, and he remembered his pledge to himself never to get hurt again. His emotional devastation was compounded by his adopted mother's reaction to the event. She became extremely solicitous and concerned about his reaction. Her solicitousness and concern was voiced daily, with inquiries about his state of mind and about whether he was still feeling depressed. This had a paradoxical effect on David. Her intense concern actually reinforced his anguish. He felt that she must know that something was really wrong with him because her concern communicated a fear that he would not be able to manage his feelings.

About 4 months into the therapy, an episode unfolded that stimulated these intense feelings of vulnerability in David's relationship with the therapist. One day David was in the waiting room and came in looking subdued and glum. He began to talk about his work at his law firm but seemed to have none of his customary enthusiasm or energy. The therapist commented on this, and at first David said that he was feeling good earlier in the day and that he could not account for his feeling of glumness. The therapist asked if anything had taken place between them. David was silent and then confided shamefully that he had heard a woman leaving the consulting room and that she had been laughing and joking with the therapist. He said that he knew that it did not make any sense to be depressed, but he did feel down. As he and the therapist explored the specific meaning of his experience, David said that he had always felt the therapist was fond of him, but that he had had a sudden feeling of competitiveness with this woman, and he began to feel that he would not interest the therapist as much as she did. After all, he said, how could he compete with a beautiful and funny woman? He felt now that he had misconstrued the therapeutic relationship and that he must be boring and vacuous. The therapist commented that the conversation between himself and the woman patient had left David feeling excluded and destitute of any concept of his value in the therapist's eyes. The therapist clarified with David how he had automatically organized the meaning of the interchange with her as a confirmation that he was not interesting or compelling in his own right. He agreed and noted how quickly this could occur for him.

As they continued to explore his family background, David and the therapist identified one aspect of his relationship with his biological father that had set the stage for this way of organizing his experience of himself. His biological father, when he was drinking, would take David with him when he went to see women. This occurred repetitively until the time the father died. The setting was usually a dingy, one-room apartment where

David would be confined to a bathroom or balcony. His father would have sexual relations with the woman while David was sequestered in the hallway or behind the door. David remembered hearing noises and that he would try to block his awareness of the sounds and smells. As he and his therapist reconstructed his feelings about these episodes, the therapist hypothesized that one of the origins of his feeling of not measuring up was the sudden loss of his father and the repeated experience of abandonment in isolated hallways. It made sense to David that this experience had repeatedly established the central theme that he would not be the one who was chosen. At various times the therapist attempted to understand the impact of his mother's leaving him, but David said that he had very few memories of her and did not feel much about her leaving the family.

As patient and therapist discussed these issues, David grew more confident and more enthusiastic about his life. This began to manifest itself in several ways. He began doing more painting, a passion that he had given up at the age of 9 or 10. He and the therapist reconstructed that his artistic nature and interest in painting had been displeasing to his adopted parents because they wanted him to have a professional career. He had thus renounced his interest in art and ended up going to law school. At this point in the treatment, he also began feeling more confident with women and began dating. Over the next year, he dated several women. Although none of the relationships worked out, patient and therapist were able to observe the recurring pattern of his feeling threatened by the women's interest in other men, and the feeling of threat began to lessen.

Soon David met a woman he truly liked. He described Ruth as funny, lively, and attractive. He had met her at a party where she was joking and being very playful. He confided that she was the type of woman that in the past he would have avoided and would have admired from a distance. He said she was just too desirable, and he knew that other men would find her attractive. The relationship proceeded, and David found himself falling in love with her. She was supportive, kind, and very interested in him. David had ongoing reactions to her vivacious and outgoing nature. She was very friendly and would start up conversations with many people. David would become intensely anxious and apprehensive and would feel as if he were losing her. On several occasions, when she was engaged in talking to a man at a party or at a restaurant, David became agitated and angry with her. She became hurt and confused and withdrew from him. David and the therapist explored these episodes and understood his reactions as a manifestation of his old way of unconsciously organizing his experience. The therapist noted David's difficulty maintaining a feeling of well-being when her interests were directed at other people. The therapist interpreted this reaction as an automatic and unconscious revival of the meaning of the experience of being suddenly abandoned by his biological father.

Soon after this discussion, David came to a session in an acute state of agitation and rage. He said that he thought his relationship with Ruth was over. Ruth had told him the night before that she was taking a walk and would be back in 10 minutes, but she actually returned in an hour. When she came home he felt enraged with her and told her that she was totally irresponsible. It was about 11 o'clock at night, and he told her that he had almost called the police. He told her that he was afraid that something dangerous had befallen her or that she had been kidnapped. She had never seen him so angry, and she broke down in tears. They did not talk about this episode in the morning, and he still felt enraged with her. He looked at the therapist incredulously and asked, "Do you want to hear the explanation of what had happened to her?" He said that she told him that she had been transfixed by the moon and the stars and had lost all concept of time because the air and the stars were so beautiful. He looked at the therapist intensely and said, "Can you believe that?!"

At this point, for the first time in his relationship with David, the therapist felt in the grip of a dilemma. David clearly was turning vigorously to him for support. David felt extremely upset with Ruth and wanted the therapist's validation for the correctness of his experience. The therapist felt conflicted because there was a bitterness in David's tone that the therapist felt masked some underlying painful feelings. The therapist also began to reflect on the tie that had developed between him and David. The therapist had always felt that David and he had developed a good rapport since their initial meeting when the therapist reassured him. The patient had developed an idealizing transference—David looked up to the therapist and admired him. The therapist wondered if the tie would be damaged if he conveyed his perception of David's vulnerability. Could David tolerate the therapist's communicating to him his understanding of the episode, which was distinctly different from David's?

The therapist decided to articulate his dilemma. He told David that he could certainly agree that what Ruth had done was an act of unreliability. He also said that it seemed clear that David wanted his support, not only as a confirmation that what she had done was unreliable but also for David's perception that this meant there was something centrally flawed about Ruth. The therapist told him that he was reluctant to support this perception because he felt there were feelings underlying David's rage that would be valuable to explore. The patient brushed aside the therapist's concerns about their relationship and said, "I trust you and I want to know what you think."

By this time, a number of memories had come to the therapist's mind of episodes, both in childhood and in adult personal relationships, in which he was blamed as a consequence for a deeply rooted insecurity in the other. He believed that something analogous was now occurring between David and Ruth. The therapist said that there was a tone in David's reaction to Ruth that he wanted to understand further, that it felt like David was reacting as if she had chosen to be with the stars and had not chosen him. The therapist told him that her action seemed to have reexposed him to a familiar feeling that he was not special and valuable. The therapist asked him what he had been thinking when she was away, if there were any other thoughts that had occurred to him. He was silent for a while and said that his other thoughts were difficult for him to disclose because they made him feel embarrassed and humiliated. While she was gone, he had imagined that she had gone to someone's house. He admitted further that the worst fantasy was that she had gone to see an old boyfriend. That thought, however, had soon become buried beneath a torrent of rage at Ruth. The therapist said that his rage seemed to be an attempt to recover his equilibrium and that his anger had been codetermined by her thoughtlessness and by his automatically and unconsciously organizing her lateness to mean that he was not compelling and special to her. The sky and the stars were equivalent to the other man in the triangle, and anything that engaged Ruth and took her away from him was experienced as a confirmation of some defect in himself. He smiled ruefully and asked plaintively, "Will this always sneak up on me; will I ever be free of this?" The therapist replied that he was confident that David would come to recognize this pattern, but that there were aspects of his reactions that awaited further understanding.

Several sessions after this, David came in feeling anxious and agitated. He had repaired the relationship with Ruth and had been feeling better, but had a dream that left him feeling shaken. He had dreamt that he was in an automobile or a machine that was going back in time. The vehicle was shaking as images flashed before his eyes and eventually stopped at some time in his past. A very young baby boy had been thrown out of the car, and he felt frantic as he looked for him. Finally, he found him at the side of the road, alive, but wrapped up in bandages.

David was clearly shaken by this dream, and the therapist asked him what he thought. He said that the dream was about an infant and he felt scared and confused, but he knew the dream was important. He said that maybe the dream had to do with his biological mother. The therapist said that he also wondered if the dream might pertain to feelings or memories that David had about his mother and her abandonment of him when he was 2 years old. He became tearful, and over the next several sessions, many memories and feelings that had been repressed began to emerge.

David did not recall his mother's leaving but did begin to remember other reactions and feelings that he had subsequently. His mother lived several blocks away from his biological father's apartment. He remembered that when he was 4 or 5 years old he would wander over to her house and play in front of her yard. He longed for her to see him and recognize him and come out and be with him. He thought that she could easily see him but that she just refused to look at him or turn toward him. He played in front of her house many times, but she never came out. He remembered feeling subdued and crestfallen and more and more depressed. He also recalled an early incident that happened with a 5- or 6-year-old girl at about that time. They were playing together in a playground, and she ran away from him to play with another friend. He felt that she had left him because he was repulsive and disgusting. Thus, his central organizing principle was established—that he could never be centrally important to a woman.

David then recalled that he had gone back to his mother when he was 16 years old. He knocked on her door, and she opened it. He told her that he was her son and tried to talk to her, and she refused to speak to him and closed the door. David then went and talked to the neighbors about his mother. They described her as reclusive and paranoid. He recalled these events tearfully and recognized the powerful role these experiences had played in shaping his core feelings about himself.

These memories supplied the foundation for an understanding that he had unconsciously organized his mother's repetitive abandonment of him as a confirmation of a central and loathsome defect in himself, leaving him feeling that he could never be central to a woman. No one, including his natural father, had ever talked to him about his experience of her abandoning him.

The new understanding of his mother's impact on him proved to be pivotal to David. He increasingly was able to recognize how he automatically assimilated Ruth's enthusiastic interest in other things as a confirmation of his defectiveness. It was Ruth's capacity for aliveness, vitality, and engagement that stimulated his own archaic organizing principles. The very qualities about her that he valued most when they were directed at him were the source of the most profound pain when exhibited outside the relationship. David now understood that his reactions to Ruth were replicating the way he unconsciously organized his experiences of abandonment by both his mother and his father. The earlier experience with his mother had been reinforced by his father's repetitively leaving him isolated and alone while his father had sexual relations. This new awareness helped David to understand his reactive rage and withdrawal as attempts to protect himself from these painful feelings. He has continued to develop a greater capacity for affect tolerance and self-reflection through the therapeutic work.

The case of David illustrates our conception of therapeutic empathy as centrally focused on the principles that prereflectively organize experience. At a critical juncture in the therapy, David had an intense experience of Ruth as unreliable and flawed. The impasse was a consequence of David's unconsciously and automatically assimilating her interest in outside activities as a confirmation of a central defect in himself. He defended himself against this painful awareness by a reactive rage and devaluation of Ruth. David's wish for the therapist to support his devaluation of Ruth was a wish for support for a defensive avoidance of the painful affective experience of not feeling special to her. The therapist's interpretations to David touched on his longing to feel special. However, the therapist primarily emphasized the repetitive organizing principle underlying David's rage—his belief that he would never be centrally important to any woman.

The distinction between empathic inquiry and supporting the patient's experience is illuminated by this case study. An attempt by the therapist to support David's experience of rage at Ruth when she had gone for a walk would have acted to cover over centrally painful archaic organizing principles. It was only by not accommodating to David's longing for confirmation of his rage that the therapist was able to facilitate the emergence of David's self-loathing.

Intersubjectivity theory does not ignore the importance of emotional responsiveness to specific longings of the patient. Therapeutic empathy, however, is not affective responsiveness but a mode of investigation. The therapeutic role of empathic inquiry parallels the developmental importance of validating attunement to the child's experience in all phases of development. This is one reason that the experience of being understood reanimates thwarted developmental longings and processes. Intersubjectivity theory emphasizes the opportunity for the patient to become aware that the legacy of recurrently malattuned responses during childhood is the constricting and limiting ways of unconsciously organizing experience. We contend that it is primarily by acquiring reflective awareness of their unique organizing principles, in concert with the powerful relational experience of being understood by the therapist, that patients can develop alternative ways of organizing their experience (Stolorow & Atwood, 1992) and be liberated from this pathogenic legacy.

REFERENCES

Atwood, G., & Stolorow, R. (1984). *Structures of subjectivity*. Hillsdale, NJ: Analytic Press.

Atwood, G., & Stolorow, R. (1993). *Faces in a cloud* (2nd ed.). Northvale, NJ: Jason Aronson.

Bacal, H. (1985). Optimal responsiveness and the therapeutic process. In A. Goldberg (Ed.), *Progress in self psychology* (Vol. 1, pp. 202–226). New York: Guilford Press.

Brandchaft, B. (1988, October). *Critical issues in regard to empathy*. Paper presented at the 11th Annual Conference on the Psychology of the Self, Washington, DC.

Kohut, H. (1959). Introspection, empathy, and psychoanalysis. *Journal of the American Psychoanalytic Association, 7*, 459–483.

Kohut, H. (1977). *The restoration of the self*. Madison, CT: International Universities Press.

Kohut, H. (1982). Introspection, empathy, and the semicircle of mental health. *International Journal of Psycho-Analysis, 63*, 396–407.

Miller, A. (1981). *Prisoners of childhood.* New York: Basic Books.

Stolorow, R. (1983). Self psychology: A structural psychology. In J. Lichtenberg & S. Kaplan (Eds.), *Reflections on self psychology* (pp. 287–296). Hillsdale, NJ: Analytic Press.

Stolorow, R. (1994a). The nature and therapeutic action of psychoanalytic interpretation. In R. Stolorow, G. Atwood, & B. Brandchaft (Eds.), *The intersubjective perspective* (pp. 43–55). Northvale, NJ: Jason Aronson.

Stolorow, R. (1994b). Subjectivity and self psychology. In R. Stolorow, G. Atwood, & B. Brandchaft (Eds.), *The intersubjective perspective* (pp. 31–39). Northvale, NJ: Jason Aronson.

Stolorow, R., & Atwood, G. (1992). *Contexts of being.* Hillsdale, NJ: Analytic Press.

Stolorow, R., Brandchaft, B., & Atwood, G. (1987). *Psychoanalytic treatment.* Hillsdale, NJ: Analytic Press.

Stolorow, R., & Lachmann, F. (1984–1985). Transference: the future of an illusion. *The annual of psychoanalysis* (Vol. 12–13, pp. 19–37). Madison, CT: International Universities Press.

Trop, J. (1994). Self psychology and intersubjectivity theory. In R. Stolorow, G. Atwood, & B. Brandchaft (Eds.), *The intersubjective perspective* (pp. 77–91). Northvale, NJ: Jason Aronson.

Trop, J., & Stolorow, R. (1991). A developmental perspective on analytic empathy. *Journal of the American Academy of Psychoanalysis, 19,* 31–46.

V

OTHER RECENT
PERSPECTIVES

14

RELATIONAL EMPATHY: BEYOND MODERNIST EGOCENTRICISM TO POSTMODERN HOLISTIC CONTEXTUALISM

MAUREEN O'HARA

In the beginning was the relationship.

Martin Buber

This chapter is intended to contribute to the fast-growing discussion of the limits of the indigenous psychology of the Western world in addressing the relational needs of its members. In particular, it will examine the limits of modernist individualism as a paradigm for understanding human experience and to bring into focus some of the ways Western psychological understandings of empathy have obscured some of the important ways empathy functions in human relationships. I also intend to show that, because of its position as a modernist, objectivist discourse, Western psychology has been slow to recognize how its modes of enquiry and expression have limited our understanding of relational realities. I want to extend our understanding of empathy beyond its present role as the "royal road to understanding" of individuals by using somewhat different frames of reference from those traditionally characteristic of psychological discussion. Although my main goal will be to expand understanding of empathy as a therapeutic process, I hope to reach further. As our world undergoes what some consider to be the birth pangs of its first truly "global civilization," in which national, ethnic, religious, gender, and class boundaries are shifting on unprecedented scales (Anderson, 1990), all of us will need new postmodern psychologies with which to navigate. The ability to empathize with other individuals and other groups may become the most important interpersonal and even political competence. Increased attention to mutual empathy could lead those of us in Western societies to recover some of our sense of connectedness to each other, our communities, and our world, a recovery that, given the West's current disproportionate impact on global realities, may prove vital to future survival.

WESTERN INDIGENOUS PSYCHOLOGY

The Modernist Worldview

In recent years a strong case has been made by many scholars that the worldview that frames mainstream Western psychology is culturally and historically situated, representing the interests, investments, and experiences of participants in a world dominated by particular ways of thinking and living (Bellah, Madsen, Sullivan, & Tipton, 1985; Berman, 1989; Gergen, 1991; Giddens, 1991; Levin, 1987a; Shweder & Bourne, 1982; Taylor, 1989). This worldview—referred to as modernity—has been shaped by, "the Copernican revolution, Newtonian physics, Cartesian epistemology and metaphysics, humanism and its political revolutions, and the beginning of the technological, industrial and commercial transformations of society" (Levin, 1987a, p. 2). The view of the person at its center also reflects the major philosophical commitments of modernism. The idea that people have something inside called "a self" or "the Self" containing a deep interiority that is contacted through introspection, self-examination, or some other form of "inward vision" would have been incomprehensible to Europeans before St. Augustine. It still is to some peoples from nonmodern societies untouched by the Western worldview.

Western psychology, particularly clinical or applied psychology and psychiatry, is a quintessential modernist enterprise. It is based in modernist views of the nature of human reality that appeared first as scientific rationalist epistemology and became culturally institutionalized though socializing processes. Its origins were the Italian Renaissance and came of age during the 19th and 20th centuries in Europe and North America (see, for example, Berman, 1989; Cushman, 1992; Gergen, 1991; Giddens, 1991; Guisinger & Blatt, 1994; O'Hara, 1984; Showalter, 1985; Shweder & Bourne, 1982; Smith, 1994; Taylor, 1989). Participants in the process of psychotherapy in Western societies, whether clients or psychotherapists, perceive and experience themselves in terms of an indigenous Western psychology. They see themselves as distinct, autonomous agents, separated from other individuals by a whole array of boundaries of identity. Whether as the European self, full of dangerous tensions between aggressive and sexual drives barely contained by the rational will, or as the American self, enthusiastic, achievement-oriented, and transcending its animal baseness through hard work and religious commitment, Western modernist society has valorized individual experience and has privileged a monadic, decontextualized person who is virtually unencumbered by any a priori external constraints. (Cushman, 1992)

Shweder and Bourne (1982) refer to the Western modernist self, at the center of its own worldview as egocentric to suggest its individualistic, abstract, and decontextualized paradigm. They contrast this with a quite different psychology found in pre-modern Europe and in nonmodernist societies such as India and Mexico, which they term sociocentric, to describe a frame of reference that sees personhood as deriving from participation in the world holistically, concretely, and contextually. I shall use Shweder and Bourne's language here.

In egocentric cultures people tend to think of themselves as possessing a self within, which they speak of in terms that are both context-free and abstract. Ideal human relationships are seen as voluntary contractual agreements between two or more individual and autonomous agents. People in America, for instance, where the individual is supraordinate to any social role or obligation, will say that they have a family. In sociocentric India the hierarchy of who belongs to what is reversed, and people say and feel at the deepest levels that they belong to their families.

In egocentric cultures people take it for granted that there is a split between their inside self and the outside world. The view of the self-as-monad becomes everywhere projected outwards, idealized, and codified. Once institutionalized in parenting habits; in religious, educational, and political traditions; or incorporated into art, language, and other symbols of consciousness, this monadic self is then reinternalized (a very modernist word). It becomes the experienced reality, the master narratives, the automatic social patterns, and the habits of life in that society. Situated within such an all-encompassing milieu, where everything mirrors the conceptual and perceptual effects of modernism, inhabitants of 20th-century Western democracies come to take this mechanistic and egocentric, atomized world as "the way things are," and it is very difficult, if not impossible, for us to imagine how it could be otherwise. We highly prize such values as the sovereign rights of individuals, celebration of individualism, egalitarianism, glorification of the solitary hero, tolerance for difference, protection of freedom, encouragement of individual creativity and expression, and idealization of reason and objectivity. At the same time, threats to sovereignty, or demands made on one solely by dint of birth, social context, or other nonchosen circumstances, make Westerners very uncomfortable. To have one's unique inner subjectivity dismissed, violated, expropriated, or as the French psychoanalyst Henri Wallon says, "confiscated" is experienced as an almost unbearable psychic loss (Berman, 1989, p. 36). Some have suggested that this self versus other dichotomy has lead to a chronic vulnerability in the Western psyche, leaving it with an insatiable need for psychic affirmation from significant others, debilitating shame if the object of insult, rejection, or abandonment, and an almost inconsolable longing for recognition and connection with significant others. The prevalence of neurotic illness, narcissism, depression, self-disorders, relationship breakdown, and addictive disorders has been linked by many authors to this fundamental rupture between selves and their contexts (Levin, 1987b).

The Rise of Mechanistic Psychiatry

Psychiatry and its descendents became a prominent aspect of Western medicine contemporaneously with the rapid and brutal industrialization of Victorian life. The exponential rise of psychiatry from the mid-1800s to the present day can be seen as a response to an epidemic of madness that Victorian psychiatrists believed to be occurring in dark, irrational counter-point to the unprecedented advances in political, scientific, and technological achievement. It should not surprise us, then, that at a time when mechanistic thinking was resulting in engineering feats the likes of which the world had never seen, that when medical men—and they *were* men—turned their attention to psychology, they would see human experience as a matter of mechanisms and would seek "to apply rigorous scientific methods to the study of insanity rather than rely any longer on . . . vague humanitarian sympathies . . . of their predecessors" (Showalter, 1985, p. 104). Henry Maudsley (1835–1918), editor of the *Journal of Mental Science* and founder of the psychiatric Maudsley Hospital in England, asserted,

> Lunatics and criminals are as much manufactured articles as are steam engines and calico-printing machines. . . . They are neither accidents nor anomalies in the universe, but come by law to testify to causality; and it is the business of science to find out what the causes are and by what laws they work. (Maudsley, 1874; quoted in Showalter, 1985)

With its emphasis on individualism, rationalism, objectivism, and instrumentalism, an emphasis that as we shall see continues to the present, modernist Western psychology, overwhelmingly views human life from within a mechanistic psychology of individuals. To modernist psychologists the clear identification of boundaries separating classes and categories of nature is vitally important, nowhere more so than in the categories that separate health from disease and rationality from irrationality. To the founders of modern psychiatry, the most important therapeutic skills were diagnostic objectivity, analysis, and instrumentalism. By contrast subjectivity, sensitivity, and compassion were seen as soft, even feminine, placing the doctor at risk of being drawn across the boundaries separating him from his patient.

Even though it might have been "just what the doctor ordered" for people suffering psychic disconnection, empathy had no place in such a psychology. Indeed, there was not even the word *empathy* in English until 1912. The opinion held by the Victorian founders of Western psychology was that it was dangerous for the healer to come too close to the patient, threatening the physician with contamination by those afflicted patients who inhabited the "borderlands" or who had traversed the boundary be-tween sanity and madness (Showalter, 1985, p. 120).

Empathy in Ego-Centric Psychologies

Empathy, the *Oxford English Dictionary* tells us, "refers to the power of entering into the experience of or understanding objects or feelings outside oneself." Originally coined as the English equivalent of the German word *Einfühlung*, when it first appeared in English, empathy had nothing to do with psychotherapy. Rather it was an epistemology—a way of know-ing—and referred to the process by which artists and poets gained access to their subjects. John Keats's empathic ability to merge the boundary between himself and his subject matter is legendary (Rollins, 1958). When first discussed as "the process . . . which plays the largest part in our understand-ing of . . . other people" (Freud, 1920/1955, p. 110), a scientifically valid method of observation by which psychiatrists could gain understanding of the inner world of their patients, it was highly suspect.

As Herbert Feigl (1959) explained,

> We recognize that, especially in the psychology of human motivation, and in psychodynamics generally, empathy is an often helpful and *im-portant heuristic tool* [italics added]. But we realize also that empathetic judgements can go woefully wrong, no matter how strong their intuitive conviction. Empathy may be a source of knowledge, in that it suggests hypotheses. But it is not self-authenticating. (p. 119)

Gradually, however, within the field of clinical, if not experimental, psy-chology, empathy came to be highly valued as a "source of analytic data" (Levy, 1985), a means of learning about the contents of other minds, partic-ularly in client-centered therapy, psychoanalysis, and other depth psychol-ogies.

Early conceptions of empathy have a decidedly modernist egocentric feel. Freud describes empathy as a "mechanism by means of which we are enabled to take up any attitude at all towards another mental life" (Freud, 1920/1995, p. 110). Of what he called one of the "necessary and sufficient conditions" for personality change in psychotherapy, Carl Rogers (1959) states,

> The state of empathy or being empathic, is to perceive the internal frame of reference of another with accuracy, and with the emotional components and meanings which pertain thereto, as if one were the other person, but without ever losing the "as if" condition. Thus it means to sense the hurt or the pleasure of another as he senses it, and to perceive the causes thereof as he perceives them, but without ever losing the recognition that it is as if I were hurt or pleased, etc. If this "as if" quality is lost, then the state is one of identification. (pp. 210–211)

At first, Rogers was the consummate modernist (O'Hara, 1995). He saw empathy as an instrument. The therapist gained access to the inner meaning world of the client to reflect these meanings back to the client for use in reconfiguring his or her authentic sense of self. He believed that empathy, like any other reality, existed in some quantity that could be accurately and quantitatively measured. The image of a clearly bounded individual discerning the inner world of another without becoming contaminated by whatever is found there clearly echoes earlier Victorian nervousness about blurring important boundaries. Truax and Carkuff, students of Rogers, took objectivism even further and developed the widely used scale for quantifying the ability for empathic understanding. The 8-point scale measured how skillful people were in paraphrasing another's statements (Carkhuff, 1969). More recently, client-centered therapists have attempted to take Rogerian empathy beyond formalizable operations to include "emergent modes of empathy." But the frame of reference is still individualistic and atomistic. Bozarth (1984) states that therapists must "develop idiosyncratic empathy modes predicated upon the therapist *as a person*, the client *as a person*, and the *therapist-client interactions* [italics added] (p. 69). Mechanistic metaphors feature prominently. One writer suggests "the therapist's understanding depends on his sensory perception of the signals the client relays" (Vanaerschot, 1990, p. 278). Whatever the metaphor, characteristic of early Rogerian conceptions of empathy is an egocentric image of two separate individuals wherein one—the therapist—attempts to discern something happening within the skin of the other—the client.

Rogerians are not the only ones who have described empathy in egocentric terms. In recent years empathy has taken center stage among psychoanalysts, particularly the object-relations analysts. Greenson describes "building up of a working model of the patient" (Greenson, 1960), and Buie (1981) suggests that "the empathizer compares . . . behavioral cues with one or more referent in his own mind which could be expressed by similar behavior. He then infers that the inner experience of the object qualitatively matches that associated with his referent" (p. 305). The work of Kohut has been particularly influential. At first Kohut, too, regarded empathy as a heuristic tool as a means, along with introspection, of knowing and understanding the inner motivations and intentions of his patients. Empathy, he said, "is the capacity to think and feel oneself into the inner life of another person" (Kohut, 1984, p. 82), and more recently Kohutians Rowe and MacIsaacs have defined empathy as the "analyst's attempt to experience as closely as possible what the patient is experiencing" (Rowe & MacIsaac, 1991, p. 16). In obvious attempts to avoid charges of being "soft," nonscientific, or nonobjective, writers about empathy go to great pains to emphasize that "empathy is neither a mystical, artistic or innate ability" (Levy, 1985, p. 373), and to distinguish between pathological and healthy forms of therapist–client connection (Buie, 1981). Concerned with protecting the ability to move into and out of an empathic state, early on Kohut resisted suggestions that empathy should be used to gratify a patient's longing for reconnection to the mother bond and emphasized the importance of analytic neutrality (Kohut, 1959). Later in his career, however, he conceded that it was "normal" for the analyst to prize the patient the way a mother might prize her infant (Kohut, 1984). As if suspicious of any psychic organization not based on the modernist ideal of individuation, psychologists from analytic, existential, and humanistic traditions have characteristically insisted that empathy be clearly differentiated from the more regressive process that Buie calls "merging."

The pervasive bias in Western modernist psychology in favor of objectivist–materialism and instrumentalism has obscured the extent to which the psyche in egocentric contexts differs from that of people in sociocentric societies. Such a bias significantly limits access by Westerners to realms of empathic knowing beyond the customary limits of objectivism.

SOCIOCENTRIC PSYCHOLOGY

Self-Assertive and Self-Transcendent States

There is good evidence that people are not all in the world in the same way and that the way people experience themselves and their phenomenal world has differed historically across time and still differs from context to context. In familial, tribal, or communitarian cultures, such as Indian peoples of South America and Indians from Asia, consciousness of self is more holistic, contextual, and concrete (Shweder & Bourne, 1982). Similar observations have been made about women in North America, whose sense of self is more holistic and concrete than American men (Belenky, Clinchy, Goldberger, & Tarule, 1986; Clinchy & Belenky, 1987; Comas-Diaz & Greene, 1994; Gilligan, 1982; Jordan, Kaplan, Miller, Stiver, & Surrey, 1991; Surrey, 1991). Similar differences have been noted for Africans and for African Americans (Jones, 1991).

Connected Consciousness

It is through the work of artists and poets that we can best grasp the differences in consciousness between sociocentric and Western modern people (Romanyshyn, 1982). The yarn paintings made by Huichol Indians of Mexico, the ephemeral sand paintings by North American Navajos and Tibetan buddhist lamas, the arabesques of Islam, the calligraphy of Taoist penmen, and Australian aboriginal art reveal a way of being in nature in which the categories, distinctions, and discontinuities common to Western consciousness are nowhere to be seen.

Such imagery provides us with an inside view of what Shweder and Bourne (1982) mean by sociocentric or holistic consciousness. It conveys the organic connections and shifting interpenetrated realities where boundaries, if they exist at all, are shown as fuzzy and situational. This is a world where reality is experienced as an emergent process, not a clearly delineated stable product. This is a fluid, sensuous, undulating world in which the mind moves from place to place and figure and ground continually shift in response to its own particular priorities. Attention is self-transcendent or holistic—directed outwards beyond the skin of individual person, involving itself in the group, community, and natural world. Viewers, like the artist, are drawn into the imagery and find themselves drawn beyond their own skin, dwelling in the swirling interconnected world. Such a state of mind, in which familiar ego boundaries are loosened, may be referred to as self-transcendent or holistic consciousness. It is not limited by fixed boundaries of time or space. Long-dead relatives or people across the globe are as real and as palpable as some solid object held firmly in hand. Self-transcendent consciousness does not experience itself standing apart from the world but as constituent parts of yet larger wholes.

The art most highly revered by modern Westerners, by contrast, strikes one immediately as far more self-assertive. From the Renaissance onwards, we see distinct images of recognizable individuals, their faces bearing the hallmarks of a complex and unique interiority. The self-portraits of European masters look directly out at the viewer as if to say, "Here am I," conveying an impression of a consciousness that pays attention to unique personhood, and identity. Modernist consciousness sees itself self-assertively—as foreground—the rest of creation set behind—as background.

I am describing here more than mere variety in conceptualizations about universal realities, but phenomenal worlds that are so differently structured and populated as to constitute different-lived versions of reality.

EMPATHY THROUGH A SOCIOCENTRIC, HOLISTIC FRAME

Now, in the last decade of the 20th century, it is clear that the extreme of Western modernism in psychology is coming under scrutiny, driven largely by cross-cultural and "cross-genderal" critiques of mainstream thought.

Beginning in the mid-1970s, Rogers's work began to shift in a sociocentric direction, as his interest moved beyond its earlier individual focus to the workings of relationships, groups, communities, and ultimately societies (Bowen, O'Hara, Rogers, & Wood, 1979; O'Hara, 1983; O'Hara, 1989; M. M. O'Hara, 1984; Rogers, 1977; Rogers, 1980). It was this work that compelled us to rethink traditional Rogerian ways of understanding empathy.

In 1977, five members of the Center for Studies of the Person of La Jolla, CA—myself and Rogers among them—were invited to convene a large community workshop in Brazil (Bowen et al., 1979). On that trip we were plunged into intensely intimate engagement with people whose world view was far less egocentric than ours. When we presented our ideas, we were chided for what Brazilian participants experienced as our exaggerated individualism. This cultural collision made it necessary to acknowledge the limitations of the egocentric worldview for addressing relational realities. Our understanding of empathy in particular became greatly enlarged.

Empathy as Contextual Awareness

Empathy has a more respected role in sociocentric human relations than it typically does in egocentric cultures. Not seen as poor relation to objective interpretation, many non-Western societies encourage the development of empathic skills and consider the ability to empathically apprehend realities—activities such as meditation, astrology, poetry, the Yogas, and so on—as an essential element of adulthood and an indispensable part of a leader's education. The Japanese *omoiyari*, for example, is characterized by a heightened sensitivity to and concern for the feelings, thoughts, needs, and moods of subordinates in hierarchical relationships such as psychotherapy (Roland, 1988, p. 82). The Japanese take it for granted that those in authority will have *omoiyari* toward subordinates. Indigenous American tribal people also consider modernist Westerners somewhat handicapped by their limited empathic abilities.

It was decidedly humbling for the Rogers team attempting to transfer to non-Western societies the importance of empathy in client-centered psychotherapy, to discover that workshop participants in sociocentric cultures were routinely more empathic than we were—sometimes to a startling degree. Time and time again people—therapists and lay-people—were able to sense feelings, thoughts, movements, and dynamics of both individuals and groups with astonishing perceptivity.

I suggest that the highly developed empathic abilities of people in sociocentric cultures is a new kind of empathy for Westerners, a full understanding of which requires a shift from egocentric to sociocentric thinking. It requires a shift from over-reliance on abstract, analytic, contractual thinking to a consciousness that is more contextual, holistic, and synthetic.

Relational Knowing

From within a sociocentric frame of reference, it becomes possible to understand empathy as a state of consciousness. It is a way of perceiving and knowing and a way of being connected to other consciousnesses by which individual human beings gain access to the inner worlds of other individuals and to the workings of relationships, and whole ecologies, of which they are but parts. It is also a way through which relationships as entities, including groups and communities, can themselves become aware of themselves as wholes. Often this is accomplished through myth, ritual, and other holistic forms of knowing.

Let me give an illustration: In one Brazilian workshop the community-building process had bogged down in a tension-filled impasse as the group tried to come to a consensus about whether Rogers should make a formal presentation of his ideas. There were many strong and conflicting feelings. Some felt Rogers owed them a presentation. They had paid for the workshop so that they could hear him speak in person about client-centered therapy. Others argued that a formal presentation was a poor substitute for a lived experience of Rogers's work and wanted the unstructured process we were engaged in to continue. On the surface, the conflict could have been easily resolved. The group could have voted on it and abided by the majority. Or those who wanted a presentation from Rogers could have heard him by themselves while everyone else did something else. But the group saw itself as a whole and could not agree to either of these positions. People resisted any moves to fragment the group. Just when one person would seem to be suggesting a reasonable solution, someone else would point out what was wrong with it. This commitment to a somewhat chaotic and frustrating process of hearing everyone out, of staying open to the participation of even the small inarticulate voices or those who spoke in poetry and metaphor, starkly contrasted the problem-solving focus more typical in groups of Europeans or North Americans. Rogers worked tirelessly to empathize with each of the individual participants, often capturing the meanings of people speaking a foreign language with exquisite accuracy. But even this was insufficient to break the impasse.

The second night people went to bed exhausted and angry. They were becoming disillusioned with the much vaunted "person-centered process." The following morning, three individuals described dreams they had had during the night. All three dreams were similar and obviously referred to the impasse within the community. One featured a battle between a white polar bear and a Brazilian *mãe do santo* or shaman. The shaman, a priestess of the Afro-Brazilian religion Macumba, was refusing to let the polar bear pass into her house. She finally consulted *exu*, a powerful spirit entity who according to Macumba tradition guards crossroads and doorways, who told her that as long as she gave *exu* his usual ration of *cachaça* (Brazilian rum), the polar bear could pass safely into her home.

All the Brazilians agreed that the reason for and the solution to the impasse was obvious. We Americans, especially big white bear Rogers, were trying to penetrate Brazilian society with our ideas. The shaman was there to help mediate the passage by insisting that traditional sensibilities be honored and that the local gods be given their due. The Brazilians interpreted the dream sociocentrically, as providing information in symbolic and metaphoric form that could be used as a guide for community action. That evening a local *mãe do santo* arrived at the workshop, presumably invited by one of the participants, and the whole company participated in a ritual of passage, giving *exu* his *cachaça* and tobacco and invoking the help of the various Macumba entities in unlocking our community's impasse. The ceremony went on well into the night.

The next morning, the community meeting began a little later than usual. The change in atmosphere within the group was apparent at once. In place of tense competitiveness, people were laughing and joking. Even Rogers, who until then had been a little uptight and stiff, was visibly looser and more playful, seated less formally, obviously enjoying his physical closeness to a couple of Brazilian voluptuaries. People talked about their experiences of the Macumba ceremony, and as we approached lunch, the group had come to an agreement about Rogers' presentation. There was a clear consensus that nothing Rogers could say in a formal presentation could come close in richness to the experience of the last 48 hours.

When we first had experiences like these, we did not know what to make of them. At first mysterious, we gradually realized that they represented holistic ways of knowing, which were commonplace among many of the world's inhabitants. The dreams and their interpretations by group members revealed an awareness of the community's "group mind," caught in a group-level identity conflict. We gradually came to see this, and other experiences similar to it, as evidence of a form of group-level empathy that was symbolic, holistic, and transindividual. The level of action based on that empathy was also holistic, involving participation, symbol, and myth or story and ritual.

To us this was a new form of empathy, which occurred on conscious and unconscious levels. It provided complex, subtle, and reliable knowledge, in imaginal, metaphoric, and narrative form, about the community as a whole that could inform appropriate, coordinated, and graceful action by the whole.

Conscious groups—groups in which many people are aware of group-level phenomena—seem also to produce more than the ordinary share of exceptional individuals, suggesting to us that when people can align themselves with the movements in the larger context without losing their unique perspective, they appear to "know" more and perform better than they ordinarily do. When a mediocre basketball player plays on a team that is flowing, he or she can play far beyond his or her own personal best. Collaborative learning can lift an individual student's performance several levels higher than usual; actors perform better when the audience is with them. It may also account for such frequently observed (and often trivialized) phenomena as "women's intuition," when a wife may have knowledge of her partner's extramarital affair even though he is going to great pains to conceal it. In one organization I consulted with, a car with Texas license plates in the company parking lot resulted in highly secret reorganizational plans being sensed by the whole organization seemingly at the same time. One employee told me, "Everything had been very normal, too normal recently. Everybody knew something was up, but nobody knew what. When we saw the Texas Lexus, we figured out we were on the auction block." A month later the company was bought out by a Texas conglomerate.

Different communities understand such phenomena in different ways. In our Brazilian group, explanations would have included the activity of the spirits of the departed. My British grandmother would have attributed such knowings to a "sixth sense." Organizational psychologists believe this to be a somewhat regressive state that recapitulates experience in the family. The group becomes "mother," and individuals merge with the group the way the infant merges with the human mother (Schein, 1985). Polanyi (1958) differentiates between focal awareness and subsidiary awareness. When we are focally aware of a whole, we are subsidiarily aware of its parts. When we focus on a part, we are subsidiarily aware of the whole. In Polanyi's view, modernist overemphasis on attention to the parts has lead to a disregard for the skills required for tacit knowing of the whole. He suggests that knowledge breakthroughs are made when scientists or poets who have retained their ability to "indwell" in the fuzzy world at the boundaries of consciousness and are able to dissolve their attention past the focally apparent particulars to gain a glimpse of some until-now unapprehended greater whole. In moments like these, we know more than we believe we know because it is possible to shift attention from the parts to the larger whole if we believe there is a reason to do so.

This ability to shift attention back and forth between the parts and the wholes to which they pertain might account for some of the seemingly magical and even paranormal breakthrough events that occur in psychotherapy, such as when the therapist and client simultaneously share the same image, when the therapist makes an statement out of the blue that proves to be profoundly appropriate, or when the therapist knows in advance that the client will soon begin to share some until-now hidden story. A sociocentric view would explain this not by suggesting that the therapist is "inside the skin" of the client, but inside the skin of the relationship, of which he or she is a part. Bozarth (1984) has referred to this phenomenon as "emergent" empathy. I prefer the term *relational empathy* to signify the sociocentric, relational nature of the process.

A RELATIONAL WORLDVIEW

Relational Empathy

When looked at through a sociocentric lense, empathy provides a means of knowing relationships not only egocentrically in terms of its particulars but also holistically as wholes that are more than the sum of their parts. In their ground-breaking work examining the role of empathy in the psychological development of women, Stone Center theorists have recently shifted descriptions of empathy in a sociocentric direction by referring to it as the "*relational* skill par excellence" (Jordan et al., 1991).

Holism, Sociocentric Awareness, and Transindividual Empathy

For psychology to make a shift from an egocentric to a sociocentric understanding of empathy requires new holistic language. Holistic thinking distinguishes between those characteristics and behaviors that give something (entity, object, thing, category, being, and so on) "wholeness" and those associated with its "partness" (Koestler, 1978). For example, a football quarterback, when known as a whole would be known in terms of features unique to him such as personal biography, sense of humor, talent, speed, throwing accuracy, and stamina—those qualities he exhibits as an individual. He can, however, also be know as a part of the team. In this case, qualities such as being able to get along with teammates, engendering team spirit, planning plays within the abilities of his team, expressing loyalty, and displaying the ability to inspire other players would be important. One familiar way to speak about this distinction in Western psychology would be to distinguish between his "self" and his "role." But in both cases, he is obviously himself. The difference is between the aspects of self we see when we look at him as a whole and those we see when we pay attention only to the way he functions as a part. For instance, his performance can be measured in terms of his individual statistics—the usual American way—or it can be assessed in terms of how well his performance contributed to the performance of the whole team—the sociocentric cultural preference. Furthermore, his unique individual characteristics, as seen egocentrically, may be true of him in any context whereas the characteristics he demonstrates as "part" will change from context to context as a function of the wholes he is a part of. A careful analysis of how he acts in one context—say on the field—will be a poor guide to how he might be in others, like at home or in church. The same distinction can be made about the team itself. How it will play against another team will be a function of both its own limits and the opportunities provided by the context.

Koestler (1987) calls those states of mind and activities that have to do with a sense of one's wholeness *individualistic* or *self-assertive*, and he calls states of mind and activities that have to do with the sense of participation and becoming one with a larger reality, *self-transcendent* or *integrative*. Wholeness is associated with sovereignty—individual identity, self-expressiveness, initiative, integrity, aggression, uniqueness, discrimination, delineation, clarity, separateness, analysis, either–or thinking, competition, distinction, specificity, and boundedness. Partness or integrative behavior is associated connection—self-transcendence, empathy, listening, under-standing, synthesis, cooperation, oneness, merging, diffuseness, participa-tion, integration, belonging, both–and, generality, love, and intuition. For any human entity, be it person, group, family, community, or tribe, both partness and wholeness are two faces of being. Like the two-eyed Buddha, who has one eye facing inwards to itself as a whole and the other facing outwards to the cosmic whole to which it belongs, human consciousness knows itself both atomistically or self-assertively and relationally or self-transcendently.

Relational Knowing

Human knowing is a relational activity. It implies both a knower and a known—we are always conscious of something or better yet *with* some-thing. It includes sensing, recognizing, making sense, and above all *meaning* of experience. Consciousness implies both self-transcendent and self-asser-tive states of mind. It requires the ability to discriminate between bounded categories and among entities, and it requires the ability to synthesize and integrate. It involves awareness of oneself in the process of knowing—how one's knowing is influenced by the contexts in which one is knowing—and it involves being swept away, out of oneself into the expanded contexts of life. By a continuous process of selection, categorization, organization, and synthesis, consciousness weaves ongoing representations of reality out of symbolic interpretations of inner and outer worlds and the dynamic relations between them.

Individual Sovereignty Versus Group Think

Participatory or relational consciousness, where individual selves are known more through the way they participate in larger wholes than as unique individuals, worries many Westerners. The idea of shifting attention away from individuals—decentering to postmodernists—looking at them only as clues to the workings of larger systems, raises fear that the intrinsic worth and sovereignty of individuals might diminish. Well-known examples of the dehumanizing effects of perverted collective consciousness such as Fascism, Communism, the Salem witch trials, or the Inquisition provide historical evidence of the dangers of "group think" and support for the importance of creative egocentric individualism. More recently, feminist critiques of the hegemonic patriarchal worldview, ethnic critiques of Euro-centrism, poststructuralist critiques of master narratives in general, and Kuhn's demonstrations of the conservative nature of scientific paradigms offer further caution about the hegemonic properties of collective thinking. Psychologists, too, resist sociocentric consciousness when they feel it disre-gards the need for people to individuate and be cherished as beings for themselves. Client-centered psychologist Barrett-Lennard (1984), for instance, despite having focused his work on families and communities, shares what he calls his "prejudice" when he admits that he has "largely by-passed" the bulk of the systems-theory discussions because he fears that "the subjectively experiencing person [may be] lost or underemphasized, in terms of agency" (p. 241).

Such critics are right. If consciousness is limited to its wide-angled, sociocentric state, the only aspects of a person's being considered important are those having to do with his or her participation in larger contexts. If human beingness is reduced to serving as mere clues to the workings of larger orders, then unique, creative selfhood and the view of self as autonomous agent may indeed become invisible. People raised in sociocentric communities are not immune from pain at having their individual needs ignored. The *ie* stem family system of Japan requires that individual selves, so sacred to participants of Western democracies, become submerged to take their place in a larger, interpenetrated kinship system. Japanese psychologists report considerable psychic costs, seen in paralyzing guilt, repressed hostility, and other psychological disturbances, that can be directly correlated with the submersion of individual expression (Roland, 1988). Across the world practices such as arranged marriages, obligatory veiling of women, forced political reeducation, censorship, ritual genital mutilation, and many others, while certainly providing a sense of psychic coherence for sociocentric peoples, strike individualistic Westerners as unbearable assaults on self.

This tension becomes resolvable not by taking exclusively either egocentric or sociocentric positions but by thinking holistically and by striving to understand persons neither as abstracted from their contexts nor as subordinated to them but as both whole unto themselves and as active participants and cocreators of the contextual wholes that they inhabit. Furthermore, every situation is unique, every context providing novel and endlessly permutational possibilities that may in turn also be known uniquely by different individuals.

What any particular person is aware of, and the degree of focus or expansion of his or her awareness, will depend on processes (physiological, neurological, conceptual, emotional) going on within that individual and on processes occurring within the larger context impinging on him or her. It will also depend on relational conditions existing at the boundary between the individual level and the higher relational level. For example, if I am physically well, alert, safe, beloved, and accompanied, I might have awareness of myself both egocentrically and sociocentrically. I may be conscious of myself as a unique, individuated center of knowledge and agency. I know what I am striving for and the meaning it has for me. At the same time, I am aware of the way I am interacting with others. I can also be aware of how others are experiencing me. I may even understand relational movements in my marriage, the organizational dynamics at work, and the political or cultural movements in my community all at once—life as a fully experienced whole. On the other hand, if I am afraid, in pain, or ill, my attention may be focused on myself, even on some isolated body part, to the exclusion of all other dimensions. This shrunken awareness might be due to dysfunctions in the larger system—such as family or political oppression—or to dysfunctions within me—such as a biochemical disorder or previous psychological trauma.

Psychological Wellness as a Function of Degree of Appropriateness in Focus or Inclusiveness of Consciousness

This leads us to the possibility of looking at psychological functioning of an individual or group not only in egocentric structural terms but also in relational and contextual terms. Healthy functioning implies that consciousness will include all contextual dimensions of concern within a given situation and at a given moment. And, if we are not to become overwhelmed by endless contexts after context, we will exclude those elements that are irrelevant to present purposes. Much pathology or dysfunction is due to awareness that is either inappropriately shrunken or restricted—a person sees only fragments but not the whole—or inappropriately inclusive, and attention is too global and life becomes overwhelming. The relational therapist's function is to help clients learn how to let their awareness focus or expand as their unique contextual situation demands.

When conflicts exist at an intrapsychic level, and many of them do, focusing consciousness at this level is appropriate in that it may yield solutions to situations of concern. But not all psychological conflicts or difficulties exist at this level. Nor do all resolutions. The individual psyche may not always be the relevant level for therapeutic attention. Some have suggested that excessive attention by psychotherapists on these intrapsychic levels of awareness has contributed to the rampant narcissism and other problems of contemporary Western life rather than their solution (Bellah et al., 1985). The following example reveals the limitations of the traditional egocentric psychological worldview for addressing relational needs.

A single father recently disclosed to his therapist that a few years earlier he had been intensely shamed by a psychologist who had interpreted as "inappropriate" his decision to cancel three weeks of twice weekly therapy appointments to drive his 18-year-old daughter across country to begin university. The trip represented an enormous sacrifice in terms of time and money for the father, and he felt intense grief about losing his daughter—although he was proud that she was to attend his Ivy League alma mater. He was inexplicably anxious about spending so much time alone with his daughter. The daughter, on the other hand, was very enthusiastic about the trip and was making elaborate plans. The psychologist suggested that the father was "co-dependent and controlling" and that his anxiety was a clear signal that he was unconsciously aware that he was being drawn into something that was not good for him. He also indicated that there might be some incestuous seductiveness on the part of the daughter in wanting to "pal along with dad" instead of taking herself off to college in an "age-appropriate" way. The psychologist tried to persuade the father that he should heed his discomfort and, in the interests of his daughter's individuation and his own psychotherapy, cancel their plans and insist the daughter take a plane. The trip proved difficult for the father, although he was glad he'd done it. However, his experience of humiliation and anxiety at what the psychologist had said was so intense that he was unable to return to psychotherapy.

The psychologist in this case was obviously interpreting the client's actions from within the egocentric bias of his training. To him, it was virtually axiomatic that interrupting psychotherapy for a month reflected resistance, that fathers and daughters do not behave as friends, and that psychological maturity required separation and individuation. A relational, sociocentric perspective enables us to look at this situation quite differently, looking at the father's decision in context. Despite some uneasiness, both father and daughter felt somehow moved to make the trip across country together. To both of them it represented an almost mythic rite of passage. After raising her since childhood, the father was seeing his daughter finally moving out into the world, and both he and his daughter wanted their final three weeks to be a time to allow their relationship to make the transition to its new adult–adult configuration. They were both naturally anxious and uneasy about how this would play out on the trip.

Although no doubt empathically accurate about the father's discomfort, what the psychologist missed, which thankfully neither the client nor his daughter did, were the needs of the relationship. Only from a relationally empathic vantage point within that specific father–daughter dyad could the relational needs be known. For some other father–daughter relationship, perhaps allowing the daughter to go it alone would have been the relationally appropriate thing to do.

Psychotherapy is a joint project of at least two participants. In holistic terms it is a multilevel, relational situation. There are whole individuals, and there are participants in relationships, dyads, or groups. These levels are also parts of larger configurations such as professions, families, classes, cultures, and genders. Attempting to understand larger system problems only from within an egocentric individualistic frame more often than not results in "blaming the victim." An example of this can be seen in the way responsibility and remedy for unwed teenage pregnancy is laid at the door of individual teenage girls or their families. Commonly absent from psychological discussions about why the girls become pregnant is consideration of larger system issues: the relationship between the rise of divorce rates among the girls' parents, the economic needs for two working parents, the biological imperative of physiological pressures, the interpersonal power inequality between fathers and teenage mothers in patriarchal society, the cultural shift to later marriage, the decrease in social abrogation, and so on. All are forces that originate outside the individual psyche and derive from larger-order dynamics beyond the influence of individual teenage girls. It is one thing to include the teenager's self-esteem, judgment, or even psychopathology in the constellation of factors that end up in a teenage pregnancy, but it is quite another to expect that she or her family will be likely to overcome easily the higher-order forces setting her up.

The origin of a client's difficulty may be on any level. The holistic psychotherapist needs to be able to bring a repertoire of techniques—from the free association of psychoanalysis and the social activism of feminist therapy to spiritual practices such as Macumba, meditation, or prayer to help bring into awareness all the components of experience relevant to a predicament.

Empathy, in both egocentric and sociocentric modes, is an essential skill of both therapist and client in this process. Egocentric empathy permits the therapist to know the client as a unique, whole individual. Sociocentric empathy provides the therapist with ways of knowing the relationships in which the clients participate, including the therapeutic relationship.

Relational psychologists may have an even more important contribution to make to the larger culture by helping society bring into consciousness and develop the necessary skills to effectively deal with higher-order relational realities so long ignored by Western cultures. Futurists are warning that many of the complex problems facing postmodern global societies will not be solved by individual genius but instead will need the coordinated efforts of diverse and creative groups (Dubos, 1981; King & Schneider, 1991). It is commonplace to suggest that nothing is so powerful as an idea whose time has come, but rarely do we consider how it is that an idea's time arrives. Our experience with relational empathy suggests that new and important ideas exist in groups in holistic, perhaps even holographic, forms as emergent properties of group consciousness. On those rare occasions when group members are empathic not only with each other but also with the group itself as a conscious entity, then vague inchoate inklings just below the surface of the group mind may crystallize into clear ideas. As the idea is articulated by one of its members, the group as a whole becomes instantly conscious of the new reality.

EMPATHY RECONSIDERED

At this point it is possible to consider empathy from outside the modernist discourse and look afresh at this ubiquitous human activity from within a relational frame. From this new vantage point, empathy ceases to be seen as the highly skilled instrumental activity of one autonomous individual—the therapist—intervening in the life of another—the client—while remaining separate and unaffected. Instead, empathy becomes understandable as an essential feature of human, relational connectedness, an expansion of a person's consciousness to include in the perceptual field the other as an individual and the relationship with the other of which he or she is a part.

Empathy is probably one of the oldest—both phylogenetically and ontogenetically—ways of orienting to self and others, predating symbolic language in both prehominid and prelinguistic human infants. One can speculate that, for social primates without symbolic language, the empathic ability to sense the feelings and intentions of others and accurately read the cues provided in the complex interpenetrated webs of actions of social groups would have given enormous advantage to those who excelled at it. Cross-cultural studies of contemporary tribal people show that, for people who live in highly structured interdependent communities, such abilities are still needed and highly valued. Symbolic and linguistic skills, as well as more recent technological advances in communication, although providing greater opportunities for complex social life, have not superseded more basic means of orientation. In fact, this may have simply added other, larger contexts in which sociocentric empathy is required. Western culture has for centuries gone to great lengths to socialize children toward egocentricism. This is in marked contrast to sociocentric patterns of childcare. Brazilian rain-forest Indian women hold their babies close to their own bodies 24 hours a day. They continue this close connection for the first 2 years of life. Every breath mother takes, every movement, aroma, or word, occurs as part of the experiential field of both mother and infant. This shared experiential reality is in stark contrast to the first experiences of infants in Western technological societies where babies are frequently enveloped in sterilized clothing and placed for long periods in solitary cots. Indian babies know nothing of separation and separateness until well after language develops, whereas a Western baby may be detached from physical contact with its mother within minutes of birth. Such contrasting early developmental contexts provide quite different psychological challenges to the child's evolving consciousness.

Some writers have suggested that individuals socialized for egocentricity make poor therapists for clients from more sociocentric communities, such as women of Asian, African, or Latin-American descent (Chin, 1994; Comas-Dias & Greene, 1994). Fortunately, though, for those egocentric Western therapists who wish to develop more relational forms of empathy, it appears the relational competences can be regained, even in adulthood. By the end of his career "big white polar bear" Rogers, after over 50 years of tuning in to the world space of others—the last 15 years or so frequently immersed in non-Western contexts such as Africa, Russia, Japan, and Latin America—said this about himself:

> When I can relax, and be close to the transcendental core of me, then I may behave in strange and impulsive ways in the relationship, ways I cannot justify rationally, which have nothing to do with my thought processes. But these strange behaviors turn out to be *right* in some odd way. At these moments it seems that my inner spirit has reached out and touched the inner spirit of the other. Our relationship transcends itself and has become something larger. (Rogers, 1986, pp. 130–131)

MUTUAL EMPATHY

The discussion, so far, has been aimed at a better understanding of empathy as a way of relational knowing, a way of, in Polanyi's (1958) words, "indwelling" in the experiential life world of individuals and groups. But there is still more that Western psychology can gain by moving beyond modernist views of empathy.

Empathy provides more than just information *about* relationships. It is an expression of *being in* relationships. It is not just a means to better healing relationship, but because it recenters relationship as a central organizing feature of psychic life, empathy itself is healing. The experience of being known and accepted deeply by another, being aware of another being aware of you, what Jordan calls "mutual empathy" (Jordan et al., 1991), is among the most psychologically important human experiences. There is ample evidence that, without a clear sense of connectedness, human beings, especially infants and children, cannot thrive. It is through mutual empathy that we develop a sense of ourselves in relationship, the security of knowing that we belong, the knowledge of who we belong to, and how we must participate if we are to be loved and recognized by our community.

Although much easier to come by in sociocentric cultures than in egocentric ones, a sense of belonging is a sine qua non of healthy psychological functioning everywhere. Such a sense, beginning in infancy and continuing throughout life, comes about by experiencing mutual empathy and by sensing oneself as part of a whole, which recognizes and accepts that one is a member.

Relational Empathy in an Era of Globalization, Narcissism, and Industrialized Health Care

The healing benefits of empathic connections are not something that the therapist can provide for the client, the way the physician gives medicines. For the full potential of therapeutic relationships as contexts in which human beings can heal and become fully themselves to be realized, relational empathy must be two-way. A common mistake made by egocentric therapists is to provide an empathic setting for their clients and interpret empathic attempts by clients as transference or as attempts at manipulation. People frequently leave therapy still operating from an egocentric frame of reference, wanting others to be empathic with them but having developed few or no relational competencies of their own. If people are to function well in the multiple relational contexts of their lives, clients need to learn how to enter self-transcendent states and to develop the capacity for egocentric and sociocentric empathy. This is best developed in a therapeutic relationship that is itself relational and in which mutual empathy can be achieved. Creation of mutual empathy takes trust. It takes commitment to creating conditions that permit emergent forms of consciousness to develop. It takes effort and time.

Ironically, and potentially disastrously, it is precisely these aspects of psychotherapy that are the first casualties in the massive changes in health care presently underway in the United States. The industrialization of health care, although intended to create economic gains for both employers and workers and to make mental health care available to a wider population, may accomplish this by forcing a return to the individualistic mechanistic paradigm of earlier periods of psychological history. Such retrograde developments may wipe out recent progress toward more holistic and relational frames of reference in psychotherapy and result in a greater emphasis on a one-size-fits-all modernist reductionistic behaviorism and on psychopharmacology. The role of empathy might conceivably return full circle to become reduced to a role only in the data-gathering and hypothesis-building stage of diagnosis. Its potential to heal disconnections and alienation and to provide access to ever-wider pluralistic realms of knowing may be left unrealized. Worse yet, through the global reach afforded by Western technology, as other societies wrestle with the demands of the new competitive global marketplace, we might export our alienating practices to those still uncommitted to modernism.

Postmodern Possibilities for a Relational Psychology

Psychology has much to gain by resisting these pressures to shrink ourselves into isolated egocentric bubbles. Now is the time to help midwife a new postmodern psychology able to meet the demands of our emerging postmodern world. It is time to reach beyond our isolated and individuated selves into the infinitely interpenetrated relational world. If able to learn more about the workings of conscious groups and how to help them form, psychology might be standing on a new threshold of knowledge. The British biologist J. B. S. Haldane (1954) suggests a nonmystical way to understand such expansion of consciousness beyond modern individualism when he states, "If the cooperation of some thousands of millions of cells in our brain can produce our consciousness, the idea becomes vastly more plausible that the cooperation of humanity, or some part of it, may determine what Compte calls a 'Great Being'" (p. 24).

Relational empathy permits individual and collective access to the wisdom contained in higher-order shared contexts and nurtures the ground out of which new creative possibilities might emerge. A new generation of Western artists are already pointing the way.

British artist David Hockney's photo collage, *My Mother, Bolton Abbey, Yorkshire, Nov. '82*, is of the artist's mother within the ancient ruins of a Cistercian abbey. The picture is composed of multiple shots; multiple camera positions; and an idiosyncratic, irregular frame. It contains an unmistakable reference, in the form of a shot of the artist's own feet peeking into the bottom of the picture, to the subject-to-subject relational connection among the artist, the artist's mother, and the viewers. Hockney, inspired both by the work of 20th-century physicists and 14th-century Chinese scroll paintings, strains to render the images of a reality yet to be created. We need, he says, "to break down borders, to entertain the interconnectedness of things and of ourselves with things; the notion . . . that it is no longer possible to have ideas about reality without taking our own consciousness into account" (Hockney, 1988, p. 87).

Should psychology choose to go in this direction and develop greater understanding of relational empathy, as a way of knowing and as a way of being connected, and should psychology learn more about the contexts in which relational consciousness can be developed and how to create communities that permit both being and belonging, psychology might yet offer some grounds for optimism in an increasingly alienated, fragmented, and pessimistic society.

REFERENCES

Anderson, W. T. (1990). *Reality isn't what it used to be.* San Francisco: Harper & Row.

Barrett-Lennard, G. T. (1984). The world of family relationships: A person-centered systems view. In R. F. Levant & J. M. Shlien (Eds.), *Client-centered therapy and the person-centered approach: New directions in theory, research, and practice* (pp. 222–241). New York: Praeger.

Belenky, M. F., Clinchy, B. M., Goldberger, N. R., & Tarule, J. M. (1986). *Women's ways of knowing: Development of self, voice, and mind.* New York: Basic Books.

Bellah, R. N., Madsen, R., Sullivan, W. M., & Tipton, S. M. (1985). *Habits of the heart: Individualism and commitment in American life.* New York: Harper & Row.

Berman, M. (1989). *Coming to our senses: Body and spirit in the hidden history of the West.* New York: Simon & Schuster.

Bowen, M., O'Hara, M. M., Rogers, C. R., & Wood, J. K. (1979). Learning in large groups: Implications for the future. *Education, 100,* 108–117.

Bozarth, J. D. (1984). Beyond reflection: Emergent modes of empathy. In R. F. Levant & J. M. Shlien (Eds.), *Client-centered therapy and the person-centered approach: New directions in theory, research and practice.* New York: Praeger.

Buie, D. H. (1981). Empathy: Its nature and limitations. *Journal of the American Psychoanalytic Association, 29,* 281–307.

Carkhuff, R. R. (1969). *Helping and human relations: Vol. 1. Selection and training.* New York: Holt, Rinehart, & Winston.

Chin, J. L. (1994). Psychodynamic approaches. In L. Comas-Diaz & B. Greene (Eds.), *Women of color: Integrating ethnic and gender identities in psychotherapy* (pp. 194–222). New York: Guilford Press.

Clinchy, B. M., & Belenky, M. F. (1987). *Women's ways of knowing: A theory and an intervention.* Unpublished manuscript, Smith College School of Social Work, Northampton, MA.

Comas-Dias, L., & Greene, B. (1994). Overview: Gender and ethnicity in the healing process. In L. Comas-Dias & B. Greene (Eds.), *Women of color: Integrating ethnic and gender identities in psychotherapy* (pp. 185–198). New York: Guilford Press.

Cushman, P. (1992). Psychotherapy to 1992: Historically situated interpretation. In D. K. Freedheim (Ed.), *History of psychotherapy: A century of change* (pp. 21–63). Washington, DC: American Psychological Association.

Dubos, R. (1981). *Celebrations of life.* New York: McGraw-Hill.

Feigl, H. (1959). Philosophical embarrassments of psychology. *American Psychologist, 14,* 115–128.

Freud, S. (1955). Group psychology and the analysis of the ego. In J. Strachey (Ed. and Trans.), *The standard edition of the complete psychological works of Sigmund Freud* (Vol. 18, p. 110). London: Hogarth. (Original work published 1920)

Gergen, K. J. (1991). *The saturated self: Dilemmas of identity in contemporary life.* New York: Basic Books.

Giddens, A. (1991). *Modernity and identity: Self and society in the late modern age.* Stanford, CA: Stanford University Press.

Gilligan, C. (1982). *In a different voice: Psychological theory and women's development.* Cambridge, MA: Harvard University Press.

Greenson, R. R. (1960). Empathy and its vicissitudes. *International Journal of Psychoanalysis, 41,* 418–483.

Guisinger, S., & Blatt, J. S. (1994). Individuality and relatedness. *The American Psychologist, 49*(2), 104–111.

Haldane, J. B. S. (1954). The origins of life. *New Biology, 16,* 12–26.

Hockney, D. (1988). *David Hockney: A retrospective.* Los Angeles: Los Angeles County Museum of Art.

Jones, R. L. (1991). *Black psychology* (3rd. ed.). Berkeley, CA: Cobb & Henry.

Jordan, J. V., Kaplan, A. G., Miller, J. B., Stiver, I. P., & Surrey, J. L. (1991). *Women's growth in connection: Writings from the Stone Center.* New York: Guilford Press.

King, A., & Schneider, B. (1991). *The first global revolution: A report by the Council of The Club of Rome.* New York: Pantheon Books.

Koestler, A. (1987). *Janus: A summing up.* New York: Random House.

Kohut, H. (1959). Introspection, empathy, and psychoanalysis: An examination of the relationship between mode of observation and theory. In P. H. Ornstein (Ed.), *The search for self* (pp. 205–232). New York: International Universities Press.

Kohut, H. (1984). *How does analysis cure?* Chicago: The University of Chicago Press.

Levin, D. M. (Ed.). (1987a). *Pathologies of the modern self: Postmodern studies on narcissism, schizophrenia, and depression.* New York: New York University Press.

Levin, D. M. (1987b). Psychopathology in the epoch of nihilism. In D. M. Levin (Ed.), *Pathologies of the modern self: Postmodern studies on narcissism, schizophrenia, and depression* (pp. 21–83). New York: New York University Press.

Levy, S. T. (1985). Empathy and psychoanalytic technique. *Journal of the American Psychoanalytic Association, 33,* 352–378.

O'Hara, M. (1983). Patterns of awareness: Consciousness and the group mind. *The Gestalt Journal, 6*(2), 103–116.

O'Hara, M. (1989). Person-centered approach as *conscientizaçao*: The works of Carl Rogers and Paulo Freire. *Journal of Humanistic Psychology, 29*(1), 111–136.

O'Hara, M. (1995). Carl Rogers: Scientist or mystic? *Journal of Humanistic Psychology, 35*(4), 40–53.

O'Hara, M. M. (1984). Person-centered gestalt: Towards a holistic synthesis. In R. F. Levant & J. M. Shlien (Eds.), *Client-centered therapy and the person-centered approach: New directions in theory, research and practice* (pp. 203–221). New York: Praeger.

Polanyi, M. (1958). *Personal knowledge: Towards a post-critical philosophy.* Chicago: University of Chicago Press.

Rogers, C. R. (1959). A theory of therapy, personality, and interpersonal relationships, as developed in the client-centered framework. In S. Koch (Ed.), *Psychology: A study of a science* (pp. 184–256). New York: McGraw-Hill.

Rogers, C. R. (1977). *Carl Rogers on personal power.* New York: Delacorte.

Rogers, C. R. (1980). *A way of being.* Boston: Houghton Mifflin.

Rogers, C. R. (1986). Rogers, Kohut, and Erickson: A personal perspective on some similarities and differences. *Person-Centered Review, 1*(2), 125–140.

Roland, A. (1988). *In search of self in India and Japan: Towards a cross-cultural psychology.* Princeton, NJ: Princeton University Press.

Rollins, H. E. (Ed.). (1958). *Keats J.: The letters of John Keats* (Vol. 1). Cambridge, MA: Harvard University Press.

Romanyshyn, R. D. (1982). *Psychological life: From science to metaphor.* Austin: University of Texas Press.

Rowe, E. C., & MacIsaac, D. S. (1991). *Empathic attunement.* Northvale, NJ: Jason Aronson.

Schein, E. H. (1985). *Organizational culture and leadership.* San Francisco: Jossey-Bass.

Showalter, E. (1985). *The female malady.* New York: Viking Penguin.

Shweder, R., & Bourne, E. J. (1982). Does the concept of the person vary cross culturally? In A. J. Marsella & G. M. White (Eds.), *Cultural conceptions of mental health and therapy* (pp. 97–137). Boston: Klewer.

Smith, B. M. (1994). Selfhood at risk: Postmodern perils and the perils of postmodernism. *The American Psychologist, 49*(5), 404–411.

Surrey, J. L. (1991). The self-in-relation: A theory of women's development. In J. V. Jordan, A. G. Kaplan, J. B. Miller, I. P. Stiver, & J. L. Surrey (Eds.), *Women's growth in connection: Writings from the Stone Center.* New York: Guilford Press.

Taylor, C. (1989). *Sources of the self: The making of the modern identity.* Cambridge, MA: Harvard University Press.

Vanaerschot, G. (1990). The process of empathy: Holding and letting go. In G. Lietauer, J. Rombauts, & R. Van Balen (Eds.), *Client and experiential psychotherapy in the nineties* (pp. 267–293). Leuven, Belgium: Leuven University Press.

15

THE EMPATHIC CONTEXT IN PSYCHOTHERAPY WITH PEOPLE OF COLOR

ADELBERT H. JENKINS

In this chapter I will discuss a perspective on empathic processes in psychodynamically oriented psychotherapy with ethnic minority clients of color[1] in America. The topic of empathy can be seen to be an important one because it is fundamental to the establishment of a helping relationship. More and more the writing on psychoanalytically oriented therapy emphasizes the quality of the therapist–patient relationship as fundamental to positive change (Gill, 1983; Luborsky, 1984; Strupp & Binder, 1984).

This is particularly true in work with ethnic minority clients of color seeking therapy. Various writers note the therapist's task of properly managing the initial sessions with these patients (Griffith & Jones, 1979). Sue and Zane (1987) note the therapist's task early on of establishing his or her "credibility" with the ethnic minority patient.[2] Gibbs (1985) suggests that African-American clients, mindful of racism, initially tend to take an *interpersonal* orientation in the therapy situation. That is, they are particularly

I gratefully acknowledge the helpful comments of Dr. Richard Bock who read earlier drafts of this chapter.

[1] In this paper when I use the terms *people of color* or *ethnic minorities* I will be referring to people of African-American, American-Indian, Asian-American, and Latino background. I will be writing from my greater knowledge of the literature on African Americans, although I will attempt to formulate what I have to say so as to make it broadly relevant to the range of people of color in America.

[2] In this article I shall use the terms *patient* and *client* interchangeably to describe the person seeking psychotherapeutic help.

sensitive to the process going on between themselves and their therapists. They are less likely than typical middle-class patients to take for granted the therapist's readiness or ability to understand them and be on their side. Thus, at first they are not ready to pursue in an *instrumental*, task-oriented phase of therapy the personal aspects of the problem that brought them to the therapist.

Such considerations raise the question of what stance to take regarding cultural differences in the therapy situation. Tyler, Brome, and Williams (1991) argue that scholarship on psychotherapy with ethnic minorities can be grouped into three categories. The first is a "universalist" perspective on cross-cultural issues that proposes there are "fundamental constructs that represent a core of human experience that supersedes the importance of other variables such as race, culture, and life circumstances in determining how individuals develop and view the world" (p. 10). A second conceptual approach, a "particularist" one, insists that the cultural ways that people are different from one another are the issues to be emphasized in tailoring mental health interventions with ethnic minority groups. Tyler, Brome, and Williams propose a third perspective, a "transcendist" one, that recognizes and respects similarities and differences among people and tries to understand the kinds of stable factors that facilitate or hinder effective service delivery in particular cross-cultural situations. This view assumes that it is possible to be helpful in these contexts by noting where patient and therapist values *converge,* by being respectful of issues where client-therapist values *diverge,* and by coming to understand and minimizing the impact of *conflictual* value positions in the therapy relationship.

There is no question that, if therapists are to be helpful to minority clients, they must bring a heightened awareness of cultural factors. An extensive literature is developing on mental health interventions with people of color that the reader should consult (e.g., Comas-Diaz & Greene, 1994; Comas-Diaz & Griffiths, 1988; Dana, 1993; Dudley & Rawlins, 1985; McGoldrick, Pearce, & Giordano, 1996; Ridley, Mendoza, Kanitz, Angermeier, & Zenk, 1994; Sodowsky, Taffe, Guitkin, & Wise, 1994; Sue & Sue, 1990). However, work with patients of color, as with many other kinds of clinical issues, raises complexities. As Enrico Jones (1985) has recently noted, it is rather easy to make general recommendations in working with the non-White client. For example, it is obviously important for the therapist to become more knowledgeable about non-White cultures, be open to a flexible use of technique, and learn to communicate acceptance of the client in terms that are meaningful within that person's cultural perspective.

However, as Jones (1985) goes on to note, even granted the salience of group identity for many non-White persons (Landrine, 1992; Tharp, 1991), treatment formulations based primarily on broad constructs such as race and social class are usually not sufficient for dealing with a given minority patient in the clinical situation. People live out their cultural and social characteristics in unique ways. There is great within-group variability among people of color. Knowledge about the general characteristics of particular groups still leaves the clinician with the task of establishing a helpful relationship with the particular individual with whom he or she is working at the moment. That is, granted a foundation of continuing sensitivity to the client's class, culture, and gender background, clinicians still have the task of, as it were, "locating" the *unique individual* within his or her particular group identity. In this chapter I will assume that the therapist's empathizing activity is one of the fundamental aspects of that process. In this sense I believe, along with Jones (1985), that empathy is an important process for all clients. This does not mean that attention to "universal" concepts such as empathy is sufficient for effective work with people of color. However, I believe there are certain aspects of the writing on empathy, illuminated by a particular approach to the human image, that can facilitate work with these clients.

With regard to the human image, there is an emerging theme in psychological and psychoanalytic theory that emphasizes a teleological and humanistic aspect of the person as a "psychological agent" (Chein, 1972; Howard & Conway, 1986; Jenkins, 1992; Rychlak, 1988, 1994; Schafer, 1976). This perspective sees persons as active in coping with the circumstances that confront them; it portrays them as being more than simply passive reactors to environmental and constitutional events that they encounter. In previous writing, I have drawn on this theme to consider the psychological issues of ethnic minorities of color in the United States (Jenkins, 1989, 1995). In this chapter I shall argue that this conception of agency can also be useful in illuminating the therapist's activity in setting the empathic context in the therapy with people of color.

The material that is particularly relevant to my discussion comes from the extensive literature on empathy in psychoanalytic and client-centered therapies (Bohart, 1991; Tobin, 1990). For my purposes here I shall concentrate on writers influenced by Heinz Kohut and some of those who take what I would call a more humanistic approach to the psychoanalytic tradition (Jenkins, 1992). I believe that heightening the philosophical issues underlying some of the recent approaches to empathy will clarify what is needed in making this a useful topic in psychotherapy with ethnic minorities.

My implicit emphasis here will be on the therapeutic situation in which there is a gap in cultural values between the ethnic minority client and the therapist of European-American middle-class background—the most likely therapeutic dyad currently. Similar considerations may apply in therapy conducted by non-White therapists with minority clients. As Sue (1988) notes, the more important issue in establishing an effective therapeutic process is probably relative convergence of *values* between patient and therapist rather than simply similarity of ethnic background. People from the same ethnic background may have conflicting value orientations.

In terms of the overall plan of this chapter, I will first begin with a broad definition of the term *empathy* as it is taken from some of the psychotherapy literature, and I shall briefly relate that notion to its function in the development of the self in the Kohutian view. Second, I shall suggest that therapists' ability to achieve empathic relationships with minority clients is potentially hampered by their personal rootedness in a racist society. I shall then argue that it is necessary to mobilize those features of the broad potential for human agency, to be defined here, that will heighten the imaginative capacities in ways useful for entering the psychological world of people who are different from them. In so doing, therapists will be able to help patients of color broaden their imaginative horizons in their efforts to achieve more satisfying directions for self-development.

THE EMPATHIC PROCESS

As various writers (Korchin, 1976; Margulies, 1989) have pointed out, the term *empathy* derives from the German word *Einfühlung,* implying a "feeling oneself into" another's experience. It refers to the ability to "put oneself in another person's shoes" emotionally, while maintaining one's own identity and perspective. It involves trying to conceptualize and experience another person's world as that person does, as much as one can. In his recent monograph on empathizing, Margulies notes four distinguishable but interrelated facets of the empathic process cited by Buie (1981):

> Conceptual empathy (emphasizing a cognitive understanding of the patient), self-experiential empathy (referring to low intensity memories, feelings, and associations experienced by the therapist), imaginative imitation empathy (imagining and imitating in fantasy an ad hoc model of the patient's inner world), and resonant empathy (an affective "contagion"). (p. 17)

It is imaginative empathy that gets the most attention in his book and is the focus for the discussion in this chapter.

The centrality of empathic processes in psychotherapy derives from their broader function in promoting human development and interpersonal relations generally. The capacity to empathize is one that evolves within the matrix of the individual's cognitive and emotional development (Buie, 1981; Hoffman, 1984). For Kohut (1977) an empathic milieu is essential to the development of healthy self processes. He notes, "Man can no more survive psychologically in a psychological milieu that does not respond empathically to him, than he can survive physically in an atmosphere that contains no oxygen" (p. 253).

As we know, the self is a central concept in Kohut's reinterpretation of certain aspects of psychoanalytic theory. The self, "an independent center of initiative, an independent recipient of impressions" (Kohut & Wolf, 1978, p. 414), has its own line of development. The quality and cohesiveness of the evolving self in the developmental situation depends on the degree to which the parents are able to understand and respond to the child's sometimes inarticulately expressed needs not only for love and physical attention but also for discipline (lest the child's impulses run out of control). When the parent's empathic contact with the child's states is adequate, it is because the parent is attuned to the child's point of view. The same must be true in the therapy relationship if the process is to be a healing one.

A problem arises when we consider the therapeutic dyad with people of color, however. The rates of attrition from and underuse of psychotherapy vary among African-American, Asian-American, and Latino groups. However, recent data continue to indicate that ethnic minorities of color could be better served than they have been by the mental health service delivery system (Sue, Fujino, Li-tze, Takeuchi, & Zane, 1991). This is not so much a manifestation of their inability to use mental health services as it is a reflection of the difficulty mental health professionals have in delivering such services in a culturally sensitive manner. Put another way, the situation with ethnic minority patients suggests that there is a considerable degree of "empathic failure" in our psychotherapeutic alliances with ethnic minority clients, a too-frequent inability to "reach" these clients and establish effective working relationships.

THE PERSONAL BASIS FOR EMPATHY

That this could be so is unfortunate but not as surprising as one would think. Interpersonal relations reflect one's participation as a person in our cultural milieu. In the United States this means a social context that has historically been problematic with regard to racial and ethnic issues. In introducing his discussion of assessment procedures in clinical psychology, Korchin (1976) notes that what he calls "informal" assessment processes are basic to clinical-judgment activities.

Empathy and Informal Assessment

Informal assessment refers to the activities of person perception characteristic of all human beings as they form impressions of others. As professionals and as laypeople, we are continually involved in our daily lives in making the judgment as to whether others are friendly or antagonistic, sad or happy, and honest or deceitful. Empathic abilities are related to these informal interpersonal operations. Formal assessment, Korchin notes, "involving interviews, tests, and systematic observation, builds on, extends, and sharpens informal assessment, but it does not replace it" (p. 144).

The relevance of these considerations here, of course, is that in considering clinical work with people of color in America we need to remind ourselves that how we function as clinicians is related to who we are as people, over and above our training. Our informal assessment activities, on which more formal work rests, develop within a sociocultural framework. Our capacity to be empathic with minority clients of color is influenced by the processes that affect person perception. The informal judgment processes that we bring to our work with people of color and on which we base our formal assessment activities are bound to be influenced by the social and historical context in which we have developed. As Jones (1985) notes regarding work with African-American patients, while

> any client can invoke in a therapist an unhelpful emotional response . . .
> black patients may evoke more complicated countertransference reactions and more frequently. The reason for this seems to be that social images of blacks still make them easier targets for therapists' projections and that the culturally different client provides more opportunities for empathic failures. (p. 178)

This is by no means a blanket indictment of therapy done in cross-cultural contexts. However, we must be highly self-reflective about how we address the psychotherapy situation. (The above discussion assumes, of course, that the ongoing process of "assessment" is part and parcel of the workings of therapy.)

Racism as Narcissistic Assault

The racial and cultural prejudice that people of color must deal with in everyday society is a special and continuing assault on the healthy aspect of their positive self-regard. Most minority people, through appropriate "self-affirming activities" (Miller, 1992), maintain a balanced sense of self and a healthy self-esteem. However, when a person's individual history has been especially troubled and the weight of events becomes too crushing, he or she may develop psychopathological symptoms. Basch (1980) argues that patients coming to psychotherapy bring the hope that they will be able to further the development of important aspects of their self-esteem that were hampered in the course of their living. Unconsciously, they hope to be able to use the therapist as a kind of "selfobject" (Kohut, 1977), a person who will respond in ways that meet the specific needs of the developmentally weakened self. However, the therapy situation is likely to be one associated for many people of color with the White establishment. This may automatically conjure up the specter of an authoritarian institution operating on the client to his or her detriment. Before he or she can make use of the therapist in the way that Basch, for example, suggests, he or she must try to become certain about what kinds of attitudes the therapist brings from the larger society.

It is in this context that we can return to Gibbs's (1985) notion of the *interpersonal* phase with African-American clients. This initial stage of treatment presumably evolves through several "microstages" in the first few sessions. For example, she suggests that often African-American clients are somewhat aloof at the outset, though watchful in an effort to "size up" the therapist. They proceed to a "checking out" phase by posing questions or statements designed to elicit the therapist's qualifications or value positions on social issues. Gibbs suggests that if the therapist fails to be sensitive to the patient's testing by responding skillfully, the relationship quickly begins to founder and the patient is likely to leave. If the therapist deals with the interaction sensitively at these points, the patient moves through the other stages that Gibbs delineates before entering the *instrumental,* task-oriented phase of therapy. From the view presented in this chapter, it is because minority patients bring their experience of social exclusion to the consulting room that they particularly need to test the therapist's empathic capacities.

Empathy: An "Outward Movement"

The typical notion of empathy is that it involves focusing inward, in a sense, and using one's own feeling states as a reference point for what another is experiencing—"vicarious introspection," as Kohut (1977) has put it. That is, I understand another's embarrassment or anger in a certain situation partly in terms of the experience of such feelings that I have had in the course of my life. However, the degree of separation among cultural groups in Western society has made it hard for well-meaning professionals, especially of Euro-American background, to establish the everyday contacts that would let them get to know people from other backgrounds personally. One has fewer grounds for relating one's own inner experience and attitudes to those of people of color. In this regard, then, Jones (1985) has suggested that in clinical situations where the cultural background of the clinician and client are different, an "outward movement of empathy" is called for, a heightening of the imagination "that would transpose oneself into an-other . . . [and thereby achieve] a more complete understanding of culturally varied predispositions . . . [and] personal constructs" (p. 178). From this view, what is needed is a different kind of effort to extend formal assessment mechanisms and override those aspects of one's informal judging process that lead to misapprehension of the minority client. It is here that I think the notion of a certain quality inherent in human agency needs to be high-lighted to reflect a particular kind of activity in the therapist's role.

In the next section of the chapter I will describe the notion of agency providing the model for therapist activity that I wish to propose here. In introducing this perspective, I am proposing that the empathic activity[3] needed with ethnic minority clients derives not only from the processes of person perception but also from other crucial characteristics of human activity.

A PHILOSOPHICAL CONCEPTION OF HUMAN ACTION

My view of the needed therapist stance stems from a particular conception of human agency found in Rychlak's (1994) logical learning theory (LLT). First, I shall give a short overview of basic tenets of the theory. Then, I will discuss these notions in enough detail to relate them to my considerations of empathic activity. In brief, the logical learning theory perspective argues that (a) "dialectical" thinking, the imaginative capacity to bring alternative conceptions of meaning to life situations, is frequently used by people to guide their behavior; (b) as human mental capacity comes at experience it actively structures, it does not just passively register, stimulus input; and (c) subjectively held intentions are as important causally as are drives and environmental forces in governing the way people behave.

Dialectical Imagination

The first component of psychological agency as conceived here has to do with how human beings impute meaning to events in their lives. A "dialectical" conception recognizes that, in deriving the meaning of a situation, human beings are inherently able to appreciate the alternative—in fact, the opposite—ways of construing what seems to be a firmly structured social or physical circumstance. As Rychlak (1988) has noted, there is always a "quality of open alternatives in experience [which] demands that the human being affirm some . . . meaning at the outset for the sake of which behavior might then take place." Which option is affirmed "is up to the individual and *not* to the environment" (p. 295). Using this capacity of the human imagination, people can, in principle, fashion conceptions of a situation that are opposed to those given by the tradition of a particular authority. From this view a person's understanding and action flow from the meanings he or she constructs in a given situation. Complementary to this dialectical mode is a "demonstrative" or, one might say, syllogistic

---

[3] My use of the term *empathic activity* is consistent not only with the definition of human agency that I shall present shortly but also with Schafer's reinterpretation (e.g., 1976, 1983, especially chapter 3) of therapist performance in his notion of psychoanalytic "action language." Elsewhere, I have shown the relationship between his work and my view of agency (Jenkins, 1992).

mode of thinking, in which an accepted basic assumption—such as "all humans are mortal"—necessarily determines the way we understand something under consideration. This is to say that once a meaning has been affirmed from among a set of dialectically conceivable possibilities it has a fixed implication for further understanding and action (see Rychlak, 1994, for further discussion of this important complementary mode of human thought). The human being's inherent "dialectical" thinking capacities are basic to psychological agency and will be particularly important to the discussion of empathy here.

The Construction of Reality

A second important aspect of this view of agency has to do with the way human mentality confronts the world. In the LLT view, mind or mentality is a *process* that meets experience "at the level of sensation (input) with a creative capacity to *order* it via patterns that constitute meaning and meaningfulness" (Rychlak, 1988, p. 326). Human mentality is active rather than passive in "coming at" experience. From birth, individuals are engaged in selecting, structuring, and framing their experience into meanings. In fact, the only way we can understand things is through the conceptual categories we bring to experience. Thus, although we can assume that there is a reality of some sort independent of our observation of it, the characteristics of reality as we come to know them depend on how we construct them mentally.

So, although recognizing the effect of experience on the individual, the LLT perspective also insists that human beings actively organize the world into meaningful units and then they relate mentally to the "reality" that they have constructed. This notion is compatible with what Howard (1991) has called a "constructive realist" point of view. It is also very much allied with the so-called narrative approaches to action being advocated and developed more and more by psychologists from diverse perspectives (Bruner, 1990; Polkinghorne, 1988; Sarbin, 1990; Schafer, 1992; Spence, 1982). From this view the order in our world hangs together as a narrative structure. Even our sense of self is a narrative product. As Schafer notes:

> So-called self-concepts, self-images, self-representations, or more generally the so-called self may be considered to be a set of narrative strategies or storylines each person follows in trying to develop an emotionally coherent account of his or her life among people. (p. 34)

To be human is to be *homo fabulans,* in Howard's (1991) terms—a storytelling being. As necessary contributors to the meaning in our lives, we are "responsible" for the constructions of reality we make and to an important degree are responsible for what we become.

Ends as Causes

Finally, this perspective takes a "teleological" view of human motiva-tion. People do not act only in response to environmental contingencies, internal drive factors, and their history of habit patterns—the typical char-acterization of causes in psychology. Just as important, they act *for the sake of* goals and intentions—reasons—that have causal power. These are *final causes* in the Aristotelian conception of causality (Robinson, 1989). Thus, an individual is not just the passive pawn of surrounding objects and forces. What is particularly important for the teleological–humanistic theorist and therapist—which includes psychoanalytic therapists in their clinical orien-tation—is to seek to understand the intentions that contribute to an indi-vidual's actions. In so doing the therapist necessarily takes an *introspective* (i.e., subjective) point of view on the patient's life, that is, the actor's perspective. In contrast, the mechanistic theorist who attempts to account for human events primarily in terms of material and efficient causation relies on *extraspective* or third-person descriptions. In human affairs such an emphasis looks for the material substance of which a thing is composed (e.g., physiological causes) and the forces acting on this matter (e.g., envi-ronmental stimuli) as the exclusive shapers of behavior. Let me now apply these notions to the therapist's empathizing activity.

AGENCY AND EMPATHIZING ACTIVITY

In addressing myself to psychotherapy with people of color, the work of some of the Kohutian theorists and others writing on empathy in the psychoanalytic situation articulates well with these views on agency. Earlier I noted the four components of empathy. In his discussion of empathy, Margulies (1989) emphasizes the third of these, imaginative empathy, or an "imaginative projection" of oneself into another's world. This perspective stresses the "active, searching quality of entering the other's world" (Margu-lies, 1989, p. 18). He emphasizes the active mode of empathic relating as distinct from the more passive mode in the "resonant" component of empa-thy. The nature of this activity seems particularly related to the concept of dialectical imagination as presented above.

The "Negative Capability"

In introducing his discussion of empathy, Margulies suggests that pre-requisites for the empathizing process can be found in both the psychoana-lytic and the phenomenological approaches to therapy. The psychoanalytic free-associative method and the phenomenological deconstructive method demand as much as possible "the suspension of preconceptions in the service of discovery" on the part of the therapist (Margulies, 1989, p. 12). To describe this process further, Margulies borrows from the poetic stance exemplified by Keats who extolled the "negative capability" in artistic creation. This is the capacity to suspend *a priori* judgments about the "truth" and live with the uncertainties and doubts of psychic life as they present themselves. This presumably allows one to see things with an "unbiased" view. In its "negativity" it is a release from one's customary ways of looking at things, an obliteration of many of one's anchor points for judgment.

On this view, then, empathizing activity is enhanced by the therapist's temporarily giving up the "knowledge" of what is "right" that anchors him or her in the world. From the view of agency presented above, this would involve reengaging a dialectic view, moving back to a "preaffirmative" position, as it were, and recapturing a sense of the alternative ways of looking at an experience. In their personal lives, therapists choose a set of social and ethical precepts derived from their backgrounds to guide their living. Although these standards feel "right" and may well be reasonable, they are nevertheless arbitrary. Accustomed cultural perspectives come to have a rather fixed implication for therapists ensuing understanding and action. Of course, they must anchor themselves in some set of conceptions to get on with their daily lives. But therapists working with persons of another culture are especially challenged to step back from their customary affirmations and become open, conceptually, to the alternative ways of framing events. That is, they must activate their dialectical imaginative abilities.

A completely deconstructive, nonjudgmental stance, one in which the therapist abandons all his or her orienting perspectives, is obviously not possible in practice. However, the more the therapist is able to activate his or her capacity to imagine alternative possibilities, the more he or she is able to take the next step of "feeling into" (*Einfühlung*) the other's experience. That is, the therapist is best able to exercise his or her imagination in constructing an image of the other person's world when he or she can be relatively free of biases about how things "are" or "should be." The "negative capability" that Margulies borrows from Keats is built into the human agent's ability to imaginatively frame a situation both in terms of a given standard and in terms of alternate possibilities. This way of formulating the process of empathy is particularly apt for building the empathic relationship with the person of color. I am suggesting here that a kind of dialectical and deconstructive attitude toward one's own cultural perspectives, perhaps necessary for the empathic act in general, particularly enables the therapist to heighten his or her imagination to enable that "outward movement" of the empathic process suggested by Jones (1985) for the work with patients of color.

Empathic Constructivism

The second defining feature of agency, that people conceptually construct the reality to which they relate, has implications for empathic activity generally and for people of color. Our imaginative empathizing constructs a "model," a conception, of the patient. Thus, as Schafer (1983) says, such a view rejects the notion

> that there is a single, unambiguously knowable emotional reality with which to empathize; and that empathizing may therefore be judged simply right or wrong on the basis of objective criteria that exist free of theoretical presuppositions. . . . That is to say, for the analyst the analysand is not someone who is somehow objectively knowable outside this model. (p. 39)

On this view, together with the patient's participation, the therapist imaginatively creates a mental model of the patient with which he or she empathizes. He or she communicates this image to the patient, thereby constantly checking the model for the patient's sense of "fit" with what the latter is struggling to achieve. In this process the model gets revised considerably over time through the therapist's interventions and the patient's responses. Margulies (1989) described a patient's retelling of a dream near the point of termination of a successful psychotherapy. In the later narration, however, the version was a revised and enriched edition that provided them with unexpected insights to explore. He notes, "there was no static truth to be found in our investigation. The therapeutic truth was a dialectic, a creation of the relationship itself, a continuous coming into being of *possibilities* requiring further exploration" (pp. 11–12).

Possible Selves

Perhaps what results from a well-functioning empathic process in therapy is the opportunity for the emergence and consideration of various "possible selves" for the patient to consider and explore. Markus and her colleagues (e.g., Markus & Nurius, 1986) have discussed this notion as a set of affective–cognitive models that the individual holds as potentialities for positive or negative development of the self. Thus,

> Possible selves are the ideal selves that we would very much like to become. They are also the selves we could become, and the selves we are afraid of becoming. . . . An individual's repertoire of possible selves can be viewed as the cognitive manifestation of enduring goals, aspirations, motives, fears, and threats. (Markus & Nurius, 1986, p. 954)

From the view here, as the therapist imaginatively "tunes in" on the patient's psychological processes and helps him or her to develop these conceptions more clearly in therapy, the patient becomes open to new possibilities for growth.

An example illustrates some of the issues I have discussed so far. Ms. D. was a single, employed, 29-year-old woman of Dominican and African-American heritage. She had grown up in a middle-class family very much concerned with propriety, and though she lived alone, she was still quite dependent on her parents. A few months into therapy, she began to muse about her wish to have a baby to assuage her feelings of loneliness.[4] She had had several disappointing romantic relationships and was not at the time involved with a man. In her fantasy she was quite content that her pregnancy and childbirth could be accomplished without her being married. From one point of view, this was an unrealistic fantasy and could be seen as an unwise thing for her to do. My tack with her was to listen to these thoughts as they came up and through my questions help her explore the various implications, both positive and negative, of such a choice. Her associations included unconditional love, the pride of motherhood, her sense of shame at being an out-of-wedlock mother, the derailment of career plans, the chance to prove she could be a better mother than she felt her mother had been, and so on. After spending a couple of intense sessions exploring these possibilities, she seemed content to move on without ever considering this topic in much detail again.

There are, of course, many facets of this that cannot be explored here. In one sense, her bringing this topic to therapy was a test to see whether I would sense her wish to have a full and free exploration of various possible selves around this topic (and eventually other subjects) without condemnation. I believe the opportunity to openly explore the possibilities of this topic began to give her a sense that this was *her* life and that she could have some control over it, beginning with the kinds of things she could allow herself to imagine. Although this particular topic receded in importance, this exchange was important in the building of the relationship with her and was characteristic of other discussions we had in a more realistic vein geared toward expanding her sense of what might be possible for her.

Awareness

For all people psychotherapy can be seen to be a process that helps them reengage their dialectical thinking regarding their lives and consider new alternatives in their self-conception and action. From one perspective, psychotherapy helps the person to become more *aware* as that term is used in LLT. In LLT, *awareness* is defined as "appreciation of the arbitrariness in experience" that is, "knowing that something else might be taking place in a life circumstance" (Rychlak, 1988, p. 354). Ideally, psychotherapy helps in the development of *self-awareness* as well: "For the person to de-

---

[4] Although the therapist was African American in the vignettes presented here, they can be used to illustrate the issues confronted in more distinctly interethnic therapy settings.

velop . . . self-awareness, he must see the contribution he *makes* to experience, depending upon what sort of meanings are affirmed [in the given situation]" (p. 355). In this sense the therapist, working empathically, helps an individual reflect on his or her meaning constructions about experience to consider alternative conceptualizations about life—new "possible selves." Therapy is useful not so much in terms of the particular *contents* of the self that are conceived and possibly adopted but in terms of the patient's taking on the *process* he or she has been involved in with the therapist, that is, coming to think more dialectically.

Although the above comments would apply to all patients, they hold special meaning for people of color. As we know, racist social practices work to limit the opportunities for self-development of minority persons and thereby encourage the individual to conceive his or her possibilities in negative and stereotypic ways. In spite of this pressure, most people of color work to sustain their dialectic capacities (Jenkins, 1995; Neighbors, 1984). However, a minority individual may well come to psychotherapy experiencing his or her social status as a constriction that is additional to the problems that have come from grappling with personal life history. The particular usefulness of psychotherapy can be that it provides an experience that not only conceptually reframes certain personality issues but also simultaneously helps the person reconceptualize the way he or she addresses the racial situation and his or her place in it. For this to happen, of course, the therapist must be open to the racial implications of the patient's struggles and must be prepared to talk about them both in the transference and in other aspects of his or her life.

The "Empathic-Introspective" View

I turn briefly to the third aspect of the LLT view of agency to illuminate the idea of empathic activity being discussed here. As noted earlier, an individual's intentions (reasons, purposes) make an important causal contribution to behavior. We cannot understand why a person does what he or she does unless we get the subjective view of behavior, through the eyes of the actor. From Schwaber's perspective, this is a defining feature of empathic activity. She stresses that empathy refers to a way of perceiving—"experiencing from *within* the patient's experience" (1980, p. 216). This "introspective" view is to be contrasted with the "extraspective" view I noted earlier (Rychlak, 1994), one that makes inferences primarily from an *external* personal or theoretical vantage point. (It is acknowledged, though, that the latter perspective is also necessary for a full understanding of an event.)

From this viewpoint, Schwaber has advocated a consideration of the transference that is different from the typical view. She conceptualizes the therapy situation as a "contextual unit" in which not only the patient's responses but also the "analyst's contribution, silent or stated, is seen as meaningfully influencing and ordering the nature" of the interpersonal "reality" in the therapy situation (Schwaber, 1980, p. 216). Thus, she assumes a mode of listening that "is characterized by my sustained effort to seek out my place in the patient's experience, as part of the context that is perceived or felt" (Schwaber, 1983, p. 523). She disavows the notion of the therapist as one whose training gives him or her the more objective, presumably "truer," grasp of reality from which to assess the patient's functioning. The therapist aligns with the patient's introspective view by clarifying what actions and characteristics of the therapist contribute to the patient's transference reactions. Feeling his or her position respected, the patient is presumably more able to explore and clarify what is being experienced.

This perspective can be concretized by a case vignette: A depressed, rather constricted but quite bright 24-year-old, single, Hispanic-American woman in therapy complied a bit hesitantly with what the male therapist thought were tactful efforts to clarify certain aspects of her sexual experience. Having completed her report, and after a brief pause, she began to reminisce about a memory of one of her friends from adolescence. It seems that this friend was dating without her very strict father's knowledge or permission. When he discovered her escapades, he had her examined by a physician to see if she was still a virgin. The therapist understood from this association that the patient had experienced his questions as a forcible exam; when asked, she acknowledged her discomfort with that inquiry. I believe the therapist's willingness at this and other points to see himself through the patient's eyes and guide his communications to her accordingly helped to sustain a willingness, generally uncharacteristic of her, to engage in exploration of various facets of her inner life in a way that gradually proved to be beneficial to her.

THE EMPATHIC CONTEXT WITH PEOPLE OF COLOR

When summarized, these notions suggest what can be useful in the therapist's empathizing as an ongoing activity in the psychotherapy relationship with people of color. First, as I have said, the agency notion used here highlights a "constructivist" position. Such a view emphasizes the idea that there are alternative ways of conceiving reality. The more one has a sense that one is looking at the world not so much the way it is, but viewing it through one's conceptualizations of it, influenced by one's own social and personal vantage point, the more open one is to recognizing the partialness of one's own truth and the possibility of other useful truths.

On this view, a therapist who takes a stance that holds philosophically that there are valid alternative perspectives on reality is likely to be able to be more open to cultural difference and allow the minority client more room for growth. One of the hallmarks of American racism has been the assumption that the Euro-American cultural vision represented *the* "reality." Other cultural perspectives were seen as distortions. People of color coming to mental health institutions have expected to be greeted from this perspective. Contact with an "authority" who believes that he or she is not the arbiter of reality should be especially liberating for these patients. Such an attitude is buttressed further by the therapist's continuing efforts to take the special introspective attitude in the relationship with the client—a rare experience in the minority person's interactions with White America.

In addition, the emphasis on the validity of alternate "takes" on reality, and the search for the patient's introspective view of the relationship, promotes an egalitarian atmosphere in therapy. Research on the impact of therapist attitudes on treatment outcome supports the importance of this variable in work with lower-class patients. Lerner (1972) found that low-income patients, many of whom were Black, showed more improvement in therapy when seen by therapists holding "egalitarian" attitudes toward low-income people in general than did clients seen by therapists not holding such attitudes.[5] Ross (1983) used the same measure of therapist attitude and found that low-income Black patients remained in therapy longer when seen by therapists with egalitarian attitudes. Within such a context as the patient communicates, both verbally and nonverbally, the therapist "feels his or her way into" the patient's emotional position by activating dialectically imaginative capacities to develop with the patient working models of the self and its cognitive and affect attributes.

The Nature of the Effects in the Empathic Context

The question is often raised as to whether empathy is primarily *facilitative* in helping the patient do the hard work of overcoming resistances and constructing usable self-conceptions in therapy or whether the therapist's empathic activity is, in and of itself, *curative*. In this context, I think the therapist's empathizing activity has both effects in a way particular to the American racial situation. In the early process of establishing credibility, Gibb's *interpersonal* phase, the therapist's sensitive and empathic responding to the patient's testing regarding the genuineness of his or her egalitarian attitudes facilitates moving into the *instrumental* stage of therapy. In addition, it is my belief that when a patient of color is treated empathically

---

[5] Lerner devised a special "authoritarianism" scale to measure psychotherapists' attitudes toward low-income people. Examples of some of her items were, "If they had had a successful treatment experience, most political radicals of both the right and the left would change their views on society and its ills" and "Involvement of the poor in programs planned for their welfare is essential, but, because they are mainly oriented to immediate gratification, it is unrealistic to give them top level decision-making powers in planning such programs because long range goals would inevitably suffer" (p. 89). Responding that one strongly agrees with such statements would presumably be toward the authoritarian side.

336   ADELBERT H. JENKINS

by a therapist of another ethnic background, especially of Euro-American background because of American history, such a process has a curative impact on the special burdens on their personal functioning that people of color carry as a result of American racism. In a psychotherapy relationship that proves to be helpful, not only does the individual experience the improvement of personal skills in coping, but he or she also learns about the possibilities for cross-cultural communication. However, such a process should also be one in which the patient feels free to examine and strengthen, if he or she wishes, aspects of his or her particular ethnic identity. For example, an African-American client might begin to feel able to revise aspects of racial identity in directions toward or away from a bicultural stance (Cross, 1991; Jones, 1991; Parham, 1989). Such an exploration would make possible the elaboration of some *diverging* values in the therapy dyad (Tyler et al., 1991).

However, of equal importance, there is the opportunity in an actively empathic context for important ameliorative effects on the therapist as well. I noted earlier the considerable separation between cultural groups in the United States. This means that most White therapists have little familiarity with nonclinical samples of people of color or with ethnic minorities as peers. Most White therapists are fated to be ignorant about this growing segment in American society. Some recent research suggests how these issues may operate in the counseling and psychotherapy process. Cross (1991) has suggested in his *nigrescence* theory that racial identity experience in African Americans can go through several stages. It starts with a stage of a lack of awareness about the African heritage for Black Americans through a stage of positive and nondefensive valuing of African-American culture. Helms (1984), drawing on earlier presentations of Cross's ideas, argues that Whites can also evolve through various stages of consciousness about their racial identity. This process begins with the awareness of Black people being different, what she calls a "contact" stage. The four subsequent stages involve guilt about societal racism, retreat from interracial contact into a defensive prejudice, emergence into a curiosity about and intellectual acceptance of Blacks, and finally a genuine emotional acceptance of racial and cultural diversity. In this last stage, Whites show a differentiated awareness of and valuing of their own identity as well as a genuine appreciation for people from other backgrounds.

Helms's view is that the stage of racial-identity development that each of the participants is in influences the therapy process in an interracial therapy. Thus, to take a problematic example, where a therapist prone to retreat from contact is working with a patient *immersed*, in Cross's (1991) terms, in a militant African-American identity, the therapy relationship would probably be characterized, at least for some period, by considerable "conflict" (Tyler et al., 1991). Ponterotto (1988) has similarly described a progression through stages of awareness of racial identity in his work with White counselor trainees.

Thus, Euro-American therapists may be more resistant to fully entering the relationship with the minority client for fear they will learn something about their attitudes that they would rather not know. However, if the therapist can become truly open to stepping back from his or her preconceptions—through self-reflection and consulting with knowledgeable colleagues—and take a dialectic stance regarding the patient's experience, he or she is bound to learn new and meaningful things about himself or herself and about the patient's world. The latter would include learning about the problematic aspects of patients' ethnic and social class roles in America, as well as some of the positive features of the way clients live out their ethnic identity. If therapists are prepared to accept the challenge of becoming more empathically introspectively engaged, the rewards for themselves as professionals and as citizens and the rewards for their patients as personal and social beings could be considerable.

CONCLUSION

In this chapter I have argued that the empathizing process in psychodynamic psychotherapy with people of color involves disciplined use of the therapist's psychological agency. Such a notion emphasizes the use of the therapist's dialectical imaginative capacities to feel into the patient's view and thereby help him or her construct a more satisfying and effective way of adapting. It calls for recognition by the therapist of the different valid cultural ways of addressing life problems and a willingness to become open to new learning about others. Such a view urges the therapist to confront the limited attitudes that he or she may have as a function of being a member of a society that is still quite restrictive racially. I suggest that when cross-racial therapy relationships are effective they do so through earnest grappling with issues such as these.

REFERENCES

Basch, M. F. (1980). *Doing psychotherapy*. New York: Basic Books.

Bohart, A. C. (1991). Empathy in client-centered therapy: A contrast with psychoanalysis and self psychology. *Journal of Humanistic Psychology, 31*, 34–48.

Bruner, J. S. (1990). *Acts of meaning*. Cambridge, MA: Harvard University Press.

Buie, D. H. (1981). Empathy: Its nature and limitations. *Journal of the American Psychoanalytic Association, 29*, 281–307.

Chein, I. (1972). *The science of behavior and the image of man*. New York: Basic Books.

Comas-Diaz, L., & Greene, B. (Eds.). (1994). *Women of color: Integrating ethnic and gender identities in psychotherapy.* New York: Guilford Press.

Comas-Diaz, L., & Griffiths, E. E. H. (Eds.). (1988). *Clinical guidelines in cross-cultural mental health.* New York: Wiley.

Cross, W. E., Jr. (1991). *Shades of Black: Diversity in African-American identity.* Philadelphia: Temple University Press.

Dana, R. H. (1993). *Multicultural assessment perspectives for professional psychology.* Needham Heights, MA: Allyn & Bacon.

Dudley, G. R., & Rawlins, M. R. (Eds.). (1985). Psychotherapy with ethnic minorities [Special Issue]. *Psychotherapy, 22*(2).

Gibbs, J. T. (1985). Establishing a treatment relationship with Black clients: Interpersonal vs. instrumental strategies. In C. Germain (Ed.), *Advances in clinical social work practice.* Silver Spring, MD: National Association of Social Work, Inc.

Gill, M. M. (1983). The interpersonal paradigm and the degree of the therapist's involvement. *Contemporary Psychoanalysis, 19,* 200–237.

Griffith, M. S., & Jones, E. E. (1979). Race and psychotherapy: Changing perspectives. In J. H. Masserman (Ed.), *Current psychiatric therapies* (Vol. 18, pp. 225–235). New York: Grune & Stratton.

Helms, J. (1984). Toward a theoretical explanation of the effects of race on counseling: A Black and White model. *The Counseling Psychologist, 12,* 153–165.

Hoffman, M. L. (1984). Interaction of affect and cognition in empathy. In C. E. Izard, J. Kagan, & R. B. Zajonc (Eds.), *Emotions, cognition, and behavior* (pp. 103–131). Cambridge, England: Cambridge University Press.

Howard, G. S. (1991). Culture tales: A narrative approach to thinking, cross-cultural psychology, and psychotherapy. *American Psychologist, 46,* 187–197.

Howard, G. S., & Conway, C. G. (1986). Can there be an empirical science of volitional action? *American Psychologist, 41,* 1241–1251.

Jenkins, A. H. (1989). Psychological agency: A crucial concept for minorities. *Theoretical and Philosophical Psychology, 9,* 4–11.

Jenkins, A. H. (1992). Hermeneutics versus science in psychoanalysis: A rigorous humanistic view. *Psychoanalytic Psychology, 9,* 509–527.

Jenkins, A. H. (1995). *Psychology and African Americans: A humanistic approach* (2nd ed.). Needham Heights, MA: Allyn & Bacon.

Jones, E. E. (1985). Psychotherapy and counseling with Black patients. In P. Pedersen (Ed.), *Handbook of cross-cultural counseling and therapy* (pp. 173–179). Westport, CT: Greenwood.

Jones, J. M. (1991). The politics of personality: Being Black in America. In R. L. Jones (Ed.), *Black psychology* (3rd ed., pp. 305–318). Berkeley, CA: Cobb & Henry.

Kohut, H. (1977). *The restoration of the self.* New York: International Universities Press.

Kohut, H., & Wolf, E. S. (1978). The disorders of the self and their treatment: An outline. *International Journal of Psychoanalysis, 59,* 413–425.

Korchin, S. J. (1976). *Modern clinical psychology.* New York: Basic Books.

Landrine, H. (1992). Clinical implications of cultural differences: The referential versus the indexical self. *Clinical Psychology Review, 12,* 401–415.

Lerner, B. (1972). *Therapy in the ghetto: Political impotence and personal disintegration.* Baltimore, MD: The Johns Hopkins University Press.

Luborsky, L. (1984). *Principles of psychoanalytic psychotherapy: A manual for supportive–expressive treatment.* New York: Basic Books.

Margulies, A. (1989). *The empathic imagination.* New York: Norton.

Markus, H., & Nurius, P. (1986). Possible selves. *American Psychologist, 41,* 954–969.

McGoldrick, M., Pearce, J., & Giordano, J. (1996). *Ethnicity and family therapy* (2nd ed.). New York: Guilford Press.

Miller, I. J. (1992). Interpersonal vulnerability and narcissism: A conceptual continuum for understanding and treating narcissistic psychopathology. *Psychotherapy, 29,* 216–224.

Neighbors, H. W. (1984). The distribution of psychiatric morbidity in Black Americans: A review and suggestions for research. *Community Mental Health Journal, 20,* 169–181.

Parham, T. A. (1989). Cycles of psychological nigrescence. *The Counseling Psychologist, 17,* 187–226.

Polkinghorne, D. (1988). *Narrative knowing and the human sciences.* Albany, NY: State University of New York Press.

Ponterotto, J. G. (1988). Racial consciousness development among White counselor trainees: A stage model. *Journal of Multicultural Counseling and Development, 16,* 146–156.

Ridley, C. R., Mendoza, D. W., Kanitz, B. E., Angerm (1994). Cultural sensitivity in multicultural counseling model. *Journal of Counseling Psychology, 41,* 125–136.

Robinson, D. N. (1989). *Aristotle's psychology.* New York: Press.

Ross, S. A. (1983). Variables associated with dropping out *Abstracts International, 44,* 616B (University Microfilm

Rychlak, J. F. (1988). *The psychology of rigorous humanism (* New York University Press.

Rychlak, J. F. (1994). *Logical learning theory.* Lincoln: University of Nebraska Press.

Sarbin, T. R. (1990). The narrative quality of action. *Theoretical and Philosophical Psychology, 10,* 49–65.

Schafer, R. (1976). *A new language for psychoanalysis.* New Haven, CT: Yale University Press.

Schafer, R. (1983). *The analytic attitude.* New York: Basic Books.

Schafer, R. (1992). *Retelling a life: Narration and dialogue in psychoanalysis.* New York: Basic Books.

Schwaber, E. (1980). Self psychology and the concept of psychopathology: A case presentation. In A. Goldberg (Ed.), *Advances in self psychology* (pp. 215–242). New York: International Universities Press.

Schwaber, E. (1983). A particular perspective on psychoanalytic listening. *Psychoanalytic Study of the Child, 38,* 519–546.

Sodowsky, G. R., Taffe, R. C., Guitkin, T. B., & Wise, S. L. (1994). Development of the Multicultural Counseling Inventory: A self-report measure of multicultural competencies. *Journal of Counseling Psychology, 41,* 137–148.

Spence, D. (1982). *Narrative truth and historical truth: Meaning an interpretation in psychoanalysis.* New York: Norton.

Strupp, H. H., & Binder, J. L. (1984). *Psychotherapy in a new key: A guide to time-limited dynamic psychotherapy.* New York: Basic Books.

Sue, D. W., & Sue, D. (1990). *Counseling the culturally different: Theory and practice* (2nd ed.). New York: Wiley.

Sue, S. (1988). Psychotherapeutic services for ethnic minorities: Two decades of research findings. *American Psychologist, 43,* 301–308.

Sue, S., Fujino, D. C., Li-tze, H., Takeuchi, D. T., & Zane, N. W. S. (1991). Community mental health services for ethnic minority groups: A test of the cultural responsiveness hypothesis. *Journal of Consulting and Clinical Psychology, 59,* 533–540.

Sue, S., & Zane, N. (1987). The role of culture and cultural techniques in psychotherapy: A critique and reformulation. *American Psychologist, 43,* 301–308.

Tharp, R. G. (1991). Cultural diversity and treatment of children. *Journal of Consulting and Clinical Psychology, 59,* 799–812.

Tobin, S. A. (1990). Self psychology as a bridge between existential–humanistic psychology and psychoanalysis. *Journal of Humanistic Psychology, 30,* 14–63.

Tyler, F. B., Brome, D. R., & Williams, J. E. (1991). *Ethnic validity, ecology, and psychotherapy: A psychosocial competence model.* New York: Plenum.

16

RELATIONAL DEVELOPMENT THROUGH MUTUAL EMPATHY

JUDITH V. JORDAN

Relational models of development posit that human beings experience a profound need for connection with other people and that isolation is one of the primary, if not *the* primary, sources of suffering. Rather than focus on development of the "separate self" characterized by internalized structure and self-sufficiency, this perspective emphasizes the integrative experience of "being in and for the relationship" (Jordan, 1992; Miller, 1976). I honor the intersubjective, relationally emergent nature of human experience. The movement of relating, of mutual initiative and responsiveness, is viewed as the ongoing central organizing dynamic of people's lives. Movement toward mutuality lies at the heart of relational development. This perspective suggests that the deepest sense of one's being is continuously formed in connection with others and is inextricably tied to relational movement. In a developmental and clinical model that stresses relational development, empathic engagement provides a compelling sense of "connected-being" or "relational self." The primary feature, rather than structure marked by separateness and autonomy, is increasing empathic responsiveness in the context of interpersonal mutuality (Jordan, 1986).

Emotional connection is established through responsiveness, often in sensing the empathic presence of the other person. In mutual empathy one gets to experience oneself as affecting and being affected by another. When one feels empathy from the other person, it provides a palpable sense that one influences and emotionally touches the other person. In empathy I am present, vulnerable, open, responsive, and concerned. This responsiveness goes against the edicts to protect oneself from the impact of another person, part of our cultural overemphasis on separation and control. Crucial to the therapist's engagement is the everpresent effort to take into account and care about the way another is going to be affected by what one says or does a kind of anticipatory empathy or empathic concern. This is at the heart of the therapy exchange. Mutual empathy enhances dialogue, a sense of connection, and the experience of human community for all participants. In mutual empathic understanding, the inner conviction of the "separate self" is deeply challenged.

WHAT IS EMPATHY?

Empathy is a complex cognitive–affective experience of joining in understanding, a feeling–resonance that leads to a more differentiated understanding of self, other, and relationship (Jordan, 1989b). It relies on an ability to tolerate the tension of opening to another's experience; as the poet Keats put it, we must be capable of being "in uncertainties, mysteries, doubt without irritable reaching after fact and reason" (Keats, 1987).

Empathy involves the capacity to perceive another's affective state, to resonate with that emotional state, and to gain some understanding or clarity about the other's subjective world. Rather than a more distance-mediated way of knowing through cognitive channels alone, empathy involves an emotional resonance that gives one a compelling psychological–physiological sense of joining with the experience of another person. Studies have documented this vicarious physiological arousal.

Empathic expansion involves moving out of a certain kind of self-centeredness into an understanding of the growth of self and other and of relational awareness. We move beyond the paradigm of self versus other and egoism versus altruism. People both contribute to and are sustained by, grow in, and depend on the relationship. People do not just come together to give and take or trade off dependencies. They create relationships to which they both contribute and in which they both can grow. Growth occurs in becoming a part of relationship rather than apart from relationship (Jordan, 1984).

EMPATHY IN THERAPY: SELF-EMPATHY AND
EMPATHY FOR OTHERS

In a relational model, therapists shift their focus from one that primarily looks at the intrapsychic and the characterological to one that focuses on relational elaboration. They engage in articulating, tracing, and getting to know relational movement from connection to disconnection and back into connection in the here and now. They foster awareness of self, other, and relationship.

Empathy is central to the process of relational psychotherapy. It diminishes the client's sense of isolation and enhances the experience of interpersonal effectiveness; being responded with increases one's sense of connectedness and relational competence.

Empathy for others and self-empathy develop in interactions with the therapist (Jordan, 1984). In this awareness-promoting relationship, the client begins to feel an appreciation for his or her inner world and its evolution, and thus, the client begins to take an empathic attitude toward his or her own feelings, thoughts, and context. The observing, often judging self then makes empathic contact with some experiencing aspect of the self. Frequently in having a memory of oneself, rather than critically judging or rejecting the experience, one finds a way to be with one's own reality in a relational context. Split-off experiences flow back into connection. The client also comes to understand the necessity of his or her particular responses and choices, given personal life circumstances.

Often, self-empathy develops along with a general increase in empathic attunement to others. This ultimately leads to enhanced relational capacity and to an increase in self-esteem as both self and other receive and give more accurate attention; this awareness allows for more appropriate representation of needs by the client. One's sense of understanding the other person and of being understood also increase significantly in this interaction. Although the need to be understood is often emphasized, the need to understand others also is important for most people.

A clinical vignette will illustrate the development of self-empathy and expansion of empathy for others: One client who was quite identified with her critical, punitive father typically spoke of herself in very derogatory terms. One day she was giving an extremely unfavorable description of herself as a child going off for her first day of school. In every comment I could hear her harsh, critical father's voice: "I was an obnoxious little kid. I wanted everyone to pay attention. No wonder my father got so mad at me!" A therapeutic intervention indicating that, of course, she wanted to feel special and safe as she went out into this new, maybe even scary, part of the world at first didn't seem to have any impact. Later in treatment, when we were looking at this same incident, however, this woman burst into tears and said, "Suddenly I saw myself as that little girl, so scared and uncertain. My heart just went out to her. I feel it now for her . . . the pain. I feel it now for me. I couldn't feel it then. But I understand why I was acting that way." It was not simply that she became more accepting and less punitive vis-à-vis certain self representations, although that was an important part of it. But she also actually connected with the affect that had been split off in the memory; both the self as object and the experiencing self were modified by this exchange. Her identification with her critical father was altered in the direction of being less punitive, and harsh inner self-judgments were softened. Although there was a momentary increase of anger at the father as he came to be seen as impatient and critical, empathically failing the child, this was not the end point of the process. Rather, as it was worked through, the woman also began to experience a deepened empathy with her father as well. As she put herself emotionally in the place of each figure, an understanding of their actions and feelings grew. Relational images, including images of self and other, changed in a direction that allowed greater empathy for both.

EMPATHIC POSSIBILITY: HEALING SHAME

Empathy is especially crucial to the healing of pathological shame (Jordan, 1989a). In shame we lose the sense of empathic possibility; we feel no one could possibly be empathically present for us. When ashamed we have great difficulty trusting that the rejected aspects of ourselves will be accepted by another. Fearing exposure, we contract and withdraw, sometimes erecting barriers to being known; our sense of ourselves as well as our capacity for relationship diminishes. At its worst, shame divorces us from the human community; we feel like outsiders, disconnected. Yet we feel we must hide these disavowed parts to maintain relationship. When someone trusted sees us empathically in a more whole way, sometimes before we are consciously able to reveal the "shameful" parts of ourselves, our capacity for relationship can enlarge. In therapy, the client develops the courage to bring herself or himself more fully into relationship and into creative action. To be "accepted" without really being known is hollow and may contribute to a sense of false self or phoniness; but to be known, in a deep and thorough way, and accepted inspires the confidence that the client can bring himself or herself more fully into relationship (Jordan, 1989a). As empathy lessens the experience of shame, there is increasing openness and self-disclosure. As one experiences the empathic presence of another, one becomes more empathic with oneself. Being joined in a process of empathic witnessing and acceptance, with a resulting decrease of harsh self judgements, opens the way for self-empathy.

As we are empathized with, and as we gain in self-empathy, we also experience an expanded empathy with others. We can then alter distorted and partial relational images that have shaped expectancies for current relationships.

MUTUALITY IN THERAPY

Rather than thinking of empathy as a one-way process, I prefer to speak of the movement of mutual empathy; in this process one is both empathizing with the other and being empathized with. In mutuality, one is both affecting the other and being affected by the other; one extends oneself out to the other and is also receptive to the impact of the other. There is openness to influence, emotional availability and a constantly changing pattern of responding to and affecting the other's state. There is both receptivity and initiative toward the other. Both the wholeness and the subjectivity of the other person are appreciated and respected. One joins in the similarities with the other and also values the qualities that make the person different. When empathy and concern flow both ways, there is an intense affirmation of the self and paradoxically a transcendence of the self, a sense of self as part of a larger relational unit. (Jordan, 1986, p. 1)

Therapy is very importantly about bearing feelings together and bearing tension together. It is about bringing frightening and shameful affect into connection and finding that someone can be with you as you try to do that. The goal is to shift and transform fixed patterns of isolation, immobilization, and denial. Mutual emotional responsiveness is central to this effort. This does not mean the therapist is simply "emoting" with the client, but in a relationship that is primarily devoted to the client's well-being, there must be engagement and considered responsiveness on the part of the therapist; this allows the client to begin to explore his or her capacity to move and value another person as he or she explores his or her own inner reality. When therapists relate in a spirit of power and control, rather than with empathy and respect, they at best impede this exploration; for those clients who are trauma survivors, therapists run the greater risk of retraumatizing them.

By suggesting that there needs to be mutuality in therapy, I am not implying that the therapeutic relationship is symmetrical. In individual psychotherapy, the therapist and client participate in differentiated roles and expectations and share the intention to assist the client with particular life problems. Mutuality in psychotherapy refers to the development of a mutually empathic relationship; both people in this relationship are emotionally open to change and to being affected by each other.

The therapist's empathy with the client has been a clear topic of interest. The mutuality involved in this process has been less obvious. In part what is involved is the capacity of the client to receive the empathy and experience the attunement of the therapist; there has to be an empathic response on the part of the client—that is, the capacity to empathically attune to the therapist empathizing with the client. Without this attunement on the part of the client, the empathy of the therapist would serve only the purpose of increasing intellectual insight on the part of the therapist. Although this increasing self-knowledge is, in fact, an important part of the therapy process, it is not the only way in which empathy contributes to the therapy process. The client's experience of feeling joined by the therapist's emotional resonance decreases a frequent sense of isolation that is often an essential aspect of the client's pain. Ultimately, the client develops an increasingly accurate empathy for the therapist; this, then, generalizes to other relationships.

It is not just the therapist's empathy that is of interest, then, but the empathy of the client as well. The client's empathy for others often expands when the client sees a relational pattern from a new perspective, and, thus, the client sees more clearly both his or her own position (for instance, "I was just a small, vulnerable child who needed this other person") and the other's position ("he was a traumatized alcoholic who picked me as a victim not because of anything I did to provoke him but simply because I was small and vulnerable"). This does not suggest forgiving or condoning the other's hurtful action, but it helps remove a tendency to personalize injury by gaining a better picture of the other person's limitations and real failure to respond empathically. A clinical vignette will capture some of this process: In therapy Diane experienced intense anger at her mother for never having been there for her because she was always busy with volunteer organizations and was quite cold and distant when she was home. Growing up, Diane was not allowed to know her anger at her mother. Instead, she felt, "I'm no good. I have done something to drive my mother away from me." In therapy, the first reworking of this relational image was: "What the hell was she doing, going out all the time and only criticizing me. And I took it all on myself. I thought something was really wrong with me." A poorly timed intervention from me (when Diane still needed to feel angry at her mother), that she might want to think some about what had led to her mother's failure to give her what she needed, was met with outrage. She felt that I had tried to rush her through her anger at her mother to empathy for her mother. I admitted my mistake and empathized with her anger that it felt like I was trying to take her feelings away, making her feel like the "bad one," something she felt had been done to her by her mother. The work we did on my intervention, experienced as a violation resembling her mother's earlier ones, became crucial to a shift in her feelings about herself. She began to feel stronger and more able to represent her feelings in relationships, and she expected to be heard by others. Her self-esteem increased dramatically. Recently, she has begun to spontaneously think about her mother's life and how the stresses of her mother's world and the failure of her mother's parenting figures compromised her mother's ability to mother. Her organization of the relational images became: "I still have a right to feel hurt and angry at my mother, but as I come to see her life, I can no longer condemn her for the way she treated me. I was not to blame, and I am sorry she could not have been a better mother for me." There is great sadness about the failure of the relationship. Therapy has allowed her to be more empathic and accepting of her mother as well as of herself and of her anger at mother. She still will occasionally playfully remind me of how "off the mark" I was in my intervention, pushing her to "understand" or, as she experienced it, "forgive" her mother. As empathy for her mother's inner experience, limitations, and context developed, however, she began to see more clearly that her mother's failure did not arise in response to her (Diane's) badness; this realization removed a great sense of unconscious shame and unworthiness, allowing Diane to build more positive current relational images. The expansion of empathy for the other, particularly someone who has been hurtful, often leads to a realization that the injury inflicted was not really personally directed at us but was a result of the other's limitations. This does not lessen the hurt, but it alters the sense of personal badness and inappropriate assumption of responsibility. This then frees people to move into more positive relationships in the present because they no longer construct relational expectations in terms of their own sense of badness and personal failure.

In viewing therapy as an expansion of empathy, I am suggesting it involves increasing empathy for self, other, and relationship. Through empathy, integration occurs. Where there has been diminished access to split-off experience and feelings, both the individual and relationships have become impoverished. Both therapist and client are moved by each other; there is a movement toward an increasingly differentiated and full representation of self-with-other. Mutual respect is essential to the therapy process.

This does not open the door for emotional acting out by the therapist or lack of disciplined attention to personal clarity (what some call boundaries and roles). Rather, a nuanced responsiveness on the part of the therapist—a kind of modulated reactivity—leads to a corrective relational experience. This approach provides the client with a powerful experience of being with someone (the therapist) who can be emotionally affected by him or her and who can still remain in safe connection. Interactions and impulses that previously led the client into isolation now can be modulated in the therapeutic connection (Jordan, 1990). The resulting return to relatedness in therapy then has a profound effect on the person's inner integration as well as on the expanding capacity to connect with others.

WORKING WITH DISCONNECTIONS

Therapy is not about being in a role; it is about creating a relationship organized around the primary task of assisting the client with self-defined problems. Therapists make themselves vulnerable to clients' impact on them; this means there must be room for mutual response, including growth-enhancing resonance and the inevitable misunderstandings followed by work on their resolution. Some of the most powerful work in therapy is on the empathic failures, the misunderstandings. Therapists must be honest regarding their mistakes and misattunements; they convey their commitment to trying to understand and to being present for the client, but they must humbly admit their limitations in this enterprise. Understanding the client, and moving into an experience of joining with the client are at the center of therapists work.

Therapists must become sensitive to their own disconnections and try to discern what is happening when they or the other person are moving away from connection. Disconnections and failures in mutuality and empathy must be named and understood.

As misunderstandings and disconnections are renegotiated and empathic failures are reworked, the client slowly develops a sense of confidence in the relationship. The very capacity of the therapy relationship not only to withstand but also to grow through the shared work on anger, hurt, and pain contributes significantly to the sense of relational confidence.

Mutual empathic attunement has an impact not just on the client but also on the therapist and on the relationship. There is an expansion of the experience of relatedness and connection. Empathy affirms the importance of "the between" and encourages relational awareness for both people. There is a reduction of an exaggerated, often-distorted notion of self-sufficiency and separateness. One of the most difficult legacies of the psychology of separation and autonomy is the notion that, as adults, people should be self-sufficient. This has distorted the psychological experience of both client and therapist. In the therapy process the centrality of relationships to people's lives is experienced in a powerful way. An appreciation of being in and for the relationships grows for both people. In therapy characterized by empathic expansion, there is an enhanced sense of personal realness or authenticity for both people as well as an enhanced experience of relationship.

We all know the deadened, bored, or anxious feelings that occur in interactions in which people cannot risk being in their truth. We also know how we resonate and come alive with another's "true feelings." Inauthenticity takes us out of real mutuality. People who have learned to manage the image of themselves that they present to others or who have suppressed true responsiveness are often relieved to let another really see them. The moments of disconnection and isolation are not just times of pain but contain possible lessons that both therapist and client must be prepared to take in. We learn from empathic failures.

Particularly for clients who have suffered severe relational violations at formative times (e.g., incest, other forms of sexual or physical abuse, and sadistic psychological abuse by parental figures), the "neutral" and "blank-screen" approach in therapy may create intense anxiety, leading the client to try to connect in increasingly maladaptive ways. With these clients, emotional availability and a certain quality of emotional authenticity on the part of the therapist may be especially important.

Dynamic psychotherapy is built on emotional, empathic knowledge; this cannot occur without emotional resonance that depends on a flexibility of boundaries and a surrender to affective arousal on the part of both participants. As crucial as clear limits are in this relationship (e.g., there should never be sexual interaction between therapist and client, the confidentiality of the client must be protected, and the therapist's own needs must never become the focus of the treatment or interfere with understanding the clients' needs), only when there is emotional responsiveness on both sides can lasting change occur for the client (Jordan, 1990).

Among therapy's central goals is the encouragement and empowerment of individuals to most fully and creatively live their own truths in a way that is respectful of others' lives. Validation of experience, which often includes directly noting the contextual factors that contribute to difficulties, assists in this process. Learning to trust that we can be ourselves, be different from one another, with the possibility that difference can lead to growth-promoting contact, is also essential to authentic relating and creative action.

In positing the development of an enhanced capacity for relationship and the desire to be in connection as central intentions in people's lives, I do not mean to overlook the importance, or very real experience, of personal clarity, productive activity, self-knowledge, or self-expression. But each person's experience broadens through participation in another's inner world that differs from his or her own; people learn and take risks with new feelings that arise in relationship. In therapy the goal is often to shift and transform fixed patterns of isolation, immobilization, and denial. The relational model suggests that relationship based on empathic attunement is the key to the process of therapy, not just the backdrop for it.

REFERENCES

Jordan, J. (1984). Empathy and self-boundaries. *Work in Progress, No. 16* (pp. 1–14). Wellesley, MA: Stone Center Working Paper Series.

Jordan, J. (1986). The meaning of mutuality. *Work in Progress, No. 23* (pp. 1–18). Wellesley, MA: Stone Center Working Paper Series.

Jordan, J. (1989a). Relational development: Therapeutic implications of empathy and shame. *Work in Progress, No. 39* (pp. 1–13). Wellesley, MA: Stone Center Working Paper Series.

Jordan, J. (1989b). Empathy revisited. *Work in Progress, No. 40* (pp. 1–14). Wellesley, MA: Stone Center Working Paper Series.

Jordan, J. (1990). Empathy and mutuality essential to effective therapeutic relationship. *The Psychiatric Times, 7*(4), 1–8.

Jordan, J. (1992). The relational self: A new perspective for understanding women's development. *Contemporary Psychotherapy Review, 7*, 56–72.

Jordan, J., Kaplan, A., Miller, J. B., Stiver, I., & Surrey, J. (1991). *Women's growth in connection.* New York: Guilford Press.

Keats, J. (1987). Letter to "My dear brothers." In R. Gittings (Ed.), *The letters of John Keats* (pp. 152–156). Oxford: Oxford University Press. (Original letter dated 1818)

Miller, J. (1976). *Toward a new psychology of women.* Boston, MA: Beacon Press.

17

VALIDATION AND PSYCHOTHERAPY

MARSHA M. LINEHAN

Perhaps nowhere is the ability to empathize with another person more important than when one is interacting with a person who is on the brink of suicide. This is true whether one views one's task as helping the individual choose continued living over suicide or, more rarely, as helping the individual make a wise choice between suicide and continued life.[1] The ability both to hold a person within life, when that is needed, and to allow a person who has chosen suicide to die, when that is needed, depend on an experiential appreciation of the other's worldview. Finding hidden or obscure ways out as well as seeing that there is no way out require both the ability and the willingness to fully enter the experience of the individual ready to suicide and, at the same time, not become that experience (that is, remain separate from the experience).

Over the past 20 years, I have been developing and evaluating an approach to treatment designed specifically for suicidal individuals, particu-

The writing of this chapter was partially supported by grant MH34486-12 from the National Institute of Mental Health, Bethesda, MD. I thank Charles Swenson, Sebern Fischer, and Kelly Koerner for their comments on previous drafts of this chapter.

[1] In my own practice I have chosen to always be on the side of life over suicide (see Linehan, 1993, for a detailed explanation of this choice), and I make this clear to clients at the beginning of therapy. However, I recognize that, in some cases—for example, in the case of a terminally ill client facing severe physical pain—others may reasonably chose a different or more flexible therapeutic stance.

larly those who are chronically suicidal. Although the treatment, Dialectical Behavior Therapy (DBT; Linehan, 1993; Linehan, Armstrong, Suarez, Allmon, & Heard, 1991; Linehan & Heard, 1993; Linehan, Heard, & Armstrong, 1993; Linehan, Tutek, Heard, & Armstrong, 1994), is now considered by many to be a general treatment approach applicable to many populations, its origins as a treatment for seriously suicidal clients had much to do with its current form. As the name suggests, DBT is firmly anchored in behavior therapy; the change strategies at its center are standard cognitive and behavioral treatment approaches. In attempting to apply standard behavior therapy to severely and chronically suicidal individuals, however, I noticed two things become immediately apparent. First, focusing on client change, either of motivation or by enhancing capabilities, is often experienced as invalidating by clients who are in intense emotional pain. In many clients, it precipitates noncompliance, withdrawal, and at times, early drop out from treatment, in other clients extreme anger and aggressive attacks on the therapist, and in still others both patterns of behavior. Second, focusing treatment on exploration and understanding, in the absence of a clear focusing of efforts to help the client change, is often experienced by these same clients as invalidating because it does not recognize the unendurability and, therefore, necessity for immediate change of the present unremitting pain. Thus, therapy approaches that focus on acceptance of the client (rather than change) also risk client withdrawal, attack, or both. Either of these client responses, attack in an attempt to change the therapist or passive withdrawal in an attempt to avoid unwanted therapist behavior, typically have a reciprocal invalidating effect on the therapist in turn. The therapist then may unwittingly respond with, at times, almost imperceptible, but none-the-less real, attack or withdrawal from the client. Although unavoidable at times, client or therapist attack or withdrawal interfere with the collaborative working relationship necessary for therapeutic progress.

It was the tension and ultimate resolution of this essential conflict between focusing on client change this very moment versus acceptance of the client as he or she is in the moment that led to the use of dialectics in the title of the treatment and to the overriding emphasis in the treatment on reconciliation of opposites in a continual process of synthesis. The most fundamental dialectic is the necessity of accepting clients just as they are within a context (and, indeed, therapy's *raison d'être*) of trying to help them to change. The emphasis on acceptance as a balance to change flows directly from the integration of a perspective drawn from Eastern mindfulness (primarily Zen) practice with Western psychological (primarily cognitive–behavioral) practice. Although acceptance and change cannot really be as clearly distinguished as I am portraying it here, for reasons of exposition, acceptance of the client in DBT is described under the rubric of three fundamental treatment-strategy groups: validation, reciprocal communication (including warmth, genuineness, and responsiveness), and environmental intervention (i.e., influencing or making changes in the environment to assist the client). These acceptance strategies are balanced by corresponding "change" strategies of problem solving (including behavioral analyses, analyses of alternative behaviors and solutions, commitment and psychoeducational strategies, basic change procedures of skills training, exposure-based procedures, cognitive modification, and contingency-based procedures), irreverent and confrontational communication, and the stance of consultant to the client (rather than to the client's personal or professional network) when interacting with the community outside of the therapeutic dyad. All strategies are applied within a context of overarching dialectical strategies and stance.

It would be difficult to overestimate the importance of validation in DBT. Together with dialectical and problem-solving strategies, it forms the triadic core of the treatment. Although validation encompasses and requires empathy, it is more than empathy. The purpose of this chapter is to describe the meaning and use of validation in DBT. I will start first with a definition of validation. Next, I will contrast that definition with definitions of empathy. I will then further discuss the meaning of validation by describing six levels of validation. Validation can also be communicated explicitly through verbal comments or implicitly by responding to the individual in a manner that implies that one takes the individual's responses to be valid. I will next discuss the importance of both types of validation. Validation can also be directed at various client responses. The importance of validating emotional, cognitive, physiological, and action response patterns (or targets of validation in behavioral terms) will be discussed next. Validation in psychotherapy is always strategic, that is, it serves particular functions. Five functions of validation are presented.

THE DEFINITION OF VALIDATION

The term *validation* is widely used in the social sciences; I found 7,927 citations for the term *validation* compared with 4,436 citations for the term *empathy* in the social sciences index. Interestingly, however, it is a term rarely found in writings on psychotherapy. The *Oxford English Dictionary* (1989) offers several definitions of validation, including, "The action of validating or making valid . . . a strengthening, reinforcement, confirming; an establishing or ratifying" as valid. It proposes synonyms for validate such as *confirm, corroborate, substantiate, verify,* and *authenticate.* The act of validating is "to support or corroborate on a sound or authoritative basis . . . to attest to the truth or validity of something." To communicate that a response is valid is to say that it is "well-grounded or justifiable: being at once relevant and meaningful . . . logically correct . . . appropriate to the end in view [or effective] . . . having such force as to compel serious attention and [usually] acceptance." Being "valid implies being supported by objective truth or generally accepted authority" (*Webster's Dictionary*, 1991), "being well-founded on fact, or established on sound principles, and thoroughly applicable to the case or circumstances; soundness and strength" (*Oxford English Dictionary*, 1989), the quality of "value or worth; efficacy" (*Oxford English Dictionary*, 1989). These are precisely the meanings associated with the term when used in the context of psychotherapy in DBT:

> The essence of validation is this: The therapist communicates to the client that her responses make sense and are understandable within her current life context or situation. The therapist actively accepts the client and communicates this acceptance to the client. The therapist takes the client's responses seriously and does not discount or trivialize them. Validation strategies require the therapist to search for, recognize and reflect to the client the validity inherent in her response to events. With unruly children parents have to catch them while they're good in order to reinforce their behavior; similarly, the therapist has to un-cover the validity within the client's response, sometimes amplify it, and then reinforce it. (Linehan, 1993, pp. 222–223)

Two things are important to note here. First, validation means the acknowl-edgment of that which is valid. It does not mean the "making" of something valid. Nor does it mean validating that which is invalid. The therapist observes, experiences, and affirms but does not create validity. That which is valid preexists the therapeutic action. Second, and I feel compelled to say this simply because my behavioral orientation may give a wrong impres-sion, the word *valid* and *scientific* are not synonyms. That is, replicable, controlled, empirical observation of events is not the only way to arrive at a determination of validity. It is, however, one way and is the preferred method when the question is indeed one of empirical validity open to scien-tific inquiry. If it alone were the criteria for validity, however, much of human experience and import would be ruled out of the therapeutic encoun-ter. Logic, sound principles, generally accepted authority or normative knowledge, and experience or apprehension of private events, at least when similar to the same experiences of others or when in accord with other more observable events, are all basis for claiming validity. In the former case, we can speak of empirical validity and in the latter of consensual validity.

WHAT TO VALIDATE

Validating the Individual

What to validate? A first question here is whether the therapist vali-dates the individual or simply the behavior or responses of the individual. Validation, at least in its purest definitions, can actually mean either. Further definitions of validation include (*Oxford English Dictionary*, 1989): "to grant official sanction to by marking . . . also: to declare [a person] elected," where sanction means to approve, support, allow, and empower. When one speaks of validating the individual person (as a whole, as it were), what is being validated? It is the authenticating of the individual as who he or she actually is. (The validation of a person's beliefs about who he or she is will be discussed below.) The question, "Who am I," of course, is a central question in almost all instances of psychotherapy. As deMello (1990) has stated, however, the question is essentially unanswerable in that any answer we give is necessarily incomplete. We are not our race, our age, our roles in life, our position, our relationships, our problems, our joys, our emotions, our actions, our thoughts, or our experiences, even in their sum total, nor are we our "self." Perhaps, as deMello says, we can only say that we are human. Even that, however, is surely a limited view. The very limitations of one's answer to this question, the boundaries on self-definition when there are no true boundaries, suggests an answer to the question. When validating the individual, one validates everything that is. That is, there is nothing that the individual experiences, feels, thinks, does, says, or "is" that is not himself or herself.

One validates the individual when the individual's existence is treated as justifiable and the person is responded to as at once relevant and meaningful, as compelling serious attention and acceptance. The person as he or she is, in the moment, is visible and seen. Therapeutic actions and reactions take into account and are responsive to the individual client rather than determined by the therapist or client roles or arbitrary rules. The person, rather than the constructs brought to the interaction by the therapist, is seen and countenanced. Validation used in this sense perhaps comes closest to the meaning of the term "unconditional positive regard" used by Rogers (1959). Of the individual, unconditional validation is required.

In DBT there is an added emphasis on balancing the therapeutic effectiveness of various interventions with the natural limits of each therapist to provide effective interventions and to weigh these two factors (i.e., the limits of providing effective interventions and therapists' personal limits) more heavily than arbitrary role definitions and arbitrary boundaries when interacting with the client. Such a stance requires responding to the client not only as he or she is in the moment but also in a manner that is responsive to one's own self in the moment. Although the therapeutic role may circumscribe therapist activities and goals, it is nonetheless the therapist as a person that is in the relationship helping the client. Thus, the therapist as a unique individual as well as the individual acting from the role of therapist are the therapeutic relationship as well as the client as a unique individual must be held valid. As I will discuss below, this sense of validation comes closest to Rogers's use of the term *genuineness*. Such a position, of course, requires utter clarity on the part of the therapist (which is why ongoing peer supervision is defined as part of DBT rather than as extraneous to it). Taking care for the client is always the responsibility of the therapist.

It is important to note here, however, that validating what is said, thought, felt, or otherwise experienced to be, but is not, is an instance of validating the invalid. Conversely, by denying that which actually is, it is also an instance of invalidation of the valid. Validation has nothing to do with social desirability and is not a synonym for praise. Therapist fears of confronting clients, of "calling a spade a spade," of acknowledging the painful, undesired, or culturally or personally "unacceptable," is often the basis of validating the invalid. Falsely telling a client who is secretly trying to manipulate you that he or she is not really manipulating you is just as invalidating as calling a nonmanipulating client a manipulator. Except in exceptionally rare instances, validating the invalid is not therapeutic. It is not genuine and, furthermore, it communicates that what is is unacceptable, unendurable, or at least, not relevant and meaningful.

Validating Behavior

As used here and in behavior therapy in general, *behavior* refers to any activity of the individual, including physiological responses (e.g., breathing, beating heart, and tensing muscles), cognitive responses (e.g., expecting, believing, thinking, and assuming), and overt actions. Contrary to what many people believe, behavior does not have to be observable by others to be important to behaviorists. From the behaviorists' perspective, behavior can be private (and observed only by the individual behaving) or public (and observed by others). Both private and public behaviors are important in DBT and in all modern behavioral treatments.

Validation of behavior is the clear and unambiguous communication that an activity, emotion, belief, sense, or other experience or response of the individual, whether private or public, is at once relevant and meaningful to the case or circumstances, and is also (a) well-grounded or justifiable in terms of empirical facts (i.e., those observed and agreed to by generally disinterested observers), logically correct inference, or generally accepted authority; and/or (b) appropriate to the end in view (i.e., efficacious for reaching the individual's ultimate goals).

As can be surmised, behavior can be valid from the perspective of one set of circumstances or for one purpose and not valid from another. In a somewhat simplified way, one can consider behavior (B) valid in terms of either: behavioral antecedents (A) where A are the facts (known empirically or by logical inference or by generally accepted authority), including previous events, responses of the individual, or current context relevant to the behavior (i.e., B is justified by or well grounded in A) or behavioral consequences (C) where B is effective in reaching C that represent ultimate goals or ends in view (B is effective at attaining C).

When considering whether behavior is valid or should be validated, a number of dialectical tensions emerge. Behavior can be valid in terms of one set of antecedents (e.g., historical events) but not in terms of another set (e.g., present events). Behavior can be valid in terms of an individual's private experience of reality (e.g., spiritual experiences) but not in terms of public events seen by the outside observer. Private experiencing, itself, can be valid in terms of the consensus of one set of authorities but not another. Behavior can be valid in terms of antecedents to behavior but not in terms of consequences (e.g., being "right" rather than effective). Behavior can be valid in terms of one set of consequences (e.g., short-term consequences) but not in another set (e.g., long-term consequences). Two points are important here. First, not all behavior is valid in every sense. Second, all behavior is valid in some sense. It is the resolution of these and similar dialectical tensions, without discounting the validity of either end of the polarity, that is at the heart of validation. The therapist may need to search for and find the grain of wisdom in a cup of sand. The guiding premise here is that in any interaction some basis for validity can be found and reflected to the client.

DIFFERENCE BETWEEN VALIDATION AND EMPATHY

There is considerable overlap between the concepts of empathy and validation, yet the two are also quite different. The overlap occurs in two ways. First, empathic communication is itself often validating. Being understood from within one's own frame of reference is inherently validating because it connotes that one is not "crazy," that one makes at least enough sense to be understood. Second, validation always involves accurate recognition, acknowledgment, and authentication of that which is. To validate the other, one must know the other. Empathy is that process whereby one knows another person more completely that the person can verbalize or communicate explicitly. It is requisite to anything but the most simple validation.

There are essential differences between empathy and validation. Although there may be many definitions of empathy, a commonly accepted one is that of Rogers, who defines it as "perceiving the internal frame of reference of another with accuracy and with the emotional components and meanings which pertain thereto as if one were the person but without ever losing the as if condition" (1980, p. 141, referenced by Greenberg & Elliott, Chapter 8, this volume). Contrast this with the definition of validation as communicating to an individual, by word or response, that he or she is heard and seen and that his or her responses and patterns of behavior have inherent validity. Validation is the answer of "yes" to the question "can this be true?" Experiencing what "this" refers to is where the first half of empathy, "perceiving the internal frame of reference of the other," comes in. Only when the therapist truly understands what the client is actually experiencing, thinking, assuming, believing, expecting, feeling, caring for and about, hoping, doing, and living within, the therapist begin to assess the validity of the "this." Assessing the truth value of "this" is where the second part of empathy, "without losing the as if condition," comes in. The therapist must be able to function as a disinterested, or at least unbiased, observer to assess whether a response is well-grounded in empirical facts, inference, or authority and is likely to be effective in moving toward the client's ultimate ends. Thus, validation in psychotherapy depends on the ability of the therapist to exercise moment-to-moment empathy during interactions with the client.

Although empathy is necessary for clinical validation, it is not sufficient. Needed in addition is an analysis of the client's response in light of its relationship to its context (i.e., the empirical situation) and its function (i.e., as a means to an end). Validation, therefore, is based on a conclusion about an empathic experience. In contrast to empathy, validation is inherently analytical, of truth, of wisdom, of effectiveness. Or, put another way, validation requires a conclusion about the validity of the person as represented (validating the individual) or the behavior or experience of the individual (validating behavior). Although all behavior can be validated at some level, it cannot all be validated at the same level. It is the differences in level that further differentiate validation from empathy.

LEVELS OF VALIDATION

Validation can be considered at any one of six levels. Each level is correspondingly more complete than the previous, and each level depends on one or more of the previous levels. The first two levels of validation encompass activities usually defined as empathic, and the third and fourth levels are similar to empathic interpretations as those terms are used in the general psychotherapy literature. Although I feel sure that most therapists use and support levels five and six of validation, they are much less-often discussed in the literature. They are, however, definitional of DBT and are required in every interaction with the client.

Level One: Listening and Observing

The first step in validation is the listening to and observing of what the client is saying, feeling, and doing as well as a corresponding active effort to understand what is being said and observed. The essence of this step is that the therapist is *interested* in the client. The therapist pays attention to what the client says and does. The therapist notices the nuances of response in the interaction. Validation at level one communicates that the client per se, as well as the client's presence, words, and responses in the session, have "such force as to compel serious attention and [usually] acceptance" (see definitions of validation above). Level-one validation requires keeping attention focused on the client and attending closely to both verbal and nonverbal content (i.e., to the manner of speaking and of responding to the therapist's communications; to the nuances of expression, and to minute changes in voice tone, posture, facial expression, and so on). It also requires paying attention to what is important to and for the client.

Listening and observing also require that the therapist be adept at maintaining the dialectical tension between unconditional listening and observing, on the one hand, and at filtering what is heard and seen through the lenses of theory and previous words and actions of the client, on the other. Preformed categories must give way to new understandings. And understanding guides further exploration and observation. The therapist lets go of theories, prejudices, and personal biases that get in the way of hearing and observing clearly the actual events unfolding, the emotions, the thoughts, and the behaviors of the client. The therapist listens unconditionally and observes things as they actually are. With no conditions set, the client is seen and countenanced as he or she is in the moment. Using what was gained from prior interactions, remembering what the client has already said and done, how he or she has reacted previously in sessions communicates powerfully that the client is important enough to remember. The client is worth one's efforts to understand. To the extent that one's theories are useful, they can assist the therapist in integrating what is heard into a picture that both informs and completes what the client is attempting to communicate. The resulting discourse validates by communicating that the client is known. Indeed, such communication—informed by theory and integration of previous knowledge—can be so powerful that it is considered a higher level of validation and is described further as a level-three validation.

Listening and observing, at level one of validation, require an engaged, reciprocal interaction pattern. "Tell me more," "I don't understand, explain that," "What were you thinking at just that point?" "What then?" communicate that both the story and the client's rendition of the story are important. Listening in such a manner requires one to stay immediate, where immediate means fully present in this one moment. Validation at the first level encompasses empathic exploration of the client's experiences as well as of the "facts" of the case. The basic idea here is that the therapist actively gets to know the client, both from the perspective of the client and from the perspective of an outside observer. The therapist attempts to understand the phenomenological experience of the client as well as the context in which the experience takes place. To use Greenberg and Elliott's words (p.

168 this volume), the role of the therapist is that of "facilitator of exploration and a companion in the search, a co-explorer." The task here is the same as actively seeking to arrive at empathic understanding of the client when such understanding is, as Rogers (1980) defined it, "perceiving the internal frame of reference of another with accuracy and with the emotional components and meanings which pertain thereto as if one were the person but without ever losing the as if condition" (p. 141). Understanding the context of the experience, including holding a sometimes more objective picture of both events and client responses, requires not "ever losing the as if condition."

The further dialectic in listening and observing is between the perspective of the client and of the observing therapist. The therapist must become a participant in the client's world as well as simultaneously remain an observer of that world. How does the therapist become a participant? The therapist must imagine the experience and perspective of the client. In DBT, therapists are encouraged to find within themselves experiences, either in memory or by way of imagination, metaphor, analogy, or story, that match the client's in some essential way. The therapist covertly rehearses stepping into the client's shoes, adopting imaginally his or her past as well as present. It goes without saying, of course, that such a stance requires moment-to-moment checking to be sure that the therapist's understanding actually does match the experience and facts of the client's experience.

How does the therapist remain an observer, not getting lost in the perspective of the client? By maintaining an overriding interest in the well-being of the client and a constant mindfulness of where the client is headed (i.e., of the client's ultimate goals). In DBT, the therapist is always focusing on both acceptance and change. Thus, at each moment, the therapist must compare the responses of the client to those that would be necessary to achieve the client's goals. The therapist is always asking the essential question: If I were the client how would I respond if I held the client's goals. That is, at each moment the therapist is noticing both what the client is experiencing and how the client is responding to that experience, asking in essence "OK, from here how do I get there?" Listening and observing is figuring out where "here" is.

Level Two: Accurate Reflection

The second level of validation is the accurate reflection back to the client of the client's own feelings, thoughts, assumptions, and behaviors. The therapist conveys an understanding of the client, a hearing of what the client has said, and a seeing of what the client does—how he or she responds. Validation at the second level sanctions, empowers, or authenticates that the individual is who he or she actually is. Generally, reflection in behavior therapy, as well as DBT, stays rather close to what is actually said by the client or observed directly by the therapist. Thus, although the therapist often summarizes patterns and uses synonyms and stories to communicate understanding and may reorganize what is said into a more coherent package, little is added to the communication of the client. Reflective accuracy, of course, requires that the therapist actually understand the perspective of the client as well as both the events that occurred and the client's responses. By back and forth discussion, with the therapist summarizing and the client correcting and adding to the summary, the therapist helps the client further identify, describe, and label his or her covert and overt response patterns. The essential goal is for therapist and client to come to a shared understanding of the material at hand. The therapist frequently says "Is that right?" testing the hypotheses that hearing is complete and understanding is accurate. The client has a chance to say the therapist is wrong.

A nonjudgmental stance, both verbally and nonverbally, is fundamental to reflection at this level. By nonjudgmental, I mean neither good nor bad. That is, validation at this level does not imply approval or encouragement. Nor does it imply judgment of effectiveness or value. The therapist does not agree that the client's perspective is the only perspective possible. Thus, for example, and contrary to many people's beliefs about empathy, when a client expresses fragility, accurate reflection does not necessarily require a sympathetic voice tone. It is the essential "isness" that is reflected. A matter-of-fact, or "but, of course" voice tone may many times be the most effective approach.

It is extraordinarily important that the therapist accurately reflect just what is being said, felt, done, or experienced by the client. Often, instead therapists confuse the responses of the client with the events or stimuli that are being responded to. Or, as I say to the therapists I train, therapists often fall into the pool with the client rather than get the client out of the pool. The therapist steps into the client's shoes but forgets his or her own shoes. In describing an interaction, the client's says in a desperate voice, "she hates me." This statement may accurately reflect what the client believes and may relate to feelings of the client that the therapist can identify and acknowledge. However the statement "she hates me" is not necessarily a statement of a fact. That is, the person in question may not hate the client. A level-two validation might be a statement such as "so, you are feeling desperate and really certain that she hates you." It is especially easy for therapists with seriously disturbed clients to pick up the client's hopelessness, helplessness, anger at the world, fears, passivity, and other responses that contribute to not reaching the client's goals. A level-two validation is when the therapist acknowledges the facts of the client's experience—that is, the therapist is so in touch with the perspective as to identify it correctly. However, it is not level-two validation to also add in word, deed, or nonverbal response that the client's responses correspond to the empirical facts when they may not. Feeling angry is different than actually being attacked. Fear is different than actually being threatened. There are any number of reasons therapists confuse the facts of a situation with the client's responses to the facts when the two are actually discrepant. With clients who are highly expressive emotionally, it may be due to emotional contagion. With clients who communicate calmly and are fluent and articulate, it may be simply that the therapist does not pay close enough attention to spot the inconsistencies. Whatever the reason, care must be taken to distinguish emotions, thoughts, and experiences as events worthy of attention and acknowledgment themselves rather than as literal statements about, markers, or signs of the world the individual is reacting to.

Level Three: Articulating the Unverbalized

In level three of validation, the therapist communicates to the client his or her understanding of aspects of the client's experience and response to events that have not been communicated directly by the client. At level three, the therapist "reads" the client's behavior and figures out how the client feels and what the client is wishing for, thinking or doing just by knowing what has happened to the client. It is when one person can make the link between precipitating event and behavior without being given any information about the behavior itself. Emotions and meanings the client has not expressed are articulated by the therapist. The therapist expresses an intuitive understanding of the client derived from all of the information and observations to date. The therapist reads the client's mind, so to speak, sometimes knowing clients better than they know themselves. In level three, the therapist may state out loud what the client observes but is afraid to say or admit. This simple act of reflection, especially when the therapist "says it first," can be a powerful act of validation because clients often observe themselves accurately in the first place, but because of mistrust of themselves, they invalidate and discount their own perceptions.

When someone knows how you are responding, how you feel or think, or what you are likely to do, without your having to tell them directly, it is almost always experienced as validating. First, and at a minimum, such validation communicates that one is known; the therapist authenticates that one is who one really is (i.e., the individual is validated as himself or herself). Articulating unverbalized responses is important for both patterns that represent client strengths as well as client weaknesses. The necessity of this type of validation, however, when the person's emotions, cognitions, or overt behavior are maladaptive, dysfunctional, or reprehensible, is often overlooked by therapists. Putting a positive cast on client behavior—refusing to acknowledge behaviors that have a tremendous negative impact on clients' lives and hopes—has the net effect often of creating in clients a sense that they really must be completely unacceptable, not to mention that the therapist is naive, uneducated, or not interested enough to figure one out. Level-three validation, when done well, can create the hope that is requisite for clinical progress to occur.

Second, being read can also communicate powerfully that, given all the contexts of the behavior, one's responses to events are normal, predictable, and justifiable. How else would the person know how you felt or thought or what you were going to do? Indeed, the feeling that someone is a soulmate who understands and accepts you is frequently based on this ability. In contrast, when a person cannot figure out how you feel or think, cannot respond empathetically unless you spell it out in detail, or expects you to do things you do not do or assumes you have done things you did not do, it is often experienced as invalidating, insensitive, or uncaring.

Reading behavior accurately requires some familiarity by the therapist with the culture of the client. By culture, here, I mean the fabric of socially transmitted response patterns that can be considered as typical of or an expression of the community or population that the client represents. For example, what is responded to with joy, interpreted as threatening and attacked, or grieved as a loss may be very different among men than among women, between individuals in one social class versus another, and in one country versus another. Similarly, responses that make sense (i.e., can be easily predictable) among individuals whose lives are marked by trauma, biological dysregulation, or specific behavioral disorder, may make little sense to others who have not experienced such conditions.

Knowing the client's current situation or the precipitating situation, together with observations of the client's verbal and nonverbal behavior, can be useful in arriving at a description of the client's emotional responses, intentions, assumptions, or otherwise private responses. The link between events and emotions or other private behaviors (e.g., thoughts and sensations) is in part universal and in part learned. Thus, to the extent that the therapist's and client's learning histories are similar (i.e., to the extent that the therapist and client share a similar culture), the therapist will be adept at reading unarticulated responses. In the absence of a similar history yourself, clinical experience, research reports, first-person accounts and autobiographies, novels, and movies about people like your client can be helpful. A very important task of the consultation group in DBT is to assist the therapist in this work. This type of level-three validation is similar to the "hermeneutics of the everyday." It seeks to articulate the private responses common to the client's own culture through a participant–observer inquiry (see Wilbur, 1995, p. 549, for a similar discussion).

At other times, the simple act of validating the nonverbalized communicates such acceptance that it gives clients permission, so to speak, to know themselves better than they did before. This is particularly likely when the therapist reads responses that the client is only minimally, if at all, aware of making. Unacceptable private responses, in particular, such as unallowable (socially or to the individual client) beliefs, intents, desires, sensations, and feelings may be unrecognized because observing and labeling accurately is inhibited so early in the chain of self-reflections that the client does not become subsequently self-aware. This is especially the case when the outcome of knowing is the experience of painful emotions such as shame, guilt, humiliation, fear, or sadness. The avoidance of observing and recognizing, as I am suggesting here, is fundamentally no different than avoidance of any other behavior whose immediate outcome is associated with pain. The acknowledgment of these private responses by a nonjudgmental outside observer whose opinion matters allows the client to validate his or her own "unacceptable" and painful experiences and behavior. Level-three validation here is similar to the "hermeneutics of suspicion" (see Wilbur, 1995, p. 549). The therapist voices the suspicion that there might be more going on than meets the eye of either client or therapist. When correct, it constitutes a level-three validation and has the potentional for enormous therapeutic value.

Level-three validation, however, is also fraught with danger and the potential for great harm. The chief danger is that an invalid or only partially valid articulation of the client's private responses will be shoved down the client's throat. A ubiquitous example of such a tendency is the proclivity of many therapists to use consequences or observed functions of behavior as proof of private intent. If the therapist feels manipulated, the client must be manipulating. If the husband who has left home returns to his wife after she cuts her wrists, then the wife must have (secretly or unconsciously) intended such an outcome. It was only a "gesture." To add insult to injury, therapists are sometimes so sure of their beliefs (often because of rigid adherence to a particular theory of motivation) that they assume that the protest at the faulty validation effort is further proof that the articulation was valid in the first place. "Thou doest protest too much." As I have discussed elsewhere (Linehan, 1993), this is the error of affirming the consequent. The best way to prevent iatrogenic level-three validations is for the therapist to have both a good understanding of human behavior, including the large variety of private response pathways to any particular public behavior, and a wealth of theoretical hypotheses that can be tested in any given case. Having more than one good theory reduces the likelihood that any one will be clung to in the face of disconfirming evidence. The dialectical necessity here is for both collaborative exploration of private behaviors and experiences, including intent, on the one hand, and courage, sophistication, and insight into what is actually going on (independently, at times, of what the client claims), on the other.

The ability to know how a client is responding to a therapeutic intervention without necessarily being told is also a requisite ability if one is to effectively communicate validation. The ability to "read" situations and people, to predict how events will make people feel, and to know how one affects others is usually discussed under the rubric of clinical sensitivity. Its accuracy, however, actually depends on accurate empathy. The more empathic therapist is marked by the ability to know not only when a client is feeling invalidated, or is likely to feel invalidated, by what one is saying but also what type of therapeutic response is likely to produce a sense of validation. Interestingly given the inherent tension between validating a response versus trying to change that response, the ability to move the client quickly through necessary changes requires a very astute moment-to-moment recognition of the client's experience of being invalidated. It is at just those moments when the client is threatened with incapacitating invalidation that the therapist must move quickly to validate and then, as quickly as the validation is experienced, move back to change. The result, at least when immediate change is of the utmost importance (e.g., when suicidal behavior is likely), is a therapy characterized by quick (and hopefully smooth) interweaving of validation with change, often oscillating phrase by phrase and sentence by sentence. Such immediacy is possible only when the therapist is able to keep one foot firmly in the client's experience and the other firmly in the reality of the astute observer.

Level Four: Validating in Terms of Sufficient (but Not Necessarily Valid) Causes

At level four, behavior is validated in terms of its causes. Validation here is based on the notion that all behavior is caused by events occurring in time and, thus, in principle, is understandable. Behavior is justified by showing that it is caused. Even though information may not be available to know all the relevant causes, the client's feelings, thoughts, and actions make perfect sense in the context of the person's current experience, physiology, and life to date. At a minimum, what is can always be justified in terms of sufficient causes. Behavior is adaptive to the context in which it is learned and to the biological responses of the human system. At level four the therapist finds the wisdom of that adaptation. The therapist, in essence, says, "Given X, how could Y be otherwise." In terms of the analyses described above, the question is "Given the antecedents (A) or consequences (C) of behavior, how could the person's behavior (B) be any different."

How does one validate behavior when it is maladaptive, dysfunctional, or ineffective for reaching the client's ultimate ends? If current behavior is destructive or leads away from a life the client can experience as worth living, how does the therapist find the grain of wisdom? When the behavior in question is invalid because of its link to invalid antecedents or its ineffectiveness at achieving life goals, there may be any one of at least three grounds for validation at level four: past learning history, present but invalid antecedents, or biological disorder.

1. *Behavior is valid in terms of historical antecedents ($A_{history}$) but may not be valid in terms of current antecedent events ($A_{current}$).* In the first type, the therapist communicates that the individual's behavior is justifiable and reasonable in terms of the past (i.e., past learning or previous goals that no longer hold). In terms of history, all learned behavior is valid. A focus on early childhood experiences as important in the development of problems as well as transference interpretation are examples (when accurate) of level-four validation. The process of exploring the past, so typical in many treatments, may be therapeutic simply because it weaves a story that makes the present make sense. It validates the present by linking it to previous events such that neither the past nor the present could be otherwise. Indeed, much of psychotherapy is involved with helping clients make just these distinctions. Responses learned in the past and appropriate to the past may no longer be needed or appropriate in the present.

   Take the following examples. A friend was raped in a dark alley one night. Some months later you are walking with your friend to meet some friends in a pub whose main entrance is down an alley. You start down the alley, and your friend says, "No! I can't. Let's go to the other entrance." You say, "But, of course! How insensitive of me. I forgot that you were raped in a dark alley. Let's go the other way." That is level-four validation. Being raped in a dark alley is ($A_{history}$); the apparent safety of the alley entrance to the pub is ($A_{current}$). Or take a clinical example: A client of mine was having marital troubles because, apparently, of her not liking sex with her husband. From all appearances, he was the ideal husband when it came to sex. He bought her lovely silk and satin negligees, put on music, lit candles, was affectionate, talked before sex, and was gentle and kind ($A_{current}$). In a previous marital therapy, it had been identified that during adolescence her parents, particularly her mother, had consistently called her a whore and chastised her whenever she showed the slightest interest in boys or sex. All agreed that her current disinterest in sex with her husband was a result of these experiences with her parents ($A_{history}$) rather than aspects of her husband's current behavior ($A_{current}$). This, too, is a level-four validation.

2. *Behavior is valid in terms of invalid current antecedent events ($A_{invalid}$) but may not be valid in terms of current antecedent events (A_{valid}).* Take the example of a client coming to a therapy appointment. Coming to the therapist's office on Thursday

at 2 p.m. could be considered invalid if the appointment is actually on Friday. The fact is there is no appointment on that day; the behavior is not justified by an empirical fact. However, suppose at the last appointment the therapist mistakenly told the patient the wrong appointment time, inadvertently saying it was on Thursday. The same behavior could be considered valid in the sense that it is based on a logically correct inference from what the therapist said. A similar distinction can be made when looking at emotional responses. Emotions can be reasonable responses to one's premises or beliefs about a situation, even though the beliefs may not be justified by the actual facts of the situation. Panic may be a justifiable response to the certain belief that one is unexpectedly in a life-threatening situation but may not be justifiable in terms of the actual facts when the facts are that one is safe and physically sound. In both cases, the therapeutic process requires one to manage the dialectics of validating and confronting a response on the basis of two independent sets of empirical facts. In the first case, the two sets of facts are the time stated by the therapist ($A_{invalid}$) versus the time actually set aside by the therapist (A_{valid}). In the second case, the two sets of facts are the premises or beliefs of the person ($A_{invalid}$) versus the actual threat value of the situation (A_{valid}).

3. *Behavior is valid in terms of disordered antecedent events* ($A_{disorder}$) *but may not be valid for achieving important desired goals or consequences* (C_{goals}). This type of level-four validation is most common when the antecedent is some type of biological disorder and the undesired consequence is some sort of disordered functioning. The goal of the client is ordinarily to alleviate the disordered functioning and enhance life satisfaction. The disease view of emotional dysfunction is an example of validating behavior in terms of biological dysfunction. Depressive behaviors, for example, can be viewed as valid response patterns to certain neurochemical brain dysfunctions ($A_{disorder}$) but ineffective in enhancing life satisfaction (C_{goals}). Overly impulsive behavior may interfere with many life goals (C_{goals}) but none the less be an inevitable response to certain genetic characteristics ($A_{disorder}$).

Level-four validation counteracts the tendency of many clients to believe that they "should not" be as they are (i.e., they "should" be different). It models validation of that which may not be admirable and teaches self-validation. The task of countering the client's shoulds is an important part of level-four validation. The first step in countering shoulds is to make a distinction between understanding how or why something happened versus approving of the event. The main resistance to believing that a particular response or pattern of behavior should have happened, given the circumstances surrounding it, is the belief that, if behavior is understood, the behavior is also approved of. The therapist must emphasize that the act of refusing to accept a given reality means that one cannot act to overcome or change that reality. Simple examples can be given here. The therapist can point to a nearby wall and suggest that, if an individual wants the wall to be chartreuse in color and refuses to accept the fact that the wall is currently purple, not chartreuse, it is unlikely that the person will ever paint the wall chartreuse. A second point is being made here: wishing reality were different does not change reality and *believing* reality is what one wants it to be does not *make* it what one wants it to be. At times, a statement that something shouldn't be is also tantamount to denying its existence. The task is to get the client to agree that neither wishing nor denying will change reality.

A useful step in countering the shoulds is to present a mechanistic explanation of causality indicating that every event has a cause. Go through a number of examples of unwanted, undesirable behavior with step-by-step illustrations of the factors that brought the behavior about. The strategy is to show that thoughts ("I don't want it") and emotions (fear and anger) are not sufficient to keep an event from happening. If wanting to be perfect would make us be perfect, most of us would have been perfect long ago. The notion to be communicated is that everything that happens should happen given the context of the world, or, in principle, everything is understandable.

Validating behavior, especially when painful or seemingly out of control, in terms of sufficient causes in a manner that is heard and accepted by the client, can require a substantial amount of time. Saying that a behavior makes sense is different than assisting the client in seeing the sense of the behavior. Although the active attempt to change the client's understanding of his or her own behavior is, itself, not necessarily validation, it can have the sum effect of validating the client's behavior. That is, it functions as a validating response. When such is the goal, the therapist may need to have many stories and metaphors at hand to illustrate the point (see Linehan, 1993, for a number of typical DBT stories).

Level Five: Validating as Reasonable in the Moment

At level five, the therapist communicates that behavior is justifiable, reasonable, well-grounded, meaningful, or efficacious in terms of current events, normative biological functioning, and the client's ultimate life goals. The therapist looks for and reflects the wisdom or validity of the client's response and communicates that the response is understandable. The therapist finds the relevant facts in the *current* environment that support the client's behavior. The therapist is not blinded by the dysfunctionality of some of the client's response patterns to those aspects of a response pattern that may be either reasonable or appropriate to the context. Thus, the therapist searches the client's responses for their inherent accuracy, appropriateness, or reasonableness (as well as commenting on the inherent dysfunctionality of much of the response if necessary). There are a number of grounds for level-five validation: inherent soundness; skillful means to long-term goals; normative behavior; and efficacious, but limited, means.

1. *Behavior is valid in terms of being well-founded on empirical facts or sound principles and thoroughly applicable to the case.* Level-five validation here focuses on the inherent validity of the behavior in the sense that the behavior is supported by objective truth or generally accepted authority, is logically derived from empirical facts, is well-grounded or justifiable and at once relevant and meaningful to the case or circumstances. The behavior makes complete sense or is verifiable in light of the facts or known truth. Although one can justify the behavior in terms of sufficient causes (such as learning history or genes), such justification is not necessary. It can be justified on its own merits in its relationship to present circumstances.

   The difficulty in much of psychotherapy is that the bias toward finding and treating clients' dysfunction can blind one to the positive aspects of their behavior. Reasonable and valid aspects of behavior are ignored in favor of focusing on that which is disordered and "crazy-making" environments go unrecognized. The nugget of gold is missed in sweeping up the sand off the floor. Go back to the first two examples given in describing level-four validations (p. 368–369). In the situation with a friend who had been raped in a dark alley, if when she says she cannot walk down the dark alley, you say "But, of course! Alleys are dangerous. Let's go the other way," that is level-five validation. In the example of the client who did not like sex, attributing it to previous dysfunctional family learning was a level-four validation. Remember, however, that the husband bought her silks and satins, played music, lit candles, and was gentle and kind during sex. Once I knew the client and this topic came up again, I said, "I don't think you are a person who does not like sex at all. You simply don't want to have a sex with a man who does not want to have sex with you. That is normal and, certainly, reasonable. You are a flannel nightgown woman and want a man who will throw you on a picnic table, "ravish" you, sweat, and be strong and commanding. You want to have sex with a man who wants to have sex with you, not with the silk and satin sex partner he has in his imagination." That was (because it was accurate) a level-five validation. (I then pointed out how her husband's behavior could be validated at level four by noting how the media kept sending him messages that what he was doing was what a woman wants. He had simply not noticed that she was not the woman in the ads.)

2. *Behavior is valid because it is an effective means to long term goals.* As I noted in the beginning of the chapter, behavior can also be valid because it is efficacious to achieving one's ultimate goals. This is validation in terms of skillful means. Much of therapy involves teaching and validating skills means. The key to this type of validation is to keep an eye on principles of shaping, especially when the client's disorder is severe or intractable. Just noticeable progress (JNPs) must be noticed, reflected, authenticated, and supported. With very difficult or chronically disordered clients, being awake to JNPs can take a lot of energy and vigilance. In DBT, one of the tasks of the consultation team is to keep an eye out for all JNPs and to hold the magnifying glass up, as it were, for the therapist to see more clearly.

3. *Behavior is valid because it is a normative and ordered response.* Communicating that behavior is due to normative biological functioning or that it is usual and normative in a given circumstance is a level-five validation. Take the example of an individual who is experiencing intense anger and is ruminating about the unfairness of being laid off from a job three months before being vested in the company pension plan. One might suggest that anger in this situation is normal. One might also suggest that ruminating about unfairness is a normative aftereffect of anger. It is similar with fear. Increased sensitivity to threat cues is a normal aftereffect. Under high arousal, attention becomes constricted and cognition gets more rigid. Clients are often surprisingly uneducated about normal psychological and biological functioning. Unfortunately, therapists are often uneducated also. This, combined with a prejudice to find at least some disorder in individuals seeking psychotherapy, can lead to pathologizing normative behavior. Not only does the therapist miss validating the valid, but the therapist may also actively invalidate the valid. Nothing, in my experience, so alienates a client as this tendency on the part of many therapists. When combined with deficits in other

types of validation, particularly level one (being awake), therapeutic progress can be seriously impeded.

4. *Behavior is valid in terms of relatively (to long-term goals) unimportant positive consequences, but these consequences simultaneously lead to important or long-term negative consequences.* This type of validation is the therapeutic "yes, but" type of validation. Validation (the "yes") of this type is often followed by confrontation (the "but"). A behavioral pattern can be effective for immediate ends but interfere with long-range ends. Although the behavior solves the immediate problem, it creates other bigger problems in the long-run. Cutting one's arms or overdosing on drugs may be perfectly valid (i.e., effective) as a way to stop unbearable tension and emotional pain in the moment, but is not a valid means to reducing overall suffering and building a life worth living. Even if only a small part of the response is valid (e.g., the expression of emotional pain or difficulty) in a sea of invalidity (trying to reduce pain in ways that cause more trouble in the long term), the therapist searches out that portion of the behavior and responds to it. By finding the validity in the client's response, the therapist can honestly support the client in validating himself or herself.

Although it is usually easy to see that parasuicidal behavior is an invalid method for building a life worth living, it may be difficult at times for others to see that the behavior is exceptionally valid for achieving the desired end of feeling better now. It is normal, however, to desire to feel better when in pain. At times, the problem in a level-five validation is that, although the therapist can see that the behavior clearly works in the short run, the therapist can't understand why the client doesn't inhibit it anyway in favor of long-term gain. What is needed here is to link together level four and five validation statements. "Using cocaine is screwing up your entire life (confrontation, or level-three validation, if true and the client experiences it but hasn't communicated it, or irreverent level five, if corroborating what the client has implied or said) even though, unfortunately, it is really effective at stopping your intense urges and even more intense emotional pain (level five), and, unfortunately, at the moment you can't resist these impulses and inhibit this behavior because you don't (yet) have the necessary self-regulation skills to accomplish the task" ($A_{disorder}$ or $A_{history}$, depending on one's perspective).

Ferreting out what to validate at level five can be exceptionally complex at times. Behavior can be valid in the sense that it is supported by relevant facts, logic, or authority but not valid in the sense of being effective. Take beliefs and opinions. It is often effective to believe certain things, even though the facts do not support one's beliefs. For example, in treating suicidal individuals, I may reinforce them for saying and believing that suicide is *not* an option (an effective belief for staying alive [C] when the chips are down and a gun is at hand [A]), when the facts of the case are that it is very much an option. Misinterpreting hurtful remarks from others as unintentional may for some ends be much more effective than finding out the truth. As with cognitions, emotional responses can also be justifiable or reasonable for the situation but not effective. Emotional behavior is valid when it is a response justified by the events that elicited it or when it is a response relevant to and effective for achieving one's goals. Take fear of falling (B) while inching along a narrow path on a sheer mountain cliff (A). The fear is certainly well-grounded or justifiable in terms of the objective risk of falling to one's death but, if it interferes with one's ability to take the next step (C), it may none the less be invalid from the point of view of effectiveness. The dialectic between being "right" and being "effective" is central in daily life and must be balanced in any attempt to validate client behavior. Mutually desirable goals can be incompatible with each other in terms of efficacious behavior (i.e., valid means). Fear and fleeing a burning building is justifiable in terms of one's own safety, but running into the fire to save one's children is equally justifiable.

The multiplicity of ends requires that the therapist always hold in mind the client's own ultimate therapeutic goals. Estimates of what constitutes positive versus negative consequences must always be tied to the client's life goals. Without initial assessment and agreement on treatment goals, validation (and the withholding of validation) in terms of effectiveness is in danger of meeting the therapist's ends rather than the client's. Without a clear understanding of what behaviors are necessary to get from the client's current state of functioning to that which the client aspires to, validation is in danger of strengthening iatrogenic outcomes, at worst, or stagnation, at best.

A number of specific validation strategies are recommended in DBT that reflect level-five validation. They can be described as follows.

Validating the "Shoulds"

Often one event must occur for a second event to also occur (i.e., the second event is conditional on the first). It is common, and appropriate, to use the term *should* in a statement when one is referring to something that must happen for something else to happen. Thus, the following phrase is appropriate: "A should happen to produce B." One must study (a) to make high grades (b). If the goal is to make high grades, then one "should" study. It is very important that therapists accept clients' preferences about their own behavior. Clients often prefer to behave in certain ways or want various outcomes that demand prior behavior patterns. In these instances, therapists must be alert to accepting the shoulds and communicate to clients the validity of their preferences (assuming the preferences are not incompatible with ultimate goals). Both therapist and client can explore together the validity of the "should" sequence. At times, a client will be making inaccurate (i.e., invalid) predictions (e.g., "A is not needed for B to occur"). At other times, a client's predictions are quite accurate. It is easy for the therapist to get caught up in validating the client's current behavior without recognizing that it is important to avoid *invalidating* the client's quite understandable disappointment in his or her own behavior. In the context of any brief discussion, it is important for the therapist to alternate between validating the events as understandable and validating the disappointment as equally understandable. Certain behaviors both should and should not occur. When this happens, an appropriate response is disappointment.

Finding the "Kernel of Truth"

The task here is to find and highlight the thoughts and assumptions of the client that are valid or make sense within the context the client is operating in. The idea is not that individuals, including clients, always "make sense" or that they do not, at times, exaggerate or minimize, think in extremes, devalue what is valuable, idealize what is ordinary, and make dysfunctional decisions. Indeed, in both popular and professional minds, individuals in therapy are, by definition, almost prone to just such distortions. But, it is essential not to prejudge the opinions, thoughts, and decisions of clients. When the therapist disagrees with the client, it is all too easy to simply assume the therapist is right and the client is wrong. In finding the "kernel of truth," the therapist takes a leap of faith and assumes that, under proper scrutiny, some amount of validity can be found or reason or sense can be make. Although the client's grasp of reality may not be complete, it is also not wholly incomplete. At times, the client's sense of what is happening, his or her thoughts on the matter, may make substantial sense. Some clients have an uncanny ability sometimes to observe or attend to stimuli in the environment that others do not observe. The task of the therapist is to separate the wheat from the chaff and focus, in this moment, on the wheat.

Respecting Differing Values

At times differences between clients and therapists are of opinions and values. Respecting these differences, while not assuming superiority, is an essential component of validation. It is easy when one is the therapist to assume a "one-up" position whereby one's own opinions and values are viewed as more respectable than the clients, thereby invalidating the client's point of view per se. For example, one of my client's believed that I should be available to her by phone any time, night or day. She herself had a job in the mental health area and stated that she was available to the people whe worked with because she believed that it was the compassionate and right thing to do. I pointed out to her that the problem here was that she was trying to get me to be like her and have broader limits on what I could give, and I was trying to get her to be more like me and to have and observe narrower limits. Although I did not change my position about my own behavior, I could appreciate the value of her point of view also.

Acknowledge "Wise Mind"

DBT presents to clients the concept of "wise mind" or wise knowing. This is in contrast to "emotion mind," or emotional knowing, and "reasonable mind," or intellectual knowing. Wise mind is the integration of both and includes an emphasis on intuitive, experiential, and spiritual modes of knowing. Thus, an important form of validation is when the therapist acknowledges and supports this type of knowing on the part of the client. The therapist takes the position that something can be valid even if it can't be proved. Just because someone else is more logical than you in an argument, does not mean your points were not valid. Emotionality does not invalidate your position any more than logic can necessarily always validate it. A further definition of wise mind is that it is the state of being where wise behavior (i.e., behavior that is just what is needed at the moment in the present context) is easy. The use and, then, acknowledgment of a construct such as wise mind is also validating in that it communicates to the client that he or she is actually capable of wise behavior. For seriously disturbed populations, this is often a sharp change in how they are usually treated. The concept of wise mind forces the therapist to search for the wisdom in what may appear to be a sea of invalidity. It is based on the ideas that what is a dysfunction for a single individual may be efficacious for the welfare of the community at large and that one's weaknesses are usually also one's greatest strengths.

Validity as Emergent

Giving the therapist the role of determining when behavior is valid in the context in which it occurs and when it is not is, at first glance, giving immense authority to the therapist. Many therapists shy away from this role (i.e., of validator), preferring instead to assume clients can best determine what is valid for themselves. This view often springs from the idea that what is true for one person may not be true for another. Truth is relative to the individual. The alternative extreme is the absolute view of truth: What is true now has always been true, will always be true, and is true for all individuals in all places. Both positions are inherently flawed.

On the one hand, the relativist view is that there is, essentially, no truth and, thus, no basis for recognizing what is valid or invalid. The universe beyond the individual does not influence what is. All roads lead to Rome. The flaw here is that all roads do not lead to Rome. Alternatively, the therapist may assume that once "conditions of worth" are removed (to quote Rogers, 1959), that which is valid will emerge and be seen clearly by the client. The therapist need not inform or intervene except to assist in sweeping away the conditions of worth imposed on the client by others. "Truth is in the air," and the client who does not see it is "resisting." The task of the therapist is to probe the resistances, assuming that once they melt away the client will see clearly and without repression of the truth that is too painful to see. The flaw in the latter is that it presupposes an inference in the absence of assessment of the individual case. It may be true, but it also may not be. The therapist who maintains this position is often experienced by the client as withholding and unwilling to give the help that is needed in the moment.

At the other hand is the absolutist view: Truth once fixed is unchanging. Not only is there truth, but it can be known with certainty. The subjective eye of the beholder can be overcome by the objective eye of the observer. The flaw here is twofold: One cannot ever divorce subject from object and, in a universe that is constantly changing and emerging, what was true in one context may indeed not hold up in another context. Thus, what is valid at one time and in one set of circumstances may not hold at another time or within a different context. The synthesis of these two views is that validity of behavior can be determined only in a collaborative manner with both client and therapist actively interacting to articulate both the fullness of the responses in question and their context at the moment and their relationship to the client's own ultimate goals.

Level Six: Treating the Person as Valid—Radical Genuineness

In level six, the task is to recognize the person as he or she is, seeing and responding to the strengths and capacities of the individual while keeping a firm empathic understanding of the client's actual difficulties and incapacities. The therapist believes in the individual and his or her capacity to change and move toward ultimate life goals. The client is responded to as a person of equal status, due equal respect. Validation at the highest level is the validation of the individual as "is." The therapist sees more than the role, more than a "client" or "disorder." Level-six validation is the opposite of treating the client in a condescending manner or as overly fragile. It is responding to the individual as capable of effective and reasonable behavior rather than assuming that he or she is an invalid. Whereas levels one through five represent sequential steps in validation of a kind, level six represents both change in level as well as kind.

The term *invalid* has two meanings. The first meaning, to be falsely based or reasoned, not efficacious, is the use of invalid as an adjective and is relevant to most of the discussion of validation so far. The second meaning of invalid, when it is used as a noun meaning one who is incapacitated by a chronic disease or disability, is most relevant here. At level six, the therapist does not respond to clients a priori as if they are invalids. Instead, the therapist responds to the client as if he or she will continue (or start) emitting valid behavior. Ability rather than disability is assumed. It is the capacity for validity that is communicated and responded to at level six. In a sense, the therapist validates the capacity for *future* validity. In contrast, at level five the therapist validates the client's behavior in terms of its validity in the present. At level four the therapist validates the client's behavior in terms of its validity in the past but not the present.

Validation at level six is closer to validating the individual than it is to validating any particular response or behavioral pattern. It implies a genuineness on the part of the therapist, the quality of being one's genuine self within the therapeutic relationship. The quality of being one's self that is alluded to here has been described by Rogers as:

> He is without front or facade, openly being the feelings and attitudes which at the moment are flowing in him. It involves the element of self-awareness, meaning that the feelings the therapist is experiencing are available to him, available to his awareness, and also that he is able to live these feelings, to be them in the relationship, and able to communicate them if appropriate. It means that he comes into a direct personal encounter with his client, meeting him on a person-to-person basis. It means he is *being* himself, not denying himself. (Rogers & Truax, 1967, p. 101)

It is described by Safran and Segal (1990) as:

> Therapists who let concepts blind them to the reality of what is truly happening for their patients in the moment are relating to the patient as an object, or in Buber's phraseology, an "It" rather than a "Thou." Therapists who hide behind the security of the conceptual framework provided here rather than risking authentic human encounters, which could lead to therapists' transcending all roles and preconceptions about how they themselves should be, rule out the possibility of the very experiences in human relatedness that will be healing for their patients. (pp. 249–250)

Such a stance of genuineness and validation of the client as he or she is in the moment, therefore, requires the ability to throw off preconceptions of client role and generalizations about psychopathology, to be aware of the present moment in all its complexity, and to respond spontaneously and completely. The ability to be compassionate, effective, and genuine or without role, all at the same time, is extremely difficult. Such naturalness is especially difficult for therapists trained in schools that emphasize the construction of strict boundaries and "professional" behaviors independent of the individual client. It is difficult for therapists who are uncomfortable with their own personal limits as caregivers, who may find it more comfortable to attribute their inability to respond empathetically to the requirements of their role as therapist rather than their limitations as professionals. It is difficult with clients who communicate unremitting emotional pain when one has only limited tools to alleviate the pain. Yet it is required. I often ask therapists to imagine in a role play that their client is their sister or their brother, coming to them in emotional agony with severely dysfunctional behavior. Invariably, they respond to the person as a whole (and usually quite differently than they respond to clients in the same plight). That is the validation that is at the heart of DBT.

At level six, almost any response to a client can be valid. The key is in what message the therapist's behavior communicates and how accurate the message is. Confrontation communicates to the client that he or she is equal to hearing the truth. Although confrontation may not validate a client's view about the behavior in question, it does validate the client's inherent capability to change. (Sometimes, at these points, it can be useful to add in a level-four validation, suggesting that it is, of course, perfectly understandable how the client would come to engage in the confronted behavior and just as understandable how the client would also not even see the dysfunctionality.) Treating the client with kid gloves, holding back on the truth as the therapist sees it, worrying excessively over timing, and so on communicate that the client is fragile and unable to function at a competent level. Therapist responses that clients experience as condescending are often validating at levels four or five but invalidating at level six.

Cheerleading is a special type of level-six validation. In cheerleading, the therapist validates (i.e., recognizes and confirms) the inherent ability of the client to overcome difficulties and to build a life worth living. Although that life may differ from what is hoped for or even expected at any given point, the potential for overcoming obstacles and for creating value is what is attended to, observed, and reflected. Cheerleading is believing in the client. For some, this will be their first experience of having someone believe and have confidence in them. In cheerleading, the therapist is validating the inner capabilities and wisdom of the client.

Cheerleading is sometimes experienced by clients as invalidating of their emotions or beliefs. If you understood how really awful it is, how really incapable they are, you wouldn't believe that they can change or accomplish anything or do what you are requesting. In cheerleading, the therapist believes the client can (at least eventually) save himself or herself. The client, in contrast, often believes that if you really understood, you would save him or her yourself. The task here is to balance an appreciation for the difficulties of making progress and realistic expectations with hope and confidence that the client can indeed move. Cheerleading has to be laced with emotional validation and a large dose of realism. Without that context, it can indeed be invalidating. Thus, the therapist must be vigilant in recognizing the difficulty of the client's problem, even while never giving up on the idea that the problem can be overcome eventually.

TYPE OF VALIDATION

There are two types of validation: topographical and functional. Topographical validation is explicit and fits the form of validation (i.e., it has the topography of a validating response). In topographical validation, the therapist responds overtly with words that say, either directly or indirectly, that the therapist believes in the validity of the client and the client's behavior: "That makes sense," "hmmm," "I agree," "of course, how could it be otherwise," and longer discussions of how the client's behavior is justifiable or effective. In functional validation the therapist responds as if the client's behavior is valid. A client says he does not want to discuss a topic, and the therapist switches topics; a client describes a problem she want to solve, and the therapist says "let's get to work." Functional validation tends to be implicit. Whereas topographical validation is validating by words, functional validation is validating by deeds. Both are very important in DBT.

In the mistaken impression that validation of all behavior is important for a client to feel accepted, many therapists inadvertently invalidate a client's central message that something has to change if life is to be endurable. An emphasis on acceptance of the client as he or she is (topographical validation), unbalanced by the focus on change that the client is saying is needed (functional validation), therefore, can also, paradoxically, invalidate. If the therapist only urges the client to accept and self-validate, it can appear that the therapist does not regard the client's problems seriously. Pure acceptance-based therapies can appear to discount the desperation of the seriously disturbed individual because they offer little hope of change. The client's personal experience of the current state of affairs as unacceptable and unendurable is thereby invalidated. Exhortations to accept one's current situation offer little solace to the individual who experiences life as painfully unendurable. It is not inconceivable that suicidal behavior in some individuals at some times functions to "wake up" the environment, including the therapist, and get the environment to take the client's problems more seriously. Thus, balancing validation with accurate invalidation is, paradoxically, a necessary validation strategy.

VALIDATING SPECIFIC RESPONSE TARGETS

Like most behavioral treatments, DBT is based on a tripartite model of human functioning that, for convenience, divides behavior into motor (i.e., action), cognitive–verbal, and physiological systems. It is important that the therapist acknowledge and validate responses across the entire system rather than focus attention on just one subsystem (e.g., cognitive representations or actions) of responding. Although emotions are viewed by many as part of the physiological system, an alternate view embraced by DBT is that they are best considered integrated responses of the total system. The form of the integration in emotional responding is automatic, either because of biological hard wiring (the basic emotions) or because of repeated experiences (learned emotions). That is, an emotion typically comprises behaviors from each of the three subsystems. Thus, emotions are a full-system behavioral response with effects on the full system. In considering what responses to validate, consideration should be given to responses in each system (actions, cognition, and physiological). When emotional dysregulation is an important part of the problem, as I hypothesize with the borderline personality disorder, emotions per se as an integrated set of responses must be attended to commonly and explicitly. For example, DBT therapists repeatedly identify and explore the primary emotions (e.g., fear, anger, sadness, shame, guilt, joy, interest, and disgust) that clients experience and express (see Linehan, 1993, for a fuller discussion of this topic). Because of the important role of emotions in all human relationships, including psychotherapy, both facilitating and inhibiting disclosure, change, and attention to client's emotional functioning is important with all clients.

Validating Action

Validation of overt behavior, or action, focuses on identifying and responding to what clients are doing, somewhat independently of what they are feeling or thinking. Actions are valid at level five when they are an efficacious means to the client's ultimate ends or are relevant and justifiable in light of the context in which they occur. The task here, therefore, is to ascertain whether indeed the client's actions are valid for those ends and then to provide feedback to the client. To use a Zen phrase, the therapist searches for instances of "skillful means" and reflects them to the client. The therapist finds the wisdom in the client's actions and notes when a response pattern is one that would be expected of most anyone in the situation. Level-five validation of action often takes the form of praise (e.g., good job) or of responsiveness (e.g., giving greater privileges to an inpatient who replaces self-destructive behavior with skillful problem solving).

Not all responses, however, are justifiable, relevant, or effective for achieving the end goals one has in mind for his or her life. For each client, therefore, behaviors not meeting that test—that they be justifiable, relevant, or effective in light of purported or agreed on goals or by the facts existing at the time of the behavior—are viewed as invalid in the moment. They are confronted or ignored. The premise here is simple: Not every road will get you to Rome. No matter how invalid a response may be with respect to its relationship to current facts or future goals, it is indisputably the case that all behavior is as it should be. That is, all behavior has a certain validity in terms of its relationship to its own history. At level four, the therapist communicates this simple fact.

Level-three validation of action is when the therapist uses the information at hand to figure out what the client has already done or is likely to do. An example of this is when a therapist can read when a client is lying about past behavior. Although one would not ordinarily think of this as validating, clients who lie, for example about drug use, often experience the therapist who does not pick up on lies as naive, not bothering to know the client, and unwilling to see and accept the client as he or she really is. A statement of the facts, without judgment of good or bad, is at once confrontational (of one's behavior) and validating (that one is who one purports to be). Knowing and communicating what behaviors are possible for a particular client or are likely to occur also validates the client as who he or she actually is. When, in addition, therapists communicate an intrinsic belief in a client's inherent capacity to emit desired behaviors and faith in a client's ability to overcome difficulties and succeed in reaching goals, level-three validation merges with level-six validation to become cheerleading (see Linehan, 1993, for a fuller description of this point). The dialectical tension here is always between knowing the client well enough to see his or her limitations while simultaneously believing in the client's inherent capacity to overcome obstacles and progress toward life goals. The ability to do both is requisite for validation.

Validating Cognition

The task of the therapist in validating cognitive responses at level five is to recognize, verbalize, and understand both expressed and unexpressed thoughts, beliefs, expectations, and underlying assumptions or rules and to find and reflect the essential truth in all or part of the client's thoughts, beliefs, underlying assumptions, rules, and so on. The strategies for "catching thoughts," identifying assumptions and expectancies, and uncovering rules that are guiding the individual's behavior—especially when these rules are operating outside of awareness—are little different from the guidelines outlined by cognitive therapists such as Beck and his colleagues (Beck & Freedman, 1990; Beck, Rush, Shaw, & Emery, 1979). The essential difference here is that the task is to validate rather than empirically refute or logically challenge. The struggle for clients, then, is to learn to discriminate when perceptions, thoughts, and beliefs are contextually valid and when they are not—when they can trust themselves and when they cannot. The task of the therapist is to assist in this process by ferreting out valid perceptions, assumptions, expectations, and so on and reflecting these back to the client. "That's reasonable," "that makes sense," "I agree" are typical validations of cognitive–verbal responses.

Level-four validations of cognitive processing must be made with great care. They can at times be quite invalidating of the clients' sense of their own ability to interpret reality (i.e., they can be "crazy making"). A heavy focus on the client's presently invalid beliefs, assumptions, and cognitive styles is counterproductive if it leaves the client unsure of when, if ever, perceptions and thoughts are adaptive, functional, and valid. For example, overinterpreting a client's perceptions as "transference" reactions, projections, or other distortions caused by unconscious processes learned in the past communicates to the client that his or her own thinking and critical evaluation of his or her own thinking is faulty or invalid. Teaching the client the therapist's rules of validating can be quite critical here. Teaching the client how to know when his or her own thinking is valid or invalid, paradoxically, validates the client's inherent capacity to critically evaluate his or her own thought processes (i.e., it is an instance of cognitive validation).

Level-three validations have to do with articulating to (and sometimes for) clients what their assumptions and expectations must be in a given situation. It is hearing and saying aloud clients' unspoken and sometimes hidden thoughts. Cognitive validation is when another person knows what you are thinking before you even say it. It is when the therapist says (with accuracy), "but you don't really believe it do you," "at that point, I'm guessing you were thinking. . . ," "and it seemed to you like. . . ." "so, you figured that. . . ," and so on. It is when the therapist figures out just how a client might interpret a situation and then acts accordingly. Empathetically, the therapist stands in the client's shoes and sees the world from that perspective. It is the essential therapeutic ability if validation efforts are to have their intended effect; validation depends on the ability to communicate to the client such that the client interprets the message as intended. The therapist must be able to simultaneously speak as the therapist, listen as the client, and use what is heard to formulate subsequent words.

Validating Physiological Responses

Like validation of any response, validation of biological functioning at level five has to do with recognition of the soundness of functioning. At this level, validation is based on whether the client's physiological responses are normative for the situation and demography of the individual. The concept of valid here is the opposite of the concept of physiological disorder, disease, or dysfunction. The individual's physiological response patterns are sufficient (i.e., are effective) for achieving outcomes the individual cares about.

The statement that one has a disease is a statement of current invalidity of functioning. Persons with serious diseases are invalids. A level-four validation of such dysfunction might be to provide a genetic-, trauma-, or learning-based explanation for such dysfunction. The biological dysfunction is understandable—it "should" be because factors necessary to impair functioning have occurred. I often tell clients their problem is that their brain (i.e., their biological system) is in love with certain thoughts. I may discuss the effects of learning on cell physiology. I also tell them that psychotherapy will work by changing neural pathways and habitual chemical reactions of the brain. I have spent a fair amount of time discussing whether certain aspects of behavior or orientation can be changed—that is, what can be changed and what cannot be changed in human behavior. Which biological systems are hard-wired and which are not?

Level-three validation of physiological functioning is when the therapist tells clients how they are most likely reacting physiologically either during the current interaction or when their problems surface between sessions. The enormous amount of psychoeducation that accompanies behavioral treatments of panic and other anxiety disorders is an example here. The ability to describe what a panic attack feels like, for example, is highly validating for the individual who experiences frequent panic. It is not uncommon in such instances for a client to exclaim "Yes! That's me." The ability to describe with and for the client the physiological experience of certain emotions or the effects of certain events (e.g., extreme trauma) can be enormously reassuring, normalizing, and, hence, validating. Predicting accurately side effects of medications or interventions is another example.

Validating Emotions

Understanding and validation of emotions is crucial in any psychotherapy. Paradoxically, this is especially the case when the focus of therapy is on helping the individual learn to better regulate (i.e., change) emotional responses. When validating emotions, the therapist communicates to the client that his or her emotional responses are valid, either because it could not be otherwise due to learning or biology (level four) or because they are reasonable or normative responses to the precipitating events; they are based on sound or logical interpretations or processing of events (level five). The role of validation here has two functions: to remove inhibitions to further processing of emotional material and to reduce environmental factors that maintain intense emotional expression. In the first instance (removing inhibitions), validation used judiciously can cut off clients' abilities to invalidate their own primary (in the sense of first in the chain of events) emotional responses to events. Self-invalidation of emotions can function as escape behavior, stopping unwanted emotions. Because the self-invalidation is often automatic and immediate, it can also cut off emotional experiences before they are sufficiently processed. When this happens, the primary emotion occurs repeatedly in response to the same precipitating events, often in a more intense fashion. The client does not learn to respond differently or to modulate the intensity of the emotion. Emotions that are no longer reasonable responses to events do not change. Although there are many theoretical positions on just what emotional processing involves, the data is accumulating that the activation of emotions appropriate to the precipitating events is crucial in decreasing dysfunctional emotional responses. For example, Foa, Riggs, Massie, and Yarczower (1995) have found that only clients who facially express fear when remembering rape improve with exposure treatments. Those who bypass fear and go straight or quickly to anger do not improve.

It is equally important that the therapist also validate the secondary emotion (i.e., the emotional response to the emotion). For example, clients often feel guilty, ashamed, and angry at themselves or panic if they experience anger or humiliation, feel dependent on the therapist, begin to cry, grieve, or are afraid. It is these emotional responses to emotions that are often the most debilitating for the client.

It is rarely useful to respond to what seems to be an unwarranted emotion by instructing the client that she need not feel that way. Therapists are frequently tempted to do this when clients are responding emotionally to the therapist. For example, if a client calls the therapist at home (according to the treatment plan) and then feels guilty or humiliated about calling the therapist, it is a natural tendency for the therapist to respond to this by telling the client that he or she need not feel this way. This should be recognized as an invalidating statement on the part of the therapist. Although the therapist may want to communicate that calling the therapist is acceptable and understandable, it is also understandable that the client felt guilty and humiliated.

In the second case (validation to reduce emotional expressiveness), understanding the communication function of emotions can be helpful in orienting the therapist to validation. Many therapists believe that validating an escalating emotion will make things only worse (i.e., the emotion will get more out of control). This is only sometimes the case, and it depends on whether the client expects the communication to allay or resolve the situation prompting the emotion. Validating sadness of an irretrievable loss may clarify the fact of the loss and thereby experiencing of sadness, thus increasing emotional intensity. Validating anger at the therapist for repeated neglect by apologizing and promising (credibly) to end the neglect serves to reduce anger. In agreeing with the client that a threatening situation is indeed fearful and backing off of urging the client to encounter the situation, the therapist expects relief from fear, not escalation. Once the emotions are heard and responded to as valid, emotional intensity will usually decrease and may disappear altogether. Validation of emotions can be self-verifying to the client when the therapeutic message is that the client's perceptions of events precipitating the emotion are valid or the emotional response is normative for the situation described. The resulting increase in a sense of predictability or control, discussed below in reference to self-verification, is often soothing and emotion regulating.

Some clients, of course, do frequently distort, sometimes exaggerate, and sometimes remember selectively. With these individuals it is common for people around them, including therapists, to assume that their thinking and perceptions are always faulty or, at least, when there is a disagreement the individual is most likely to be incorrect. Such assumptions are especially likely when full information about events precipitating the individual's emotional response is not available—that is, the stimuli setting off the individual's reaction is not public. Especially when a person is experiencing intense emotions, it is easy for others to assume that the individual is distorting, somehow. Things are not, or could not be, as bad as the person says. The trap here is that assumptions take the place of assessment; hypothesis and interpretations take the place of analysis of the facts. The other person's, including the therapist's, private interpretation is taken as a guide to public facts. Such a scenario replicates the invalidating environment that many individuals have or currently experience in their lives.

Intense emotions can precipitate emotion-congruent thoughts, memories, and images. Conversely, thoughts, memories, and images can have powerful influences on mood. Thus, once an intense emotional response starts, a vicious circle is often set up where the emotion sets off memories, images, and thoughts and influences perceptions and processing of information that in turn, feed back into the emotional response and keep it going. In such instances, distortions of perceptions, memories, and interpretations of information can take on a life of their own and may color many, if not most, of the individual's interactions and responses to events. Not all mood-related thoughts, perceptions, expectancies, memories, and assumptions, however, are dysfunctional, misinterpretations, or distorted. This point is crucial in conducting psychotherapy.

Most often, therapist invalidation of feelings will arise from therapists' over-anxious attempts to help the client feel better immediately. Such tendencies should be resisted because they are counter to an important message that the therapy is attempting to communicate, namely, that negative and painful emotions are not only understandable but also tolerable. Additionally, if the therapist responds to negative emotions on the part of the client by either ignoring them, telling the client he or she need not feel that way, or too quickly focusing the client on changing the emotions, the therapist runs the risk of behaving in a manner identical to others in the client's natural environment. The attempt to control emotions by will power or to "think happy" and to avoid negative thoughts is a key characteristic of the invalidating environments. The therapist must be sure not to fall into this trap.

WHY VALIDATE?

Within this wide rubric of what to validate, more specific guidelines for targeting of validation will depend always on the intended function of validation at the particular time it is used. That is, therapeutic validation should be strategic. The strategic floor of therapy is one of the characteristics that differentiates therapy from ordinary other relationships. Thus, the therapist must at all times have a clear view of a number of factors described more fully below but including: the client's fears that change in therapy will not be possible or will make matters worse (validation as acceptance to balance change); the client's level of self-validation or, conversely, self-invalidation, castigation, or attack (validation to strengthen self-validation); the relationship of the behavior currently occurring or being reported to the client's life goals (validation to strengthen clinical progress); the client's understanding of his or her own behavior and knowledge about behavior in general (validation as feedback); and the client's sense of being understood by the therapist (validation to strengthen the therapeutic relationship).

Validation as Acceptance to Balance Change

First, as noted above, validation in psychotherapy functions to balance psychotherapy change strategies. Validation functions as both acceptance and verification of clients' views of themselves and their own world. As such, it likely has the twin effects of bolstering client perceptions of predictability and control and, at least when the verified self-views are positive, tends to increase positive affect (Swann, Stein-Seroussi, & Giesler, 1992) An unremitting focus on change, in contrast, can increase perceptions of unpredictability and loss of control, increasing fear, anxiety, and anger to such an extent that processing of new information is shut off and therapy comes to a virtual standstill. The amount of validation needed per unit of change focus will vary among clients and for a particular client over time. At the beginning of therapy, before a strong relationship has been formed, validation may be the principal intervention. Later, once the client feels secure with the therapist and with the methods and direction of therapy, a sustained focus on therapeutic change may be possible with only minimal attention to active validation. Self-disclosure, important in all psychotherapies, however, can occur only when the client does not feel threatened or overwhelmed by the therapist's emphasis on change. Generally, the client who is nonverbal, unassertive, and tends to withdraw when confronted will need a higher validation-to-change ratio than the combative client who, while equally vulnerable and sensitive, can "stay the course" when feeling attacked. For all clients, when stress in the environment (both within and outside of the therapy relationship) goes up, the validation–change quotient must also go up accordingly. Similarly, when addressing particularly sensitive topics, particularly topics where the client is vulnerable to loss of emotional control, validation must be increased. Even within a particular session, the need for therapist validation can be expected to vary. Validation can be a brief comment or digression while working on other issues, or it can be the focus of most of the session with only a small effort devoted to eliciting or strengthening change. Therapy with clients can be likened to pushing an individual ever closer to the edge of a sheer cliff. As the back of the person's heel rubs the edge, validation is used to pull the person back from the precipice towards the safe ground near the therapist is in the service of resuming (ASAP!) moving back to the edge.

Validation to Teach Self-Validation

Second, therapeutic validation functions as a first step in the acquisition and the strengthening of skills in nonjudgmental self-observation and nonpejorative descriptions of self (i.e., to teach self-validation). The experience of mistrusting oneself is intensely aversive when it is either longstanding and pervasive or occurs with respect to a topic of life and death importance where there is no more authoritative source of information. At a minimum, as noted by G. Mark Williams (personal communication, May 3, 1991), you have to at least trust your own decision on who to believe—yourself or others. The goal here is to help clients learn to trust themselves and their own reactions to events. I often point out to clients that a major goal in therapy is to help them learn to trust (rather than change) their own responses. This goal is based on the notion that many of the primary or initial responses of clients are in fact valid; often, it is the secondary response of invalidating the initial response that creates so much pain and trouble for individuals. This point of view is very similar to points Greenberg has frequently made about the roles of primary and secondary emotions and will be discussed further below. This function of validation is similar to the function of empathy in client-centered psychotherapy noted by Greenberg and Elliott in chapter 8 of this volume.

Therapist validation of clients' responses works in two ways to increase self-validation. In the first place it models appropriate validation (i.e., how to respond to one's self in a validating manner). At times, it may simply model how to nondefensively and noncritically think through one's own opinions, emotions, or actions to arrive at a conclusion about their validity. Second, to the extent that therapeutic validation is reinforcing, it can also be used to reinforce client self-trust. It is very important, however, to recognize that validation of client responses does not *ipso facto* teach self-validation. It is possible to inadvertently use validation as a reinforcer for self-mistrust. This is most likely to occur when self-denigration or other acts of self-mistrust are regularly followed by therapist validation. In particular, it is important that the therapist not use validation strategies immediately following dysfunctional behaviors that are maintained by their tendency to elicit validation from the environment. Validation is best used when it follows an instance or report of behavior that is both valid and to be strengthened. In this case, therefore, validation is a response to the client's own acts (however tentative at first) of self-trust or indications of confidence in his or her own veracity or judgment.

Validation to Strengthen Clinical Progress

Third, validation functions to reinforce behaviors other than self-trust that the therapist wishes to strengthen. This is true, of course, only when therapist validation is a reinforcer for the individual. Although it is likely to be reinforcing for most, it is crucial to assess its functions for each client. When reinforcing, it is important that the therapist provide validation contingent on behaviors that represent clinical progress and not validate immediately following dysfunctional behaviors that are maintained by their tendency to elicit validation from the environment. The question arises, can one validate behavior one does not want to reinforce? That is, does it make sense to validate behavior that is dysfunctional or that you and the client want to change? The answer is yes and no. It depends on how you deliver the validation and, especially, what you surround it with. Take the case of the employed woman who tells me about becoming angry and crying when her boss refuses an important request, blocking once again her ability to succeed in her job. I might validate her crying behavior by saying that it is reasonably common for women to respond that way. Whereas men when angry are more likely to escalate their verbal aggression, women are more likely to cry. Therefore, I may comment that her behavior is a "normal" expression of frustration (which, I might add, was also understandable given the behavior of her boss) and expectable; she is not "pathological" or weak. (Parenthetically, I might also say to her that verbal aggression may be more acceptable in the workplace than crying only because men made up the rules for acceptable workplace behavior in the first place.) However, I would then most likely go on and validate her frustration with herself over crying, confirming her view that, if she does not learn another way to handle anger, she is not likely to progress as far as she wants to go in her company. In summary, the message would be "your behavior is perfectly understandable and it is not pathological, but it has to change anyway." So what patent behaviors are being reinforced here? I would analyze the interaction above as follows. First, both telling me about crying and crying when frustrated are being reinforced when I communicate in essence "but, of course! women cry when they are frustrated; that is normal; don't worry about it." That communication also serves to weaken (or punish) her tendency to castigate and judge herself negatively when she cries. I am validating crying as part of a normal biological response to frustration and anger. Next, when I communicate, in essence, "but, of course, I agree with you also that this is frustrating and has to change!" I am strengthening her resolve to stop crying during interactions with her boss and am also reinforcing her assessment of the effectiveness of her own behavior. I am validating her business judgment: Women crying at the office is not a recipe for breaking through the glass ceiling. What is not being reinforced here is a non-self-accepting stance on the part of the client. I could, however, even validate that by commenting that it is completely understandable in light of her previous learning history. The first validation (crying is normal) is an instance of level-five validation, and the second validation (so is self-blame because of faulty learning) is a level-four validation.

Validation as Feedback

Closely related to validation as strengthening, yet slightly different, is the role of validation in giving clients feedback about themselves and their behavior. Although all behavior can be validated at level four (i.e., all behavior is in principle understandable), not all behavior is valid at level five (i.e., not all behavior is justified by current events or by its effectiveness at achieving desired goals). Both communications (level four and level five) are exceptionally important, however. Both give information. Validation at level four teaches clients a nonjudgmental way of thinking about themselves and also helps them ferret out the probable development factors that influence their current behavior. Such stories (i.e., those that tell us how our behavior was learned or influenced by biological factors) are important for many in constructing meaning to their lives. In this fashion, validation is a change process rather than a purely acceptance strategy. In level-five validation, the therapist is informing the client that specific responses and response patterns are efficacious for achieving desired outcomes or life goals (i.e., they are "appropriate to the end in view") and that cognitive behaviors (e.g., beliefs, opinions, expectations, are perceptions) are "well-founded, in fact, or established on sound principles, and thoroughly applicable to the case or circumstances." Validation of physiological responses gives information about the "soundness and strength" of the individual's biological functioning; normal physiological responses of the client to events and their influence on other response systems are identified and highlighted. For many clients, information about the appropriateness, normality (in the sense of normative or expected), and reasonableness of their behavior is sorely needed. Many have either not received such information while growing up or are currently living in crazy-making environments where it is difficult to keep their bearings in relation to their own behavior. For some clients, indeed, this information-giving function of validation is all that is really needed from therapy. This might be especially true for clients who are isolated or different from those around them, for example, the only women in an all-male work environment, the liberal who has just moved to a very conservative region, and the only highly emotional member of a very mellow family.

Validation to Strengthen the Therapeutic Relationship

Finally, validation functions to create a positive, attached, therapeutic relationship. This function of validation is primarily a by-product of the previous functions. As noted above, when the therapist validates responses and characteristics of the client that he or she finds admirable and desirable, some increase in positive affect can be expected. Similarly, when the therapist validates the client's own negative views of himself or herself, particularly when some hope of positive change as a result of therapy is also provided, the client's sense of control and predictability is also increased and, thus, also leads to more positive emotional states. Validation here soothes and calms the client. A similar result can also be expected when the therapist validates the client's perceptions of problems in the therapy per se or with aspects of the therapist's behavior. Validation in such instances is the first step in offering hope that favorable changes can be made. The attachment in each case is by way of associating the therapeutic relationship with more positive affect. From a reinforcement perspective, the therapist becomes associated with positive outcomes, thereby becoming positively valenced and moved toward.

REFERENCES

Beck, A. T., & Freedman, A. (1990). *Cognitive therapy of personality disorders.* New York: Guilford Press.

Beck, A. T., Rush, A. J., Shaw, B. F., & Emery, G. (1979). *Cognitive therapy of depression.* New York: Guilford Press.

deMello, A. (1990). *Awareness.* New York: Doubleday.

Foa, E. B., Riggs, D. S., Massie, E. D., & Yarczower, M. (1995). The impact of fear activation and anger on the efficacy of exposure treatment for PTSD. *Behavior Therapy, 26,* 487–499.

Linehan, M. M. (1993). *Cognitive behavioral treatment of borderline personality disorder.* New York: Guilford Press.

Linehan, M. M., Armstrong, H. E., Suarez, A., Allmon, D., & Heard, H. L. (1991). Cognitive–behavioral treatment of chronically parasuicidal borderline patients. *Archives of General Psychiatry, 48,* 1060–1064.

Linehan, M. M., & Heard, H. L. (1993). Impact of treatment accessibility on clinical course of parasuicidal patients: In reply to R. E. Hoffman. [Letter to editor]. *Archives of General Psychiatry, 50,* 157–158.

Linehan, M. M., Heard, H. L., & Armstrong, H. E. (1993). Naturalistic follow-up of a behavioral treatment for chronically parasuicidal borderline patients. *Archives of General Psychiatry, 50,* 971–974.

Linehan, M. M., Tutek, D. A., Heard, H. L., & Armstrong, H. E. (1994). Interpersonal outcome of cognitive behavioral treatment for chronically suicidal borderline patients. *American Journal of Psychiatry, 151,* 1771–1776.

Rogers, C. R. (1959). A theory of therapy, personality, and interpersonal relationships, as developed in the client-centered framework. In S. Koch (Ed.), *Psychology: A study of a science* (Vol. 3, pp. 184–256). New York: McGraw-Hill.

Rogers, C. R. (1980). *A way of being.* Boston: Houghton Mifflin.

Rogers, C. R., & Truax, C. B. (1967). The therapeutic conditions antecedent to change: A theoretical view. In C. R. Rogers (Ed.), *The therapeutic relationship and its impact* (pp. 97–108). Madison: University of Wisconsin Press.

Safran, J. D., & Segal, Z. V. (1990). *Interpersonal process in cognitive therapy.* New York: Basic Books.

Simpson, J. A., & Weiner, E. S. (1989). *Oxford English dictionary* (2nd ed.) [On-Line]. University of Washington Information Navigator.

Swann, W. B., Stein-Seroussi, A., & Giesler, R. B. (1992). Why people self-verify. *Journal of Personality and Social Psychology, 62,* 392–401.

Webster's ninth new collegiate dictionary and thesaurus. (1991). [On-Line]. University of Washington Information Navigator.

Wilbur, K. (1995). *Sex, ecology, spirituality: The spirit of evolution.* Boston, MA: Shambhala Press.

18

EMPATHY AND THE ACTIVE CLIENT: AN INTEGRATIVE, COGNITIVE–EXPERIENTIAL APPROACH

ARTHUR C. BOHART AND KAREN TALLMAN

In this chapter we present an integrative view of psychotherapy based on the idea that the client is an active, self-healing agent and, as such, is the primary agent of change in psychotherapy. The therapist is an important and useful adjunct to the client's self-healing change process, and empathy is the basis from which therapists provide their assistance. Whether or not one agrees with our view of the client as active self-healer, we believe that the view of empathy we develop provides a basis for effective therapeutic practice from any perspective and is particularly important for those who wish to practice integratively. We first present our therapeutic perspective and then our view of empathy.

A CREATIVE COGNITIVE–EXPERIENTIAL VIEW OF THERAPY

The Active Client as Self-healer

We believe it is clients who are the primary agents of change in psychotherapy. They create change through a cyclical process of thinking, exploring, and experiencing, which leads to the creation of new meaning and of new ways of being and behaving in their personal worlds. This is a metatheoretical view of how change occurs. One can adopt it and still practice from any of a variety of perspectives. This perspective particularly fits with integrative practice, where the therapist tries to provide what the client needs, rather than what the therapist's theory says the client needs. This perspective is expressed in the therapist's attitude toward the client and in the subtle alterations in interaction and dialogue that accompany this attitude. As long as the therapist realizes that it is not his or her procedures or interventions that create the change, but rather the client who uses them to make change, the therapist may operate from any theory or use any set of procedures. The only prerequisite is that the therapist's interactions and suggestions must be empathically compatible and join with the client's self-healing process.

This perspective is derived from our roots in client-centered theory, from the emphasis in brief strategic approaches on client resourcefulness and creativity (Hoyt, 1994; Rosenbaum, 1990), and from research considerations. It is compatible with others who emphasize the client as the major locus of change (Duncan, Solovey, & Rusk, 1992; Gold, 1994). We believe that the research supports the idea that therapy is ultimately clients' helping themselves. Our view contrasts to the more typical "medicallike" view (Orlinsky, 1989), in which it is the therapist and the therapist's interventions that are the "potent" and primary agents of change.

The Medicallike Perspective

In the medicallike view the therapist is analogous to a doctor: an expert who diagnoses and then treats. Treatments consist of strategies, techniques, or "interventions" that "operate on" whatever is dysfunctional in the client to remedy it. Stiles and Shapiro (1989) have referred to this as the "drug metaphor." For instance, challenging dysfunctional cognitions is portrayed as modifying schemas and transference interpretations as strengthening egos.

Medicallike thinking includes the assumption that different client problems require different "treatments" (Marten & Barlow, 1993; Paul, 1967). The medicallike view has a mechanistic flavor in that the power of therapy is seen as residing in the therapist's interventions that presumably bring about changes *in* clients, analogous to how medications or back exercises precipitate change in medicine. It, therefore, puts the emphasis on therapist-chosen technique over client creativity, and it tends to minimize the relationship *as* relationship. The relationship between therapist and patient is either (a) a "nonspecific" factor that makes clients more willing to comply with the therapist's treatment prescriptions or (b) an "intervention" to be manipulated by the therapist. Empathy, therefore, becomes a nonspecific relationship-building background characteristic or a technique to be differentially applied. The flavor of empathy as a genuine form of human meeting and of deeply "knowing" another person is lost.

The medicallike model of the therapist as expert interventionist who assesses client problems and then prescribes differential treatments influences theorists from many different orientations. It is highly compatible with managed care and represents how some in the American Psychological Association currently think about therapy (e.g., Task Force on Promotion and Dissemination of Psychological Procedures, Division of Clinical Psychology of the American Psychological Association, 1995). It also leads to an emphasis on manualization of therapy. However, we do not believe it is an accurate portrayal of the true nature of therapy.

The Active-Client Perspective

We believe that all power to effect change comes from the client. Interventions by therapists are impotent and useless until active clients invest their own creative energies in them to make them work. Interventions are really tools that are handed to clients by therapists, but it is clients who use them to fashion their own idiosyncratic solutions (e.g., Gold, 1994). Empathy is fundamental to the enterprise, in that what is important is less what technique is chosen and more how it is sensitively and dialogically offered to the client. Interventions do not operate *on* clients to effect change, but rather are used *by* clients for exploring, thinking, and creating. There is no necessary one-to-one relationship between an intervention and the kinds of outcomes clients may generate. The client is the important "common factor" in therapy (Bohart & Rosenbaum, 1995; Bohart & Tallman, 1996; Duncan & Moynihan, 1994; Gold, 1994). The role of the therapist is more like that of a research assistant (O'Hara, 1986). The client is the "lead investigator."

Our point of view is derived from consideration of research findings that do not make sense from the medicallike view (Bohart & Tallman, 1996). First, the idea of "differential treatment" for different client problems has not, with some exceptions, generally been supported (Bergin & Garfield, 1994; Greenberg, Elliott, & Lietaer, 1994; Stubbs & Bozarth, 1994). Second, there is evidence that the expertise of the therapist, as defined by professional training and advanced degree, either does not make one a better therapist (Christensen & Jacobson, 1994; Jacobson, 1995; Strupp & Hadley, 1979; Svartberg & Stiles, 1991), or at best has only a modest effect (Stein & Lambert, 1995). Third, self-help resources, such as books, groups, journaling, and computer-provided therapy, appear to work as well as professionally provided therapy (Christensen & Jacobson, 1994; Goodman & Jacobs, 1995; Segal & Murray, 1994).

These findings all suggest that the power for change comes largely from the client. To quote Bergin and Garfield (1994):

> it is the client more than the therapist who implements the change process. . . . Rather than argue over whether or not therapy works, we

could address ourselves to the question of whether or not the client works. . . . As therapists have depended more upon the client's resources, more change seems to occur. (pp. 825–826)

We assume that it is clients who provide all the impetus of change; who take inert techniques and invest life in them; who creatively modify techniques to find personally relevant answers in ways sometimes undreamed of by their therapists; who, for most problems, are able to use practically *any* learning environment provided by their therapists, be it psychodynamic, cognitive, behavioral, or experiential, as long as it is not fundamentally intrusive and counter-therapeutic; who, even when learning highly specific techniques from their therapists, are the ones to creatively use them to solve their individual problems in their everyday life spaces; and who, if given half a chance, can frequently generate their own appropriate goals and their own learning strategies. *If* we are right, *then* it makes sense that different procedures are not necessarily needed for different problems, 400 different therapies can all work, and many clients can use self-help procedures as effectively as professionally provided therapy.

What Therapists Provide

The experiences provided by therapy are resources for clients to use in their own active thinking–exploring–experiencing and creating process. Therapists most fundamentally are prosthetic devices to aid client thinking and exploring and to help them be able to think more intelligently about their own problems (Snyder, 1994; Zimring, 1990). The most basic resource provided is a time and a place for clients to do this. The single most important common factor in successful therapy is the provision of a good "working space." Empathy forms the basis for this "work space" and is the basic experience that facilitates clients' thinking more intelligently (Snyder, 1994).

Clients often come into therapy feeling overwhelmed and threatened. Such a state narrows thinking, creates dichotomous thinking, and interferes with creative problem solving. The provision of an empathic interaction gives clients an opportunity to take a deep breath, step back from their problems, and gain perspective. Therapists also provide "tools" for the work space by offering techniques and their own responses. Techniques provide structured opportunities for exploration. Clients may be able to use many different techniques (or therapeutic approaches) to solve a given problem. For other problems, certain exercises or procedures may be particularly useful (e.g., sex therapy). Different clients will be drawn to different approaches as their preferred style for working things through, just as some individuals prefer jogging to swimming as a form of exercise.

The active client perspective differs from the medicallike view in that the therapist holds a genuine belief that the client is an expert—on his or her own experience. In addition, the therapist believes that the relationship is, at its core, collegial, dialogic, and democratic. Techniques are empathically offered to clients as possibilities for them to use, not as prescriptions. It is clients who are ultimately the experts on whether a technique will work for them and on how it will work, and an empathic interaction creates a climate where clients will ultimately begin to feel they have this power.

Therapists practicing under the medicallike rubric also believe that client collaboration is essential. However, for them collaboration is seen as client *compliance*. Clients must be willing and able to implement the procedures prescribed by the therapist for therapy to work, just as medical patients must be willing to take the medication or do the back exercises.

In contrast, our view emphasizes the power of the client—the client's enormous capacity for resilience and self righting (Masten, Best, & Garmazy, 1990)—when it is given a context in which to operate. An empathic climate is the best "place" for clients' resiliency to operate.

Change is Cognitive–Experiential

Learning and discovery that leads to change is experiential and not just intellectual. Experiencing is a different way of knowing than knowing through conceptual analysis or through thinking about (Bohart, 1993). Experiencing is basically perceptual but can include thought, emotion, and the inner referents associated with action. Perception is different than conceptual knowing in that it is immediate and recognitional. In everyday life people primarily operate by *recognizing* meanings, not by conceptually analyzing what is going on.

Perceptual–experiential recognition of patterns is represented internally by a "sense" or a "feeling." An outfielder chasing a fly ball has a "feel" of where to run. Even learning how to do mathematical proofs is a matter of getting a "feel for" the process. Gendlin (1964) has called this internal kind of feeling a "felt sense." Such a feeling is not an emotion but a bodily based perception of meaning (Bohart, 1993).

In therapy, conceptual knowing without recognitional knowing is unlikely to lead to change. Change occurs when one attains experiential recognition of meanings. One may conceptually analyze one's experience and conclude that one's self-esteem problems are based on how one was treated as a child. However, this will have far less impact than vividly recalling incidents where one was criticized by one's parents—where one now directly recognizes the connection between that criticism and feeling inadequate. True insight is perceptual and recognitional (Bohart & Associates, 1996; Schooler, Fallshore, & Fiore, 1995) and only secondarily conceptual. Therapists, therefore, never impart "truths" to clients. Rather they provide opportunities for, or *point* clients in the direction of, experience that allows insight and perceptual recognition of such meanings. It is always clients' own recognition and discovery of new meanings that leads to change. As such, all therapy is ultimately experiential self-discovery (Bohart, 1993; Bohart & Wugalter, 1991; Todd & Bohart, 1994) of new meanings or behaviors. Even two different clients practicing "the same" assertion skills will have their own unique experiences as they practice and will, therefore, end up with different perspectives on what assertion means to them.

Thinking and conceptualization function in two ways in therapy. First, thinking generates hypotheses that guide experiential exploration until new experiential insights occur. In cognitive therapy a client acquires the hypothesis that his or her negative self-image is not accurate. This hypothesis guides his or her attention to his or her own experience in such a way that he or she begins to directly recognize and notice that he or she can be competent. Second, thinking and conceptualization helps to consolidate insights and to guide further exploration and action. Through experience a person who is having panic attacks can directly recognize how he or she is reacting to and thinking about bodily sensations in a way that creates further panic. Understanding how he or she is creating his or her own panic can then help him or her deal with incipient feelings of panic the next time they occur.

The process of thinking, experiencing, and exploring provides clients with the opportunity to perceptually discover new meaning relationships in their life spaces and, thus, to institute new changes. They search not only in therapy but also outside of therapy and coordinate what they learn in therapy with what they discover by way of their own personal creative efforts in their everyday life. Clients can make this back-and-forth process of thinking, experiencing, and exploring happen in a wide variety of settings using a wide variety of "spaces" and techniques offered by therapists. Therapists' theoretical frameworks are "scaffoldings" that clients use for exploring their experience.

This back-and-forth thinking–experiencing–exploring process is the core process by which clients "self-right" even when the therapist is teaching skills. Skills training is not the mechanistic implantation of "habits." Rather, practice provides experiences leading to new recognitions and increasingly deepened knowledge of a skill domain. Clients who apply assertion skills in a rote, mechanistic fashion will not fare well. Learning that is rote and algorhythmic does not generalize well to new situations (Nickerson, 1994), nor do solutions that are told to clients (Dominowski & Dallob, 1995). Ideas will help clients change only when they see the "sense" in them for themselves.

Creative problem solving is enhanced when clients feel free to engage in "play" with new ideas. This is facilitated by an empathic atmosphere. An empathic atmosphere also allows clients to suspend old ways of viewing things. A core process in therapy is to encourage clients to suspend preconceptions as much as possible and to adopt a "phenomenological attitude"

(Todd & Bohart, 1994). This is because ordinary ways of viewing things often get in the way of gaining a new perspective (Isaak & Just, 1995), and one of the major processes involved in helping individuals find creative solutions is to help them remove the blocks from their old ways of thinking (Schooler et al., 1995).

In summary, a good therapeutic context is an open nonjudgmental empathic "space" in which clients feel safe. This helps clients reduce stress and cognitive overload. This facilitates experiential exploration, higher-level thinking, reduction of dichotomous thinking, and creative problem solving. In such a context, clients mobilize their own agentic potential to solve their own problems. Therapists help by providing support, interactive experience, and tools or structured opportunities for exploration and discovery. The client is the most important common factor in psychotherapy, and therapists who are skilled at empathically joining with client potential will be most helpful.

EMPATHY

The therapeutic relationship is, in contrast to medicine, an intensely human enterprise in which meanings are continuously sharpened, evolved, and cocreated through ongoing dialogue. No matter how manual-driven, the "art" of therapy lies in the ability of the therapists to dialogue—to continually hear how that other agent involved in the interaction, the client, is experiencing the therapist and the therapist's interventions, and to respond accordingly. Therapists who mechanistically apply manuals will not fare well, and good therapists are flexible, continuously improvising within their manual- or theory-driven framework and departing from the manual or theory when the client and their empathic connection with the client dictates. This is because therapy is more so a matter of two humans interacting, with techniques being part of the interaction, than it is *primarily* a technique-driven enterprise. Differences among therapists and relationship variance account for considerably more of therapeutic outcome than do technique factors (Lambert, 1989, 1992).

Empathy is therefore the "glue" that holds the collaborative relationship between therapist and client together and facilitates communication. We will first define empathy and explore its nature. Next we will discuss how the therapist attains empathic understanding. Then we will examine the function of empathy.

Definition and Nature of Empathy

Empathy is first and foremost an orientation toward trying to understand the other person's communications and actions in terms of his or her frame of reference. This is different than knowing from an external perspective, where another person's behavior is understood in terms of the observer's presumed "objective" perspective. For therapists, this "objective" perspective usually consists of the therapist's personal opinions about what is normative and appropriate, the therapist's utilization of professionally sanctioned systems for evaluating others (i.e., DSM–IV) and the therapist's preferred theoretical orientation. Deciding that someone is thinking irrationally or is splitting is based on observing from an external perspective. Trying to understand why an individual has engaged in self-mutilation in terms of his or her own experience is empathic. This distinction is similar to one made between "connected" (empathic) and "separate" (external) knowing by Belenky, Clinchy, Goldberger, and Tarule (1986).

Empathy is a fundamental part of ordinary interpersonal interaction and conversation and can be used for better or for worse (see Shlien, Chapter 3, this volume). One must be able to empathize to accurately perceive "where other people are coming from"—what they appear to be thinking, feeling, intending, and so on. Empathy involves basic developmental processes of learning to read "other minds" (Baron-Cohen, 1995). Empathy also involves the process of understanding what other people mean when they say something. That involves establishing a "common ground" (Clark & Brennan, 1991) and engaging in a complex and ongoing process of conversational repair when there are failures in understanding (Schegloff, 1991).

During ordinary interactions, people do not necessarily focus on being empathic. Understanding the other is often a secondary intention in the service of other, more primary intentions. People try to navigate their social worlds, and it can help to have a sense of where other people are coming from. However, it is only on occasion that their primary focus is on trying to understand another person. Furthermore, their understanding may often consist only of a quick superficial reading of the other's intentions, emotions, and motivational state. It is rare that people take the time to deeply grasp and understand the experience of another.

For purposes of doing psychotherapy, we therefore define empathy as having a *primary intention* to try to understand the client in terms of the client's frame of reference. The intention to understand is even more important than whether or not the therapist actually does understand. This intention guides the therapist to: (a) persistently and carefully try to catch client meanings; (b) take seriously what clients say, and to not just dismiss client responses as rationalizations, defensive maneuvers, or products of dysfunctional thinking (though they might also contain elements of these); (c) continually check understanding of how the client is experiencing; (d) struggle to understand when a technique is not working for a client or when the therapist's communications seem not to click; (e) try to attain a deep and complex grasp of the client's experience, more so than just a superficial conceptual understanding of what they are saying; (f) try to get a real, operational "feel for" what it is like to be the client; and (g) continually check to see how the client is perceiving and understanding what the therapist communicates.

If the therapist holds this intention, it will get communicated over time. There will be no one kind of response or sequence of responses that would be labeled as *empathic*. Clients might experience interpretations, questions, advice, suggestions of a technique, silences, or even occasional confrontations as empathic. Understanding, and the intention to understand, will be conveyed through the *pattern* expressed during an interaction: perhaps remaining silent at this time, interpreting at that time, suggesting something at another time, and seeking clarification at still another time. The client's perception of the therapist's empathy during a given sequence is, therefore, an invariant (Gibson, 1979) that is extracted from the pattern of interaction. Furthermore, empathy is not equivalent to a technique; it is not just a paraphrase, a basic level or advanced level empathic reflection, or compassion. Rather, it is a fundamental attitude (Bozarth, Chapter 4, this volume).

Empathy, therefore, cannot be equated with a set of "therapist operations or behaviors." There are virtually an infinite number of possible combinations and sequences of therapist behaviors that could convey empathy. Research by Bachelor (1988) has lent support to this contention. She found that clients did not equate the experience of being understood with any particular therapist responses or behaviors. Similarly, Elliott et al. (1982) found that client perceptions of feeling understood correlated more highly with sequences of therapist responses than with individual responses.

Achievement of Empathy

Empathy is achieved through careful listening and attending, through "hearing" and "seeing" what the other person has to say and what he or she seems to be experiencing, through careful listening to oneself and to what "comes up" in oneself in response to the other person, and through continual checking to make sure one is on the right track.

Most definitions of empathic understanding stress the idea of "putting oneself in the other's shoes." However this idea is only one possible metaphor for empathy. People often achieve a complex experiential understanding of another's perspective by carefully listening to what they have to say without ever trying to put themselves in the other's shoes. Most of us have had conversations where we felt a deep sense of resonance with another person. If we reflect on such conversations, we will note that we were *not* trying to put ourselves in their shoes. In fact, we weren't focusing on their state of mind at all. What we were focusing on was the *topic* about which we were dialoging. We detected their perspective from noting how they responded to the topic and to our responses to the topic. Our understanding came from a deep, total involvement and sharing in the conversation.

Careful experiential listening is, therefore, more basic than any conceptual activity of putting oneself into the other's shoes. A better metaphor is reading. If one reads with an open, receptive mindset, trying to experience and absorb what one is reading, rather than with a critical, analytic mindset, one can at least at times pick up what the author has to say without the intellectual effort of putting oneself in the shoes of the author. In fact, if one "thinks too much," one may actually block one's ability to directly read and absorb what the author is saying. As long as we are experiencing a "felt sense" (Gendlin, 1964) of understanding, we continue to read smoothly. This felt sense arises from a continual, rapid, "automatic" checking process where what we thought we understood in one moment is compared to what comes next. If it matches, we have a sense that we are on the right track, and we continue to read smoothly. We deliberately "think" and try to project ourselves into the author's frame of reference only when (a) we suddenly realize that we have misunderstood the author or (b) we find something confusing and unclear.

Empathic listening is similar. If we listen openly and carefully, with an orientation toward grasping how the other is experiencing the world, we can often directly grasp their frame of reference without any intellectual, inferential activity. This is because people can "directly" perceive and recognize meanings in another's communications and behaviors without deliberate conscious activity. In this regard, Neisser (1988) has given an example of how animals can "read" each other's behavior and "understand" what each is up to:

> As Darwin put it, "When two young dogs in play are growling and biting each other's faces and legs, it is obvious that they understand each other's gestures and manners" (1904, p. 60). . . . Darwin's use of the term "understand" in this context should not be misunderstood. He does not claim (or at least I do not claim) that puppies have an *intellectual* understanding of each other's behavior; their interactions do not necessarily involve a conceptual self or a conceptual other. What is going on between them is sometimes called "non-verbal communication," but even that term can be misleading; it tends to suggest that each participant is somehow telling the other about his/her own mental states. If that were true, the achievement of intersubjectivity would depend on the accuracy with which we attribute thoughts and feelings to other people. While we do sometimes attempt such attributions in adult life, they can hardly be the basis of the smooth and immediate interpersonal coordination I am considering here. (p. 44)

In a similar manner, Trevarthen (1993) has referred to the "universal immediacy of human interpersonal understanding" (p. 159). Trevarthen notes that "the core of every human consciousness appears to be an immediate, unrational, unverbalized, conceptless, totally atheoretical potential for rapport of the self with another's mind" (p. 121). He also notes that "it is simply untrue that human mental states are unobservable, to humans. We can detect the mind states of other people instantly from their expressions" (p. 122).

Such immediate reading, of course, by no means happens all the time. First, it is more likely when we share a common experiential–cultural background. Second, particularly in therapy, people are often trying to articulate what has never previously been articulated. Psychodynamic therapists call this the unconscious; experiential therapists refer to the implicit, tacit, or experiential dimension. No matter how it is conceptualized, it may be difficult for the therapist to "read off" what the client's frame of reference is because the client is unclear about it. It is at this point that the therapist's empathic attempts may be particularly useful, as therapist and client together "co-create" an articulation of implicit or unconscious experience.

Adopting the intention to empathically understand as a listening vantage point does not mean one has to give up one's own perspective. But it does mean that one must listen with "dual attention"—both to one's own internal reactions and to the other. What comes up in the listener in response to the other can be used as a basis for empathic responding. In a good dialogue, what one thinks to say to the other is often "in tune" with what the other has said. Bohart and Rosenbaum (1995) have called this "empathic resonance." However, although others have used the term *resonance* to mean "experiencing a similar feeling to the client," Bohart and Rosenbaum mean something more akin to dictionary definitions of resonance, which stress "vibrating in harmony with" and "amplifying on" something. The therapist's own reactions can be responses that are in harmony with, but not identical to, the client's experiential state, in the sense that the therapist's reactions are aligned with or parallel to the track of meaning the client is following. Furthermore, they can empathically amplify on what the client has said. The therapist's reactions and responses can build on, follow up on, or carry forward implications in the client's frame of reference. These responses need not be simple paraphrases or low-level summaries of what the client has said. Rather, these responses can reflect the listener's own perspective, as long as they include and coordinate with the other's vantage point. Such responses can lead to a mutually empathic dialogue and to each person sharpening his or her understanding of the other and the development of a shared structure of mutual understanding.

In this sense empathy ultimately is a two-way street. Bohart and Rosenbaum (1995) have suggested that it is more like a "dance," and Trevarthen (1993) has observed that, what we would call an empathic conversation, is like

> a musical duet, in which two performers . . . seek harmony and counterpoint on one beat to create together a melody that becomes a coherent

and satisfying narrative of feelings in a time structure that they share completely. In a good performance by two or more musicians each partakes of, or identifies with, the expression of the whole piece, the ensemble. Each gains musical understanding or satisfaction from the actions of the other(s), as well as separately from within themselves. (p. 139)

Johnson (1993) has noted the same resonant, dancelike reciprocity in the fundamentally empathic nature of a shared sexual experience:

I must experience your touching of me as both expressing your desire and as directed toward me and my desire. I must take up and carry forward your desire in my active response to you. In happy cases the result is a reciprocal play between partners, a kind of erotic dialectic in which we share in each other's experience. (p. 201)

Empathy is, therefore, ultimately a shared achievement.

Our view that empathy is empathic listening implies that the most important thing the therapist must do is to continually check to make sure that he or she is accurately experiencing and understanding the client. Checking means that one will be on the alert for signs that one has missed something. It is particularly important that therapists continually check because the ordinary processes of conversational repair may fail to operate in therapy. Because of the power differential between therapist and client, clients may defer to therapists and keep their feelings of having been misunderstood to themselves (Rennie, 1990). Therefore, therapists need to be sensitive to clients' nonverbal signals of having felt misunderstood. They also need to be able to prove to clients that they can tolerate correction—that they value understanding over "being correct."

Shared Attention and Resonant Responding

Empathic listening involves attempting to maintain a *shared focus of attention* with the client. We have suggested that the listener focus his or her attention not on the other person's mental perspective but on the *topic* to which the client is attending (see also Mahrer, chapter 9, this volume). Supporting this, research has found that the most important component in an empathic therapist communication is that it respond to the centrality in the client's message (Elliott et al., 1982; Sachse, 1990). The therapist needs to respond in terms of what *concerns* the client (i.e., what he or she is explicitly focusing attention on) as well as all the connected implicit aspects.

Empathic failures occur when one person arbitrarily or unilaterally shifts the shared focus of attention. Consider a 14-year-old girl who comes to therapy and tells you about an incident with her mother. She had gone home from school and had told her mother, "I got in a fight with my teacher today. I thought I had the right answer, but my teacher wouldn't listen to me. So I got mad. And then she sent me to the principal." The mother had said in response, "You know, you should never get angry at your elders. You must respect them." The 14-year-old girl reports that she felt misunderstood by her mother. Why? Because the mother has arbitrarily shifted the focus of attention from the daughter's feeling that she was unfairly treated to the mother's focus on proper behavior towards elders.

As the client relates this story to you, her focus of attention is on her distress at her mother's not understanding her feelings about her teacher. If *we* say to the client, "You were angry with your teacher because she reminds you of your mother," we, too, have shifted the focus of attention (to a causal explanation). The client will most likely not feel understood. However, if we say, "I wonder if you felt just as unlistened to by your mother as you did by your teacher," then our response maintains a shared focus of attention (on the feeling of not being listened to) and the client will be more likely to experience it as empathic.

Both the poor response and the good response above are interpretative. Yet one maintains a shared focus of attention and one does not. Therapists will provide the experience of feeling understood to the extent that they are able to maintain with clients a shared focus of attention, even if offering an alternative perspective.

Communicative "completions" (Wilkes-Gibbs & Clark, 1992) are an important part of empathy and occur as a result of the therapist and client maintaining a shared focus of attention. A completion is where a person is struggling to explain what he or she is saying, and the other person "completes" it. Thus, a person might say, "When she left me, it felt like a. . . a. . ." And the other person might say, "A punch in the stomach?" And the first person might say, "Yes!" Such interactions are coconstructive in that the referent being talked about ("feeling like a punch in the stomach") is a joint product of both participants. Completions are akin to good empathic responses by client-centered therapists or effective insight-providing statements by psychodynamic therapists; they serve to help clients articulate what has previously been unarticulated. They also fit in with the idea that therapy is ultimately a process of cocreating new meaning (Mahoney, 1991).

In summary, therapists can respond "in resonance" with clients if they maintain and respond from a shared focus of attention. If the therapist responds in such a fashion, then the client will be more likely to feel understood, no matter what theoretical perspective the therapist comes from, and no matter what therapeutic practices the therapist uses.

How Empathy Helps Provide a Good Problem-Solving Context

The therapeutic atmosphere must foster *cooperation* and *open communication.* In an interaction, attempts to empathically grasp "where the other person is coming from" help one individual coordinate his or her frame of reference with that of the other so that there can be good communication across frames of reference. In a cooperative relationship, each party tries to see the other's point of view, even if they ultimately come to disagree with it. I will feel more willing to try to hear what you have to say if you have tried to hear what I have to say. Trying to see the other's point of view is respectful and sends the message that the other person is worth listening to. It implies that he or she has some intelligence and wisdom and is not a complete "dodo."

In addition, to the degree that I accurately hear you, I can respond in a fashion that encourages us to compare and contrast our ideas in a productive fashion, rather than in a fashion that encourages us to rigidly hold to and defend our perspectives. My ideas can be expressed in a way that encourages you to productively hear them and use them. Similarly, you will then be better able to come back with communications more attuned to what I am trying to get at. Furthermore, even if we disagree, if we feel we are on "the same side," we will be more likely to treat disagreements as possible sources of productive convergence and insight.

In addition, therapists who strive to hear where their clients are coming from will be better able to offer feedback and suggestions that are sensitively attuned to what the client wants and needs. Even therapists who go in with a "program" (such as behaviorists or cognitive therapists) must be able to sensitively hear from clients how they are using what the therapist is offering if they are to fine-tune, adjust, and facilitate the process. Supporting this contention, some unpublished research we have conducted on films of famous therapists such as Hans Strupp, Carl Rogers, Albert Ellis, Donald Meichenbaum, and Fritz Perls found that all were rated by undergraduates as at least somewhat empathic, and a study by Raskin (1974) also found that six famous therapists of different orientations were all rated as at least "somewhat" empathic by professional therapists.

If a therapist offers a technique that makes a client feel misperceived, the odds go up greatly of the technique not being helpful. A shared context of understanding allows the therapist to sensitively time the suggestion of a technique and the client to perceive how to use it and how it might be relevant to what the client is focusing on. In essence, the therapist is handing the client the right tool at the right time as the client engages in his or her active search. Empathy also helps create a safe environment where clients feel free to "open up." Clients who are worried about being judged from an "outside" perspective will become "performance-oriented" (Tallman, 1996). They will focus more on how they are presenting themselves to the therapist than on exploring the components of their problem. In contrast, a client who feels that the therapist is trying to accurately hear and perceive them will feel safe to go further, to say more, to confront more, and to take more chances. The client will feel that she or he is in "good hands" (if you don't feel accurately perceived by another person, it is hard to trust what they have to say, even if they are an "expert"—this holds true for doctors, lawyers, parents, and others besides therapists).

In essence, empathy is the core component in the "art" of therapy—the art of sensitively responding to the client in a facilitative manner, no matter from which point of view the therapist is coming. In contrast to medicine, where a treatment can be "applied" to a disorder, therapy is a complex interactive *process* of continual trying out, getting feedback, and retuning. Rather than being primarily a *mechanical and technical* process, it is most basically an *intelligent* process involving continual listening, thinking, fine-tuning, and dialoging. Even if one is following a manualized approach to therapy, there is still an "art" in how one applies the manual in a given moment (Beutler, 1995), and we believe that empathy underlies that art.

How Empathy Facilitates Exploring, Experiencing, and Thinking

For some clients therapy is primarily a process of their having a place to "tell their story" (Harvey, Orbuch, Chwalisz, & Garwood, 1991; Pennebaker, 1995). Careful empathic listening and responding can help clients search experience, clarify beliefs and perceptions, make needed differentiations in meaning, discover new perspectives, develop new conceptual frameworks, and try out new behaviors. Three of the major ways therapists can join the client in this process are through empathic reflections, empathic interpretations, and empathic self-disclosures.

Empathic reflections could almost be said to be a form of "joining" the client's process of thinking and exploring out loud. Good empathic reflections fit in so well with the client's train of thought that when the client responds to the therapist it is almost as if the client is responding to himself or herself. When such a sequence gets started, clients will often look like they are talking more to themselves than to the therapist. One may even notice clients staring off as if they are thinking and reflecting, rather than focusing attention on the therapist. Therapists' empathic reflections can, therefore, help the client make differentiations in experience. They can also help the client pay attention to potentially relevant information, such as neglected feelings, emotions, and perceptions and to bring that into the thinking–exploring–experiencing process.

Clients can also use empathic understanding responses by therapists to question and disrupt their own self-critical activities and to challenge dysfunctional thoughts (Safran & Segal, 1990). They may model the therapist and begin to listen to themselves in more empathic, useful, problem-solving ways, rather than in judgmental, self-critical ways (Barrett-Lennard, Chapter 5, this volume; Bohart, 1991).

Empathic interpretations, sensitively offered at the right moment, can provide a piece of information that helps clients reorganize their perspective in new, more productive directions. Empathic self-disclosures can similarly provide information to clients. In addition, empathic self-disclosures can have a reassuring effect, increasing the client's feeling that "I'm not alone" and "I'm not all that weird or different." Bachelor (1988) found that clients identified therapist self-disclosure as a major form of empathy.

Many clients want more than just to tell their story. They want more active strategies. Here, too, therapist empathy is crucial. The more fine-tuned the therapist's response is to "where the client is at in the moment" in terms of his or her struggles to understand and master the problems, the more facilitative of thinking, experiencing, and exploring the therapist's response will be. For instance, a "deeply empathic" suggestion of a technique will help the client make important distinctions in experience, just at the point where the client is struggling to make such distinctions.

Finally, empathy is itself something the client experiences. Over time the client will recognize, through the therapist's body language and sequence of responses, that the therapist is really interested in understanding the client's perspective. The client will also recognize and experience the implicit respect for the client implied in these efforts. An empathic attitude intrinsically recognizes the client as an "equal" in some sense—as an active problem solver. As Jenkins (Chapter 15, this volume) has pointed out, this will help clients reinstitute their own dialectical thinking process. In addition, the experience of the therapist's efforts to share the client's attentional focus, and to not "rape" the client by forcing another attentional focus on them (especially a judgmental one), helps the client feel safe to explore painful material. The client may also have the corrective experience of having another person listen very carefully, something many people have only infrequently in everyday life. Furthermore, the therapist's ongoing ability to develop a shared frame of reference with the client communicates to the client that he or she is not so crazy or out of touch, that his or her experience is understandable by another human being.

In summary, therapist empathy provides a facilitative context for the process we believe to be important in therapy: client thinking, exploring, experiencing, and problem solving. It not only facilitates clients' own self-healing processes but also is an important basis for therapeutic interaction from all perspectives.

CASE

Art was a graduate student in psychology in 1968 when he entered therapy with Dr. Bonham because he was experiencing a recurrence of generalized anxiety. The original "attack" occurred in 1966 when Art was a college senior.

Art had always struggled with a conflict between his desire to live a creative life and his self-perception that he was shy and afraid to take chances. When he entered college, his ultimate dream was to go to Paris and become a writer. Yet he chose to double major in mathematics and psychology.

Art's plan had been to try writing on graduation. However, as he approached graduation, he felt totally inadequate to "chucking it all" and going off to Paris. Instead, he envisioned himself getting a job as a computer programmer and living a lonely life in a little apartment. It had been at this point that, reading a novel by Henry Miller (who had been in Paris during the 1930s), he began to experience pervasive anxiety.

Art originally had gone to see Dr. Root once a week in psychoanalytically oriented psychotherapy. Dr. Root was friendly before sessions started, but once they had started, the "blank screen" came down. The atmosphere became cool and very intellectual. On the one hand, Dr. Root provided a relatively open "working space" in which Art could explore. On the other hand, Dr. Root's style was not empathic. He listened in a distanced, analytic way, responding to Art's communications by intellectually looking for patterns of meaning rather than by trying to grasp Art's experience. If Art talked about his shyness in asking a girl out, the focus would be on trying to intellectually analyze what this must mean. By focusing on what the behavior must mean from an external perspective. Dr. Root missed what Art was focusing *his* attention on: how frustrated and critical he felt of himself for not being more free, creative, and outgoing.

Art took his cue from the therapist and intellectually tried to figure out what was wrong with him. He speculated that his problems were due to his relationship with his mother. Art achieved a picture of how his relationship with his mother might have influenced his behavior, but this picture was intellectually deduced rather than being based on any actual experienced recognition of patterns in his history. Art also concluded that his interest in writing was a compensatory defense for being unable to take chances in real life. However, these conceptual speculations did not lead to any actual changes in Art's behavior or experience.

Nevertheless, therapy was somewhat helpful. Having someone listen in a nonjudgmental way let him calm down sufficiently so that he was able to think through an important decision. Instead of seeing his choice as "either I go to Paris and become a writer or I get a job as a computer programmer," a completely new direction dawned on him. He decided to go to graduate school in psychology. He thought that being a psychologist would be a profession spiritually close to being a writer. Then he could take his time deciding if he wanted to pursue writing. He applied and was accepted into a doctoral program in personality psychology. That fall he started the program.

Despite nagging residual anxiety, the level of Art's anxiety gradually declined, and after a year in graduate school, Art decided to terminate therapy. Six months later, however, he attended a party of graduate students. During 1968 virtually everyone Art knew was experimenting with psychedelic drugs. However, Art had resisted trying them. At this party he was the only person who was not on either marijuana or LSD. This reawakened his perception of himself as afraid to fully live and take risks, and he began to experience anxiety once again. It was at this point that he sought out therapy with Dr. Bonham.

Dr. Bonham was also psychodynamic, and the therapy atmosphere was superficially similar to the one Art had had with Dr. Root. However, Art experienced Dr. Bonham as much more actively empathic. Dr. Bonham carefully listened and tried to hear Art in terms of Art's frame of reference. For instance, Dr. Bonham zeroed in quickly on Art's self-criticism: "You really get frustrated with yourself when you're not as spontaneous as you think you should be, don't you?" This recognition of what Art was focusing on helped Art begin to realize that part of his problem was how critical he was of himself *for* being shy. Over time, this would lead him to recognize that his self-criticism for being shy created so much anxiety that he would then act shyly.

Dr. Bonham's responses seemed to usually take into account Art's focus of attention and frame of reference. Art experienced Dr. Bonham as empathic, even though Art could not for the most part identify particular empathic things that Dr. Bonham said or did. In general, Dr. Bonham's empathic way of responding provided a good "work space" in which Art creatively explored, experienced, and thought. Art "followed his own nose" in exploring his childhood. He recognized, felt, and experienced that his chronic asthma as a child had had more impact on him than had his relationship to his parents. Chronic asthma had led him to develop a negative self-perception as weak and fragile. Recognizing this led Art to feel more self-accepting.

There were two incidents in therapy that stood out. The first incident occurred early. Art said that he was feeling suicidal. After a brief discussion, Dr. Bonham responded in a concerned but inquiring tone of voice, "Are you serious? Because if you are, I'd have to have you hospitalized." Although the response may seem confrontive, Art experienced it as empathic because Art in fact was not seriously suicidal. Rather, he was feeling very weak and fragile about himself—*worried* that he could be suicidal. Dr. Bonham had correctly perceived that Art's attentional focus was on his *worry*. In thinking through his response to Dr. Bonham's empathic question–confrontation, Art realizing that he really wasn't suicidal. Art then carried this further by examining how he tended to catastrophize about himself, to focus on some of his negative feelings to the exclusion of more positive, strong feelings, and to thus magnify the negative. Art used Dr. Bonham's response to creatively explore his tendency to think negatively about himself.

The second incident was one in which Dr. Bonham self-disclosed that he, too, wanted to be a writer. He and Art spent several minutes discussing the excitement of writing and their mutual aspirations. Dr. Bonham went on to disclose his own conflicts over being a psychologist while wanting to be a writer. Finally, Dr. Bonham mentioned that he had provisionally resolved it by deciding to do both at the same time. He did not offer this as advice to Art, simply as information.

Art experienced this self-disclosure as highly empathic. First, Dr. Bonham's interest in Art's writing had the effect of validating Art's interest in writing (and providing what Kohut would have called a "twinship" experience). Prior to this, Art had been thinking, along with his prior therapist's help, that his interest in writing was probably a compensation of some sort for his feelings of being shy and not a risk taker. Dr. Bonham's response helped Art to feel that his interest in writing was not merely a defense but had some internal integrity.

Dr. Bonham's response helped Art further think through how he was making himself anxious. He began to consider the possibility that, in general, there was some sensible purpose to his behavior, some coherence, and that his choices were not necessarily based on something being wrong with him. Over the next several sessions, Art extended this into other areas. He began to recognize that his own behavior made sense to him. For instance, he realized that his not taking drugs at the party was because *he* did not want to alter his consciousness in those ways. He also began to realize that *he* did not actually want to go to Paris. He discovered that he had a desire to be in a profession where he could make a "substantive" contribution, such as psychology. He thought that Dr. Bonham's solution therefore made sense to him—to pursue a professional career and write on the side. He began to realize that this choice actually fit him better than a choice to abandon it all and go to Paris.

Over a period of 5 months, Art was gradually able to change his negative self-perceptions and to feel more confident. The anxiety attack abated, and after another few months, Art terminated therapy.

This case illustrates many of the points discussed previously. The client actively used therapist responses to work through problems. Empathy was generally not conveyed by particular classes of therapist responses but embedded in context-dependent sequences. If the therapist's response was in empathic resonance to where the client was focusing his attention, even a confrontation could be experienced as empathic. Finally, the client used empathic responses to validate his basic "okayness," to reduce distress, and to sharpen his self-exploration and self-understanding.

The client, of course, was the first author. As with all case presentations, this one is slightly fictionalized to protect the privacy of the parties involved (namely, him. P.S. If you want some of his poetry, just write).

REFERENCES

Bachelor, A. (1988). How clients perceive therapist empathy: A content analysis of "received" empathy. *Psychotherapy, 26*, 372–379.

Baron-Cohen, S. (1995). *Mindblindness: An essay on autism and theory of mind.* Cambridge, MA: Massachusetts Institute of Technology Press.

Belenky, M. F., Clinchy, B. M., Goldberger, N. R., & Tarule, J. M. (1986). *Women's ways of knowing: The development of self, voice, and mind.* New York: Basic Books.

Bergin, A. E., & Garfield, S. L. (1994). Overview, trends, and future issues. In A. E. Bergin & S. L. Garfield (Eds.), *Handbook of psychotherapy and behavior change* (4th ed., 821–830). New York: Wiley.

Beutler, L. (1995, August). *What works with whom: Developing effective treatment plans.* Workshop presented at the annual convention of the American Psychological Association, New York.

Bohart, A. (1991). Empathy in client-centered therapy: A contrast with psychoanalysis and self psychology. *Journal of Humanistic Psychology, 31*, 34–48.

Bohart, A. (1993). Experiencing: The basis of psychotherapy. *Journal of Psychotherapy Integration, 3*, 51–68.

Bohart, A., & Associates. (1996). Experiencing, knowing, and change. In R. Hutterer, G. Pawlowsky, P. F. Schmid, & R. Stipsits (Eds.), *Client-centered and experiential psychotherapy: A paradigm in motion* (pp. 199–211). New York: Peter Lang.

Bohart, A., & Rosenbaum, R. (1995). The dance of empathy: Empathy, diversity, and technical eclecticism. *The Person-Centered Journal, 2*, 5–29.

Bohart, A., & Tallman, K. (1996). The active client: Therapy as self-help. *Journal of Humanistic Psychology, 36*, 7–30.

Bohart, A., & Wugalter, S. (1991). Change in experiential knowing as a common dimension in psychotherapy. *Journal of Integrative and Eclectic Psychotherapy, 10*, 14–37.

Christensen, A., & Jacobson, N. S. (1994). Who (or what) can do psychotherapy: The status and challenge of nonprofessional therapies. *Psychological Science, 5*, 8–14.

Clark, H. H., & Brennan, S. E. (1991). Grounding in communication. In L. B. Resnick, J. M. Levine, & S. D. Teasley (Eds.), *Perspectives on socially shared cognition* (pp. 127–149). Washington, DC: American Psychological Association.

Darwin, C. (1904). *The expression of emotion in man and animals.* London: John Murray.

Dominowski, R. L., & Dallob, P. (1995). Insight and problem solving. In R. J. Sternberg & J. E. Davidson (Eds.), *The nature of insight* (pp. 33–62). Cambridge, MA: Massachusetts Institute of Technology Press.

Duncan, B. L., & Moynihan, D. W. (1994). Applying outcome research: Intentional utilization of the client's frame of reference. *Psychotherapy, 31,* 294–301.

Duncan, B. L., Solovey, A. D., & Rusk, G. S. (1992). *Changing the rules: A client-directed approach to therapy.* New York: Guilford Press.

Elliott, R., Filipovich, H., Harigan, L., Gaynor, J., Remischuessel, C., & Zapadka, J. K. (1982). Measuring response empathy: The development of a multicomponent rating scale. *Journal of Counseling Psychology, 29,* 379–387.

Gendlin, E. T. (1964). A theory of personality change. In P. Worchel & D. Byrne (Eds.), *Personality change.* New York: Wiley.

Gibson, J. J. (1979). *The ecological approach to visual perception.* Boston: Houghton Mifflin.

Gold, J. R. (1994). When the patient does the integrating: Lessons for theory and practice. *Journal of Psychotherapy Integration, 4,* 133–158.

Goodman, G., & Jacobs, M. (1995). The self-help, mutual support group. In A. Fuhriman & G. Burlingame (Eds.), *Handbook of group psychotherapy* (pp. 489–526). New York: Wiley.

Greenberg, L. S., Elliott, R., & Lietaer, G. (1994). Research on experiental psychotherapies. In A. E. Bergin & S. L. Garfield (Eds.), *Handbook of psychotherapy and behavior change* (4th ed., pp. 509–542). New York: Wiley.

Harvey, J. H., Orbuch, T. L., Chwalisz, K. D., & Garwood, G. (1991). Coping with sexual assault: The roles of account-making and confiding. *Journal of Traumatic Stress, 4,* 515–531.

Hoyt, M. F. (1994). *Constructive therapies.* New York: Guilford Press.

Isaak, M. I., & Just, M. A. (1995). Constraints on thinking in insight and invention. In R. J. Sternberg & J. E. Davidson (Eds.), *The nature of insight* (pp. 281–326). Cambridge, MA: Massachusetts Institute of Technology Press.

Jacobson, N. (1995). The overselling of therapy. *Family Therapy Networker, 19,* 40–51.

Johnson, M. (1993). *Moral imagination: Implications of cognitive science for ethics.* Chicago: University of Chicago Press.

Lambert, M. J. (1989). The individual therapist's contribution to psychotherapy process and outcome. *Clinical Psychology Review, 9,* 469–485.

Lambert, M. J. (1992). Psychotherapy outcome research. In J. C. Norcross & M. R. Goldfried (Eds.), *Handbook of psychotherapy integration* (pp. 94–129). New York: Basic Books.

Mahoney, M. (1991). *Human change processes.* New York: Basic Books.

Marten, P. A., & Barlow, D. H. (1993). Implications of clinical research for psychotherapy integration in the treatment of anxiety disorders. *Journal of Psychotherapy Integration, 3,* 297–312.

Masten, A. S., Best, K. M., & Garmazy, N. (1990). Resilience and development: Contributions from the study of children who overcome adversity. *Development and Psychopathology, 2,* 425–444.

Neisser, U. (1988). Five kinds of self-knowledge. *Philosophical Psychology, 1,* 35–59.

Nickerson, R. S. (1994). The teaching of thinking and problem solving. In R. J. Sternberg (Ed.), *Thinking and problem solving* (pp. 409–450). New York: Academic Press.

O'Hara, M. (1986). Heuristic inquiry as psychotherapy: The client-centered approach. *Person-Centered Review, 1,* 172–184.

Orlinsky, D. (1989). Researchers' images of psychotherapy: Their origins and influence on research. *Clinical Psychology Review, 9,* 413–442.

Paul, G. L. (1967). Outcome research in psychotherapy. *Journal of Consulting Psychology, 31,* 109–118.

Pennebaker, J. W. (Ed.). (1995). *Emotion, disclosure, and health.* Washington, DC: American Psychological Association.

Raskin, N. J. (1974). *Studies of psychotherapeutic orientation: Ideology and practice,* (Research Monograph No. 1). Orlando, FL: American Academy of Psychotherapists.

Rennie, D. L. (1990). Toward a representation of the client's experience of the psychotherapy hour. In G. Lietaer, J. Rombauts, & R. Van Balen (Eds.), *Client-centered and experiential psychotherapy in the ninenties* (pp. 155–172). Leuven, Belgium: Leuven University Press.

Rosenbaum, R. (1990). Strategic therapy. In R. A. Wells & V. J. Gianetti (Eds.), *Handbook of brief psychotherapies* (pp. 351–404). New York: Plenum.

Sachse, R. (1990). The influence of therapist processing proposals on the explication process of the client. *Person-Centered Review, 5,* 321–344.

Safran, J. D., & Segal, Z. V. (1990). *Interpersonal process in cognitive therapy.* New York: Basic Books.

Schegloff, E. A. (1991). Conversation analysis and socially shared cognition. In L. B. Resnick, J. M. Levine, & S. D. Teasley (Eds.), *Perspectives on socially shared cognition* (pp. 150–171). Washington, DC: American Psychological Association.

Schooler, J. W., Fallshore, M., & Fiore, S. M. (1995). Epilogue: Putting insight into perspective. In R. J. Sternberg & J. E. Davidson (Eds.), *The nature of insight* (pp. 559–588). Cambridge, MA: Massachusetts Institute of Technology Press.

Segal, D. L., & Murray, E. J. (1994). Emotional processing in cognitive therapy and vocal expression of feeling. *Journal of Social and Clinical Psychology, 13,* 189–206.

Snyder, M. (1994). The development of social intelligence in psychotherapy: Empathic and dialogic processes. *Journal of Humanistic Psychology, 34,* 84–108.

Stein, D. M., & Lambert, M. J. (1995). Graduate training in psychotherapy: Are therapy outcomes enhanced? *Journal of Consulting and Clinical Psychology, 63,* 182–196.

Stiles, W. B., & Shapiro, D. A. (1989). Abuse of the drug metaphor in psychotherapy process-outcome research. *Clinical Psychology Review, 9,* 521–544.

Strupp, H. H., & Hadley, S. W. (1979). Specific versus nonspecific factors in psychotherapy: A controlled study of outcome. *Archives of General Psychiatry, 36,* 1125–1136.

Stubbs, J. P., & Bozarth, J. D. (1994). The dodo bird revisited: A qualitative study of psychotherapy efficacy research. *Applied and Preventive Psychology, 3,* 109–120.

Svartberg, M., & Stiles, T. C. (1991). Comparative effects of short-term psychodynamic psychotherapy: A meta-analysis. *Journal of Consulting and Clinical Psychology, 59,* 704–714.

Tallman, K. (1996, April). *Goal-orientation: Applying educational research to psychotherapy.* Paper presented at the Convention of the Society for the Exploration of Psychotherapy Integration, Berkeley, CA.

Task Force on Promotion and Dissemination of Psychological Procedures, Division of Clinical Psychology of the American Psychological Association (1995). Training in and dissemination of empirically-validated psychological treatments: Report and recommendations. *The Clinical Psychologist, 48*(1), 3–23.

Todd, J., & Bohart, A. (1994). *Foundations of clinical and counseling psychology* (2nd ed.). New York: HarperCollins.

Trevarthen, C. (1993). The self born in intersubjectivity: The psychology of an infant communicating. In U. Neisser (Ed.), *The perceived self: Ecological and interpersonal sources of self-knowledge. Emory Symposia in Cognition* (Vol. 5, pp. 121–173). New York: Cambridge University Press.

Wilkes-Gibbs, D., & Clark, H. H. (1992). Coordinating beliefs in conversation. *Journal of Memory and Language, 31,* 183–194.

Zimring, F. (1990). Cognitive processes as a cause of psychotherapeutic change: Self-initiated processes. In G. Lietaer, J. Rombauts, & R. Van Balen (Eds.), *Client-centered and experiential psychotherapy in the nineties* (pp. 361–380). Leuven, Belgium: Leuven University Press.

VI
CONCLUSIONS

19

EMPATHY: WHERE ARE WE AND WHERE DO WE GO FROM HERE?

ARTHUR C. BOHART AND LESLIE S. GREENBERG

In this chapter we analyze and attempt to integrate different ideas about empathy and its functions in therapy. First, we consider issues about the definition and nature of empathy. Second, we examine the diverse functions that have been postulated for empathy in therapy. Finally, we present our own integrative model of therapeutic empathy.

DEFINITION AND NATURE OF EMPATHY

As others have observed (e.g., Eagle & Wolitsky, Chapter 10, this volume; Feshbach, Chapter 2, this volume; Gladstein & Associates, 1987), there are multiple definitions of empathy. When referring to psychotherapy, we believe it is best to think of it as a multidimensional construct. What all the definitions of empathy in psychotherapy have in common at a super-ordinate level is that they involve trying to sense, perceive, share, or conceptualize how another person is experiencing the world. There are different dimensions involved in this. First, empathy includes a cognitive or *understanding* dimension. Second, empathy includes an affective or *experiential* dimension. Third, empathy can involve *action*—especially *communication*. Fourth, empathy is a way of *being together* in relationship. Finally, empathy overlaps with the construct of interpersonal confirmation, or *validation*. We consider each of these dimensions in turn.

Empathy Involves Understanding

Others have observed that there is a cognitive and an affective dimension to empathy (Feshbach, Chapter 2, this volume; Gladstein & Associates, 1987). We have chosen to use the terms *understanding* and *experiencing* instead of cognition and emotion because we want to emphasize the complexity of both the kind of understanding involved and the kind of experiencing. The kind of understanding may consist of what we typically think of as cognition (i.e., thinking and conceptual inference). Or it may involve more affective, perceptual, experiential, or tacit kinds of understanding. Similarly, experiencing is more than just experiencing the same emotion as the client. It overlaps with understanding and includes tacit, perceptual, and affective ways of contacting and being attuned to another's experience. It also includes one's own experiencing in response to the client. In general, experiencing is a complex cognitive–affective process (Greenberg & Safran, 1987).

Understanding is emphasized by virtually all of our contributors. Shlien specifically draws a distinction between empathy per se and empathic understanding. Trop and Stolorow, distinguish between empathic inquiry, which is a method of investigation for illuminating a client's unconscious organizing principles and affective responsiveness. Others see empathy as a mode of knowing or observing (Rowe), careful listening and understanding (Bozarth, Bohart & Tallman), apprehending the implicit meanings in the client's experience (Barrett-Lennard, Greenberg & Elliott, Vanaerschot, Warner), social intelligence (Shlien), interpersonal perception (Jenkins), role-taking (Eagle & Wolitsky), and attunement (which involves perception; Greenberg & Elliott, Rowe).

Schematizing these, there are two general modalities of empathic understanding. The first is through immediate perception of the client and of the interaction; the second is through cognitive operations such as conceptual analysis and imaginative role taking. Therapists can perceive the client's affect, actions, body language, and speech. This can result in a kind of tacit–experiential way of knowing or sometimes in an immediate "reading" of what the client is saying or experiencing. Therapists may deliberately attune to clients to achieve this. Therapists can also cognitively project themselves into the client's world, and use conceptual analysis to try to understand the client's perspective. A key therapist skill here is the ability to temporarily suspend one's own frame of reference in service of taking the role of the other, as well as being able to go beyond this to be able to empathically grasp the larger context in which the experience of both therapist and client in interaction is taking place (Selman, 1980). We consider the two different ways of achieving understanding below. We also consider other dimensions of empathic understanding, as well as the issue of its validity.

Conceptual and Experiential–Tacit Knowing

One way of trying to understand the experience of the other involves active cognitive operations such as imaginative role taking and conceptual analysis. The therapist observes the client's experience, observes his or her own reactions to the client, or imagines himself or herself into the client's shoes and then draws inferences about the client's internal states. This view of empathy characterizes some of the psychodynamic views discussed by Eagle and Wolitsky, and also to some extent the work of Trop and Stolorow. This view also characterizes Kohut (MacIsaac) to the extent that they used empathy in the service of explaining unconscious patterns to the client. Some psychodynamic writers (e.g., Buie, 1981) have argued that inference is *the only* way to know the mind and experience of another person. Inference may use and be based on more experiential, tacit ways of knowing, discussed next.

The second way of attaining understanding is based in experiential or tacit ways of knowing. In this form of knowing, there is a tacit synthesis of a variety of levels or aspects of information to arrive at understanding, and this does not involve a conscious, conceptual thinking process. Such knowing is more perceptual, recognitional, and affective. Jenkins uses the word "intuitive." Rowe calls this "expanding attunement." Greenberg and Elliott state that empathy is a felt, experiential way of knowing more so than being conceptual understanding. For Shlien, empathy is based in direct perception, such as in the immediate (and nonconscious) noting of and reacting to things like the dilation of another's eyes. This is echoed by Bohart and Tallman, who argue that we can often fairly immediately perceive what another person is meaning or experiencing without effortful conceptual activity. Others who argue for a tacit, perceptual, or experiential type of knowing include O'Hara and Mahrer. On the other hand, these more experiential, tacit ways of understanding are not magical. Both Shlien and MacIsaac object to the idea that empathy involves any kind of magical intuition.

An observational, inferential way of proceeding has been more emphasized by psychodynamic therapists, while client-centered and experiential therapists have more emphasized tacit and experiential ways of understanding. We suspect that this difference has reflected different goals of empathic understanding. As we noted in our introductory chapter, for psychodynamic therapists empathy is ultimately to help them understand the client's *general* frame of reference, how he or she *characteristically* construes and experiences the world, and how that is based in his or her experiential history—thus a focus on imaginative role taking and conceptual inference. In contrast, for client-centered and experiential therapists, the first and foremost goal is communicative attunement—to grasp the immediacy of the client's experience, the frame of reference from which the client is operating in the moment—thus a focus on immediate, tacit, experiential apprehension of the client's present state. However, both approaches use both modalities of knowing. Psychodynamic therapists base their conceptual inferences in part in their immediate, tacit–experiential ways of knowing, and client-centered and experiential therapists use at least low levels of inference to guess at aspects of the client's experience that are implicit and not yet verbalized. They also use inference to test out their understanding of what the client is trying to communicate. From a psychodynamic perspective, Rowe has particularly emphasized the tacit aspect of empathy in this volume. Therefore, for both, empathic understanding is a complex cognitive–affective kind of understanding. How the two modes of knowing—conceptual and tacit—are used by therapists as they pursue their selective goals, and how they may differentially lead to clients' experience of feeling understood, merits further theoretical and empirical elaboration. We note in this regard that Feshbach's developmental model, although not explicitly including a fully fleshed-out experiential–tacit dimension, does include both affect perception (both of self and of other) and cognitive role taking.

Depth of Empathic Understanding

Empathic understanding has been referred to either as deep or as superficial. Depth, however, is defined differently for different approaches, leading us to suggest that empathy is better viewed as consisting of different types rather than along a depth continuum. For psychodynamic therapists, "deep" means the use of empathy to gain a complex understanding of the patterns in the client's experience and to gain insight into underlying unconscious experiential determinants. For client-centered and experiential therapists, "deep" means grasping the subtlety and organizational complexity of clients' immediate, here-and-now felt meanings and experience. It also means being deeply in tune with their process of experiencing. For Mahrer, "deep" means grasping the client's deep experiencing potential—a not-yet-actualized set of possibilities for new ways of being and behaving. For self-in-relation theorists such as Jordan, "deep" refers to the depth of empathic connection, which invites and allows the client to bring into relationship experiences that have heretofor felt too vulnerable to be shared. Linehan's levels of validation also include a "depth" dimension. In level-three validation, the therapist goes beyond what the client has expressed to "mind read" and to capture some of what is implicit for them. In levels four and five, the therapist helps to validate the implicit "sense" in the client's behavior.

The concept of "deep" understanding distinguishes those who view empathy as central in therapy from those who see it as more of a relationship-building or background characteristic. As we have discussed in the introduction, empathy as rapport consists of a general acknowledgement of what is fairly obvious in the client's experiential state. It is recognizing what the client already recognizes and is aware of. This can be therapeutic at times. In general, however, the function of such recognition could be little more than relationship building because there is nothing to the empathic response that facilitates further processing. We discuss the relationship between empathy and compassion in more detail below.

Focus of Empathic Understanding

A third aspect of empathic understanding involves its targets. The first target to be considered is whether understanding is focused on experience that is conscious or unconscious. Client-centered and experiential therapists focus on understanding of the client's conscious, immediate, moment-by-moment experience of relating, dialoging, and struggling to articulate. They try to stay attuned to the ongoing, emerging, active client process of thinking, exploring, and feeling. They are less-focused on the specific content or issues the client is struggling with. This involves an immediate, connected, and experiential mode of knowing, which is believed to help symbolize and confirm inchoate experience and promote exploration. Such articulation often deals with implicit meanings, but implicit meanings that are nonetheless consciously available.

In contrast, psychodynamic theorists such as Trop and Stolorow, Rowe, and MacIsaac include moment-to-moment responses to and understanding of the client's experience, but their ultimate goal is to explain to the client how the client is unconsciously organizing his or her experience. They hope to help clients understand how unconscious adjustments and accommodations to early childhood experiences are still providing the basis for how they organize their adult experience.

This raises an important theoretical issue: Can one empathize with the unconscious? There is evidence that clients can experience interpretations as empathic (e.g., Bachelor, 1988, Elliott et al., 1982). Conceptually, however, is there such a thing as an "empathic interpretation?" Eagle and Wolitsky draw a distinction between broad and narrow conceptions of empathy. A narrow view of empathy focuses on understanding conscious experience, whereas a broad view includes a focus on the unconscious. Eagle and Wolitsky note problems with the idea of empathizing with the unconscious. For instance, how can one empathize with theoretical mechanisms that are postulated to operate unconsciously, such as defense mechanisms or schemas? Eagle and Wolitsky conclude that it makes sense to talk about empathizing with the unconscious only if one has in mind empathizing with things that can in principle be experienced. This view is echoed by Warner.

Nonetheless, we still wonder: Can one actually *empathize* with the unconscious (i.e., with that which is not available to experience)? Or does one use empathy to make inferences about the unconscious? There are those who might argue that one actually can empathically apprehend what is unconscious (e.g., Berger, 1987), who might claim that through one's use of one's own imagination that one can intuit oneself into the client's unconscious meanings. On the other hand, as we read Trop and Stolorow, MacIsaac, and Rowe, empathic immersion or empathic inquiry helps the therapist make experience-near *inferences* about the client's unconscious, and these are shared through the form of explanation or interpretation. These are presumably empathic to the degree to which they are derived from the analyst's empathic understanding of the client's conscious experience and to the extent to which they address things that are in principle experienceable.

In traditional psychodynamic theory, conscious experience is often seen as a compromise formation, and the purpose of interpretation is to explain the psychogenesis or components that constitute it. As Eagle and Wolitsky note, the analyst observes the client and uses theory to draw inferences about links between various aspects of the client's behavior and his or her dynamics. Interpretations are based on these inferences and are, in principle, not directed toward anything that is in experience. So they are, by definition, not empathic. An empathic interpretation, in contrast, is an attempt to bridge the gap between conscious and unconscious by making inferences about what must be potentially there but is not being experienced. Theoretically, therefore, we suggest that one can not directly *empathize* with the unconscious and unconscious needs. Rather, one can use empathic understanding to *guess at* what is in the unconscious, but the target must be something that can be experienced. If one makes a good guess, one "brings forth" some kind of experiential recognition that seems right to the client, and the client "feels understood." In addition, empathy helps in timing interpretations so that they are given when clients are ready to receive them (MacIsaac).

We borrow an example from Wachtel (1993), which he discusses in terms of accusatory versus facilitative interpretations. The first, nonempathic interpretation is: "You avoid acknowledging sexual feelings." This is not, in principle, experienceable. It encourages the client to adopt a distanced analytical stance toward himself or herself and to look for a pattern across his or her experience—that of a general dispositional state of defensive avoidance. The second is: "You seem rather harsh with yourself when you sense any hint of sexual feeling." This is more potentially experienceable; this interpretation could direct the client's attentional search to his or her actual experience so that he or she can see if he or she really is harsh with himself or herself when he or she senses sexual feeling.

In addition to conscious and unconscious targets, there are other possible foci for empathy. Empathy can target thoughts, feelings and needs, or both. As Greenberg and Elliott have noted, there is a difference between being empathically attuned to the client's excitement (targeting an emotional reaction) and empathically understanding the client's belief that he is over the hill (targeting a cognition). Finally, there is the distinction between targeting what is explicit in the client's conscious experience and what is implicit, but still consciously available although not verbally articulated. A simple acknowledgement of a client's concern about losing his or her job targets what is explicit. Going beyond this, one could respond to the client's implicit (but still consciously available) worry that if he or she loses his or her job he or she may have to stay in the bad relationship he or she is in.

Experience-Near Attempts to Understand the Client's World Versus Communicative Attunement

In the introduction we noted a distinction between communicative attunement, which is the client-centered target of empathy, and experience-near attempts to understand the client's world, which is more like the psychodynamic target of empathy. With communicative attunement the therapist tries to enter into the client's *immediate* emerging and ever-forming frame of reference as the client struggles to articulate his or her experience and to dialogue with the therapist. The therapist may even try to find the "leading edge" of this ever-forming and moving internal frame of reference and to help the client continue its articulation—and in the process help the client "make meaning." In contrast, psychodynamic therapists are ultimately interested in gaining an understanding of the client's general internal frame of reference, how the client characteristically interprets experience, and how his or her experiential history has led to the client's current perceived life situation. Put another way, one kind of empathy is targeted at what it is like to be the client in a general sense: What is it like to be someone who has had repeated failed relationships, who self-mutilates when he or she gets depressed, who is married to an unempathic partner, or who had parents who were cold, neglectful, and abusive? The other kind of empathy is targeted at what it is like to be the client right now. What is it like to be this person trying to form this experience into words, communicate his or her sense of hopelessness and frustration and sense of the problem to the therapist, while experiencing that sense of helplessness and frustration in this moment as he or she tries to do it?

These appear to be two different kinds of empathic activity, although they feed into each other. It is likely that they create different experiences and function somewhat differently, as well. Immediate, moment-by-moment careful tracking of the client as the client refers inward and struggles to articulate experience in words supports the client's attempts to form inchoate or implicit experience into verbalizable concepts and supports the client's further exploration process of examining these concepts. Communicative attunement is more likely to create an immediate "feel" of being listened to and a sense of immediate contact. The client is liable to feel "I am able to make sense of my experience right now." It thus is validating, but validates the client as an active "sense-making" agent. Experience-near attempts to grasp the client's whole frame of reference create more of a "feel" that the therapist understands the whole picture of the client's experience. These attempts are more likely to serve an explanatory function, helping the client put problems and life experiences into context. They also help the client make sense of experience, but in a broader sense, more in the form of "narrative reorganization and repair" than in the form of facilitating immediate articulation. The client is liable to feel "it is not surprising that I am having the problem that I am having. It makes sense. I am not so weird."

As we have noted, these two types of empathy feed into each other. A psychodynamic style can include understanding a client's immediate experience and communication (e.g., MacIsaac, Rowe), but usually this is used as a way of going beyond the immediate to try to understand the general way the client contrues experience. A client-centered style may use knowledge of the client's broader experiential context to more deeply understand how the client is immediately experiencing in this moment. However, the therapist operations for these two types of empathic understanding are somewhat different. Because the purpose of communicative attunement is to check understanding of the client's immediate frame of reference, empathic reflections of various types are probably the prototypical response, although other responses might also be appropriate. In contrast, to gain a more general understanding of the client's experience of his or her situation, the therapist may not only focus on moment-by-moment attunement to the client's communications but also on asking questions to elaborate on his or her understanding of the patterns involved in the client's experience. In addition, the therapist may make test interpretations to explore his or her understanding or to demonstrate his or her comprehension of the links in the client's experience. In the case of both kinds of empathic understanding, the therapist may imaginatively project himself or herself into the client's shoes, but again, in different ways. To heighten communicative attunement, the therapist may ask himself or herself, "what would I be feeling/experiencing now, and what would I be trying to say, if I were in his shoes?" To heighten empathic understanding of the client's general frame of reference, the therapist might ask himself or herself "what kind of problems or experiences have I had in the past that allow me to relate to someone who is in a cold marriage and had neglectful parents?"

The Issue of the Validity of Knowing Through Empathic Understanding

Eagle and Wolitsky raise the issue of the validity of what is understood through empathy. They point out that there is nothing magical about empathic understanding and its truth value needs to be validated in the same manner as any other constructs arrived at by the therapist. They also note that even the client's experience of a therapist's comment as understanding does not necessarily guarantee its validity. Even inexact therapist interpretations might make clients feel understood. This assumes that the goal of empathic understanding is to establish some sort of "truth" about the client's experience.

In contrast, although some writers refer to "accuracy," for them accuracy means that an empathic response (a) fits the client's experience in some reasonable fashion, or (b) helps them articulate or construct their experience (e.g., Jenkins, Warner, and Vanerschot). It is assumed that there are alternative possible ways to construe experience. The usefulness of an empathic response lies not in its objective accuracy so much as in its ability to help the client carry forward his or her experiencing and to create new and more functional narratives or meaning structures or to facilitate the client's ongoing self-exploration, self-structuralization, and self-actualization. Those who hold this view are more likely to adopt intersubjective views of empathy in general (see below) and to see therapy as a process of cocreating meaning.

Empathy Involves Experiencing

The therapist not only conceptualizes but also actively experiences. This dimension includes several components: mood congruence, experiencing as one listens to and interacts with the client, and experientially responding in an empathically complementary way. The key therapist skill is the ability to tune into and accurately identify his or her own experience.

Mood Congruence

Developmental psychologists define empathy as having the same emotional reaction as the other person (e.g., Feshbach). Having an emotional reaction similar to that of the client can be an aspect of therapeutic empathy and can be used to help achieve understanding. In addition, it may strengthen the bond between therapist and client. Therefore, when the client feels sad the therapist may experience a taste of sadness. Feshbach has even argued that it is the shared affective component of empathy that makes it more genuine. However, an important distinction drawn by most of the authors in this volume (with the exception of Mahrer) is that the therapist must be careful not to confuse his or her experience with that of the client's or get lost in the client's experience. One is to enter the client's experience on an "as if" basis but never to lose the sense of distinction between self and client. A difference between developmental and therapeutic views of empathy is that, for developmentalists, mood congruence *is* empathy, with understanding of the other's frame of reference a component contributing to mood congruence. On the other hand, for therapists, empathy focuses more on achieving understanding, with mood congruence helping the therapist to understand the client's experience and frame of reference.

Experiencing as One Listens to and Interacts With the Client

More broadly, empathy includes a complex kind of experiential apprehension. First, one may feel or understand the complexity of what the client is undergoing. This includes sensing the complexity of what the client is up against and how the client is viewing his or her situation, in addition to sensing what emotion the client is feeling. This consists of experiencing a complex felt meaning (Gendlin, 1967).

In addition, one can experience the feeling of *trying to understand* the client. Greenberg and Elliott claim that one need not experience the same state as the client, but that to be empathic one must be experiencing one's understanding of them. That is, understanding needs to be more than sheer intellectual understanding. Several writers (e.g., Vanaerschot) also stress the idea of "tuning" one's experience so that it becomes more in accord with that of the client. Mahrer believes that one can carry this to the point where one actually "becomes" the experience of the client. This includes getting in touch with the client's deep experiencing potential for new ways of being and behaving. For both Vanaerschot and Mahrer this involves a complex resonating with and sharing of the client's whole experience. Vanaerschot says that the therapist becomes a "surrogate experiencer" for the client, and Mahrer would probably agree.

Responding in an Empathically Complementary Way

One may respond in a way that is empathically complementary to the experience of the client. Empathic complementary means that one's response is "in tune" with the central meaning the client is focusing on. The therapist responds in a way that signals that he or she has heard the client, recognized the client's meaning, understands it, but offers back something that *shows* understanding by being a *response to* the client, rather than a mirroring of what the client has just said. This is how empathic understanding often functions in everyday communication (MacIsaac). What is offered back may be a disclosure of the therapist's own thoughts or experience (e.g., Bozarth, 1984) or the suggestion of a technique. Bohart and Rosenbaum (1995) have used two jazz musicians empathically improvising in response to each other's solos as an example. This kind of empathy also is compatible with Mahrer's approach. Mahrer tries to tune into what the client is experiencing and then carry it forward, going beyond what the client is experiencing in the process.

Issues Concerning the Relationship of Empathy to the Experience of the Therapist

An important issue is to what degree the experience of the therapist as a person is a vital part of the empathic process, and thus of therapy in general. A number of writers (e.g., Bozarth, Vanaerschot, Mahrer, Trox, & Stolorow) stress the usefulness of therapists' experience for providing helpful clues to clients' experience. Others (e.g., Jordan & O'Hara) stress therapists' experience as important because therapy is an intensely personal encounter in which empathic experience is cocreated. Eagle and Wolitsky discuss how therapists' counter-transferential feelings, or experience of patients' projective identifications, can be used for empathic purposes. Thus, therapists may use their personal experience to understand the client, or to make contact with them. Several authors suggested self-disclosure as one way of achieving these aims, and Bachelor (1988) found that clients experience therapist self-disclosure as one contributor to empathy.

However the relationship between therapists' personal experience and clients' experience is complex. Psychoanalysts (e.g., Eagle & Wolitsky) caution therapists against mistaking their own experiential reactions for those of their clients. They point out the pitfalls in assuming that one's own reactions can provide "infallible" knowledge about the patient. Just because the therapist feels anger as a client describes an incident of abuse does not mean that is what the client is experiencing. In that regard, Leitner (1995) has proposed the concept of "optimal therapeutic distance." The therapist must be close enough to the client's experience to taste some of it and to experientially react, but maintain enough distance so as not to confuse his or her experience with that of the client. This is a complex, ongoing task. It involves continuous attempts by the therapist to discern what is "me" (i.e., the therapist's own reactions to the client's issues), what is "not me" (i.e., what is a reflection of the client's experience), and what is "us together" (i.e., therapist experiential reactions that are a joint product of therapist and client interactive experience in the session). This means that therapists must be engaged in an ongoing process of self-understanding as well as that of trying to understand the client.

In our view, therapists can protect themselves against confusing their experience with that of the client if they use their personal experiential reactions in the following ways. First, they use them as probes to further and deepen their understanding of the client's experience (psychoanalytic, client-centered, experiential). Second, they use them to facilitate clients' exploring and processing of their experience. Third, they use them as a basis for connecting with clients, "co-experiencing" and being in relationship with them (Jordan, O'Hara, Mahrer). The case of Mahrer is complex because Mahrer believes that he can "become" the experience of the client. However, an examination of how Wahrer actually uses his experience in therapy reveals that it is used to join with clients and facilitate their own experiencing rather than as a basis for making authoritative judgments about their experience.

Empathy Involves Action and Communication

A third major dimension of empathy is that it leads to action and interaction in one form or another. This includes empathy as attunement or immersion, empathy as an active attitude, empathy as communication, and empathy as a basis for other therapeutic actions. Related to the communication of empathy is the issue of whether empathy can be harmful or not.

One form of action is when the therapist communicates an active, attuned, or immersed stance toward the client's experience (MacIsaac, Rowe, and Greenberg & Elliott). Empathic attunement or immersion are trial and error processes that one must continually work at (MacIsaac), and rest on developing one's perceptual sensitivity (Rowe). These active efforts to try to pick up, recognize, and resonate with the client's experience communicate empathic involvement to the client, even if the therapist is not always on target. Similarly, for Bozarth and other client-centered therapists, empathy is ultimately an active attitude that can be manifested in a variety of ways.

A particular form of action is verbal communication. Trop and Stolorow, Greenberg and Elliott, and Barrett-Lennard (1993) make a distinction between the therapist's experiencing empathy with the client and the communication of empathy. Client-centered therapists also make this distinction but have stressed the communication of empathy. What has changed for client-centered therapists (e.g., Bozarth) is the increased flexibility in the manner in which empathy is communicated to the client. Greenberg and Elliott note the differential use of different kinds of empathic responses at different times. For others, empathy and the communication of empathy are intimately intertwined. This is true of Jordan, Mahrer, and O'Hara. Mahrer's whole technique is the communication of his "aligned" sense of joining with the client. For Jordan the fundamental therapeutic act is the active, mutual, open sharing of empathy. For O'Hara it is the mutual sharing of experience that occurs through the medium of imagery, dreams, and nonverbal modalities, as well as through verbal modalities. For Eagle and Wolitsky, the therapist's empathic communicative style might be more important in enhancing the client's experience of empathy than the therapist's *experience* of empathic understanding.

The equation of empathy with communication reminds us of the tradition, started by Truax and Carkhuff (1967), of equating empathy with active *skills* that can be trained. Although treating empathy as a response skill undoubtedly has made a contribution, the views of empathy presented in this book go beyond viewing it as listening and responding skills. We believe, as Bozarth and others have emphasized, that the attitudes and intentions underlying empathic communications are at least as important as the skillfulness of the communications themselves. Recently, Phillips, Lipson, and Basseches (1994) have argued that there are different cognitive–developmental levels of listening. The kind of empathic listening practiced by some therapists, that being at the level of paraphrase and tolerant understanding, is at a lower cognitive–developmental level of listening complexity than what most of the writers in this book are advocating. We believe the level of listening and understanding complexity is more basic and crucial than empathic response skills.

Finally, empathy can be communicated through a variety of therapeutic actions. For instance, one's empathic understanding may lead to the suggestion of a technique or even to remaining judiciously silent for a time. With some clients, empathy may mean keeping an empathic distance (see our discussion below concerning the issue of whether empathy can be harmful or not). For Bohart and Tallman, as well as for Eagle and Wolitsky, all good therapy responses should be conveyed empathically.

Is Empathy in Therapy Ever Harmful?

Some writers have suggested that empathy can be harmful. Burns (1980), in commenting on empathically based, nondirective therapy, says, "When you do feel better as a result of achieving emotional release with an empathic and caring therapist, the sense of improvement is likely to be short-lived if you haven't significantly transformed the way you evaluate yourself and your life." He also notes, "If the therapist does not provide objective feedback about the validity of your self-evaluation, you may conclude that he agrees with you . . . As a result you probably will feel even more inadequate" (p. 60). And Hammond, Hepworth, and Smith (1980) have said,

> With emotionally overexpressive individuals . . . empathic responsiveness, especially that which focuses on the feelings presented, may indeed foster cathartic and temporary symptomatic relief, but it may also defeat the aims of therapy by permitting, reinforcing and perpetuating the client's dysfunctional mode of coping. Such clients need more to encourage their rational processes than to express their emotions freely. (p. 155)

Elsewhere, Wachtel (1993) has expressed concerns that the therapist's empathic immersion in the experience of the client may preclude the therapist from offering an alternative, objective perspective and challenging the client to overcome resistances when needed. Beutler, Crago, and Arizmendi (1986), citing several research studies, draw the conclusion that therapists who are actively empathic, supportive, and involved are actually countereffective with clients who are reactant against authority, poorly motivated, suspicious, and highly sensitive.

We believe that whether empathy can be harmful or not involves several issues. The first is whether it is always good to actively, forcefully, and directly communicate empathy to the client. Trop and Stolorow, among others, would say no. Client-centered therapists (e.g., Bozarth) would probably also say a qualified no because, for them, empathy most fundamentally is an attitude. In cases where they sensed that the client wanted space, their expression of empathic understanding would be indirect—by providing that space. In keeping with this, Bohart and Tallman, as well as Eagle and Wolitsky, suggest that empathy underlies all sensitively offered therapeutic interactions. The most "direct" expression of empathy may be to express it indirectly at times, through silence, through the suggesting of a technique, or through keeping one's distance. With some clients to focus on showing that one "understands" them may paradoxically demonstrate a lack of understanding. If the client is very businesslike and task-focused, the best way to enact one's understanding is to stay focused on the task. There are also clients who find talking about their emotions and inviting another into their experience as terrorizing at a physiological level (Lynch, 1985). Therapists who "force" an emotional focus in the name of empathy may be harmful. It may be more empathic to keep a respectful distance.

A second issue concerns the target of empathy. The above quotations dwell on empathy's potential for harm when the therapist is focusing on affect. If the therapist responds with simple empathic reflections that acknowledge the client's affective state (e.g., "You're feeling sad," "That really made you angry") and does not go further, it is possible that such responses may have negative effects. First, they may provide only temporary relief through clients' getting their feelings off their chests. Second, they could serve to reinforce negative affect. There is evidence that cathartic expression is not always helpful (Bohart, 1980; Greenberg & Safran, 1987). There is further evidence that with "alexithymic" individuals forcing a focus on talking about feelings and on having intense emotional experiences can be counterproductive (Lynch, 1985).

However, as we have previously noted, affect is only one potential target of empathic responses. More typically for our contributors, empathy targets attempts to deeply understand complex aspects of experience that are presumed to carry forward clients' work in rearranging their modes of perceiving self and world. With some clients, affect may not play a particularly important role in this. Or empathy involves developing the capacity for a deep, mutual, experiential meeting between persons. These presumptions need to be empirically researched, but the point is that empathy is more complex than an affective focus alone.

Furthermore, whether or not an empathic response is helpful or harmful may depend on how it is phrased and how it is timed. To a very hurt client who is not accepting his or her feelings, empathic recognition of his her pain (what Greenberg and Elliott call "empathic prizing at a vulnerability marker," e.g., "You feel very hurt") may be very therapeutic. To a client who has moved beyond acceptance and recognition of his or her pain into potential for exploration of it, the same response might be counterproductive, keeping his or her attention stuck on the pain.

A third objection is that the therapist may get "lost" in the client's experience and lose the advantage of offering an "objective" perspective. This is also indeed a danger. The therapist could get so immersed in the client's feelings that negative attitudes and ways of being and behaving inadvertently get reinforced. Linehan has noted the paradoxical quality of totally accepting a client's experience *and* expecting them to change. But is the only alternative for the therapist to provide an external perspective? Neither Rogers (Bozarth) nor Mahrer would agree. For Rogers, the danger that empathy would reinforce a dysfunctional subjective state in the client would appear to depend on the degree to which the therapist loses the "as if" quality (Bozarth). Rogers's goal was to show the client that he understood the client's frame of reference, not that he agreed with it. This is a crucial distinction. In effect, Rogers was helping to articulate the internal dialogue between the articulate, reflective self and the immediate, experiential self (Barrett-Lennard). In so doing, he was presumably strengthening *two* client skills: (a) the skill of empathically listening to the self and allowing in previously disowned aspects of experience and (b) the ability to reflect on the self (analogous to the observing ego in psychoanalytic theory). By strengthening the observing side, the therapist is, in effect, helping the client to develop the client's own ability to break out of dysfunctional subjective traps. Bohart and Tallman would agree, arguing that, given a good "workspace," clients are capable of extricating themselves from traps on their own. This depends on the therapist's not losing the "as if" quality. Otherwise the therapist might "side" with the experiential side and get lost in the client's experience.

Mahrer tries to empathize with the client's deep experiencing *potential* and, thus, draw out client potential for change. Thus, he, too, believes that therapist empathy can facilitate client change without a need for the therapist's offering an "objective" perspective. It is an important empirical question whether a very good Rogerian therapist or a very good experiential therapist in the Mahrer tradition would inadvertently reinforce dysfunctional client states by virtue of their not offering an objective perspective.

Even Rogers (with his emphasis on genuineness in his later years) did not totally advocate the therapist's surrendering of his or her own perspective. None of the rest of our authors advocate this either. In fact, most emphasize achieving a kind of coordination of the "two poles" of the client's experience and the therapist's experience or observation, with the dialogue between those two different poles being that which is therapeutic. The issue of whether or not the therapist's perspective is the "objective one," implied by the views of both Burns and Wachtel, is another matter. Theorists who adopt relational and intersubjective perspectives, such as O'Hara and Trop and Stolorow, might question the idea that the therapist is in the "objective" position vis-à-vis the client. Rather, although the therapist's point of view may be different than the client's, it is an equally subjective one.

In summary, the issue of whether empathy can sometimes be harmful is extremely important and needs to be researched further. It may depend on (a) whether empathy is expressed or not, (b) what the target of empathy is, (c) how it is expressed, (d) and to what degree clients are capable of extracting themselves from their own subjective traps if given the proper working environment. Finally, Duan and Hill (1996) have suggested that clients' needs for empathy may change from time to time and, therapists need to "empathically" sense when and what kind of empathic communication clients want.

Empathy is a Way of Being Together

Extending the idea that empathy is a form of action, empathy is also a fundamental way of being in psychological contact with another person. It is a way of "deep" meeting (see Shlien's discussion of Buber versus Rogers). This contrasts with the traditional view of empathy as one separate self trying to infer or intuit itself across the gulf separating it from another. For Jordan empathy involves a willingness to be open, vulnerable, and present to the other person. Empathy in a relationship is mutual—a two-way street. Not only does the therapist gain empathy for the client, but the client develops empathy for the therapist through a mutual sharing of experience. O'Hara extends these sentiments to groups and to cultures. Empathy is a contextual, nonrational, intuitive way of knowing, which, if we are reading her correctly, is more "right brain" than "left brain." It involves the sharing and cocreating of meaning through analogical, nonverbal channels; through imagery; through stories, dreams, and narratives; and through verbal communication. It is through this that groups (and therapy is a two-person group) can operate in harmony, as a larger "group mind," and can, under the right circumstances, act intelligently. This is all very foreign to the way egocentric cultures view the self and processes of knowing but is accepted in sociocentric cultures. It is compatible with views that cognition is socially shared (Maturana & Varela, 1987; Resnick, Levine, & Teasley, 1991).

These perspectives suggest that empathy is a fundamental mode of interpersonal knowing, valued more by women than by men and by people of other cultures than by Euroamerican culture. Furthermore, it is a way of sharing and of being together in experience, or almost one of "coexperiencing." It is in such relationships that the deepest sense of self is continuously being formed. Empathy, as such, is far more than a therapeutic tool wielded by the therapist. Rather, it is the very essence of personal relatedness and growth. Technique comes in a distant second to a real relationship in such approaches. This fits with Jenkins's view that for people of color who have been oppressed by society being with an empathic other is intrinsically therapeutic.

Furthermore, there is some empirical evidence that this sense of connection may be biologically based. Lynch (1985) has argued that human dialogue has a physiological impact on the participants. Lynch maintains that

> Human beings are biologically interrelated . . . we can understand and cope with illness only when we are able to view ourselves as part of a complex world beyond the confines of our own individual skin. The response of our hearts, blood vessels, and muscles when we communicate with spouse, children, friends, colleagues, and the larger community has as much to do with our cardiovascular health as do factors such as exercise or diet. (p. 10)

The intersubjective nature of the therapeutic relationship and, hence, of empathy is emphasized by many of our authors. However, some emphasize the dimension of psychological contact—the idea of a true meeting of persons—less than others. For the psychodynamic theorists, this dimension is less prominent because their emphasis is more on seeing themselves as serving a transferential selfobject function for their clients, subject to later explanation or interpretation. The intersubjective element of therapy is perhaps most eloquently illustrated by Shlien's story of being with his patient who was feeling sad and crying. The patient blows his nose in his handkerchief, and then when he notices that Shlien has tears in his eyes, offers it to Shlien. Both suddenly become aware of the fact that the handkerchief has been used, and both are aware of each other's awareness of this, of the generous meaning of the gesture of offering the handkerchief, and of the reasons for the declining and withdrawing of the offer. An important sharing of experience has taken place in an instant, without a word being spoken.

Empathy and Validation

Linehan's concept of validation overlaps with, but is not identical to, empathy. In her scheme one must be able to empathize to validate. Validation is communicating to the client that the client's responses make sense or that the client is a being worthy of attention. Validation is inherently valuational, whereas empathy is not (most authors see empathy as involving the suspension of judgment). As Linehan portrays it, validation is a higher-order construct that involves all three of Carl Rogers's therapeutic conditions. One must have unconditional positive regard for the client, one must be able to empathically grasp the meanings in their communications and actions, and one must be able to respond genuinely (validation will work only if it is genuine). At the same time, validation is more than just a synthesis of Rogers's three therapeutic conditions in that it is also, as conceived of from Linehan's behavioral perspective, a therapeutic strategy.

Linehan's validation model is integrative in that it subsumes and includes both client-centered and psychodynamic views of empathy. Levels two and three are similar to Rogerian "communicative attunement" empathy, and level four is akin to psychodynamic attempts to understand the client's experience in terms of history. Level five, validating by trying to see the sense in the client's behavior right *now*, is similar to the client-centered notion of finding the "positive thrust" in the client's behavior (Gendlin, 1967) as a way of being empathic. Linehan's model thus provides a coherent framework and rationale for using different types of empathy. However, empathy is not central for her, but rather is in service of validation. Her model suggests we look at empathy from a different angle, and suggests the possibility that validation may be at the heart of some of the positive effects we have heretofore attributed to empathy.

Aspects of Linehan's construct of validation have an affinity with Buber's ideas of confirmation and also the importance of the interpersonal affirming process (Greenberg, Rice, & Elliott, 1993). For Buber, in particular, confirmation is recognizing the uniqueness of the other person and affirming both his or her existence and his or her potential for growth (Friedman, 1994).

Empathy Versus Compassion, Sympathy, or Unconditional Positive Regard

A consideration of validation raises the issue of the relationship of empathy to other constructs such as sympathy, compassion, and unconditional positive regard, all of which involve liking or "feeling for" the client. Many writers on psychotherapy have distinguished between empathy, as an effort to perceive and comprehend the subjective world of the client, on the one hand, and liking and prizing the client, or feeling sympathy and compassion for the client's plight, on the other. Sympathy and compassion have been seen as particularly suspect because they might erroneously cause the therapist to inappropriately take the client's side, lose objectivity, and perhaps try to "rescue" the client rather than help clients help themselves. Yet Bachelor (1988) found that clients perceive therapists' compassion as empathic. In addition, in social psychology, the measure of empathy used by Batson and his colleagues (e.g., Batson & Weeks, 1996) is essentially a measure of compassion. In fact, compassion can be empathic. To feel compassion for someone, one must comprehend his or her point of view and experience to some degree. However compassion alone without sustained empathic understanding can be countertherapeutic. It is not uncommon in everyday life for people to feel compassion based on apprehending the fact that the other person is suffering but completely misperceive and misunderstand what the person is really trying to communicate about what is bothering them and what it is like to be them. Therapists, too, can do this, believing they are being empathic because they feel compassion for the client's plight, but misunderstand the complexity of the client's experience because the therapist is primarily seeing the client through the therapist's theoretical preconceptions.

On the other hand, as Shlien has noted, empathy *without* some kind of sympathy or compassion could be used in a manipulative or cruel fashion. Perhaps it is fair to say that empathic understanding without compassion can be manipulative and dangerous, and compassion without empathic understanding can be shortsighted and of limited therapeutic value.

With respect to holding unconditional positive regard for the client, Bozarth has argued that this is inextricably bound up with empathy. Although empathy and regard can be distinguished conceptually, they go hand in hand in therapeutic practice. It is worth noting that unconditional positive regard is not conceptually the same as sympathy and compassion. It is prizing the whole person—having respect for them and not necessarily feeling sympathy or compassion for their plight in life. It is more akin to Linehan's concept of validation. We agree that empathy, to function benificiently, must be coupled with genuine positive regard and respect for the client.

All of this raises the issue of what is the healing element of empathy: Is it the fact that the therapist *understands* the client's subjective world or is it that the therapist *understands and validates* some aspects of the client's subjective world, *prizes and respects* the client, and has some *sympathy and compassion* for what they are going through? Perhaps empathy works in part because it makes the therapist's validation, prizing, and feeling for the client more believable and more real. This is certainly implied in Linehan's concept of validation and in Bozarth's view. An important empirical question is thus: Is it empathic understanding per se, or is it validation, prizing, and compassion, backed up by deep empathic understanding, that is healing?

Conclusions

Integrating the above together, empathy is a higher-order construct and includes a number of different dimensions. It involves the most basic aspect of person perception, the perception that there are other minds (Eagle & Wolitsky). A minimal level of empathy appears to be a universal human necessity for functioning in an interpersonal world, and empathy skills can enhance interpersonal functioning in a variety of ways (Feshbach). Those who cannot read the mind states of others (Baron-Cohen, 1995), at least to some degree, would be unable to function in an interpersonal context. In addition, empathy can involve more complex forms of interpersonal understanding as well as the ability to "taste" and share the experience of the other to at least some degree.

We believe it is helpful to define a construct of *therapeutic empathy* and to distinguish it from empathy per se. Therapeutic empathy is an ongoing, interactive process of coming to know and understand another person for the purpose of facilitating their growth, development, and problem resolution. This definition emphasizes the process nature of therapeutic empathy and distinguishes it from the kind of empathy studied by developmental psychologists (e.g., feeling the same feeling as another person). It further explicitly includes the intention to help another person as part of its definition, whereas empathy per se could be used malevolently (Shlien, Chapter 3, this volume), such as in the service of manipulating another person.

Therapeutic empathy consists of the following components. First, it is most basically an attitude or stance toward the client. It includes regard for the client and a genuine respect for the client's point of view. It also includes a belief that there is a kind of validity to clients' feelings, behaviors, and experience when seen from their point of view (Linehan). Second, it is an experience. Therapists directly perceive and experience the *client* in relationship to themselves, *themselves* in relationship to the client, and the *relationship* itself. These experiences can provide clues to what the client is experiencing. One of these experiences may consist of having a similar emotional reaction to that of the client. In addition, therapists experience their efforts to attune to and understand the client. They may be able to "taste" or vicariously experience some of the complexity of the client's life and problems. Therapists may specifically try to vicariously attune their experience to that of the client, and then, by imaginatively reaching inside, help the client access new potentials for experiencing or function as "surrogate experiencers" and help carry forward the client's experiencing. Therapist may also tune into their own reactions in response to the client's experience and use those to gain an empathic sense of the client.

Based on their immediate perceptions and experience, therapists can develop inferences concerning the client's subjective world. These can be targeted at the client's immediate here-and-now communications (what is the client saying) and associated experience (what it is like to be the client right now) or can be targeted toward getting a "background" sense of the client's whole situation (what it is like to be the client in a more general sense). These may be relatively "immediate-level" inferences directed toward aspects of the client's experience that are presently available or inferences directed at the hidden experiential world of the client—the world of early childhood experiences and the implicit and unconscious organizing principles that make up that world.

Empathy may or may not be directly expressed. Empathy may also be communicated indirectly. Therapists may self-disclose in ways that show an empathic awareness of the client's experience. Or they may respond with a suggestion or a comment that demonstrates an empathic grasp of how the client is feeling and experiencing. For some clients the best expression of empathy will be for the therapist to *not* directly share empathic understanding but to demonstrate it through respecting the distance between them or through suggesting task-focused interventions. An intense empathic focus on joining, meeting, conveying understanding, and emoting may be, paradoxically, invasive and nonempathic for some clients. In this, empathy and respect for "where the client is at" must go hand in hand to be *truly* empathic.

Empathy also can be a way of being, and not just an intervention, or a basis for interventions. Mutual empathy, consisting of the struggle to empathically meet each other, includes sensitive openness, and self-disclosure, and a willingness and desire for the client to empathically know the therapist. This provides the relational base for the development of genuine psychological contact between persons.

Finally, validation, as a behavioral strategy, overlaps with many aspects of empathy. It can include immediate-level recognition of what the client is saying and feeling, as well as inferences about what is implicit. A particular focus is on the potential "wisdom" in whatever the client may have done.

FUNCTIONS OF EMPATHY

The functions of empathy in therapy can be broken into (a) the function in the therapeutic relationship and (b) functions for the client. The functions for the client can be further subdivided into process and outcome functions. We conclude this section by discussing the function of empathy and its relation to diversity issues.

Function in the Relationship

Empathy is hypothesized to play a significant role in forming a helpful therapeutic relationship. It promotes safety, it can lead to greater client openness and self-disclosure, it can lessen resistance (Jenkins), and it can dissolve fear and denial (Barrett-Lennard). In addition, feeling understood increases clients' confidence in what the therapist has to offer and is an essential part of a collaborative, cooperative relationship (Bohart & Tallman). Finally, therapists' and clients' working through misunderstanding experiences can have a number of positive benefits for the relationship (Jordan). Such working through can also result in several beneficial outcomes to the client, such as greater client self-acceptance of imperfection and greater client trust in others.

But the function of empathy can be even more basic. For O'Hara and Jordan one could say there really is no "therapeutic" relationship if it is not empathic. Questioning Western culture's emphasis on the idea of separate selves, they argue that selves *are* selves-in-relationship. Empathy is fundamentally and essentially *mutual meeting*. These authors, as do Trop and Stolorow, hold the idea of relationship is an emergent, higher-order unit of human existence. The views of O'Hara and Jordan are compatible with those who see therapy as a creative process of coconstructive dialogue (e.g., Neimeyer & Mahoney, 1995; Snyder, 1994). Therapy is primarily discovery rather than the application of treatment. Empathy is crucial because it is the process by which therapist and client dialogue, share, codiscover, and cocreate new meaning.

Function for Clients

For clients, empathy serves two sets of functions. The first set deals with the process of therapy: How does empathy facilitate the client processes that are presumed to result in change in therapy? The second set concerns client outcomes: How might empathy directly lead to changes in client functioning? Process and outcome are interconnected, and some of the effects presumed to be due to empathy are both processes and outcomes (e.g., changes in how clients listen to and explore themselves).

Facilitation of Client Process

Empathy is postulated to facilitate client process in a number of ways. By helping put experiencing into words, empathy facilitates self-exploration, the development of self-understanding, client dialectical thinking, and clients' telling their story. By reducing interpersonal anxiety, it facilitates openness to intrapersonal experience, the accessing of deep experiencing potential, and the unblocking of the process of experiencing. By directing attention internally, it facilitates the recognition and owning of one's own experience. By attending and symbolization, it facilitates clients going deeper, exploring the edges of their experience, and accessing aspects that have heretofore been implicit. It can also facilitate emotional processing by arousing emotion and then helping to put previously inchoate experience into words, which allows it to be more easily assimilated into existing meanings. It can also lead to therapist interpretations that can help clients access unconscious aspects of experience. By empathically dealing with clients' perception of therapist's empathic failures, empathy can facilitate the working through of self–object transferences. By becoming aware of and symbolizing what is felt, it facilitates clients' moving out of a helpless orientation, heightens perceptions of control, and helps them adopt a more mastery-oriented stance toward their problems. Finally, by contacting the other and providing an experience of meeting, empathy confirms people's experience and possibilities and thereby reduces feelings of vulnerability and isolation.

In Linehan's scheme, empathy is part of the validation process. Validation is postulated to facilitate the therapeutic process through facilitating the development of: the therapeutic relationship, acceptance (particularly self-acceptance), and an understanding of ones' own behavior and of behavior in general. Furthermore, it is postulated to strengthen clinical progress by reinforcing positive changes.

A large number of different complex effects of empathy are thus postulated. Much investigation is needed to subject these to empirical test.

Facilitation of Client Outcome

Empathy is postulated to lead to changes in the self and in how the self relates to others. It is suggested that empathy leads to increased self-acceptance, increased self-congruence and self-harmony, lessened self-criticism, lessened shame, heightened self-validation, changes in how one represents one's needs and one's self in relation to others, and the development of a more functional self-concept. In more general terms, it can lead to self-actualization (Bozarth), to self-structuralization (Rowe, MacIsaac), and to the development of the relational self (Jordan, O'Hara).

Self-Empathy. Several authors, Barrett-Lennard in particular, have targeted increases in client self-empathy as a major therapeutic outcome. Self-empathy involves two major processes. The first is self-acceptance. Self-acceptance means a nonjudgmental acknowledging of one's own thoughts, feelings, and experiences. It also means allowing into awareness one's experience and being able to recognize one's experience (Warner). Clients move from a generally critical, self-rejecting, self-distrusting stance, in which they are liable to feel intense shame, toward a more self-accepting stance. This, in turn, facilitates self-exploration and discovery. This results in greater self-understanding and a new, more functional view of the self and, ultimately, to problem resolution.

The second major process is the development of the ongoing ability to refer inwardly to experience and to articulate it. Symbolizing experience in words gives clients a greater sense of control of their experience by helping them to know what they feel. In addition, it helps them formulate new directions and behavioral alternatives. This could be called developing a capacity to be open to experience, and leads to more fluid experiencing and a greater capacity to make flexible decisions. Barrett-Lennard particularly develops a view of how the ability of the "articulate self" to listen to and relate to the experiential self facilitates personal problem solving and growth.

Self-Validation. In a similar manner, Linehan has suggested that therapist validation can lead to client self-validation. This means that one comes to recognize that (a) there is some "sense" in one's own responses and (b) one is, in general, a person worthy of attention. Other therapists, too, see empathy as leading to self-validation. However, Linehan has explicitly articulated different levels of validation. She has also differentiated it from empathy (although empathy is needed as part of validation). She notes that empathy is presumably nonjudgmental, whereas validation specifically makes a judgment—a positive one. We suspect that for many authors the concept of validation is *implicit* in their views of empathy. Yet they have not worked out how a presumably nonjudgmental activity—empathy—can be validating. Further theoretical and empirical work clarifying the relationship of empathy to validation is needed.

The concept of validation goes to a deeper level of empathy than some therapists pursue. For instance, it does not fit with the way empathy is used in cognitive therapy. While a cognitive therapist such as Beck may be empathic in recognizing a client's emotional experience (Linehan's levels one and two), Beck does not "dig for" what could be called the "implicit logic" in the client's experience (Linehan's level five). Rather, it is assumed that the client's experience is being created by dysfunctional cognitions and the focus is on identifying and modifying these cognitions.

Along with Linehan, we particularly want to highlight an important function of empathy, that of the respectful *empathic recognition* of the client as a unique other person, and along with this, the acceptant recognition of his or her right to have his or her own experience. This is fundamentally validating of the client's personhood, and we believe, a fundamentally important outcome of therapy.

Self-Actualization and Accessing Deep Experiencing Potential. Client-centered therapists believe that empathy (along with unconditional positive regard and congruence) provides a condition in which clients' own intrinsic actualizing tendencies can operate. Clients will naturally and spontaneously confront issues that are important to them, struggle to understand and master them, and evolve idiosyncratic but personally meaningful solutions if given this kind of climate. Although Mahrer does not call it self-actualization, for him empathy can help the client access deep experiencing potential, which is the potential for idiosyncratically creating meaningful new ways of being and behaving.

Self-Structuralization. Self-psychologists believe that empathic understanding, interpreting, and explaining will help with client self-structuralization. Clients gradually develop the capacity to take initiative and to have ambitions, and they develop the capacity to choose personally meaningful values and set meaningful goals. They also develop capacities to deal with stress, to self-soothe, and to hold themselves together. Therapist empathy helps the client develop self-coherence and a sense of vitality. Finally, clients develop a capacity for self-empathy. Although there is no empirical evidence for these speculations, some developmental research (Feshbach) has found that parental empathy facilitates children becoming high achievers, compatible with the idea that therapist empathy could facilitate the development of the ability to take initiative and to set meaningful goals.

Facilitation of Empathy Toward Others. Both Barrett-Lennard and Jordan hold that the experience of empathy in psychotherapy facilitates the development of client relational skills, particularly the client's ability to empathize with others. This seems plausible on the basis of developmental findings (Feshbach) that parental empathy contributes to the development of empathy in children. Going further, Feshbach argues that the development of empathy skills can enhance social functioning in a variety of ways, including the ability to identify emotions in oneself and others, the ability to take the perspective of others, and the ability to articulate and express emotion. This position is compatible with the views of Synder (1994) who, following Mead, has argued that "the ability to put oneself in the role of the other and perceive reality as the other perceives it, is the foundation of [social] intelligence" (p. 87). If so, development of client empathy is an important potential outcome of therapist empathy.

Ethnocultural and Gender Issues and the Function of Empathy. Jenkins, O'Hara, and Jordan each comment on the importance of empathy for working with diverse populations. Jenkins notes that empathy is particularly important in working with people of color, who tend to distrust professionals. Although many people of diverse cultures prefer approaches to therapy that emphasize instrumental activities to approaches that emphasize open-ended self-exploration, empathy nonetheless is essential in establishing a good working relationship, so that the instrumental phase of therapy can be implemented. In addition, it can have an especially curative function if a White professional can empathize with a client who is a person of color. Jordan and O'Hara both suggest an alternative way of conceptualizing human beings, based on the experience of groups traditionally underrepresented in American psychological theorizing—women and people of other cultures. For these groups empathy is a more fundamental mode of relating and knowing than the rational, conceptual, inferential processes favored in this culture. The implication of this is that empathy may be far more important than North American (male) psychotherapists realize, being perhaps the dominant communicative modality and way of being together for many women and many people of other cultures.

Conclusions

The functions postulated for empathy in therapy are multiform. Empathy contributes to the therapeutic relationship in major ways, building the therapeutic bond and reducing defensiveness. However, empathy is postulated to be a far-more-potent ingredient than simply a contributor to the relationship. First, it actively facilitates important client processes such as dialectical thinking, working through of self–object transferences, emotional reprocessing, and so on. Second, it is postulated to lead to important outcomes, such as changes in the self. Clearly what is needed at this point is research to explore if these effects of empathy do indeed occur.

IMPLICATIONS

On the basis of the above, we present an integrative summary of therapeutic empathy. Therapeutic empathy is first of all a complex *process* (see also Bozarth; Duan & Hill, 1996) that includes different aspects. It is a way of helping people to explore their experience, both inner and outer, and to create new meaning. We feel that the focus on empathy as a single thing rather than to appreciate it as a process with a complex set of operations has led to a sort of oversimplified and restricted view of empathy that often breaks out into a dichotomous debate. Thus, we have the dichotomy of cognitive versus affect, attitude versus behavior, momentary experience versus life situation, shallow versus deep, and expressed versus unexpressed. The empathic *process* contains all these and more. In therapy we need to articulate the empathic process and get away from restrictive dichotomies. Empathic process in therapy involves a feedback cycle in which one attends to the client with a genuine interest in understanding the world from the client's point of view and has respect for the client's subjective world and for the client as an authentic source of experience. In this process one needs to perceive what the client is feeling, attempt to understand their communications, imaginatively enter their world, and engage in a complex process of comprehending what it is like for that person to be that person. This is a full-bodied integrative experience in which multiple sources of information, including cognition and affect, are used, possibly including one's own feeling, one's own prior experiences, as well as any current reverberatory feeling one might have through the process of imaginative entry. This comprehensive process is both a conceptual process and an experiential process. It is not a singular act but varies according to that which is being understood in the moment—it may be understanding a feeling ("you felt really alone") or a complex narrative of a person's perception of an event ("it was somehow the way he looked at you that led you to feel so small and led you to react so angrily"), or at another time a high level synthesis of complex experience ("and this was the final rejection"), or at still another time identifying an idiosyncratic meaning ("this meant: 'I've finally proved it.'"). The type of processing the therapist is involved in at each point differs—at one point it is affect perception, at another narrative reconstruction, at a third articulation of the immediate and emerging implications in what the client is saying, and at still another more of an abstract synthesis. The empathic process is not a simple or singular thing.

Therapeutic empathy is also a coconstructive process that includes the client, in essence, forming a "joint mind." Each party is building on the other—the two individual processes, that of the client's exploration, experiencing, and cogitation and that of the therapist's, joint to create a larger emerging gestalt, based on two people focusing on the same thing. In this effort nobody is trying to control; it is one of coexploring. It involves constant checking and rechecking and reconstructing. This therapeutic process is an ongoing dynamic one, like navigating when one is sailing a boat. The client helps the therapist sharpen understanding, and the therapist helps the client sharpen understanding. Both are converging towards a coconstructed new meaning.

This process can involve all different kinds of therapeutic responses, including reflection, empathic inquiry, experience-near interpretations, empathic conjectures, keeping an empathic distance when necessary, empathic silence, openness and dialogue, and the responsive use of techniques. It can lead to a wide range of outcomes, including the development of a stronger therapeutic alliance, sensitive application of technique, the facilitation of clients' articulation of their experience, insight into unconscious aspects, working through of transference issues, and development and strengthening of various aspects of the self and of self-relationship and interpersonal-relationship skills.

Training

A topic we have not considered in this book is the training of empathy. In the past, empathy training for therapists has largely consisted of training in empathy response skills, along the lines of programs such as those of Carkhuff (Cash, 1984) and Egan (1984). As we have pointed out, therapeutic empathy is a complex cognitive–affective interactive process. We believe new training programs need to be developed that emphasize the complex set of cognitive and affective skills involved (see, for instance, Phillips et al., 1994). We believe it is not enough merely to learn how to respond. Future therapists, especially in an increasingly pluralistic society, must really learn how to enter into another's world and walk in their shoes. How they respond and what they say from that ability is really secondary. As we have repeatedly emphasized in our introductory and in this chapter, genuine empathy is not merely a mechanical skill, be it the use of empathic reflections or even the ability to cognitively role take. It must involve a genuine *interest* in entering another's world, gaining a real "feel for" what it is like to be them, and in essence, developing some sense of a "we" feeling with them. This is really the key element of the therapeutic bond—the sense that the client can rely on the therapist because the two of them are "in it together" and because the therapist *really* understands them, not just in some cognitive, intellectually deduced fashion. We believe future empathy-training programs for therapists should involve some of the skills Feshbach and her colleagues have developed for training empathy in children—exercises designed to increase accurate perceptual awareness of the other's emotional states, exercises designed to facilitate internal self-awareness, and exercises designed to give extensive practice in walking in the other's shoes. For instance, in a recent program, Feshbach and Feshbach (in press) have built empathy training into the school curriculum. When children study Columbus's arrival in the New World, they are asked what it would have been like to have experienced it through the eyes of a Native American. Such exercises could profitably be included in clinical training programs whenever a graduate student is asked to evaluate a case and develop a treatment plan. Such exercises could also be designed to sensitize therapists to their implicit cultural assumptions and how those assumptions affect understanding of their clients.

Future Directions in Research

Empirically, a deeper study of empathy is required with an emphasis on both discovery-oriented research that probes both therapists' experience of being empathic and clients' experience of receiving empathy to help understand the nature and functioning of empathy. As well, research on the specific and more global effects of empathy is needed. Novel views need to be tested such as the effects of empathy on clients' empathic abilities. The possibility (not discussed in this volume) that empathy has direct physiological effects, on both client and therapist (e.g., Lynch, 1985), bears investigation. The differences between empathy targeted at moment-to-moment experience and empathy targeted at making interpretations of the unconscious also warrents investigation. The old hypothesis that empathy leads to increased depth of self-exploration and, in turn, to outcome was too undifferentiated and failed to gather sufficient support. What is required are more probing attempts to understand and demonstrate the effects of empathy in human relating. Such questions as when is empathy most helpful, with whom, and what preceeding conditions (such as a good alliance) need to prevail for it to be helpful need to be investigated.

To achieve this, it will be necessary for researchers to specify exactly what component of empathy they are measuring. It will no longer be useful simply to say that one is measuring "empathy." For instance, if "feeling understood" is one outcome of therapist empathy, what components produce the experience of feeling understood? Are these components the same or different than those that might lead a client to feel psychologically contacted and empathically "met"? In addition, new operational definitions are needed. For instance, someone studying empathy from Trop and Stolorow's perspective might wish to measure empathy by using an Interpersonal Process Recall (Elliott, 1986) with the therapist after the session because the function of empathy is primarily data collection for the therapist. A researcher studying relational empathy, postulated to be a process occurring between the two participants, might want to look at the development of "fluency" in understanding between the two and the fluency and ease with which the two work towards correcting misunderstandings. In particular, the idea of empathy as "meeting" or as the making of psychological contact needs further specification and operational definition. Related to this, Mahrer's claim that he is able to empathically align with the client and "become" the voice of the client's deep experiencing potential also needs to be investigated. Tapes of therapy sessions could be played for clients, and they could be asked whether they felt a response by Mahrer was empathically attuned to their experiencing, or whether they felt it was Mahrer who was actually suggesting a new direction for experiencing.

After having developed good operational definitions, the next order of business will be to look at types of empathy and their relationships to various hypothesized functions in therapy. For instance, affective empathy (sharing the same emotion) and empathic understanding may not serve the same functions (Duan & Hill, 1996). We suspect that affective empathy may particularly help build a therapeutic bond and provide safety for many clients, whereas complex experiential understanding may particularly facilitate self-exploration and self-reorganization processes. The kind of empathic relatedness emphasized by O'Hara and Jordan may be especially helpful in facilitating the development of client relational skills.

The importance of validating some of the hypotheses concerning empathy presented in this book cannot be overstated. In a managed-care era where some see therapy as nothing more than the technological application of certain procedures and where the humanness of the relationship is minimized, those who believe that empathy is more than merely a background contributor will have to demonstrate that trying to deeply understand another human being has important effects of its own.

REFERENCES

Bachelor, A. (1988). How clients perceive therapist empathy: A content analysis of "received" empathy. *Psychotherapy, 25,* 227–240.

Baron-Cohen, S. (1995). *Mindblindness: An essay on autism and theory of mind.* Cambridge, MA: Massachusetts Institute of Technology Press.

Barrett-Lennard, G. (1993). The phases and focus of empathy. *British Journal of Medical Psychology, 66,* 3–14.

Batson, C. D., & Weeks, J. L. (1996). Mood effects of unsuccessful helping: Another test of the empathy–altruism hypothesis. *Personality and Social Psychology Bulletin, 22,* 148–157.

Berger, D. M. (1987). *Clinical empathy.* Northvale, NJ: Jason Aronson.

Beutler, L. E., Crago, M., & Arizmendi, T. G. (1986). Therapist variables in psychotherapy process and outcome. In S. L. Garfield & A. E. Bergin (Eds.), *Handbook of psychotherapy and behavior change* (3rd ed., pp. 257–310). New York: Wiley.

Bohart, A. (1980). Toward a cognitive theory of catharsis. *Psychotherapy: Theory, Research, and Practice, 17,* 192–201.

Bohart, A., & Rosenbaum, R. (1995). The dance of empathy: Empathy, diversity, and technical eclecticism. *The Person-Centered Journal, 2,* 5–29.

Bozarth, J. D. (1984). Beyond reflection: Emergent modes of empathy. In R. F. Levant & J. M. Shlien (Eds.), *Client-centered therapy and the person-centered approach* (pp. 59–75). New York: Praeger.

Buie, D. (1981). Discussion. In J. Lichtenberg, M. Bornstein, & D. Silver (Eds.), *Empathy* (Vol. 1, pp. 129–136). Hillsdale, NJ: Analytic Press.

Burns, D. D. (1980). *Feeling good.* New York: William Morrow.

Cash, R. W. (1984). The human resources development model. In D. Larson (Ed.), *Teaching psychological skills* (pp. 245–270). Monterey, CA: Brooks/Cole.

Duan, C., & Hill, C. E. (1996). A critical review of empathy research. *Journal of Counseling Psychology, 43,* 261–274.

Egan, G. (1984). Skilled helping: A problem-management framework for helping and helper training. In D. Larson (Ed.), *Teaching psychological skills* (pp. 133–150). Monterey, CA: Brooks/Cole.

Elliott, R. (1986). Interpersonal Process Recall (IPR) as a psychotherapy process research method. In L. S. Greenberg & W. M. Pinsof (Eds.), *The psychotherapeutic process* (pp. 503–528). New York: Guilford Press.

Elliott, R., Filipovich, H., Harrigan, L., Gaynor, J., Reimschuessel, C., & Zapadka, J. K. (1982). Measuring response empathy: The development of a multi-component rating scale. *Journal of Counseling Psychology, 29,* 379–387.

Feshbach, N. D., & Feshbach, S. (in press). Aggression in the schools: Ethnic conflict, ethnic identity, and ethnic understanding. In P. K. Trickett & C. Schellenbach (Eds.), *Violence against children in the family and in the community.* Washington, DC: American Psychological Association.

Friedman, M. (1994). Reflections on the Buber–Rogers dialogue. *Journal of Humanistic Psychology, 34,* 46–65.

Gendlin, E. T. (1967). Therapeutic procedures in dealing with schizophrenics. In C. R. Rogers, E. T. Gendlin, D. J. Kiesler, & C. B. Truax (Eds.), *The therapeutic relationship and its impact* (pp. 369–400). Madison: University of Wisconsin Press.

Gladstein, G. A., & Associates. (1987). *Empathy and counseling: Explorations in theory and research.* New York: Springer-Verlag.

Greenberg, L. S., Rice, L. N., & Elliott, R. (1993). *Facilitating emotional change: The moment by moment process.* New York: Guilford.

Greenberg, L. S., & Safran, J. D. (1987). *Emotion in psychotherapy.* New York: Guilford Press.

Hammond, D. C., Hepworth, D. H., & Smith, V. G. (1980). *Improving therapeutic communication.* San Francisco: Jossey-Bass.

Leitner, L. M. (1995). Optimal therapeutic distance: A therapist's experience of personal construct psychotherapy. In R. A. Neimeyer & M. J. Mahoney (Eds.), *Constructivism in psychotherapy* (pp. 357–370). Washington, DC: American Psychological Association.

Lynch, J. L. (1985). *The language of the heart: The body's response to human dialogue.* New York: Basic Books.

Maturana, H., & Varela, F. J. (1987). *The tree of knowledge: The biological roots of human understanding.* Boston: New Science Library.

Neimeyer, R. A., & Mahoney, M. J. (Eds.). (1995). *Constructivism in psychotherapy.* Washington, DC: American Psychological Association.

Olmstad, B. L. (1995). *Cognitive appraisal, emotion, and empathy.* Mahwah, NJ: Erlbaum.

Phillips, A., Lipson, A., & Basseches, M. (1994). Empathy and listening skills: A developmental perspective on learning to listen. In V. Sinnott (Ed.), *Interdisciplinary handbook of adult lifespan learning* (pp. 301–324). Westport, CT: Greenwood Press.

Resnick, L. B., Levine, J. M., & Teasley, S. D. (Eds.). (1991). *Perspectives on socially shared cognition.* Washington, DC: American Psychological Association.

Selman, R. L. (1980). *The growth of interpersonal understanding.* New York: Academic Press.

Snyder, M. (1994). The development of social intelligence in psychotherapy: Empathic and dialogic processes. *Journal of Humanistic Psychology, 34,* 84–108.

Truax, C. B., & Carkhuff, R. R. (1967). *Toward effective counseling and psychotherapy.* Chicago: Aldine.

Wachtel, P. (1993). *Therapeutic communication.* New York: Guilford Press.

AUTHOR INDEX

Guerney, B. G., 7, 27, 117, *120*
Guisinger, S., 296, *317*
Guitkin, T. B., 322, *340*
Gurman, A. S., 17, 18, 28, 235, *243*
Guzman, R., 26, *185*

Haase, R. F., 22, *30*
Hadley, S. W., 395, *414*
Hagen, R. L., *54*
Haldane, J. B. S., 315, *317*
Ham, M. A., 22, *28*
Hamilton, J. W., 223, 238, *243*
Hammond, D. C., 431, *449*
Hargrove, D. S., 16, *28*
Harigan, L., *413*
Harrigan, L., 27, 243, *448*
Hart, J., 7, *28*
Harvey, J. H., 6, 28, 407, *413*
Harvey, S., 20, *30*
Havens, L. L., 11, 28, 188, 190, 193, 194, 200, 208, *212, 213*
Heard, H. L., 354, 391, *392*
Hefferline, R. F., 66, *80*
Heinz, S. P., 268, *277*
Helms, J., 337, *339*
Henderson, V., *80*
Henry, W. P., 22, *28*
Hepworth, D. H., 431, *449*
Hess, E. H., 78, *80*
Hill, C. E., 15, 26, 170, *186*, 434, 444, 447, *448*
Hill, D. E., 21, *29*
Hines, M. H., 114, *120*
Hockney, D., 316, *317*
Hoffman, M. L., 23, 24, 28, 35, 36, 37, 38, 40, 43, 46, 57, 58, 59, 218, 219, 226, 243, 244, 324, *339*
Holt, R. R., 219, 226, 229, *243*
Hopkins, J., *55*
Horvath, A. O., 13, 19, *28*
Houlihan, D., *55*
Howard, G. S., 323, 329, *339*
Howard, J. A., 46, 47, 49, 54, *58*
Howes, C., 42, *57*
Hoyt, M. F., 394, *413*
Hughes, M. A., 49, *58*
Hummel, T. J., 114, *120*
Humphrey, A., 26, *185*
Hunt, E. J., 48, *59*

Iannotti, R. J., 46, 49, *58*
Isaac, D. S., 200, *213*
Isaak, M. I., 399, *413*

Jacobs, M., 395, *413*
Jacobson, N. S., 12, 26, 395, *412, 413*
Jacobson, R. S., *59*
Jaffe, D. S., 188, *212*
Jaffe, J., 24, *25*
Jahoda, M., 112, *120*
Jenkins, A. H., 323, 328, 334, *339*
Johnson, B., 16, 21, *28*
Johnson, M., 404, *413*
Johnston, W. A., 268, *277*
Jones, E. E., 321, 322, 323, 326, 327, 331, *339*
Jones, J. M., 337, *339*
Jones, R. L., 301, *317*
Jordan, J. V., 301, 307, 314, *317*, 343, 344, 345, 346, 347, 349, *351*, 351
Josephs, L., 225, 226, 227, *244*
Joyce, A. S., 169, *186*
Just, M. A., 399, *413*

Kagan, N., 16, *28*
Kanitz, B. E., 322, *340*
Kaplan, A. G., 301, *317, 351*
Kasari, C., 49, *58*
Katz, R. L., 111, 113, *120*
Kay, D., 20, *30*
Keats, J., 344, *351*
Kemeny, V., 18, *27*
Kiesler, D. J., 20, *28*
Kieth, B., 48, *53*
King, A., 312, *318*
King, L. M., 46, *54*
King, R., *40*
Kirschenbaum, H., 72, 73, 80, 84, 85, 86, 94, 95, *100*
Kissna, K. N., *80*
Klein, M., 20, 28, 106, *120*
Kleinberg, J. L., 117, *120*
Kluver, H., 71, *80*
Knight, G., 35, *55*
Koch, S., 73, *80*
Koestler, A., 307, *318*
Koestner, R., 43, *58*
Kohut, H., 10, 28, 45, 58, 81, 100, 113, *120*, 127, 128, 138, *140*, 188,

Mindell, A., 92, *101*
Mitchell, K. M., 4, 17, 18, *29*, *31*, 114,
    121
Mitchell, S., 10, *29*
Moore, M. K., 219, *244*
Moynihan, D. W., 91, *100*, 395, *413*
Murphy, G., 70, 80, *244*
Murray, E. J., 395, *414*
Murray, H. A., 199, *213*
Mutchler, R. D., 48, *59*
Mutchler, T. E., 48, *59*

Neighbors, H. W., 334, *340*
Neimeyer, R. A., 12, *29*, 440, *449*
Neisser, U., 402, *413*
Neufeldt, S. A., *26*
Neville, B., 92, *101*
Nickerson, R. S., 398, *413*
Nolen-Hoeksema, S., 18, *26*
Nurius, P., 332, *340*

Oberlander, M., 106, *120*
O'Hara, M. M., 296, 300, 302, *317*,
    318, 395, *414*
Olden, C., 200, *213*
O'Leary, E., 38, 44, *57*
Olinick, S., 148, *164*
Olmstad, B. L., 24, *29*, *449*
Olsen, K. H., 48, *59*
Orbuch, T. L., 6, *28*, 407, *413*
Orlinsky, D. E., 7, 15, 18, *29*, 394, *414*
Ornstein, P. H., 247, *264*

Paivio, S., 6, *27*, 169, *186*
Parham, T. A., 337, *340*
Parks, B. K., 7, *29*
Pascual-Leone, J., 184, *185*, *186*
Patterson, C. H., 18, *29*
Paul, G. L., 394, *414*
Pearce, J., 322, *340*
Pennebaker, J. W., 6, *29*, 169, *186*,
    407, *414*
Perls, F., 66, *80*
Pettit, G. S., *242*
Phillips, A., 431, 445, *449*
Phinney, J., 40, *59*
Piaget, J., 267, *277*
Pigman, G. W., *244*
Piper, W. E., 169, *186*

Polanyi, M., 306, 314, *318*
Polkinghorne, D., 329, *340*
Ponterotto, J. G., 337, *340*
Pound, A., 44, *55*
Powell, A. L., *54*
Puckering, C., 44, *55*

Quintana, S. M., 112, *121*

Racker, H., 232, *244*
Radke-Yarrow, M., 35, 36, 39, 40, 46,
    59
Rappaport, J., 18, *26*
Raskin, N. J., 7, *29*, 88, 94, *101*, 111,
    121, 406, *414*
Rawlins, M. R., 322, *339*
Raylor, C. A., *29*
Reik, T., 226, *244*
Reimschuessel, C., *27*, *243*, *413*, *448*
Rennie, D. L., 22, *29*, 404, *414*
Reno, R., *55*
Resnick, L. B., 434, *449*
Rhodes, R. H., 16, 21, 28, *29*
Rice, L. N., 8, 9, 20, *27*, *29*, *31*, 128,
    133, 134, *139*, *140*, 148, *164*,
    167, 180, *186*, 436, *448*
Ridgeway, D., *54*
Ridley, C. R., 322, *340*
Rief, A., 38, *58*
Riggs, D. S., 385, *391*
Robinson, D. N., 330, *340*
Robinson, E., 20, *30*
Robinson, J. L., *59*
Roe, K., 37, 38, 47, 51, *57*
Rogers, C. R., 6, 7, 8, 15, *30*, *59*, 68,
    73, *80*, 81, 82, 83, 84, 85, 86,
    87, 88, 89, 90, 91, 93, 94, 95,
    96, 97, *101*, 104, 105, 106, 110,
    111, 112, *121*, 127, 134, *140*,
    145, *164*, 188, 200, 201, *213*,
    221, *244*, 299, 302, 313, 314,
    317, *318*, 357, 362, 377, 378,
    392
Roke, E. J., 46, *58*
Roland, A., 303, 309, *318*
Rollins, H. E., 299, *318*
Romanyshyn, R. D., 301, *318*
Rose, A., 42, *57*
Rosenbaum, R., 91, 99, 394, 395, 403,
    412, *414*, 428, *448*

SUBJECT INDEX

mutual empathy, 314
origins of pathological process,
137–138, 253
parental empathy, 41–43, 325
psychoanalytic, 10, 24
psychotherapist versus psychologist
models, 24–25
racial models, 337
relational, 343
self psychology, 239, 240–241
significance of empathy in, 23,
24–25
socialization process, 41–45, 105
See also Children and adolescents
Dialectical behavior therapy
applications, 353–354
articulating unverbalized experience
in, 364–367
causal validation of behavior in,
367–370
contextual considerations, 387
empathy in, 359–360
feedback, 390–391
listening and observing in, 360–362
mechanism of change in, 354, 355
model of behavior, 380–381
reflection in, 362–364
strategy groups, 354–355
strengthening clinical progress,
389–390
teaching self-validation in, 388–389
theoretical basis, 354
therapeutic relationship, 391
therapeutic stance, 357–358
therapeutic validation in, 356–359
types of validation, 380
validation of action, 381–382
validation of behavior as reasonable
in moment, 370–377
validation of client in, 377–380
Dialectical thinking
definition, 328
empathic listening, 403
for psychological agency, 328–329
for relational empathy, 307–308
therapeutic mechanism, 333
in therapeutic validation by listening, 361
for work with ethnic minority
clients, 331, 332, 338
See also Dialectical behavior therapy
Didactic intervention, 115

Distortions or exaggerations, response to
client's, 382, 386
Distress behavior
empathy as, 35
infant response, 219

Eclectic practice, 13
Empathic attunement
communication of, 175
mechanism of change, 185
in mutual empathy, 347, 350
in process-experiential therapy,
173–175
therapist experience in, 174
See also Expanded attunement
Empathic checking, 21, 404
Empathic complementarity, 428
Empathic conjecture, 175, 178
Empathic exploration, 20, 175,
176–178, 185
clinical example, 181–183
process-experiential tasks, 180–181
Empathic identification, 73
Empathic joining, 12
Empathic prizing, 20
Empathic-process functioning, 147–148
Empathic rapport, 13, 15
Empathic recognition, 442
Empathic reflection, 4
action of, 407
in dialectical behavior therapy,
362–364
See also Reflection of feelings
Empathic resonance, 403
clinical examples, 148–162
eliciting a felt sense in, 145–146
in empathic-process functioning,
147–148
empirical validation, 236–237
incongruence as obstacle to,
146–147
mechanism of change in, 141
therapeutic process, 162–163
therapist preparation for, 146
as way of knowing, 144–145
Empathic understanding, 67, 73, 75, 85
affective–cognitive nature of, 420,
422
client, 116
as common feature of therapeutic
conceptualizations, 420, 421

depth of, 422–423
empirical validation, 237, 426–426
experiential-tacit knowing for, 420
forms of, 423–425
Kohut's conceptualization, 250
mechanism of change in, 137–139
modalities of, 420
as observational method, 220,
      222–227, 281–282
process-experiential view, 172–172,
      175
therapist skills for, 420
Empathic-understanding response process, 94
Empathy Training Program, 50–51
Empathy Training Study, 46
Ethnic minority clients
      challenge for psychotherapy, 325
      clinical conceptualizations, 322, 443
      consideration of possible selves,
            332–333
      development of therapist in work
            with, 337–338
      developmental models, 337
      effects of empathic context,
            336–338
      empathic assessment, 325–327
      establishing relationship with,
            321–322, 326–327
      racism as narcissistic assault,
            326–327
      role of empathy, 323, 324–325
      salience of values, 323–324
      social pressures for, 334
      therapeutic self-awareness, 333–334
      therapeutic stance, 331, 335–336,
            338
      therapist preparation for work with,
            322
      within-group differences, 322–323
      See also Cross-cultural practice
Evocative empathy, 20, 175, 176
Excessive empathy
      clinical conceptualizations, 433
      overidentification, 218
      in parenting behavior, 41
      perceptions of traditional mechanistic psychiatry, 298–299
      in therapeutic sharing, 39
Existential psychology, 65
Expanded attunement
      case vignette, 270–275

clinical goals, 270
conceptual basis, 265
definition and characteristics,
      269–270
rationale, 267–268, 275–276
as tacit knowing, 421
Experience-near empathy, 14, 15, 127
      client experience of, 426
      communicative attunement and,
            425–426
      conceptual development, 246
      distinctive features, 252
      in expanded attunement, 270
      psychoanalytic conceptualizations,
            266–267
      versus experience-distant mode, 266
Experiencing
      affective-cognitive nature of, 420
      client-centered therapeutic goals,
            168
      clinical conceptualizations of empathy as, 427–428
      creation of meaning in, 143
      empathic exploration of, 180–183
      in empathic-process functioning,
            147–148
      empathic resonance as, 144–146
      felt sense in, 142–143
      felt sense-symbol interaction, 143
      focus of empathic understanding,
            423
      group thinking in sociocentric cultures, 303–306
      healthy mental functioning in,
            143–144
      of mutual empathy, 343–344
      process model, 142–144
      right to, 160
      structure-bound functioning,
            146–147, 160
      temporal orientation, 144
      therapeutic empathy as experience,
            408
      therapist's, in client-therapist alignment, 193–194
      validation of behavior as reasonable
            in moment, 370–377
      validation of behavioral causality,
            367–370
      validation of client behaviors, 359
      as way of knowing, 397
      See also Self-experience

Experiential recognition
  as empathic understanding, 421
  empathy and, 132–134
  felt meaning and, 131–132
  forms of, 130–131
  fragile style of processing life narratives, 137–138
  interpersonal responding, 131
  life narrative construction, 137
  therapeutic change in, 130
Experiential therapies
  client perspective of, 150–153, 156–162
  clinical examples, 148–162
  conceptual basis, 7
  depth of empathic understanding in, 422
  empathic understanding in, 421–422
  empathy in, 8–9
  focus of empathic understanding, 423
  integrative models, 8, 444–445. *See also* Cognitive-experiential psychotherapy; Process-experiential therapy
  levels of change, 163
  measurement of empathic processes, 20
  model of experiencing, 142–144
  process-enhancing intervention, 141
  recognition of process signals, 163
Eye contact, 189

Fear, 76, 103, 374
  accurate reflection of, 363–364
  of expressing intense emotions, 184
  prognostic indicator, 385
  of therapeutic change, 387–388
  therapeutic validation of, 385–386
Feedback, 444
Felt experience, direct reference to, 105–106
Felt meaning, 131–132
Felt sense
  in empathic-process functioning, 147–148
  in empathic resonance, 145–146
  in experiencing process, 142–143
  nature of, 397
  premature conceptualization, 148
  stimulating, in therapy, 153–162

therapeutic experience, 151
  therapist experience, 169
Feminist thought, 308–309
  empathy in, 4
Freud, S., 9, 222–224, 266, 299
Fully functioning person, 104–106

Gender differences
  clinical implications, 443
  in empathy, 43, 44–45, 434
  in empathy–aggression linkages, 46–47
Genetic capacity for empathy, 219, 402–403
Genuineness, 4, 15, 17, 18, 19, 357–358
Gestalt therapy, 12
  integrated with experiential therapies, 8
Goodman, Paul, 66
Group work, 95

Health care system, 315
Hermeneutics
  empathy as process of, 5
  of suspicion, 366
Holistic thinking, 307, 309
  in psychotherapy, 311–312
  therapeutic techniques, 312

Iatrogenic effects, 13
  articulation of client's unverbalized experiences, 366
  clinical conceptualizations, 431–434
  invalidation of client feelings, 386–387
  reinforcement of client self-mistrust, 389
  See also Excessive empathy
Imagination, 37
Imaginative empathy, 324, 330–331
Individual differences, 36
  communication of empathy, 438–439
  effects of empathy, 432–433
  within ethnic minority groups, 322–323
Inference, 421
Insight, psychoanalytic, 9

Interpersonal empathy
    characteristics, 343–344, 400
    dancelike quality, 403–404
    definition, 125–126
    as developmental need, 343
    in egocentric modernist cultures,
        296–297
    forms of, 33–34
    group intuition, 306
    healing capacity of, 314
    as measure of mental health,
        112–113
    measures of, 300
    natural tendency, 402–403
    nature of mutuality in, 346–347
    as postmodernist project of psychol-
        ogy, 295–296
    as product of therapeutic empathy,
        443
    relational view, 312–313
    self-empathy and, 104, 110–111
    self-shame as obstacle to, 346
    significance in cross-cultural prac-
        tice, 327
    significance of empathy, 434–435
    social benefits, 313
    in sociocentric cultures, 303–306
    sociocultural obstacles to, 295
    therapeutic change in, research find-
        ings, 114–117
    training, 51
    understanding as secondary goal of,
        400
    as value neutral, 249
    See also Therapeutic relationship
Interpersonal Process Recall, 16
    case examples, 149
    features, 149
    research into misunderstandings in
        therapy, 21–22
Interpretation
    accusatory, 424
    degree of inference in, 171
    empathic, action of, 408, 424
    empathy as enabling agent for, 223,
        238–239
    empathy-based, 175, 178
    empathy versus, 167, 170–172. See
        Interpretation versus empathy
    facilitative, 424
    nature of, 169–170
    premature, 148

    psychoanalytic approach, 9,
        126–127
    psychodynamic formulations, 424
    in self psychology, 10
    therapeutic goals, 170–171, 173
    therapeutic relationship in, 171–172
    validation as, 360
Interpretation versus empathy, 7, 167
    clinical conceptualizations, 423
    degrees of inference, 171
    nature of interpretation, 169–170
    therapeutic goals, 170–171
    therapeutic relationship, 171–172
    therapeutic targets, 171
    therapist perceptions, 172
Intersubjective approach
    case example, 283–290
    empathic inquiry in, 280
    in expanded attunement, 269
    principles of self-organization,
        279–280
    significance of empathy as psycholog-
        ical contact in, 435
    sustained empathic inquiry in,
        282–283
    theory and practice, 279
    therapeutic goals, 290
    therapeutic stance, 290
    transference conception, 280
Intuitive knowing as tacit knowing, 421

Kluver, Heinrich, 70–71
Kohut, Heinz, 68, 81
    abstract definition of empathy,
        247–248, 280
    case of Mrs. M., 254–262
    clinical concept of empathy,
        248–250, 280, 300–301
    contributions of, 262–263
    developmental conceptualizations,
        239
    on drive concept, 247–248
    on experience-near mode of observa-
        tion, 138–139, 266, 267, 281
    on explaining, 250–252
    on operation of empathy, 221–222,
        227–228
    optimal failure concept, 239–240
    professional development, 245–246
    selfobject concept, 240–241
    theory of pathology, 253

theory of self, 252–253, 301, 324–325

theory of therapeutic change, 113, 128, 253–254

on understanding, 250

Language of empathy, 64–65

Listening, 108, 112, 167–168
    clinical conceptualizations, 431
    empathic attunement, 173–174
    empathy as, 220–221, 401–404
    experiential, 401–402
    process-experiential view, 172–172
    psychoanalytic conceptualization, 217–218
    shared focus of attention in, 404
    therapeutic validation through, 360–362

Logical learning theory
    conceptual basis, 328
    construction of reality in, 329
    dialectical thinking in, 328–329
    self-awareness in, 333–334
    teleological conception, 330

Margulies, A., 330–331

Mead, George Herbert, 67, 70

Measurement of empathy, 115, 300
    challenges in, 34–35
    in children, 37–39
    client empathic understanding, 116
    client-therapist correlation, 16
    comparison of therapy models, 207–208, 209
    depth of patient processing, 20–21
    experiential assessment, 20
    ontogenetic pattern, 39–41
    in outcome research, 17–19
    research needs, 117–118, 446–447
    response modalities, 38
    self-empathy, 118
    stimulus modalities, 37–38
    techniques, 15–17
    temporal orientation, 21
    types of therapist responses, 175–176, 179

Medical model, 394–395

Minnesota Couple Communication Program, 115–116

Minnesota Multiphasic Personality Inventory, 116

Misunderstandings in therapy
    client experience, 21–22
    in-session checking, 404
    invalidation of client feelings, 386–387
    recognition of, 350
    reinforcement of client self-mistrust, 389
    as shift in shared focus of attention, 404–405
    therapeutic benefits, 350
    therapist attunement to, 175

Morality, empathy and, 67

Mother–child relations
    developmental outcomes, 42–43
    maternal depression, 44
    psychoanalytic models of development, 24
    in sociocentric cultures, 313
    See also Parenting behavior

Motivation
    empathy as, 23, 37
    in logical learning theory, 330

Myths, 304

Narcissistic behavior or disorders, 127, 128, 138, 220
    racism as, 326–327

Narrative construction, 136–137, 329
    empathy for, 6
    See also Contruction of meaning

Negative capability, 148, 330–331

Nondirective attitude, 87–88

Nondirective therapy, 84

Nonjudgmental stance, 363

Nonverbal behavior, 229, 230
    empathic attunement, 174
    significance of, 110
    therapist, 22
    therapist's expanded attunement, 270

Nurturant empathy, 20

Object relations theory, 300

Objectivity
    clinical conceptualizations, 433–434
    comparison of therapy models, 207–208

in conceptualization of therapeutic
empathy, 400
of material elicited in therapist–
client alignment, 207–209
as therapist quality, 84, 86
Opening session, 189–190
with ethnic minority clients,
321–322, 326–327
expanded attunement approach,
273–275
Optimal failures and frustrations,
239–240, 253
Organismic self, 105
Outcomes
change in empathy, 114–117
empathy research, 17–19
empathy training program, 50
potential negative effects of therapeutic empathy, 431–434
research needs, 23
Rogerian empathy, 90–91
See also Therapeutic change

Parenting behavior, 24
child–parent empathy intervention,
117
developmental role of empathy,
41–43, 221, 325
empathy training, 49
excessive empathy, 41
infant experience of empathic interaction, 135–136
mother–child relationship, 42–43,
44
Pathological process
in egocentric modernist cultures,
298
empathic failures in childhood, 253
as impairment of empathy, 103,
113, 119, 220, 221
inability to hold experience in attention, 137–138
intersubjectivity theory, 279
medicallike perspective, 394–395
origins of neurosis, 266
relational model, 310–312
Rogerian concept, 82
in sociocentric cultures, 309
validation of physiological responses,
383–384

Perception
developmental capacities, 267–268
divided attention in analytical situation, 268
in empathic understanding, 420
in experiencing, 397
psychoanalytical, development of,
268–270
Perls, Fritz, 66
Person-centered therapy. *See* Client-centered therapy
Perspective taking
aggressive behavior and, 47
situational determinants, 48
skills training, 50
Physical space considerations, 189
Poignant experiences, 173, 176, 178,
180
Popular culture, 66
Postmodern thought
conceptualizations of empathy in,
12–13
opportunities for relational psychology, 315–316
psychological project, 295–296
Problem–solving, empathy as context
for, 405–407
Process-experiential therapy, 8
affirmation of intense vulnerability,
183–184
concept of self in, 184–185
empathic attunement in, 173–175
empathic communication, 175
empathic exploration of experiencing, 180–183
empathic tasks, 180
empathy in, 172–173
growth orientation, 173
measurement of therapist responses,
175–176, 179
reflection of feelings in, 173
targets of empathic responding,
178–179
types of empathic responses,
176–178
Projective identification, empathy and,
231–234
Prolonged empathic immersion, 282
Prosocial behavior
empathy and, 23, 24, 45–46
empathy training for, 50–51
in infants and children, 40

Protective factor, empathy as, 49
Psychoanalytic theory and practice
    communication of empathy, 250
    concept of understanding, 250
    conceptualization of empathy, 9–11,
        126–127, 217–220, 241–242
    countertransference and empathy,
        230–231
    countertransference challenge,
        280–281
    development of perception in analyti-
        cal situation, 268–270, 275–276
    developmental theories, 24
    divided attention in analytical situa-
        tion, 268
    drive concept, 247–248
    egocentric conceptualizations of em-
        pathy, 300–301
    empathy as negative capability,
        330–331
    empathy as observational method,
        220, 222–227, 281–282
    empathy as therapeutic agent,
        238–241
    empathy with defensive processes,
        227
    empirical validation of empathic
        claims, 233–238
    experience-near mode of observa-
        tion, 266–267
    explaining process, 250–252
    extended conception of empathy,
        225–227
    intersubjective investigation,
        282–283
    intersubjectivity theory, 279
    listening in, 217–218, 220–221
    process of empathy, 227–230
    projective identification and empa-
        thy, 231–234
    research needs, 265
    significance of therapist experience,
        429
    theory of unconscious, 224–225
    See also Expanded attunement
Psychodramatic doubling, 115
Psychodynamic therapy
    depth of empathic understanding in,
        422
    empathic understanding in, 421–422
    experience-near empathy in, 425

focus of empathic understanding,
    423, 424
interpretation in, 424
outcome research on empathy,
    17–18
relational approaches, 10
significance of empathy as psycholog-
    ical contact in, 435
use of empathy, 11, 14
validation in, 436

Race and ethnicity
    interventions for conflict reduction,
        52
    See also Cross-cultural practice; Eth-
        nic minority clients
Recipathy, 199
Reflection of feelings, 7, 8, 81, 84–85,
    88–89
    empathy and, 92–93
    empathy beyond, 163
    as level of validation, 362–364
    in process-experiential view, 173
Reframing, 12
Relational approaches, 3
    current psychoanalytic practice, 10
    developmental conceptualization,
        343
    evidence for, 301–302
    mutuality in therapy, 346–348
    postmodernist, 12–13
    role of empathy in, 345
    therapeutic change, 350–351
    therapeutic focus, 344–345
    therapeutic relationship, 349–350
    therapist responsiveness, 349
Relational empathy
    conceptions of psychological health
        and dysfunction, 310–311
    conceptual basis, 309–310
    current cultural obstacles to, 315
    dual consciousness for, 307–308
    healing capacity of, 314–315
    in postmodern psychology, 315–316
    self-development and, 344
    self-empathy and, 345–346
    social benefits of psychotherapy
        based on, 311–312
    sociocentric basis, 306–307
    therapist's capacity for learning,
        313–314

Relationship Inventory, 16, 19, 115
Research on empathy
    client factors, 22
    client perspective, 19–20
    current state, 23
    developmental issues, 51
    developmental models, 34
    empathic communication, 185
    empirical validation of empathic
        claims in psychoanalysis,
        233–238
    empirical validation of empathic con-
        structs, 426–426, 447
    future opportunities, 446–447
    gender differences in empathy, 43,
        44–45
    measurement, 15–17, 117–118
    in naturalistic settings, 51
    obstacles to, 34–35, 209
    outcomes, 17–19
    self-empathy, 114, 119
    therapist–client alignment, 209
    therapist misunderstanding, 21–22
    therapist response modes, 20–21
    trends, 15
    See also Measurement of empathy
Resonant empathy, 11
Respectful inner listening, 108
Reverberative empathy, 75–79
Ritual, 304
Rogerian concept of empathy, 67
    answering direct questions, 93
    as-if clause, 73, 75, 86, 299
    communication of empathy to
        client, 73, 81, 93–97
    concept of sympathy in, 70
    congruence in, 83, 96–97
    definition of empathy, 6, 359
    definition of unconditional positive
        regard, 83
    distinctive features, 6–7, 39, 81–82,
        83, 98
    implicit meanings in, 110
    nondirective attitude in, 87–88
    origins and development of, 68–75,
        83–86, 94–95, 98–99, 221–222,
        300
    reflection and, 92–93
    research findings, 90–91
    sociocentric content, 302–303
    theoretical framework, 82–83,
        97–98

therapeutic attitude versus therapeu-
    tic technique in, 86–87, 88–89,
    92–93
therapeutic change in, 82, 85, 86
therapist attunement in, 110
therapist experience in, 127
therapist objectivity in, 84, 86
as unconditional positive regard,
    81–82, 89–90
as understanding, 73
See also Rogers, Carl
Rogers, Carl, 66
    Buber and, 69–70, 71, 74–75
    concept of self, 106
    etiological concept, 82
    on fully functioning person,
        104–105
    group work, 95
    idiosyncratic practice, 96–97
    intellectual characteristics, 68
    Kohut and, 81
    personal characteristics, 70
    on sociocentric relating, 313–314
    stressful period with hallucinating
        client, 71–73, 86
    therapeutic style, 21
    on therapist qualifications, 84
    See also Rogerian concept of em-
        pathy
Role taking, 37
    for therapeutic understanding, 420,
        421

Safe therapeutic environment, 7
Sartre, Jean-Paul, 76
Schizophrenia, 251
Self-actualization, 442
Self-empathy
    clinical conceptualizations, 441
    in creation of meaning, 112
    formative recognition in, 109
    interpersonal empathy and, 104,
        110–111
    measurement, 118
    nature of, 108–110, 119
    received empathy in, 109–110
    recovery of, through therapy,
        111–114
    relational empathy and, 345–346
    research findings, 114, 119
    respectful inner listening in, 108

therapeutic development, 345
therapeutic significance, 103
Self-experience
acceptance of intense emotions, 184
in client-centered therapies, 7, 8
client's self-reported empathy,
19–20
complexity of self, 106–108
consideration of possible selves,
332–333
construction of reality in logical
learning theory, 329
empathy as, 126
empathy training for, 50
experiential recognition in, 131–133
in experiential therapies, 8–9
as focusing, 106
fragile processing, developmental
origins of, 137–138
in fully functioning person, 104–106
impairment of empathy, 103
internalization of capacity to hold experience in attention, 134–136
intersubjectivity theory, 279–280,
290
Kohut's theory, 252–253
learned self-validation, 388–389,
441–442
mechanistic models, 298–299
modernist egocentric conceptualizations, 296–298
openness to experience, 104, 134
in organismic self, 105
phenomenological reduction,
199–200
process-experiential view, 184–185
processing of life narratives,
136–137
in recipathy, 199–200
relational empathy for, 344
in relational knowing, 308
relational model, 343
Rogerian concept of psychopathology, 82
self-awareness in logical learning theory, 333–334
self-invalidation of emotions,
384–385
sociocentric view, 301–302
therapeutic goals, 170–171, 351
therapeutic mechanism of empathy,
6, 441

therapeutic validation, 356–358
therapist self-understanding, 84
therapist's, for relating to client, 362
therapist's, for therapeutic congruence, 146
therapist's, in client–therapist alignment, 194–195, 200–201
therapist's, in traditional empathic
intervention, 200–201
therapist's, significance of, 429–430
Self-help interventions, 395, 396
Self-in-relation theory, 4, 5
depth of understanding in, 422
Self–other differentiation, 36, 37
Self psychology, 4
case example, 254–262
change theory, 253–254
concept of empathy in, 127–129,
280
conceptual basis, 10
empathic communication in, 169
integrated with client-centered therapy, 8
mechanism of change in, 239–241
self-structuralization as change in,
442
selfobject concept, 240–241
selfobject functions, 134, 138–139
selfobject transference, 253
Self-structuralization, 442–443
Shame, 346
Shared empathy, 19–20
excessive, 39
Simmel, Georg, 71
Situational variables, 48
Skills-training for empathy
for adults, 52
attachment outcomes, 51
child–parent intervention, 117
for children, 49–51
in client-centered therapy, 7–8
clinical conceptualizations, 430–431
rationale, 51–53
research findings, 115–117
six-stage model, 49
for therapists, 445–446
Social psychology, 23
Socialization processes
antecedents of empathy in, 41–43
clinical implications, 44–45
organismic valuing in, 105
sex differences in empathy, 43,
44–45

goals of therapeutic interpretation versus empathy, 170–171

healing of shame, 346

internalization of capacity to hold experience in attention, 134–136, 138–139

in interpersonal empathy, 114–117

levels of interaction, 163

mechanism of empathy in, 5–6, 15, 125, 128–130, 137–139, 141, 169, 185, 221–222, 253, 336–338, 349, 405–408, 437, 444

medicallike perspective, 394–395

optimal frustrations for, 253

outcome research on empathy, 17–19

physiological metaphor, 384

psychoanalytic conceptions of empathy, 238–241

as recovery of self-empathy, 111–114

relational empathy for, 314–315

as self-actualization, 442

self-empathy and, 110–111, 345

in self psychology, 10, 239–241, 253–254

as self-structuralization, 442–443

therapeutic alliance for, 13

therapist–client alignment for, 196–198, 201

through unconditional positive regard, 82, 89–90

as transmuting internalization, 253

validation of client capacity for, 377

validation of client experience for, 351

Therapeutic relationship

affective component of empathy in, 39

affective responsiveness, 281

affirmation of intense vulnerability, 183–184

analyst's divided attention, 268

attending to feelings in, 21

attention to client's topic versus client's mental perspective, 404–405

behaviorist approach, 11–12

benefits of empathy in, 53

boundary definition, 11, 39

in client-centered therapy, 6–7, 168

client experience of empathy, 19–20, 116

client factors in empathy processes, 22

in cognitive-experiential psychotherapy, 395, 396–397, 399

communication of empathy, 73, 168

conceptualizations of empathy in, 439–440, 444

congruence in, 146

correlates of empathy in, 19, 22

countertransference, 230–231

in dynamic interpretation, 169–170

in dynamic interpretation versus empathic responding, 171–172

empathic-introspective view, 334–335

empathic resonance in, 144–146

empathic responding in Rogerian model, 93–97

with ethnic minority clients, 321–322, 326–327, 335–336

Freud on, 266

goal-determined choice of empathic form, 176

goals of empathy in, 188

in-session checking, 404

intersubjective approach, 290

measuring empathy in, 16–17

medicallike perspective, 394–395, 397

as mutual empathy, 343–344, 347–349, 439

nonjudgmental stance, 363

nonverbal expressions, 22

performance-oriented client, 406–407

in postmodernist thought, 12–13

projective identification, 231–233

psychoanalytic conceptualizations, 9–10, 11

psychoanalytic theory of empathy process, 228–230

in psychodynamic therapy, 11

recognition of client as self-healer, 393–394

relational conditions, 3

relational therapy, 349–350

resonant empathy, 11

reverberative empathy in, 75–79

in Rogerian concept of empathy, 84–85

in self psychology, 10
significance of empathy in, 3–4
significance of sociocentric cultures,
     303–306
socialization antecedents of empathy
     and, 44–45
strengthened by validation of client,
     391
structures of consciousness model of
     empathy, 92
sympathy in, 25
synthesis of absolutist and relativist
     views, 366–367
as therapeutic alliance, 13, 19
therapist flexibility, 399
therapist misunderstandings, 21–22
therapist response modes, 20
therapist self-disclosure, 408, 411,
     429
therapist's empathic stance,
     167–168
therapist's negative capability, 331
traditional mechanistic psychiatry,
     298–299
transparency in, 96–97
types of empathy in, 13–15
for validation of client as person,
     378–379
validation of client through listening
     and observing, 360–362
Therapist–client alignment
advantages of, 187, 207–209, 210
client qualities for, 192
definition of empathy as, 188
discovering and using deeper poten-
     tial in, 197–198, 208–209
ending session, 198
eye contact, 189
limitations of, 202
necessary and sufficient conditions
     for, 191–192, 210
obstacles to, 192
opening instructions to client,
     189–190
outward focus, 190–191, 196,
     198–199
recipathy in, 199–200
research opportunities, 209
seating arrangement for, 189
significant features, versus face-to-
     face intervention, 198–209, 210
sustained throughout session, 195

therapeutic change in, 196–198,
     201
therapeutic material elicited by,
     202–209
therapist experience, 188, 191,
     193–195, 200–201
therapist expression of client experi-
     ence, 195–196
therapist qualities for, 192–193
Titchener, E. B., 65, 69
Training of clinicians, 53, 445–446
Transference
empathic-introspective view,
     334–335
intersubjectivity theory, 271
selfobject, 253–254
Types of empathy, 13–15, 175
client perspective, 19–20
common features of, 419
frames of reference, 175
imaginative, 30
research needs, 447
therapeutic goals in selection of, 176
See also Clinical conceptualizations
     of empathy

Unconditional positive regard, 4, 7, 15,
     19, 436
definition, 83, 437
empathy and, 437
in Rogerian concept of empathy,
     81–82, 89–90
Unconscious processes
broader psychoanalytic conceptions
     of empathy, 225–227
in dynamic interpretation versus em-
     pathic responding, 171
empathic understanding of, 423–424
experiential conceptualization, 403
intersubjective model of empathic in-
     quiry, 280, 283
intersubjective model of self-organiza-
     tion, 280, 282
therapeutic role of empathy, 5, 11
traditional psychoanalytic concep-
     tions of empathy, 224–225

Validation, 11–12
acceptance of client's intense emo-
     tions, 183–184
accurate reflection as, 362–364

ABOUT THE EDITORS

Arthur C. Bohart is Professor of Psychology at California State University, Dominguez Hills, and is in part-time private practice. He has published articles on psychotherapy integration, experiencing in psychotherapy, empathy, constructivism, couples therapy, and the role of the client as self-healer. He is the coauthor of two textbooks, *Foundations of Clinical and Counseling Psychology* (with Judith Todd) and *Personality* (with Seymour Feshbach and Bernard Weiner). Along with Karen Tallman, he is currently writing a book to be published by the American Psychological Association called *The Client as Active Self-Healer*.

Leslie S. Greenberg is Professor of Psychology at York University in Toronto, where he is Director of the Psychotherapy Research Centre. He also has a part-time private practice. He is coauthor of a number of books, including *Emotion in Psychotherapy* (with Jeremy Safran), *Emotionally Focused Therapy for Couples* (with Susan Johnson), and *Facilitating Emotional Change: The Moment-By Moment Process* (with Laura Rice and Robert Elliott). He is past president of the Society for Psychotherapy Research, and has published extensively on research on the process of change.